Siegfried Goebel

The Parables of Jesus

A methodical exposition

Siegfried Goebel

The Parables of Jesus
A methodical exposition

ISBN/EAN: 9783744795845

Printed in Europe, USA, Canada, Australia, Japan

Cover: Foto ©Lupo / pixelio.de

More available books at **www.hansebooks.com**

CLARK'S

FOREIGN

THEOLOGICAL LIBRARY.

NEW SERIES.
VOL. XV.

The Parables of Jesus.

EDINBURGH:
T. & T. CLARK, 38 GEORGE STREET.
1883.

PRINTED BY MORRISON AND GIBB,

FOR

T. & T. CLARK, EDINBURGH.

LONDON,	HAMILTON, ADAMS, AND CO.
DUBLIN,	GEO. HERBERT.
NEW YORK,	SCRIBNER AND WELFORD.

THE

PARABLES OF JESUS:

A METHODICAL EXPOSITION.

BY

SIEGFRIED GOEBEL,

COURT-CHAPLAIN IN HALBERSTADT.

Translated by

PROFESSOR BANKS,

HEADINGLEY.

EDINBURGH:
T. & T. CLARK, 38 GEORGE STREET.
1883.

PREFACE.

THE immediate occasion of the following exegetical work on the Parables of Jesus was a want which I felt in the exercise of the ministerial office. The homiletic and catechetical treatment of the Parables of the Lord is a task to which every minister of the word finds himself ever called afresh. And this not merely because many of them form part of the public lessons, but because the unchanging attraction and popularity of their form, along with the depth and fulness of their contents, necessarily give them unique importance in relation to the edification of the Christian Church and the instruction of Christian youth. All the more to be regretted is the unlimited caprice with which they are often, and one must almost say traditionally, handled and interpreted. Under cover of an appeal to the infinite many-sidedness of the word of God, expositors think themselves justified in straining the figurative form of the Parables for any purpose and to any extent, and in foisting on them all imaginable references and comparisons. But in reality such a mode of treatment by no means accords with the reverence due to the language of Holy Scripture and the words of our Lord. Not, indeed, that the preacher or teacher is to be denied the right of a free application and many-sided employment of the Parables for the purposes of edification and instruction in general. But he is only justified in doing this, and able to do it, after he has, first of all, assured himself of their true, original, and simple meaning, and thus laid a firm basis for his application, defined the simple bearing of the Parables, and fixed the limits of sobriety. And here the want mentioned above makes itself felt. Any one who desires to avoid the usual arbitrariness in the treatment of the Parables, and to investigate their original meaning under the guidance of a thorough, methodical, and exact exposition, will at present seek in vain in modern exegetical literature for a work that meets this desire. At least such is my experience. I therefore attempted to help myself, and undertook the present work. I publish it in the hope that it may render the same help to one or another of my ministerial brethren which it has rendered to myself, perhaps also that here and there among non-theological readers of the Greek New Testament it may find a friend to whom it may prove instructive, and not without pleasure. Beyond this the design of its publication does not extend. But should it turn out that the work is not without value, even in a scientific aspect, in opening the way to a methodical treatment of the Parables in general, and to greater certainty in their still very divergent interpretation in detail, I shall especially rejoice in this as a welcome addition.

It will be self-evident that in what has been just said no disparaging judgment is meant to be passed on the works which have previously treated monographically of the Parables of Jesus in one way or another. Only they cannot satisfy the need of a methodical and exact exposition, because they do not even propose to do this. I quote them here, so far as they are known to me. Older ones are: Unger, *De Parabolarum Jesu natura, interpretatione, usu*, 1828 (an elaborate treatise, but without thorough exposition); Lisco, *Die Parabeln Jesu*, ed. 4, 1841 ("exegetico-homiletic"), in it is also found an elaborate list of still older works, from 1717 onwards; de Valenti, *Die Parabeln des Herrn*, 1841 (a practical exposition "for Church, School, and Home"); Arndt, *Die Gleichnissreden Jesu Christi*, 1842 (sermons). In more recent days: Thiersch, *Die Gleichnisse Christi nach ihrer moralischen und prophetischen Bedeutung* (Bible hours); Behrmann, *Die Gleichnissreden des Herrn*, first half (Bible hours); Mangold, *Populäre Auslegung sämmtlicher Gleichnisse Jesu Christi* ("in catechetical order").

The modern exegetes on the synoptical Gospels have been everywhere compared, even where not specially quoted by name.

TRANSLATOR'S NOTE.

THE following work has won considerable favour in Germany. Dr. Weiss commends the "solid exegesis, sound judgment, and sober, skilful interpretation" of the author (*Theol. Literaturzeitung*, Aug. 28, 1880). His adverse criticism relates to three points. He blames the author for his inadequate discussion of the nature of the parabolic mode of teaching, his disregard of the results of "Criticism," and his diffuse, involved style. The first point might be conceded without detracting from the value of the work as a whole. The author's discussion of the nature of parabolic teaching in the Introduction is quite subordinate to his main purpose. The views there expressed on this general question have comparatively little influence on the detailed exegesis of the individual parables. The second fault in the critic's eyes will be a merit in the eyes of many. Until two members of the advanced "Critical" school can be found to agree, the expositor may justly decline their guidance. The truth of the third charge is freely conceded. The translator has done what he could so far to modify this feature as to secure clearness.

To English students the absence of all reference to English works of exposition may appear a more considerable defect. On the other hand, this very circumstance gives the work a freshness and independence which it could not otherwise have.

The method of interpretation sketched at the close of the Introduction should be especially noticed, as it is the one applied to each parable in succession.

TABLE OF CONTENTS.

INTRODUCTION.

	PAGE
The Word "Parable" in the New Testament,	1
The Parables in the strict sense,	3
Distinction between Symbolic and Typical Parables,	4
Parable and Fable,	6
Fable and Parable in the Old Testament,	9
Rabbinical Parables,	13
Purpose of Parables,	14
Distribution of the matter in the Gospels,	17
Classification of the Parables according to their Import,	20
Method of Exposition,	24

PART I.

THE FIRST SERIES OF PARABLES IN CAPERNAUM.

The Parables to the People by the Sea,	29
The Sower, or Divers Soils,	37
The Tares in the Wheat,	57
The Fruit-bearing Earth,	80
The Grain of Mustard Seed,	93
The Leaven,	99
The Parables in the Conversation with the Disciples,	106
The Hidden Treasure,	107
The Pearl of Great Price,	111
The Fishing-Net,	115
Review,	122

PART II.

THE LATER PARABLES ACCORDING TO LUKE.

Introductory,	124
The Merciful Samaritan,	127
The Importunate Friend,	140

The Rich Fool,	149
The Fig-Tree,	159
The Great Banquet,	169
THE THREE PARABLES IN LUKE XV.,	190
The Lost Sheep,	191
The Lost Coin,	197
The Lost Son,	200
The Unjust Steward,	215
The Rich Man,	232
The Unjust Judge,	257
The Pharisee and the Publican,	269

PART III.

THE PARABLES OF THE LAST PERIOD.

General View,	281
The Unmerciful Servant,	281
The Labourers in the Vineyard,	298
The Wicked Vinedressers,	324
The Royal Marriage-Feast,	349
THE ESCHATOLOGICAL DISCOURSE UP TO THE ESCHATOLOGICAL PARABLES,	379
The Ten Virgins,	382
The Talents in Trust,	405
The Pounds in Trust,	432
ARRANGEMENT OF THE PARABLES IN SYSTEMATIC ORDER,	457
LIST OF SCRIPTURE PASSAGES DISCUSSED,	459

THE PARABLES OF JESUS.

INTRODUCTION.

THE word "parable" has in the New Testament, in its application to the discourses of Jesus, a considerably wider meaning than the one in which we speak of the parables of the Lord in the current phraseology of the Church. The designation παραβολή, from παραβάλλειν (therefore = placing side by side, comparing), belongs to every utterance containing a comparison of any kind. Thus, in Luke v. 36 the maxim of the old garment, which does not fit in with a new patch, is introduced as a parable.[1] In the same way, in Luke vi. 39, the maxim, "If the blind lead the blind, will not both fall into the ditch?" is called a parable (εἶπε παραβολήν). Further, in Mark iii. 23 ff., the appeal of Jesus to the impossibility of a kingdom or household at variance within itself standing, is described as a speaking "in parables." And in Matt. xxiv. 32, Mark xiii. 28, Jesus Himself calls His allusion to the budding of the leaves on the fig-tree, which announces the approach of summer, a parable.[2] All these maxims are called parables, because in a visible fact, belonging to the sphere of physical or human life, they picture a corresponding truth in the sphere of religious life. Thus, in the incompatibility of an old garment with a new patch, they depict the incompatibility of the old Pharisaic legal system with the new nature and life manifested in Christ; in the obvious impossibility of one blind man leading another, the impossibility of one who is himself impervious to divine truth guiding others in divine things; in the notorious impossibility of a kingdom at variance within itself standing, the impossibility that Satan's kingdom, strong as it is,

---

[1] "Ἔλεγε δὲ καὶ παραβολὴν πρὸς αὐτούς; cf. also the two following maxims of the new wine and old skins (vv. 37, 38), and the old and new wine (ver. 39), which, placed on a parallel with the first, are also clearly parables in the same sense as the first.

[2] Ἀπὸ δὲ τῆς συκῆς μάθετε τὴν παραβολήν.

should stand, if hostile to itself; and finally, in the infallible certainty with which the bursting leaves of the fig-tree announce the approach of summer, the infallible certainty with which the events foretold by Jesus indicate the approach of His second coming.

A still more general use of "parable" is seen in the passage Matt. xv. 15, where it refers to the utterance of the Lord in ver. 11 (cf. vv. 16–20): "Not what enters into the mouth (food) defiles the man; but what proceeds out of the mouth (evil speech), this defiles the man." Here, therefore, it refers to a *concrete maxim* without a properly figurative character, simply of an enigmatical stamp. A similar use under another aspect is found in the passage Luke iv. 23, where the *proverb*, "Physician, heal thyself," is called a parable, and that, as it seems, not so much because of its figurative, as rather merely because of its proverbial character. Both passages follow the correspondingly general use of the word parable as a translation of מָשָׁל in the Septuagint, where not merely abstract and concrete maxims (Prov. i. 6), but also in general every favourite saying that has passed into popular use is called a parable, whether figurative in form (Ezek. xviii. 2, 3) or not (1 Sam. xxiv. 14; Ezek. xii. 22). But if, passing by this latter use of the word, in which it has departed far from its fundamental meaning as "comparison," we direct our attention merely to all those utterances of Jesus which, as embodying comparison and figure, come under the category of parable, it is self-evident that a separate exegetical treatment of all Christ's utterances and brief discourses, which might be called parables in this wider sense of the word, is an impossibility. They are so numerous and, moreover, so interwoven with the structure of Christ's discourses, that an attempt at their complete treatment must inevitably swell into a treatment of His discourses in general. Let any one, for example, consider the following parables in the Sermon on the Mount merely: the Salt that has lost its Savour (Matt. v. 13); the City on a Hill (v. 14); the Light, not under the Bushel, but on the Stand (v. 15); the Two Adversaries on the Way to the Judge (v. 25, 26); the Plucking out of the Eye, etc., for the good of the whole body (v. 29, 30); the Treasures which neither Moth nor Rust consume (vi. 19, 20); the Eye the Light of the Body (vi. 22, 23); Serving Two Masters (vi. 24); the Censorious Man (vii. 3–5); the Swine and Pearls (vii. 6); the Children asking Bread or Fish (vii. 9–11); the Two Gates and Two Ways (vii. 13, 14); the Wolves in Sheep's Clothing (vii. 15); the House built on Rock or Sand (vii. 24–27).

Accordingly, we have in the first instance to limit our matter by distinguishing the parables in the stricter sense, known by this name in the phraseology of the Church, from the parables in the wider sense, corresponding to the Biblical use of the word parable. It is incorrect to say that the parables of Christ, so called κατ' ἐξοχήν, are merely detailed comparisons,[1] which would leave no characteristic mark distinguishing them from other figurative discourses and utterances of Jesus. For no one, for example, assigns the very detailed figurative discourse of the Good Shepherd in contrast with the thieves and hirelings (John x. 1–16) to the stricter circle of parables, whereas the parable of the Costly Pearl (Matt. xiii. 45, 46), although consisting of but two brief sentences, without doubt belongs to the circle. Thus, there must be a definite distinguishing element constituting the idea of the parable in the stricter sense. The correct view is as follows:—It is the distinction obvious to the eye, between the figurative language occasionally interwoven and the figurative history expressly imagined, which is the cause of the latter only being called the parables of Jesus by pre-eminence. Accordingly, the character of a complete figurative history or narrative is to be regarded as the distinguishing mark of the parables strictly so called. Not merely an allusion to some fact belonging to the sphere of physical or human life, or to some relation obtaining there, but the invention and narration of a connected series of particular events, combined into a single whole, serves here as a pictorial representation of doctrine belonging to the religious sphere. Certainly there are some among the parables, bearing this name universally in Church usage, to which the *narrative*-form is wanting, *e.g.* the two parables of the Lost Sheep and Lost Coin (Luke xv. 3–10). But still both, although merely clothed in the form of a question referring to an imagined case, give in the contents of the parabolic question the *matter* for a narrative so definite in detail and complete in itself, that the absence of the narrative-*form* is lost to the consciousness of the hearer and reader. The same is true of the parable of the Importunate Friend (Luke xi. 5–9). Introduced merely in the form of a parabolic question, it still gives as to substance a narrative completely worked out. On the other hand, again, among the parables so

[1] Cremer, *Biblico-Theological Lexicon*, p. 125 (Clark).

called κατ' ἐξ. there are some which, regarded as to their *contents*, present less the *narration* of a specially imagined history that once happened under definite conditions, than a *descriptive picture* of events actually taking place daily by necessity of natural law, or else by a necessity grounded in the nature of the case. This holds good of the parables of the Sower, the Mustard Seed, the Leaven, the Fishing Net. But, nevertheless, in all these, not the descriptive, but the *narrative-form* is chosen (in that of the Mustard Seed, Matthew drops it in the second part, while Luke retains it to the end). Thus, not the entire body of events of the same kind is comprised in a descriptive picture, but—in order to picture the subject with greater directness to the hearers (for only in the special can the general be contemplated)—out of the series of events of the same kind a particular one is selected, and this is narrated independently as a particular event that somewhere took place. And it is precisely this retention of the narrative-form which in usage has given to this class of parables also a place among the parables in the stricter sense. But by far the greatest number of the parables coming under this head, along with the narrative-form, exhibit also as to their contents the character of a history specially imagined for the didactic purpose present to the author's mind. The incidents of the history, while borrowed from actual life, form in this particular arrangement and combination into a whole, an event, unique in kind, which, as the fiction supposes, once took place somewhere.

Accordingly, the idea of the parable may in the first instance be generally defined to this effect: *A narrative moving within the sphere of physical or human life, not professing to communicate an event which really took place, but expressly imagined for the purpose of representing in pictorial figure a truth belonging to the sphere of religion, and therefore referring to the relation of man or mankind to God.*

But then, in reference to the manner of the figurative representation, an essential distinction is observable among the parables of Jesus lying before us in the Gospels. To commence with a definite designation, they are either *symbolic* or *typical*. The first class forms by far the greatest number. The general background here is the presupposition of an all-pervading harmony between the entire sphere of the physical world and man's physical life on the one hand, and the higher sphere embracing the relations of man to God on the other, so that in virtue of this divinely-established harmony, states and relations, incidents and operations, belonging to the former sphere of life, mirror something of a like kind in the latter sphere. In this way, not by accidental similarity, but by the inner coherence subsisting, the visible becomes a symbol of the invisible, the earthly of the heavenly, the temporal of the eternal. Viewed from this standpoint, the nature of the symbolic parable is to represent in figure those truths belonging to the religious sphere which it wishes to illustrate, in a narrative freely composed out of symbolically significant relations, incidents, and operations in physical or human life. In order, therefore, to ascertain the true meaning, the hearer or reader first needs the *interpretation*, *i.e.* the translation of the figure into the thing symbolized, of the image into the counterpart, to which, however, in most cases some interpreting word of the narrator himself gives a clue. Sometimes, again, allegory is mixed with the symbol forming the basis of the symbolic parable, namely, wherever particular features are added to the figurative history, which, without having symbolic significance in themselves, or at least blending as more precise details with the main symbolic circumstances of the parable, only shadow forth something of like kind in the higher sphere in virtue of an outward similarity. But in such cases the chief circumstances always remain of a symbolic nature, and *purely* allegorical features occur but rarely. It is not allegory, but symbol, when sowing, growth, ripening, and reaping in the field, or the operations of the fisherman in fishing, or the toil of the shepherd about his sheep, are used as figurative representations of similar incidents and operations in the sphere of God's kingdom; or when earthly treasures are made an image of spiritual blessings, an earthly feast of spiritual happiness, or the relation between king and subjects, master and servants, proprietor and steward, father and son, bridegroom and bride, creditor and debtor, judges and administrators, etc., is made an image of the relation between God and man, or Christ and the people of God, and incidents moving within the lines of such a relation serve as a figurative representation of what takes place between God and man. On the other hand, it is no longer symbol, but allegory, when (for example) the interpretation of the parable of the Sower places over against the coming of the birds of heaven to devour the seed, the coming of the devil to carry off the word from man's heart; or when in the parable of the Tares the devil is described as an enemy who of set purpose sows tares among the wheat; or when in the parable of the Mustard Seed the birds nesting in the branches of the tree are made an image of the nations of the earth entering into the kingdom of God. Many other traits, mostly allegorical, which have been assumed in the parables of Jesus, rest on arbitrary explanations.

But alongside these symbolic parables we find a number of others, which we have called *typical;* "type" here, however, being taken, not in the specific sense of Rom. v. 14, as a prophetic representation of something future, but in the usual sense of *exemplum,* either as a model summoning to imitation (Phil. iii. 17; 1 Tim. iv. 12), or as a warning and terror (1 Cor. x. 6, 11). These are the parables which illustrate the teaching they wish to give, not in the way of symbolical clothing, but in that of direct exemplification. Such are the parables of the Merciful Samaritan, the Rich Fool, the Rich Man, the Pharisee and Publican (Luke x., xii., xvi., xviii.). In all these cases a παραβάλλειν, or comparative setting side by side, takes place in so far only as the author introduces a particular case in the shape of an artificial history by way of comparison with the general truth meant to be taught. The particular case so confirms the truth that the religious truth in question is intuitively recognised in the history as in a striking example. Thus the narratives themselves as such bear a religious character. Their chief personages, after whom they are named, are not symbolic images, but are themselves the typical representatives of an ethico-religious disposition. And, on the other hand, the name and person of God may enter directly into the narrative without figurative clothing; divine acts, invisible to sense, may form an essential ingredient of the action (both hold good of the parables of the Rich Fool and the Pharisee and Publican); or, as in the parable of the Rich Man, the history of human persons may be followed into the next world,—all which is impossible in the symbolic parable by its very nature. Here, what is necessary in order to give expression to the moral of the narrative is not the interpretation of a symbol, but merely the generalizing application of what is said and narrated of a particular case to all cases of a like kind, so that the special events of the history related are traced back to the universally valid law executed and the universally valid truth confirmed in them.

In the profane literature of antiquity the Æsopian *fable* is very similar as regards rhetorical form to the New Testament parable in the stricter sense.¹ Like the parable, the fable also is a history, not professing to communicate an event that really took place, but expressly imagined for the purpose of representing a general truth in pictorial figure. Certainly the form of representation in the two is for the most part different, but by no means always so. In respect to the form of representation, parable and fable may also perfectly coincide, so that no really *decisive* distinction exists between them in a formal respect. The following common definition of the distinction is not to the point: The fable moves in the sphere of fantasy, because it introduces irrational creatures (beasts, trees, etc.), thinking, speaking, and acting rationally; whereas the parable always borrows its matter from actual life, and never transgresses the limits of the possible.² Here it is overlooked that there are also purely human fables, in which only rational creatures are the actors;³ that there are other fables which hover, indeed, between man and beast, but without anything being said of the latter but what really lies within the animal nature;⁴ and finally, such fables as treat, indeed, only of beasts, but without attributing to them other properties than those which they really possess.⁵ Thus the first-named class of fables agrees as respects its means of representation with the numerous parables taken from the relations of man's natural life, the second with those treating of the relations between man and beast (the Lost Sheep, the Fishing Net), and also a parable corresponding to the third class of fables, although not actually met

---

[1] The distinction drawn by Aristotle (*Rhetoric*, ii. 20) between parable (παραβολή) and fable (λόγος), in contrasting them with each other as two different species of artificial proof-example (παράδειγμα), does not come into view here, because his παραβολή, of which for the rest he does not speak, as it is different in his view from λόγος, is in any case something quite different from the New Testament parabolic narrative. The two examples which he gives of his "parable" are the following: οἷον εἴ τις λέγοι ὅτι οὐ δεῖ κληρωτοὺς ἄρχειν· ὅμοιον γὰρ ὥσπερ ἂν εἴ τις τοὺς ἀθλητὰς κληροίη μὴ οἳ ἂν δύνωνται ἀγωνίζεσθαι ἀλλ' οἳ ἂν λάχωσιν, ἢ τῶν πλωτήρων ὅν τινα δεῖ κυβερνᾶν κληρώσειν, ὡς δέον τὸν λαχόντα ἀλλὰ μὴ τὸν ἐπιστάμενον. Here, therefore, we have no narratives at all, but simply the alleging of conceivably possible cases from other spheres in proof of a political principle.

[2] Unger, Lisco, de Valenti, Cremer, *et al.*

[3] *E.g. Fab. Æsop.*, Trübner's ed., by Halm, 98, 169, 351, 412: The Countryman and his Sons, the Physician and Invalid, the Thief and his Mother, the Miser, etc.

[4] *E.g. Fab. Æsop.* 97, 111, 192, 374: The Countryman and the Serpent, the Woman and the Hen, the Dog and the Gardener, the Sheep and the Wolf.

[5] *E.g. Fab. Æsop.* 21, 228, 233, 421: The Two Fighting Cocks and the Eagle, the Dog and the Horse, the Dog with the Bone, the Geese and the Cranes.

with, is at least not absolutely unthinkable, as is seen in the symbolic-parabolical allusion to the act of the hen in gathering her chickens under her wings (Matt. xxiii. 37; Luke xiii. 34).

There is, in fact, a decisive distinction between the parable of the New Testament and the fable of antiquity, but it is of an inward, not outward kind. It lies primarily in the difference of the didactic matter represented, not in the different mode of representation. *The New-Testament parable is religious, the Æsopian fable profane.* There, the truth represented always refers to the relation of man to God, and only refers to the moral relation between man and man from the standpoint of religious obligation to God; here, it is merely rules and precepts of natural utility and morality, and therefore either rules of a virtuous but natural prudence, or rules of common worldly policy, or even mere precepts of experience, often of a thoroughly trivial nature, which constitute the "moral" of the fable. From this difference of the matter follows next a manifold diversity in the outward mode of representation, which, however, is not without exceptions. Thus the parable is predominantly symbolic, only occasionally merely typical; whereas the fable is for the most part typical, and therefore presents its teaching only in the form of example, for which reason it chooses animals by preference, not as symbolic, but as typical figures.[1] Only when its moral is not a universal precept, but simply refers to a historically given case, *may* it also be allegorical,[2] but never symbolic in the sense in which the parable mostly is; because the higher, invisible world, of which the parable sees and exhibits the symbol in the visible world of nature and man, lies far from it. Hence arises a further difference, that the parable which illustrates its religious truth either by means of the symbol, and therefore of a symbolic fact found in the life of nature or man, or by means of direct example, which must itself, as an example of a religious truth, be of a religious nature, can never work with mere fantastic figures like thinking and speaking animals, trees, etc.; whereas the fable, to which the diversified nature of its precepts gives the widest scope in the choice of examples, takes them, not always indeed, but still by preference, from the world of fantasy.

---

[1] The fox is not a symbol, but a type of policy, the lion of strength, the wolf of gluttony, etc.

[2] Cf. the fable of the Horse and Stag in Aristotle, *ut ante*, and Halm, *Fab. Æsop.* 175.

Finally, it follows from the sacredness of the subject-matter of the parable, that the character of severe simplicity and sober earnestness is everywhere appropriate to its narrative; whereas again the purpose of the fable, bearing merely on natural worldly prudence and experience, implies that its narrative frequently has a ludicrous, not seldom even a licentious character.[1]

Outside the New Testament the parable is found also in the Old Testament and in the Rabbins of the Talmud.

In the Old Testament we meet both with fable and parable. Of the former we have only one example, Jotham's fable of the trees and the bramble, Judg. ix. 7—15. The trees, so Jotham tells the Shechemites, wished to anoint a king over them. The olive, the fig-tree, and the vine, to whom they applied, declined. Through their own worth they had enough reputation both with God and man. Why should they leave their useful work for a tottering authority over the trees? But the useless, wretched bramble, having nothing to give up and nothing to lose, accepts the royal dignity, and promises them its shadow, in which, however, they find no protection against the sun, but merely stinging prickles; or fire may easily break out in it, and spreading from it consume them. It is a fable of political wisdom, warning against the perilous ambition of political adventure, and is directed against the folly of the Shechemites, who, although none of the great heroes of Israel had hitherto stretched out his hand to the royal dignity, and a Gideon had even declined it, made the cruel adventurer Abimelech their king.[2] Some have attempted to find another Old-Testament fable in the passage 2 Kings xiv. 9 (= 2 Chron. xxv. 18), where Joash king of Israel replies scornfully to the challenge of Amaziah king of Judah: "The thistle that was in Lebanon sent to the cedar that was in Lebanon, saying, Give thy daughter to my son to wife; and there passed by a wild beast that was in Lebanon, and trode down the thistle." But the fable here lacks the essential character of narrative as a connected series of events combining to form a single whole. Instead of this we have simply a scornful contrasting of two unconnected occurrences, namely, of the proposal for a marriage alliance, implying the claim of equality, made by the thistle to the cedar,

---

[1] Cf. the Prologue of Phædrus to his revision of Æsop's *Fables: Duplex libelli dos est: Quod risum movet. Et quod prudentis vitam consilio movet.*

[2] Cf. the not dissimilar fable of Æsop of the fox impaled by the bramble, when he wished to hold on by it, Halm, *Fab. Æsop.* 8.

and of the thistle being trampled on by the wild beast, to which fate it was exposed because of its little height.

On the other hand, the parabolic narrative is found in two Old-Testament examples, and indeed one of each of the two classes of typical and symbolical parables, which we have distinguished from each other. The first is the parable (2 Sam. xii. 1–6) uttered by the prophet Nathan to King David, when the latter had taken Bathsheba, the wife of Uriah, to wife. The prophet there tells of a rich man, possessed of sheep and cattle in great abundance, who nevertheless took from a poor man his only lamb, tenderly reared and beloved, to make provision for a guest. The requisite conclusion of the narrative is given in the words of King David himself, when he says angrily to the prophet: "As the Lord liveth, the man that hath done this thing shall surely die," etc. (vv. 5, 6); upon which the prophet at once makes the application of the parable to the historically given case in the words: "Thou art the man," and in the further address which follows (vv. 7–12). But it is not a symbolic, partially allegorical parable which we have here before us, but merely an exemplary, typical parable. By the example of a particular case, it exhibits directly the general truth of the great guilt incurred by the rich man, who, not content with all the possessions which God has given him, with insatiable avarice robs even the poor man of the trifling possession which is dear to his heart because it is all he has. Solely to exemplify this general truth, the applicability of which to the case given here of David's sin is obvious of itself, is the parable invented, and it is only adapted to this end. But it is not an allegorical and figurative representation of what took place between David and Uriah, as if the many sheep and cattle of the rich man were meant to "signify" the many wives at the disposal of the king, and the solitary lamb of the poor man the one wife of Uriah, in which case one would be compelled also to ask who are to be understood by the children of the poor man mentioned in ver. 3, and the guest of the rich man in ver. 4.

The other parable of the Old Testament, Isa. v. 1–6, is of a symbolic nature. There the prophet tells of a friend of his, who had a vineyard in the best situation, and, having spent all conceivable toil and care on it, expected it to bring forth grapes, when it brought forth wild grapes (vv. 1, 2). Upon this the master of the vineyard, suddenly introduced speaking in the animated style of prophetic speech, himself calls on the people of

Jerusalem to judge between him and the vineyard, announcing that he will withdraw his hand from the vineyard and abandon it to desolation (vv. 3-6). And after the last clause in ver. 6: "And I will command the clouds that they rain not thereon,"—no longer a word of man, but a word of divine power,—has broken through the figurative shell of the language, in ver. 7 the interpretation follows at once: "The vineyard of the Lord of Hosts is the house of Israel, and the men of Judah His pleasant plant: and He looked for judgment, but behold oppression; for righteousness, but behold a cry." The relation of the human cultivator to his field or vineyard, in virtue of which he justly expects it to bear fruit in return for all the toil and care expended on it, is symbolic of the justice of the divine demand on man, that he now bear the moral fruit of righteousness in return for all the benefits and care he has received from God. This generally symbolic relation is here applied especially to the relation of Jehovah to His covenant-people, from whom, after all the great things which He has done for them, He now expects the fruit of righteousness. But instead of this he only finds the evil fruit of unrighteousness. What else can follow, but that He will withdraw His hand from them and abandon them to destruction? In what relation Christ's parables of the Fig-Tree and the Wicked Labourers in the Vineyard stand to this parable will be shown in the exposition of the former.

No parabolic *narratives* are found elsewhere in the Old Testament, but only, apart from the very numerous figurative sayings and phrases occurring everywhere, a number of detailed parabolic *passages* of a predominantly allegorical kind, resting, however, partially at least on a symbolic basis. There is an example of this, when in the parabolic discourse, Ezek. xv., just as in Isaiah's parable of the vineyard, the degeneration of the noble vine into an unfruitful, useless trunk, as a symbol of the moral degeneracy of Israel planted by God, is made the basis of the announcement of judgment;[1] or when in Ezek. xvi., xxiii., the marriage-covenant between man and wife, as a symbol of the relation of God to His people, serves as a basis for the elaborate allegorical descriptions of the adultery of the people of God, or of the two sisters, Samaria and Judah;[2] or when the prediction, Ezek. xvii. 22-24, uses and allegorizes the growth of the tender shoot into a

---

[1] Cf. the parabolic exposition of Christ, John xv. 5, 6.
[2] See on the counterpart in the discourses of Christ in Matt. xxii. 1.

great tree in reference to the extension of the theocratic kingdom of the Messiah;[1] or when the allegory in Prov. ix. 1–6 makes the nourishment and refreshment of the feast a symbol of the spiritual blessings prepared by God for man's enjoyment.[2] On the other hand, other parabolical passages of the Old Testament move exclusively in the sphere of allegory, and have therefore next to no affinity with the parables of Christ. Thus the vine becomes a mere allegorical figure of Israel in the figurative discourse, Ezek. xix. 10–14, and of Zedekiah the king of Judah in the figurative account of the two great eagles, one of which planted the vine, which then grew and strengthened and stretched toward the second eagle, Ezek. xvii. 1–8. Here, therefore, we have a formal, figurative history, which yet has next to nothing in common with the parabolic narratives of Christ, because it is not an artificial, didactic narrative, like the fable and parable, but a historic narrative, only loosely veiled in an allegorical garb as picturesque as it is transparent; it is, in short, a historic picture with allegorical figures.

But, finally, there is one parabolic description in the Old Testament which, while it lacks the form of narrative, stands very near to those parabolic narratives of Jesus which, as regards their contents, are merely descriptive pictures of the circumstances of husbandry. It is the description of the conduct of the husbandman in ploughing and threshing, Isa. xxviii. 23–29. The description aims at two points. First, at showing that in scoring the earth with the sharp ploughshare, the husbandman merely prepares it for the good seed of various kinds, which he then sows (vv. 24, 25); and secondly, at showing that in threshing the grain he does this with no more severity, and no longer, than the grain in question will bear without bruising (vv. 26–28). In this the prophet sees, not merely an accidental similarity, but a divinely-appointed symbol of what God does in His dealings with men, for he expressly refers this conduct of the husbandman to God's ordinance (ver. 29, and also in ver. 26, if we translate there, "and he prepares it according to the law which his God teaches him;" cf. Drechsler here). In the proceedings of the husbandman in the field he sees the truth symbolized, that God causes His blessings to follow the sharp chastisements with which he visits men, after the way of the one has been prepared by the

---

[1] Cf. Christ's parable of the Mustard Seed.
[2] Cf. Christ's parables of the Great Supper and Royal Marriage-Feast.

other; and in the proceeding of the thresher with the grain, that God will not chastise men longer and more severely than they are able to bear, and than is needful for the purpose of chastisement. Here, then, is a twofold symbolic parable which, without deserving the name of parable in the strict sense, shows, next to the two parabolic narratives of the Old Testament already quoted, most affinity with the parables of Christ.

A series of parabolic narratives is found also in the Rabbins of the Talmud, exceedingly like the parables of Christ in form, save, of course, that they bear no sort of comparison with the latter either in depth and truth of meaning, or in simplicity and convincing force of representation. This applies even to those among them which show a striking resemblance to certain parables of Christ. This circumstance has been explained by supposing either that Christ used current Rabbinical parables, improving and deepening their meaning for His purposes, or that the authors of the Rabbinical parables knew and used the Gospels, or again from mere accident, and therefore from the mere accidental employment of the same figurative circumstances as instruments of representation for a like didactic purpose. The latter supposition, however, is not sufficient everywhere. To me the supposition, that certain leading forms and phrases in several parables of Christ passed over into Rabbinical tradition without consciousness of their origin, seems best to correspond to the mutual relations of the parables in question. Two instances may be given here, in which the resemblance is the most striking. They may serve, as examples of the Rabbinical parables generally, to show the vast distance which, with all the conformity, exists between them and the parables of the Lord. The one certainly is merely related to a comparison of Christ, not to a proper parabolic narrative; but just here the similarity is closest. Compare with Christ's parabolic saying of the wise man who built his house on the rock, and the foolish man who built on the sand (Matt. vii. 24–27), the following one of Rabbi Nathan from the treatise Aboth:[1] "Si quis opera bona habet multumque in lege didicit, is similis est homini, qui domum ita exstruit, ut inferius saxa ponat, iis vero postea laterales imponat. Licet postmodum aquæ multæ veniant et ad latus ipsorum consistant, tamen illa loco movere non possunt. Homo vero, qui non habet

---

[1] Quoted by Unger, *De Parabolarum Jesu natura*, p. 157, from Schoettgen, *Horæ Talm.*

bona opera multumque legi operam dedit, similis est ei, qui inferius lateres collocet, iis vero saxa imponat; si aquæ sensim tantum adveniunt, statim illam evertunt." Whereas, therefore, Jesus simply contrasts building on the sand with building on the rock, here the scarcely conceivable "bricks below and stones above" is artificially contrasted with the " stones below and bricks above." And as concerns the thing compared, hearing and doing (in reference to hearing and not doing the words of Christ) are mechanically changed into multum in lege discere and bona opera habere (or non habere). Further, compare with Christ's parabolic narrative of the Labourers in the Vineyard the following one from the treatise Berachoth (*Gem. Hieros.*):[1] "Cum R. Abia f. Chiæ mortuus esset, R. Seira adventans concionem habebat, quod R. Abia paucis diebus tantum profuerit, quantum alii vix multis annis. Subjecit parabolam hanc: Erat rex qui conduxit operarios. Eratque ibi operarius rectius agens in opera sua præ omnibus. Ecquid fecit ipsi rex? Secum eum tulit, atque cum eo ambulavit hinc illinc. Tempore vesperæ congregabantur operarii ad auferendam mercedem, atque hic etiam mercedem suam accepit, æque ac ipsi. Murmurarunt autem operarii, dicentes: nos defatigati sumus toto die, et hic nonnisi duabus horis.[2] Respondit Dominus: hic duabus horis plus laboravit, quam vos toto die." Here too, with all the similarity, what a distance between this parable and that of Christ! Whereas Christ contrasts the sovereign freedom of divine grace, which gives to the last as to the first, with all such mechanical reckoning as would make the more or less of human performance the standard for measuring the divine reward, in the Rabbinical parable this thought is so superficialized and distorted as, with the mechanical measuring of the reward by the standard of the *time* of labour, to contrast, as the professedly divine standard, merely the just as mechanical measuring of the reward by the standard of the *amount* of labour done. Other Rabbinical parables, which have been ranked with the New-Testament ones of the Merciful Samaritan, the Rich Man, the Ten Virgins, etc., have, in fact, merely incidental traits in common with them.

After thus defining the idea of the parable as a narrative expressly imagined for the purpose of representing a religious truth in a pictorial figure, we need not specially inquire into the *purpose* of the parabolic form of teaching. It is one lying in the

[1] Unger, *ut ante.*   [2] Cf. Matt. xx. 10–12.

nature of the parable, namely, *to present directly to the hearer's view the teaching to be imparted*, either by exhibiting it in the concrete image of the individual case (typical parables), or in a symbol taken from the world of nature or man (symbolic parables). The parable is therefore essentially pictorial instruction. But there are two different cases, which make the employment of the parabolic mode of teaching necessary or useful, in place of the abstract and direct. Either an inadequate degree of the power of apprehension is presupposed in the hearers, incapacitating them for understanding the teaching to be imparted, or an evil tendency of the will, disclining them to receive it. In the former case, the parable serves the purpose of facilitating the apprehension of the teaching even to feeble power of intelligence; and in the second case, of convincing even the reluctant will of its truth. The former purpose naturally predominates in the parables spoken by Jesus to His disciples, the second in those spoken to His enemies. It is self-evident that the two coalesce in so far as the intellectual is combined with a moral defect, or conversely the moral with an intellectual. But whichever of the two preponderates, the primary end everywhere is to place the doctrine, as yet unknown to the hearers, so directly before their eyes, that they shall *intuitively* recognise its truth. And as to the other ends alleged, as, for example, that the parable is meant to excite attention, awaken reflection, impress the memory, or even to soften the harshness of unwelcome truths by temperateness of form,[1] these are only single elements, subordinate to that general and everywhere identical end. The last-named element especially is only present in so far as the parable, even where it speaks most harshly to opponents, always does this with the intention of convincing them, and is therefore never absolutely repellent, but always appeals to a remnant of susceptibility to the truth in their own conscience.

Certainly another purpose of the parable, which has been put on a level with that first and primary one, as if it held good just as generally and were just as necessarily grounded in the nature of the parable, is of a directly opposite kind. The parable, it is supposed, is meant to do two things, namely, to reveal the truth to the receptive, and to conceal it from the unreceptive.[2] But,

[1] Cf. Lisco, de Valenti, Lange in Herzog's *Encycl.*, art. "Gleichniss."
[2] So Weiss, *Zeitschr. f. christl. Wissenschaft*, 1861, p. 322, and Lisco, de Valenti, Lange, *ut ante;* Keil, etc.

stated thus generally, this assertion is incorrect, for it is far from applying to all the parables. Under this head, of course, merely the symbolic parables can come into account at all, since the merely typical ones possess no figurative veil, such as might operate as a means not merely of illustration, but also of concealment, and might serve the author for this end. How, for example, can any one conceive to himself that in the example of the Merciful Samaritan, by which the Lord so strikingly illustrates the true meaning of the command to love one's neighbour, He also meant to conceal it? But even among the symbolic parables, which actually clothe what they wish to say in a figurative dress, so that along with the purpose of illustration an intention of concealment is also possible and conceivable, there is still a series, in which as matter of fact no intention of this kind is present along with the other. Such is the case with all those which Jesus uttered, not before a mixed circle of hearers, but simply before a narrower circle of His disciples, as, for example, that of the Treasure in the Field, the Costly Pearl, the Fishing Net, and a series of others; for here, while the narrative does not lack the figurative veil, which might serve to conceal, the persons are wanting among the hearers, to whom the purpose of concealment could apply. But even those parables, in which Jesus does not address His disciples and adherents, but His opponents,—the Pharisees or Sanhedrists,—in order to strike at their conscience and convince them (as, *e.g.*, that of the Great Feast, the Wicked Labourers in the Vineyard, the Royal Marriage-Feast, etc.), cannot possibly mean also to conceal from them what is meant to be said to them. Moreover, in many parables the symbolic veil is so transparent, or it is so directly drawn aside by the appended explanatory statement of the Lord Himself, that for this reason there can be no question of an intention to conceal anything by them. The former, *e.g.*, is the case in the parable of the Lost Son, the latter in that of the Importunate Friend, the Unmerciful Servant, etc. On the other hand, certainly the intention to conceal is definitely expressed in the first series of parables, which Jesus spoke both to His disciples and a mixed crowd of people on the shore of the Sea of Tiberias. Here He purposely chose the parabolic form of teaching, for the double purpose of disclosing the mysteries of the kingdom of heaven to His disciples on the one hand by means of symbolic illustration, and on the other hand of hiding them from the dull-minded populace by means of the figurative dress. That this was His intention, He says Himself to His disciples in the answer to the question : " Why speakest Thou unto them in parables ? "[1] But both question and answer primarily refer merely to the case in hand, which is very significantly distinguished from all other cases in which Jesus uses the parable, by the circumstance, that here only does Jesus give a series of parables in continuous discourse, without prefixing to them any introductory saying, or linking them together by any intermediate remarks, or appending to them any explanatory statement. That this method of speaking exclusively in a series of unconnected, closely successive parables was peculiarly strange in Christ's teaching at that time, is shown by the special concluding remark recurring in all three evangelists :[2] ταῦτα πάντα ἐλάλησεν . . . ἐν παραβολαῖς τοῖς ὄχλοις καὶ χωρὶς παραβολῆς οὐδὲν ἐλάλει αὐτοῖς. It is certainly true that the same intention, which according to the Lord's own saying then led to the choice of the parabolic form of teaching, may have influenced Him also in other similar cases. But, at any rate, it only follows from this, that in *special cases before a mixed circle of hearers* Jesus combined with the above-mentioned chief end, lying in the nature of the parable, the other end of concealing by figurative clothing from the unreceptive and impenitent, disclosures suited only to receptive and earnest hearers, in the spirit of His saying : " Give not that which is holy to the dogs, neither cast ye your pearls before swine " (Matt. vii. 6).

Let us now come nearer to the matter lying before us for treatment. This matter embraces the parables of Jesus in the strict sense of the word already explained. It offers itself to us in the synoptical Gospels exclusively. The Gospel of John contains no parabolic narrative. Even here, indeed, more or less extended symbolic comparisons are not wanting in our Lord's discourses. This holds good in one passage of the mysterious blowing of the wind (iii. 8), in another of the refreshing power of water (iv. 10-14), and again of nourishing bread (vi. 27-35, 47-58), or the grain of wheat deposited in the earth (xii. 24), or the work of sowing and reaping (iv. 35-38), or the relation of the vine to the branches (xv. 1-8), or that of the shepherd to the sheep (x. 1-16), etc., as symbols of like things in the sphere

---

[1] Matt. xiii. 11-17 and parallels.
[2] Matt. xiii. 34 and parallels. Cf. the exposition.

of the spiritual life. But everywhere these comparisons only occur in the shape of parabolic maxim or more extended parabolic discourse, without anywhere assuming the shape of parabolic narrative. All the more frequently does the latter meet us in the first three Gospels, especially in Matthew and Luke. And here, indeed, three groups at once strike the eye, embracing all the parables of this kind. First, the first series of parables delivered together by Jesus, according to the account of Matthew, chap. xiii., on one day at Capernaum, and to which the accounts of the other evangelists supply partial parallels. Secondly, the series of parables recorded by Luke as examples of the teaching of Jesus in the section forming the centre of his Gospel, and usually, although erroneously, taken as the account of Christ's last journey to Jerusalem. They are almost all peculiar to Luke's Gospel. Finally, the series of parables belonging to the Last Period of Christ's teaching and work, and contained in chaps. xviii.–xxv. of Matthew's Gospel,—these again, for the most part, are peculiar to this Gospel. Thus, if we simply follow the order of the parables in the accounts of the evangelists, a chronological point of view naturally presents itself from which to arrange the matter, namely: 1. *The First Series of Parables at Capernaum;* 2. *The Later Parables according to Luke;* 3. *The Parables of the Last Period.* To the first series we also add in its place the parable (Mark iv. 26–29) of the Growing Seed, or, more correctly, of the Fruit-bearing Earth, which takes the place in Mark's parallel account of the parable of the Tares in Matthew. For although the character of narrative, which we have seen to be the distinctive mark of the parable in the strict sense, is wanting to the former parable peculiar to Mark, not only as regards contents, but also as regards form, still it cannot be passed over in a connected investigation of the first series of parables in Capernaum. Standing as it does midway between the parable of the Sower and that of the Mustard Seed as a description of a similar kind, it yet forms a whole of itself as original as it is complete. This one being added to the seven in Matthew, the first series will embrace eight parables. With the second series, beginning with the parable of the Merciful Samaritan (Luke x.), that of the Two Debtors, found in Luke vii., might have been connected. But it is so closely interwoven with the narrative of the woman that was a sinner, who anointed the Lord's feet in the house of Simon the Pharisee, and, consisting only of the one trait that a creditor forgave his two debtors their debt,—to the one a great debt, to the other a small one (vv. 41, 42),—it forms so clearly the mere basis of the longer address delivered thereupon by Jesus to Simon (vv. 43–47), that it cannot with propriety be treated apart as an independent passage. Thus the second series of the Later Parables, according to Luke, will be composed of the following: the Merciful Samaritan (chap. x.), the Importunate Friend (chap. xi.), the Rich Fool (chap. xii.), the Fig-Tree (chap. xiii.), the Great Feast (chap. xiv.); then the group of five parables in chaps. xv., xvi.: the Lost Sheep, the Lost Coin, the Lost Son, the Unjust Steward, the Rich Man; finally, in chap. xviii. follow the two parables of the Unjust Judge and the Pharisee and Publican,—altogether, therefore, twelve parables. The parable of the Pounds, given by Luke in chap. xix., after he has actually begun in chap. xviii. 31 a continuous account of the last journey of Jesus through Jericho to Jerusalem, belongs to the parables of the Last Period, and thus to the third series. And since this parable, although belonging in Luke to another and somewhat earlier situation, is very similar both as regards its figurative form and its contents to Matthew's parable of the Talents, which forms in the latter evangelist the conclusion of the series of parables of the Last Period, in this third series, which will comprise the parables of the Last Period, we follow first of all the chronological lines of Matthew's account, in order next in the last place to combine with the exposition of the Talents in Matthew that of Luke's parable of the Pounds. Accordingly, the third series will consist of the following parables: the Unmerciful Servant (Matt. xviii.), the Labourers in the Vineyard (chap. xx.), the Wicked Labourers (chap. xxi. with parallels in Mark and Luke). Immediately before the last-mentioned in Matthew stands the short and simple parable of the Two Dissimilar Sons of a Father (xxi. 28–30), with the explanatory application made at once by Jesus Himself (vv. 31, 32), which will be touched on in the introduction to the exposition of the parable of the Wicked Labourers. Next follows the Royal Marriage-Feast (chap. xxii.), so essentially different from the similar parable in Luke of the Great Supper belonging to the second series, that we leave each one in its own place. Finally, in chap. xxv. we have the parable of the Ten Virgins and the Talents, and along with the latter Luke's parable of the Pounds (Luke xix.),—altogether seven parables in this third series. Sometimes also Christ's prediction of the Judgment of the Son of Man at His coming in glory (xxv. 31–46), which follows immediately upon those two last parables in the twenty-fifth chapter of Matthew, has been reckoned among the parables, and in the wider sense rightly, since it is a prophetic parabolic discourse. But it does not belong to the parabolic *narratives* with which we have to do. For the same reason also parabolic discourses like that of building on rock and on sand (Matt. vii. 24–27), the cost of building a tower (vv. 31, 32), the servants looking for their lord (Luke xii. 35–38), the good or bad steward (vv. 42–46 ; Matt. xxiv. 45–51), etc., are excluded from discussion, because they are either not narrative or furnish no connected narrative. It is thus, for example, with the first-mentioned one of building on rock and on sand, which certainly assumes a narrative-form, but not in order to give a connected history, but only to place in contrast the proceedings of two builders and the different result of their proceedings, without the two men being otherwise placed in any relation to each other.

In following the division just indicated, we renounce the attempt to take as the basis of our discussion of the parables a classification of them according to their contents. Such attempts indeed have been made in various forms.[1] But in all attempts of this kind one is compelled first of all to acknowledge that they lack a scientific aim, and therefore scientific value. They would only have such value if the end in view were to formulate on Biblical and theological grounds the special doctrinal system of the parables of Jesus. But in relation to the work of Biblical theology the parables can only come into view as an integral constituent of the synoptical discourses of Jesus generally. If Biblical theology desired to settle the doctrinal system of the latter, it is impossible to separate the parables delivered by Jesus

---

[1] *E.g.* by Lisco, de Valenti, Arndt, Lange, etc., and by each in a different manner. Lisco distinguishes three main classes of parables : 1. Such as describe the kingdom of heaven as a divine force ; 2. Such as represent it as a Church founded by the divine forces of the Word ; 3. Such as consider the members of the kingdom as regards disposition, walk, and destiny. In de Valenti there are two main classes: 1. Such as treat of the kingdom of heaven in the proper sense as a vast moral association ; 2. Such as treat of it in the improper sense, and represent it as the inner moral condition of the members of the kingdom. Arndt comprises his studies of the parables under three heads: 1. The glory of the kingdom of heaven ; 2. Conditions of entrance into the kingdom ; 3. Hindrances. Finally, Lange tries to point out a threefold cycle : 1. The seven parables showing, as is supposed, the historical development of the kingdom of God from the beginning to the end ; 2. Such as depict the government of divine grace ; 3. Such as depict God's judicial righteousness.

at different times and on various occasions from the non-parabolic discourses. Thus, the only scientific justification for a separate treatment of the parables, apart from practical needs, is simply their peculiar *form*, which requires a correspondingly peculiar method of exposition; but this does not justify us in assuming a doctrinal *import* peculiar to them in contrast with the other discourses of Jesus. It is said, indeed, that the kingdom of God is the central idea of the parables, and consequently Christ's teaching about the kingdom of God is contained in them. But the kingdom of God is precisely the central idea of Christ's teaching generally. And a direct reference to the idea of the kingdom of God is wanting not merely in many non-parabolic discourses, but just as much also in many parables. The only value, therefore, of such attempts is, that they give a synopsis of the parables, arranged in the order of their contents with more or less success; and in this sense such an attempt may be made here. While retaining the central idea of the kingdom of God, we distinguish between such parables as describe the kingdom of God in its nature and development, and such as refer to the conduct of its members, either exhorting to what is right, or warning against the opposite. The first class, again, falls into—1. Such as have for their subject the founding of God's kingdom by the actual labour of Jesus; 2. Such as describe the progressive development of the kingdom actually founded; 3. Such as relate to the future completion of the kingdom at the end of its temporal development. In the same way the second class, bearing on the conduct of the members of the kingdom, falls again into—1. Such as relate to their conduct to God; 2. Such as relate to their conduct to the world. The scheme here given is certainly simple and clear, and all the parables enumerated above may without difficulty be included in it as follows:—

I. Nature and Development of the Kingdom of God.

1. Founding of the Kingdom.
    The Sower, or Divers Soils: The result of preaching dependent on the hearers.
2. Development of the Kingdom.
    a. The Immediate Future.
        The Fig-Tree: Last respite for Israel.
        The Great Supper: } From the Jews to the Gentiles.
        The Wicked Labourers:

b. The Entire Development to the End.
   The Fruit-bearing Earth (Mark iv.): Through the personal labour of members of the kingdom.
   The Tares: Intermingling of impure elements.
   The Mustard-Seed: } Growth until the whole world is
   The Leaven: } embraced, Interpenetration.
   The Fishing-Net: First gathering, then sifting.
   The Royal Marriage-Feast: First called, then nevertheless rejected.

3. Completion of the Kingdom.
   The Ten Virgins: Exclusion of those not found ready at the hour of Christ's coming.
   The Labourers in the Vineyard: Strange adjudging of the reward in the future kingdom.
   The Pounds in Trust: } The reward of faithfulness and
   The Talents in Trust: } punishment of unfaithfulness in the future kingdom.

II. The Right Conduct of Members of the Kingdom.

1. Towards God.
   The Pharisee and the Publican: Humility before God.
   The Treasure in the Field: } Such delight in God as
   The Pearl of Great Price: } sacrifices everything for the highest good.
   The Importunate Friend: } Perseverance in prayer to
   The Unjust Judge: } God.

2. Towards the World.
   a. To Men.
      The Merciful Samaritan: Practical proof of love for one's neighbour to one needing help.
      The Unmerciful Servant: Unlimited placability towards wrong-doers.
      The Lost Sheep: }
      The Lost Coin: } Unselfish delight in the sinner's conversion.[1]
      The Lost Son: }
   b. To Earthly Goods.
      The Rich Fool (Luke xii.): Folly of reliance on perishable goods.

---

[1] The justification of this classification as to this and all the other parables can, of course, only be supplied by the exposition.

The Rich Man (Luke xvi.): Selfish employment of earthly wealth criminal.

The Unjust Steward: Wise employment of temporal means in reference to eternity.

But however attractive such a classification may be in appearance, it must always be unsuited to be the basis of an exegetical treatment of the entire material. Directly this is done, two evil results follow, which place such a course at a disadvantage beside the one proposed by us. In following the path marked out for him by an arrangement according to the matter, the exegete is compelled, whenever he approaches a new parable, to assume its doctrinal import, and therefore to assume the result which is the aim of his entire work beforehand as a text. The only use in this case of the exposition itself is to serve as a supplementary proof of a result already given, instead of, as it ought, interesting the reader in the work, perhaps conducting him step by step to new results, and enlisting his convictions on their side. But even if this is not thought mischievous, the other evil result remains, which is certainly more serious in character, namely, that in following such a systematic division the exegete is compelled to break up the connected groups found in the Gospels in favour of the scheme laid down by himself, and thus to tear a considerable number of single parables from the relation in which they stand to each other. Thus, in de Valenti, the parable of the Fishing-Net in the group Matt. xiii. is placed beside that of the Ten Virgins in the eschatological discourse Matt. xxv.; and finally, the parable of the Sower, the first in Matt. xiii., is placed among the last on his scheme, side by side with that of the Unjust Steward in the group Luke xv., xvi. And on the scheme advanced by Lisco, the parable of the Tares in Matt. xiii. is placed beside that of the Royal Marriage-Feast in chap. xxii. Even a Lange has not succeeded, although plainly he has not kept this aim in view in the interest of his scheme of division, in framing an arrangement of the parables according to their contents which coincides with the groups found in the Gospels and with the order of the particular parables there given. Even he (*e.g.*) is compelled to pass by two of Luke's parables—that of the Rich Fool and the Fig-Tree—and place them at last among the final parables in Matthew. And so, on the classification attempted by us, it was impossible to avoid dislocating and throwing into confusion the groups of parables joined together in the text. And if, nevertheless, the context in which the particular parable stands is to have justice done to it, considering its essential importance so often to the exposition, wearisome repetitions are unavoidable, without compensation being really obtained for the loss of a coherently progressive exposition of the groups of parables given in the text.

Before passing to the exposition itself, it still remains to settle its *method*. The fact that fixed principles and a certain method are still for the most part wanting in the exposition of the parables is incontestable.[1] Certainly the general principle, that every particular ingredient in a parable must not be interpreted separately, that, on the contrary, in explaining a parable, its essential elements must be held fast, is too obvious for general agreement to be wanting on this point; and every expositor is compelled occasionally to appeal to such a principle. Chrysostom early gave apt expression to this general rule with special reference to the parable in Matt. xx. 1–16: οὐδὲ χρὴ πάντα τὰ ἐν ταῖς παραβολαῖς κατὰ λέξιν περιεργάζεσθαι, ἀλλὰ τὸν σκόπον μαθόντες, δι' ὃν συνετέθη, τοῦτον δρέπεσθαι καὶ μηδὲν πολυπραγμονεῖν περαιτέρω. But however great the agreement on this general principle, the manner and extent in which it is applied differ in almost every parable and every expositor; and thus, considering the want of unity and certainty existing in the explanation of the parables, scarcely anything has been gained by the acknowledgment of this canon.

We have accordingly to seek *more definite rules* for interpreting the parables, and for this end take into consideration the two bypaths into which interpretation may fall. The first of these bypaths, and the most commonly frequented one, is the *transgression* of the due bounds of interpretation by confounding the edifying application of a parable with the simple original sense which the parable had in the mouth of Jesus in relation to those to whom He delivered it. Although particular features in a parable may here and there lend themselves obviously to a definite application to Christian life, or serve suitably and strikingly as a figurative representation of definite Christian truths or particular facts of the sacred history, this by no means proves that they had this sense originally in the context of the

---

[1] Cf. Weiss, *Marcus-evangelium*, preface, p. v.

parable. On the contrary, the interpretation of a parable is often led grievously astray through an expositor at the outset isolating a certain particular, assigning it a meaning perhaps exceedingly probable, although not in fact originally intended, and then finding himself compelled to bring everything else into unison therewith. In opposition to such a course, the simple principle is to be most rigidly maintained: "Nihil amplius quærendum est quam quod tradere Christi consilium fuit."[1] In interpreting a parable, we must first of all ask what Jesus meant to say to those to whom He delivered it, what doctrine, exhortation, or warning He meant to give; and with strict reservation of this point of view, we must judge how far the particulars in the parable require, according to the fundamental plan, a definite counterpart in the interpretation, and, in effect, how they are to be interpreted.

But, of course, we must not make too light of such judgment. Were we to be content with the general purpose of the parable, and then lightly to pass over its particulars, so far as their interpretation did not readily fit into the compass of the general purpose, simply taking them for byplay and ornament, we should merely fall into the opposite bypath. *Strictly understood, there is no mere byplay and empty ornament in the parables of Jesus.* This second principle must be everywhere maintained as a supplement to the first one. For we can nowhere seriously accept the opinion that Jesus wove particular ingredients into His parables which serve no purpose, or no other purpose than to give the narrative a more pleasing outward form. On the contrary, it must be presupposed that all particulars in a parable, in so far as they are not meant to find a special counterpart in the interpretation, have nevertheless some important position of their own in the connection of the whole, and thus serve the end of the whole, either helping by delineation in detail to picture a truth vividly, or fitting as essential ingredients into the systematic structure of the narrative. The expositor must therefore never say that this or that particular lies outside the compass of the intended comparison, and therefore cannot be explained, without at the same time indicating what purpose it serves in its place in the connection of the whole.

But if, in the application of these principles, the problem of ascertaining the original meaning of a parable with equal purity

[1] Calvin on Matt. xx. 1-16.

and completeness is to be really solved with approximate certainty, the exposition must pursue such a *logical course* as is dictated by the nature of the problem. And the course which seems to me to be prescribed to the expositor of a parable by the nature of his task, because leading most accurately and certainly to the goal, is the following.

Before approaching the parable itself, we must first of all settle with the greatest possible exactness, so far as the text supplies indications on the point, on what occasion, or in what connection, and to whom Jesus uttered the parable. Next, we must follow the figurative history itself in its natural course, word by word and step by step, seeking in the first instance everywhere to understand the simple verbal sense lying in the sphere of physical or human life, without entering at present, as is commonly done, on the field of interpretation, without asking in every verse and at every step what is meant to be symbolized,—to speak generally, without letting ourselves be disturbed and misled in the understanding of its course and connection by thoughts of the interpretation and its supposed difficulties. For only by thus putting aside prejudice, and letting the narrative in its natural course up to the conclusion, on which everything depends, influence us, is a secure basis laid for a consistent interpretation of the parable. Now, in such a consecutive study of the text as to its verbal sense, those ingredients in the figurative history, which decisively influence its inner course, and therefore form its essential contents, and also those which merely serve the purpose of pictorial delineation or the formation of its outward structure, will spontaneously stand forth before the expositor in their true character; and thus the necessary postulates will be gained for solving, in the next place, easily and surely, all *merely apparent* difficulties in the work of interpretation on the basis of such previous labour. And, on the other hand, in this way the danger will be avoided at the outset of getting rid of *real* difficulties, which the interpretation perhaps presents, by forcing on the text of the narrative a sense which its literal meaning of itself does not give, for the sake of the interpretation which we think ourselves bound to bring out.

But even after having thus laid the secure basis for interpreting the parable, we cannot yet enter immediately on its specific interpretation, but must first ascertain, in the third place, its general didactic purpose, by comparing the course and contents of the narrative thus discovered with what may previously have been settled respecting the connection in which Jesus delivered it, and the persons to whom it was delivered. In the case of most parables an interpreting statement of Jesus, appended to the figurative history, aids the exposition.

And now only, after we are certain of the purpose lying at the basis of the whole, and of the point of view under which the whole must be placed, can the proper interpretation be carried out in detail, and that with unbroken continuity. The exposition will again strike back to the beginning of the figurative history,[1] and, following it once more step by step to its conclusion, will estimate each one of its particular elements in its significance for the whole, and set the thing symbolized in definite contrast with the symbol.

[1] [Figurative history or figurative story is always, of course, = figurative narrative.]

PART I.

THE FIRST SERIES OF PARABLES IN CAPERNAUM.

The Parables to the People by the Sea.

(Matt. xiii. 1, 2, 10-17.)

IN the thirteenth chapter of St. Matthew's Gospel we meet with the first series of parables, to which the fourth chapter of St. Mark's Gospel supplies an obvious, although incomplete, parallel both as to situation and contents.[1] And indeed, in agreement with Mark iv. 1, Matthew (vv. 1, 2) relates the precise circumstances in which Jesus spoke the following parables, *i.e.*, according to him, first of all the four recounted in the paragraph vv. 3–33. But in beginning to give this account the evangelist expressly mentions that what follows took place "on that day," therefore on the same day to which the events related previously belong. If, then, we inquire what these events were, the way in which both the paragraph chap. xii. 46–50 and that reaching from vv. 38 to 45 are closely connected with the preceding vv. 22–37—the former by ἔτι αὐτοῦ λαλοῦντος, the latter by τότε ἀπεκρίθησαν αὐτῷ—refers us back to ver. 22. Regarded from this standpoint, Matthew's account gives us the following picture of the previous events of the day: Jesus had healed one possessed with a devil in the presence of the people, upon which the Pharisees, in order to suppress the commotion thus excited among the people, spread abroad the charge, that He only cast out devils through Beelzebub, their prince, vv. 22–24. Jesus had then rebuked the Pharisees for this blasphemy in severe

---

[1] The parallel in St. Luke (viii. 4 ff.) gives only the first of the parables, and according to ver. 4 represents it as merely addressed to a great crowd of people in general.

language, which culminated in the warning against the sin of blasphemy against the Holy Ghost, for which there is no forgiveness, vv. 25–37. And when some of them demanded of Him a special miraculous sign in evidence of His authority, ver. 38, His complaint had extended from them over the entire contemporary generation as one which merely asked after signs (in this taking up the keynote of its leaders), more impenitent than the heathen Ninevites in the days of Jonah, and less earnest about salvation than the Queen of the South in the days of Solomon, vv. 39–42; a generation, therefore, whose merely superficial and transient awakening from wickedness would end in a far worse state than the one in which it was before, vv. 43–45. But while He was yet speaking to the people, word was brought Him that His mother and brethren stood without desiring to speak to Him, vv. 46, 47, which gave Him occasion—in notable contrast with the previous language of rebuke to the people and to His tempters—to acknowledge His disciples (in the wider sense, cf. Mark iii. 33–35) as His mother and brethren, because they did the will of His Father in heaven, vv. 48–50.

This glance at the previous events of the day, suggested to us by the evangelist himself by the words "on that day," sets in a clear light the kind of success which Christ's public work had so far met with, and indicates the feelings of Jesus at this time, and especially on the day on which He uttered the following parables. It was a time of division and decision. On the one side stood the Pharisees, who had already well-nigh advanced to the extremest degree of obduracy, and the mass of the people, who, while crowding around Him from curiosity and eagerness after miracles, showed themselves increasingly insensible to His call to repentance, and increasingly unsusceptible to His preaching of the kingdom; and, on the other side, a little band of disciples, separating themselves from the rest and gathering around Him, with whom He knew and felt Himself to be in intimate union, because they were ready to do the will of His Father.

We have thus to think of Jesus as under the influence of these circumstances when it is said of Him (xiii. 1): "On that day went Jesus out of the house (*scil.* out of the house where He was accustomed to dwell, and where also the events of this day previously related took place [1]), and sat by the (Galilean)

---

[1] Cf. the ἔξω, xii. 46 and Mark iii. 19.

sea." This going out, however, is not viewed as following immediately on the events related in chap. xii. In that case a different mode of connection with what precedes would have been chosen from the actual one, which merely notices the identity of the day. Nay, Jesus has meantime dismissed the people, as ver. 2 shows. On going out He is not from the first accompanied and beset by a multitude of people, but at first is only followed by the small band of disciples so intimately united with Him. To give Himself up to friendly converse with them will be a refreshment to Him after the toilsome, exciting work of the day. For this reason He sits down in their midst by the seaside. That we are right in understanding the ἐκάθητο (ver. 1), not of taking a seat apart in order to rest, but of a teacher sitting amid a circle of hearers, follows from ver. 2 : καὶ συνήχθησαν πρὸς αὐτὸν ὄχλοι πολλοί, ὥστε αὐτὸν εἰς πλοῖον ἐμβάντα καθῆσθαι, καὶ πᾶς ὁ ὄχλος ἐπὶ αἰγιαλὸν εἱστήκει. The καθῆσθαι in ver. 2 plainly resumes the ἐκάθητο in ver. 1. The ἐκάθητο there must therefore be understood in the same sense as the καθῆσθαι here, which is a taking a seat in order to teach. So many people gathered round Him—such is the meaning of the account—that He found Himself compelled to exchange the seat taken at first on the sea-shore for another more suited to the increased number of hearers. And thus He went into a boat lying near the strand,[1] and sat down there, where He was saved from the pressure of the crowd, whilst the latter, spreading along the shore (ἐπὶ τὸν αἰγιαλόν), were able to keep the speaker in view. Thus, sitting opposite the people, He discoursed to them.

But before the evangelist repeats the discourse of Jesus, he calls attention to its peculiarity, ver. 3 : "And He spake to them many things in *parables*." And, in fact, a glance at the discourse thus introduced makes the "speaking in parables," such as is found here, seem strange enough. Without any preparation in the hearers for the subject to be treated of, the discourse begins at once with a figurative history ; and when this is finished, Jesus does not even add any word of interpretation or application, such as might be likely to give the hearers a key to the hidden meaning of the figurative language. Rather, in merely adding, ver. 9 : ὁ ἔχων ὦτα ἀκουέτω (*i.c.* he that has capacity for doing so, let him mark and learn the meaning of

[1] Cf. Mark iv. 1.

the discourse), it is as if He wished expressly to put aside their eager desire for explanation. And the strangeness of this observation is enhanced when, looking beyond the paragraph (vv. 10–23) interposed here (as will be shown afterwards merely for incidental reasons), we consider the discourse of Jesus up to its conclusion. For alongside the first parable appears at once a second (vv. 24–30), unconnected with the former by remark between; and just in the same unconnected way a third follows on the second (vv. 31, 32), and a fourth on the third (ver. 33), each one merely linked to the preceding one by the remark of the narrator: "Another parable set He before them" or "spake He unto them," and introduced by the speaker himself simply by "the kingdom of heaven is likened," or "is like," and then worded in such figurative form that the veil of the figurative language is nowhere lifted. And that we must not put this strange way of speaking in parables, and in parables loosely joined together, to the account of a redaction by the evangelist, who desired to weld a number of parables into one collection, that this strange method of teaching was rather just the distinctive feature of Christ's speaking to the people at this time, is expressly emphasized at the close of the discourse, ver. 34: ταῦτα πάντα ἐλάλησεν ὁ Ἰησοῦς ἐν παραβολαῖς τοῖς ὄχλοις, καὶ χωρὶς παραβολῆς οὐδὲν ἐλάλει αὐτοῖς. The emphasis of the first clause lies wholly on ἐν παραβολαῖς—how much, is shown by the second clause, in which the evangelist, still more minutely describing the mode of teaching referred to, and therefore continuing in the imperfect, says, that He spoke only in parables without any exception.[1] And this mode of speech is so significant to him, that he sees in it a fulfilment of Scripture, an

---

[1] The imperfect ἐλάλει, which Weiss (*Marcusev.* p. 165) finds so strange here, is, on the contrary, thoroughly in place. It might also stand in ver. 34a, and even in ver. 3, instead of the aorists there, because in both these passages as well the subject is not merely that Jesus spoke and what He spoke, but also the nature of His speaking. When, therefore, in Mark we actually find the imperfect in all the three parallel passages, we ought not, with Weiss, to draw the marvellous conclusion, that according to Mark the parables were not spoken in the situation definitely marked out in ver. 1, but are only introduced as an example of Christ's method of teaching generally. What then becomes of the picturesque situation described in ver. 1, which is left altogether floating in the air? And why should not Christ's method of teaching in a situation already definitely marked out be just as well described by the imperfect as His method of teaching generally? The language must then be supplementarily limited in some way, and that arbitrarily, because the χωρὶς παραβολῆς οὐκ ἐλάλει αὐτοῖς, ver. 34, does not apply absolutely to Christ's general mode of teaching.

antitypical analogue to the mode of speech in the seventy-eighth Psalm (ver. 35).

But if, as we are obliged to suppose after the express and unanimous declarations of the evangelists, this method of speaking exclusively in loosely-connected parables—we may even, with Strauss, call it an " overwhelming with parables "—was really the character of the discourse of Christ delivered to the people in the situation described in vv. 1, 2, a definite purpose on the part of the speaker must necessarily have underlain such a course; and it will not be without value for the understanding of the parables themselves, if we first assure ourselves why Jesus then spoke to the people in precisely this manner and no other. When, then, we compare the present method of parabolic speech with Christ's method of speaking in parables elsewhere, this difference at once strikes us, that everywhere else Jesus uses the parable, as its very nature implies, primarily as a means of illustration, in order by the figurative dress to bring the subject in hand directly home to the understanding and heart of His hearers, whether friends or foes. Hence the figurative history for the most part runs out into a non-figurative saying helpful to interpretation; whereas in the present method of speaking parabolically and only parabolically, passing rapidly from one figure to another in appearance without uniformity and connection, the primary purpose is not to bring the subject in hand home to the understanding of the hearers, but the very opposite purpose seems to prevail, namely, *to conceal the true subject by a veil of figurative language that is never lifted, and remove it to a distance from the understanding of the hearers.* And that this purpose was really the motive for choosing the present mode of teaching, we are assured by an express declaration on the point given by Christ to His disciples.

After the two evangelists Matthew and Mark have set down the first parable, they hasten to interrupt the recording of the discourse delivered to the people from the boat for the purpose of mentioning a later conversation between Jesus and His disciples, in which Jesus gave them information respecting the reason and aim of this parabolic teaching (vv. 10–17).[1] To this they naturally join the explanation of the first parable given by Jesus to the disciples in the same conversation (vv. 18–23).[2] Mark, moreover, adds two sayings of Jesus in reference to the

---

[1] Mark iv. 10–12. [2] Mark iv. 13–20.

information given to the disciples (iv. 21–25). Only then do the evangelists resume the discourse broken off after the first parable. That the conversation here mentioned only took place as matter of fact afterwards, is not merely specially noted by Mark, when he puts it in the time "when Jesus was alone" (ver. 10), and therefore after Jesus had ended His discourse to the people and dismissed them;[1] but it is also obvious from the question of the disciples introducing the conversation, because the wording of the question presupposes the delivery of a number of parables. According to Mark, the reason of Jesus giving the explanation in question was, that the disciples "asked Him about *the parables.*"[2] In Matthew the wording of the question introduces the answer more distinctly and with greater logical precision: "Why speakest Thou unto them (*scil.* unto the people) in parables?" (ver. 10). Thus questioned, Jesus replies to His disciples, that He does it because knowledge of the mysteries of the kingdom of heaven is vouchsafed by God only to them—the questioners, not to those, *i.e.* the multitude (ver. 11). The meaning then is, that in hiding the mysteries of the kingdom of heaven from their understanding by a figurative form of language, He is fulfilling a divine behest, according to which the knowledge of these mysteries is vouchsafed only to the disciples, but refused to the rest. This divine behest is based, as is explained in ver. 12, by $\gamma\acute{a}\rho$ on the general maxim, borrowed from the circumstances of earthly possessions, but also embodying a divine appointment: "Whosoever hath, to him shall be given, and he shall have more abundance; but whosoever hath not, from him shall be taken away even that he hath." The $\delta o\theta\acute{\eta}\sigma\epsilon\tau a\iota$ evidently explains the divinely-appointed $\delta\acute{\epsilon}\delta o\tau a\iota$ in ver. 11; and in the same way the still more intense $\dot{a}\rho\theta\acute{\eta}\sigma\epsilon\tau a\iota$ $\dot{a}\pi$' $a\dot{v}\tau o\hat{v}$ corresponds to the $o\dot{v}$ $\delta\acute{\epsilon}\delta o\tau a\iota$ in ver. 11. The sense, therefore, in which that general rule applies here is this: They who possess and manifest receptiveness and capacity of understanding for the word of the kingdom, shall be increasingly placed in a position for knowing the mysteries of the kingdom; while they who show themselves unreceptive and incapable of understanding, will be confirmed and hardened in their spiritual obtuseness until they reach the extremest degree of ignorance. This is God's appointment, and

---

[1] Cf. Matt. xiii. 36.
[2] The reading of the Rec. τὴν παραβολήν is clearly a correction for the strongly attested and original τὰς παραβολάς.

because it is God's appointment, "*therefore*" proceeds Jesus in ver. 13, recurring with the διὰ τοῦτο to vv. 11, 12, " Therefore speak I to them in parables, because they seeing see not, and hearing they hear not, neither do they understand." Thus, on the ground of the divine appointment declared in vv. 11, 12, He conceals from them—those incapable of understanding—the mysteries of the kingdom of heaven by figurative language, which apparently depicts before them merely sensuous things in confused succession, thus aggravating their state of seeing and yet not seeing, of hearing and yet not hearing, to the highest degree. And so the prophecy of Isaiah finds its fulfilment in them (vv. 14, 15),—quoted after the wording of the LXX., which differs from the original text,—in which the people are threatened with a state of hearing with the ears without hearing, and of seeing without seeing, because by hardening their hearts and stopping their ears and blinding their eyes they resisted conversion and the healing which it brings. It is now obvious of itself that when Mark (and Luke also in his wake), in whom the answer of Christ runs differently and more briefly, describes the inability to see and hear by ἵνα as the *end* which Christ has in view in the parabolic mode of teaching (iv. 12),[1] he does not thereby really contradict Matthew, in whom in ver. 13 it is described by ὅτι as the *reason* impelling Christ to this mode of teaching. For even in Matthew this state of inability to see and hear is not *merely* described as the reason of such teaching, but in its aggravation is also viewed as its end, according to the rule: " Whosoever hath not, from him shall be taken away even that he hath ; " and only by means of an utter exegetical perversion can we find in Matthew the opposite thought,—a thought, moreover, least of all compatible with the form which the parabolic discourse takes in him,—namely, that Jesus adapted Himself by the parabolic mode of teaching to the people's feebleness of apprehension in order to their further understanding and final conversion.[2] After Jesus has thus disposed of the question why He speaks to the people in parables, in contrast with the people given over to judicial blindness He pronounces the disciples all the more blessed (vv. 16, 17), because their eyes are permitted to see and their ears to hear what many prophets and righteous men desired in vain to see and hear, namely, those mysteries of the kingdom of heaven which it is

[1] Cf. Luke viii. 10.   [2] Meyer.

given to *them* to know. For this reason in ver. 18 He begins to explain to them, and only to them (ὑμεῖς οὖν), the figures concealing these mysteries.

To sum up the results of the previous investigation: when we remember the circumstances detailed in chap. xii., under the influence of which Jesus stood at that time, and especially on that day, on one hand seeing opposite Him His foes, the Pharisees, and the impenitent populace so unreceptive to His words, and on the other, embracing with all the greater affection, the small band of disciples gathered around Him; when we remember, further, the more precise circumstances in which this discourse of His was spoken,—how, sitting at first by the sea, surrounded by His disciples, He saw Himself compelled by the gathering of great numbers of people to address His discourse to them from the boat; and finally, when we compare herewith the strange, purely parabolic form of the discourse and the declarations on the subject given by Christ Himself to the disciples, declarations based entirely on the contrast between the disciples and the people,—from all this the purpose becomes clear with which Jesus begins to deliver the series of parables lying before us. Jesus wishes to unfold to His disciples—to the Twelve, and to those who, like them, have gathered round His person with penitent desire for salvation—the mysteries of the kingdom of God. But wishing to do this, He finds Himself, through the pressure of the crowd, in presence of listeners already hardened in impenitence against His former preaching of repentance and the kingdom, and therefore wholly unfitted to grasp with inner intelligence teachings which go farther and deeper. In order, then, to give the disciples the intended teachings, while still professing to be speaking to the people, who are unprepared for such teaching, He says what He wishes to say entirely in a series of parables, so that on one hand the multitude hear something without hearing or understanding, whilst the disciples on their part can either understand or fall back on the interpretation. Thus the exclusively parabolic form of the discourse here is designed for the multitude, whilst the contents belong to the disciples, and to them only. He desires to impart to them " the mysteries of the kingdom of heaven," *i.e.* the parables are meant to unfold to them new, previously unknown and unknowable truths respecting the nature and development of the kingdom of God.

We proceed, therefore, to consider the first of these.

The Sower,[1] or Divers Soils.

(Matt. xiii. 3–8, 18–23, and parallels.)

Arousing attention with "Behold," Jesus begins to narrate: "*Behold, the sower went forth to sow.*" Ὁ σπείρων is he whose calling it is to sow.[2] Hence we may translate "the sower," but not "a sower" (Luther), nor, which comes to the same thing, "the sower whom I have in view" (Meyer). The thought is not that of a certain individual sower, who did so and so in distinction from others, and who fared so and so. The subject is simply a sowing done by one whose business it is to sow.[3] In the sequel, also, the person of the sower is left out of sight. The narrative speaks simply of the fate of the seed sown, the different kinds of soil on which it fell, and the corresponding effect it produced. This account begins in ver. 4: "and as he sowed, some *seeds* fell by the wayside." Now this must not be understood to mean that as he sowed some grains of seed fell beyond the limits of the field *upon* the way leading past,[4] and therefore upon ground altogether outside the purpose of the sower,—a meaning also which παρὰ τὴν ὁδόν could not have, but which would require παρὰ τὸν ἀγρόν. It is self-evident that by παρὰ τὴν ὁδόν a portion of the field itself is meant to be characterized in accordance with the nature of its soil, namely, the strip of soil lying alongside the boundary-path, usually trodden hard and smooth by the feet of passers-by, so that the seed falling there is left lying on the hard surface. The consequence which may be expected is: "*and the birds came and devoured it.*" The hard-trodden edge of the field, because unable even to admit the seed dropped there into the bosom of the earth, exposes it by this very fact to speedy destruction; for, attracted by the grains lying exposed, the birds come and eat it up. And no less certain is its destruction in the other way, of which mention is made in Luke (viii. 5), along with and previous to the being eaten by birds, in the words καὶ κατεπατήθη. The seed beside the path must necessarily be crushed by the feet of the people passing and repassing afterwards as before.

---

[1] It will be seen in the following exposition that the author objects to this title. It is prefixed here simply in deference to English usage.

[2] Cf. 1 Cor. ix. 13: οἱ τὰ ἱερὰ ἐργαζόμενοι.

[3] On τοῦ σπείρειν, "to sow," cf. Winer, *Gram. N. T. Greek*, p. 408.

[4] Weiss, Lange, *et al.*

Of a different kind was the soil upon which another part of the seed fell (ver. 5): "*and others fell ἐπὶ τὰ πετρώδη*," *i.e.* upon the rocky parts of the field,—with the article, because the existence of such soil is assumed as something not unusual. This pregnant description is then more fully explained by the addition: "*where they had not much earth.*" Therefore, such soil is meant as under a slight layer of earth conceals massive rock, a kind of soil frequently met with on such shelving coasts as lay before the eyes of the speaker, which is therefore characterized in Luke (ver. 6), sufficiently for the hearers, by the brief ἐπὶ τὴν πέτραν without explanatory addition. The fate of what was sown there is what might be expected from soil of this kind: "*and straightway they sprung up, because they had no deepness of earth.*" Because the soil is wanting in depth, the grain is unable to strike root vigorously into the bosom of the earth before emerging into the light, but comes out and up forthwith, as is very strikingly described by the double compound ἐξανέτειλεν. With this apparently favourable beginning its ultimate fate stands in sad contrast (ver. 6): "*and when the sun was risen, they were scorched.*" The ἀνατέλλειν of the sun is here, as everywhere else, the sunrise, and cannot be arbitrarily changed into the higher ascent of the sun at mid-day or in summer.[1] The thought is simply this: The grain, so quickly sprung up, is unable to bear the risen sun, but, tender and weak as it is, is scorched by the sun's rays. "*And,*" so it is said further, "*because they had no root, they withered away.*" Thus, this second clause says that the grain, once scorched, is unable, having no vigorous roots in the bosom of the earth, to recover itself by drawing new moisture from the earth, but of necessity withers away utterly and for ever. Luke emphasizes the want of moisture (ver. 6) when, without mentioning the sun, he briefly says: καὶ φυὲν ἐξηράνθη διὰ τὸ μὴ ἔχειν ἰκμάδα.

The grain again finds another hindrance in the soil characterized in ver. 7: "*and others fell upon the thorns.*" As in Luke ἐπὶ τὴν πέτραν stood for ἐπὶ τὰ πετρώδη, so also here the hindrance to prosperity, hidden in the soil, is put for the soil itself. "Upon the thorns," is the same as "upon the thorny ground," under the surface of which a crop of thorns lies already concealed. The article is to be taken as in ver. 5. And in this way the fate of the seed is again decided, as the second half of the verse tells: "*and the thorns grew up and choked them.*" The word ἀναβαίνειν,

[1] Lange, Stier, *et al.*

like ἀνατέλλειν, of itself signifies primarily the coming up of the grain simply, not the shooting aloft.¹ But certainly as regards the thought, thorns being the matter in question, shooting up in rank luxuriance after the manner of thorns naturally joins on to the ἀναβαίνειν, so that καὶ ἀπέπνιξαν αὐτά may be at once added to ἀνέβησαν as its effect. Alongside the thorns, growing up and multiplying luxuriantly after their manner, the good grain is unable to spring up, it is choked. At what stage of its development this choking is viewed as taking place, is not clearly evident from the text in Matthew. But according to Luke's text (ver. 7), καὶ συμφυεῖσαι (i.e. grown up along with) αἱ ἄκανθαι ἀπέπνιξαν αὐτό, a previous growth in common is to be supposed; and when in Mark (ver. 7) it is added: καὶ καρπὸν οὐκ ἔδωκεν, when, therefore, as the consequence of the choking of the grain, it is said that it bore no fruit,—this implies the thought that the growth of the grain had already approached the point of fruit-bearing. Accordingly, in the description so far the progress must not be overlooked, that in the hard-trodden soil first-named, the seed perishes without coming up at all; that in the second loose but not deep soil it springs up indeed, but only at once to wither again; that, finally, in the third deep but not pure soil, it grows up indeed, but is again choked before bearing fruit.

And this threefold advance in the description reaches its goal when, in the fourth place, that kind of soil is mentioned which permits the seed to attain to actual fruit-bearing (ver. 8): "*and others fell upon the good ground;*" good in opposition to the three kinds of ground previously mentioned, namely, loose in opposition to the first, deep in opposition to the second, pure in opposition to the third, and thus raising hindrance neither to the coming up nor growth, nor to the final fruit-bearing. Hence of the seed sown there it can be said: "*and it yielded fruit.*"² But this fruit-bearing of the seed which fell upon the good ground is again different in respect of its multiplication. The ἄλλα is here in turn divided into a threefold ὃ μέν ... ὃ δέ ... ὃ δέ: "*and yielded*

---

¹ Cf. below on Mark iv. 8, where the ἀναβαίνειν is expressly distinguished from the αὐξάνεσθαι.

² Cf. Mark iv. 8, where also the special contrast with the fate of the seed sown on the first and second kinds of soil is indicated by the participles ἀναβαίνοντα καὶ αὐξανόμενα added to ἐδίδου καρπόν, i.e. "*and yielded fruit, springing up and increasing.*" Such is the reading according to א B, instead of αὐξάνοντα or αὐξανόμενον. Cf. Weiss here.

fruit, some a hundred, some sixty, some thirty," i.e. grains. Thus, even in the good ground again, there is diversity in the nature of the ground, which shows itself in a corresponding variety in the fruit-bearing, so that some bears a hundred-fold, another merely sixty-fold, and even merely thirty-fold. Or, as the thought in Mark is reversed: It bore up to thirty (εἰς τριάκοντα), and even to sixty, and still more to a hundred; whereas in Luke this feature is wanting, the hundred-fold wealth of fruit being simply set in contrast with fruitlessness (ver. 8): καὶ ἐποίησεν καρπὸν ἑκατονταπλασίονα.[1]

On a review, then, of the entire parable, the first thing arresting attention is that, although delivered in narrative form, the parable is not as regards contents a real narrative, not an account of special events which happened but once in a certain order, but a description of what often, nay always, takes place by necessity of nature under the same conditions. It is a description, clothed in narrative form, of that order of nature, according to which, when a sowing takes place, the effect of the sowing depends on the actual nature of the ground sown, and is therefore just as widely different as the actual difference in the nature of the ground necessarily involves. Since, then, we know from the declarations of Jesus Himself that He meant by this parable to unfold "mysteries of the kingdom" to His disciples, we must first of all ask: What new truth it is in reference to the nature and growth of the kingdom of heaven which Jesus wishes to set before His disciples by His description of this order of nature. And the right answer to this question has been already suggested by the insight we have gained from chap. xii. 22–50, into the different kinds of success which Christ's Messianic work had hitherto met with among the people, and into the corresponding influences under which Christ stood when He spoke this parable. As we have seen, His preaching of repentance and the kingdom had its designed effect in the case of a small band of disciples only. In the case of the great multitude and of their leaders, the Pharisees, it either remained without effect altogether, or was only attended by transient success. This, then, is the phenomenon, just then becoming clearer and clearer, which Jesus wishes to point out to His disciples in the present parable, that they may not be deceived

---

[1] On the hundred-fold increase, in which the exuberant fertility of Galilee is to be taken into account, cf. also Gen. xxvi. 12, and Winer, *Biblisches Real-Wörterbuch*, art. "Ackerbau;" Smith's *Bible Dict.* "Agriculture."

by it as if it had its reason in the nature of the kingdom of heaven, and in the manner of its realization determined by that nature. For this end, in opposition to the prevailing expectation, that when the Messiah appears He will set up the kingdom of heaven in glory by means of a display of outward power, certain and universal in effect, He discloses the mystery, that the kingdom of heaven must be realized by means of a sowing which is dependent for its effect on the actual nature of the soil, and therefore by no other means than the insignificant one which they have previously seen in operation—*of preaching the gospel of the kingdom* (iv. 23, ix. 35), *the effect of which by its very nature as a purely spiritual agency is dependent on the condition of heart of those to whom the preaching comes, and must be just as widely different as the actual condition of heart in the hearers.*[1]

But, then, we must not think that in indicating this or any similar fundamental thought we have exhausted the original meaning of the parable, or reject a special interpretation of the four different kinds of soil, and the correspondent fourfold effect of the sowing, as a construction having no basis in the original plan of the parable.[2] On the latter view the explanation given, according to the account of all three evangelists, by Jesus Himself must be regarded as originating in a later misunderstanding, and wrongly ascribed to Jesus Himself by tradition. For in the first place this at least is certain, that in the interpretation we must distinguish between the fourth kind of ground mentioned in the parable on the one hand, and the first three on the other, as between a condition of heart which allows the word preached to have its full effect unhindered, and one which does not allow this through one or another hindrance contained in it. But then, the description itself is not so arranged, either as to form or contents, that the class of soil which proves fruitful is simply contrasted with that which proves unfruitful; but it is so arranged that each one of the three unfruitful classes of soil stands in contrast with the two others and with the fourth fruitful class just as definitely as the fourth with the first three. For, as regards first the form, we see the description everywhere

---

[1] Certainly this also indirectly implies an intimation to the disciples "of what they are to expect as to the success of *their* preaching of the word," but not as the real design of the parable (so Hofmann on Luke viii. 4 ff.). For here the matter in question is primarily the strange fact lying before their eyes, and therefore merely the very diverse results of Christ's own labour.

[2] So especially Weiss.

pass from one class of soil to the other uniformly with an ἄλλα δὲ ἔπεσεν, and thus from the third to the fourth in no other way than from the second to the third, and from the first to the second. And as regards contents, the description of each successive class of soil exhibits a definite advance on the preceding one in respect of its nature, and the effect of the seed dependent thereon; and this is done in uniform succession, ascending from the first to the second, and from the second to the third, in just the same way as from the third to the fourth. Thus the whole is seen to fall, as regards form and contents, into four co-ordinate parts, each one of which claims a special interpretation.

For these reasons the parable just as definitely requires a special interpretation of the first three kinds of soil as of the fourth in distinction from the first three; and our confidence is justified that we do not go beyond its original design in asserting that every one of the four kinds of soil is meant to symbolize a condition of heart of like nature, which allows to the preached word an effect like that of the seed. And, according to the designed construction of the parable, this takes place in such order that in the first case the condition of heart in question makes any effect of preaching altogether impossible, whereas in the second case it permits to the preaching an initial but quickly vanishing effect, in the third an effect apparently more permanent, but at last coming to nought, and only in the fourth case a right effect.

Thus there is no ground whatever for violently setting aside by a critical verdict the fourfold interpretation which, according to the account of the evangelists, Jesus Himself gave to the disciples, and which even a critic like Ewald finds "so full of life, so pregnant and distinctive," that "with good reason we may recognise therein the words of Christ Himself." Rather in the interpretation of particulars we may confidently commit ourselves to the guidance of Christ's interpretation—of course not without independent examination. For it must always be taken into account, that when Jesus, Himself the author of the parable, interprets it to His disciples, His standpoint is not that of the exact expositor, who aims at ascertaining the meaning of the parable, at exactly defining it to the extent to which it belongs to the figurative history, and reproducing it without any additions. His is the higher standpoint of the practical expositor, who desires to impress the meaning of the parable, of which He is sure, on the hearts of others, in which course He is at liberty to avail Himself, in the interpretation of further details, of concrete applications, and also of using additional analogies, provided only the original sense of the parable is not deranged and confused.

We turn then to the interpretation, which, as we saw, Jesus first gave to His disciples afterwards in a special conversation. After explaining to them the reason and aim of His parabolic discourse (vv. 10-17), He proceeds in ver. 18: "*Hear ye then the parable of him who sowed.*" So it is said, according to the true reading τοῦ σπείραντος, in allusion to the σπείρειν used at the opening of the parable, and not according to the altered reading τοῦ σπείροντος: "*The parable of the Sower,*" with mistaken reference to ὁ σπείρων. The parable is named after the sowing, which is the subject, and not after a particular person supposed to be treated of. Hence, too, in the interpretation now following, in noteworthy distinction from the interpretation of the second parable (ver. 37), the person of the sower is not specially taken into consideration.

Whereas, now, in the other evangelists the detailed interpretation of the parable is preceded by the general statement, prefixed by way of theme, that the seed sown is the word (Mark, ver. 14), or the word of God (Luke, ver. 11), the text of Matthew begins at once with the special interpretation of the first of the four parts of the parable. But this is done in such a form, that in the first words of the passage referring to the question, the seed sown is here also described, and that more definitely than in Mark and Luke, as "the word of the kingdom," the word having the kingdom of God for the subject of its announcement.[1] Thus, at the very outset of the interpretation, the same is affirmed as we indicated above to be the fundamental thought of the parable: The only way in which the kingdom of heaven is realized is, that word of it comes to men, and this word by its nature exercises different effects, according as the hearers to whom it comes are different. This is seen in the first case (ver. 19): παντὸς ἀκούοντος τὸν λόγον τῆς βασιλείας καὶ μὴ συνιέντος, ἔρχεται ὁ πονηρὸς καὶ ἁρπάζει τὸ ἐσπαρμένον ἐν τῇ καρδίᾳ αὐτοῦ. This construction is usually but wrongly pronounced anakoluthic, which it could only be if the evangelist had meant at first to write in

---

[1] Cf. τὸ εὐαγγέλιον τῆς βασιλείας, iv. 29, ix. 35, xxiv. 14.

as complicated a manner as *e.g.* Meyer (and Keil) supposes: παντὸς ἀκούοντος τ. λόγ. τ. βασ. καὶ μὴ συνιέντος, ἐκ τῆς καρδίας ἁρπάζει ὁ πονηρὸς τὸ ἐσπαρμένον. On this theory, in order to make such an intention at all conceivable, the ἐν τῇ καρδίᾳ belonging to ἐσπαρμένον is always arbitrarily changed into ἐκ τῆς καρδίας, which is joined to ἁρπάζει. Rather the genitive παντὸς ἀκούοντος κ.τ.λ. is to be taken with the following ἔρχεται, as every reader or hearer is inclined at first to take it, as a genitive absolute prefixed to the finite verb. Thus: "*When any one heareth the word of the kingdom and understandeth it not, then cometh the evil one and snatcheth away that which hath been sown in his heart.*" Certainly this mode of expression is not quite correct logically, but every one at once understands its meaning, namely, that it is the same as saying: When any one hears the word and understands it not, *in every case* the evil one, etc. Τὸ ἐσπαρμένον ἐν τῇ καρδίᾳ is that which is present in the heart through the sowing which has taken place, or without figure, through the preaching which has taken place. The occurrence of figurative language again within the interpretation is a phenomenon lying in the nature of popular interpretation, and hence always recurring in the sequel.

Let us then compare this interpretation with the text of the first part of the parable. The hindrance which the seed sown encountered in the first kind of soil was the inability of the soil, due to its having been trodden hard, even to admit the seed into the body of the earth. The like hindrance, which the preaching of the word meets with in one class of hearers, is plainly meant to be described by the words καὶ μὴ συνιέντος added to παντὸς ἀκούοντος. Thus the hearers of the word, corresponding to the first kind of soil, are they who are ἀσύνετοι, without the qualification for receiving with the inner intelligence the word which falls on their ears.[1] The natural consequence in relation to the seed not received into the earth, but left lying on the surface, was that it perished without having any effect, being either trodden to pieces or devoured by birds. The like fate befalling the word, which was not admitted into the heart with inner

---

[1] According to this view, the words καὶ μὴ συνιέντος are so essential and indispensable in the interpretation, that, although Mark and Luke have nothing corresponding, they must be held to be, not an explanatory addition by Matthew, but original. They have disappeared elsewhere because of their seeming unimportance in addition to what is said of the devil taking away the seed.

intelligence, but remained outside the understanding, is indicated in the apodosis: "Then cometh the evil one, and taketh away that which was sown in his heart," namely, the word, which, although not understood, was at all events present in the heart. But we must not, on the ground of this clause, say that the birds of the air in the parable signify the devil or his angels,[1] or his delegate spirits—evil thoughts.[2] The birds which devour the seed can just as little signify anything special as the people who tread it to pieces. Both traits simply describe in a plastic way how the seed, not admitted into the earth, must necessarily perish. The interpretation is: The word, not understood, is lost to the hearer, as if he had never heard it. And when in the interpretation this general thought of the parable is more precisely explained to mean, that the devil at once[3] carries away the word present in the heart, "that," as the text of Luke (ver. 12) further adds, "they may not believe and be saved" (an explanation unmistakeably allied to what is said of the birds in the parable),[4] the analogy is one not taken from the parable itself, but drawn from the actual circumstances of the case, and first added in the interpretation. For, as matter of fact, the case is just this, that as the seed not admitted into the earth is liable to be eaten by the birds, so the word lying in the heart without being understood is liable to be carried away by the devil, because, busy as he is everywhere in neutralizing the effect of the word, he is able in this case to carry it away from the heart, i.e. to cause the man to forget it. Here, then, we have, it is true, an allegorizing explanation, but one consciously given as such on good grounds, and such an one as must always be open to the practical expositor, because, while it goes beyond the original and general meaning, it really exists in fact, and adds an analogy thoroughly suiting the framework of the parable, without introducing confusion into the sense.

Thus, leaving out of sight this explanation, the meaning of the first part of the parable is this: Just as in the first case the seed falls on hard-trodden soil, which does not allow it to penetrate the earth, so in one class of hearers the word of the kingdom preached lights on inability to understand it. And just as on such soil the seed must perforce perish, so will the word,

---

[1] Bengel. [2] Stier. [3] Mark, ver. 15 : εὐθύς.
[4] Cf. ver. 4 : ἦλθεν τὰ πετεινὰ καὶ κατέφαγεν, with ver. 19 : ἔρχεται ὁ πονηρὸς καὶ ἁρπάζει.

because not understood, be again lost to such hearers, as if they had never heard it.

But before the interpretation of the second part of the parable is entered upon, it is specially remarked by way of supplement, that what has just been said is meant for an interpretation of the first part of the parable, in the words: οὗτός ἐστιν ὁ παρὰ τὴν ὁδὸν σπαρείς. That is, literally: "*This one*," to whom it happens as has just been said, "*is he who was sown by the wayside*," plainly (and this without formally supplying ὁ σπόρος παρ. ὁδ. σπαρείς[1]) a compressed form of expression for: He is the counterpart of the seed sown by the wayside. Certainly at the first glance it must seem extremely singular that the seed, which was just now the word preached, is here at a stroke identified with the person of the hearer, who was just now the counterpart of the field. Nor can it avail to take ὁ σπαρείς, as many do, to be the counterpart here, not of the seed sown in the field, but of the field sown with seed; because while σπείρειν in itself may also have the latter meaning, it can never have this meaning when the place where the seed falls is added with a preposition like παρά, ἐπί, εἰς. In the same way it is an inadmissible expedient to paraphrase: "This is he, in whose case the seed was sown upon the road."[2] One might perhaps acquiesce in such inaccuracy of expression as this paraphrase supposes, if the identification of the seed with the persons occurred only in this one passage. But a glance at the sequel shows that this identification recurs in the interpretation of each one of the four parts of the parable. Not only is the interpretation of each separate part introduced in just the same way as here the interpretation of the first part is concluded (with ὁ δὲ ἐπὶ τὰ πετρώδη ... ὁ δὲ εἰς τὰς ἀκάνθας ... ὁ δὲ ἐπὶ τὴν καλὴν γῆν σπαρείς, οὗτός ἐστιν κ.τ.λ.[3]), but also in the detailed interpretation what is said of the seed sown is often transferred direct to the persons.[4] If we add, further, the preliminary observation, that in the parable immediately following, which treats in like manner of the sowing of seed and its growth, the seed is from the first expressly interpreted of persons and persons only,[5] it remains without doubt that the present passage can only be

---

[1] Weiss.   [2] Meyer, Keil.   [3] Vv. 20, 22, 23, and parallels.
[4] Cf. ver. 21 and parallels: οὐκ ἔχει δὲ ῥίζαν; ver. 23 and parallels: καρποφορεῖ καὶ ποιεῖ ὁ μὲν ἑκατόν κ.τ.λ.; and in Luke, ver. 14: συμπνίγονται καὶ οὐ τελεσφοροῦσιν.
[5] See ver. 38.

explained in the light of this general phenomenon. But we need only carefully consider the relation of the occurrence used as a figure in the sphere of nature to the occurrence symbolized in the spiritual sphere, in order to see that this identifying of the seed first with the word preached and then with the person of the hearer, and again the identifying of the person of the hearer first with the soil of the field and then with the seed itself, lies in the nature of this relation, and does not spring from any incongruity between the interpretation given and the figure.[1] Where the act of sowing is compared to that of preaching, there, of course, the seed as the means and instrument of the sowing corresponds primarily to the word as the medium of the preaching, while the person on whose ear the preaching falls corresponds to the field on which the seed is strewn. But the relation is changed directly the effect of the sowing is further compared to the effect of preaching. In the natural sphere the effect of sowing is not an effect on the soil itself, which receives the seed, but the very seed, which in the first case was the means of the sowing, now appears on the other hand as its effect. From the same grains of seed, which served as the means of sowing, springs also the grain, the production of which is the aim of the sowing. But the field is and remains merely the soil which keeps the grain concealed, and then according to its own nature puts it forth and causes it to develope as something distinct from itself. But in the spiritual sphere the effect of the preaching is an effect on the person of the hearer himself, and consists, so far as it is realized, in a transformation of his most peculiar and intimate personal life. It is therefore realized and manifested nowhere but in and upon himself. Hence the man, who as the hearer of the word is in the first instance the soil which receives the seed, on the other hand, inasmuch as he does not put forth the effect of what he has heard as something different from and alien to himself (this effect rather being nothing else than a transformation and re-creation of himself), may also be identified with the grain which is the product of the sowing. And the seed, which is in the first instance the word, may also, where it no longer appears as the means, but as the result of the sowing,—the grain which is the aim of the sowing, —be just as well identified with the persons in whom the word heard is effective as the principle of a new personal life. When

[1] So Weiss.

this general relation of the natural occurrences used as a figure to the thing symbolized is taken into account, everything strange in the identification in the present passage of the seed sown by the wayside with persons of the kind described vanishes. True, in this case the word heard exercises the same as no effect on the person of the hearer. But at all events, after he has once heard the word, he carries in himself the potent principle of a new personal life, how long makes no difference. For this reason the hearer of this kind also may be identified with the seed, but only with that sown by the wayside, *i.e.* which perishes before it reaches any stage of development.

With ver. 20 begins the interpretation of the second part of the parable, and in such a form that this time ὁ ἐπὶ τὰ πετρώδη σπαρείς (*i.e.* he who answers as counterpart to the seed sown on the rocky ground) is made from the first the subject of the following description: ὁ δὲ ἐπὶ τὰ πετρώδη, οὗτός ἐστιν ὁ τὸν λόγον ἀκούων καὶ εὐθὺς μετὰ χαρᾶς λαμβάνων αὐτόν. In this case, therefore, not simply a mere passive hearing, but also an active reception, takes place; and, indeed, the word is received straightway with joy (εὐθύς belongs to μετὰ χαρᾶς). But with this is set in contrast in ver. 21 the inner nature of a hearer, who receives the word straightway with joy, as a nature which must of necessity bring to a speedy end the commencement that seemed so full of promise: οὐκ ἔχει δὲ ῥίζαν ἐν ἑαυτῷ ἀλλὰ πρόσκαιρός ἐστιν. In the first clause the inner nature of such a hearer is characterized first of all negatively by transferring what was said of the grain in the second case—namely, that it had no root in the rocky ground, which failed to afford room for such roots because of its want of depth—immediately to the hearer, without changing the figurative form, and in such a way that in one and the same sentence he is identified just as well with the grain as with the soil—a striking illustration of what was said in ver. 19. The figurative saying as to the grain having no root in the soil is transferred thus: He has no root *in himself,* *i.e.* without figure: As a believing follower of the word, in which capacity he corresponds to the grain, he is not firmly grounded, because, as a hearer of the word, in which capacity he corresponds to the soil, he has not allowed the word to penetrate deeply enough into his heart. Hence now the antithesis: "*but endureth only for a while.*" He is, of course, the subject of this statement in the same capacity in which he was the subject of the first clause, to which the second forms the antithesis. As a believing follower of the word, he is not firmly grounded in himself, "but endureth only for a while." It is obvious that πρόσκαιρος in this its literal and ordinary sense is here quite in place, supplying a thoroughly pertinent antithesis to the first clause; and, accordingly, there is not the slightest reason for foisting on the word in this connection a special and elsewhere undemonstrable signification like "fickle."[1]

In what case the falling away of such a hearer, which is to be expected in these circumstances, follows, is then stated in the sentence joined on by the metabatic δέ: namely, γενομένης δὲ θλίψεως ἢ διωγμοῦ διὰ τὸν λόγον εὐθὺς σκανδαλίζεται. By ἤ the narrower idea "persecution" is distinguished from the more general "tribulation." For although the idea "tribulation" is limited by the qualification διὰ τὸν λόγον belonging to γενομένης (and therefore referring just as much to θλῖψις as to διωγμός), to a signification similar to that of the latter word, still the distinction remains, that θλῖψις embraces everything bad, which a follower of the word has to submit to indirectly or directly for the word's sake (e.g. evil report, disrespect, isolation, etc.), whereas διωγμός includes only the sufferings inflicted on the followers of the word with conscious intention by its enemies.

Σκανδαλίζεσθαι, although passive, has not here really a purely passive signification, "to suffer an offence,"[2] but means "to take offence."[3] And this here indeed, as also in the exactly corresponding passage xxiv. 9, 10, in the pregnant sense of some one actually falling through taking offence, letting himself be led to apostasy thereby. Hence we must translate, with Lange: "*When, then, tribulation or persecution ariseth because of the word, he straightway falls at the offence.*" Instead of this whole sentence, Luke has more briefly: καὶ ἐν καιρῷ πειρασμοῦ ἀφίστανται, but without a really divergent meaning. For πειρασμός there is not so much temptation (as in 1 Tim. vi. 9) as rather hostility, assaults of an outward kind,[4] by which any one is put to the test. Thus here also as to substance nothing is thought of but the tribulation with which the follower of the

---

[1] Luther, Lange, Stier.   [2] As e.g. in 2 Cor. xi. 29.   [3] As e.g. in ver. 57.
[4] As almost everywhere in the New Testament; cf. xxvi. 41 and parallels; Acts xx. 19; 1 Pet. iv. 12; 2 Pet. ii. 9.

word is attacked from without by way of test. Luke's expressing himself merely in this brief, general way is in keeping with the circumstance, that in his text of the parable nothing at all was said of the heat of the sun, which occasioned the withering of the grain. In him, therefore, the words ἐν καιρῷ πειρασμοῦ are merely an explanatory addition to the interpretation, whereas in Matthew (and similarly in Mark) the mention in the parable itself of the scorching heat of the sun, in allusion to the figurative language of the Old Testament,[1] points definitely to the pressure of tribulation, by which the follower of the word must be tested just as necessarily as the grain by the heat of the sun. Hence the interpretation here: γενομένης δὲ θλίψεως κ.τ.λ., exactly corresponding to ἡλίου δὲ ἀνατείλαντος.

Thus the interpretation given of the second case, in exact conformity with the meaning of the parable everywhere, is as follows: Like as the seed in the rocky ground, while not encountering impenetrable hardness in the soil, falls into too shallow earth, so in other hearers the preached word meets with, not indeed entire want of understanding, but such superficiality of mind as does not allow the word to live and be treasured deep in the heart. And like as it is involved in the nature of the too shallow earth, that the effect of the sowing there comes at first quickly to light in the grain springing up forthwith, while the grain, directly its capacity of life is tested by the heat of the sun, withers away, because it has no root; so it is implied in the nature of superficial hearers, that in virtue of the excitability peculiar to them the effect of the word comes quickly to view, since they receive it with visible joy; but when it becomes necessary to approve themselves its followers under the pressure of the tribulation or persecution inevitably befalling them for the word's sake, then they at once fall away, because in their character as followers of the word they are not firmly grounded in themselves.

Now begins the interpretation of the third case in perfect analogy with that of the second, ver. 22: "*And he that was sown among the thorns,*[2] *this is he that heareth the word*" ... And now the cause is forthwith mentioned, which in this third case

---

[1] Ps cxxi. 6; Isa. xxv. 4, xlix. 10, etc.

[2] Here the ἐπὶ τὰς ἀκάνθας, ver. 7, is exchanged for the better form εἰς τὰς ἀκάνθας, which Mark has already in the text of the parable.

also at last neutralizes the effect of the word, when it is said immediately: καὶ ἡ μέριμνα τοῦ αἰῶνος[1] καὶ ἡ ἀπάτη τοῦ πλούτου συμπνίγει τὸν λόγον, i.e. literally: "*and the care of the age and the deceitfulness of riches choke the word.*" Ἡ μέριμνα τοῦ αἰῶνος is the care pertaining to the present age, inasmuch as its object does not lie beyond the sphere of the age, thus care for the earthly and perishable. To this care καί subjoins ἡ ἀπάτη τοῦ πλούτου, i.e. the deceit practised on man by riches, when that which is an empty, because a merely earthly and perishable good, palms itself off on him as an exceedingly desirable good. In so far as the man allows this deceit to be played on him, there awakens in him the desire for the possession of riches, and for all the worldly enjoyments offering themselves in that possession. Thus, "the deceitfulness of riches," awakening the worldly *lust* slumbering in the heart, stands beside worldly *care* as a correlative; and there is no need to recur to the other meaning of ἀπάτη, undemonstrable elsewhere in the New Testament, and only in appearance more suitable in the present passage— delight (passing delusion). The two—care and lust—συμπνίγει τὸν λόγον. What was said in the parable of the seed being choked is therefore again immediately transferred, both here and in Mark, to the preached word, without being divested of the figurative form, in so far as the word produces an effect in the heart. In Luke it is transferred to the persons of the hearers themselves (συμπνίγονται, see below), in so far as they exhibit the effect of the word in their own person.

Mark, hitherto almost identical with Matthew, now adds by way of supplement a third subject of the verb (ver. 19): καὶ αἱ περὶ τὰ λοιπὰ ἐπιθυμίαι εἰσπορευόμεναι. So according to ℵ.[2] Thus, in Mark, "the deceitfulness of riches" is not understood of worldly lust kindled by riches, but only of the particular lust

---

[1] According to B D Sin. τούτου must be erased as a needless addition, although a correct explanation; cf. vv. 39, 49.

[2] The reading of the *Sinait.* must here be taken as the original: καὶ αἱ μέριμναι τοῦ αἰῶνος καὶ ἡ ἀπάτη τοῦ πλούτου συμπνίγει τὸν λόγον, καὶ αἱ περὶ τὰ λοιπὰ ἐπιθυμίαι εἰσπορευόμεναι. For it is easy to suppose that the halting addition καὶ αἱ περὶ ... εἰσπορευόμεναι was inserted after ἡ ἀπάτη τοῦ πλούτου, and the singular of the verb, which appears strange after the plural αἱ μέριμναι, changed accordingly into the plural συμπνίγουσι; whereas the origination of the Sinaitic reading out of the usual one is well-nigh impossible. We must in that case, with Weiss, suppose that the words καὶ αἱ περὶ ... εἰσπορευόμεναι dropped out by accident; then—utterly without reason, in the most surprising way—the plural of the verb was changed into the singular: and finally, those omitted words were then restored after the verb.

referring directly to riches as a possession, and therefore of avarice. Hence by way of supplement he describes "the lusts referring to other things" (*i.e.* to good living, sensuous enjoyment, power, honour, etc.) as belonging to the same class, joining them to the verb συμπνίγει already prefixed by the supplementary participle εἰσπορευόμεναι. Accordingly, we must translate: "and also the lusts referring to other things, entering" (*i.e.* the man), *scil.* choke it. But the expression "entering" does not imply the notion that the desires come into the man *from without*,[1] which would, of course, be incompatible with the meaning of the parable; but here again the man is viewed equally as the soil from which the thorns spring, and the grain into which they rankly penetrate. Awakened and kindled by the goods and joys of the world, the desires spring from the heart of the man himself, where they slumber in secret, and penetrate into him while under the influence of the word.

Luke also has a triple division of the choking factors in substantial agreement with that of Mark, since he says in freer language, less closely following the structure of the parable (ver. 14): καὶ ὑπὸ μεριμνῶν καὶ πλούτου καὶ ἡδονῶν τοῦ βίου πορευόμενοι συμπνίγονται. Nevertheless the ἡδοναί are not here, like the ἐπιθυμίαι in Mark, viewed subjectively as desires, as the qualification τοῦ βίου shows, but are viewed objectively. Side by side with the riches as the outward worldly possession, appear the ἡδοναί as the sensuous enjoyments of life. The meaning therefore is: "And coming under the influence of care and riches, which awaken avarice, and of the pleasures of life, which awaken in them the corresponding desires, they are choked."

After it has been stated how the effect of the word is neutralized in this case also, according to the analogy of the first and second cases, the interpretation would seem to be exhausted. But as in Mark we found already in the parable (ver. 7) the special clause: καὶ καρπὸν οὐκ ἔδωκεν after συνέπνιξαν αὐτό, so in the interpretation in all three evangelists a corresponding clause is found, the figure being retained. This is done with the difference, that in Matthew and Mark it is said of the *word* καὶ ἄκαρπος γίνεται, not of the man,[2] since in Mark the allusion to οὗτοί εἰσιν κ.τ.λ. would require the plural, whereas Luke says of the hearers themselves: καὶ οὐ τελεσφοροῦσιν. But as in the parable in Mark the clause "and it yielded no fruit" started from the idea that

---

[1] Weiss, Meyer.   [2] Meyer.

the seed in this case was near bearing fruit, so the corresponding clause in the interpretation rests on the supposition that in the hearers of this class, in distinction from those previously described, the word seemed to be about to have its full effect. This supposition is seen in the mode of expression: "*and it* (the word which is on the point of yielding fruit) *becomes* (γίνεται) *unfruitful*." And in Luke also the fruit is clearly viewed as already set, when it is said: "and they bring no fruit to perfection," *i.e.* they bring not the fruit already set to maturity. Thus stripped of its figurative form, the clause affirms: Although in such hearers, in distinction from those previously described, the word may have a more enduring effect, still even in them it fails finally to accomplish the end at which the preaching of it aimed, the effect being neutralized in the way indicated.

Accordingly, the interpretation of the third part of the parable is this: Like as the seed this time falls, not indeed upon soil trodden hard or wanting in depth, but upon impure soil,—impure through the thorns and weeds concealed in it,—so in hearers of another kind the preached word meets with, not indeed entire want of understanding or superficiality of mind, but the impurity of heart which secretly cherishes sinful inclinations. And as it is involved in the nature of such soil that the seed grows up indeed, but still yields no fruit, because the thorns grow up thickly with it and choke it; so it is involved in the state of heart of such hearers, that the word has in them a more enduring effect, but still even in them does not finally accomplish its end, because the sinful inclinations cherished in their hearts gradually increase in strength, and finally gain such complete possession of the man, that the new direction of thought produced by the word has no room by their side, and is choked by them. Thus the thorns, as the weeds which pollute the soil, symbolize generally the sinful inclinations polluting the heart.[1] That these appear and dominate the man in the form of care about what belongs to the world, or of lusts kindled by the goods and enjoyments of the world, is not, of course, thus definitely contained in the figure, but is stated independently in the interpretation in accordance with the actual circumstances of the case.

Now begins the interpretation of the fourth part of the parable, again in conformity with that of the second and third parts (ver. 23): "*And he that was sown upon the good ground, this is he that*

[1] Jer. iv. 3.

heareth the word." The good reception which the word finds in the hearer now in question, in distinction from the one previously pictured, is described by the clause καὶ συνιῶν.[1] The other reading συνιείς arose out of συιέντος in ver. 19. Thus, although it was only in the hearer of the first class that it was pointed out as a distinctive peculiarity that he understood not the word, still even in those of the second and third class the understanding really befitting the contents of the word is regarded as wanting. Only of the hearer of the fourth class can it be said in the full sense: *"he that hears and understands it."* The same full sense is also meant when such hearers are characterized in Mark (ver. 20) as they who "hear the word and accept it" (καὶ παραδέχονται). It is true that in the second (λαμβάνειν μετὰ χαρᾶς) and in the third case a reception of the word in some sense took place. But only the hearers of the fourth class actually receive it in the way in which it seeks to be received and ought to be received according to its nature. The contrast with the hearers of the second and third classes appears more sharply marked only in Luke, when the hearers of the last kind are defined as they οἵτινες ἐν καρδίᾳ καλῇ καὶ ἀγαθῇ ἀκούσαντες τὸν λόγον κατέχουσιν, "which in an honest and good heart," corresponding in nature to the fourth kind of soil, because concealing none of the hindrances to the effect of the word previously described, "having heard the word, keep it," without again becoming apostate at once, as in the second case, or at last, as in the third case.

The result attained in such a case is introduced by the evangelist in a different form from the one adopted in the first three classes of hearers—namely, by the relative construction, and with a certain solemnity: ὃς δὴ καρποφορεῖ, *i.c.* "*who verily beareth fruit.*" Here, then, again what is said of the grain in the parable is transferred to the person of the hearer himself. And this transference is carried out farther in reference to the different degrees of fruitfulness mentioned. To this end certainly an independent sentence was necessary, since the singular ὅς, although denoting not a single hearer, but the species, could not fitly be divided immediately into a threefold ὁ μέν ... ὁ δέ ... ὁ δέ. For this reason the interpretation concludes with a separate sentence: καὶ ποιεῖ ὁ μὲν ἑκατόν κ.τ.λ., *i.c.* "*and bringeth forth one a hundredfold, another sixty, another thirty.*" Because of their rhythm with the last words of the parable (ver. 8), the words form a conclusion

[1] On this form, comp. Winer, *Gram.* p. 97.

full of emphasis. But this emphasis, which consists in the rhythm of something corresponding and yet different, would be utterly spoilt if the view were right, that the transference preserved hitherto of what is said about the grain is here broken off, that the conclusion is a mere repetition of the last words of the parable,[1] and that we must here accentuate not, as the context in this passage requires, ὁ μέν ... ὁ δέ as the masc. of the art., but as in ver. 8, ὃ μέν ... ὃ δέ, as the neuter of the relative.[2]

In Mark, too, what is said of the diverse fruit-bearing is transferred to the person of the hearers, only in reverse order, in accordance with his text of the parable, since we must write there thrice, not ἕν, but ἐν: καὶ καρποφοροῦσιν ἐν τριάκοντα καὶ ἐν ἑξήκοντα καὶ ἐν ἑκατόν. On the other hand, in Luke, who only mentions in the parable the hundredfold fruit-bearing, this is simply explained by καὶ καρποφοροῦσιν ἐν ὑπομονῇ. The ὑπομονή is not to be referred to the perseverance, in virtue of which they bring forth fruit simply,[3] which would be a mere repetition of the τὸν λόγον κατέχουσιν, but, with Weiss, to the perseverance which they show in fruit-bearing, the fruit becoming richer and richer.

Accordingly the interpretation of the fourth part of the parable is this: Like as the seed in the fourth case falls upon good ground, and therefore on soft, deep, and pure ground, in opposition to the first three kinds; so the preached word in other hearers finds a well-prepared heart, *i.e.*, in opposition to the first three classes of hearers, a heart capable not only of the first understanding, but also of the deeper apprehension of the word, and unpolluted by hidden propensity to sin. And as in such ground the grain springs up, grows, and actually bears fruit unhindered; so such hearers allow the word to have not merely an initial, but also an enduring and finally abiding effect in them, and allow it to produce in and upon them that transformation of life at which the preaching of the word of the kingdom aims, *i.e.* the righteousness of the kingdom of God. But as, again,—this is the concluding feature of the parable,—even the fruitful grain differs in fertility according to the relatively different goodness of the soil, so even in such hearers the relatively different preparation of heart has for its consequence, that the transformation of life, at which the word aims, is carried into effect in a different degree, falling more or less short of perfection (the descending

---

[1] Bengel, Meyer, Weiss.   [2] Tischendorf, Lachmann.   [3] Bengel, Meyer, Godet.

order of Matthew), or more or less approximating to it (the ascending order of Mark).

We are at the end of the interpretation of the parable. But another general remark is necessary in order to guard it against misunderstanding on one side. If our interpretation is right, the fourfold difference of soil in the parable represents not merely a fourfold difference in the attitude of the hearers to the word, but also a fourfold difference in the state of heart which the preached word already finds, so that the different attitude to the word always has its ground in the already existent inner nature of the hearer. The non-understanding of the word had its ground in the already existing incapacity to understand it; the speedy falling away after a joyous reception at first its ground in the already existing superficiality of mind; the final falling away through complete subjection to worldly and sinful inclinations seemed determined beforehand by the existing impurity of heart; and finally, even the holding fast of the word up to a more or less perfect accomplishment of its end seemed determined beforehand by already existing preparation of heart. But at the same time we must not leave out of sight the distinction necessarily presupposed in the comparison between the relations and events borrowed from the unconscious life of nature on the one hand, and those moral relations and events compared with them on the other, which are based on the self-consciousness and self-determination of man. There, the ground to be sown is in an unconscious and involuntary way always of the same nature as it now is; here, the inner nature of the hearer of the word has not become what it now is without conscious self-determination. And again, there the different reception which the seed finds in the soil, and its further fate in this soil, is merely the consequence of the different nature of the soil, following by unconditional physical necessity; here, on the other hand, while the different attitude of the hearers to the word is determined beforehand by the difference of their inner nature, this is not so in the sense that the former must follow from the latter by irresistible necessity, but in the sense that man's own self-determination is exerted in reference to the word in the direction which it has given to itself. On this view, the possibility at least of another attitude than the one to be expected after what has been said can never be regarded as entirely precluded.

The Tares in the Wheat.

(Matt. xiii. 24-30, 36-43.)

After the interpolation reaching from ver. 10 to ver. 23, inserted here for incidental reasons only, the words ἄλλην παραβολὴν παρέθηκεν αὐτοῖς λέγων (ver. 24) resume, in Matthew's account, the discourse begun in ver. 3, and consisting exclusively of parables. Thus the persons before whom another parable is "set" (*i.e.* delivered) are they to whom the first parable was spoken, namely, the people assembled on the shore. When the parable begins this time with the formula : ὡμοιώθη ἡ βασιλεία τῶν οὐρανῶν ἀνθρώπῳ σπείραντι κ.τ.λ., the comparison, of course, must not be taken so literally as to make the ἄνθρωπος alone symbolize the kingdom of heaven, but the comparison applies to the whole narrative. The meaning of the formula, often recurring in Matthew, is, that the following narrative is one which the kingdom of heaven is like, that it represents corresponding circumstances and events in the sphere of the kingdom of heaven. And the articulation of the phraseology is so loose, that the subject or main idea of the first sentence is isolated from the narrative beforehand, and set over against the kingdom of heaven—the thing compared. Next, the narrative itself usually begins with a relative sentence joined on to the isolated subject or main idea (vv. 31, 33, chaps. xviii. 23, xx. 1, xxii. 2, xxv. 1), or as here and vv. 45, 47, etc., with a participial sentence occupying the place of the relative sentence. But while in all the succeeding parables of this chapter and xx. 1 the formula simply runs : ὁμοία ἐστὶν ἡ βασ. τῶν οὐρ. κ.τ.λ., here and in xviii. 23, xxii. 2, it is said : ὡμοιώθη ἡ βασ. τῶν οὐρ. κ.τ.λ.,[1] *i.e.*: "The kingdom of heaven has become like." Whereas, therefore, the first formula says only generally that the kingdom of heaven is like what follows, the second says definitely, that in the then stage of its development the kingdom of heaven has assumed the shape in which it is delineated in the following narrative. In this sense it is said : *The kingdom of heaven has become like* ἀνθρώπῳ σπείραντι[2] καλὸν σπέρμα ἐν τῷ ἀγρῷ αὐτοῦ. The preposition ἐν is to be observed. It does not stand here for εἰς, nor does it

---

[1] Cf. xxv. 1 : ὡμοιωθήσεται ἡ βασ. τῶν οὐρανῶν.
[2] So we must read, with Lachmann and Tischendorf, instead of σπείροντι.

anywhere.[1] Ἐν τῷ ἀγρῷ is not indeed for that reason to be applied, with Bengel, to the person of the sower (*in quo ipse est*), but it denotes the place where the seed now remains and rests, after coming there through sowing.[2] But the use of the preposition ἐν was especially apposite in the present passage, because from the first the seed is viewed here, not as the means, but as the result of the sowing.[3] The point in question is not what kind of seed the man scattered as he sowed *in the field*, but what kind of grain he had in view in sowing *in and on the field*. That σπέρμα, as it signifies the sum-total of the seed first to be sown, may also just as well signify the seed (*sata*) lying in the ground and developing there, which is the aim of the sowing, is implied in the nature of the case. Compare passages like 1 Sam. viii. 15, Isa. xxiii. 3, where the LXX. uses σπέρμα, and Job xxxix. 12, where they use the synonymous σπόρος to reproduce the Heb. זֶרַע in this sense, and also all passages where σπέρμα is used of human seed = "posterity." And that σπέρμα here too has this meaning is clear from the antithesis in ver. 25: ἐπέσπειρεν ζιζάνια ἀνὰ μέσον τοῦ σίτου. For what is here called καλὸν σπέρμα is there called σῖτος, and the antithesis to the sowing of the καλὸν σπέρμα is there not the sowing of bad seed, but of a bad crop—darnel. In the same way καλὸν σπέρμα and ζιζάνια are opposed to each other in ver. 27, and in the interpretation ver. 38. The translation therefore is: "*The kingdom of heaven has become like a man who sowed good grain in his field.*" The emphasis of the sentence lies on "good." The fact above all to be kept in view is, that it was a crop of pure wheat which the man's sowing aimed at.

This being premised, the narrative now proceeds (ver. 25): ἐν δὲ τῷ καθεύδειν τοὺς ἀνθρώπους ἦλθεν ὁ ἐχθρὸς αὐτοῦ καὶ ἐπέσπειρεν[4] ζιζάνια ἀνὰ μέσον τοῦ σίτου, καὶ ἀπῆλθεν, *i.e.*: *But at the time when men sleep, his enemy came and sowed tares thereon among the wheat, and went away*. The owner of the field, therefore, had an enemy, as tacitly implied in the narrative. This enemy "came and sowed tares thereon," *i.e.* on the pure wheat. Ζιζάνιον = darnel or wild corn (*lolium temulentum*), "is the only grass which also in the East very frequently grows as tares

---

[1] Winer, *Gram.* p. 514 (Clark).
[2] Cf. *e.g.* vv. 19, 31; Luke viii. 7; 2 Cor. viii. 16.
[3] See the previous parable, on ver. 19.
[4] So we must read, with Lachmann and Tischendorf, instead of ἔσπειρεν.

among the wheat, and is very similar to the latter, especially while still young. The Talmudists take the *lolium* as degenerate wheat."[1] The separation being troublesome even afterwards, the full-grown darnel not seldom gets into the bread, spoiling it, and making its use injurious to health. The malicious design of the enemy is thus, by mingling darnel with the wheat, to destroy the grain in the field and the fruit expected from it. With this intention he does not even sow darnel in straight line merely, as if he only desired to see darnel growing in the field in addition to the good grain, but he sows it with such premeditation, as the words ἀνὰ μέσον τοῦ σίτου specially emphasize, that it appears among the good grain now definitely called wheat. Of set purpose the enemy aims in the act of sowing at so intermingling the two—wheat and darnel—that a separation of the one from the other shall be made as hard as possible. But in order that he may not be seen and disturbed in this wicked action of his, he chooses the time when men sleep (ἐν δὲ τῷ καθεύδ. τοὺς ἀνθρ.); and as soon as he has finished his work he makes off again (καὶ ἀπῆλθεν), as unnoticed as he came. Only by adjusting the meaning of the narrative to an interpretation settled beforehand has it been possible to limit the quite general expression: ἐν τῷ καθεύδ. τοὺς ἀνθρ., to the sleeping of the field-watchers,[2] or, as modern writers also wish, to the sleeping of the owner's servants mentioned afterwards (ver. 27). For neither does the outward wording furnish the slightest support to such a limitation, nor the tenor of the narrative any actual occasion for it. The words simply denote the general, therefore the nocturnal, sleeping-time of men, which as such is especially favourable to one who desires to remain unseen and undisturbed in what he does.

To καὶ ἀπῆλθεν Bengel well appends the note: "Inde aliquantisper latuere zizania." The secrecy in which the enemy succeeded in veiling his action necessarily had for its consequence,

---

[1] Winer, *Bibl. Wörterbuch*, Zeller's *Bibl. Wörterbuch*, and the Calwer *Bibl. Nat. Gesch.*, would take ζιζάνιον not as darnel, but as creeping wheat or couch-grass (*triticum repens*), especially with reference to ver. 29, because the couch-grass penetrates the ground with its creeping roots, and intertwines with the roots of the wheat, which makes its extirpation impossible. But that the supposition of the couch-grass is needless for the understanding of ver. 29, see on the passage. On the contrary, the confidence with which the servants (ver. 28) seek permission to root up the zizanium shows that the uprooting of these tares was neither impracticable nor unusual in ordinary circumstances.

[2] Chrysostom, Bengel.

through the great likeness of the young darnel to the wheat, that even on the sprouting of the blade, the presence of the former among the wheat remained concealed. But in contrast with this concealment of the tares at first, such as is implied in what is said in ver. 25, it is now said in ver. 26 : ὅτε δὲ ἐβλάστησεν ὁ χόρτος καὶ καρπὸν ἐποίησεν, τότε ἐφάνη καὶ τὰ ζιζάνια. The καρπὸν ποιεῖν here, in distinction from Luke viii. 8, can only be meant to signify the first fruit-forming, the setting of the fruit, since, according to ver. 30, there is still a considerable time to harvest. But in the forming of the fruit appear the definite signs distinguishing the tares from the wheat. "The distinction becomes easier, so soon as the slender, bearded stalk is formed, with the single ears crowning the stem."[1] Thus the meaning of the sentence is: "*But when the grass*[2] (here without distinction the grass of the field generally) *sprang up and brought forth fruit, then appeared* (whereas hitherto all seemed to be wheat) *the darnel also*" (*i.e.* was recognised as such).

This appearance of the darnel then forms the subject of a conversation between the owner of the field or householder and his servants, who now figure in the narrative for the first time. The scene of this conversation is immaterial, nor is it anywhere definitely indicated. Neither προσελθόντες, ver. 27, nor ἀπελθόντες, ver. 28, contains such an indication,[3] the former simply denoting the coming of the servants to the master to ask a question, the latter simply the going away to carry out a command. The occasion of the conversation is the extreme surprise of the servants at the appearance of the darnel. They know, or at least assume, that their master sowed good, exclusively good, grain in his field. And yet amid the good grain they find the darnel grown so thickly, that it can only have been sown of set purpose, thus rendering their assumption questionable, although, of course, in an incomprehensible way. This utterly helpless perplexity of theirs at the fact lying before their eyes finds apt expression in their inquiry, ver. 27: "*And the servants of the householder came and said unto him: Didst thou not sow good grain in thy field? Whence then hath it darnel?*" By the first negative question, expecting therefore an affirmative answer, they themselves reject as inconceivable, even while stating, the only possible explanation, in their opinion, of the present phenomenon,

---

[1] Riehm, *Bibl. Handwörterbuch.*   [2] [Of course the green corn.]
[3] Olshausen: the house of the householder.

namely, that their master sowed anything but good grain, and all that is left to them is to proceed to the second question of helpless surprise: "Whence then hath it darnel?"[1] But the householder, who is of course conscious of only having sown good grain, at once perceives the true origin of the present phenomenon, and is therefore able to give to the perplexed inquirers the simple explanation of the mystery, ver. 28: "*A hostile man* (ἐχθρὸς ἄνθρωπος) *has done this.*" Such is the answer, and not as Luther translates: "The enemy hath done this." The person of the doer is not definitely indicated, as if the work of his enemy, related in ver. 25, had been known to the householder from the first,[2] a supposition only possible by taking the interpretation into account beforehand,—a course out of harmony with the natural course of the narrative. All that is said is, that the sowing of the darnel was the act of a man of *hostile* disposition. Accordingly, the entire emphasis of the answer lies on the ἐχθρός prefixed as an adjective. To the conjecture expressed, although only in negative form, that he himself perchance in some way was the cause of the present state of things, the householder opposes as the only possibility, and therefore by inference as matter of fact, the statement that it was a man *hostile* to him who had done this, with the malicious intention of injuring him.

But all the more the servants now think they are right in concluding that he will desire the darnel sown out of enmity to him to be at once pulled up. Hence their second question, ver. 28: θέλεις οὖν ἀπελθόντες συλλέξωμεν αὐτά. The conjunctive of deliberation συλλέξωμεν is here, as is usual in verbs of wishing or permitting,[3] connected directly with θέλεις, which may be reproduced in German thus: "*Also du willst, wir sollen hingehen, und ihn zusammenlesen? Wilt thou then we go* (ἀπελθόντες, go from here on the instant) *and gather it up?*" They speak only of *gathering* the darnel, not of rooting it up, which must of course come first, nor of the burning which usually follows. The choice of this and only of this word shows, that they are not so much concerned for the destruction of the darnel as for the purity of the wheat. Their eager regard is directed to gathering the darnel

---

[1] This question and the following answer should properly have restrained any one from asserting that originally the parable mentioned only an everyday phenomenon, and the sowing by an enemy (ver. 25) is a later addition (Weiss), instead of being bold enough to propose at the same time simply to expunge vv. 27, 28.

[2] Stier.   [3] Cf. xxvi. 17; Luke ix. 54; Winer, *Gram.* p. 356.

from amid the wheat by itself, so that the good may be purified from the bad grain intermingled with it; and this, they think, must also be their master's will. But in this they are mistaken. The answer of the householder runs, ver. 29: οὔ, scil. οὐ θέλω. Little as the growth of the darnel among the wheat lay in his intention, on the other hand, after the darnel has come into existence, it is by no means his will that a premature attempt be made to pull it up. Why not, the appended sentence says: "*Lest haply while ye gather the darnel, ye root up the wheat with it.*" Thus they are forbidden to gather the darnel, because they could not do so without at the same time plucking up the wheat. But this danger to the wheat does not lie in the impossibility or difficulty of distinguishing the two growths from each other, since their similarity at first has already, according to ver. 26, given place to a definite distinction. The servants have already distinguished the two; and in the harvest, ver. 30, the reapers also must distinguish the two, to whom a higher gift of discrimination can only be ascribed in comparison with the servants by an inadmissible anticipation of the interpretation. The danger lies rather in the fact that, after the darnel has been carefully sown among the wheat for the very purpose of making separation difficult, ver. 25, it has intertwined its roots with those of the wheat in the twice-sown earth, and, mingling everywhere thickly among the latter, and as it were identified with it, has overspread the whole field. Thus the uprooting of the darnel, although it may be done without material injury where tares are found here and there by chance in the wheat-field, would be impossible in the present case, without at the same time uprooting the genuine wheat, unripe as it still is, and thus destroying it while in process of development.

What, then, is to be done? What is to be the final outcome of this mixing of the bad with the good grain? The householder's answer to this question, unexpressed indeed, but necessarily following from what precedes, forms the conclusion of the parable. He first gives the servants instructions as to how long the mingling of the darnel among the wheat, once it exists, is to last, and secondly as to when and how the separation is to take place; and this in so certain and thoroughgoing a manner, that all anxiety about the final issue must needs disappear. He says first, ver. 30: "*Let both grow together until the harvest.*" The emphasis lies on the last words, which add something new, saying as they do how long the present state of things is to last. Until the harvest (i.e. as long as the time of growth and ripening lasts) they are to let both—darnel and wheat—grow together, and let each one separately bring forth the fruit already set according to ver. 26. And then, when the harvest comes, will be the time when alone the separation can and will take place with certain, thoroughgoing completeness. That it will then take place, and how, he says in the second place: καὶ ἐν καιρῷ τοῦ θερισμοῦ ἐρῶ τοῖς θερισταῖς κ.τ.λ. Then, ἐν καιρῷ τοῦ θερισμοῦ, he—the householder himself—will provide for the severance of the bad grain from the good; then will he himself issue orders to separate the two. The article before καιρῷ is to be erased on decisive testimony. But it is not on this account necessary to apply here the usual meaning of the formula ἐν καιρῷ, "at the right time,"[1] in which case the genitive τοῦ θερισμοῦ, as a more precise definition added appositionally, would be grievously limping. For, that the article may be absent before καιρός not only when, standing alone, it has the above general signification, but also when, as here, it is a time more precisely defined by a genitive or adjective, is proved by passages like Luke viii. 13; 1 Pet. i. 5; Heb. ix., xi. 11. Ἐν καιρῷ τοῦ θερ. is therefore simply "at the time of the harvest." But that this particular time of the harvest is not fortuitously chosen, but is alone the *right* time for effecting the separation, which is most closely connected with the work of the harvest, is implied of itself in the wording of the householder's command, nay, even in the naming of the persons to whom the command is addressed. It is not issued to servants at random, but to those to whom the work of harvest belongs, "to the harvesters."[2] And indeed for this reason, because, as the command itself shows, the separation is to be effected by them in connection with their harvest-work. The command thus runs: "Gather up *first* the darnel and bind it in bundles[3] to burn it; but gather the wheat into my barn." The harvest then is come, the reapers stand ready to do the work (*i.e.* to gather the corn from the field, where it stood hitherto, into the barn); this is the situation in which the command is issued. But when the harvesters stand ready to do what belongs to their office, the householder's command intervenes with its πρῶτον. The grain is not to be gathered into the barn without thought and

---

[1] Bengel, Stier, Lange.   [2] Ὁ θεριστής here and in ver. 39 is = ὁ θερίζων.
[3] The τις before δεσμάς is to be erased, with Tischendorf.

discrimination. For only the genuine grain, which he himself sowed, belongs to *his* barn (εἰς τὴν ἀποθήκην μου), not the bad, which his enemy sowed. *First*, therefore, the reapers must gather together the darnel, an act no longer dangerous to the wheat which is fully ripened and only awaits the barn,—and, binding it into bundles, prepare it for the fire, to which it belongs by reason of its thoroughly worthless, even harmful nature. But the wheat, and the wheat only, they are to gather into his barn. With the promulgation of this command the parable has reached its conclusion, there being no need to mention that the reapers will do as they are commanded.

If, then, we review the entire course of the figurative history, there meets us at once, as the one fact treated of from beginning to end, the appearance of the darnel among the wheat crop. The entire parable groups itself around this one fact; the first part, vv. 24–26, giving information as to its real origin, whereas in the second, vv. 27–30, the fact becomes the subject of a conversation in which the householder first of all brings to light the concealed fact of its origin, then intimates the conduct to be pursued in relation to the mixed state, and finally, explains the when and how of the final severance. Accordingly, the gaining of the right standpoint for the explanation of the parable all depends on ascertaining what fact in the sphere of the heavenly kingdom is meant to be represented by the appearance of the darnel among the wheat.

And we shall learn this without difficulty by considering the context in which the parable stands, by comparing it with the one which it follows in Christ's discourse according to Matthew's account. The first thing meeting our view in this comparison is, that the figurative setting, within which the two narratives move, is exactly the same. Here as there, a sown field, in which the wheat crop grows and ripens, is equally pictured—an identity of background in the two parabolic figures, which not merely justifies us in starting from the interpretation of the first one in interpreting the second, but even compels us to do so. But the characteristic feature, presented in the process of the growth of the grain, consisted in the first case in this, that it attained full ripeness only in one part, because disturbed and spoilt sooner or later in the process of development by various hindrances. In the development of the heavenly kingdom, the fact corresponding to this physical occurrence is, that only in a portion of those called through the preaching of the word to the kingdom of heaven is the issue that form of life which makes them actual members of the kingdom. Comparing with this the contents of the present parable, we find that those various hindrances to the development of the grain are here left quite out of sight. On the contrary, the uniform undisturbed development of the grain in natural course up to the harvest is presupposed; and thus, in distinction from the first parable, the crop forms a united whole, springing from the same soil, going through the same development, ripening to the same end. For this reason it cannot, as in the first parable, be meant to symbolize merely those called to the heavenly kingdom as hearers of the word, but the calling to the kingdom here coincides with belonging to it, the hindrances to the effect of the call being ignored. And thus the counterpart of the grain here is a united whole, it is the members of the kingdom absolutely, the body of members or the community of the kingdom of heaven. And to the other phenomenon attracting attention in this second parabolic figure, namely, that a second and different crop appears among the wheat-crop, everywhere intermingled with it, which, similar as it seems, has really nothing in common with it, being mere darnel, a worthless, nay, harmful weed,—to this phenomenon the only possible corresponding fact in the development of the heavenly kingdom is, that amid the community of God's kingdom, everywhere intermingled with its true members, there are found those who belong to it in appearance, but in reality have nothing in common with it, being inwardly alien and hostile to the nature of the heavenly kingdom.

The way in which we saw Jesus introduce the parable with the preterite $\omega\mu οιώθη =$ " has become like," shows that this fact of a mingling of alien elements in the circle of disciples gathered round Him was not merely foreseen by Him as something future, but was already experimentally present to His consciousness. With the glance of the Heart-searcher He had discerned among those who passed as His disciples, nominal disciples, like the darnel among the wheat. On the other hand, it is scarcely to be supposed that this fact had then occurred to the disciples themselves; in any case it was reserved for them to learn it soon enough by experience. And they all the more needed to be forewarned in reference to it, as it stood in opposition to their expectations of the Messianic kingdom presently to be set up, just as much as the fact of the conditional and therefore diverse success of Christ's Messianic work, that formed the subject of the first parable. For not merely did the language of the prophets seem to them to sanction the expectation that the community of the Messianic kingdom, in opposition to the blending of righteous and unrighteous, true and false members, existing previously in the Israelitish national Church, would be exclusively pure and holy in form,[1] but also the voice of John the Baptist, scarcely as yet silent, definitely foretold that the Messiah coming after him would thoroughly carry out the purifying work requisite for such an end (Matt. iii. 12). Thus the truth, *that righteous and unrighteous, true and false members, would again exist together even in the Church of the Messianic kingdom,* was in fact to them a mystery, respecting which they needed instruction, —and to give this to them we recognise as the one aim of the present parable. But the way and order in which this instruction is given, according to the structure of the figurative narrative explained above, is, *that first the origin of this state of things is disclosed to them, then instruction is given as to the conduct to be pursued in relation to it, and lastly, it is shown when and where this state of things will find its final solution.*

In proceeding to gather these disclosures from the parable one after another by interpreting the details, we have again, as in the first parable, the help of an explanation given afterwards, according to the evangelist's account, by Jesus Himself to His disciples. In the conversation of Jesus with the disciples in private after the dismissal of the multitude, the contents of which have been partially anticipated by the interpolation vv. 10–23 for incidental reasons, and which is further related in the place (from ver. 36 on) to which it belongs in order of time, the disciples requested an interpretation of the second parable, probably in allusion to the extended one given them of the first parable. They rightly name it after the subject of which it treats throughout. In ver. 36 they ask: φράσον ἡμῖν τὴν παραβολὴν τῶν ζιζανίων τοῦ ἀγροῦ. Φράζειν is such a telling as makes another know or understand something, thus here: "*Explain to us the parable of the tares of the field.*" On this request Jesus gives them the explanation, vv. 37–43. True, the originality of this explanation has been denied,[2] and it has been called the work of the evangelist, both because of the style of

[1] Cf. Isa. lx. 18, 21.   [2] Ewald, Holtzmann, Weiss.

the explanation and because of the alleged discrepancy between it and the parable itself. What is to be thought of this assertion can only be seen from a complete examination. We have accordingly first of all to take this explanation into consideration, without, of course, thinking that we are thereby raised above the necessity of independent investigation and explanation.[1]

The assistance given to the interpretation of the first part of the parable (vv. 24–26) embraces ver. 37 up to the words in ver. 39 : ὁ δὲ ἐχθρὸς ὁ σπείρας αὐτά ἐστιν ὁ διάβολος. The *assistance* to the interpretation—we say advisedly. For a glance at this section shows that the method of interpretation here differs considerably from the way in which we saw Jesus interpret the first parable. Whereas there from beginning to end He placed the corresponding *events* in the sphere of the kingdom of heaven over against the *events* described in the sphere of nature, thus giving an interpretation in the proper sense, expressing and working out the thoughts of the parable; here at first He merely selects the particular ideas occurring in the figurative history, and leaves the hearers to construct for themselves the proper interpretation of the events from the material thus given into their hands. The motive for this course is His wish to lead the disciples, after completely explaining the first parable to them, to an independent and spontaneous interpretation of His parables. This design is especially apparent from the fact, that He forthwith delivers to them a number of new parables (vv. 44–50), without any explanation whatever, and at the end asks them, ver. 51 : " Have ye understood all these things ? " to which they are able to reply with a simple " Yea." The man in the parable, the field, the good grain, the darnel, the enemy, —these are the five ideas taken from the parable, over against which a counterpart is placed in succession. First of all it is said : " *He that* (according to the narrative delivered) *soweth the good grain is the Son of man.*" This is not the place to investigate more carefully the meaning of Christ's designation of Himself as " the Son of man," as it would contribute nothing to the understanding of the parable. Suffice it to recall the fact, which may pass as undoubted, that it is a designation of Himself as the manifested Messiah. He says that He—Jesus—in His character as the manifested Christ, is He who sowed the good grain, that to do so is His Messianic calling, in the performance

[1] Cf. what was said on the interpretation of the previous parable.

of which He is *engaged*. For such is the meaning when, instead of the σπείραντι in ver. 24 being simply resumed in ὁ σπείρας, the aorist is changed into the present ὁ σπείρων. "*And the field*"—so it is said further in ver. 38, that field therefore which is mentioned in the parable of the Sower, and in which He sows the good grain—"*is the world*," ὁ κόσμος, viewed according to New-Testament usage as the abode of mankind in the present aeon. And of the good grain, standing on the ground of the world, it is said in the third place: τὸ δὲ καλὸν σπέρμα, οὗτοί εἰσιν οἱ υἱοὶ τῆς βασιλείας. On account of the plural predicate the singular subject is again resumed with οὗτοι. Υἱός, as often, denotes the relation of belonging to; οἱ υἱοὶ τῆς βασιλείας are therefore the adherents of the kingdom of Messiah or of heaven, belonging to it in so far as the word and will of God have become the ruling principle of their life. But as members of the one organized kingdom—this lies, of course, in the case—they are not merely an aggregate of individuals, but an interconnected whole, the community of the kingdom or the Church of the kingdom of God. But their being identified with τὸ καλὸν σπέρμα confirms to us the fact, if it needs further confirmation, that "the good seed" in the figurative story was not meant as the means, but as the result of the sowing, as the grain to be produced in and upon the field. Then, again, the bad crop of the tares is placed beside the καλὸν σπέρμα and explained in parallelism with it, and is then for the first time traced back to the enemy who sowed it; for, so it is said in the fourth place: τὰ δὲ ζιζάνιά εἰσιν οἱ υἱοὶ τοῦ πονηροῦ. The genitive τοῦ πονηροῦ is not here, as is almost universally supposed, to be taken as a genit. masc., but as a genit. neut., hence with Luther: "*but the tares are the children of wickedness.*" *Per se* both senses are equally possible. For as ὁ πονηρός is a designation of the devil (ver. 19, etc.), so also τὸ πονηρόν = wickedness, moral badness, is an expression common in the New Testament.[1] Moreover, the combination υἱοὶ τοῦ πονηροῦ presents just as little difficulty in the neuter acceptation of the genitive as in the masculine.[2] But decisive in favour of the neuter acceptation here is first the parallel οἱ υἱοὶ τῆς βασιλείας, and again principally the circumstance that a special sentence is added for the purpose of mentioning the devil, in

---

[1] Chap. v. 37; Rom. xii. 9; 1 John v. 19.
[2] Cf. υἱοὶ τῆς ἀπειθείας, Eph. ii. 2, v. 6; Col. iii. 6; τέκνα ἀδικίας, Hos. x. 9.

correspondence with the enemy in the parable, as he with whom the distinctive nature of the class of men symbolized by τὰ ζιζάνια originates. If, then, τὰ ζιζάνια may here be already interpreted of the children of the devil, the following sentence becomes thoroughly tautological. Accordingly, "the sons of wickedness" in the present sentence is meant to describe the class of men corresponding to the tares, not according to the person from whom they spring, but merely according to their own distinctive nature, in virtue of which they are the counterpart of the tares. To the bad darnel-growth correspond the children of (moral) badness or wickedness, the latter being regarded as a substantive principle, by which their distinctive nature is determined. Then only does the following sentence come in easily and naturally, giving the fifth explanation, ver. 39 : "*And the enemy that sowed them is the devil.*"

With the aid of these hints, then, let us work out the interpretation of the first part of the parable, which reveals in the form of a narrative of definite events the *origin* of the fact, that true and false members are found together in the Church of the Messianic kingdom. As the sowing of the man in the parable aims only at a *good* crop, which is to stand in his field, so the Messianic work of the Son of man is only directed and adapted to establish for Himself on the ground of this world, which is His world, a *holy church and kingdom,* consisting of such members as are constituted members in the true sense by the righteousness of the kingdom of heaven distinguishing them. It is evident that this interpretation of the first statement of the parable, as on one hand it assigns its proper force to each of the single hints given by the Lord with respect to the interpretation, so on the other hand it corresponds exactly to the wording of the figurative story. Only in one point have those important hints added something new, not lying directly and necessarily in the parable, namely, in relation to the interpretation of the field. Of course the field, which is set down in the narrative as the property of the man, which he has a right to sow, requires a definite counterpart in the interpretation. But whether it is to be explained of the nationality of Israel, or of the human world generally, the narrative of itself does not say with certainty; and from their standpoint the disciples might, without opposition from anything in the parable, be inclined to understand the former. Christ's explanatory words have made it certain that He wished the human world generally, not Israel, to be understood. Not the Israelitish nationality, but the world generally, so far as it is the dwelling-place of men, is to Him the field *to be sown, i.e.* the ground to which He has a right, and on which He is about to establish for Himself a holy Church and kingdom. But the field *sown*, in which the pure crop already stands, is the world, inasmuch and in so far as at any time it has become in fact the ground of God's kingdom; and, where the field occurs further in the parable (cf. ver. 27), in the nature of the case it can only be "the world" in the latter reference and limitation, *i.e.* only so far as upon and in it the kingdom of heaven has come to realization.

But as the man in the parable, so the interpretation continues, had an enemy, so the Son of man has in the devil an antagonist, who is bent on destroying His work. For, like the enemy of the householder, who sowed darnel—so like wheat, and yet so bad—in the midst of the pure wheat, so the devil strives with earnest zeal to bring even into the new Church of the heavenly kingdom false members, who outwardly belong to it, whereas in truth they have nothing in common with the kingdom of heaven and its righteousness, being determined and ruled by the opposite principle of sin. And again, like as the enemy sowed the darnel so secretly that, at first unknown, it was only known on the growth of the blade by the setting of the fruit, so Satan is able to veil his evil action in such secrecy that its effects remain concealed in the beginning, and the introduction of false members into the Church is first known as an accomplished fact by the fruit of evil works found in its midst. All special interpretations assigned to the words ἐν τῷ καθεύδειν τοὺς ἀνθρώπους beyond the general thought of the secrecy of the devil's action, either by trying to find in them a special accusation against the ecclesiastical office,[1] or an image of indifference to God's word and of a state of spiritual indolence generally,[2] have been already rendered questionable by settling the sense of these words in the context of the narrative, where the sleeping involves neither a special nor a general reproach. On the other hand, in the circumstance that the recognition of the darnel is placed expressly in the forming of the fruit (ver. 26), and in the often-recurring emphasis of the good or evil fruit as the mark of the good or evil nature of the tree in other figurative speeches of the Lord,[3] we believe we see a special allusion to the truth, that the existence of false members

---

[1] So the ancients. [2] Keil. [3] Cf. vii. 16–20, xii. 33; Luke vi. 43, 44.

in the kingdom will be known by the scandal arising from wicked works.[1]

After the origin of the state of things in question has been revealed in the first part of the parable in the form of an account of definite occurrences, the further teachings to be communicated on the point are given in the second part in the form of a conversation of the householder with his servants. If we observe the remarks of Christ in His interpretation on this second part of the parable, we find that He makes the interpretation of the "harvest" and the "reapers" follow immediately on the five single indications in ver. 39 already noticed, thus passing at once to the last declaration of the householder, which forms the conclusion of the conversation, and thus of the entire parable. And this cannot surprise us in view of the character of the interpretation which bears only on the single ideas, such as we have observed hitherto. For apart from the servants, who do not interfere in the action of the parable itself, but merely appear on the scene as persons astonished at and receiving instruction on the fact lying before them, up to that concluding declaration of the householder, no new persons or ideas emerge in the conversation, which proceeds exclusively on the basis already given in what precedes. We have accordingly to continue the interpretation exclusively on this basis.

As concerns first the servants, who figure in the narrative as persons needing and receiving instruction in reference to the appearance of the darnel, the disciples of Jesus who listen to the parable, without needing any special indication of the Lord, must in them have recognised themselves as the persons to whom the instruction of the parable is addressed, and who called it forth. In the first twofold question of the servants (ver. 27), they find striking expression given to their surprise at the state of things disclosed in the parable as something of which they will soon enough have experience. For like as the servants, in their astonishment at the appearance of the darnel, were almost deceived respecting the householder and respecting the aim of his work being a *good* crop, so the appearance of the children of wickedness amid the Church of God, established by Jesus in the world, may expose them to the danger of mistake respecting Him, their Lord, and respecting the aim of His Messianic work being the restoration of a *holy* kingdom of God. But let them not be deceived!

[1] Cf. τὰ σκάνδαλα, ver. 41.

Such is the answer of the householder (ver. 28), setting the explanation of the origin of the strange phenomenon, already given in the matter-of-fact account in the first part of the parable, once more before them in the form of a retrospective inference from the existing state of things. In these words of the householder, Jesus once more expressly testifies to His disciples: The impure form, in which the kingdom of heaven is manifested, has so little to do with His own Messianic labour, whose only aim of course is to establish a holy kingdom of God, that, on the contrary, it can only be referred to the agency of a being *hostile* to Him, one diligently bent on counteracting His work.

But they must not allow the certainty that the authorship of the existing mixed state is as stated, to hurry them away to a mistaken and premature line of action. The danger of this is disclosed in the second question put into the mouth of the servants, according to which, with apparent reasonableness, they expect to be empowered to separate the darnel from the wheat forthwith. For, if the introduction of false members into the Church is only to be referred to the irregular agency of an enemy of Christ and His kingdom, how probable seems the inference, that the enemy's pernicious work should be counteracted, the false members removed from the midst of the Church, and the Church restored to unsullied purity! In this way the transition is made to the second instruction contained in the parable, relating to *the attitude of the disciples* towards the form of the development of the kingdom under consideration. With the οὔ (ver. 29), Jesus commands them to abstain from their well-meant purpose to sever the false from the true members of the kingdom forthwith, and to renounce the attractive notion of an immediate restoration of the kingdom of God in unsullied purity. For what reason He wills this, is said in the telic sentence appended. As it would be an impossibility to gather the darnel, everywhere thickly intermingled with the wheat, out of the midst of the grain, growing and intertwining its roots as it does in and upon the same ground, without at the same time uprooting the wheat itself, still unripe, so it would be impossible to exclude from the midst of the Church the false members everywhere thickly interspersed with the true members of the kingdom, and closely connected and intertwined with them on the same ground in all the concerns and relations of natural life. It could only be done by withdrawing the Church itself at the same time from the soil of worldly life, upon which, however, it has to develope, and from the sphere of the natural relations of life, within which it has to gain strength, a course which would cut it off from the possibility of continuous development, and hand it over to decay. If, then, we have rightly unfolded the thought of the parable, it has nothing in common with the notion that the Church must not arrogate to itself penal authority over the person and life of its false members,[1] for the zeal forbidden in the parable was not directed so much to the destruction of the darnel, as rather merely to its severance from the wheat. But the prohibition is not opposed to any kind of Church discipline, exercised on individual members for their training, or as an atonement for a special public scandal; but it is simply directed against the fundamental attempt, by summary and absolute exclusion of all false members, to establish the Church of God's kingdom in complete purity and sanctity during the stadium of its development on the ground of the cosmos. And the reason of the prohibition is not placed in the danger of confounding the false with the true members,[2] so that one might go on with the exclusion without scruple, so far as no such danger existed,—for the similarity of the darnel to the wheat no longer came into account in this passage,—but the prohibition is simply based on the close intermingling of the false among the true members, and the close connection of the two, which cannot be broken up without a pernicious effect on the Church itself.

But how long the Church of the kingdom of heaven is to remain in this mixed state, and when and how its restoration to full purity and sanctity is to take place, this is stated in the final words of the householder (ver. 30), where the third instruction is given respecting the *issue* which the present state of things will have. But here again the interpretation of the Lord strikes in, and we have first of all to direct our attention to it.

The interpretation (ver. 39*b*) continuing just as heretofore, in the first place two new ideas, which appear here in the action of the parable, are explained, each one by itself—the harvest and the reapers. It is said first: ὁ δὲ θερισμὸς συντέλεια αἰῶνός[3] ἐστιν. The harvest in the parable came into view as the temporal end of the period of growth and maturity, and in this sense "*the consummation of the* (current) *age*" corresponds to it in the sphere of the kingdom of heaven. It is said secondly: οἱ δὲ

---

[1] As many suppose, in the train of Luther.
[2] So Jerome, Bengel, Bleek.   [3] Rec.: τοῦ αἰῶνος

θερισταὶ ἀγγελοί εἰσιν, *i.e.* the *reapers,* who appear in the parable at harvest-*time* as the official agents of the harvest-*work,* in the sphere of the kingdom of heaven are *angels.* But now the discourse of Jesus rises from the previous method of interpreting single ideas to a proper and complete interpretation of the last thought of the parable, which is accordingly expounded with solemn emphasis in elevated language and elaborate detail in vv. 40–43. Ver. 40 serves to introduce what follows: "*As then the darnel is gathered and burned with fire, so shall it be in the end of the world.*" The protasis is not to be taken as reminding of what is usually done with darnel, but according to the context, as a definite reference to what will be done, according to the words of the householder in the parable, at the time of harvest with the darnel sown by the enemy. What was there said (ver. 30) of the gathering together of the darnel is here resumed with συλλέγεται, and what was said of preparing the darnel, πρὸς τὸ κατακαῦσαι αὐτά, is resumed with πυρὶ καίεται,[1] the πυρί being added plerophorically to prepare for the intended explanation, in which the idea of fire occurs expressly. But no stress must be laid on the replacing of the compound verb κατακαῦσαι (ver. 30) by the simple verb καίεται, even if this reading is the right one in ver. 40, because καίεσθαι may, and here must, signify "*be consumed,*" just as well as κατακαίεσθαι, since it is impossible to say of the darnel, "it is set on fire with fire."[2] Thus something analogous to the gathering and burning of the darnel will take place in the consummation of the age. And this is more fully explained ver. 41: "*The Son of man will send His angels,*" *His* angels, because standing at His command as their Lord, for the execution of His will, as in the parable the reapers at the command of the lord of the harvest. But the mandate is not mentioned, for the execution of which they are sent, as in the case of the reapers in the parable, the execution itself being assumed, but conversely, the mandate being assumed, its execution is at once affirmed. On the ground of their mission they will do two things—the first corresponding to the συλλέγειν of. the darnel, the second to the πυρὶ καίειν. To the former corresponds ver. 41*b*: καὶ συλλέξουσιν ἐκ τῆς βασιλείας αὐτοῦ πάντα τὰ σκάνδαλα καὶ τοὺς ποιοῦντας τὴν ἀνομίαν. The kingdom of the Son of man (ἡ βασιλεία αὐτοῦ), to which this is done, is

---

[1] Or, according to another likewise well-attested reading: πυρὶ κατακαίεται.
[2] Meyer.

the kingdom founded by Him, and existing in the present æon on the ground of the cosmos, not the one set up at the συντέλεια τοῦ αἰῶνος.[1] For what transformation the present state of things is to undergo at the συντέλεια τοῦ αἰῶνος remains still to be told. Hitherto, in the æon now ended, the kingdom of God had only come to realization in such a form that, according to its empirical appearance, such as was presented in the Church standing on the ground of the world, it included σκάνδαλα and workers of ἀνομία. To this present state an end is now put by the angels gathering out of the kingdom πάντα τὰ σκάνδαλα καὶ τοὺς ποιοῦντας τὴν ἀνομίαν. But τὰ σκάνδαλα must not be taken as a designation of persons. The appeal to Matt. xvi. 23 [2] does not warrant this, for when Jesus there says of Peter that he is a σκάνδαλον, the word is still merely the predicate attached to a person,[3] by no means the designation of a person. Moreover, if the σκάνδαλα are meant to be persons, we must either distinguish those thus designated from the ποιοῦντες τὴν ἀνομίαν, as specially scandalous evil-doers, from those sinning merely *pro sua parte* (Bengel), which distinction is altogether destitute of support in the parable, and, if intended, would have been more clearly expressed, or we must concede a tautology.[4] But the force of the periphrastic expression τοὺς ποιοῦντας τὴν ἀνομίαν is, that the language advances from the actual scandals to their personal authors, from the scandalous acts to their doers, so that the scandals are rather to be identified with ἀνομία than with ποιοῦντες. What was scandalous in the outward appearance of the kingdom was not primarily the false members themselves, but the evil works by which the existence of the former was made known.[5] For this reason also here, where the point in question is the restoration of the kingdom to an appearance corresponding to its inner nature, the removal of these actual scandals is primarily considered, and so a difference is made between the fruit of the tares and the tares. Every sinful work and thing in antagonism to God's holy will (called σκάνδαλα, because calculated to lead to error respecting God's holy nature, and the divine origin of the kingdom itself, where found within the Church of the kingdom), and those who do τὴν ἀνομίαν, that which is in opposition to God's ordinances, and therefore the authors of those scandals, the angels will *gather* out of the kingdom of their Lord, the

---

[1] Meyer.   [2] Meyer, Keil, Weiss.   [3] As *e.g.* also in 1 Cor. i. 23.
[4] Meyer.   [5] Cf. ver. 26 and its interpretation.

expression being preserved which is used of what the reapers do to the darnel, *i.e.* they will remove and exclude them all from the kingdom. And, in the second place, they will do with them, the ποιοῦντες (for in the punishment, of course, merely the persons come into view), what corresponds to the πυρὶ καίειν (ver. 42) : "*They shall cast them into the furnace of fire.*" Ἡ κάμινος τοῦ πυρός is Gehenna. But this appellation is not, as we might be inclined to suppose, specially used here in allusion to the image of the tares, which are cast into a furnace to be burnt, for it recurs (ver. 50) in a parable without a groundwork of this kind, still less is there any reference to the fiery furnace, into which, according to Dan. iii., Daniel's friends were cast,[1] which has not the most remote relation to Gehenna; but the designation of Gehenna as the "fiery furnace" follows naturally on the ground of the general conception of Gehenna as the place of punishment of the condemned burning with fire.[2] But the choice of this particular designation was specially appropriate, because it clearly emphasizes the point of comparison between the fate of the evil-doers and that of the tares. Finally, that the furnace of fire means, as matter of fact, nothing but the well-known place of punishment of the condemned, is shown by the words often recurring in similar connections elsewhere in the discourses of Jesus: "*There shall be the weeping and the gnashing* (biting together from pain) *of teeth.*" Here, as wherever this formula occurs, the article stands before κλανθμός and βρυγμός, because the pain of the condemned is not described, but something well known to the hearers is simply brought to recollection.

But with this addition the explanatory language of Jesus has already outstepped the limits of what was said in the parable, in such a way, however, as merely to add something directly resulting from what precedes. In the same manner he now further expounds the subject under the other aspect, when, finally turning from the unrighteous to the righteous, He says of the latter (ver. 43) : τότε οἱ δίκαιοι ἐκλάμψουσιν ὡς ὁ ἥλιος ἐν τῇ βασιλείᾳ τοῦ πατρὸς αὐτῶν. In the parable, after the description of the measures to be taken in regard to the tares, it was merely said of the wheat—what is already implied in the idea of reaping— that it is to be gathered into the barn. The interpretation does not reproduce this circumstance of the reaping, but mentions the

[1] Lange. [2] Cf. xxv. 41 ; Rev. xix. 20, xx. 15.

counterpart of the barn—the place in which the righteous will be gathered: ἐν τῇ βασιλείᾳ τοῦ πατρὸς αὐτῶν. This expression is notably different from the one used in ver. 41 : ἐκ τῆς βασιλείας αὐτοῦ, scil. of the Son of Man ; and under this difference of expression here lies a difference in the thing described. As certainly as the βασιλεία there could only be the kingdom of God founded by the Son of Man on the ground of the world, and developing on this ground until the end of the current age, so certainly can the βασιλεία here, as the dwelling-place of the righteous after the συντέλεια τ. αἰῶν., only be the divine kingdom of the future æon. And just to characterize it as such is the purpose of the expression : ἡ βασ. τοῦ πατρὸς αὐτῶν. Similarly in xxvi. 9 Jesus calls it ἡ βασ. τοῦ πατρός μου, and in xxv. 34 He foretells that *the Son of man*, when He comes in His glory *with His angels* (ver. 31), will invite *the righteous* (vv. 37, 46), as the blessed *of his Father*, to take possession of *the kingdom prepared for them (by the Father) from the beginning of the world.* Accordingly there can be no doubt in what sense the expression : ἡ βασ. τοῦ πατρὸς αὐτῶν, is chosen in the present passage. It describes the divine kingdom of the future world as the eternal home prepared for the righteous by their Father. Their gathering there being presupposed, it is now said of the state in which they will be found : "*They shall shine forth* (ἐκλάμψουσιν) *like the sun.*" The words are perhaps used in allusion to the prophecy of Daniel in similar terms,[1] but their meaning is not therefore quite the same in the present context as there. There the meaning is, that the good, after their deliverance from the darkness of affliction (ver. 1), and their awakening from the night of death (ver. 2), will shine for ever in the celestial transfiguration of their natural life, כְּזֹהַר הָרָקִיעַ ; here, that, after the exclusion by the angels of everything and every one impure, the righteous will rise out of the obscurity to which their righteousness was subject through the σκάνδαλα, and the unrighteous found among them, and "will shine forth like the sun ;" shine forth, therefore, in their character as righteous with a brilliance in a moral respect pure and bright as the sun. Or, in other words, the subject here is not the glorious reward consisting in the celestial glorification of their natural life, in which the good are one day to partake, which would introduce into the interpretation an element quite new and altogether foreign to the strain

[1] Dan. xii. 3 ; cf. too Wisd. iii. 7.

of thought in the parable; but the subject is the glorious effect which the removal of the σκάνδαλα and their authors, previous to the righteous being brought into the kingdom of the Father, will have on the state of the righteous there, namely, a shining forth of their righteousness with unsullied purity. Thus, the thought added in the interpretation is again merely one directly resulting from the final events of the parable.

It remains for us, founding on these explanatory words of Jesus, to carry out the interpretation of the last teachings of the parable itself respecting the issue of the present state of things. How *long* the present blending of opposite elements in the Church of the kingdom is to last, is first stated in ver. 30*a*? As long, namely, as the period of the development of the heavenly kingdom on the ground of the cosmos lasts, so long righteous and unrighteous will remain together, and in this state of conjunction, moreover, unfold their different characters,[1] until this period finds its end in the consummation of the age. This is what is said figuratively in the words: "Let both grow together until the harvest." On the other hand, the figure of the darnel and wheat growing together gives no support to the thought, that this conjunction with the unrighteous is a training-school, and thus a means of growth, to the righteous;[2] and it must therefore be excluded from exact interpretation, however suitable it may be for homiletic purposes. Finally, ver. 30*b* says when and how the severance of the unrighteous from the righteous, and thus the restoration of the Church to complete purity and holiness, will take place. Like as the householder at the time of harvest issues orders to the harvesters, whose business it is, to gather the ripe grain into the barn; so the Son of man at the consummation of the age will issue orders to the angels, whose office it is, to bring the Church, which has attained the goal of its development, into the eternal kingdom of the future world.[3] They are not, without thought and discrimination, to bring the Church, in the mixed form belonging to it on the ground of the cosmos in the present æon, into that kingdom; but previously (συλλέξατε πρῶτον) they are to exclude all the unrighteous from its midst,

---

[1] Cf. Rev. xxii. 11.   [2] Augustine, Stier, Nebe (*die evang. Perikopen*).

[3] Weiss overlooks this in supposing that the reapers, as the regular agents of the harvest, are not to be interpreted of the angels. But the angels are just as much the regular, official agents of the future συναγωγή of believers (xxiv. 31), and for this precise reason correspond to the reapers.

and commit them to the fire of Gehenna, and then bring the righteous, and the righteous only, into the eternal homes prepared for them, into the kingdom of their Father. This is all the meaning of the συλλέξατε πρῶτον, which is certainly emphatic. On the other hand, all such thoughts as that the righteous will behold the punishment of the unrighteous,[1] or that the former will remain masters of the field,[2] lie quite outside the figure. The same holds good of the opinion, that the binding into (several) bundles, which simply pictures the manner in which the accumulated mass of tares is committed to the fire, is meant to symbolize different punishments according to the different degrees of wickedness.[3]

It is evident of itself that the teaching of the final words of the householder substantially agrees with Christ's own interpretation, only that the latter by additions still further expounds the subject of the figurative discourse on both sides, with respect to the unrighteous as well as the righteous. But the motive by which Jesus was led, in interpreting the conclusion of the parable, not merely to break off the previous mode of interpreting only single details, but to pursue the subject with such emphasis beyond the limits of what was symbolized in the parable, is not hard to perceive. The reason is not, that Jesus here gives expression to the proper theme He has in view,[4] for the teachings given at the beginning and in the middle of the parable respecting the origin of the state of things in question and the conduct to be pursued towards it stand on a footing of equal importance with the teaching given at the close respecting its issue, both as regards their formal exposition in the parable and also their intrinsic weight. Nevertheless, the Lord must have been anxious to set this last disclosure respecting the separation, which the Son of man will one day effect through His angels, with special emphasis before the eyes of the disciples; for only by keeping this firmly in view could they be saved from being deceived by the phenomenon itself and the statement first made to them as to its origin, as well as from being hurried away to a premature line of action in reference to it. We have thus found nothing, either in the manner in which the interpretation proceeds in the beginning and at the close, or in its contents, to justify the assertion that it did not originate with Jesus Himself.

[1] Bengel.   [2] Nebe.   [3] Augustine, Nebe.   [4] Meyer.

The Fruit-bearing Earth.

(Mark iv. 26-29.)

Before proceeding to the parable of the Mustard Seed, standing next in Matthew's account, we have first to direct our attention to the parallel account in the fourth chapter of Mark. How this account runs parallel with that of Matthew, has been already shown above.[1] Just like Matthew, Mark first describes the situation of the discourse of Jesus, vv. 1, 2, next records the parable of the Sower as the first, vv. 3-9, but then breaks off the account of the discourse *to the people* in order to interpolate from a subsequent conversation with the disciples alone the explanation of Jesus respecting the design of His strange mode of teaching and also His interpretation of the first parable, vv. 10-20. At this point, diverging from Matthew, he subjoins to this interpolation two sayings of Jesus, of which the first imposes on them the duty of disseminating the truths disclosed to them, vv. 21-23, and the second calls on them to take heed to what they hear, because the amount of further instruction will be measured by the degree in which they take heed, vv. 24, 25. In the case of both sayings the καὶ ἔλεγεν αὐτοῖς intimates that they are to be taken as addressed to the disciples especially, just as much as the preceding paragraph, vv. 11-20. Here the interpolation in Mark must be regarded as having come to an end. For when in ver. 26 with καὶ ἔλεγεν without αὐτοῖς he gives another parable, and with a second καὶ ἔλεγεν, ver. 30, without further connection yet another parable, and thereupon in vv. 33, 34 concludes the entire section (in correspondence with Matt. xiii. 34, 35) with the statement, that Jesus preached the word to them (the people) in many such parables, and without a parable spake not to them, but simply explained everything to His own disciples in private, it is clear that with ver. 26, like Matthew with ver. 24, he resumed the interrupted account of the parabolic discourse of Jesus from the boat. But Mark does not resume the interrupted discourse, like Matthew, with the parable of the Tares in the Wheat, but with another parable; and the two evangelists again coincide in giving the parable of the Mustard Seed as the third. Thus, the parable Mark iv. 26-29

[1] Cf. "The Parables to the People by the Sea."

stands in this evangelist in exactly the same place as that of the Tares in Matthew. But that it is in no way identical with the latter, at least in the form in which it lies before us, but is a quite different parable, the very first glance leaves no doubt. Here also, it is true, a sown field is placed before the view; but whereas in the parable in Matthew from beginning to end only the appearance of the tares is treated of, in the present parable nothing at all resembling this occurs. It requires, accordingly, separate and independent investigation.

This parable is introduced, like those related in the same context in Matthew, by prefixing the kingdom of heaven as the thing compared, only that here the expression ἡ βασιλεία τοῦ Θεοῦ, usual elsewhere, is found in place of ἡ βασ. τῶν οὐρανῶν, common in Matthew. But the manner in which the subsequent description is used for the purpose of comparing the kingdom of God is peculiar. It is said, ver. 26 f.: Οὕτως ἐστὶν ἡ βασιλεία τοῦ Θεοῦ ὡς ἄνθρωπος βάλῃ τὸν σπόρον ἐπὶ τῆς γῆς, καὶ καθεύδῃ κ.τ.λ., i.e.: It is with the kingdom of God as if a man had done this and that, and then should do so and so. The ὡς, or according to another reading ὡς ἐάν,[1] with the conj. aorist for the purpose of comparing the relations of the kingdom of God, puts a case which the hearers are to suppose has already occurred, and with the following present conjunctive a case which they are to suppose occurring afterwards. The case to be conceived as having occurred already is this, that "*a man had cast the seed upon the earth.*" Σπόρος has the article in the very beginning, because the figurative use of the seed was the basis of the first parable in the discourse. As this second parable also treats of seed, it continues within the limits of the figure already employed and familiar to the hearers. The expression "cast" instead of "sow" sets forth the comparative insignificance of what the man did with the seed; it was a mere "casting" of the seed. And the case which is represented as occurring afterwards is this, that the man then καθεύδῃ καὶ ἐγείρηται νύκτα καὶ ἡμέραν, καὶ ὁ σπόρος βλαστᾷ καὶ μηκύνηται ὡς οὐκ οἶδεν αὐτός, ver. 27. These words characterize the attitude which the man assumes to the development of the seed, after he has thrown it down, the first clause describing his *conduct* in reference to the development of the seed, whilst the second discloses his *relation* to the development, by which his

[1] But ἐάν is not necessary. Cf. e.g. Homer, Il. v. 161, ix. 323, etc.

conduct is regulated. "*And* (as if he) *should sleep and rise night and day*" (according as it is time to sleep or wake) is the first statement. Thus his mode of life is described as determined by the natural succession of time, and therefore as not disturbed in its regular course by trouble and toil about the progress of his work as sower. In the description καθεύδῃ precedes ἐγείρηται, and correspondently νύκτα precedes ἡμέραν, because the unconcern which he permits to himself in reference to the work commenced appears chiefly in the circumstance, that he surrenders himself to the rest of sleep whenever summoned to do so in the natural course of things. And that this unconcern, to which he surrenders himself, is not arbitrary, but thoroughly in keeping with his actual relation to the natural order of his work, is stated in the next clause: "*and* (as if) *the seed should sprout and become long* ὡς οὐκ οἶδεν αὐτός," *i.e.* literally = "in what way," or "*in a way which he himself knows not*," thus not: so that the sower has no knowledge of the fact of the growth, but: so that he has no knowledge of the how, the manner of the growth, so that he himself (αὐτός), the man who yet sowed it, does not even know how this springing and growth of the seed come about. The choice of the unusual μηκύνεσθαι (not *mid.* but *pass.*) = "to be prolonged, increase in length," intimates already something mysterious in the circumstance of growth, a proof that the words ὡς οὐκ οἶδεν αὐτός, placed emphatically at the end, are kept in view from the first in the whole sentence. That the springing and growth of the seed take place in a way of which the sower himself has no knowledge, and thus the springing and growth of what he himself has sown lie altogether outside his sphere of influence, since he does not even know the how of this occurrence (to say nothing of its being his business to bring it about), this and only this is the thought expressed. But ὁ σπόρος is not placed in emphatic contrast with ἄνθρωπος in order to state what the seed on its side does *altogether of itself*, whilst the man is idle.[1] For, in the first place, the "altogether of itself," upon which in that case the emphasis of the thought would lie, is not even found here; and, in the second place, the break now made in the construction with ver. 28 (the construction dependent on ὡς, and proceeding to the close of ver. 27 in *one* flow, being here broken off and continued with an independent indicative sentence), shows that here and here first

[1] Weiss.

the description is varied in order to state by what factor the development of the seed lying altogether outside the sower's sphere of influence is brought about.

According to the correct reading, the sentence runs (ver. 28): αὐτομάτη[1] ἡ γῆ καρποφορεῖ, πρῶτον χόρτον, εἶτα στάχυν, εἶτα πλήρης σῖτος[2] ἐν τῷ στάχυϊ. The want of connection with what precedes marking the sentence, after the γάρ has been erased, is a new proof that the sentence is by no means a mere confirmation or detailed explanation of what, it is supposed, was said *implicite* in ver. 27, but that it contributes a new, independent statement. Αὐτομάτη stands first with strong emphasis: "*Spontaneously* the earth beareth fruit." The καρποφορεῖν, affirmed of the field or the earth, is to be taken in the most general sense. Where the grain is the subject of the fruit-bearing, the fruit, of course, can only be the wheat. But where the earth is the subject, the springing blade also stands as its product, its fruit. But the fact of the fruit-bearing being here attributed to the earth as an independent action, does not need to be explained by the remark that the earth conditions the productive power of the seed,[3] as if what is said applied properly, not to the earth, but to the seed. For the seed has just as little productive power without the earth as the earth without the seed; and what might have been said of the seed,—which, however, is not said here,—that it bears fruit spontaneously, whereas it cannot do so without the earth in which it is sown, may just as well be said of the earth, on the assumption that it is sown with seed. Add to this, that the latter fact is not silently assumed, but was already expressly mentioned in ver. 26. But when here the productive power of the earth, not of the seed, is spoken of, we must not pass it by unnoticed upon the pretext that this feature is in conflict with ver. 27[4] (whereas there the efficient factor of the growth was spoken of, not in positive, but in negative terms), but we must keep the circumstance steadily in view, that in the present parable, in contrast with the inactivity of the man, not the spontaneous action of the seed, but that of the earth is made prominent.

The spontaneous action of the earth is now further expounded in the three stages of its results. It brings forth "*first the blade, then the ear, then—full wheat* (wheat-seeds developed to their full extent) *in the ear.*" The first two accusatives are dependent on

---

[1] γάρ is to be erased on weighty grounds, with Lachmann and Tischendorf.
[2] The πλήρη σῖτον of the Recepta is an obvious correction. [3] Meyer. [4] Weiss.

the φέρειν contained in καρποφορεῖν; but at the third stage, when the end of the entire process is seen to be reached, the standpoint of living contemplation leads the narrator of the parable to exclaim with wondering delight: "Full wheat in the ear!" But these words are not meant to emphasize the law of progression, to which the spontaneous fertility of the earth is subject, because it must of necessity bring forth the blade before the ear, and the ear before the fully ripe corn; and still less is it true that the proper point of the parable must be sought in this progression.[1] Taken in this sense, the effect of the words would simply be to qualify and tone down the spontaneous activity ascribed with such emphasis to the earth, which would need at least to be expressed by a δέ added after πρῶτον. But in reality they serve rather to enhance still more what is said of the spontaneous fertility of the earth by indicating the extent to which the αὐτομάτη καρποφορεῖν holds good of the earth. What the words say is, that the earth spontaneously brings forth corn at one stage of development after another, first the blade, then the ear, up to the completed stage of the full wheat, and that therefore the entire process of the growth of the grain in the beginning, middle, and end, is the uninterrupted, independent work of the earth.

But everything which we have observed in this sentence—the way in which the construction of the clauses hitherto dependent on ὡς is given up, its want of connection with the preceding sentence, the strong emphasis with which it opens, the exposition of the καρποφορεῖν rising climactically from one stage to another, and finally, the emphasizing of the spontaneously reached end by an exclamation of joyous wonder,—all this gives such emphasis and weight to the statement made in the sentence, that in that statement, standing outwardly in the heart of the description, we must seek the central meaning, to which what precedes is merely preparatory, and of which what follows gives the conclusion.

Over against the statement, that the earth spontaneously brings the wheat to full maturity, enters, now that this end is reached in ver. 29 with δέ, as a conclusion to the whole, the statement of what is then done on the sower's part: ὅταν δὲ παραδοῖ[2] ὁ καρπός, εὐθὺς ἀποστέλλει τὸ δρέπανον, ὅτι παρέστηκεν ὁ θερισμός. In translating the disputed παραδοῖ we must keep

---

[1] Weiss.

[2] This unusual conjunctive, formed after the analogy of verbs in -όω, must be held to be original, παραδῷ (Rec.) to be a correction.

to the usual signification of παραδιδόναι, the only one occurring in the New Testament: "to give up, offer, hand over," only that we take it in the present passage intransitively: "to offer oneself." The counter remark, that no "quite certain" example of this intransitive use of παραδιδόναι,[1] even if it should apply universally,[2] does not seem decisive in presence of the fact that in Greek many verbs unite the transitive and intransitive significations (and compounds of διδόναι with special frequency).[3] For this reason it seems easier to assume the intransitive signification than, with Klostermann, to take the word in the present passage as an elsewhere unknown *term. technicus* = "to give up, let go," *scil.* the grains as they become loose. And as to the other signification "to allow,"[4] even if one overlooks the fact that it is rare and only demonstrable outside the New Testament, as well as that the object of the verb must in that case be supplied from what follows, the inner connection of thought of the whole sentence is decisive against it, because, in face of the corresponding meaning of the protasis: "but when the fruit shall have permitted it" (the sending forth of the sickle), the justifying clause ὅτι παρέστηκεν ὁ θερισμός does not receive its due. This clause, as a logical middle term between the protasis and apodosis, first makes known that which justifies the man in at once sending forth the sickle on the occurrence of the παραδιδόναι of the fruit. Therefore—so it is said—he at once applies the sickle on the occurrence of the παραδιδόναι of the fruit, because with this παραδιδόναι of the fruit the harvest (*i.e.* the time for reaping the corn) is come. But if we translate: "when the fruit permits (it), he at once sends forth the sickle," we make the act of sending forth the sickle find its justification directly in the παραδιδόναι itself, the effect of which is, that the clause: "because the harvest is come," which professes to justify the timeliness of the sending forth of the sickle, is deprived of meaning. Accordingly we must translate thus: "*But when the fruit offers itself*" (*scil.* to the sower waiting for it), "*he at once sends forth the sickle, because the harvest is come.*" Thus, by the fact of the fruit offering itself, he knows that it is *time* to gather in the grain; and because

---
[1] Meyer.
[2] In the passage 1 Pet. ii. 23, παραδιδόναι is not to be taken intransitively, with Winer, but transitively; cf. Huther here.
[3] Cf. Krüger, *Griechische Sprachlehre*, § 52, ii. 8; Buttmann, *Griechische Grammatik*, § 130, v. 2; Winer, *Gram.* p. 314.
[4] Accepted by Bleek, Weiss, Lange, Grimm, after the example of Meyer.

the harvest-*time* is come he does the harvest-*work*, he sends forth the sickle. This is the only interpretation which explains the strange circumstance that, after the action of the earth has been treated of with such weighty emphasis, no remark is made on the recurrence of the description to the action of the sower, an ἀποστέλλειν being at once mentioned without the subject being named, just as if the sower only had been spoken of throughout. The sower is again silently present to the thought in the protasis: "but when the fruit offers itself," because this statement rests on the presupposition that, although inactive, the sower followed the development of the grain with interest, and eagerly awaited the fruit now offering itself to him.

With ὁ καρπός the idea πλήρης σῖτος ἐν τῷ στάχυϊ is resumed, the fruit being viewed in its full maturity. The expression ἀποστέλλει τὸ δρέπανον is formed after the Hebrew כִּי שָׁלַח,[1] and is therefore not to be taken as the act of sending forth the reapers,[2] but, according to the secondary meaning of שָׁלַח: "to stretch out, apply," transferred by a Hebraism to the Greek ἀποστέλλειν, as the personal stretching out and application of the sickle. But the circumstance that, when the fruit offers itself to him, the man *at once* applies the sickle, shows anew that his previous inaction was not owing to want of concern about the grain, but was prescribed to him by the nature of the case. When the time comes for him to intervene, he acts without delay.

A glance back at the course and contents of the description enables us at once to discern with certainty its single thought. The element in the process of the growth of the corn to which the present description calls attention is this, that the earth, once sown with seed (left to itself by the farmer who sowed it, because the carrying on of the growth of what is sown lies altogether outside his sphere), then brings forth fruit by spontaneous action, and this continuously and without break through every stage of growth, until the end is reached, until the wheat in the ear has attained full development, so that the agency of the sower has only to intervene again at the harvest. Or, in other words, after the work of sowing, the sower's only business is to reap. All that lies between the sowing of the seed and the gathering of the fruit (namely, the unfolding of the seed and its development through every stage of growth up to the ripe fruit),

---

[1] Joel iv. 13, Sept.: ἐξαποστείλατε τὸ δρέπανον; cf. Rev. xiv. 15 : πέμψον τὸ δρέπανον.
[2] Matt. xiii. 30, 41.

is the business of the soil to which it is committed.¹ This simple and yet peculiar thought is so clearly and certainly expressed in the words of the description, that a different conclusion is only comprehensible on the supposition that the interpreter allows himself to be prematurely influenced in interpreting the words, either by partiality for the explanation he desires, or by interest in the critical question as to the relation of this parable to that of the Tares. The opinion of Strauss, moreover, who calls the parable "a thing without hands and feet," can only be pronounced altogether inconsiderate.

In order to answer the question, what mystery of the kingdom of God, ver. 11 (*i.e.* what truth hitherto concealed in reference to the nature and growth of the kingdom of God), is presented to view in the description of this side of the process of the growth of corn, it is necessary to go back, as in Matthew's second parable of the Tares, to the first parable in the discourse to the people, that of the Sower. For what holds good of the second parable in Matthew, that the lingering of the discourse on the natural process of the development of the seed marks it out as related to the first parable, and *mutatis mutandis* to be interpreted in a similar way, holds good still more of this second parable in Mark, —"still more" for this reason, because the second parable in Matthew is essentially distinguished from the first as to its parabolic character by the fact, that it is not again a bare description of the natural circumstances of husbandry, but a narrative of a definite case, in which the development of the grain took a special form through human interference, whereas this second parable in Mark, exactly like the first, is confined to the natural course of the development of the grain. That first parable in the discourse and this second parable in Mark are only distinguished in their parabolic character by this, that they emphasize different sides of one and the same natural process,— the first emphasizing the fact that the actual result of the sowing is naturally dependent on the actual character of the ground sown, and the second parable the other fact, that—the good character of the ground being assumed—the seed scattered by the sower is not developed to fruitfulness by any exertion of power on the sower's part, but by the spontaneous action of the ground sown. The parables thus bear upon elements related in their very diversity, because they both in like manner bear upon

¹ Cf. also Klöpper, *Jahrb. f. deutsche Theol.* 1864, p. 141 ff.

the dependence of the development of the seed on the soil to which it is entrusted. But if the mystery of the kingdom set forth by emphasizing that first element, according to Christ's own explanation,[1] was this, that the result of Christ's work in founding the kingdom is dependent by its very nature on the state of heart of those whom the preaching reaches, on the other hand nothing can be meant to be set forth by emphasizing this second and different element in the process of the development of the grain but this—*that the development of the new principle of life implanted in believing hearers of the word by the founding work of Jesus, which consists in preaching the word of the kingdom, and the working out of that principle until it issues in a form of life in perfect correspondence with the nature of the kingdom of God, are not to be looked for from an exertion of power by Christ, but are the work of the independent moral activity of the believing hearers.* And it is now clear that this second revelation is in opposition to the same error in the prevailing expectation respecting the kingdom as the first, only under another aspect. Just as, in opposition to the expectation that the coming Messiah would establish the kingdom of God in glory by means of an exercise of outward power, the first parable showed that Christ's Messianic work by its very nature rejects all outward constraint, and, on the contrary, depends from the first for its success upon the receptiveness of human hearts; so the second parable now shows that even where this receptiveness is present, and where, therefore, the development of the kingdom is not hindered from the first by a wicked state of heart, the progress and carrying through of the foundation-work begun by Christ are not to be expected from an exercise of Messianic power on His part, but in the nature of the case are the work of the independent activity of those in whom the kingdom of God has made a beginning. Thus, the parable does not so much counteract an erroneous expectation in reference to the *time* of the establishment of the kingdom in glory,[2] as rather an erroneous expectation in reference to the manner in which this will be done, namely, not by means of an exercise of Messianic power, but by the independent moral labour of those called to the kingdom of God by the Messiah. It is only *indirectly* implied that the final establishment of God's kingdom in glory, which can only be accomplished in this way, will be still delayed.

[1] Cf. vv. 13–20.   [2] Weizsäcker, Klöpper.

From this point of view the significance of the particular features of the parable may now be estimated. The statement respecting the earth's spontaneous action, which forms the centre of the parable, was prepared for by the sower's manner of life being described as undisturbed by any further anxiety about the growth of the corn after the seed was sown. The corresponding fact in the sphere of the kingdom of God is, that after Jesus, by the preaching of the word of the kingdom, has implanted in the hearts of receptive hearers the principle of a new life which submits freely to God's kingly will, He has finished the work of His historic Messianic calling, and His mode of existence will be no longer conditioned by any historic mission on this account. This general thought is all that is expressed by the "sleeping and rising night and day," ver. 27. There is thus only an indirect allusion to His approaching departure from the world. No clear and definite prediction of this fact in the future, such as is given in other and later parables,[1] occurs in the present parable. Nor, again, is anything said in ver. 29 of a coming again. There is therefore no definite allusion to the Parousia as such.[2] Moreover, ver. 27b shows that the nature of the case implies that the work of Christ's historic calling does not extend beyond the implanting of the new principle of life in the hearts of men. For just as the process of the development of the grain is withdrawn by its very nature from all influence of the sower to such a degree that he knows not even the how of the process; so, too, the process of the gradual unfolding of the principle of life implanted in men's hearts by God's word is withdrawn by its inward nature from all influence from without, and therefore even from Christ's, so far as it is exerted through human means. We have intentionally refrained from making the sower's non-*knowledge* of the manner in which the seed grows part of the comparison. For the reason why the ὡς οὐκ οἶδεν αὐτός in the parable is so strongly emphasized is not that the non-*knowledge* has of itself an independent significance, but simply that this circumstance in the sphere of natural events is the one which most strikingly illustrates the sower's impotence with regard to *influence* upon the growth. Hence in the interpretation it is only to be applied under this aspect. The dogmatic objection which may perhaps suggest itself here, to the effect that an influence even upon the inner progress of His

---

[1] Matt. xxv. 15 ; Luke xix. 12.   [2] In opposition to Weizsäcker.

work in the human heart must in point of fact be ascribed to the Lord because of the divine character of His person, is irrelevant, because the purpose here is not to define the degree of the influences of divine grace upon man's inner life, but merely to mark out the mission which Jesus has to fulfil towards receptive hearers within the limits of His historic, human course. In the nature of the case the limits of this mission coincide with the limits of the possibility of His influencing them as a man by means of human discourse.

When Christ, following up what has been already said, makes known to the disciples that they themselves, like the spontaneously fruit-bearing earth, must by their own moral effort unfold the new germ of life implanted in them by His word, He does not mean this in contrast with the influences of divine grace generally, but with the influences upon the disciples issuing at present from His personal manifestation through the word of His mouth. The disciples must do so, not for half the way merely, but through every stage of inner growth until their entire inner and outer life has been shaped into correspondence on all sides with God's holy will, and thus into ripeness for God's kingdom in the future world ($\pi\lambda\acute{\eta}\rho\eta\varsigma$ $\sigma\hat{\iota}\tau o\varsigma$ $\acute{\epsilon}\nu$ $\tau\hat{\omega}$ $\sigma\tau\acute{\alpha}\chi\upsilon\ddot{\iota}$). And this does not mean simply the working out of the principles of God's kingdom in the life of the individual disciple; but the statement of the parable is such that in conformity with the nature of the figure used, in which the development of the single stalk is one with that of the entire field of corn, the working out of those principles in the individual life coincides with their working out in the body of the disciples, in the community of the kingdom.

We must take this circumstance into view in order to understand the temporal connection in which the prospect opened out in ver. 29 stands with what precedes. The whole concludes with a promise annexed to the actual attainment of the goal of the development, and meant therefore to encourage and strengthen the disciples for fulfilling the duty that rests upon their own spontaneous effort. Just as the sower who follows the development of his crop with eager interest makes no delay when the fruit offers itself to him, but at once applies the sickle, so will the Son of Man, who watches over the development of His Church, make no delay in what will again be the business of His Messianic calling as soon as He sees the Church arrive at the goal of its development, and ripe for the kingdom of God in the future world. On the contrary, because now the time of consummation is come, He will at once accomplish it, *i.e.* He will gather the righteous into the kingdom of His Father.[1] Thus, the disciples of Jesus, who as *hearers* of the word were hitherto represented in the parable under the figure of the earth receiving the seed, here at the conclusion appear also as the counterpart of the living corn-crop now fully ripe and awaiting the sickle, because the hearers of the word do not put forth its effect as something different from themselves, as the earth puts forth the effect of the seed, but work out and exhibit its effect in their personal life. It is the same natural interchange of figurative representation which we have already observed in the parable of the Sower and its interpretation in a still more striking form.[2]

The original meaning of the parable, as thus set forth, certainly differs materially from the exposition of it current in the Church. According to the latter, Jesus is supposed to exhort His disciples, with reference to their future calling as preachers of the gospel, to wait patiently for the fruit of their preaching, trusting in the living productive force inherent in God's word, which operates in the human heart secretly and slowly, but not on that account the less certainly, and in due time will bring forth fruit to the light of day,—instead of doubting of the fruit of their preaching, because it is not visible forthwith, or wishing with over-hasty zeal to supplement the secret operation of the Word by artificial means. But against such an interpretation lies the objection, first, that everywhere—in the preceding parable of the Sower, in the following one of the Mustard Seed, and in that of the Tares standing in Matthew between those two in the place of the present one—Jesus refers in the sowing to His own work in founding the kingdom; secondly, that the application of the sickle to the corn now fully ripe, because the harvest is come, has no analogy at all in the work of the preacher of the word, but instead all the more plainly points to the action of the Son of Man at the end of the world; finally, that in the parable neither is any emphasis laid, as is done in Jas. v. 7, on the *patience* with which the farmer waits for the fruit, nor on the living productive force inherent in the seed as such, but simply on the spontaneous fruit-bearing of the earth in contrast with

---

[1] Cf. the parable of the Tares, Matt. xiii. 30, 43.
[2] Cf. on Matt. xiii. 19.

the inactivity of the sower. The sole element in the text, which seems to favour the former interpretation, namely, that the ὡς οὐκ οἶδεν αὐτός has no application to the Lord, has already been explained in the course of the interpretation. On the other hand, it must be conceded that the thoughts expressed above, although not constituting the original meaning of the parable, lie sufficiently near it to permit of their being deduced from it by a pertinent transference of what is affirmed respecting the limits of Christ's official work to the like official work of the disciples as preachers of His word. Those thoughts are also pre-eminently suited for practical use.

While, accordingly, we must not overlook the connection in which the present parable stands with the first one in the discourse to the people, and also indirectly with the parable of the Tares occupying the second place in Matthew, on the other hand there are no adequate grounds for the conjectures which deny to it all independence and originality, alleging that it simply arose out of the parable of the Tares, either as a spiritless dilution[1] or a recasting of that parable.[2] For as regards, first of all, substantive purpose, this one has no affinity whatever with the parable of the Tares, except in the general circumstance that both parables deal with the development of the kingdom of God. The one speaks of the appearance of children of evil among the disciples (Matt. xiii. 38), the other of the duty of spontaneous effort on the part of the disciples for the realizing of God's kingdom. That a parable with the latter meaning should be derived from one with the former either by dilution or recasting, must be regarded as more than improbable. And as regards outward form, after putting aside the general circumstance, that in both parables, as also in the first parable in the discourse to the people, the growth of corn is used to represent in figure the growth of the kingdom, and the recurrence naturally following of words like βλαστάνειν, χόρτος, καρπός, θερισμός, or synonymous ideas like σπόρος here and σπέρμα there, γῆ here and ἀγρός there, with a parabolic reference partially similar, but also partially, especially in the latter case quite, different,—only one thing is left, namely, that in both parables a sleeping is spoken of in one place,[3] but still in a quite different relation, which must therefore be regarded as a pure accident. There is nothing therefore to justify us in departing from the supposition suggested

[1] Hilgenfeld.   [2] Weiss.   [3] Cf. ver. 27 with Matt. xiii. 25.

from the first by the relation of Matthew's account to that of Mark, that *both* parables form an integral part of the discourse of Jesus to the people by the sea, beginning with the parable of the Sower. And if we are to venture still further on the uncertain ground of conjecture, the especially close connection explained above in which the present parable stands with the first in the discourse—the former dwelling on the *spontaneous action;* the latter, on the *diverse nature* of the soil of the field—would seem to suggest that the original place of the former was immediately after the latter, and before the parable of the Tares.

The Grain of Mustard Seed.

(Matt. xiii. 31, 32, and parallels.)

We now return to Matthew's report of the parabolic discourse. Matthew introduces (ver. 31) the third parable of the Mustard Seed, just like the second parable of the Tares, with the words: ἄλλην παραβολὴν παρέθηκεν αὐτοῖς λέγων, whereas Mark (ver. 30) joins it to the parable of the Fruit-bearing Earth merely by καὶ ἔλεγεν. Luke, on the other hand, does not give the parable of the Mustard Seed along with that of the Leaven, which follows it also in Matthew, in one context with the parable of the Sower, which, according to him, too, was delivered to a great multitude of people (viii. 4 ff.). Nor does he give it in another context, but merely in another place (xiii. 18–21) as a separate and independent paragraph, without specifying in any way when and in what circumstances it was spoken. For by the ἔλεγεν οὖν (ver. 18) he simply joins one example of the teaching of Jesus to another, without chronological connection, and even without any certainly discernible connection in matter with the preceding paragraph (vv. 10–17). The assertion that in him the two parables stand in their original context, whereas the place which they occupy in Matthew is merely the result of systematic arrangement, is therefore doubtful, because in Luke they are not placed in any definite historical context at all.

Matthew begins the parable again in the way already noticed in reference to the parable of the Tares;[1] *i.e.*, the chief idea of the

---

[1] See on ver. 24.

first sentence, which in this case, as also elsewhere in the smaller parables, is the chief idea of the entire parable, is singled out beforehand and likened to the kingdom of heaven as the thing compared, after which the narration of the event begins with a relative sentence joining on to this chief idea, the relative sentence presenting a corresponding event in the sphere of the kingdom of heaven. "*The kingdom of heaven*," it is said in ver. 31, "*is like a grain of mustard seed which a man took and sowed in his field.*" The prefixing of the participle λαβών to the verb ἔσπειρεν merely sets forth the action of the man in pictorial circumstantiality.[1] It does not imply that he was obliged to take up the small grain carefully because of its almost impalpable minuteness,[2] as is shown by comparison with the λαβοῦσα (ver. 33). He sowed the grain of mustard seed ἐν τῷ ἀγρῷ αὐτοῦ, *i.e.* so that it came to lie in his field (cf. vv. 19, 24). In Luke it is said in different yet similar terms: ἔβαλεν εἰς κῆπον ἑαυτοῦ, "he cast it into his garden." Thus, according to both evangelists, the field- or garden-plot where he sowed the mustard seed is definitely described as belonging to the sower, just like the field in the parable of the Tares, ver. 24. In Mark, on the contrary, no mention whatever is made of the concrete circumstance, that a man took a grain of mustard seed and sowed it in his plot of ground. The only reference there is a general one to the mustard seed sown in the earth,[3] in order at once to describe the peculiarity in regard to the size distinguishing it at first and in the course of its growth.

Then Matthew, giving up his previous narrative style, passes on with ver. 32 to a similar description. Whereas Luke proceeds calmly to relate what became of the particular mustard grain[4] which the man sowed in his garden, without entering into a

---

[1] Cf. Meyer here.   [2] Lange.

[3] iv. 31: ὡς κόκκῳ σινάπεως, ὃς ὅταν σπαρῇ κ.τ.λ. The reading here is with Tischendorf and Weiss, ver. 31 f.: ὡς κόκκῳ σινάπεως, ὃς ὅταν σπαρῇ ἐπὶ τῆς γῆς, μικρότερον ὂν πάντων τῶν σπερμάτων τῶν ἐπὶ τῆς γῆς,—καὶ ὅταν σπαρῇ, ἀναβαίνει κ.τ.λ. The anakoluthon seems to me to be most simply explained as follows. According to the plan at first the sentence should run: ὅς, ὅταν σπαρῇ ἐπὶ τ. γ., ἀναβαίνει καὶ γίνεται κ.τ.λ., *i.e.* the first ὅταν σπαρῇ already suggests ἀναβαίνει κ.τ.λ. as the apodosis. But the appositional participial clause: μικρότερον ὂν πάντων τῶν σπερμ. τῶν ἐπ. τ. γ., having been appended to the protasis to lead up by the contrast to the point of the apodosis, the need now arises to resume the protasis before ἀναβαίνει κ.τ.λ., in order to preserve the close connection between ὅταν σπαρῇ and the apodosis now unduly separated from it; and this is done by inserting the words καὶ ὅταν σπαρῇ.

[4] Ver. 19: καὶ ηὔξησεν, καὶ ἐγένετο εἰς δένδρον μέγα.

comparison of the mustard grain as such with other kinds of seed on the one hand, or other garden herbs on the other, Matthew leaves off the narrative which he has begun of the particular mustard grain, and turns aside to a description of the distinctive peculiarities of the mustard seed generally, from which the hearer or reader may learn for himself what became of the grain first-mentioned. He continues, ver. 32: ὃ μικρότερον μέν ἐστιν πάντων τῶν σπερμάτων. The relative connection with what precedes is only loose, as is shown by the circumstance that the relative is governed in its gender not by the κόκκος, ver. 31, but by the following πάντων τῶν σπερμάτων. The relative therefore does not resume the particular κόκκος, ver. 31, but borrows from it the generic idea of a σπέρμα σινάπεως. Hence the translation is: "*a seed* (a kind of seed) *which is smaller than all seeds.*" Of course this statement in reference to the special smallness of the mustard seed is made, not from the standpoint of scientific botany, but merely from that of practical gardening, comparing the kinds of seed most usual at the time. Its precision is less to be dwelt upon as the mustard grain served among the Jews, on account of its smallness, to describe proverbially the insignificance of anything.[1] In contrast with this special smallness of the mustard seed is now set in what follows its conspicuous magnitude when grown: "*but when it is grown, it is greater than the herbs.*" Thus the same mustard seed, which as a seed is distinguished from other seeds by its smallness, as a plant (ὅταν αὐξηθῇ) excels all plants belonging to the same category [2] in magnitude. Nor does it stop at the size of a λάχανον of conspicuous size, but in its growth assumes a form which makes it seem to belong to a different class of plants from that of λάχανα. This it is which the words say: καὶ γίνεται δένδρον, *i.e.* although belonging to the class of herbs, it becomes a plant like a tree.[3] Without using the word δένδρον, Mark says the same in the words: καὶ ποιεῖ κλάδους μεγάλους, for the branching of large boughs from the main trunk is just that which makes the high-grown mustard plant look like a tree. When, on the other hand, it is said in Luke: καὶ ἐγένετο εἰς δένδρον μέγα, it is assumed that, where a mustard plant is the subject spoken of, no one will

---

[1] Cf. xvii. 20: ὡς κόκκος σινάπεως, and the proverbial כְּחַרְדָּל among the Rabbins.

[2] Cf. Mark: πάντων τῶν λαχ.

[3] That the mustard plant in the East really shoots up so high as to take the form of a tree, see the detailed proof in Winer, *Handwörterbuch*, art. "Senf."

understand "a tree, great in proportion to other trees," but that every one will understand "a tree, great as such in proportion to the usual size of plants, or to what the mustard plant may reach in other cases;" for to the very end Luke speaks of the particular mustard-grain sown by the man in his garden. The δένδρον μέγα does not on this account need to be explained by the supposition that in Luke, not the mustard plant, as in Matthew and Mark, but the mustard tree is meant[1] (*Salvadora persica*), especially when by this supposition, if the meaning is "a tree great in comparison with other trees," the δένδρον μέγα would not really be explained, since the *Salvadora persica* is but a tree of very moderate size. Moreover, this tree, if at all native in Palestine, in any case is only rare, and its designation by σίναπι without proof.[2]

The consequence of this δένδρον γίνεσθαι, stated now as the conclusion of the whole, is, "*that the birds of the heaven come and nest*[3] *in its branches*" (in the branches of the mustard-seed now become a tree). These branches, because like boughs, are large enough to afford them the shelter requisite for building their nests. Mark specially emphasizes this state of things by subjoining to his ποιεῖ κλάδους μεγάλους as a consequence: ὥστε δύνασθαι ὑπὸ τὴν σκιὰν αὐτοῦ τὰ πετεινὰ τοῦ οὐρανοῦ κατασκηνοῦν, where σκιά is not merely a shelter from the heat of the sun, but in the wider sense a shelter from wind and weather in general. Finally, Luke mentions also the dwelling of the birds in the narrative style; and he does not relate it, we should observe, in subordination to the ἐγένετο εἰς δένδρον μέγα as a mere consequence of the same, but in a separate, independent clause joins on this circumstance, as the last which he has to tell, to what he has previously related: καὶ τὰ πετεινὰ τοῦ οὐρανοῦ κατεσκήνωσεν ἐν τοῖς κλάδοις αὐτοῦ.

In the present parable, accordingly, a different, although similar physical event is used in figurative representation from that used in the first parables. True, at first the subject spoken of (according to Matthew and Luke) is a man who *sowed;* but what he sows this time is a grain of mustard seed. Here, therefore, what is pictured is not a field of wheat developing from the seed to ripe fruit, as in the first parables, but the process of growth of a mustard plant. And the peculiarity pointed out in the growth

---

[1] So *e.g.* Weiss. [2] See Winer, as before.
[3] κατασκηνοῦν, pitch their tent, build their nest.

of such a plant consists, on the one hand, in the diminutive smallness of the mustard grain, which has passed into a proverb, and on the other hand in the astonishing, tree-like magnitude of the plant springing from it, a magnitude excelling that of all plants of like kind. Thus the rule, *e minimo maximum*, which, of course, is the rule of all growth in nature, is here illustrated by the process of growth of the mustard seed particularly, because it can be illustrated in it by reason of its proverbial peculiarity with specially striking effect. In this way the choice of the mustard plant as the means of parabolic representation is perfectly explained; and it is empty trifling to refer here to the seasoning virtue of the mustard.[1] The mystery of the kingdom, then, here revealed to the disciples, can be no other than this, *that the kingdom of God founded by Jesus presents indeed at first an outwardly insignificant form; but this very beginning, small to diminutiveness, possesses an inherent force of extension, in virtue of which it will grow unceasingly until it attains the vastest size,* —a revelation designed to solve for the disciples the contradiction existing between their expectation, based on the prophetic word, of the mighty extent of the Messianic kingdom, and the fact that merely a small company of sincere adherents had gathered round the person of Jesus.

In detail, the course of thought in the parable is as follows. Just as what the sower deposits in his field is but a diminutive mustard-grain, so the kingdom of God in the beginning, imposed upon it by the founding work of Jesus on the ground of the world, presents an outwardly insignificant form, being realized at first merely in an exceedingly narrow and small circle of men, in the diminutive band of disciples gathered round the Lord. The sowing of the man must here (according to Matthew and Luke) be referred, as in the preceding parables, to the work of Jesus in founding the kingdom. And when it is not merely said generally that the man sowed the seed in the earth, but in *his* field (Luke, "in his garden"), a definite parabolic reference must underlie this feature, just as in the case of the similar feature in the parable of the Tares, ver. 24. And indeed Christ's own explanation in reference to the parable of the Tares[2] must be taken as fixing the sense here, namely, that He meant to describe not merely, as one might suppose, the Israelitish nation, but the world in general, as the ground belonging to Him, on which He was

---

[1] Stier, Olshausen.   [2] See on ver. 38 there.

about to establish the kingdom of heaven. But as the small mustard-grain, so the thought continues, in virtue of the power of growth inherent in it, attains an astonishing, tree-like magnitude on the ground in which it is planted, so the kingdom of God, narrowly limited at first, will, in virtue of the power of unceasing growth inherent in it, extend to a size transcending all expectation at its beginning. That it will at last embrace all mankind is certainly not said expressly. But what the last feature of the parable says looks in this direction, so far as the nature of the figure permits.

When at the conclusion we read of the birds nesting in the branches, or under the shadow of the mustard plant that has grown into a tree, at the first glance one might feel tempted to suppose that this statement, as a mere illustration of the magnitude of the tree-plant, is not meant to have a special interpretation.[1] But a more careful consideration makes this supposition seem doubtful. First of all, the formal circumstance should be noted that, despite the otherwise not inconsiderable diversity of the accounts, this feature recurs in all three evangelists,—in the narrative of Luke, not in subordination to, but co-ordinately with the previous events,—and everywhere its position as the conclusion of the whole gives it unmistakeable emphasis. In the second place, unless it really required a definite counterpart in the interpretation, it would not as to its substantive meaning even contain an illustration of the main thought; for after the plant has been once called a tree, its greatness receives in fact no new light from emphasizing the circumstance that birds make their nests in it. This feature would then be an incidental ornament of the description, possessing no value at all in reference to the thought expressed in the parable. And again the repeated occurrence of this feature in precisely similar connections in the figurative language of the prophets, and that with an undoubtedly definite meaning, is decisive. When Ezekiel predicts of the Messianic Branch of David's royal house, that He will grow from a tender shoot into a great tree, that therefore His regal power will extend far, he adds, xvii. 23: "And under it shall dwell all fowl of every wing, in the shadow of the branches thereof shall they dwell."[2] And the prophet connects a quite definite thought with this dwelling of the birds under the shade of the branches

---

[1] So Weiss.

[2] בְּצֵל דָּלִיּוֹתָיו, cf. ὑπὸ τὴν σκιάν in Mark, and ἐν τοῖς κλάδοις in Matthew and Luke.

of the tree, meaning thereby the dwelling of the *nations* under the shadow of the regal power of the Son of David. This is proved by comparison with xxxi. 6, 12, where, in a similar description of the kingdom of Assyria under the figure of a great tree, it is said: "All the fowls of heaven made their nests in his boughs;" and this figure is at once expressly interpreted thus: "Under his shadow dwell all *great nations.*" Compare also Dan. iv. 9, where, in the description of the royal power of Nebuchadnezzar under the figure of a great tree, the addition again is not wanting: "The fowls of the heaven dwell in its boughs." When therefore here, in a similar description of the extension of God's Messianic kingdom under the figure of a tree, the coming and dwelling of the birds of heaven [1] in its branches and under its shadow is spoken of, the prophetic figure implied for the hearers of the parable, to whom its meaning was well known, is the definite promise that the kingdom of God in its extension will embrace the nations, that the nations of the earth will enter it and partake of its blessings.

The Leaven.

(Matt. xiii. 33; Luke xiii. 20, 21.)

With the words ἄλλην παραβολὴν ἐλάλησεν αὐτοῖς, only slightly different from the formula used in vv. 24, 31, Matthew makes the transition (ver. 33) to the fourth and last of the parables constituting the discourse to the people,—that of the Leaven,—which is wanting in Mark, whilst Luke puts it in the same place as the parable of the Mustard Seed, appending it to the latter, xiii. 20, 21; and does so with a πάλιν εἶπεν, which intimates that the discourse lingers on a subject previously discussed, so that in Luke the two parables join to form an independent and mutually related pair.

The incident employed in figurative representation is introduced (ver. 33) in the same way as in the preceding parables:[2] ὁμοία ἐστὶν ἡ βασιλεία τῶν οὐρανῶν ζύμῃ, ἣν λαβοῦσα γυνὴ

---

[1] Not here, as in Ezek. xvii. 23, "*all* birds," simply because the figure of the mustard plant does not suffice for this.

[2] See on vv. 24, 31.

ἐνέκρυψεν εἰς ἄλευρον σάτα τρία, ἕως οὗ ἐζυμώθη ὅλον. In Luke, apart from the somewhat different introduction, and the reading ἔκρυψεν preferable there, the words have just the same tenor. Here, then, the kingdom of heaven is compared to a lump of leaven, "*which a woman took and hid in three sata of meal.*" Three sata of meal make exactly an ephah, an ordinary quantity of meal.[1] Although the measure of such a quantity cannot be determined with full certainty, so much is established that it is a very considerable amount of meal. Thus an ordinary, and at the same time the greatest possible quantity is chosen to define the amount of the meal. Bengel: "Quantum uno tempore ab homine portari, vel ad pinsendum sumi soleret." The word ἐγκρύπτειν, occurring only here in the New Testament, describes as the business of the woman a simple working of the leaven into the mass of the meal, so that it is hidden therein. There is therefore here no intimation that a continuous and strenuous mixing and kneading of the leaven into the meal takes place. Hence we must not translate: *knead in.*[2] And in this case also the clause ἕως οὗ ἐζυμώθη cannot mean that the woman persevered in her work "*until it* (τὸ ἄλευρον) *was entirely leavened.*" Neither the expression ἐγκρύπτειν, nor the meaning of ζυμοῦσθαι, countenance this meaning. For ζυμοῦσθαι cannot denote the blending of the meal with the leaven, which takes place during the act of mixing, but is the process of the leavening of the meal taking place gradually in the fermentation after the act of mixing is ended, by which the meal assumes the properties of the leaven, and itself becomes leaven. The clause ἕως οὗ ἐζυμώθη ὅλον cannot therefore be meant to define the duration of the act of ἐγκρύπτειν, but merely the duration of the state thereby induced. The woman hid the leaven in the meal, and left it hidden until the meal was thoroughly leavened.

In order to ascertain the thought of the parable, the relation of this parable to that of the Mustard Seed must chiefly be taken into consideration, forming, as they do, a pair of parables in Matthew, and still more plainly in Luke. And this all the more, that their close mutual relation plainly appears also in the parallelism of the figurative incidents in the two parables. For although the figure used in the second parable is quite different from that of the first, still the two chief incidents finding

---

[1] Gen. xviii. 6; Judg. vi. 19; 1 Sam. i. 24.
[2] van Oosterzee.

expression in the two passages are unmistakeably parallel. There, a mustard grain which a man took and sowed in his field (ὃν λαβὼν ἄνθρωπος ἔσπειρεν κ.τ.λ.); here, a lump of leaven, which a woman took and hid in a mass of meal (ἣν λαβοῦσα γυνὴ ἐνέκρυψεν κ.τ.λ.). And whereas there it is shown how the small mustard-grain, when sown in the field, grows to vast size on this ground; so here, how the small lump of leaven, when inserted in the great mass of meal, exerts a transforming influence on this mass, communicating to it its own nature, until the entire mass has become a great leaven. Here, therefore, the rule *e minimo maximum*—the chief thought of the parable of the Mustard Seed—as such recurs, only with the difference that there the small thing becomes great in virtue of the power of self-extension inherent in it; here, on the other hand, in virtue of an assimilative power inherent in it, which converts the surrounding mass into its own nature. This parallelism of the figurative events in the two parables, which form a pair, requires then of necessity for the second an interpretation running parallel with that of the first. And if the first was intended to teach the disciples that this very beginning—small even to insignificance,—belonging to the kingdom of God at present on the ground of the world, possesses a power of extension, in virtue of which it will grow to a vastness embracing all nations, the second is meant to show them *that this very beginning—small almost to the vanishing-point—assigned to the kingdom of God in the broad human world, possesses a transforming power, in virtue of which, becoming more and more pervasive, and advancing without interruption, it will exert a transforming influence on humanity, communicating to it its own nature, until the whole of humanity has assumed the nature of the kingdom of God.* Thus the thought here expressed is not in fact essentially different from the one expressed in the parable of the Mustard Seed. The distinction is simply this, that there the world appears in a merely general sense as the ground on which the kingdom of God is founded and extends; here, on the other hand, as the material which the kingdom of God concealed in its midst pervades with its own nature, and thus absorbs into itself. Both parables serve likewise to remove the surprise of the disciples, arising from their intense expectation of a mighty extension of the Messianic kingdom in the world, at the beginning of that kingdom outwardly so insignificant and limited; and they do this by bringing to view the truth, that this very beginning, so slight at present, is the condition and security of its greatness in the future. And precisely for this reason the contents of the two parables are especially appropriate to the situation,[1] which was characterized by a thoroughgoing severance between a small band of sincere disciples of Jesus on the one hand, and the body of the people receding more and more into inveterate unbelief on the other.

Accordingly, the exact interpretation of the parable is as follows. Like a small lump of leaven which a woman hid in a great heap of meal, so Christ's founding work plants the kingdom of God in an inconsiderable, insignificant form amid the great, wide human world, so that it disappears in that world. But as that slight quantity of leaven, in virtue of its assimilative power, appropriates and works in the great mass of meal until the latter is thoroughly leavened, so the kingdom of God, in virtue of the renewing and transforming forces inherent in it, will exert an unceasingly progressive influence on the human world surrounding it, pervading it with God's word, and subjecting it to God's holy will, and by this means transforming it, until in its entirety it shall have assumed the nature of the kingdom of God, until humanity as a whole shall have become the community of God's kingdom. Thus, in the hiding the leaven, as the act which gives the impulse to the subsequent development, Jesus refers to His own Messianic work as in the former parables in the sowing. The reason why the founding work is here ascribed, not to a man, but to a woman, is plainly the obvious one, that an employment commonly falling to woman in domestic life is referred to, not a work falling to men. This circumstance, therefore, gives no right whatever in the interpretation to make the Church at once the subject of the "hiding." And just as little as the woman is the Church, is the leaven the word of God or the gospel. The leaven is not merely the means and instrument for leavening the mass of the meal, it is itself a small quantity of already leavened matter in the midst of a vast mass of matter to be leavened by it in the way of assimilation. Hence the word of God may be called the leavening virtue in the leaven, but not the leaven itself. The latter, in exact correspondence to the mustard seed, is rather the kingdom of God in the still limited form in which it was established by Jesus, or in other words, the small circle of the disciples of Jesus planted in the great, wide human world,

[1] Cf. "The Parables to the People by the Sea."

to whom the word and will of God have become the governing principle of life, and from whom the influences above described do and will issue.[1] Further, not without intention is the working of the leaven into the meal described by the unusual expression "hiding," which makes prominent the vanishing of the leaven in the mass of meal. It is thereby intimated that the kingdom of God in the world is at first hidden and unmarked. Because of its insignificant appearance it vanishes, so to speak, in the mass of the human world, in whose midst it is set up. Finally, the three sata of meal are not, as might be interpreted in consonance with the wording, the situation, and the standpoint of the disciples, to be referred merely to the Jewish nation, but in conformity with the œcumenical design of Jesus Himself, as it appeared in the interpretation of the field in the parable of the Tares, to the human world in general. But this gives no sort of warrant to the amusing references of the *three* sata—which, however, are only mentioned as the usual amount of a large baking—to the three parts of the world then known, or to the three sons of Noah,[2] or to the Greeks, Jews, and Samaritans;[3] and still less does it warrant references to the three orders, or the heart, soul, and spirit,[4] or the body, soul, and spirit.[5]

The interpretation given certainly differs materially from the view not unusual in practical exposition. According to the latter, the leaven is said to be the word of God, and the woman the Church, whose duty it is to mix the word, so to speak, in the world and in worldly life, until that life is permeated by it.[6]

---

[1] Cf. Matt. v. 13: "Ye are the salt of the earth;" Matt. xxviii. 19: μαθητεύσατε πάντα τὰ ἔθνη.

[2] Stier.   [3] Theodore of Mopsuestia.   [4] Augustine, Melanchthon.

[5] See Olshausen. Hofmann (on Luke xiii. 20, 21) declares not merely against the Jewish-national reference of the meal disclaimed above, but also against the œcumenical reference. The object of appropriation and transformation is said to be merely those "destined to be the Church of God at last." But humanity as a whole is destined to this. That in the present æon it includes such elements as oppose themselves with invincible obstinacy to the appropriating and transforming virtue of God's kingdom, that therefore the positive assimilative virtue will not attain its goal without the purifying judicial catastrophe of the end,—this other side of the question might remain outside the view of the present parable, which condenses into one brief sentence, and under one great single point of view, the entire development of God's kingdom from its smallest beginnings up to its great final goal, because the necessary exclusion of individuals, however great their number, makes no change in the certain attainment of the goal itself, namely, humanity as a whole becoming the community of the kingdom of God.

[6] Cf. *e.g.* Stier.

That this view misinterprets both the woman and the meal itself, has been already shown. Moreover, something is deduced from the "hiding" which it does not contain, namely, the idea of strenuous, continuous kneading, and with this kneading again is combined the process of leavening as its immediate and contemporaneous effect, whereas in reality it is an independent effect, to which the hiding of the leaven merely gives the impulse. And again, on this interpretation, the obvious parallelism of the figurative events in the present and the preceding parable is left quite out of sight, which is enough alone to make it impossible.

Moreover, this latter point is decisive against the interpretation advanced by older expositors, and advocated recently by Thiersch, according to which the meal is said to be the corruption in doctrine and life invading the kingdom of God. On the other hand, there is no force in the objection that the meal is likened by ὁμοία ἐστίν to the kingdom of heaven,[1] for this by no means affirms that in the parable thus introduced the leaven is intended as a single idea to symbolize the kingdom of God.[2] It is, however, decisive against the interpretation of Thiersch, that in this way the meal receives an interpretation altogether unlike that of the Mustard Seed, whereas it is obviously put on a parallel with that parable. And in what glaring incongruity the entire thought of the parable would stand with that of the parable of the Mustard Seed! By the side of the comforting promise that the kingdom of heaven will grow from its small beginning to a greatness embracing the nations, would be placed the gloomy, fateful prediction, that corruption will invade and permeate the kingdom of God until it falls a complete prey to this corruption. Nothing else could be the meaning of the parable, without even an intimation being given respecting the solution of so dark a mystery. No analogy for a prediction of such baleful meaning can be anywhere found in the discourses of Jesus, least of all in the parable of the tares, where only a temporary combination of false with true members in the Church was spoken of, which will come to an end with the complete, thoroughgoing exclusion of the former. And thus the only plausible support which this interpretation finds in the circumstance that the influence issuing from the leaven is used figuratively in three passages of the New Testament[3] in a bad sense, is thoroughly precarious. In itself

---

[1] *E.g.* Stier, Lange.   [2] Cf. the parable of the Tares, on ver. 24.
[3] Matt. xvi. 6 ; 1 Cor. v. 6–8 ; Gal. v. 9.

this influence may be used figuratively just as well in a good as in a bad sense, or rather more aptly in a good sense, because within the figurative incident the influence on the baking is not bad, but good. The more frequent use of the influence of the leaven in a bad sense only needs the explanation readily presenting itself in the allusion to the legal prohibition of the leavened bread in the Paschal Feast, to which the chief passage (1 Cor. v.) expressly refers. But such a reference is altogether foreign to the present passage, because here the intention of the woman is certainly represented to be not the corrupting of the meal, but the preparation of a wholesome baking.

We have now reached the end of the series of parables delivered to the multitude gathered near the sea. If we glance back once more at the disclosures made therein to the disciples respecting the nature and growth of the kingdom of heaven, they arrange themselves in the following order. The teaching of the first parable is, that the founding of the kingdom of God takes place, not by the exertion of an outwardly compelling power, but in the spiritual way of a preaching of the word of the kingdom, the effect of which depends on the character of the hearers. The second parable in Mark adds, that the continuous development of the kingdom of God founded by the labour of Jesus, until it reaches the goal of consummation, is not to be looked for from an exertion of the Messiah's power, but rests with the personal moral effort of the hearers of the word. This continuous development of the kingdom of God from the basis laid by Jesus' Messianic work, up to the goal of its consummation, forms then the subject of the remaining parables. This development indeed will be stained by the intrusion of false members,—such is the teaching of the second parable in Matthew, giving the needful revelations and instructions respecting this strange fact. But, on the other hand, the third parable says, that this development will exhibit a continuous progression from a small beginning on to world-embracing magnitude, in virtue of an impulse of self-extension inherent in the kingdom of God once founded, or, according to the fourth parable, in virtue of the power peculiar to it to permeate the surrounding world and transform it into its own nature.

THE PARABLES IN THE CONVERSATION WITH THE DISCIPLES.

AT Capernaum, on the same day on which Jesus had uttered the first parables by the sea, the disciples were permitted to receive a second series of parables from His lips in the course of the conversation, already mentioned several times, which took place in private after the dismissal of the people.

The previous course of investigation has already led us to consider the initial portion of the conversation. When Jesus, having dismissed the crowds of people and returned to the house, was alone with the Twelve and other disciples, the latter had questioned Him as to the reason of His parabolic method of teaching, and also requested from Him the interpretation of particular parables.[1] Hereupon Jesus had first instructed them respecting the reason of His parabolic mode of teaching (vv. 11–17), then explained at length the first of His parables (vv. 18–23), and finally, at their request, given an explanation of the second (vv. 37–43); this time, however, briefly naming the counterparts of the particular persons and ideas in the narrative, and leaving to them the interpretation proper of the figurative incidents on the same lines. He expressly interpreted merely the incident concluding the whole narrative—for what reason has been investigated before. Accordingly, if the previous course of the conversation appears governed by the intention to lead the disciples on to an independent understanding of the parables, this intention emerges clearly to view when we now hear Jesus, founding on the first complete and the second incomplete interpretation, deliver to the disciples a new series of parables (vv. 44–50), and then see Him address the question to the disciples: Have ye understood all these things? (ver. 51),—a question to which the disciples can now reply with the simple affirmative. Therefore the Lord is able to say to them in the concluding saying, which is clothed in figurative form (ver. 52): "Because of this acquaintance with

[1] Cf. Matt. xiii. 36 with ver. 10 and Mark iv. 10.

the mysteries of the kingdom of heaven (διὰ τοῦτο), a treasure of new knowledge lies at the service of every teacher who is a disciple of the kingdom," in addition to the traditional teaching to which the scribes of Israel were previously limited; and this treasure he is to use in free and independent activity.

The Hidden Treasure.

(Matt. xiii. 44.)

Ὁμοία ἐστὶν ἡ βασιλεία τῶν οὐρανῶν θησαυρῷ κεκρυμμένῳ ἐν τῷ ἀγρῷ; thus begins the first parable of the new series (ver. 44). The πάλιν before ὁμοία (Rec.) is (with Tischendorf) to be erased on weighty authority. In allusion to the immediately preceding interpretation of the parable of the Tares, the word is borrowed from vv. 45, 47, the new independent start made here by the discourse being overlooked. The kingdom of heaven is compared to "*a treasure hid in the field.*" To paraphrase the article before ἀγρῷ, " in the (definite) field,"[1] or to take it without further ado as generic,[2] is not to explain it, but to render it unintelligible. The use of the article rests on the assumption, that to the hearers with the notion of a treasure not merely preserved,[3] but hidden, the notion of a garden or field where it is buried is naturally associated, burial being the usual way of securely concealing a treasure of gold or silver. The following relative sentence says of this hidden treasure: ὃν εὑρὼν ἄνθρωπος ἔκρυψεν. Thus, a man found the treasure, in what way is not said, the conjunction of circumstances which caused him to find the treasure being left out of view. With the participle aorist the narrative passes quickly over the finding to state what he did with the find: εὑρὼν ἔκρυψεν. One might feel tempted to take this ἔκρυψεν as identical with the κρύπτειν already mentioned in κεκρυμμένῳ, and therefore in the sense of the pluperfect as a supplementary explanation of that participle, so that the treasure would not be found in the field, but somewhere else, and then buried by the finder in the field.[4] But this attempt is inevitably wrecked on the confusion thus

---

[1] De Wette. [2] Meyer, Keil.
[3] In opposition to Weiss. [4] Fritzsche.

introduced into the simple flow of the narrative. For when a treasure hidden in the field, which some one found, was first spoken of, the finding could not possibly be meant to refer to any other than the hiding-place just described; and when a second κρύπτειν is spoken of, in the circumstances of the case this can only be a second hiding of the treasure, and, no other place being mentioned, in the same field in which it was hidden before. The apparently enigmatical character of this act is explained so soon as we learn from what follows that the intention of the finder is directed to the acquiring of the *field*. He leaves the treasure in its hiding-place in order that he may be able to acquire it for himself in this its hiding-place. He cunningly says to himself that it would be dangerous were he to publish his find before he is able really to call it his own; and that, buried as it is, the treasure will remain secure to him whilst he goes to make it his own.

In what follows the relative construction is given up, the narrative continuing in an independent sentence with a vividly descriptive present tense. Moreover, the action stated in this final sentence is specially emphasized by the introductory clause: καὶ ἀπὸ τῆς χαρᾶς αὐτοῦ ὑπάγει, a plain indication that the special emphasis of the narrative lies on this final sentence. In connection with emotions like χαρά, φόβος, λύπη, the preposition ἀπό denotes the inner motive of an action, in which case the article may be absent (Luke xxi. 26), but is more frequently present (Matt. xiv. 26; Luke xxii. 45, xxiv. 41; Acts xii. 14). But even when the article, wanting in the corresponding German[1] expressions, "from joy, fear," etc., is present, the αὐτοῦ added here has still nothing strange about it, and there is no reason for depriving it of its obvious reference to the finder as the subject of the joy, and referring it, as many do, to the treasure as the object of the joy. Hence: "*And moved by his joy he goes,*" καὶ πωλεῖ πάντα ὅσα ἔχει καὶ ἀγοράζει τὸν ἀγρὸν ἐκεῖνον. In addition, then, to prudence and cunning, in his joy he exhibits a determination that renounces and sacrifices everything in acquiring the treasure. It is no difficulty to him that he must pay a price which he can only command by selling the whole of his possessions. He acts without hesitation, "*sells all that he possesses and buys that field,*" thus putting himself, at the sacrifice of all the rest of his property, in possession of the hidden treasure.

[1] So too in English.

The design of the parable is plain. For when a description is given here of the way in which a man gets a treasure he has found into his own possession, the intention can only be to say *in what way we must appropriate the kingdom of God, which Jesus brings to men, and make it our own possession.* Thus the kingdom of heaven or of God stands over against the individual man, not so much as an order of things fixed by the divine will, to which the individual has to submit, and of which he has to become a member, but as an order of things replete with divine blessings, and therefore as a state of blessedness, a precious good which offers itself to his possession, and summons him to make it his own.

When, then, the description of the way in which the man obtains the treasure is introduced in the parable by the statement that the treasure which the man found is hidden in the field, and therefore buried, this can only mean that the blessings of the kingdom of heaven are not, as the Jewish expectation in its externalizing conception of the Messianic promises was inclined to suppose, blessings obvious to sense, and lying on the surface of things, but that they belong to the sphere of the inner life of the spirit hidden to the outward gaze—they are the purely spiritual blessings of the divine fellowship offering itself to man in Jesus. This interpretation of the buried state of the treasure, so opposed to the Messianic hopes of the age which looked for a kingdom of public, outward glory, is clearly the only natural one; whereas the interpretation, favoured by many, of the hiding of the treasure in the bosom of the Church, falls to the ground with the erroneous reference of the field to the Church;[1] and the reference, favoured by others, to the concealment of the treasure before the appearance of Christ[2] is irrelevant, because the treasure in the parable was not merely hidden previously, but is found hidden, and remains hidden even after it is found. When, then, the blessing of God's kingdom, hidden in that sense, is so brought home to a man that the blessing is made known to him (*i.e.* that he sees and feels its inestimable worth), this is a piece of good fortune, like the finding of treasure buried in a field. But whoever enjoys such good fortune (as was the case with the hearers of the parable—the disciples of Jesus) must turn it to profit. For as one cannot call a buried treasure his own simply because he has found it, but must first acquire it for himself, so also it is

---

[1] See below. [2] Kuinoel.

not enough to have received an impression of the kingdom of heaven and its priceless worth; on the contrary, it must be made a personal possession. And to this end there is needed, on one hand, thoughtful prudence; on the other hand, and chiefly, a moral determination which foregoes and sacrifices everything. Just as the man in the parable prudently leaves the treasure in its hiding-place until he can really call it his own, so also the man to whom the hidden blessing of God's kingdom has presented itself is not to boast and brag prematurely, before he really possesses it, else he would be in danger of losing it before he has it; but he is to leave the costly blessing of God's kingdom, so secret and inward in nature, in this its hiding-place, by allowing the impression of it which he has received to nestle in the hidden depths of his heart, and by cherishing it in quiet feeling. Thus will it remain assured to him while he strives for its possession with all his strength. This definite interpretation of the circumstance, that the finder again hides the treasure, and acquires it for himself in its hiding-place, is required, because the strange addition of so peculiar a feature—by no means indispensable to the rest of the context—is only explained by the reference to such an interpretation. Nevertheless, the chief purpose has reference to the last thought, to the all-sacrificing determination by which the kingdom of God must be acquired. For as the man in the parable goes and sells all that he has in order, instead, to buy the buried treasure, so whoever would secure the treasure of God's kingdom must inwardly give up every other possession, everything otherwise dear to him to which his heart clings, must inwardly renounce affection for every other possession whatever, in order instead to gain that highest good; for at no lower price will it become his. It can only be possessed by one who renounces the desire to possess anything else beside it. Thus it is an inward act that is expressed and required by the selling of every possession in the parable, as is implied in the nature of a comparison representing the inward by the outward; but it is not for this reason a mere depreciation of everything else in comparison with the blessing of the gospel that is meant,[1] but an act of renunciation which, although inward, is none the less actual and complete. After this act is done, the outward, literal giving up of any possession, wherever requisite, is no longer a matter of hesitation.

[1] Kuinoel.

If, then, we have correctly reproduced the original meaning of the parable, every special interpretation of the twice-mentioned field is excluded. And this rightly. For at the beginning of the parable the mention of the field merely served to intensify the idea of hiding by the more definite and picturesque idea of burial, which is the surest, and therefore the usual, way of concealing a treasure. Its second mention at the close of the parable, where the field is bought as containing the treasure, was unavoidable, if the thought was to be carried out, that the hidden treasure of God's kingdom also must be acquired as a hidden one. Especially must we reject the frequently attempted reference of the field to the *Church*, because the relation of the Church to the blessings of God's kingdom treasured by it in no way corresponds to the relation of a field to the treasure buried in it. For instead of concealing and hiding the blessings of God's kingdom, the Church's calling is rather in every way to make known and publish those blessings, which in themselves are of a hidden nature. And if we attempt to apply the field to the secularized Church, in which the true blessings of salvation are buried under the rubbish of external worldly aims and human ordinances, the re-burying of the treasure in the field and the buying of the field at the conclusion will not at all harmonize with such a view. For on no account can the meaning be, that, in order to obtain the blessings of salvation, one must accept a church, which has perverted its true calling into its opposite, into the bargain. To accept this interpretation is to attribute to the parable *ex eventu* a prophetic signification, having reference to particular periods in the history of the Church, to which the text gives no manner of support.

The Pearl of Great Price.

(Matt. xiii. 45, 46.)

Beside the parable of the Hidden Treasure now appears (ver. 45 f.) a second, resembling the former in the main—that of the Pearl of Great Price. Its resemblance to the former is indicated at the outset by the introductory πάλιν suggestive of repetition. Πάλιν ὁμοία ἐστὶν ἡ βασιλεία τῶν οὐρανῶν ἀνθρώπῳ ἐμπόρῳ. That the kingdom of heaven is not at once likened to the pearl as the parallel-idea to the treasure, but that instead of this an ἔμπορος is put first, cannot surprise us after what has been already remarked on ver. 24 of this chapter. Whether then the single idea put first as such answers to the kingdom of heaven or not, the meaning of the introduction is simply this, that the following narrative is meant to serve as a comparison to corresponding circumstances and events in the sphere of the heavenly kingdom. Ἀνθρώπῳ is prefixed to ἐμπόρῳ as an antithesis to τῶν οὐρανῶν. Thus special attention is called to the fact that the nature of the kingdom of *heaven* is meant to be illustrated from the sphere of the natural life of *man*.[1] Ἐμπόρῳ is in apposition, thus: "*The kingdom of heaven is like a man* (namely) *a merchant*." An ἔμπορος is a *merchant*, then more precisely a wholesale dealer, whose work lies principally in the *purchase* of goods, the procuring of transmarine or other foreign wares, whilst leaving the sale to the retailer. Then to the designation as ἔμπορος corresponds the kind of mercantile activity ascribed to the one so designated. It is so in the appended participial sentence, which here, as in ver. 24, takes the place of the relative sentence occurring elsewhere in similar introductions to parables: ζητοῦντι καλοὺς μαργαρίτας. Thus, the mercantile activity here considered does not relate to the disposing of wares, but lies in the region of inquiry. The object which his inquiry has in view is pearls, an article of trade of great importance in the ancient world,—and pearls of special beauty and excellence. The adjective καλούς cannot be meant in the present context to describe pearls generally as excellent in comparison with other things, but distinguishes the pearls, which are the objects of his search, as excellent from pearls of inferior order. The merchant is therefore a man skilled in the value of pearls, making it his special business to seek pearls of pre-eminent excellence.

Then in what follows the finding at once responds to the seeking; for, putting εὑρών first with emphasis, and opposing it by δέ to ζητοῦντι, the narrative proceeds, ver. 46: εὑρὼν δὲ ἕνα πολύτιμον μαργαρίτην. Such is the correct reading, which, in order to give this emphasis to the εὑρών, somewhat harshly breaks off the construction scarcely begun, and begins an independent sentence; whereas the reading ὃς εὑρὼν κ.τ.λ. (Rec.),

---

[1] Just so in ver. 52, xviii. 23, xx. 1, xxii. 2.

which perhaps arose from a reference to the ὃν εὑρών in the parallel parable, ver. 44, is smoother, although less pregnant. But that which he found is nevertheless highly surprising to the finder, leaving his expectation far behind. The seeker after goodly pearls found "*one pearl of great price.*" The excellence of this pearl, far surpassing all other pearls, is expressed not merely by the adjective πολύτιμος, still further heightening the designation καλός, but chiefly by the prefixing of the numeral ἕνα. Not merely has he found a pearl of special costliness, but a unique, costly pearl, which presents itself to him—a connoisseur on this subject—as unique of its kind, alone and incomparable in its costliness. And after he has found the costly pearl, and finding it has perceived its unique value, he acts accordingly: ἀπελθὼν πέπρακεν κ.τ.λ. The introductory ἀπελθών, corresponding to the introductory clause ἀπὸ τῆς χαρᾶς αὐτοῦ ὑπάγει in the parallel parable, ver. 44, signalizes the following act as specially worthy of notice. And at the same time in the present connection it denotes the instantaneous breaking off and giving up of his previous work of seeking. Now that he has found the one pearl of great price, his search after goodly pearls is at an end; he has but one thing to aim at, actually to possess the one of great price. And this possession he strives after with the same all-renouncing, all-sacrificing determination with which the man in the previous parable puts himself in possession of the treasure: πέπρακεν πάντα ὅσα εἶχεν καὶ ἠγόρασεν αὐτόν. Here the narrative does not, as in the previous parable in the corresponding place, pass into the present of vivid realization. But here also the perfect πέπρακεν before the aorist ἠγόρασεν lays a specially vivid emphasis on the decisive act, the selling of all his property: *He has sold all that he had, and bought the same.* It only corresponds to the incomparable value of the pearl, that it cannot be purchased at a lower price than the sale of every other possession. And thus the merchant, perceiving its unique value, without delay pays this price in order to become possessor of the one pearl.

The general design of the parable is obviously the same as in the preceding parable. For as there the point in question is the acquiring of a treasure found, so here it is that of a pearl found. Thus, here as there the way is explained *in which man must acquire and make his own the blessing of the kingdom of heaven offered to him in the person and words of Jesus.*

GOEBEL.

But the way in which this final thought is prepared for is materially different here from what it is there. For whereas there the finding of a treasure was at once spoken of as an unexpected piece of fortune happening to a man, here, while a similar find is spoken of, the personality of the finder is briefly and sharply characterized, so that we see what enabled him to find it. The intention here, therefore, is to intimate what is requisite on the part of man in order even to find the costly blessing of God's kingdom. What caused the merchant to find the one costly pearl was this, that he, a man skilled in the pursuit, instituted zealous search with critical intelligence after pearls of special worth. Had he not been what he was, and had he not done what he did, he would not have found the pearl of great price, or, what amounts to the same, would not have perceived its worth. In the sphere of the heavenly kingdom this merchant can only be the man who finds no satisfaction in the blessings of life offered him by the world, but, recognising their insignificance, with critical intelligence and earnest spiritual longing seeks after better, more precious blessings, whose possession will yield true, abiding satisfaction. Accordingly, the goodly pearls as such have no definite reference, as often supposed, to the blessings of intellectual culture, science, art, and the like. They are objects of search merely, and therefore still indefinite. Only such a man is able to find the kingdom of heaven, for only such an one is able to estimate its worth. Like as the merchant in his search meets with a pearl, which he perceives to be of unique costliness, so to the man who seeks and inquires with earnest longing for salvation the kingdom of God presents itself as the one supreme good of absolute, infinite worth, beside which everything else which a man may possess appears worthless. But it is not enough, when we have found the kingdom of God, to recognise it in its absolute worth as the one supreme good, but, in order to become its actual master, moral action corresponding to such knowledge is required. Thus, at the close the parable reverts completely to the line of thought in the previous parable. Like as the merchant, after he has found the pearl of great price, sells everything in order to obtain it, so the costly blessing of the kingdom of God, as alone precious, is to be acquired by renunciation of every other possession. (Cf. the interpretation of the corresponding passage in the previous parable.)

A comparative retrospect of the two parables shows, that they not merely run up into the same principal and concluding thoughts, but that they have also something in common in their first introductory portion. For when Jesus at first describes the kingdom of heaven as a hidden good, which is found in the same way as a buried treasure, and then adds by way of climax, that, in order to be able to find it at all, a deeper longing for salvation must be present, such as is able to distinguish the precious from the worthless, the two statements suggest in common the difficulty which man finds in arriving at an inner perception of the supreme good presented to him in the kingdom of heaven. The difficulty laid bare in the first comparison is one having its ground in the nature of God's kingdom itself; the difficulty laid bare in the second is the one lying in the pre-condition requisite on the part of man. This is the only distinction between the two parables, not (as *e.g.* Olshausen supposes [1]) that the one pictures a more receptive nature, the second a noble, self-active nature,—a view which would unwarrantably deprive the parables of their generality of application. Accordingly, the two parables remind, in their introductory portion, of the first parable of the Sower. For, like that one, these parables also serve to explain to the disciples why the word of the kingdom finds an intelligent reception with so few, whilst remaining a mystery to the multitude.

The Fishing-Net.

(Matt. xiii. 47-50.)

Upon the pair of parables—the Treasure and the Pearl—follows now a third parable, joined to the former by πάλιν only, without any connecting words. The connection by πάλιν, indicative of repetition, we have already found twice in pairs of parables closely related in meaning, namely, in addition to the twin parables of the Treasure and Pearl just noticed, in those of the Mustard Seed and Leaven in Luke xiii. 20. We are therefore warranted in expecting that here also the πάλιν will not refer in a purely formal way to a second comparison of the kingdom of heaven, but is also meant to intimate, in reference to the

[1] And Keil in like manner.

third parable, a similarity in contents to the preceding pair of parables.

In ver. 47 it is said: πάλιν ὁμοία ἐστὶν ἡ βασ. τῶν οὐρ. σαγήνῃ. Here, then, the first thing in the symbolic narrative is a fishing-net, and that a large drag-net, intended to catch fish in masses, according to the special meaning of σαγήνη, in distinction from the more general δίκτυον. And, in the first place, the participles, which supply the place of a relative sentence, recount the circumstances bearing upon this net: βληθείσῃ εἰς τὴν θάλασσαν καὶ ἐκ παντὸς γένους συναγαγούσῃ. The participles stand in the aorist. The occurrence is therefore not depicted, as might indeed have been done also in the present case, as one often repeated, but is related as of a particular definite fact, "*the net was cast into the sea, and gathered of every kind.*" The word "gathered," chosen to describe the act of catching, signalizes in this act the element of bringing together, collecting. What the net collects is very diverse, it gathers "of every kind," *scil.* of fish. The right exposition of the words "of every kind" is of special importance for the understanding of the entire parable. First of all, it is certain that the meaning cannot be, that every kind of fish in existence was caught,—an inconceivable thing,—but every kind of fish offering itself to the net. The net cast into the sea —such is the thought—makes no distinction between the fish, admitting the one sort and leaving the rest outside, but without distinction gathers of every kind coming in its way. The only doubt possible is, whether in those words we are to think simply of different *genera* of fish in the scientific sense, or of different kinds in the general sense, without regard to what their difference of kind consists in, whether in scientific species, or in size or excellence, or aught else. But whilst the literal meaning of γένος = " race " by no means necessitates the former view,—for elsewhere also it expands into the meaning "different kind" in the general sense,[1]—the context decides for the latter. For obviously the indiscriminate gathering here spoken of is meant to form a contrast to the separation between the good and the bad related afterwards. But this contrast only actually exists if the "gathering of every kind" refers, not merely to different scientific species, but to any difference of kind whatever, inclusive of those described afterwards by the distinction of good and bad. The narrative then continues with an independent

[1] *E.g.* 1 Cor. xii. 10, 28, xiv. 10.

sentence, although one joined on to the preceding by the relative pronoun, ver. 48: ἦν, ὅτε ἐπληρώθη, ἀναβιβάσαντες ἐπὶ τὸν αἰγιαλὸν καὶ καθίσαντες συνέλεξαν τὰ καλὰ εἰς ἄγγη, τὰ δὲ σαπρὰ ἔξω ἔβαλον. This reading must here be adhered to as by far the best attested, in opposition to Lachmann's and Tischendorf's: ἦν ... ἀναβιβάσαντες αὐτὴν καὶ[1] ἐπὶ τὸν αἰγιαλὸν καθίσαντες κ.τ.λ. Therefore: "*This, when it was full, they drew up on the beach.*" It is self-evident that the words "when it was filled" cannot mean, as Stier supposes: "When the whole sea is fished out, and all the fish that swam therein are in the net," a thought just as impossible as the reference of ἐκ παντὸς γένους to every kind of fish in existence, and still more inconceivable. But Stier's exposition is worthy of mention, because it strikingly shows what the effect is when one lets himself be guided in the exposition of the literal meaning of a figurative narrative by an interpretation previously decided on. Of course the words "when it was filled" can only denote the point of time when the space in the net was filled up, when therefore it had received the number of fish it was designed to hold, which is made known by the weight dragging down the net. When this point of time came, they drew the net to shore, "*and sat down and gathered the good into vessels, but threw the bad away.*" The καθίσαντες put first intimates the thoughtful care with which the work of separation is performed. It is just as needless and forced to think of other things present in the net beside the fish caught,[2] because of the generality of the expressions τὰ καλὰ ... τὰ δὲ σαπρά, as it is with others to supplement the expressions by ἰχθύδια. In examining the catch, consisting of course of fish, the sitters direct their attention merely to the distinction of good and bad; hence the general expression, "the good, the bad." The latter, according to the literal meaning of σαπρός, are the corrupt, dead fish, in a state of rottenness, not "the unclean marine animals,"[3] and in contrast with them τὰ καλά are here the sound fish, and therefore fit for use. The latter they gathered into the vessels standing ready; the former they cast ἔξω, i.e. instead of *into* vessels, they cast them *out* and away, as one throws away worthless things.

Just, then, as in the former parables of the Sower, Mustard Seed, and Leaven, it is the description of an oft-recurring event which serves as a comparison to the kingdom of heaven, so here the description of a draught of fish does the same. But the pro-

---

[1] Tischendorf omits καί.   [2] Kuinoel.   [3] Lange.

ceeding characteristic of such a draught, to which the description is directed, was the final "casting out" of that which is bad after the indiscriminate "gathering of every kind" at the beginning. Here is the point of the entire description. Accordingly, the design of the parable can only lie in the warning allusion to the fact *that everything gathered at first indiscriminately into the kingdom of God will at last be subjected to a careful testing, by which the precious will be rigidly severed from the worthless, and the latter will be excluded.* Such is the meaning of the interpreting word, which the Lord at once appends to the parable, vv. 49, 50: "*So*"—as in the conclusion of the parable—"*will it be at the end of the dispensation. The angels will go forth*"—*scil.* from their heavenly abode, for the purpose of carrying out the work entrusted to them—"*and sever the wicked from among the righteous.*" The expression ἐκ μέσου τῶν δικαίων, instead of the simple ἀπὸ τῶν δικαίων, brings before us the state which the angels will find at the end of the world,—the unrighteous present among the righteous. They will bring this state to an end by excluding the former, "*and will cast them into the furnace of fire. There shall be the wailing and gnashing of teeth.*" On this image of ἡ κάμινος τοῦ πυρός for Gehenna, and also on the sentence ἐκεῖ ἔσται κ.τ.λ., cf. the interpretation of the parable of the Tares on ver. 42. Here also both are independent additions to the interpretation, carrying the explanation of the figurative language of the parable beyond the limits of the figure.

In detail, therefore, the parable is to be interpreted in the following way: the kingdom of God, like a great net cast into the sea, is planted in the midst of the world, with the design of drawing men within its compass, and folding them in its bosom. The sea only comes into view here as the element inhabited by and crowded with fish. Hence its counterpart is the κόσμος merely as the dwelling-place of mankind;[1] the sea is not the masses of the people themselves. The figurative representation of the latter by waves of the sea and floods of water in several passages of the Old Testament, often introduced here,[2] has nothing in common with the present passage. As, then, such a net gathers fish of

---

[1] Cf. the field in the parable of the Tares, and the œcumenical interpretation given by Jesus Himself in ver. 38.

[2] *E.g.* Ps. lxv. 7; Isa. viii. 7; Jer. xlvii. 2; cf. also Rev. xvii. 15, where the point of comparison lies in the restless roar of the waves, or in the force of the flood carrying everything with it.

every kind,—for it stands open to all indiscriminately, whatever their character,—so the kingdom of God gathers men of every kind. However different they may be in other respects, either outwardly in descent, rank, race, etc., or even inwardly in difference of capacity or difference of moral worth, the kingdom of heaven lies open to all without distinction. If we have rightly understood the words "gathered of every kind," in the context of the narrative, this and nothing else must be the meaning of the first part of the parable. And this interpretation must also have suggested itself to the hearers in presence of the motley throng of Christ's disciples, made up of all kinds of people— fishermen and publicans, sinners and righteous. But we must not try to find in the words ἐκ παντὸς γένους an image of all nations,[1] if, at least, the πᾶν cannot be referred to every γένος existing in the sea, but only to every one coming in the way of the net, and if γένος here expresses not merely the scientific species, but difference of kind in the general sense. And just as little can the words "when it was filled" here, according to their only possible meaning in the context of the figurative description, mark the time of the end as the time when the kingdom of God shall embrace all nations, but only as the time when it shall embrace the complement which it is meant in God's purpose to embrace, and thus the time when its mission in and to the world shall be perfectly fulfilled. Accordingly the comparison then proceeds: Like as the net, when full, was drawn to the beach, so the kingdom of heaven, when in the above sense it shall have perfectly fulfilled its mission in and to the world, shall be withdrawn from the sphere of the present world-life, and at the same time —such is the presupposition—the present dispensation shall find its end. But by no means—thus follows now the main thought of the parable prepared for in what precedes—shall all that was enclosed by God's kingdom in the present dispensation be gathered into God's kingdom in the future world, as indiscriminately as it was collected in the present world. Just the contrary! Like as the mixed multitude of fish in the net drawn to the shore is then submitted to a careful testing and separation, the good and useful being gathered into vessels, while the bad and useless are cast away, so there will take place then a careful testing of all those who belonged to the kingdom of God as to its outward form in the present dispensation. And only they

[1] Meyer.

who in this severe testing prove themselves fit by their moral character, because the righteousness of the kingdom of heaven is found in them,—only they shall be gathered into God's kingdom in the future world, while they who are found morally corrupt (σαπροί), these " wicked," severed from among those " righteous," as unfit for the kingdom of heaven, shall be excluded from it for ever. Thus " the gathering into vessels " is the same here as the gathering into the barn in the parable of the Tares, *i.e.* the bringing of the righteous into the future kingdom of God.[1] On the other hand, no sort of allusion is found in the present parable to the circumstance that that sifting and this bringing are the business of the *angels*, whereas it was expressly symbolized in the parable of the Tares by the emphasis laid on the reapers in distinction from the servants. Here also, indeed, the interpreting word of Jesus (ver. 49) mentions the angels, but in this mention He just as definitely goes beyond the limits of what is symbolized in the parable itself as in the mention of the furnace of Gehenna. For the question who the persons are who perform the act of sifting, was just as little thought of in the figurative description as the question who the persons are who cast out the net,—so little, that neither in the former nor in the latter act were the agents so much as named.

But the difference between the two parables in this particular point is simply an outcome of the difference of their general purpose. A special reference to this design here will not seem superfluous if we have regard to the surprising resemblance between the thoughts finding expression here and there. The resemblance is in the excision, predicted in both parables for the end of the world, of the ungodly from the midst of the righteous, with whom they were associated during the earthly development of God's kingdom. But the fore-announcement of this fact takes place here and there under quite different points of view. There a different and longer exposition precedes, and only as the conclusion of this exposition is that fact of the future held up before the disciples *for their comfort and the strengthening of their faith* in face of the temptation which the strange appearance of the ungodly amid the righteous might present to their faith in the newly founded kingdom of God. In this sense, after the disciples had been told that it was not their business to carry out the excision of the ungodly within the present æon, the prospect is

[1] Cf. on ver. 43.

spread before them at the close that this excision will be the work of the angels of God at the end of the world. When, on the other hand, here simply the general fact is held up before the disciples, that at the end a strict testing and sifting according to their moral worth lies before the mixed multitude of those who were included in the kingdom of God as to its outward form in the present æon, this is done *for their own warning*, in order that they may not fancy themselves sure of entering into God's kingdom in the future world by reason of their belonging to God's kingdom at present, but may strive with unwearying earnestness to be able for their part to stand in that severe testing and sifting.

We have now reached the end of the second series of parables delivered on one day at Capernaum, and forming a part of the supplementary conversation of Jesus with the disciples. If we glance back at the three parables constituting this series, there can no longer be any doubt, after what has been said, as to the point of view under which the third is so closely linked with the first two, to which at first sight it seems so unlike. That which the third has in common with the first and the second is the hortatory purpose suited to the then state of their inner life. All three parables join on to the present standpoint of the disciples as those who, in distinction from the unbelieving masses of the people, have already in some way personally entered into the fellowship of God's kingdom. They it is who have had the happiness of finding the hidden good of God's kingdom (1); they it is who, with the keen discrimination of a heart thirsting for salvation, have recognised in the kingdom of heaven the supreme good (2); they it is who in motley throng have been already enclosed by the net of God's kingdom (3). But to find a costly good, and recognise its worth, does not render one sure of its possession,—they must now acquire God's kingdom for themselves, even at the cost of sacrificing every other possession (1 and 2). And the fact that they are enclosed by the net of God's kingdom in this world does not make them sure of salvation for the future,—they must strive not to be put to shame in the testing and sifting reserved for the end (3). Thus, whereas an objective didactic purpose ruled in the first series of parables by the sea, seeing they were meant to give the disciples a series of objective revelations in reference to the present founding and future development of the kingdom of God, in this second series of parables a subjective hortatory purpose rules, seeing they are meant to set the personal relation of the disciples to God's kingdom in its right light before them, and to admonish and warn them in reference to the moral duty binding upon them in consequence of that relation.

Review.

In conclusion, a word must be said respecting the theory advanced, in the wake of Bengel, by expositors like Stier, Thiersch, Lange (certainly by each one in a different shape), to the effect that the seven parables in Matthew are meant to set forth prophetically seven historical Church-periods in the future, following each other in the same order. The most attractive form of this theory is given by Lange, when he arranges and characterizes the seven supposed historical periods thus: 1. The Sower = the apostolic age; 2. The Tares = the early Catholic Church flourishing amid heresies; 3. The Mustard Seed = the Universal Church of Constantine; 4. The Leaven = the transforming action of Christianity in the mediæval Church during the national migrations; 5. The Treasure in the Field = the period of the Reformation; 6. The Pearl = the antithesis of Christianity and the blessings of modern civilisation; 7. The Net = the concluding Judgment. But, instructive as such an exposition may seem to many, it fails altogether to hold its ground upon sober examination, if, that is, the exposition is meant to imply that Jesus Himself, in uttering these seven parables in their present order, had regard prophetically to a corresponding succession of historical Church-periods in the future. In the first place, the text, as regards its form merely, affords no justification for speaking of a continuous cycle of seven interconnected parables, for we do not find in Matthew a continuous series of seven parables, but first a series of four complete in themselves, and then a second independent series of three. The latter are part of a conversation held at a later time and in a different place, a conversation occasioned by subsequent inquiries of the disciples. Thus there is nothing to warrant the notion that Jesus there broke off His line of thought with the fourth parable, and resumed and continued it here with the fifth. But if we wish to combine the four and the three parables, we must at least add St. Mark's second parable of the Fruit-bearing Earth, of which no notice is taken in those theories, put it in its original place among the rest, and assign to it a corresponding period in Church history. And in the second place, as concerns the substance of the seven particular parables, their investigation has shown us that they all equally have their starting-point in the condition of God's kingdom at the time,—the first in the want of success then attending the Messianic work of Jesus among the multitude, the second in the mixture of impure elements in the circle of the disciples, obvious at least to the eyes of the Lord,[1] the third and fourth in the insignificance of the beginning made by God's kingdom, the three belonging to the second series in the condition of the inner life of the disciples. And where a prediction of the future really contrasts with these starting-points taken from the present,[2] the prediction everywhere covers the entire development of God's kingdom from its beginnings in the present up to the end of the present dispensation, so that this entire development is merely placed under another single point of view and exhibited in another light. But the first, fifth, and sixth (Sower, Treasure, Pearl) contain no prediction at all. In relation to these it is only possible to claim an intended prophetic reference to definite historical events in the future, by assuming, with Bengel, a *sensus reconditissimus* behind the *communis ratio*, which robs the exposition of all certainty, and hands it over to the ingenious caprice of the expositor. But of course we must not deny, but acknowledge the truth lying at the basis of these theories, namely, that the disclosures made in these parables respecting the nature and growth of God's kingdom in the course of its historical development upon earth find ever new confirmations, and also that especially striking confirmations of one or the other of these parables may be pointed out in particular periods of Church history in the past. Only it is not the province of exposition, but of free application, to point out such historical confirmations and fulfilments of the universally applicable truths contained in particular parables, and such application again will not allow the freedom which is its right to be limited by the demands of a particular order of succession.

---

[1] Cf. the ὡμοιώθη in ver. 24.
[2] As in the second, third, fourth, and seventh parables (Tares, Mustard Seed, Leaven, Fishing-Net).

PART II.

THE LATER PARABLES ACCORDING TO LUKE.

INTRODUCTORY.

THE parables peculiar to Luke's Gospel, of which this second section is to treat, are found all together in the portion of the Gospel usually called Luke's *journey-narrative*, because it is asserted that with chap. ix. 51 the evangelist begins to describe the last journey of Jesus to Jerusalem, all that follows up to the account of the entry into Jerusalem (xix. 28 ff.) being on this view nothing but a continuous description of the journey. Were this supposition correct, all these parables of Luke would fall within the last period of the life and teaching of Jesus, and would all belong to a later period than the first one of the last parables in Matthew which are to be treated of in the third section,—we mean the parable of the Unmerciful Servant, Matt. xviii. 23 ff., which the latter evangelist makes to have been spoken in Capernaum immediately *before* the beginning of the last journey (cf. xix. 1). But the supposition is wrong. First of all, it stands in strange contrast both with the space taken up by the section reaching ostensibly from ix. 51 to xix. 27 in the evangelist's treatise, and with the character it bears. This description of the last journey of Jesus would then fill no less than ten chapters, thus constituting well-nigh half the entire Gospel, whilst only five chapters would remain for the description of the entire public work of Jesus previously. And looking at the contents of this section as a whole, we are met by a comprehensive collection of discourses and sayings of Jesus on the most diverse occasions, some of which indeed combine into groups on chronological grounds, while the different groups combine with each other and with the intermediate passages in such a way that no continuous chronological connection can be made out. This does not give the impression that we have to do here with a single unbroken description of a journey, and only very cogent reasons can compel us to accept such a notion. Certainly we can scarcely insist that in that case a number of incidents and sayings of Jesus, which Matthew places definitely in an earlier period, would, according to Luke, belong to that last journey; and that an occurrence, the scene of which, according to John's Gospel, can only be Bethany, would be transferred by Luke (x. 38 ff.) to some Galilaean village,—we can scarcely, we say, insist on this without exposing ourselves to the suspicion of harmonistic fanaticism. Nevertheless, by those who are not hunting with critical fanaticism after contradictions in the evangelists, this should at least be taken into account as an element in forming a judgment on the present question. But it is a decisive consideration that the sole basis on which this entire supposition, so strange in itself, rests is altogether inadequate. It rests solely on the fact that in that section, comprehensive as it is, three isolated passages occur in which mention is made of a journey of Jesus to Jerusalem: ix. 51, xiii. 22, xvii. 11. These three passages, it is thought, must be so understood that the first forms a turning-point in the account of the evangelist, chronologically separating everything which follows from what precedes, and that in the two others the evangelist for the sake of clearness reminds the reader of the circumstances in which he finds himself in the journey-narrative there begun.[1] But in reality these passages have not the meaning ascribed to them. When the passage (ix. 51) says that Jesus, when the days of His taking up (to God) were fulfilled, set His face directly towards Jerusalem, and therefore directed His journey straight through Samaria, the design of these words, as is clear from ver. 53, is specifically to introduce the account of the occurrence that follows, vv. 52–56. For because His face was directed to Jerusalem, the Samaritans refused to receive Him, ver. 53, and the fiery anger of the disciples at the Samaritans is set in sharp contrast with the disposition which makes Christ encounter suffering and death, ver. 54. But the words: καὶ πορευομένων αὐτῶν ἐν τῇ ὁδῷ εἶπέν τις πρὸς αὐτόν, ver. 57, at least leave it doubtful whether Luke here means to give a continuance of the

[1] Cf. e.g. Ewald, Meyer, Godet.

journey mentioned, vv. 51–56, or whether he does not rather simply link this other incident of a journey to the first on internal grounds—to say nothing of the question whether it would be right to take all that follows as a continued account of that journey. It is just the same with the second passage, xiii. 22, as is clear from ver. 33. Because, on the day to be here spoken of, ver. 31, Jesus uttered a saying, ver. 33 (beside other sayings, vv. 23–30), having special reference to His journey to Jerusalem and His death, which He could undergo nowhere but in Jerusalem, therefore the remark is specially prefixed to the account of the sayings of this day, that He was then on the way to Jerusalem. And when, finally, in the third passage, xvii. 11, to the narrative of the ten healed lepers, among whom the Samaritan alone showed himself grateful, thus giving occasion to the Lord's sorrowful complaint of the ingratitude of the rest (vv. 17, 18),—the statement is prefixed by way of introduction that Jesus then went through the borders of Samaria and Galilee on His (last) journey to Jerusalem, here also there is no justification for giving the remark an application reaching beyond the particular incident thus introduced, not even to what follows, ver. 20 ff., to say nothing of what precedes, as if the purpose were to remind that this also belongs to the period of the last journey to Jerusalem. On the contrary, the expression: "And it came to pass, as He was on His way to Jerusalem," etc., plainly is so worded that it must be referred to what follows in distinction from what precedes.[1] Accordingly, this entire section of Luke's Gospel, which begins, not with ix. 51, but in ver. 46, after the conclusion of the preceding section, with the announcement of the Passion, vv. 44, 45, and ends with xviii. 30 (from which point Luke then really describes the last journey to Jerusalem, thus beginning the history of the Passion in the broad sense), is simply to be regarded as a collection of sayings and teachings of Jesus, the combination of which was not governed by a chronological point of view. That such a conception is inconsistent with the declared intention of the evangelist to write $καθεξῆς$ (chap. i. 3),[2] could only be asserted if it were proved, which is impossible, that the $καθεξῆς$ cannot apply to any grouping of material from any point of view, but only to a strictly chronological enumeration of every particular. That this section contains so much that is peculiar to Luke, can-

---

[1] Cf. also Hofmann on all three passages, Luke ix. 51 ff., xiii. 22 ff., xvii. 11 ff.
[2] Meyer.

not surprise us, because he here expressly makes room for the employment of the material which his careful researches (i. 3) have brought within his reach beyond the well-known material found in written and oral tradition. At most it might be said by way of conjecture, in regard to the three passages in which mention is made of the journey to Jerusalem, that, in the case of the present collection of discourses and sayings of Jesus, Luke perhaps had at command, beside others, an authority treating of this last journey in detail.

After what has been said we must renounce the attempt, in treating of the parables peculiar to Luke's Gospel, to define exactly the chronological position of each individual parable.

The Merciful Samaritan.

(Luke x. 25-37.)

The first of the parables peculiar to Luke's Gospel meets us in chap. x. 30-37,—that of the Merciful Samaritan, forming part of a conversation of Jesus with a scribe. We must therefore first of all, in order to understand the parable, glance briefly at the previous course of the conversation.

According to ver. 25, a lawyer[1] arose, putting Jesus to the test with the question: τί ποιήσας ζωὴν αἰώνιον κληρονομήσω; i.e. literally: *Having done what, shall I inherit eternal life?* therefore: What must I do in order to inherit eternal life? With this question he desires to put Jesus to the test (ἐκπειράζων αὐτόν), i.e. to see whether He will not give some answer contradicting the law, and thus afford opportunity to refute Him from the law. But Jesus at once saw through the man's intention, and therefore, instead of Himself pronouncing an opinion on the question proposed, calls upon him to take the answer to his question from the law, with which he is acquainted. In this sense he puts the counter-question (ver. 26): "*What is written in the law? how readest thou?*" The answer to this question, which the scribe takes from the law (ver. 27), contains the same peculiar collocation of the command to love God (Deut. vi. 5), with the command to love our neighbour (Lev. xix. 18),

[1] νομικός, as to substance synonymous with γραμματεύς, current elsewhere.

which we find in another place (Matt. xxii. 37 ff.; Mark xii. 29 ff.) in the mouth of Jesus Himself,—there as *His* answer to the question put to Him by another lawyer: Which is the greatest commandment of the law? And that the combination in this way of those two passages of the law, as a summary of the entire law, was a novelty, and by no means something already current, is clear there from the joyous surprise at the answer on the part of the questioner (Mark xii. 32 f.). Accordingly, we cannot suppose that the lawyer here framed the answer simply from his own knowledge,[1] or that he gave it in the well-known meaning of Jesus;[2] but we must suppose (which may be done without difficulty) that in the inquiry of Jesus as to the relevant statements of the law (an inquiry summarily condensed by the narrative into the words: What is written in the law? how readest thou?), He more definitely referred the scribe to those two passages of the law. This view, on the other hand, does not preclude the thought that the scribe proved his exact knowledge of the law by a quick and correct apprehension of the hints given him. And now, in response to his question, what he must do to inherit eternal life, Jesus is in a position to give him, instead of, as he had expected, an answer disputable on the ground of the law, an answer in undeniably strict agreement with the law according to his own words. He does so in the words (ver. 28): "Thou hast answered right; this do, and thou shalt live." Here the question put has found its solution in a manner disconcerting to the scribe. For not only is his attempt to involve Jesus in conflict with the law completely baffled, but, the question proposed being shown to be one scarcely open to discussion for a man acquainted with the law, the questioner's impure intention is also laid bare, namely, that something else than a real desire to learn led him to ask the question.

But just because the man learned in the law plainly feels the reflection cast on him by such a solution of the question, he will not let the conversation drop, as it might do here (ver. 29): "Ὁ δὲ θέλων δικαιῶσαι ἑαυτὸν εἶπεν πρὸς τὸν Ἰησοῦν, καὶ τίς ἐστίν μου πλησίον; The first words: "*But he, desiring to justify himself,*" expressly state the reason why the conversation, which otherwise would have been at an end, is continued by the scribe. Consequently, he cannot from the very beginning have had the question in view: "Who is my neighbour?"[3] And his attempt at justifica-

---

[1] van Oosterzee, Nebe. [2] Meyer. [3] Meyer.

tion can only refer to the suspicion of a dishonest intention in his first question,—the suspicion arising from the previous course of the conversation,—and not to the reproach, that he had not fulfilled the command to love his neighbour,[1] a reproach not even cast upon him in the previous discussion, which is purely objective in character. Moreover, the question which he now brings forward, merely seeking to point out a difficulty supposed still to lie in the reply given by Jesus, is only in keeping with an effort to disarm such a suspicion, not with an effort to meet such a reproach. The subject in hand, he objects, cannot be settled so simply, *i.e.* with a bare reference to the legal command to love God and love our neighbour, for all depends still on the questionable meaning and limit of the idea "neighbour." The καί prefixed to the question is not passionately defiant: "Now then, who is my neighbour?"[2] but a mere combative interruption, behind which combativeness the questioner quickly and cleverly hides his sense of shame. In the question itself some have wished to take πλησίον, after Winer's example, as a mere adverb, because of the absence of the article ("Who is near me?"); wrongly, for the substantivizing of the adverb πλησίον by the article prefixed is so common, that the word may retain the substantival meaning even with the occasional omission of the article, when the context of the discourse implies it. And here it must retain the meaning, because the question itself is taken direct from the command: "Thou shalt love thy neighbour." But certainly the omission of the article is noteworthy, the question thereby acquiring the more distinct colour of a controversial question proposed for discussion. With the article: Who is my neighbour? the question would simply ask for some other appellation of him to whom love is to be shown according to the command. But in the anarthrous question: *Who is neighbour to me?* the desire is expressed for an investigation of the idea "neighbour," such as will show who falls under this idea. The comparison with Matt. v. 43, where "and hate thy neighbour" is cited as a traditional appendix to the command to love one's neighbour, shows how the Rabbinical exposition of Scripture not merely applied the command exclusively to members of the Israelitish nation, but even tried to limit it to the relations of private personal friendship, or at least to exclude from it every personal enemy. The proposal of such a question was therefore

---

[1] Stier, Godet, *et al.*   [2] Stier.

natural enough for a man like the scribe. And in reply to this question: Who falls under the idea "neighbour"? Jesus now begins the narrative of the Merciful Samaritan.

"*Then Jesus answered*[1] *and said, A man went down from Jerusalem to Jericho*" (ver. 30). The much-discussed question, whether the man was a Jew, as supposed by most, or even a heathen,[2] or what else, is a strange question to ask, if, as must be at present assumed according to the analogy of the other parables of Jesus, we have to do merely with an imaginary person in an imaginary narrative. All that can be said in reference to this point is,—if the narrator had thought it important for a definite notion to be formed of the man in this respect, he would not have omitted a statement on the subject. The road taken by the man, from Jerusalem in direct line down to Jericho, went through the wilderness of Judæa, which had an ill reputation for insecurity, and was gladly avoided. For this very reason, as is shown in the sequel, this road is chosen as the scene of the narrative, whereas the definite indication of the direction of the man's journey down from Jerusalem to Jericho in the Jordan valley, and not conversely up from Jericho to Jerusalem, is simply suggested by the need of concrete description. On this road, then, there happened to the man what is told in the next words : καὶ λῃσταῖς περιέπεσεν, i.e.: *He fell among robbers,— οἳ καὶ ἐκδύσαντες αὐτὸν καὶ πληγὰς ἐπιθέντες ἀπῆλθον.* The καί before ἐκδύσαντες is neither to be taken in correlation to λῃσταῖς, as though it were meant to mark the conduct of the robbers as in harmony with their trade, nor is it to be taken as a climax to the tacitly assumed stealing of the money on the man's person, but is most simply explained, with Meyer, as corresponding to the second καί before πληγὰς ἐπιθέντες. By καί ... καί = et ... et, prominence is given to the twofold injury inflicted on the man; for ἐκδύειν must not be limited to the violent stripping off of the clothes in distinction from a previous stealing of other objects. In the absoluteness in which it stands here, it expresses generally, like the Latin *exuere*, and even the German "ausziehen,"[3] utter, reckless plunder, even to what he wore on his person. This plunder, however, was only the least injury done the man by the robbers. Hence ἐκδύσαντες comes first, and πληγὰς ἐπιθέντες follows by way of climax. The

[1] ὑπολαβών only here in the New Testament in this sense.
[2] Olshausen.   [3] And the English "strip."

question, whether as to time the man was first wounded and then stripped, or conversely,—and whether and when he made resistance, although most expositors occupy themselves with it, is just as singular in the case of a merely imaginary narrative as the question whether he was a Jew, since the narrative itself makes no reference of any kind to minute details. But the worst thing done to the man by the robbers is reserved for the finite verb still remaining: "*who, after they had both stripped him, and also inflicted blows* (scil. on him)," ἀπῆλθον ἀφέντες ἡμιθανῆ τυγχάνοντα, *i.e.* "*went away, leaving him when he was just half dead.*" Τυγχάνοντα does not stand simply for ὄντα, rather is ὄντα to be understood along with it. It is the participial form of τυγχάνω ὤν, I am just, as *e.g.* τυγχάνω ἔχων, I have just; ἔτυχον παρών, I was just then present, etc. Emphasis is laid on his abandonment coinciding with the occurrence of a state perilous to life, and we are thus made to feel more sensibly, not indeed the unconcernedness of the robbers,[1] whose disposition is not noticed, but the misfortune of the plundered man. Utterly stripped and sorely beaten as he is, the unhappy man is abandoned just when he is exhausted and half dead. He thus seems left to a terrible death in the lonely wilderness, for it is not to be expected that another traveller will come in the nick of time by this dangerous, unfrequented road. If, however, this took place, as is now to be further related, it was a συγκυρία, *i.e.* a special coincidence of circumstances not to be looked for in the usual course of things, certainly a special call to render instant help for one whom such a συγκυρία led this way. In this sense the narrative proceeds (ver. 31): "*And by a coincidence* (κατὰ συγκυρίαν) *a certain priest went down that way.*" The "went down" certainly gives the same direction from Jerusalem towards Jericho to the journey of the priest as to that of the plundered man, which, however, is just as satisfactorily explained by the need of concrete description as in the other case. It is importing too much into the narrative to wish to find in this an intimation that the priest is coming from ministering in the temple, which aggravates his guilt, or that he was not on the way to, but on the way from his priestly ministry, and that therefore he had not even a plausible excuse, such as ministerial urgency, or the fear of pollution.[2] If we can find nothing special in ver. 30 in the indication of the direction, so definite there, how much less here, where the

[1] Meyer.   [2] Nebe.

"from Jerusalem" does not even appear! What, then, will the priest do when he comes to the scene of the crime? His conduct is briefly and sharply characterized in the words: καὶ ἰδὼν αὐτὸν ἀντιπαρῆλθεν. The double compound ἀντιπαρῆλθεν makes the absence of mercy lying in the παρέρχεσθαι specially prominent, namely, that *over against*, i.e. *in face of* one so unfortunate, lost without his help, he was able to pass by. And a Levite followed just the same course, ver. 32: ὁμοίως δὲ καὶ Λευίτης γενόμενος κατὰ τὸν τόπον, ἐλθὼν καὶ ἰδὼν ἀντιπαρῆλθεν. Ὁμοίως is not to be joined to γενόμ. κατ. τ. τόπ., but to the finite verb ἀντιπαρῆλθεν, fixing attention at once on the like *conduct* of the Levite. The participial clause: γενόμ. κατὰ τὸν τόπον intervenes merely as a more precise explanatory definition in apposition to Λευίτης, whilst the two following participles: ἐλθὼν καὶ ἰδών, introduce the finite verb. Therefore: "*And in like manner a Levite also, who had come*[1] *towards the place* (κατά with the accus. "in the direction to"), *after he had come* (by the way) *and seen* (scil. him), *passed by on the other side.*" Some writers have wrongly found in the part. ἐλθών here the suggestion of a nearer approach in order to a closer inspection,[2] which latter must in this case be expressed by ἰδών. This is forbidden, however, by the consideration that, according to the analogy of ver. 31 (καὶ ἰδὼν αὐτόν), the ἰδών here can only express the catching sight of the unhappy man, not a subsequent closer inspection of the facts of the case (cf. also the order of the expressions, vv. 33, 34: ἦλθεν . . . ἰδών, and then only the προσελθών following). Accordingly, the part. ἐλθών merely depicts the nearer approach on the road,[3] in vivid realization of the scene as it unfolds itself in the successive approach of the Levite, his catching sight of the unhappy man, and his unmerciful passing by.

Thus, priest and Levite have left the unhappy man lying without help. From whom could he still expect help? And yet a third one comes by the way. Certainly it is no priest or Levite, not even a Jew, but a Samaritan, ver. 33: Σαμαρείτης δέ τις ὁδεύων ἦλθεν κατ' αὐτόν. The name Σαμαρείτης stands with emphasis at the head of the sentence. The participle ὁδεύων is perhaps to be referred back adjectivally to Σαμ., therefore: "*But a journeying Samaritan came*," not: "But a Samaritan, as he journeyed, came." It is a half-heathen foreigner who now approaches the sufferer. The

---

[1] γινόμενος, as in chap. xxii. 40. [2] Kuinoel, Meyer, *et al.* [3] De Wette.

foreign character is emphasized in "journeying." Moreover, as a Samaritan, he is regarded with hate and enmity of the bitterest kind by the inhabitants of the land through which he is journeying. And yet, where priest and Levite had closed their hearts in cruelty, this Samaritan feels compassion: "*He came to him, and when he saw* (him), *he had compassion on him.*" And where priest and Levite had passed by (ἀντιπαρῆλθεν), he goes near (προσελθών) in order to render quick, effectual help, ver. 34: "*And he came to him, and bound up his wounds, pouring on them oil and wine.*" To bind up the gaping wounds of the man lying there half dead was the first, most essential requisite. In doing so, he pours on them oil and wine, which he carries with him as part of the outfit of his journey. Oil was much used by the ancients as an external remedy, serving, in the case of open wounds, to assuage the pain (cf. Isa. i. 6). The use of wine as an external remedy for wounds is also mentioned elsewhere.[1] Here it may perhaps serve to cleanse the wounds and stanch the blood. Having taken the first, most essential steps, the Samaritan proceeds unweariedly in his rendering of help: ἐπιβιβάσας δὲ αὐτὸν ἐπὶ τὸ ἴδιον κτῆνος ἤγαγεν αὐτὸν εἰς πανδοχεῖον καὶ ἐπεμελήθη αὐτοῦ. Ἐπιβιβάζω in itself, indeed, does not signify "lift up" (Bengel: imponens cum labore), but only "make ascend" generally. But of course here, where a half-dead man is in question, the idea of *lifting* up is supplied by the context. He lifts him on *his own* beast; but this does not imply that several such beasts were at hand. The adjective ἴδιον is simply meant to point out that, in placing the wounded man on *his own* beast, he thereby renounces the wonted use of it himself. Thus "*he brought him* (himself going on foot) *into an inn.*" Πανδοχεῖον denotes one of the caravanserais, which in those days were set up on the roads, especially in uninhabited districts. Usually they supplied travellers with shelter only, and that gratuitously, but often also with board for payment. So here, according to ver. 35. They may perhaps have been designed rather for non-Jews on their way through the country. In the case of the Jewish inhabitants of the land, there was less need to use such houses, because of the generally prevailing hospitality, from which, of course, Samaritans were strictly excluded. Accord-

[1] Cf. the passage in Wetstein and Nebe.

ing to Winer, the hosts also in such caravanserais were undoubtedly Gentiles.[1] This being so, all ground is removed for any reference to the supposed Jewish nationality of the host, and his presumed heartlessness to a Jewish fellow-countryman.[2] Such reflection is also without support in the text of the narrative, in which the host, like the robbers, comes into notice only in the exercise of his business, and is a thoroughly subordinate figure. Therefore, without any reference to the host first named in ver. 35, it is said of the Samaritan, in simple continuance of the description of his charity: "*and he took care of him.*" Thus he is not satisfied with saving the unhappy one for the moment from death in the wilderness, and bringing him under roof and shelter, but he continues to show him care. The persistent, opportune, self-sacrificing character of his thoughtfulness, bent as it is upon not leaving his work incomplete, but doing it thoroughly, is especially depicted in the conclusion of the narrative which follows, ver. 35: καὶ ἐπὶ τὴν αὔριον ἐξηλθών, ἐκβαλὼν δύο δηνάρια ἔδωκεν τῷ πανδοχεῖ καὶ εἶπεν, Ἐπιμελήθητι αὐτοῦ, καὶ ὅ τι ἂν προσδαπανήσῃς ἐγὼ ἐν τῷ ἐπανέρχεσθαί με ἀποδώσω σοι. The genuineness of the participle ἐξελθών before ἐκβαλών, although apparently doubtful as regards external attestation, must be maintained, since the dropping out of an apparently difficult word is easily conceivable, while the subsequent insertion could scarcely be explained. It serves to characterize the scene of the following conversation, namely, that it transpired when the Samaritan had issued from the caravanserai to begin his journey, and thus after the actual departure. Hence we must translate: "*And on the morrow,*[3] *when he had started, he took out,*" etc. The meaning is: Even when he is about to resume his journey, interrupted for the sake of the sufferer, and to leave him behind, he does not cease to feel concern for him. He took out (*scil.* from his girdle) "*two denarii, and gave them to the host, saying, Take care of him; and whatsoever thou spendest more, I,*[4] *when I come back again, will repay thee.*" The denarius, about equal to ninepence, corresponded

---

[1] *Handwörterbuch*, cf. the arts. "Herbergen" and "Reisen."
[2] Stier, Nebe.
[3] ἐπὶ τὴν αὔριον = towards the break of day, Acts iii. 1; Mark xv. 1.
[4] ἐγώ emphatic.

to the amount of a day's wages at that time (cf. Matt. xx. 2). The two denarii would therefore only suffice for two days' maintenance. But the assessment of the amount at so low a sum can neither be explained by the supposition of a speedy recovery,[1] since the man was represented as suffering under dangerous wounds; nor by the supposition of the Samaritan's speedy return,[2] since there is no intimation of a return to the sufferer himself. The only thing entering into view is a conversation with the host in reference to a subsequent discharge of the expense incurred. The two denarii are merely meant as a payment, to which the promise: ὅ τι ἂν προσδαπανήσῃς κ.τ.λ., forms the necessary supplement. Again, certainly we must not, with Luther, render ὅ τι ἂν weakly: "If thou shalt prove anything more," but correctly: "Whatever thou shalt expend more." While making a payment just now as high as he is able to make for the present, he at the same time pledges himself to bear the entire cost of maintenance, however great it may be. When he comes again by the road, on his return from his present journey, he will reimburse the host.

Here, then, the didactic story has reached its end. It was delivered as a direct reply to the question of the scribe: "Who is my neighbour?" But in what sense it is meant to serve as a reply to this question is shown in the sequel, when Jesus, having laid a basis by repeating the story, as it were gives the lawyer his question back again, calling upon him to decide the general question proposed by him in the light of the particular case now put, ver. 36: τίς τούτων τῶν τριῶν πλησίον δοκεῖ σοι γεγονέναι τοῦ ἐμπεσόντος εἰς τοὺς λῃστάς; Here also, in resuming the question of the scribe, πλησίον stands again without the article: "*Which of these three seems to thee to have become neighbour to him who fell among the robbers?*" But it at once strikes us as peculiar, that these words do not simply give back the lawyer's general question in its bearing on this particular case, but contain also an amendment of the question. A simple giving back of the question by way of application must needs have gone to show to which of these three the unhappy sufferer was neighbour, with which of them as neighbour he stood in the relation which involves the duty of exercising love. But this is not

---

[1] Nebe. [2] Meyer.

the tenor of Jesus' question, and the narrative supplies no ground for a question in this form. But He asks, *Which of the three became neighbour to the sufferer?* therefore, *which of them on his part entered into the relation of a neighbour with him?* To the question so put, the answer was unavoidable. The Samaritan must of necessity be described as he who became neighbour to the sufferer. And this even the scribe concedes, ver. 37: ὁ ποιήσας τὸ ἔλεος μετ' αὐτοῦ. The preposition μετά is here used Hebraistically = עִם.[1] The conjecture may be right that the scribe used this periphrasis in order not to be compelled to mention the Samaritan by name; but this only makes the answer more pertinent, because the Samaritan now receives his name from the action by which he became neighbour to the sufferer. And now, finally, the entire conversation finds its conclusion in the direction given by Jesus to the lawyer: εἶπεν δὲ[2] αὐτῷ ὁ Ἰησοῦς, Πορεύου καὶ σὺ ποίει ὁμοίως, i.e., "*Go and do thou also* (καὶ σύ) *likewise.*" The precept ποίει ὁμοίως points back to the words ὁ ποιήσας ἔλεος. The first meaning therefore is: Do thou *also* show mercy like the Samaritan. But since the complete meaning of the answer of the scribe, to be supplied from ver. 36, is: He that showed mercy on him became thereby neighbour to the man that was robbed, the complete meaning of the direction based on these words is: Do thou in like manner show mercy, and thou too wilt by this means become neighbour to him to whom thou showest it. From this it is clear how by this direction the question (τίς ἐστίν μου πλησίον) by which the scribe had tried to make a difficulty of the definition of the idea "neighbour," has in fact found its conclusive solution. For if it is true, as he himself was compelled to allow, that one becomes neighbour to another by the mere fact of exercising love, whoever it may be, the only thing necessary to the fulfilment of the precept to love our neighbour is an act of love, no matter to whom.

From this conclusion of the conversation, added by Jesus as a sequel to the parable, the moral of the parable is now clear. *It is meant to show how the divine command,* "*Thou shalt love thy neighbour as thyself,*" *is to be fulfilled, namely, by assiduous endeavour to unite ourselves through helpful acts of love to any one needing help, without asking first who he is, and in what relation*

---

[1] Cf. chap. i. 58, 72. [2] Not οὖν, Rec.

he stands to us; and therefore by actively becoming neighbour to him, without asking first, Is he also my neighbour?

If we review the narrative from this point, the first general observation striking us is, that the mode of pictorial representation here is not, as in all the parables hitherto expounded, that of symbolic clothing, but simply that of exhibiting a concrete example. It is the first *typical* parable, in distinction from the *symbolic*,[1] which here meets us, for it illustrates its subject not, as most of the other parables of Jesus, by means of symbol, but simply by means of example. On the other hand, we must not go so far as to say that the present narrative is not imaginary, but that it gives an account of actual occurrences. There is nothing to suggest that it differs in this respect from the other parables of Jesus. On the contrary, in keeping a definite purpose in view from beginning to end in every part, the narrative plainly exhibits the narrator's productive hand, and, just as much as the other parables, bears throughout the character of a narrative invented in order to set forth a particular doctrine. And now we have specially to direct our attention to the way in which all the separate occurrences, of which the narrative is made up, set forth the doctrine already stated in the form of example, whereas the task of working out an interpretation of the figurative occurrences in the proper sense falls aside because of the merely exemplary nature of the narrative.

When then, in ver. 30, we read of a man who, on his journey through the wilderness of Judæa, fell into the hands of robbers, was stripped of everything, wounded and left in his half-dead state, the image is presented to us of a sufferer whose condition demands loving and effectual help from any one becoming aware of it. In fact, what condition could be pictured more imperatively demanding help of all passers-by than that of a man stripped naked, with bleeding wounds, in an untenanted wilderness? The narrative then leads three persons in succession past the unfortunate one. First of all a priest, and it makes this priest pass by without mercy in sight of the sufferer, ver. 31. If we wish to gain a clear view of the import of the narrative, we must here ask: Why does Jesus make a priest in particular come that way? and how is it conceivable psychologically that he should pass by such wretchedness without pity? The right answer is

[1] See the Introduction.

forthcoming when we remember the grossly legal proclivity of the man to whom the narrative primarily refers, and especially his interpretation of the command to love our neighbour, as indicated by his question, "Who is neighbour to me?" an interpretation which gave occasion to the whole narrative. The priest is introduced as a representative of this proclivity and this hair-splitting interpretation of the command, such as was characteristic of the Jewish hierarchy and scribes of those days. Like the lawyer, he only deems himself under obligation to those whose character as "neighbour" has been first of all settled. What course of conduct follows from such a standpoint in a case like the one described in ver. 30, the example of the priest is meant to show. And, in fact, this course of conduct can be no other than unmerciful want of concern. For as to the man lying there naked and wounded, of course nothing was certainly known but the crying need of help; and so he remains a stranger to the priest,—Who knows who he is, and how he came here? it does not concern him, no kind of obligation can be proved,—he passes by. That this want of mercy is not meant in the light of a simply individual fault of the priest in question, but really in the light of an interpretation of the command to love our neighbour prevalent in the circles of the Jewish hierarchy, is confirmed by the addition of the second, quite analogous example of the Levite, who passes by the sufferer with the same unmerciful hardness, ver. 32. Thus the truth strikingly exemplified in these two occurrences, both separately and in their mutual harmony, is this, that the prevailing interpretation of the command to love our neighbour, which requires the definition of the relation of neighbour as a postulate of showing love, leads practically to a hardness and unmercifulness in glaring contradiction with the divine meaning of that command. Straining out a gnat leads to swallowing a camel, Matt. xxiii. 24.

But the narrative then turns to a new and third example, in contrast with the first two, meant to show in what way the command to love our neighbour alone finds its fulfilment. It is a journeying Samaritan whom the narrative now makes to approach the sufferer, that he may serve as an example of this truth. Thus, he is not merely a foreigner, but, in addition, one belonging to that Samaritan race which was an object of special hatred to the Jew. But precisely as such he was specially suited to be an example of a fulfilment of the command quite independent of the question, "Who is neighbour to me?" For if the man lying on the road in the heart of the Judæan country seemed a stranger even to the priest and Levite, how much more must he have been a stranger to the Samaritan, if the thoughts of the latter had been of a like narrow-hearted kind! If he had been of the same mind as the two others, he would have said to himself, that he probably had before him a child of the country, a son of that Jewish nation so bitterly hostile to his own, and would, like the priest and Levite, only with a greater appearance of justice, have turned coldly from him. But when, instead of this, it is told of the Samaritan, how he pities the sufferer, renders him instant and effectual help, and beyond the momentary assistance cares for him with patient, skilful thoughtfulness, himself becoming security for him until he is fully restored, we are taught that the crying need of the man as such goes *near* this Samaritan. Whoever and whatever the sufferer may be, his need brings him near the Samaritan's heart; because of his misfortune the Samaritan feels for him as a neighbour; because of his misfortune he acts to him as a neighbour. And although everything which can separate men existed between these two, by acting in this way to the sufferer the Samaritan really became neighbour to him, and fulfilled to him the command to love our neighbour. This it was which even the scribe was obliged to concede. And thus the aim of the didactic story is reached. By means of the example given in the history related, it is proved, alike graphically and incontestably, that only such a disposition really fulfils the command to love our neighbour as shows love to every one needing help, simply because he needs help, without asking who he is; whereas the opposite disposition, which would make the fulfilment of the command dependent on the previous question: "Who is neighbour to me?" puts itself in glaring contradiction with the divine meaning of the command. The direct consequence following from the parable is, that according to the divine meaning of the precept the idea "neighbour" will brook no kind of limitation, but is, on the contrary, to be extended to every fellow-man. But Jesus Himself, avoiding all theoretical discussion, does not give expression to this consequence. It is rather left to the scribe, as to every hearer and reader of the parable, to draw this inference for himself.

A series of ancient expositors, from Origen down to Luther

and Melanchthon, and also moderns like Stier, de Valenti, Thiersch, Lange, have ascribed yet another and second meaning to the present parable. Taking it not merely as an exemplary, but in addition as a properly figurative history, they say, the Samaritan is Christ Himself, and the man who fell among robbers is humanity lying in the misery of sin and death; in compassionate love Christ came to its succour. This main thought is then worked out in the most extraordinary way as regards every particular, *e.g.* Jerusalem is Paradise, the robbers are the devil and his angels, priest and Levite are the law and the prophets, the inn is the Church, the two pence are baptism and the Lord's Supper, etc. Against this view it is sufficient, while appealing to the preceding exposition, to remark, that neither the wording of the narrative, nor the context in which it stands, gives any sort of justification for the notion of such a double meaning. As regards especially the allegorical interpretation of the particulars, we must agree with Calvin when he remarks on this point: Scripturæ major habenda est reverentia, quam ut germanum ejus sensum hac licentia transfigurare liceat. Certe præter Christi mentem has speculationes a curiosis hominibus fuisse confictas, cuivis perspicuum est. But, on the other hand, it must of course be acknowledged to be quite within the limits of a legitimate *application* of the narrative to point out how, in the person of the *Samaritan*, Jesus not merely *pictured* a graphic example of true fulfilment of the command to love one's neighbour, but also in His *own* person *gave* us a corresponding example *in act*, when He, the Son of God, became neighbour to us—children of men—by the pitying, self-sacrificing love with which He came to relieve our wretchedness. But it is obvious at once that such a thought only has its pure and potent influence when it is added in the way indicated as an independent application of the parable, instead of being made part and parcel of the parable itself as a supposed deeper, hidden meaning.

The Importunate Friend.

(Luke xi. 5–10.)

The parable of the Importunate Friend, meeting us in chap. xi. 5–10, is preceded by the section vv. 1–4, which tells how

Jesus, at the request of one of His disciples to teach them to pray, communicated to them the Lord's Prayer. But the words "and He said unto them" join the following parable to this section in so general a manner, that no chronological connection is indicated, and, considering the compilatory nature of this entire portion of the Gospels, none is to be supposed. The parable, and its sequel up to ver. 13, form accordingly an independent paragraph, which the evangelist combines with the preceding one (vv. 1–4) simply on account of their common reference to prayer. Thus, nothing being said respecting the occasion and original connection of the parable, we are remitted for its interpretation simply to the text itself.

The parable opens this time not in the form of calm narrative, but in the more graphic form of question. The matter treated of is not a particular incident which took place; but the hearers are simply asked whether, in a particular case into which they are to put themselves in thought, any one of them would not do so and so. For this must be taken into view at the outset, that the question left afterwards unexpressed in consequence of the anacoluthic construction, since it is introduced by "Which of you," and appeals, therefore, to the personal decision of each one of the hearers, can only apply primarily to something which they would have to decide in the case supposed, and therefore only to something which they would do or not do, not to something which another would decide to do or not to do to them. (See analogous questions in ver. 11 f., xiv. 5, 28, xv. 4; Matt. vii. 9–11, etc.) In this sense the parable begins, ver. 5: *Τίς ἐξ ὑμῶν ἕξει φίλον καὶ πορεύσεται πρὸς αὐτὸν μεσονυκτίου.* It is obvious that the futures ἕξει and πορεύσεται do not contain that to which the question is meant properly to apply, a view which would give the absurdity found here by Winer:[1] "None of you would go to his friend at midnight; such importunity would never occur." Rather, since the futures here express, as often, not the actual future, but merely a case possibly occurring in the future, they stand primarily in the mere sense of a hypothetic protasis, they simply put a case to which the final question is meant to refer. Therefore correctly:[2] "*Who of you will be in circumstances to have a friend, and to go to him at midnight?*" . . . Certainly this mode of inserting the description of the case, to which the question is meant to refer, in the interrogative form itself, is only

[1] *Gram.* p. 350.   [2] See Meyer here.

feasible so long as the question proper may be expected to follow immediately. But since the speaker here passes on to present a vivid picture of the case in question by repeating a detailed dialogue, the language naturally falls out of the interrogative future into the hypothetical conj. aorist, more appropriate to such a preliminary description of the logical position; and this logical position of the picture spontaneously suggests to the reader an ἐάν governing the conjunctive. Hence it is continued: καὶ εἴπῃ αὐτῷ, Φίλε ... κἀκεῖνος ἔσωθεν ἀποκριθεὶς εἴπῃ ... Therefore: "*Who of you will be in circumstances to have a friend ... and (supposing) he say to him ... and he answer him from within and say*" ... This interpretation, which takes the first εἴπῃ of the dialogue just as hypothetically as the second corresponding to it, seems to me more natural than the one which makes the first εἴπῃ, as an interrogative *conj. deliberativus*, just like the futures ἕξει and πορεύσεται, depend immediately on τίς ἐξ ὑμῶν.[1] The latter interpretation must afterwards, in the case of the corresponding κἀκεῖνος εἴπῃ, suppose a change to the hypothetical construction, and take this second conjunctive, correlative to and synonymous with the first, in a different sense from the first.

The first καὶ εἴπῃ, then, introduces a *request* with which the hearer must imagine himself coming at midnight to his friend, vv. 5, 6 : "*Friend, lend me three loaves, for a friend*[2] *is come to me from a journey, and I have nothing to set before him.*" Bengel's remark on the triple number of the loaves:[3] "Unum pro hospite, unum pro me, unum *supernumerarium*," is too fine-spun in conception, the number of the loaves being merely placed at the amount necessary for the intended meal along with the guest. The *answer*, which the hearer is to imagine himself receiving to this request from his friend within, runs, ver. 7: "*Trouble me not! The door is shut, and my children are with me into bed;*[4] *I cannot rise and give thee.*" The circumstances therefore into which each hearer is required to transport himself are these, that he has nothing to set before a guest who has come to him unexpectedly and late from a journey, and accordingly finds himself compelled to ask from a friendly neighbour, in the middle of the night, the loan of the necessary bread, but encounters reluctance in this

---

[1] Meyer, Winer.   [2] Φίλος, without μου, Tischendorf.
[3] Cf. also Stier, Godet, van Oosterzee.
[4] Εἰς τὴν κοίτην εἰσί, the verb of rest joined with εἰς, because the rest is viewed as the result of the previous motion.

neighbour on account of the disturbance to the repose of his house, which compliance with the request would entail. We see that the case is so planned in all the several circumstances composing it, that on one side a great and unpleasant perplexity imperatively compels to the making of a request, all the more when we consider how inviolable the duties of hospitality were to the Israelite; whilst, on the other side, compliance with the request encounters a hindrance in the no less difficulty which such compliance would occasion to the person asked.

Thus, according to the original plan of the discourse, in τίς ἐξ ὑμῶν ἕξει φίλον καὶ πορεύσεται πρὸς αὐτόν a question is intended in this sense, whether any one of the hearers in the circumstances of such a petitioner would not follow such and such a particular course,—not a question in the sense whether any one, approached with such a request, will do so and so, in which case the hearer would not have been required to transport himself into the circumstances of the petitioner, but (as in ver. 11 and Matt. vii. 9, 10) into those of the man petitioned. Accordingly, that which the question begun is intended to set forth as the sequel to be expected in every case cannot be the final compliance with the request by the person petitioned, of which we then read in ver. 8, and still less can it be, as Meyer supposes, the first negative answer given already in ver. 7, which rather belongs entirely to the description of the case to which the question was meant to refer. But the question must have reference to a course of conduct on the petitioner's part, which will be the necessary consequence of this first negative answer, and be the postulate of the final compliance. And if, nevertheless, a question of this kind is omitted, the construction here breaking off without coming to a conclusion, the reason of this is indeed, in the first place, that the vivid picture of the situation interposed has grown to such a size as to leave the original plan of the discourse behind, and also not less, that the conduct to be expected of every one found in such a situation is so clear, that its further express description may be omitted as superfluous. It is evident that no one would readily remain quiet in such circumstances, but every one would strive by continued and strenuous repetition of the request to secure its being complied with, — so evident, that the final sentence of the parable now following expressly recurs to this conduct, although its description is omitted; nay, even bases the declaration which concludes the whole simply upon this course of conduct to be expected on the petitioner's part. Just as if the question begun in τίς ἐξ ὑμῶν had found complete expression, Jesus continues, ver. 8 : λέγω ὑμῖν, εἰ καὶ οὐ δώσει αὐτῷ ἀναστὰς διὰ τὸ εἶναι αὐτοῦ φίλον, διά γε τὴν ἀναίδειαν αὐτοῦ ἐγερθεὶς δώσει αὐτῷ ὅσων χρῄζει. The εἰ καί introducing the protasis is here concessive, like the Latin licet. In the same protasis the participle ἀναστάς follows the δώσει, although preceding it in time, and stands immediately before διὰ τὸ εἶναι αὐτοῦ φίλον, because the person petitioned does not need a special motive to giving in itself, but merely to rising up. Observe the repeated mention of the rising (ἐγερθείς) in the apodosis also,—there, immediately after the words specifying the motive (διά γε τὴν ἀναίδειαν), and before δώσει. The protasis is therefore to be translated : "*I say to you, although he will not give, rising up because he is his friend*" . . . Here the possibility is again conceded in the case put in the preceding description, that the simple relation of friendship to the petitioner will not lead the one petitioned to grant the request, not, however, without its being intimated in the emphasis laid on the motive disregarded in the present case, that friendship itself might and should have led to compliance with such a request. This concession then gives all the more emphasis to the assurance in the apodosis, that even in the case given, where the more obvious and nobler motive is disregarded, the petitioned will nevertheless find himself compelled to comply with the request: "*Still, on account of his impudence at least* (διά γε), *he will rise and give him as much as he needs.*" It is the words διά γε τὴν ἀναίδειαν, standing first with emphasis, which recur to the conduct imposed on the petitioner by the nature of his circumstances, and therefore to the question not completed, but naturally suggested by the meaning, whether in such a case any one would not steadily persevere with his request. By this natural conduct of the petitioner the intentionally strong expression signalizes the element which ensures his final success—the importunity that knows no shame ; for this importunity must in the course of time become more irksome to the petitioned than the slight trouble of rising up. And having once risen, he will then give him ὅσων χρῄζει, without stint, *as much* as he needs, for only thus will he be quickly rid of his importunity. What Jesus therefore expressly asserts in this final clause by "I say to you" is this, that an asking so persistent and strenuous, such as no one would omit in these circumstances, must at last of necessity lead to success.

For the one petitioned will find himself compelled, if not by a feeling of friendship for the petitioner, yet certainly by the annoyance arising from his importunity, to give him everything he needs.

With κἀγὼ ὑμῖν λέγω, in ver. 9, Jesus annexes to the parable a doctrine of His own for the disciples. There is neither necessity nor warrant for asserting that κἀγὼ ὑμῖν λέγω is put inexactly for "and so say I to you,"[1] but it means and must mean, "*I* also say *to you*." Standing next to ἐγώ, and before λέγω, ὑμῖν also is emphatic. Of course it is impossible, logically, to make the doctrine introduced by Jesus in these words simply identical with the final assurance δώσει αὐτῷ κ.τ.λ. (ver. 8), which, however, Jesus Himself gave with "I say to you." Rather it is the doctrine lying in the whole of the parable which Jesus now *Himself* confirms, and especially *to them*, His *disciples*. In first of all clothing the designed instruction in the form of a parable, He first left the nature of the case pictured in the figurative description to speak for itself. But having done this, He now intervenes with His own personal authority in behalf of the truth set forth, as a truth especially to be laid to heart by them, His disciples. And the doctrine which He thus draws from the parable with the intervention of His authority, consists in an exhortation, strengthened by a promise annexed, ver. 9: αἰτεῖτε, καὶ δοθήσεται ὑμῖν· ζητεῖτε, καὶ εὑρήσετε· κρούετε, καὶ ἀνοιχθήσεται ὑμῖν. It is self-evident that the exhortation, couched in general terms, has special reference to the relation to God. The exhortation is in three parts: Ask—seek—knock! The last two imperatives repeat the meaning of the first in figurative form. An allusion to the figurative form of the previous description scarcely lies at the basis of the exhortation,[2] because the description contains no mention at all of seeking, and none of knocking, at least expressly. On the other hand, it is certainly the last two imperatives which give complete expression to the exhortation implied in the parable. For not every asking, but only a patient, persevering one can be figuratively called a "seeking;" and in the same way, not any asking whatever, but an energetic, persistent one, is denoted by "knock," which, standing thus absolutely and independently, cannot mean a timid tapping,

[1] De Wette.   [2] Godet.

but only a vigorous knocking. The additional imperatives, "seek—knock," therefore, enlarge and strengthen the exhortation "ask" in such a way as to demand a patient, persevering, an energetic, persistent asking. To this must be added, that the threefold utterance of the exhortation is in itself a demand for an ever-repeated, unwearied asking. Again, the threefold exhortation is supported by the threefold promise annexed; and this in such a form that the threefold promise, each time in correspondence with the preceding exhortation, sets before the asking the prospect of receiving, before the seeking that of finding, before the knocking that of the door being opened. And that the disciples may, in fact, absolutely reckon on the correspondent hearing in the case of such an asking, seeking, and knocking, is now confirmed (ver. 10) by the emphasizing of the *infallibility* with which the correspondent hearing is vouchsafed to *every one:* "*For every one that asketh receiveth; and he that seeketh findeth; and to him that knocketh it shall be opened.*" The emphasis rests throughout on the "every one" standing at the head, in which word the confirmatory element lies. This being duly considered, it is impossible to say that reference is here made to an experience of daily life,[1] the "every one," which shuts out every exception, not agreeing with such experience. Moreover, this confirmatory assurance, just as in ver. 9, is an instruction given independently by Jesus to the disciples in reference to their relation to God, and in harmony with the parable. Thus the doctrine which Jesus, building on the parable, Himself gives to the disciples in vv. 9, 10, consists in *the exhortation to persevering, persistent prayer in prospect of the hearing then infallibly certain.* And a glance back at the contents of the figurative description shows at once that this statement embodies the purpose of the parable. The divergent opinion, that the purpose of the parable lies not in this exhortation, but exclusively in the promise of certain hearing,[2] is in conflict both with the words of Jesus, vv. 9, 10, which, above all, deduce an exhortation from the parable, to which the appended promise serves as a mere support, and also with the plan of the parable rightly understood. For the graphic question, Which of you? with which it began, has in view first of all the persevering importunity to be expected on the part of the petitioner; and only of such

[1] Godet. [2] Meyer.

importunity was it then said in ver. 8, that it must at last find a hearing.[1]

In what way the exhortation, which we have seen to be the purpose of the parable, along with the promise annexed to it, finds effective expression, can only be shown by a more precise interpretation. To find the correct method of interpretation, we observe again, above all, that we have not before us here a formal figurative history, but merely a question proposed to the disciples, whether any one of them in a particular case will not do so and so to a friend, and then, by way of addition, an assurance as to what, in such a case, the friend will do to them. If then, according to the purpose of the parable, such as appears in the words of Jesus, vv. 9, 10, we know already that through that question and this assurance the hearers are meant to receive instruction as regards their relation to God, it is self-evident in what way alone the interpretation of such a parable can be carried out, namely, by an inference *a minori ad majus*,—in the same way, therefore, as in ver. 13, where, to the three parabolic questions directly following the present parable, and similar to it, although briefer, Jesus Himself expressly adds the interpreting conclusion: $εἰ\ οὖν \ldots πόσῳ\ μᾶλλον \ldots$ Therefore the allusion to what they would do to a *human* friend is meant to encourage the disciples *all the more* to pursue a like course towards God; and the assurance as to what such a *human* friend would then do to them, is meant to inspire them with confidence that *all the more* would they experience the like from God. Accordingly, the first thought of the parable is this: If any one who had at first encountered a refusal from a human friend, to whom he had gone with a petition of extreme urgency, instead of easily desisting from his request, would only continue to ask with all the greater earnestness, how much more does it become the disciples of Jesus, who have God for their friend, if at first they seem to find no hearing with their petitions

---

[1] This, too, against Hofmann, who would take the $κἀκεῖνος\ εἴπῃ$ in ver. 7, like the $καὶ\ εἴπῃ\ αὐτῷ$ in ver. 5, as a continuation of the question begun with $τίς\ ἐξ\ ὑμῶν$, which now requires a negative answer; the final meaning, according to him, being, that such an excuse as is uttered in ver. 7 is in no case to be expected from a friend. But why then so detailed an exposition of the excuse here? In reality it is by no means improbable, still less—impossible; and not the friendship of the one petitioned, but the impudence of the petitioner, is therefore, according to ver. 8, the element which finally ensures compliance.

to Him, — petitions with which none made to men can compare in urgency, — instead of growing weary in asking this divine Friend, to ask with all the greater constancy and persistence! Should they exhibit less energy and patience in prayer in presence of God's fatherly love than in presence of the friendship of a man? In this final inference lies the complete interpretation of the first part of the parable. Every attempt to give a definite reference to each detail in the figurative description goes beyond the original meaning of the question, and mars its simple force. To this class belongs not merely the attempt to refer the three loaves to three particular spiritual gifts of some kind,[1] but also the attempt often made to see in the friend who came at midnight the neighbour for whom intercession is to be made. We cannot even say offhand that the friend inside the house is God. Rather, all details of the description serve only to depict with concrete vividness a situation between friend and friend which, whilst causing the person petitioned to delay complying with the request, drives and forces the petitioner to persistent asking. From this picture the hearers at once recognise the final inference before mentioned, bearing upon their relation to God. And just in the same way is the interpreting conclusion to be drawn from the assurance appended in ver. 8. If a human friend finds himself compelled by patient, persistent asking to grant the petitioner his request, and to grant him all he needs, if not out of friendship for him, yet to rid himself of the annoyance caused by his importunity, how much more will God hear one who calls on Him with persistent earnestness, and give him all he needs, — God, whose unchangeable fatherly love does not need, like man's precarious friendship, to be reluctantly constrained, but willingly and gladly lets itself be compelled. Thus the comparison, ascending here also from the less to the greater, must be correctly limited. The meaning is not, that what God will not give from loving goodwill to the petitioner, He will give in order to be rid of his irksome importunity; but from the compelling influence exercised by patient, persistent asking on the precarious friendship of man, the inference must be drawn to the certain, infallible influence which it must have in presence of God's unchangeably faithful love.

Thus the parable has in the first instance shown that the ask-

[1] De Valenti

ing, seeking, knocking, to which Jesus, building on the parable, exhorts in His own name, ver. 9, are prescribed by the nature of the case; and, in the second place, has proved that the promise of an infallible hearing, annexed by Jesus in vv. 9, 10, is guaranteed by the nature of the case.

The Rich Fool.

(Luke xii. 16-21.)

The occasion of the parable of the Rich Fool was supplied to the Lord by the request of one of the people, ver. 13 : " Teacher, bid my brother divide the inheritance with me." It is true, the man himself, who makes this request, is curtly dismissed with the answer, ver. 14 : " Man, who made me a judge or a divider over you ? " But from this incident Jesus takes occasion to warn the listeners generally against the disposition that prompted the man's request, ver. 15 : ὁρᾶτε καὶ φυλάσσεσθε ἀπὸ πάσης[1] πλεονεξίας. The persons addressed are the listening "multitude," ver. 13.[2] The warning is directed against "covetousness." Covetousness had made the disputed question of inheritance so important to the man, that he thought he must bring it to the Lord. Starting from this particular expression of covetousness, attaching itself to a disputed inheritance, Jesus pointedly warns the hearers[3] against covetousness in *every* (πασῆς) shape and form. And He further confirms this warning of His by the words : ὅτι οὐκ ἐν τῷ περισσεύειν τινὶ ἡ ζωὴ αὐτοῦ ἐστὶν ἐκ τῶν ὑπαρχόντων αὐτῷ.[4] The emphatic position of the οὐκ before ἐν τῷ περισσεύειν τινί will not allow the latter words to be taken in the sense of a protasis, and the negation to be referred merely to what follows, making the sense to be : Though any one has superfluity, his life is not a part of his possessions,[5] or : Nevertheless life will not come to him from his possessions.[6] Rather,

---

[1] The correct reading instead of τῆς.
[2] Cf. ver. 22, where it is specially noticed that the sayings of Jesus, following there, are again addressed to the disciples.
[3] Cf. the twofold imperative ὁρ. κ. φυλ.
[4] Instead of αὐτοῦ, according to Tischendorf, Lachmann ; cf. viii. 3 ; Acts iv. 32 : τὰ ὑπάρχοντά τινι = opes alicujus.
[5] De Wette. [6] van Oosterzee.

from the position of the οὐκ, the negation must be referred directly to ἐν τῷ περισσεύειν τινί. The negation must be meant to affirm that something, which according to the fancy of covetousness is contained ἐν τῷ περισσεύειν τινί, is really not contained therein. But this being established, we can no longer connect the words ἡ ζωὴ αὐτοῦ ἐστίν with the following ἐκ τῶν ὑπαρχόντων αὐτῷ. The attempt, while rightly referring the negation to ἐν τῷ περισσεύειν τινί, to retain such a connection, has led to the translation: "*Not by the fact of a man's possessing abundance does his life consist in his possessions,*" which must mean, Superfluity is not necessary in order to sustain life by that which one possesses, One can live on little. But what a round-about way of expressing an almost trivial thought! And how little would such an interpretation agree with the following narrative, the theme of which is not, whether one needs much or little in order to live, but, that life does not depend at all on possessions! Accordingly, the words ἡ ζωὴ αὐτοῦ ἐστίν must be independently and directly connected with οὐκ ἐν τῷ περισσεύειν τινί alone, as is inevitably suggested on the first reading. Thus, the first statement runs in its simple and complete form: "*For by no means is a man's life included in the superfluity belonging him,*" so that the one is secured and guaranteed to him with the other. The emphasis lies first on οὐκ and next on ζωή. Then certainly ἐκ τῶν ὑπαρχόντων αὐτῷ is left over as an addition no longer fitting into this already complete statement. But the solution of the difficulty is found in taking these words by themselves as a supplementary explanation, separated from what precedes by a comma. It is easily made a complete and independent sentence by a repetition of the οὐκ, understood from what precedes, while preserving the subject ἡ ζωή and the copula ἐστίν. No express repetition of the οὐκ was necessary, because the strong emphasis with which it stands at the head of the entire statement naturally extends its influence to the second supplementary clause. In German, of course, the negation must be repeated, because the copula ἐστίν must be repeated in the second member, thus: "*By no means is a man's life included in the superfluity belonging to him,—it springs not from his possessions.*" Thus the first statement, to the effect that the possession of life is not included in the possession of riches, finds its explanation in the second supplementary statement, to the effect that a man's life has not its ground and origin in the wealth which he possesses; and we get now a fully pertinent and striking sense without necessity or even occasion to interpret "life" here otherwise than of bodily life, and to understand thereby *felicitas*[1] or "true life."[2]

In the words: "And He spake a parable unto them, saying," ver. 16, the evangelist makes the transition to the recital of a parable delivered by Jesus on such an occasion. It is beyond question that these words do not form a transition to a new and independent paragraph, but to a parable delivered on the occasion related in vv. 13, 14, and in reference to the utterance of ver. 15, because "unto them" here, just as in ver. 15, can only refer to the people then gathered round the Lord, according to ver. 13. We are therefore justified in expecting that the parable will serve as a more precise illustration of the warning against covetousness in ver. 15, and of the utterance respecting the relation of the possession of life to the possession of riches, added in confirmation of the warning.

Ἀνθρώπου τινὸς πλουσίου ηὐφόρησεν ἡ χώρα,—thus begins the narrative, ver. 16. Χώρα here (as in xxi. 21; John iv. 35, *et al.*) is the land. The notion of special magnitude does not lie necessarily in the word, but is here supplied by the context, vv. 17, 18. It is needless to take the aorist ηὐφόρησεν, in distinction from the following aorists, in the sense of the pluperfect, "had brought forth well." On the contrary, it is the simple rendering: "*A certain rich man's land brought forth well,*" which gives an effective background to the following description. The man is not represented as not knowing what to do with the exuberant produce of the harvest already reaped, but as observing an unusual fertility in his ground, and, directly that he perceives this, beginning anxiously to ask, as we read in ver. 17: "*And he reasoned with himself thus, What shall I do, for I have not where to gather my fruits?*" He utters the anxious question, what is to be done, and names as the ground of his anxiety, that he has not room enough to lay up his fruits. The outward reason of his anxiety is therefore his comparatively limited rooms, as to which he fears that they will not hold the unusually rich produce of his ground; but the true, inner reason is nothing but his covetousness. Because of his covetousness he at once calls the fruit still standing in the field his own (τοὺς καρποὺς μου; cf. ver. 18: τὰ γενήματά μου), forthwith, so to speak, laying

---

[1] Kuinoel. [2] Ewald, Olshausen.

his hand on the growth of the field as his property. Because of his covetousness he directs his attention by anticipation only to laying up the entire mass of the produce in secure keeping, that nothing of it may be lost. And thus from his covetousness springs the anxious question: "What shall I do?" It is covetousness then which guides him in his further deliberations, and suggests to him the plans mentioned in ver. 18. Instead of deciding to limit his greed by the extent of his rooms, and to hand over the probable superfluity for the comfort of others more needy, he resolves to meet the hindrances standing in the way of his covetousness with special and unusual arrangements: "*This will I do*,"—καθελῶ μου τὰς ἀποθήκας καὶ μείζονας οἰκοδομήσω, καὶ συνάξω ἐκεῖ πάντα τὰ γενήματά μου καὶ τὰ ἀγαθά μου. Καθελῶ stands first with emphasis, expressing the violence with which he has determined to get rid of every hindrance to the gratifying of his avarice, thus: "*Pull down—will I my barns, and greater will I build, and there will I gather all my products.*" The new barns are to be so large that he will be able really to bestow therein all his produce (πάντα τὰ γενήματα), leaving out nothing, and, as he involuntarily adds, with a still further enlargement of his schemes, "*and my goods.*" The storehouses are to be such that he will be able to lay up in them, along with the fruits of the field, his goods in general. And then, when he shall have collected his entire possessions in safe custody, he thinks he may surrender himself to rest and the enjoying of his treasures, as he pictures to himself in ver. 19: καὶ ἐρῶ τῇ ψυχῇ μου· Ψυχή, ἔχεις πολλὰ ἀγαθὰ κείμενα εἰς ἔτη πολλά· ἀναπαύου, φάγε, πίε, εὐφραίνου. In thus objectifying to himself his soul as the animating, and therefore sensitive and enjoying, principle in him, and resolving to summon it to undisturbed enjoyment, he paints to himself the full consciousness, and the consequent delight, with which he will then surrender himself to enjoyment. The summons is preceded by the assurance: "*Thou hast much goods laid up for many years.*" He intends to refer his soul to the mass of goods well and safely laid up in the new large storehouses, intimating that these goods will suffice for many years, and ensure long enjoyment. Hence the unconnected imperatives, on the ground of this reference, rushing from one enjoyment to another: "*Rest, eat, drink, be merry.*" To give oneself up to delightful rest after all the toil of building and collecting, to feast to the full on the gathered treasures, to surrender oneself without reserve to the merriment of such feasting,[1]—to this the first, second, third, and fourth imperatives rush one after another.

Thus the man stands before his fruitful fields, anxiously pondering how he is to manage everything, swelling with vast plans for securely laying up all his treasures, and revelling beforehand in the enjoyments they will give him. To this description the conclusion of the parable, now suddenly striking in, presents the sharpest and most effective contrast, ver. 20: εἶπεν δὲ αὐτῷ ὁ Θεός, Ἄφρων κ.τ.λ. The point in question is a speaking on the part of God, where the subject is pushed to the end for the sake of emphasis, because the stress of the words lies in the fact that they are words of *God*, who effects what He says by simple speech, according to the canon: He speaks, and it is done; He commands, and it stands fast. And when these words are described as spoken to the rich man, and clothed in the form of an address to him, one must even then bear in mind that they are words of God. They are not spoken to the rich man in the way in which one man speaks to another in conversation, but in the way in which God speaks to men, namely, in the sense that in what they *do* they aim at him, in their *effect* come to him as a divine reply to his plans, and are perceived by him in the way of experience. This is a sufficient explanation of the form of address. We do not need the supposition, to which the words literally taken must certainly lead, that a verbal revelation was made to the rich man by God in a supernatural way; which would be a fiction strange in the highest degree, and destitute of all analogy in the other parables of Jesus,[2] and, moreover, quite superfluous, contributing nothing whatever to the moral of the parable. Nor do we need the supposition, to which some then retreat, that God awakened in the rich man a warning presentiment of approaching death.[3] This is a dilution, with nothing to justify it, of the divine address to the rich man in the second person in quite definite words, and would also entail an essential dilution of the contents of the divine words themselves, since they would no longer simply initiate a fact,

---

[1] Εὐφραίνεσθαι here, as often, with special reference to the pleasures of the table; cf. e.g. xv. 23, 24, et al.

[2] In opposition to Meyer, who, overlooking the sober character of the parables of Jesus, repeats, after Theophylact: πλάττεται ταῦτα ἡ παραβολή.

[3] van Oosterzee, Godet.

but only express a presentiment awakened in the rich man, which certainly has something of a vague character about it. Accordingly this final sentence of the parable is not meant to relate a new incident in the rich man's life in continuation of the previous narrative, but, the description of the rich man being concluded, Jesus now lifts before the hearers of the parable the veil hiding the future from the rich man, in order to delineate with concrete distinctness the blindness of his course of thought. Jesus does this by informing them of a divine judgment pronounced on the blinded man in reply to his covetous schemes, and whilst he is revelling in the illusive prospect of future enjoyments. The aim in communicating this divine judgment is to disclose the rich man's infatuated folly. For this reason the attention is fixed on this point, and is intensified by the Ἄφρων prefixed, i.e. "Thou fool."[1] The announcement of the fate impending follows: ταύτῃ τῇ νυκτὶ τὴν ψυχήν σου ἀπαιτοῦσιν ἀπὸ σοῦ. "This night" is the night following the day on which the rich man's observing the fruitfulness of his fields led him to form such plans. The divine judgment is represented as an immediate reply to this scheming, and therefore contemporaneous with it. The expression chosen for the suffering of death (τὴν ψυχήν σου ἀπαιτοῦσιν ἀπὸ σοῦ) receives its illustration from the analogous expressions τὴν ψυχὴν διδόναι (Matt. xx. 28), τιθέναι (John x. 11, et al.), παραδιδόναι (Acts xv. 26). As the latter denote a willing pledging and surrender of life, so the former denotes a reluctant suffering of death, so that the animating ψυχή, which the living man would fain retain, is *required* from him as something which he is bound to give (ἀπαιτεῖν = *debitum reposcere*). It lies on the surface, that as the former may take place just as well in the form of a violent as of a natural death, so the latter may take place just as well in the form of a natural as of a violent death; and thus the word ἀπαιτοῦσιν by no means justifies us in adding in thought, without further support in the text, robbers and murderers as its subject.[2] Nor must we even think of the angels of death as the subject of ἀπαιτοῦσιν,[3] since the notion that angels require the ψυχή from the departing one, although within the Biblical mode of contemplation, is certainly not so common[4] as to warrant us in at once understanding the

---

[1] Cf. on the nominative instead of the vocative, Winer, *Gram.* p. 227.
[2] Paulus, Bornemann, van Oosterzee. [3] Stier, von Gerlach.
[4] xvi. 22 is certainly different.

angels, even where they are not mentioned. Rather, the supply of a definite subject is not requisite either on grounds of language or fact. The impersonal active is simply a periphrasis for the passive, like the German periphrasis "man."[1] Finally, the putting of the object τὴν ψυχήν before the verb ἀπαιτοῦσιν is not to be overlooked. Advisedly and emphatically, dying is paraphrased as a loss of the "soul." To the man who dreams that with his treasures heaped up for a long time his life is secured to him and sets before his soul the prospect of long enjoyment, the reply comes from God: "*This night* (this very) *thy soul is required of thee.*" So fearfully is the address "Fool" confirmed by the fateful announcement following it, after which the disclosure of the man's infatuation is completed in the question still to be added: ἃ δὲ ἡτοίμασας, τίνι ἔσται; The metabatic δέ passes over from the loss of *life* to the *property*, in order to raise the question, how it will fare with the latter. In ἃ ἡτοίμασας the latter is described as the provision he *prepared* for himself, *scil.* to enjoy it, the supposition being that in gathering his riches his aim was the same as in the plans for the future in ver. 19. "*Whose shall it be?*" is asked in regard to what is thus prepared, without any intimation of an answer. Nor, in fact, is the question one meant to receive an answer, so that its meaning could only be gathered from the answer supplied, such as: "It will not be thine, but another's;"[2] but what is meant to be affirmed lies complete in the answerless question itself. Precisely in the statement that it is uncertain who will possess his treasures, lies the affirmation that, when he is compelled to give up his soul, all his treasures will be *ownerless* property, belonging to no one knows what possessors.[3] And thus the intimation of the divine judgment exposes the rich man's mode of thought in all its folly. Whilst he dreams of his life being secure for many years because of his multitude of goods, sufficient for a long time, and amuses his soul with the picture of long-lasting enjoyment, in reality his life will be required of him the same night, and that moment all his treasures will be lost to him.

Οὕτως ὁ θησαυρίζων ἑαυτῷ καὶ μὴ εἰς Θεὸν πλουτῶν,—in these

---

[1] English, *one;* French, *on.* [2] Meyer.
[3] Cf. with the entire narrative Ecclus. xi. 18, 19. Despite the great diversity between the vividly concrete narrative of the present parable and the general didactic sentences of the Son of Sirach, it is unmistakeable that a reminiscence of and allusion to the passage in the latter writer are felt in the parable.

words Jesus makes the application of the parable, ver. 21. Οὕτως is to be referred back to the *folly* of the rich man, such as has been exhibited by the intimation of the divine sentence pronounced on him. Thus it signifies not so much: to fall victim to the like fate,—which really would not even be a pertinent generalization of the particular case given,—as rather: entangled in like folly. The description of him to whom the οὕτως applies then follows in a twofold manner, first positively: ὁ θησαυρίζων ἑαυτῷ, then negatively: καὶ μὴ εἰς Θεὸν πλουτῶν. The meaning of the former words is clear: "*He who gathers treasures for himself,*" aiming at his own possession and enjoyment. This first positive characterization is now completed and intensified by the second on the negative side. Πλουτῶν is the correlative idea to θησαυρίζων, before which εἰς Θεόν stands with emphasis in antithesis to ἑαυτῷ. Accordingly πλουτῶν cannot be taken in a different sense from θησαυρίζων, namely, of temporal, earthly riches, or the preposition εἰς otherwise than as meaning the same as the *dat. commodi* ἑαυτῷ, therefore = *in commodum alicujus.* And in the present connection it can signify nothing else. Πλουτεῖν εἰς τινά can only mean "to be rich *for* some one, so that the riches benefit the latter" (cf. Rom. x. 12). Especially it cannot mean "to be rich in reference to some one, so that the latter preserves the riches for one,"[1] a meaning obviously forced upon the simple words, because it is thought the πλουτῶν must perforce be understood of heavenly treasures. Ὁ θησ. ἑα. καὶ μὴ εἰς Θε. πλου. is therefore he who in his conduct in regard to earthly goods only has *himself, not God,* in view, whose sole study is to *augment* his treasures for *his own* possession and enjoyment, not to place his possessions at *God's* service, to employ them "for divine ends,"[2] especially in the practice of mercy (cf. ver. 33).[3] From this it is clear why the θησαυρίζων could not be resumed in the second clause, but had to be replaced by πλουτῶν, namely, because the restless *gathering* and heaping up of treasures is of course appropriate to one who has only his own possession and

---

[1] Meyer.   [2] De Wette.

[3] According to Hofmann (who finds the meaning: "without possessing riches which are such for God, in God's eyes"), the simple antithetical interpretation of the two clauses is precluded by the connection by means of καὶ μή (instead of καὶ οὐ). Καὶ μή, it is supposed, adds something which is denied in relation to θησαυρίζων ἑαυτῷ. But καὶ μή may also, as a more precise, intensive, and complemental definition, very well annex merely the denial of the opposite to the preceding θησαυρίζων ἑαυτῷ. Cf. *e.g.* i. 20: ἴσῃ σιωπῶν καὶ μὴ δυνάμενος λαλῆσαι.

enjoyment in view, not to one who places his possessions at God's service. Accordingly the wording and context here do not allow the εἰς Θεὸν πλουτῶν to be understood of those treasures in heaven of which Jesus speaks in other places, *e.g.* ver. 33; Matt. vi. 20. Nevertheless, the thought of those imperishable treasures in heaven is not on this account alien to the present passage. On the contrary, the εἰς Θεὸν πλουτεῖν is viewed here as a means and way to secure an abiding possession beyond the attacks even of death. For when the μὴ εἰς Θεὸν πλουτῶν is represented here as a fool like the rich man in the parable, and therefore a fool in presence of always imminent death and the loss of all earthly goods consequent thereon, this also implies the converse, that a rich man, who is such for God, has no reason to fear death, and would not be impoverished by the loss of earthly possessions. In so far the present passage certainly compares with those passages in which beneficence (ver. 33), or the selling of earthly property for the good of the poor (xviii. 22 and paral.), or the renunciation of earthly possessions for the Lord's sake (xviii. 29, 30, and paral.), is mentioned as a means of gaining an imperishable treasure in heaven, but especially with the passage (xvi. 9) where, according to the correct exposition, the exhortation urges to a gaining of God's friendship by means of mammon, and therefore in the most real sense to an εἰς Θεὸν πλουτεῖν, in order, when mammon ceases, to be received by God into eternal habitations.

If, then, from this final application of the parable we glance back at the utterance of Jesus (ver. 15), which formed its starting-point, and at the narrative lying between, it is clear at once how the narrative serves to illustrate that utterance. The Lord there warned against all covetousness, by representing it as an illusion that life depends on the multitude of goods, as if life arose from possessions. In the example of the rich man, which according to ver. 21 is to be applied to him that gathers treasures for himself, and therefore to the covetous generally, a vivid picture is presented of how, on the one hand, the covetous man really lives in that illusion, and of how, on the other hand, he is terribly deceived. Thus there can be no doubt respecting the purpose of the parable. It is this,—*to characterize the perilous folly of the illusion in which covetousness lives, as if life depended on possessions.* And to this purpose the narrative in its two parts is faithful, describing in the first part the manner in which covetousness forms pictures of the future, and calculates upon it, and disclosing in the second the perilous blindness in which it is entangled. In keeping with this purpose, therefore, we have to work out the application indicated in ver. 21 in the light of the entire narrative. For the only point in question here is the working out of an application, not the filling up of an interpretation, seeing that without doubt we have before us here (as in x. 37 ff. already) not a symbolic, but merely an exemplary narrative, and therefore not a symbolic, but a typical parable.

First of all, in the first part of the narrative Jesus sketches in the example of the rich man a vivid picture of a peculiar kind of avarice, anxious about the future, framing plans for it, and eagerly painting it to oneself. As the rich man, in presence of the fertility of his ground, begins at once to be anxious how ever he is to manage so as to lose nothing, so for the covetous man anxiety is inseparable from the possessions belonging to him, as to whether and how he can succeed in securing everything and avoiding all loss. And as the rich man does not let himself be limited by the extent of his barns, but forms plans for pulling them down and building new and large storehouses in which to lay up all his goods, so it is natural to the covetous man with boundless greed to frame plans for heaping up treasure in superfluous abundance, without letting himself be limited by any hindrances whatever, such as naturally oppose the heaping up of treasures in the hand of an individual, and without turning his thoughts to an unselfish use of the superfluity. And as, finally, the rich man pictures to himself as the end of his plans, how he will show his soul the goods stored up for many years, and summon it to rest, enjoyment, and pleasure, so it is natural to the covetous man to dream how, when he shall have heaped up treasures enough for all the future, he will surrender his soul wholly to their enjoyment.

So far the description of the covetous man's train of thought in reference to the future. There follows in the second part the disclosure of the foolish illusion in which such a mode of thought lives. When Jesus concludes the narrative by communicating a divine judgment that passed sentence of death on the rich man for this very night, we see suddenly in grimmest illustration the foolish, perilous infatuation in which avarice of the peculiar kind, anxiously planning for the future, and forming pictures of it, is entangled. As the doom is pronounced on the rich man, that this night his soul and life are required of him, whilst he is planning the collection of provision for many years, and promising his soul enjoyment in life of corresponding length, his treasures falling to no one knows whom; so the rich man, amid his anxieties, plans, and fancied enjoyments in the future, is not sure of his life for a single day, upon which he calculates for so many years, or of his soul, to which he promises enjoyments so far ahead, nor even of his goods, which, instead of securing him life, are lost to him with life, an ownerless possession, scattered no one knows where.

The Fig-Tree.

(Luke xiii. 6–9.)

With the words: "And He spake this parable" (ver. 6), a parable is joined to the foregoing paragraph (vv. 1–5). The absence of any information respecting the hearers of the parable, shows that it is meant to be taken in connection with the foregoing discourse. The words just quoted simply intimate that a parable now follows, the discourse in the context from ver. 1 being directly continued. According to ver. 1, some among the bystanders had told of the Galileans whom Pilate slew while they were sacrificing,—an event not mentioned elsewhere. The words: παρῆσαν δέ τινες ἀπαγγέλλοντες, suppose a greater number of persons present, among whom some are found who relate the incident. Perhaps the way in which this news was mentioned and discussed gave Jesus a special occasion for interfering in its discussion, as He does in vv. 2–5. He warns against the inference, only too congenial to popular Jewish ideas, that those Galileans were special sinners above all Galileans, because they suffered such things (ver. 2), and confronts this opinion with the prediction: "*Unless ye repent, ye shall all in like manner (i.e. just as terribly) perish*" (ver. 3). And by adding another similar case, belonging also presumably to the immediate past, in which eighteen persons had perished by the fall of a tower in Jerusalem, He repeats and enforces what He says by this second example. In regard to this case also He opposes the notion that those eighteen were specially guilty above all dwellers in Jerusalem, and again confronts such an opinion with the prediction: "Unless ye repent, ye shall all likewise perish" (vv. 4, 5). But who are the "all" to whom Jesus predicts such things? In the first instance, of course, the bystanders; but these again not as individual persons, but—since what is applied to them holds good both of all Galileans and of all dwellers in Jerusalem—as members and representatives of a collective body, including both classes, the dwellers in Galilee and the dwellers in Jerusalem, therefore as members of the Jewish people lying under like common guilt. The partial divine judgments—this is the truth expressed—which the present generation sees executed here and there are not grounded in the special guiltiness of individuals, but are meant to remind the members of the nation of their common, heavy guilt, and are to them, unless they repent, mere precursors of a general divine sentence of destruction that will burst over the entire present generation.

And here the parable strikes in (ver. 6 ff.): συκῆν εἶχέν τις πεφυτευμένην ἐν τῷ ἀμπελῶνι αὐτοῦ,[1] i.e.: "*A fig-tree a certain man possessed, which was planted in his vineyard.*" The express mention of its being planted asserts that it was not a tree which the owner met with by chance, but one specially planted and reared. And the statement that it was planted *in his vineyard*, signalizes a peculiar privilege that had fallen to this tree. Vineyard-soil is pre-eminently favourable to fruit-trees. The legal enactment (Deut. xxii. 9) forbidding the sowing of the vineyard with divers seeds, does not necessarily prohibit the planting of single trees, while the comparison with that passage shows that it was a privilege for the tree to stand in its possessor's vineyard. And so the owner was certainly justified in expecting much and good fruit from this tree planted in his vineyard. Nevertheless, it is now said further: "*And he came seeking fruit in it, and found none.*" Then, in presence of the vinedresser (εἶπεν δὲ πρὸς τὸν ἀμπελουργόν), who is consequently represented as accompanying the owner in his inspection, he gives expression to his disappointment in the words (ver. 7): Ἰδοὺ τρία ἔτη, ἀφ' οὗ ἔρχομαι ζητῶν καρπὸν ἐν τῇ συκῇ ταύτῃ καὶ οὐχ εὑρίσκω. The words wanting in many manuscripts (ἀφ' οὗ), are all the more certainly genuine, as they are apparently dispensable. But in reality they first give to the words preceding them (τρία ἔτη)

---

[1] This order of the words is preponderantly attested.

the full emphasis which they are meant to have, these words now becoming an independent exclamation, to which the declaration proper is then added in the form of a relative clause: "*Behold*, (it is) *three years since I came* (again and again) *seeking fruit*," etc. But the meaning of this complaint cannot be the one obtained by unduly pressing the words, to the effect that since he came for the first time, looking in vain for fruit on the tree, to the present moment three complete years have elapsed. Then the present year would be the fourth year of fruitlessness, which certainly is not meant. But the meaning of such a phrase is this, that the present fruit-season, in which he again sees his expectation disappointed, is the third in which the tree has refused fruit, the current year being the third one of fruitlessness. From what has been said, it is evident that the remark sometimes made in explanation of the "three years," that as a rule the tree bears fruit within three years of its being planted,[1] is out of place here, because the owner has expected and sought fruit for three years already. On the other hand, the remark of Baumgarten-Crusius is all the more pertinent: "Three years' fruitlessness is proof of barrenness." When a tree refuses fruit, not merely the first and second, but also the third year, we are justified in inferring its complete barrenness. The owner does so here, and therefore naturally gives expression to his disappointment in the command to the vinedresser: "*Cut it down.*" He adds, however, a special reason for this command: ἵνα τί καὶ τὴν γῆν καταργεῖ; *i.e.* "*Wherefore does it* (useless in itself) *also make the ground useless?*" Because already useless in itself, it would deserve the axe; but in addition—and this is an especial offence to the speaker—it makes useless the soil of the vineyard in which it is planted. His vineyard is too valuable to bear a barren tree. He will have a fruitful tree—this lies unexpressed but plain in the background—planted in its stead.

But then the vinedresser, to whom the owner of the vineyard has thus spoken, makes intercession for the tree. The motive influencing him in this intercession, notwithstanding that the command to cut it down appears thoroughly well-grounded objectively, can only be a special fondness for this tree, leading him still to hope concerning it, even where, according to ordinary judgment, there is nothing to be hoped for. Hence ver. 8: "*But he answered and said:*" κύριε, ἄφες αὐτὴν καὶ τοῦτο τὸ ἔτος,

[1] Wetstein, Meyer.

i.e. "*Let it alone this year also.*" For this present year also, although as the third year of fruitlessness it seems to decide the tree's barrenness, the gardener asks the same patience that was shown to it the two former years. His request is to the effect that it be not cut down, but left standing this year also. It is self-evident that, if not cut down this year, the tree is to remain standing till the return of the fruit-season next year. This is the presupposition when, further explaining and confirming his request, he more exactly defines the time up to which he desires the tree to remain: ἕως ὅτου σκάψω περὶ αὐτὴν καὶ βάλω κόπρια:[1] "*till I shall dig about and dung it.*" He thus expresses the purpose to do everything possible to the tree in the way of digging and dunging, and until this shall be done (*i.e.*, according to the meaning, until the effect of his action is seen, therefore until next year's fruit-season) he implores respite for the tree. Then, as he now adds in conclusion, according to the success or failure of these efforts of his, let the fate of the tree be decided (ver. 9): κἂν μὲν ποιήσῃ καρπόν· εἰ δὲ μή γε, εἰς τὸ μέλλον ἐκκόψεις αὐτήν. In ἐὰν μέν ... εἰ δέ the two cases—that of success and that of failure—are contrasted with each other.[2] But in the case of success first taken into consideration, the apodosis is absent, and this not because it can be supplied from the foregoing by an ἄφες αὐτήν repeated,[3] for in the case of bearing fruit supposed no such special intercession for the tree is needed, and were there need of it, it would not be self-evident, but must be expressly repeated. Rather, the apodosis is absent simply because in the case supposed the tree's remaining is entirely matter of course. Therefore, with Meyer *et al.*, something like καλῶς ἔχει must be supplied, thus: "*And in case it shall bear fruit, well!*" Even in the classics such aposiopeses are not rare, and are especially frequent, as here, after the first of two parallel conditional sentences, the speaker leaping forward to the second sentence as the principal.[4] So here, by the aposiopesis of the first apodosis, the second one, in which the petitioner himself proposes the tree being cut down in the opposite case, acquires all the greater emphasis: "*But if not,*" *i.e.* if even then it bears no fruit, "*cut it down the next year.*"

---

[1] So, according to the best witnesses, instead of κοπρίαν.

[2] Respecting the interchange of ἐάν and εἰ in parallel conditional sentences, see Winer, *Gram.* p. 363 f.

[3] Kuinoel, *et al.*   [4] Cf. Winer, *Gram.* p. 627.

The words εἰς τὸ μέλλον must not here be taken in general indefiniteness = "afterwards," as *e.g.* in 1 Tim. vi. 19; but, since the words εἰς τὸ μέλλον ἐκκόψεις αὐτήν here plainly stand in contrast with ἄφες αὐτὴν καὶ τοῦτο τὸ ἔτος as a supplement and limitation, the context necessarily requires the completion by ἔτος, therefore "in the next year." The gardener does not in his request desire the cutting down of the tree to be postponed to an indefinite future, but definitely proposes the next year for doing this, if fruitlessness then ensues.[1] Something special has been found in the fact of ἐκκόψεις, not ἐκκόψω, being used at the close;[2] but wrongly, for since the words are still a part of the gardener's request to the master, it is obvious that he speaks in the second person in the way of mere proposal, and does not in an unbecoming manner give expression to independent resolutions in the first person. And this request, now brought to a conclusion, forms the close of the entire narrative. It is not even said that the request was granted. We certainly see that the request is conceived to be effectual from the mere fact that only as such does it really form a conclusion; but, on the other hand, this mode of concluding the narrative strengthens the impression, how the fate of the tree trembles in the balance. Nothing stands between the tree and the axe that is to cut it down save the prayer of the gardener, who desires to make a last trial. And even this prayer extends only to a brief measured respite, and in case the respite passes away without effect, merges into the proposal: "But if not, thou shalt cut it down."

As soon as we compare these contents, and especially this result of the narrative, with the words of threatening prediction, to which it directly refers, it is clear that those words of Jesus contain the very theme of the parable. There Jesus twice foretold to the bystanders that, unless they repent, they all, namely, the entire body of the Israelitish nation, will perish in like manner as those Galileans and Jerusalemites, therefore that they will incur a divine judgment, involving in destruction not merely individuals, but the entire generation. And it is precisely this judgment, only enlarged and intensified into the destruction of the nation in its national existence, which presents itself as the theme of the parable. *That the nation of Israel,*—for we are warranted

---

[1] On the use of the preposition εἰς of a future time, in which something will or ought to take place, cf. i. 20; Acts xiii. 42.
[2] Bengel, Stier, *et al.*

by the context in provisionally assuming that Israel is represented by the image of the fig-tree,—*unless it now repents, will fall victim to God's sentence of destruction without further delay,*—to exhibit this solemn truth as unchangeable is the design of the parable. In other words, the design of the figurative history is to show that what Jesus first of all merely held up before the bystanders as a menacing prediction, with the weight attaching to His own testimony,[1] is also a fact inseparably bound up with the peculiar nature of the present circumstances of Israel, so that it must itself be recognised as such. Let us see more closely how this is done in detail.

"A fig-tree a certain man possessed, planted in his vineyard;" in these words the object, of which the narrative is to treat, is put first. Even in the Old Testament the fig-tree is an image of the people of Israel (Joel i. 7). Nevertheless, since the same is certainly true of the vineyard,[2] the attempt has been made to apply the fig-tree not to Israel, but to the individual Israelite, and then the vineyard to the nation.[3] But the fig-tree cannot be the individual Israelite as a member of the nation, because throughout the narrative it is single and alone, not an individual tree among many, which even when taken together do not make a vineyard. We must therefore adhere to the view that the fig-tree is Israel. This is required alike by the connection with what precedes, and by the figurative signification of this tree in the Old Testament. Then the words: "A certain man had," intimate the relation in which God stands to this nation. It is that of owner to the property belonging to Him in a peculiar sense. This relation is figuratively described in its distinctiveness by "planted." Israel is not a nation that has grown in a purely natural way, but, like a tree specially planted, it was called into existence as a nation by special extraordinary acts of God.[4] And it is just this privilege belonging to it above other nations, in regard to its relation to God, which now finds complete figurative expression in the words: "in His vineyard." There is no necessity, because the fig-tree is Israel, to interpret the vineyard in which it is planted of the world in general,[5] in which case nothing would be affirmed of Israel but what is just as true of all other nations, that the world is its dwelling-place. Rather, the figurative signification of the vine-

---

[1] Cf. the λέγω ὑμῖν, vv. 3, 5.   [2] See the passage quoted, and Isa. v. 1–7.
[3] Stier.   [4] Cf. Ps. lxxx. 8, 15.   [5] van Oosterzee.

yard found elsewhere must here be simply adhered to, only, of course, with the modification it receives in other figurative discourses of Jesus. In the Old Testament, where the theocracy on earth is identical with the Israelitish nationality and constitution as such, the vineyard, because signifying the kingdom of God, signifies also, of course, "the house of Israel" (Isa. v. 7). But not so in the figurative language of Jesus. In the parable (Matt. xx. 1 ff.) Jesus symbolizes by the vineyard the kingdom of God in itself, without special reference to the Israelitish nation;[1] and in the parable Matt. xxi. 33 ff., He distinguishes between the vinedressers as the representatives of the Jewish nation and the vineyard as the kingdom of God, which indeed they previously held in possession, but which hereafter will be taken from them and handed over to others. It is the same here. When it was affirmed here of the fig-tree as a special privilege, that it was planted in its owner's vineyard, this can only mean the privilege belonging to Israel as the nation designed and educated by God from the first to be the people of His kingdom, and encircled in the entire course of its growth with all the blessings of the theocracy.

From this standpoint we can now interpret without difficulty the single incidents of the narrative. In the first place, this is certain: As the owner of the fig-tree has a right to expect fruit from the tree planted in his vineyard, so has God a right to expect the moral fruit of righteousness from the chosen people of His kingdom. And as the owner seeks fruit in the tree without finding it, so does God in His people. Nay, as the owner is forced to complain respecting the fruitlessness of the tree lasting through three years, so has God to complain respecting the lasting impenitence of Israel, — so lasting, that the nation must be regarded as utterly hardened and incapable of repentance. Here we arrive at the true interpretation of the "three years." Against the often attempted application to the three official years of Christ,[2] it is decisive that, if this interpretation of the three years is accepted here, it must also be accepted in the interpretation of vv. 8, 9, which would lead there to the impossible result, that Jesus places the occurrence of the judgment on Israel within the space of a year. Moreover, the work of Jesus in Israel was not at all in question previously, but merely the relation of God

---

[1] See on that parable.
[2] *E.g.* Bengel, Wieseler, Weizsäcker, similarly van Oosterzee.

to Israel as the people of His possession. We should then be compelled, as Stier does consistently, from the first to interpret the lord of the vineyard of Christ, thus involving the whole in utter confusion. But on the supposition that what is here said of the physical life of a tree is to be transferred to the moral life of a nation, how could the three years as such be incorporated mechanically in the interpretation? Three years were named in the parable, because the fruitlessness of a tree through this number of seasons seems to prove its incurable barrenness. Transferred to the moral development of a nation, the correspondent period can only be a period of moral corruption and obduracy, of such prolonged duration as to form a just basis for inferring the utter incapacity of the nation as such for moral reformation,— an inference which cannot be based, as with a tree, on years, but only on centuries or millenniums. Thus, in the present case, the period corresponding to the three unfruitful years of the fig-tree is the entire historical past of Israel from its beginning to its present, during which the nation had never experienced a thoroughgoing moral reformation, so that its incurable obduracy seems proved. It is clear that, after the thought underlying the mention of three years has thus found its complete application in the interpretation, the attempts of older expositors to point out a corresponding triplicity of periods within the past of Israel [1] must be relegated to the domain of arbitrary conjectures. And, to proceed with the interpretation, as now, on the ground of the proved barrenness of the tree the owner issues the command to cut it down, so Israel, after the centuries of its history up to the present have established its incurable obduracy, lies exposed to the divine judgment. The decree of God, giving it up to judgment as an obdurate nation, incapable of repentance, is already pronounced. And even the special reason for the command: "Cut it down," added by the owner in the parable, ought not to be passed over, since the otherwise superfluous addition is only explained by supposing a corresponding interpretation to be aimed at. But after the planting of the tree in the *vineyard* has been rightly explained, as above, the corresponding interpretation of this feature easily follows. The cutting down of the tree is necessary for a double reason, because it is not only useless in itself, but also makes useless the rich soil, where other fruitful

---

[1] *E.g.* the age of the Law, the Prophets, and Jesus, or of the Judges, Kings, and High Priests.

trees might be planted. So Israel lies under the doom of destruction for a double reason, because it is not only in itself unworthy to exist, but also, as the chosen people of God's kingdom, enjoys in vain the blessings and prerogatives which might be given instead to other peoples hitherto at a distance from the kingdom of God.

In the foregoing interpretation of the complaint as to the barrenness of the tree, and of the command to cut it down, we have made no reference to the circumstance, that both—the complaint and the command — are in the narrative uttered in presence of the gardener. And this with good reason. For the fact that the owner's disappointment, and his resolve to cut the tree down, find expression, not in another and simpler form (*e.g.* in that of a soliloquy), but as a complaint and command to the gardener, is without independent significance. This circumstance obviously has its significance merely as a preliminary to the conclusion of the narrative, where this very gardener, in replying to the complaint and command, himself decisively intervenes in behalf of the tree already condemned to the axe. Here, then, we must inquire as to the interpretation of the gardener. Without doubt Jesus intends in the gardener to typify Himself, and in what the gardener does for the tree to set forth what He does for Israel. And this not merely in the indefinite generality, that His work is the last attempt on Israel.[1] To express only this thought an essentially simpler construction of the figurative history would have sufficed, namely, instead of the express command ἔκκοψον, crossed and delayed by the prayer ἄφες αὐτήν, a simple intimation to the gardener to do for the tree whatever was possible again and for the last time. That the *intercession* of the gardener, which delays the cutting down of the tree, imperatively requires a definite interpretation, is proved decisively by the analogous historical incidents in the Old Testament, especially the repeated intercession of Moses for the people, which delayed the divine judgment,[2] an intercession which must necessarily have occurred to the Jewish hearers in the present case. Accordingly, without going beyond the original meaning of the narrative, we have to continue the interpretation to the end as follows: Like a gardener who, despite persistent fruitlessness, cherishes to

---

[1] Meyer.

[2] Ex. xxxii. 7–14; Num. xiv. 11–19; cf. 1 Sam. vii. 9; Amos vii. 2; Dan. ix. 16–19.

the last the hope of causing a tree dear to him to bear fruit, so Jesus, in love to His people, is unwilling even now utterly to abandon hope of them, despite their moral obduracy proved again and again up to the present moment. As, therefore, the gardener prays the master, who has already decreed the cutting down of the tree, to let it stand yet another year, so is Jesus seeking by His intercession before God to delay for the present the divine judgment already passed upon Israel. And as the gardener further explains his request to mean, that at least the effect may be awaited of a last extraordinary attempt to be made with the use of every means, with digging and dunging about the tree, so the inner purport of the prayer of Jesus for Israel is, that at least a respite may be granted it, until the final effect of His present work shall decisively show itself,—work in which everything possible will be done in a way never seen before to arouse the nation to repentance. That mercy will take the place of judgment in case of actual success is self-evident, in regard both to the fig-tree and Israel. But as in case of renewed failure the gardener sees himself compelled to propose the cutting down of the tree next year (namely, as soon as the failure shall be confirmed), so even Jesus' prayer for mercy to Israel neither will nor can extend beyond the time when the failure of His present toil shall be decided, and therefore in no case—this is plainly implied —beyond the time of the present generation, for which He has toiled. When the fruitlessness of His present toil shall be manifest in them, then the divine sentence of destruction, so long threatening Israel, will and must infallibly be executed on this generation, which has filled up the measure of the sins of its fathers (Matt. xxiii. 32). It will see bursting upon it a penal catastrophe, involving it in destruction, and inflicting on the nation as such the dissolution of its national existence. And thus the meaning of the parable merges at last into the threatening prediction which precedes it, and the unavoidableness of which follows from the peculiar nature of the present circumstances of the nation: "Unless ye repent, ye shall all likewise perish."

The Great Banquet.[1]

(Luke xiv. 15-24.)

The parable of the Great Banquet was uttered by Jesus when He was dining with one of the heads of the Pharisaic sect on a Sabbath day, xiv. 1. This "ruler of the Pharisees" (ἄρχων τῶν Φαρισαίων) and his brother-Pharisees sitting with him at table, were the hearers. The friendly association into which they had drawn Jesus was used by them as a cover for watching Him (ver. 1b). In keeping with this relation of the rest of the guests to Jesus, His conversation with them assumes the form of a series of admonitions which He gives them. First of all, the presence of a man with the dropsy, brought about as it seems by set arrangement, leads Him to heal the man, and to justify in a striking manner His act of healing on the Sabbath to the spies and secret murmurers, so that they are unable to answer Him, vv. 2–6. Again, when He sees how the guests affect the chief places at table, He reproves the arrogant longing for vain honour in the figurative form suggested by the occasion (ἔλεγε παραβολήν, ver. 7), and exhorts to the modesty which without ostentation gives way to others, instead of trying to raise itself above them, vv. 7–11. Again, apparently, it was the exclusiveness of the host in the selection of the guests which led Jesus (at the same time suggesting the figurative form) further to admonish the host to show his liberality, not so much to those from whom recompense might be expected, as rather to those who could make no return, ver. 12 ff. "And thou shalt be blessed, because they have not *wherewith* to recompense thee; for thou shalt be recompensed in the resurrection of the just," ver. 14, —with this promise Jesus concluded the exhortation. These words decide the meaning of the exclamation, into which one of the guests breaks out directly after this discourse of Jesus (ἀκούσας δέ), and which gives the Lord the special occasion of the following parable. Μακάριος ὃς φάγεται ἄρτον ἐν τῇ βασιλείᾳ τοῦ Θεοῦ, so runs the exclamation, ver. 15. Ἄρτον ἐσθίειν (אָכַל לֶחֶם,

---

[1] Respecting the mutual relations of this parable and that of the Royal Marriage-Feast (Matt. xxii. 1 ff.), which are supposed, according to the judgment of modern critics (most recently by Weiss), to have been originally identical, see at the close of the exposition of the last-named parable. This point can only be decided when each of the two parables has been independently expounded in its context.

e.g. Gen. xxxi. 54, xliii. 32, *et al.*) means "to take a meal," in the general sense, "to partake of a meal."[1] Here, therefore: "*Blessed is he who shall partake of food in the kingdom of God.*" The exclamation presents itself at first sight merely as an affirmative repetition of the last words of Jesus. For, when it was said, "And thou shalt be blessed, . . . for thou shalt be recompensed in the resurrection of the just," this recompensing was there represented, in keeping with the figurative form of the whole section, vv. 12–14, as a return-invitation[2] to the feast in the future kingdom of God which is set up at the resurrection of the just. And yet what seems and is meant to seem merely an affirmative repetition of the last words of Jesus in a somewhat altered form, is in reality a complete perversion. For whereas Jesus had commended the blessedness of God's future kingdom to His Pharisaic host in the light of a recompense for the fulfilment of a perfectly definite command,—a command involving for the Pharisee and all like him an essential change of mind,—the Pharisee, seizing simply upon the last words of Jesus, emphatically commends merely the blessedness in general of partaking in the feast of God's kingdom, without so much as mentioning that command of the Lord. This relation in which the Pharisee's exclamation stands to the preceding words of Jesus as an apparently affirmative repetition of the blessing pronounced, while omitting the condition to which it was attached, makes plain the meaning in which the otherwise unobjectionable and edifying words are viewed here. The Pharisee commends participation in the feast of God's kingdom, not as a lofty, attractive goal, worth every sacrifice and only to be attained by thorough change of mind, but as a possession supposed to be secure to him and those like him, and to which he has a right without further condition, to say nothing of his needing a change of mind in order to reach the goal. To this statement the parable gives the answer. For in the story of the parable Jesus especially addresses Himself to the guest who made this statement, ver. 15 (ὁ δὲ εἶπεν αὐτῷ). And thus we are warranted in expecting that the purpose of the parable will be directed against this Pharisaic security, which glories in the blessedness of God's kingdom as a right.

"*A certain man made a great banquet,*" so the narrative begins, ver. 16. Δεῖπνον here is "banquet" generally. At least no

---

[1] Cf. ver. 1; Matt. xv. 2; Mark iii. 20.
[2] Cf. ver. 12: μή ποτε καὶ αὐτοὶ ἀντικαλέσωσίν σε καὶ γένηται ἀνταπόδομά σοι.

stress is laid on the difference between the principal evening meal and ἄριστον as the morning meal,[1] because in the following narrative the time of day is nowhere alluded to. A banquet is called great or small according to the greater or smaller number of guests for whom it is prepared, not according to the number of viands,[2] of which there may be many even in a small meal, or according to the costliness of the viands [3] and the dignity of the host.[4] The word "great" only expresses the festive magnitude of the meal indirectly, namely, in so far as a meal for unusually numerous guests requires also unusually large preparations, and is generally set out with special pomp. To the greatness of the feast in preparation corresponds exactly the following: "and He called many." To the magnitude of the preparations intended for a multitude of guests corresponds the invitation addressed to a multitude of guests. This first calling is consequently viewed merely as a preliminary announcement, contemporaneous with the preparation of the feast, by which those to whom it is addressed become "called," *i.e.* invited guests, without the hour of the feast being as yet precisely indicated to them. Only on this assumption can it be said further, ver. 17: καὶ ἀπέστειλεν τὸν δοῦλον αὐτοῦ τῇ ὥρᾳ τοῦ δείπνου εἰπεῖν τοῖς κεκλημένοις, "Ἔρχεσθε, ὅτι ἤδη ἕτοιμά ἐστιν πάντα, *i.e.* "*And he sent his servant at the hour of the feast,*" etc. In the words "his servant" a specially near relation of the servant to his master has been supposed to be intimated.[5] But this view is based only on a preconceived interpretation of the servant. The article is the simple generic article,[6] and the servant only comes into consideration here as bearing the message to the guests, again as reporting their answers, and finally, as executing other commissions, without his person having independent significance in the context of the narrative apart from the execution of these commissions. "*At the hour of the feast,*" *i.e.* at the hour when the feast was ready, word is again sent to the guests, in order actually to call those who before were only invited preliminarily and without exact specification of time. That such is the meaning is put beyond doubt by the wording of the message to be addressed to the guests: "*Come, for all things are now ready.*" The little word "*now*" implies that those invited did not expect the feast to be ready just now. The only other possible rendering of the order,

---

[1] Cf. on Matt. xxii. 4. [2] van Oosterzee *et al.* [3] Luther. [4] De Valenti.
[5] Nebe. [6] Cf. *e.g.* Matt. viii. 9, λέγω . . . τῷ δούλῳ μου.

"all things are now ready," as a reminding exhortation because of the negligence of the guests who failed to appear at the hour already announced to them on the first invitation,[1] is inappropriate, because so important and strange a circumstance as the non-appearance of all the invited guests at the appointed hour could not have been passed over in silence in the narrative. When, accordingly, proof is found that a second invitation to festal guests is customary in the East, this is simply a confirmation of the only meaning admissible here.[2] The answers also, which the invited ones give to the order, ver. 18 ff., represent them as taken by surprise by the summons: "Come, for all things are now ready," at a time when they did not expect it. That in which all the invited ones agree in their answer is placed first, ver. 18: καὶ ἤρξαντο ἀπὸ μιᾶς παραιτεῖσθαι πάντες. Παραιτεῖσθαι, as the immediately following request: ἔχε με παρῃτημένον, places beyond doubt, has here the signification "praying to decline," or "to ask to be excused," therefore what we call "to excuse oneself" from an invitation. But ἤρξαντο παραιτεῖσθαι is not a mere pleonasm for "they excused themselves," but the apparently superfluous "began" suggests the new and wonderful thing implied in the invited guests meeting the call now actually to come to the feast with excuses. Whereas hitherto, so long as the invitation was merely preliminary, they seemed to view it as an honour and delight, *now* (when they are actually to come) *they began to excuse themselves!* And this is all the more strange as they do it ἀπὸ μιᾶς πάντες, "*all with one consent.*" Ἀπό with the genitive stands here [3] with the adverbial significance of the manner in which something is done. Whether καρδίας or ψυχῆς or γνώμης is to be supplied to μιᾶς is not worth disputing. Precisely because the supplement follows of itself in either of these ways, but always with the same sense of unanimity, the μιᾶς may stand thus absolutely. Thus their excusing themselves with one consent certainly means in the first instance: they showed unanimity in excusing themselves. But really their unanimity goes still farther, without, however, there being a trace of concert beforehand.[4] While the excuses which they offer differ according to the different situation in which the call to the feast finds the individuals, they are all alike as regards the

---

[1] Winer, *Realwörterbuch*, art. "Gastmahl;" Nebe.
[2] Meyer quotes Rosenmüller, *Morgenland*, v. p. 192 f.
[3] As *e.g.* in Matt. xviii. 35; 2 Cor. i. 14, ii. 5.   [4] Godet.

meaning expressed in them. When, then, in what follows the refusal of the first, that of a second, and that of a third of the guests are quoted literally, the intention of this threefold exemplification may either be to characterize three different classes of guests by three essentially different grounds of excuse, or in the intrinsic resemblance of the three answers given by way of example to indicate the deeper cause lying beneath the reluctance of all the guests alike, which thus explains the unanimity of their reluctance. Let us now look at the three examples, vv. 18b–20.

The first said to him :—

| Ἀγρὸν ἠγόρασα | καὶ ἔχω ἀνάγκην ἐξελθεῖν καὶ ἰδεῖν[1] αὐτόν· | ἐρωτῶ σε, ἔχε με παρῃτημένον. |

And another said :—

| Ζεύγη βοῶν ἠγόρασα πέντε | καὶ πορεύομαι δοκιμάσαι αὐτά· | ἐρωτῶ σε, ἔχω με παρῃτημένον. |

And another said :—

| Γυναῖκα ἔγημα, | . . . . . . | καὶ διὰ τοῦτο οὐ δύναμαι ἐλθεῖν. |

Thus each of the three men invited intimates, in the first place, that he has acquired a piece of property: the first, "*I have bought a field;*" the second, "*I have bought five*[2] *yoke of oxen;*" the third, "*I have married a wife.*" For it is plain that in this juxtaposition the marrying of a wife is regarded as the acquisition of a piece of property equally with the buying of a field and of five yoke of oxen.[3] To this prefatory statement the first and the second then add the more precise intimation to what extent the object acquired has claims on them; the first, "*and I must needs go and see it*" (the field); the second, "*and I go to prove them*" (the pairs of oxen). Because of these words appended, it has been believed, without reason, that the preceding aorist ἠγόρασα must be taken in the sense of a present or future (Kuinoel: emere volo agrum), or that the purchase is not finally concluded.[4] Certainly it is a dictate of prudence for any one to see and test a thing before

---

[1] Or also, according to good witnesses, ἐξελθὼν ἰδεῖν.

[2] The frequent use of the number five, due to the need of concrete, vivid narrative, is worthy of notice; cf. xvi. 28.

[3] Cf. Ex. xx. 17.   [4] Stier, van Oosterzee, von Hofmann.

buying it. But this kind of seeing and testing is not here in question. Here the point is the seeing and proving a newly-acquired object with the contented feeling of possessing it as property, which, without being a dictate of prudence, still answers to a natural want based on the relation of the possessor to the thing acquired, and yields the possessor all the greater enjoyment the more he has been wont to attach his heart to the objects of his possession. Therefore, somewhat as a miser can scarcely wait to see a newly-acquired treasure, to count it over again and again, toss it to and fro and test the single coins, so the one is eager to see his field, and the other to test his five yoke of oxen. But the strong expression ἔχω ἀνάγκην, which the first one gives to this eagerness, is on one hand grounded in his subjective attachment, in virtue of which he must do what he cannot leave, and on the other hand is the result of his courteous effort to represent the ground of excuse as compulsory, and therefore conclusive; whereas the second, in merely stating the fact, "I go to prove them," without alleging necessity, shows a less degree of courtesy. And in this respect the third again is different from the second, since he curtly and pettishly says nothing in detail as to the extent of the claim made on him by his possession, but contents himself with the statement: "I have married a wife." As matter of fact, it is clear that here also the preventing element lies in the need of enjoying the object of his possession, the wife whom he has taken to himself as his own.[1] To the statement of the ground of refusal all three again expressly add the refusal itself; and this also with diminishing courtesy, the first and the second in the courteous form of the same request: ἔχε με παρῃτημένον (i.e. by a Latinism, habe me excusatum, "*hold me excused*"[2]); the third, with contempt for such courteous forms of request, refusing out and out: "*I cannot come.*" Accordingly, as regards the more or less courteous form, the refusals certainly vary in a diminishing degree. But as regards the preventing element on which they insist, they are thoroughly alike. The three examples do not present three essentially different grounds of excuse, characteristic of three classes of guests different in disposition; but they show that all those invited equally decline to leave their property in field or cattle, farm or house, and prefer enjoying it to partaking in the pleasures of the feast offered them by the giver of the feast,

[1] Deut. xxiv. 5.
[2] Cf. the similar use of ἔχω, Matt. xiv. 5, xxi. 26; Phil. ii. 29.

so that the distinction of field, cattle, and wife is simply the necessary interchange of the threefold exemplification. Upon this correct interpretation we have no longer to ask whether the particular excuses are more or less cogent; but it is clear that all these answers, whether more or less courteous in form, involve one and the same culpable contempt for the householder's feast.

"*And the servant*[1] *came and reported these things to his lord,*" so we hear further, ver. 21. The fact that in these words the reporting of the guests' answer to the householder, which for its own sake might just as well have been passed over as the reporting of the latter's message to the guests, is nevertheless expressly related, is not due merely to the circumstantial style of narrative; but these words are meant to remind the hearer of the eager curiosity resulting at this point from the course of the previous narrative: What will the giver of the feast now do, when these contemptuous answers are reported to him? Will he leave his table empty, and reserve their places for those who still were once invited? And if not, in what other way will he fill his table? To this question of eager curiosity an answer is given in what follows: τότε ὀργισθεὶς ὁ οἰκοδεσπότης εἶπεν τῷ δούλῳ αὐτοῦ κ.τ.λ. The householder is transported with just anger at the report of the scornful answers of his guests, and in anger at them (ὀργισθείς . . . εἶπεν) gives the servant the following commission: ἔξελθε ταχέως εἰς τὰς πλατείας καὶ ῥύμας τῆς πόλεως, καὶ τοὺς πτωχοὺς καὶ ἀναπήρους καὶ τυφλοὺς καὶ χωλοὺς[2] εἰσάγαγε ὧδε. The ταχέως after ἔξελθε is to be explained from ὀργισθεὶς εἶπεν. He does not urge to haste, as many take it, from the hospitable thought of the long-waiting meal,—then the ταχέως must rightly have stood in the case of the second ἔξελθε, ver. 23, where it is wanting,—but wrath at those invited makes him take speedy measures for their punishment. Without troubling himself further about them, or waiting for them, or wasting another word upon them, he gives the servant orders to go quickly after other guests to take the place of the former ones at his table. And he is to go out εἰς τὰς πλατείας καὶ ῥύμας τῆς πόλεως, i.e. "*into the* (broad) *streets and* (narrow) *lanes of the city.*"[3] Consequently a city appears here as the scene, if not necessarily of the feast, yet of the invitations, so

---

[1] Ἐκεῖνος after δοῦλος (Rec.) is too weakly attested.
[2] The reverse order χωλοὺς καὶ τυφλούς (Rec.) is taken from ver. 13.
[3] Cf. Isa. xv. 3, LXX.

that the guests first invited, whom we see from their excuses to be owners having fields, cattle, and households, are pictured as resident citizens of the city.[1] The only possible meaning of the order given by the host is that, after the citizens of the city have despised the invitation, the servant must now seek the homeless populace of the city, gathering them, so to speak, from the streets and lanes, namely, "*the beggars, and cripples, and blind, and lame.*" Just as in ver. 13, alongside the cripples,[2] the blind and lame embraced under that designation are specially mentioned as the classes of such unfortunate ones most commonly met with. The heaping together of such expressions indicates that no class of wretchedness, whatever it be, is to be passed over. And indeed they are not simply to be summoned, but the direction runs: $εἰσάγαγε$ $ὧδε$, "*bring them in here*," scil. into this my house,[3] certainly a form of direction such as naturally follows from the situation here. For if beggars and cripples, such as lie about streets and lanes, are really to be brought, not merely as recipients of alms to the door, but as guests into the house and to the festive table of the wealthy, noble householder, a mere summons, which they will scarcely understand, to say nothing of their venturing to obey it, is not enough, but they need to be brought in. But, on the other hand, it is also clear that, besides the shame and diffidence to be overcome in presence of so honourable and unexpected an invitation, no other objection, like that of the guests first invited, is to be anticipated from these unhappy, homeless people, and that therefore the direction "bring them in here," while necessary to overcome their shame, is certain of success. For this reason the execution of the commission itself may be passed over in silence, the fact of its execution being at once announced, ver. 22 : "*And the servant said, Lord, it is done as thou didst command.*" Certainly it has recently been contested[4] that the execution of the commission may be supplied between vv. 21 and 22. The servant, it is supposed, in immediate response to the order of the householder, answers that he has already done spontaneously as the master orders him.[5] But in this case the action of the servant would merely have to be supplied between vv. 20 and 21, instead of between vv. 21

---

[1] Cf. Matt. xxii. 7.   [2] $ἀνάπηρη$, "mutilated."
[3] Cf. ver. 23 : $μου ὁ οἶκος$.   [4] Meyer, van Oosterzee.
[5] In the newest (6th) edition of Meyer's commentary, edited by Weiss, the latter has again set aside this interpretation.

and 22, and this with impossible harshness. Then, too, even if we are willing to refrain from emphasizing the essential element, that the servant did it *spontaneously*, His words at least should have run γέγονεν ἤδη ὡς ἐπιτάσσεις, instead of γέγονεν ὡς ἐπέταξας.[1] And how is it possible to conceive that, because a servant has received refusals from the invited guests of his noble, wealthy lord, he should hit upon the expedient of gathering the beggars and cripples from the streets and bringing them as guests to the table, and that without further inquiry he should carry this suggestion out on his own responsibility? This view so entirely contradicts the natural tenor of the narrative, that its advocacy can only be explained as an adaptation of the text to an interpretation settled beforehand.[2] And even when the servant, after announcing the execution of his master's commission, makes the addition: "and yet there is room," this by no means implies an element of initiative on the part of the servant, such as some have once and again tried to find in the interests of a preconceived interpretation. Directly we keep in view the situation created by the previous course of the narrative,—a *great* feast is made ready, *many* were invited, *all* refused, the servant was sent forth to fill the empty table with the beggars and cripples of the streets,—it is evident that as the servant hitherto was everywhere merely the messenger going and returning to carry out the behests of his lord and bring him back word, so here also he remains in this position, since in simple duty he announces the fact that, although he has done his lord's command and brought in the beggars and cripples, the design of the command is only imperfectly accomplished, the table instead of being full is still partially empty. As to place, this announcement of the servant to the householder is not to be pictured as made within the banquet-room itself; but after the analogy of the parable, Matt. xxii. 1 ff.,[3] we have to think of the giver of the feast here as a great lord, who does not receive the guests directly within the banquet-room, but awaits their assembling without. The last words of the servant: "*and still there is room*," bring the narrative again to a similar point of expectancy as at his first announcement, ver. 21. Will not the householder now at least pay regard to the men who were

---

[1] Nebe.

[2] The truth supposed to be signified thereby is, that Jesus executed the commission of ver. 21 before His return to God.

[3] Cf. ver. 11.

the invited ones; will he not at least reserve the room still left for them, and if not, in what other way will he *fill* his table? This is the question resulting from the situation in the form it has taken. The question finds its answer in ver. 23 : καὶ εἶπεν ὁ κύριος πρὸς τὸν δοῦλον, Ἔξελθε εἰς τὰς ὁδοὺς καὶ φραγμοὺς καὶ ἀνάγκασον εἰσελθεῖν, ἵνα γεμισθῇ μου ὁ οἶκος. In contrast with εἰς τὰς πλατείας καὶ ῥύμας τῆς πόλεως, ver. 21, it is said here: εἰς τὰς ὁδοὺς καὶ φραγμούς. The ὁδοί accordingly are here meant in the stricter sense as highways, and καὶ φραγμούς is subjoined for the purpose of more exactly defining the general, indefinite expression by emphasizing a peculiarity characteristic of *country*-roads. Accordingly we are not to think of hedges enclosing the vineyards, gardens, and fields,[1] or farm-premises,[2] nor yet of hedges in general, because vagrants, beggars, etc., usually haunt such places,[3] for they do this only when such hedges directly occur in the road. But, according to the context, we are to think of hedges and fences, inasmuch as they run along and bound the highways in contrast with the rows of houses forming the bounds of city-streets. In this sense it is said: "*Go out into the highways and hedges, and compel to come in.*" Whom, is not said. But the very fact of the command : "compel to come in," being put down absolutely without object, says in the strongest way that the servant is to do so to every one whom he meets in the road. He is to *compel* them to come in, of course in the only way open to him, by pressing entreaty and urgent address, which may just as well be signified by ἀναγκάζειν as compulsion by threat and violence.[4] The words: "compel to come in," therefore mean essentially the same as "bring in here," ver. 21, save that the expression is strengthened. If the beggars and cripples of the *city* need to be *brought in*, in order to their appearing as guests at the festive table of the great lord perhaps unknown to them, certainly the strangers of the country roads must be *compelled to come in*, if they are to be gathered as guests at the table of the householder hitherto unknown to them. It is the timid diffidence grounded in the nature of the case which here as there needs to be overcome, and any other resistance, springing from contempt, is as little to be thought of here as there. Hence the "compel to come in" is as certain of success as the "bring in." The telic sentence which then follows

---

[1] Kuinoel. [2] von Hofmann.
[3] De Wette, Meyer. [4] Cf. *e.g.* Matt. xiv. 22 ; Mark vi. 45.

does not belong specially to "compel," which, being grounded in the nature of the case, does not need a special definition of aim. The meaning is not, "In order that my house may be full, even compulsory means are to be employed," a misunderstanding which results in essential errors. But the telic sentence belongs to the entire commission: "Go out into the highways," etc. The words: "that my house may be filled," plainly correspond to the words of the servant: "and yet there is room," ver. 22. Because the householder desires to see no empty room in his house, because, despite the scorn on the part of those invited, he desires to see his table *filled* with guests, therefore, without even now paying any regard to those first invited, he commands the servant to go forth the second time and compel the strangers of the highways to come in,—"*that my house may be full.*"

At this point, then, the course of the narrative has reached a thoroughly complete conclusion. How those who were first invited to the feast despised it, is told in the first part; upon which the second part has shown how the householder replied to this contemptuousness with the commission to fetch in the beggars and cripples from the streets, and next, when the existence of more room was patent, with the further commission to compel even the wanderers of the highways to come in, that his house might be full. It has shown, therefore, how the despising of the feast on the part of those invited had for its consequence their final and complete exclusion from the feast on the part of the householder. When, then, to the narrative thus brought to a conclusion, ver. 24, the asseveration is added: λέγω γὰρ ὑμῖν ὅτι οὐδεὶς τῶν ἀνδρῶν τῶν κεκλημένων γεύσεταί μου τοῦ δείπνου, the introduction to this asseveration, which is specially used, peculiarly in Luke's parables, for the purpose of appending a confirming declaration of Jesus after a narrative is closed,[1] ought to prevent the attempt to embody the asseveration here in the narrative itself as an asseveration added to the commission addressed to the servant, ver. 23.[2] To whom could such an asseveration of the householder be addressed? Because of the plural ὑμῖν resort must be had to such obvious makeshifts as this, that the servant is addressed as a collective individual, or that other chance bystanders, or the beggars already brought in, are included among those addressed, whereas the colloquy of the master with the

---

[1] Cf. xi. 9, xv. 7, 10, xvi. 9, xviii. 14, and Matt. xxi. 43.
[2] De Wette, Olshausen, Meyer, Godet, Nebe, von Hofmann.

servant does not even take place in their presence (see *e.g.* ver. 22). And even if this were the case, what sort of meaning could such a solemn asseveration have for the body of servants or the beggars ? What could they gather from it ? As an asseveration of the householder, it would be just as unsuitable to them as it is forcible considered as an asseveration of Jesus to the Pharisaic hearers of the parable. Some writers, indeed, say that the words : " none of those men that were called," must necessarily have this meaning,[1] without, however, showing why. Would they require that on the lips of Jesus " none of you " should have been said to His Pharisaic hearers in direct address instead of " none of those men " ? But this would be something quite different. In this way Jesus would have pronounced an absolutely exclusive judgment on each individual among the guests actually present; whereas He pronounces, indeed, an absolutely and universally exclusive judgment on the category of " the men invited " because of their conduct described in the parable, but withal leaves it to each individual hearer to take the judgment to himself, and, as far as he is concerned, to withdraw from solidarity with " the men invited." There remains only the statement, that after Jesus had just been the inviting servant in the parable, He could not immediately describe the feast as *His* (" my supper "). But this, again, is to base the exposition of the words on an interpretation previously settled, whereas, logically, the latter must be based on the former. Accordingly, the words are to be taken here merely as an asseveration of Jesus confirming (hence "*for* I say to you") the import of the narrative to the hearers, like the declarations of Jesus similarly added in other parables. What Jesus related of the householder at the conclusion,—that on the announcement, " there is still room," the latter, without regarding those invited first, sent forth the servant anew to fill his house with the wanderers of the highways,—this He now confirms to the hearers with the asseveration : " *I say to you, None of those men who were invited shall taste of my banquet.*" He pledges His word to the hearers, that none of the category of those men who were originally invited, but refused to come, shall taste His banquet because of room being subsequently found for them. Bengel well remarks on ἐκείνων : *Pronomen removendi vim habet.* But the same expositor goes too far in paraphrasing the γεύσεται by gustabit, nedum perfruatur, since the verb

[1] De Wette, Olshausen.

γενέσθαι does not retain its fundamental signification, "to taste," in contrast with full enjoying, but merges altogether into the general signification of enjoying, eating, partaking.[1]

Consequently the declaration of Jesus added here serves not so much to interpret the figurative form of the narrative as rather simply to confirm its result. It interprets only in so far as Jesus now describes the banquet of the householder in the parable as *His* feast. But He does so as the Messianic Son of God, the King of the Messianic kingdom. As the kingdom of God is *His* kingdom,[2] so also the banquet of God's kingdom is *His* banquet.[3] "My supper" is therefore the feast of God's Messianic kingdom. And so with this declaration Jesus expressly recurs to that utterance of one of the guests which furnished the occasion of the narrative. "Blessed is he that shall eat bread in the kingdom of God," the guest had said, meaning that this enjoyment was indefeasibly certain to him and his brethren, like a natural right. To this Jesus replied with the narrative of a banquet, in which the attitude of those originally invited was such that they were all excluded from the feast, and then, in conclusion, pledges His word that at *His* feast—the feast of God's Messianic kingdom—this general exclusion of the originally invited will in fact take place. The purpose of the parable is now clear. It is this, to tell His Pharisaic hearers, who think they have a right to enjoy the blessings of God's kingdom in virtue of their belonging to God's chosen nation, *that the chosen nation, instead of possessing an indefeasible claim in its separate vocation to the blessedness of God's kingdom, will, on the contrary, be excluded in its entirety from this kingdom in favour of others because of its present attitude to the message of the kingdom of God.* And to this purpose, as a review of the course of the narrative at once shows, the parable is faithful, exhibiting in its first part, in figurative form, the present attitude of the chosen people to the message of God's kingdom, and in its second part describing the consequences which will and must accrue to the nation from this attitude.

From this point of view the interpretation of the course of the narrative must now be worked out in detail. The fundamental idea of the parable standing at the head, as supplied to the Lord by the general situation and the special utterance of the Pharisaic guest, ver. 15, is that of a banquet. Meat and drink, satisfying

---

[1] Cf. ix. 27; Acts x. 10, xx. 11, *et al.*   [2] Cf. *e.g.* Matt. xiii. 41.
[3] Cf. xxii. 30 and Matt. xxii. 2.

man's hunger and thirst, and rejoicing his heart, serve already in the Old Testament as a figure for the spiritual blessings of divine communion, satiating and filling with joy the hungering, thirsting souls of the good.[1] In accordance with this view, the predictions of the prophets represent the blessedness of the future kingdom of God and the Messianic salvation under the figure of a rich, costly banquet,[2] which God prepares in order to satisfy the souls of men.[3] This representation suggests, on one hand, the current Jewish notion of the banquet of Messiah's kingdom, ver. 15, and, on the other, the corresponding figurative language of Jesus.[4] Thus, the banquet prepared by the householder in the parable is the entire sum of the spiritual blessings offered by God in His kingdom to men in order to confer perfect satisfaction and blessedness on the souls starving and perishing in estrangement from Him (xv. 17). It was a *great* banquet which the householder prepared, *i.e.* God's preparatory arrangements aimed from the first at embracing a great number of men in His kingdom, and at making them happy through its blessings. But when, according to the narrative, one part of the great preparations made by the householder was that, before the feast itself was ready, he "invited many," and when we add that these "many" figure everywhere in the sequel as "the invited" in the sense of a privileged class, and, further, in contrast with the homeless in the streets and the foreign aliens, figure as the resident citizens of the city, there can no longer be any doubt who the "many" are, and what is to be understood by the preliminary invitation addressed to them,—they are the members of the chosen nation, the citizens of the Old-Testament theocracy, to whom the establishment of God's Messianic kingdom was previously announced through the word of prophecy, and before whom the prospect of participation therein was spread. And as, when the hour of the feast is come, the householder sends the message to the invited ones: Come, for all things are now ready, so now, that with the appearance of Christ the hour of the realization of God's kingdom has struck, the call goes forth to the members of the chosen nation with divine authority to enter by repentance and faith into the divine kingdom promised of old, but now realized. In this statement the meaning of ver. 17 is fully reproduced, and there

---

[1] Cf. Ps. xxiii. 5, xxxiv. 10, xxxvi. 8, cvii. 9; Prov. ix. 1-6, *et al.*
[2] Isa. xxv. 6.   [3] Isa. lv. 1-3.
[4] Cf. xiii. 29, xxii. 30; Matt. v. 6, viii. 11, xxvi. 29.

is no occasion to apply the servant carrying the message to one or several definite persons. For indispensable as was the introduction of his person for the construction of the narrative as the agent of the message, ver. 17, the bringer of the answer, ver. 21, the organ of the commands, vv. 21, 23, on the other hand, his importance entirely ceases with the execution of these commissions. The only point treated of everywhere is the execution of the commissions, never anywhere the character of the person who executes them. It is not then to be wondered at that all attempts to assign a definite interpretation to the person of the servant prove unsatisfactory. The most popular application to the person of Jesus,[1] which in ver. 17 at least seems really appropriate, is untenable, because in ver. 23 the apostles must be suddenly substituted for Jesus Himself.[2] The application to several persons[3] is impossible, because the servant in the parable is only *one* person, and least of all a "collective individual." Only by transgressing the limits of exact interpretation, indeed, can we say, in more precisely expounding the import of the parable: To the servant really correspond at each point of the narrative those persons who at different times, as matter of fact, executed the divine commission given; and therefore in ver. 17 John the Baptist and Jesus Himself, in ver. 21 again Jesus Himself, and in ver. 23 the apostles, especially a Paul and all missionaries to the heathen.

But over against this message of the realized kingdom of God, as it now goes forth to Israel, appears a strange attitude on the part of the chosen nation, resembling that of the "invited" in the parable. The latter gratefully accepted the preliminary invitation. But in presence of the call actually to come, they all began with one consent to excuse themselves. So, too, the members of the chosen nation in the theocracy. The promise given them of the *future* kingdom of God they gratefully accepted, glorying in its blessedness as a possession reserved for them, to which they have a claim. But when the announcement of the kingdom of God *already in existence*, and the call to enter it, *now* reach them, they are deaf to the announcement, and harden themselves against the call. And this is not simply the attitude of a portion of them,

---

[1] Stier, Meyer, van Oosterzee, Nebe.

[2] Cf. Meyer: "This commission to the servant was fulfilled by Jesus through the apostles."

[3] Luther, Lisco (John the Baptist and the apostles).

with which the willing obedience of another portion stands in contrast, but it is the unanimous attitude of the whole theocratic hierarchy, and of the entire nation subject to its influence and within the theocratic ordinances. This unanimity of the entire official Israel in rejecting the message of the kingdom was therefore clearly perceived by Jesus when He related this parable. Certain individual exceptions, simply because of their isolated character, and therefore not affecting the national unanimity, do not come into account in the figurative representation.

What the inner reason of this strange phenomenon is, the narrative now further shows, in the three refusals which it puts into the mouth of three individuals among the invited ones by way of characterizing all. The common meaning of the three answers was this: They feel themselves inconveniently disturbed in their comfortable occupation with the properties they have acquired by the call to the feast of the householder, and, in order to enjoy this possession of theirs, treat the feast with contempt. Thus, apart from figure, the inner reason of the unanimity of Israel in rejecting the message of God's kingdom is this: They have acquired worldly wealth and earthly possessions, and have become inwardly identified with them; they have made themselves comfortable and thoroughly at home in the world, like a landowner who has made a purchase, or a farm proprietor who has filled his stalls with cattle, or a householder who, with his wife beside him, has set up housekeeping. They feel themselves inconveniently disturbed in the enjoyment of these earthly possessions of theirs by the call to God's kingdom; they neither can nor will tear their heart from these things, as that call demands of them. And because they are so captivated by their earthly possessions, because they prefer the temporal gratification which these things give them to the supreme good of God's kingdom offered by divine grace, therefore they refuse to enter into God's kingdom, therefore they despise the call of divine grace. And this despising is everywhere the same, whatever the form in which it appears, whether as a courteous, cool declining, or as an open, hostile contradiction. This it is which Jesus wishes the hearers to understand by the more or less courteous form in which He clothes the substantially quite similar answers of the three invited ones. And He does this, as we may suppose in conformity with the situation, not without special reference to the relation to Himself of the Pharisaic host and his guests, who thought they could unite the outwardly courteous forms of social intercourse with their inwardly negative attitude to the Lord and His preaching of the kingdom of God. Therefore it is not three classes of men, distinguished by essentially different causes of resistance to the divine call, which are meant to be typified by the three speakers among the guests,—as Stier supposes, who distinguishes property, trade, and lust as three grounds of refusal; and Nebe, the thorns of care, riches, and lust; while older expositors refer the three answers to three classes: the priestly class as cultivators of land, the class of worldly governors as oxen, according to Ps. xxii. 17, and the family state.[1] The investigation of the wording of the narrative has already cut away the ground from beneath all attempts in this direction. They are wrecked, if on nothing else, on this circumstance, that the distinction between the first and the second of the answerers, which ought, of course, to be just as sharply carried out as that between the first two and the third,—if any distinction at all is to be made,—is obviously a forced one. Rather the purport of the threefold exemplification is simply to show that, amid the certainly more or less sharply-manifested opposition, it is everywhere the same inward attachment to objects of earthly possession which causes Israel to despise the invitation to become possessors of the supreme good of the kingdom of God.

After the first part of the parable has thus exhibited the present attitude of Israel to the message of God's kingdom as a unanimous despising of the salvation offered by God, the second part pictures the consequences which such an attitude must entail. Like as the despising of his feast on the part of those invited excited the wrath of the householder, so must such a despising of His grace on the part of those called before all others to His kingdom, excite the just wrath of the holy God. And like as the householder in his wrath quickly sends out into the streets of the city, and instead of the resident citizens commands the beggars and cripples of the streets to be brought in, so the punishment threatened by divine wrath to the citizens of the Israelitish theocracy, and following directly at the heels of their scorn, is this, that the message of God's kingdom will be taken from them and sent to those unhappy classes who, although living within Israel, and belonging to it in the natural sense, are yet destitute of civic rights in the theocratic commonwealth—there-

[1] Augustine, Luther.

fore to the numerous classes of "publicans and sinners," who, although Israelites in blood, were excluded from the theocratic community, and put on a level with the heathen (Matt. xviii. 17). God's will and commission is that they be "*brought in*," *i.e.* that the timid diffidence in regard to the gospel of God's kingdom, natural to them in their circumstances hitherto, be overcome by friendly instruction and guidance, and that they be thus brought to the blessedness of this kingdom—for no other resistance, no contempt like that of the called citizens of the theocracy, is to be feared on the part of these unhappy ones. That we have rightly interpreted the beggars and cripples of the streets is evident from the twofold antithesis in which they stand, on one hand, as the homeless *street*-populace to the resident citizens, and, on the other, as the *city*-populace to the aliens of the high-roads, ver. 23. The latter antithesis, so plainly indicated in the narrative, is effaced, if by the beggars and cripples we understand the heathen.[1] But even the usual distinction made between the invited ones and the beggars, as between the representatives of the theocracy—the *leaders* and *heads* of the people—on the one hand, and the *poor* nation itself on the other,[2] does not in this form exactly correspond to the parable. For as certainly as the "called many" (ver. 16) meant the calling of the *nation* of Israel in its entirety (which is undisputed), so certainly the "called" afterwards cannot be limited merely to the leaders and heads of the nation, and thus to the classes of the Pharisees and scribes ruling in the days of Jesus; but we must distinguish, as above, between the nation of Israel as the body of citizens of the theocratic commonwealth on the one hand, and the excluded, homeless classes, in the theocratic sense, on the other. Consequently the corresponding fact in the historical development to this turn in the narrative is, that in the same degree in which the message of God's kingdom encountered resistance and contempt in the theocratically intact Israel, Jesus addressed Himself with this message to the rejected, despised classes of "publicans and sinners."[3] But we need not on this account seek two periods in the ministry of Jesus, periods separated by a definite point of time.[4] The succession of two missions, in order of time, is

---

[1] Gerlach: "The heathen dwelling near the place and time of the appearance of Christ;" Lisco: "The proselytes from the heathen, or the heathen dwelling among the Jews."

[2] Cf. *e.g.* Meyer, Nebe, van Oosterzee.   [3] Cf. xv. 1 ; Matt. xxi. 31.

[4] *E.g.* Nebe: The first ministry in Judea and Jerusalem, and the later in Galilee.

merely the figurative form of the narrative necessary in order to describe pictorially the inner connection of the second divine commission with the failure of the first. And if we have rightly interpreted the angry words of the householder ("Go out quickly") to mean, that the divine wrath makes the bringing in of the publicans and sinners follow directly upon the scornful resistance of the citizens of the theocracy, then the narrative itself contains here an intimation of the historical circumstance, that the fulfilment of the first divine commission in the theocratic Israel, and that of the second in the rejected classes of the nation, directly interlace with each other in the ministry of Jesus, since the calling of the latter takes place already, whilst the contempt of the former is still consummating itself in inveterate malignity.

Consequently, according to what has been said, the calling of the despised, outcast classes of the Jewish nation had for theocratic Israel the significance of a threat of exclusion by divine wrath from the Messianc salvation. But that this exclusion of theocratic Israel, which with one consent despised the invitation to the kingdom of God, will be final and universal,—this is the meaning of the second sending forth of the servant, forming the conclusion of the narrative, ver. 23. Like as it appears, after the beggars and cripples are brought in from the streets, that the great table of the householder still contains room for more guests, so the calling of the despised outcasts of the Jewish nation will not suffice to conduct to God's kingdom that complement of members which it is meant in the divine plan to embrace and bless. But like as the householder on the announcement of the fact sends the servant away from the city into the high-roads to find guests for his food, so, after the rejected unhappy classes of Israel are gathered, the gospel of God's kingdom will address itself to the heathen, its messengers will by the divine commission traverse "the ways of the Gentiles" (Matt. x. 5), who hitherto, outside the preparatory Old-Testament theocracy, and without contact with it, had gone their own ways—the ways of aliens, without knowing the God of Israel, or being aware of the promises of His kingdom. And just this distance and estrangement of theirs, which must needs make it hard for them to believe and obey the invitation so unexpectedly given them to partake of the salvation of God's kingdom manifested in Christ, are to be overcome by the "compulsion" enjoined. Seeing that in their case it is not merely a surprise, as it is to the outcast of

Israel, that the gospel of God's kingdom is addressed to *them*, but that this message itself is something new in every respect, and the God who sends it to them is a God hitherto unknown, the "compel" enjoins a calling and inviting, friendly and urgent, in a heightened degree, in order to give them courage to believe and obey. Every interpretation of the command: "compel to come in," which goes beyond this point, with a view to justifying the use of *outward* compulsion in the sphere of foreign or home missions, is just as unwarranted by the meaning of these words given in the context as the certainly worse misinterpretation which Augustine gave them in the strife with the Donatists in reference to the force to be used in case of necessity against the disobedience of heretics. Thus the circumstance, that the gathering of the despised and outcast of the Jewish nation merely into God's kingdom, does not satisfy the comprehensive purpose of divine love, will not benefit the theocratic Israel, which with one consent despised the call of God; but, the latter being finally and utterly excluded, the divine end will be realized by the calling of the heathen. That is, the complement of members, corresponding to the comprehensive plan of divine love and to the means devised for its execution, will be gathered into His kingdom and made partakers of the Messianic salvation. Finally, when at the close, in order to confirm the import of the narrative, Jesus added the asseveration, that none of those men invited should taste of His feast, the meaning, apart from figure, is that none of the members of theocratic Israel called in the first instance, who, under the leading of the Pharisees, with fixed unanimity despised the call to God's kingdom, shall partake in the Messianic salvation. To this theocratic Israel therefore, in its entirety, He expressly announces the doom of exclusion from the kingdom of God. But to the individual hearers of the parable it is declared, in allusion to the utterance of the particular guest (ver. 15), that instead of having an indefeasible claim to the blessedness of God's kingdom in virtue of their belonging to the chosen nation, they can only hope to become partakers in it by withdrawing, as individuals, from solidarity with their fellow-countrymen, and having the courage to break with the chosen nation of the theocracy in its inner condition at that time.

A comparison of this parable of the Great Banquet with that

of the Fig-Tree (chap. xiii.), previously examined, is suggested by the similarity in their purport. That which is common to both is the announcement of the divine judgment upon Israel, the chosen nation of the old covenant,—there, positively as a penal judgment fatal to the national existence of the people; here, negatively as the exclusion of the nation from the Messianic salvation. On the other hand, the purport of the two parables differs in this respect, that there the possibility is retained, although only with faint hope, of a conversion of Israel taking place at the eleventh hour in consequence of the ministry of Jesus; while here, on the other hand, the starting-point is Israel's unanimous obduracy against the message of salvation coming to them, as an already accepted fact. To this correspond the further differences, that there the divine judgment is proclaimed to the nation conditionally; here, on the other hand, the penal sentence of exclusion from the salvation of God's kingdom is expressed unconditionally,—and again, that there the thought, that room must be made by hewing down the fig-tree—Israel—for planting other nations in its place in the vineyard of God's kingdom, is only briefly and enigmatically hinted in the words: "Why does it also cumber the ground?"[1] whereas here the calling of the heathen to the kingdom of God instead of Israel is predicted in the plainest and most definite manner. For these reasons we must believe that the parable of the Great Banquet in chap. xiv. belongs to a later period in the life and teaching of Jesus than that of the Fig-Tree in chap. xiii., a conclusion which presents no difficulty upon the correct view of the section of Luke's Gospel, reaching from ix. 46 to xviii. 30, as a collection of sayings and discourses of Jesus not professing to be a chronologically consecutive account of a journey.

[1] See on xiii. 7.

THE THREE PARABLES, LUKE XV.

The first two verses of chap. xv. tell us the occasion of the parables which follow, and, in the first place, of the three contained in this chapter. It is said: ἦσαν δὲ αὐτῷ ἐγγίζοντες πάντες οἱ τελῶναι καὶ οἱ ἁμαρτωλοὶ ἀκούειν αὐτοῦ. The πάντες cannot be a mere hyperbole of the narrative, for to say "all" instead of "many" would be an inadmissible exaggeration. Still less may we translate "publicans and sinners of every kind," for πάντες is not "of every kind." Rather πάντες is to be left in its ordinary literal sense: "*all publicans and sinners were drawing near to Him*," i.e. there was a general streaming on the part of this class of people to Jesus. The meaning also of ἦσαν ἐγγίζοντες is thus exactly reproduced. For if the coming near to Jesus on the part of this class of people was general, of course it was also continuous, which is meant to be expressed by ἦσαν ἐγγίζοντες. Then "*the Pharisees and scribes murmured*" at the reception which these publicans and sinners found with Jesus, saying: "*This man receives sinners and eats with them*," ver. 2. Thus we have here an altogether similar situation to the one in Matt. ix. 10, 11, of which passage we are reminded by the objection, "eateth with them." Certainly it must be left undecided whether these words here, as well as there, are spoken with reference to the situation at the moment, so that we should have to think of Jesus here also as sitting at table with people of that class, or whether they refer to what Jesus usually did at other times. In any case, we here see the Lord occupied with publicans and sinners, and, at the same time, certain Pharisees and scribes who are offended at the spectacle, and who murmur so loudly that it reaches the ears of Jesus. Jesus then turns to these Pharisees and scribes, and utters to them, as ver. 3 tells us, the parable following in vv. 4–7, to which a second similar one is immediately linked, vv. 8–10. Then a third parable is joined to the former ones by a mere εἶπεν δέ, vv. 11–32, whereas the fourth parable and its sequel, chap. xvi. 1–13, are introduced with the phrase: ἔλεγεν δὲ καὶ πρὸς τοὺς μαθητάς. Only in this fourth parable, therefore, does the Lord turn from the Pharisees and scribes to "the disciples," and consequently the three parables of chap. xv. are all addressed to the Pharisees as the answer of Jesus to their murmurs. It is in this direction that we have to seek the central point of the parables.

THE LOST SHEEP.[1]
(Luke xv. 4-7.)

"What man among you will not do so and so in such and such a case?" In this way the Lord begins His first parable (ver. 4).[2] He does not begin a formal figurative story, but calls on each one of the murmuring Pharisees to transfer himself in thought into the position depicted in the two participial clauses: ἔχων ἑκατὸν πρόβατα καὶ ἀπολέσας ἓν ἐξ αὐτῶν, and therefore into the position of an owner of a flock who has lost one of his hundred sheep. The Lord then asks: τίς ἄνθρωπος ἐξ ὑμῶν— finding himself in this position—οὐ καταλείπει τὰ ἐνενήκοντα ἐννέα ἐν τῇ ἐρήμῳ, καὶ πορεύεται ἐπὶ τὸ ἀπολωλός, ἕως εὕρῃ αὐτό, i.e. whether any one of them will not leave the ninety and nine in their pasture in the wilderness, and go after the lost one (ἐπὶ τὸ ἀπολωλός) until he find it. The number a hundred, which we see here, is chosen as a round number readily suggesting itself for the entire number of the sheep forming a numerous flock, and is put so high in order to contrast a great number of sheep not lost with the one lost. And yet—so the persons interrogated must allow—every man would do as the Lord says for the sake of the one lost, because love of his property would impel him to such a course. In what follows (ver. 5 f.) the form of interrogation used at first is given up, the language, however, continuing without change in the direction marked out by the question. The narrative no longer speaks of a particular man who did so and so, but simply describes what it would be natural for a man to do in the circumstances here given, partly from the love of his property, which must be presumed to exist in every man, partly from the special tender feeling which a shepherd usually has for each individual sheep in his flock.[3] In this sense

---

[1] Respecting the relation of this parable to Matt. xviii. 12, 13, see at the close of the exposition.

[2] Cf. on chap. xi. 5 ff.

[3] That love of property does not enter into the question at all in this parable as the motive for seeking the lost one, but only tender sympathy for the stray sheep in

the description proceeds, ver. 5: "*And after he hath found it, he layeth it on his own shoulders*" (ἐπὶ τοὺς ὤμους ἑαυτοῦ), which is not meant to emphasize the fact that he did not give it to another—a servant—to carry, as many explain, but simply emphasizes the trouble he took in carrying it more strongly than would be the case with the simple ἐπὶ τοὺς ὤμους without ἑαυτοῦ. And, indeed, he submits to this trouble "*joyfully* (χαίρων), *and after he has come home*" he again does what a man cannot but do who has met with great cause for joy, "*he calls together his friends and neighbours*," and calls upon them to share in his joy with loving sympathy: "*Rejoice with me, for I have found my sheep which was lost*," ver. 6.

When, then, Jesus adds to this close of the parable, ver. 7: λέγω ὑμῖν ὅτι οὕτως χαρὰ ἐν τῷ οὐρανῷ ἔσται ἐπὶ ἑνὶ ἁμαρτωλῷ μετανοοῦντι κ.τ.λ., it is clear that with this οὕτως He refers back expressly to the συγχάρητέ μοι (cf. vv. 9, 10). In allusion to the sympathetic joy so graphically requested from the assembled friends and neighbours, Jesus testifies that a like joy, a thrill, therefore, of loving sympathetic delight, will run through the inhabitants of heaven over a repenting sinner. Of course this declaration of Jesus, as will be shown in investigating it more closely, does not give the interpretation proper, but merely a special application of the parable. But this we may already learn from it, that the theme of the parable is the conversion of sinners, and that an essential element of its purpose lies in the summons to sympathetic joy expressed at the close. And this is placed beyond doubt when we combine with the declaration the occasion of the parable, which, according to vv. 1, 2, lay in that which is the opposite of such sympathizing joy —the murmuring of the Pharisees at the intercourse of Jesus with sinners. Consequently the purpose of the parable is this— to tell the Pharisaic hearers *that, instead of having a right to murmur at the trouble which Jesus took with sinners, they ought rather to rejoice with Him over the conversion of sinners.*

Let us see how this purpose is worked out in the parable. We observed at the outset that in the present parable we have,

its misery (so Godet, similarly von Hofmann), is saying too much, and is not warranted in the text. Rather the seeker's effort in ver. 4 is plainly directed to the recovery of the property that he has lost, and it is in ver. 5 that we first meet in his action with signs of the tender feeling for the sheep that is lost, such as the figure used suggested. Accordingly, the inferences drawn from this view to the specific difference of this parable from the following one are without ground.

as to form, no narrative before us, but a question relating to a supposed case, a question which then takes the form of a description of what in this case every one would feel himself impelled to do. But the question with which the parable opens is obviously quite similar to the question of Jesus on another occasion, Matt. xii. 11: "What man shall there be of you that shall have one sheep, and if this fall into a pit on the Sabbath day, will he not lay hold on it, and lift it out?" And the very words added there by Jesus Himself: πόσῳ οὖν διαφέρει ἄνθρωπος προβάτου· ὥστε ἔξεστι τοῖς σάββασιν καλῶς ποιεῖν, point us to the right way of interpreting the present parabolic language. "How much better is a man than a sheep!" Here is the key to the interpretation. To the Pharisees who murmur at His intercourse with publicans and sinners, Jesus replies by an inference *a minori ad majus*. What any one would do for his sheep, justifies what Jesus does for the children of men. Accordingly, the first thought of the parable is this: If for the sake of a lost sheep a man will leave behind ninety and nine not lost, and take every pains to seek and bring back the lost one, how should not Jesus take every pains in going after the lost children of men, *i.e.* sinners, and restoring them; and how can it be made a reproach to Him that He interests Himself in personal intercourse about each individual among them, and for that individual's sake leaves behind those not lost? In this comparison it is assumed that sinners are God's property; nay, strictly taken, that they are the property of Jesus; that they are lost *to Him* through their sin, and hence that He seeks lovingly to win them back to *Himself*. Moreover, a testimony of Jesus Himself to His divine dignity lies hidden in this and the following parable. Further, the occasion of the parable puts it beyond doubt to whom the Lord refers in contrasting the ninety and nine sheep not lost with the one lost sheep, so that His seeking the lost one becomes also a leaving behind the ninety and nine. He can only refer here to the murmuring Pharisees, into whose thoughts He pierces. To their pride, the disparagement with which they were treated in comparison with the publicans and sinners seemed the greatest scandal. The consideration that the impenitent Pharisees appear as not lost in comparison with the penitent publicans and sinners ought not to mislead us, since the Lord, in arguing with the Pharisees, was obliged in the first instance to speak from their point of view. Add to this, that as regards the righteousness of outward morality, the contrast was not without real ground. Further, the fact that Jesus not merely speaks of such a man seeking the sheep until he finds it, but also of his personal toil in bringing it back, does not warrant the supposition that He meant by this to symbolize a twofold activity in reference to the sinner. It simply depicts all the trouble which such a man will take with the lost sheep, so far as the nature of the figure permits, in order to justify in the manner explained above all the trouble which Jesus takes with the conversion of the sinner.

So far, therefore, the parable is a *self-justification* of Jesus against the attacks of the murmuring Pharisees. But by this *refutation* of the murmurers He has prepared the ground for the *rebuke* of them to which He now advances. After showing them that they have no right to murmur, He then says that, if they were in a right state, the precise opposite would be natural to them, namely, the joy of loving sympathy. For in what follows, ver. 6, it is not so much the personal joy of the owner of the sheep that is spoken of,—this is self-evident after what has been said, and is only cursorily mentioned even in the χαίρων, ver. 5,—but a summons to others to sympathizing joy. Accordingly, the thought of the parable continues thus: If such a man claims the sympathizing joy of his neighbours and friends because he has found his sheep, how should not Jesus call on us to share His joy at the conversion of sinners, instead of murmuring? Thus, with the συγχάρητέ μοι this and the following parable pass over into a reproachful admonition to the Pharisees.[1]

Incomparably striking and humiliating is the special application which Jesus now makes of the parable in the declaration introduced by the emphatic "I say unto you." The last sentence of the parable has shown how just is His demand on others to rejoice with Him over the conversion of sinners. He might now have applied this thought expressly and directly to the Pharisees in some such words as: "I say to you, you ought also to rejoice," and so on, which certainly would have been the smoothest ending of the parable. But He does not do so. On the contrary, His words run, ver. 7: λέγω ὑμῖν ὅτι οὕτως χαρὰ ἐν τῷ οὐρανῷ ἔσται ἐπὶ ἑνὶ ἁμαρτωλῷ μετανοοῦντι κ.τ.λ. Instead, therefore, of saying to the Pharisees that it was their duty to

[1] In the third parable the entire concluding section corresponds to the present conclusion.

share His joy, He prefers to remind them where His joy over the conversion of sinners is really shared, namely, in heaven by the angels of God; and it is evident what a humiliating effect this language must have had on the murmurers. That the angels are referred to in the expression "in heaven," is proved by the parallel, ver. 10, where the expression is somewhat varied: "in the presence of the angels of God."[1] Certainly the joy of God also is self-evidently included, since it is the necessary postulate for the joy of angels. The future ἔσται is used, because the case of a sinner's conversion is viewed as one constantly repeated in the future. It gives, therefore, no materially different sense from that in the parallel passage, ver. 10, where a present γίνεται occurs. To suppose ourselves obliged to search for a deeper reason in such diversities of expression, without considering how natural such slight changes of phraseology are in a statement recurring after an interruption, is to embark on misleading paths. The humiliating effect of this application is then essentially strengthened when to the words: ἐπὶ ἑνὶ ἁμαρτωλῷ μετανοοῦντι the Lord adds, with a backward glance at what was said in the beginning of the parable, ver. 4: ἢ ἐπὶ ἐνενήκοντα ἐννέα δικαίοις οἵτινες οὐ χρείαν ἔχουσιν μετανοίας. That by the "ninety and nine righteous persons" only righteous persons of the class of the Pharisees so solemnly addressed in "I say unto you," and thus the righteous in the outwardly legal sense, are meant, cannot remain doubtful to us after all that has been said above in interpreting the parable generally, and especially the leaving behind of the ninety and nine sheep not lost, to which figurative trait there is clear reference here. And when Jesus calls them righteous persons, "*who* (οἵτινες) *need no repentance,*" He says this again just from their point of view. From His point of view He would speak of no class of men at all in this way.[2] As has been remarked, this is said with a sort of sacred irony. Accordingly, in His application to the Pharisees, Jesus reminds them of two things which may humiliate them,—first, that *joy* (χαρά put first with emphasis) is in heaven over that very thing from which

---

[1] Cf. on ver. 10.

[2] The expression of adherence to the assumption of the opponents lies precisely in the word οἵτινες, indicating motive, which Weiss quotes against the above interpretation (in his revision of Meyer's *Commentary*). Also in opposition to Hofmann, who understands such as have already yielded obedience to the call to repentance, it may be remarked that they who have become what they are by means of repentance cannot possibly be spoken of as those who do not need it.

they took occasion to murmur—the conversion of the sinner; and secondly, that the angels of God have more joy in one sinner who repents than in ninety and nine righteous persons like them.

The parable of the Stray Sheep in Matthew (xviii. 12, 13) resembles Luke's parable of the Lost Sheep almost feature by feature, and yet is essentially different from it. For it not merely stands in quite a different context, but is also of essentially different meaning from Luke's parable. There (Matt. xviii. 10) the parable is preceded by a testimony to the providential care exercised by God over every believer in Jesus, even the least:[1] "*I say to you, their angels in heaven (i.e. the angels charged to watch over them) always behold the face of my Father in heaven*," so that everything which concerns them is always brought before God. To this assurance is then joined the parabolic question,[2] vv. 12, 13: "*How think ye? If any man have a hundred sheep, and one of them be gone astray, doth he not leave the ninety and nine, and go unto the mountains, and seek that which goeth astray? And if so be that he find it, verily I say unto you, he rejoiceth over it more than over the ninety and nine which have not gone astray.*" And the interpreting words of Jesus at once say in what sense the figurative language is here meant, ver. 14: "*Even so it is not the will of your Father which is in heaven, that one of these little ones should perish.*" We see that while the same figurative circumstances are worked out in almost the same way, they are employed to set forth quite a different point of doctrine. In Luke's parable the matter in hand is, first, a justification of the special trouble taken by Jesus in winning and converting each individual of the morally low class of publicans and sinners, while disparaging the morally righteous who thought they had no need of repentance; and secondly, His claim on others to rejoice with Him, instead of murmuring, at the conversion of every sinner. Here, on the contrary, the matter in hand is a testimony, first to the special care which God takes even of the least believer in Jesus, to save him from being misled and lost; and then to the special divine joy at the preservation of such a "little one" who was in danger of being lost—both in comparison with those believers who do not need

[1] Cf. ver. 6.
[2] Even if the eleventh verse: "for the Son of man is come to save the lost," should be genuine, contrary to the opinion of Lachmann and Tischendorf.

care of this kind in the same degree, and for this reason are less an object of such joy. The position of things, therefore, is not that Matthew's parable of the Stray Sheep merely occurs in a different context from the one in Luke, or the converse; but Luke's parable of the Lost, and Matthew's of the Stray Sheep, are two quite different parables in purport. This is the actual state of the case which exegesis discovers directly that it does justice to each of the two passages in their connection. And with this actual state of the case criticism ought to reckon, instead of pronouncing critical judgment in the usual hasty, off-hand critical way on a mere similarity of sound, without the essential preliminary toil of independent exegesis.

The Lost Coin.

(Luke xv. 8-10.)

We return to the fifteenth chapter of Luke's Gospel. In ver. 8 Jesus addresses a second question to the Pharisees, similar to the one put in ver. 4, and joined to the latter by a simple "or." We are thus confirmed in the view that the description of vv. 5 and 6 was only meant to be a continuation of the question asked in ver. 4; for only on this supposition could a second question be so directly joined to the first, after the description has intervened. Further, this connection of the second question with the first by a simple "or," leads us to expect that in the following parable Jesus will merely present the same subject in another manner, and forbids the attempt to find a special distinction in the contents of the two parables. And so, in fact, we find this second parabolic question similar to the first in every respect. As Jesus then put the case of a man having lost one of a hundred sheep, so here He puts that of a woman having lost one of ten drachmæ; and then asks here, as there, whether such a woman will not take every pains in seeking the lost piece of money; whether she will not light a lamp (in order to illuminate even the dark corners and rooms of the house) and sweep the house, and seek diligently until she find it. The fact of the trouble of seeking being delineated here in vivid detail, otherwise than in the first parable, is due to the nature of the figure used. The effort put forth in recovering a lost coin can only consist in seeking it, and is at an end when it is found. On this account, the stress of the thought lies simply on the trouble of seeking; whereas, in the first parable, where the labour of bringing back was added to the trouble of seeking, any special delineation of the latter was unnecessary. To the same circumstance it is also due that Jesus here speaks of a woman, not of a man. This has merely the psychological reason that such unwearied zeal in seeking for a lost piece of money is far more natural to a woman than a man; and we ought justly to admire this psychologically fine feature, instead of seeking a special interpretation of the woman in distinction from the first parable, and understanding the Church or even the Holy Spirit.[1] And the reason is similar of the number of the drachmæ being put much lower than the number of the sheep in the first parable. There the number might be placed so high, because to the owner of a flock even the single lost sheep has a value in itself, and not merely as a part of his entire property. But the value which a small piece of money like a drachme[2] has in the eyes of the owner is measured simply by the number of such pieces forming the entire amount of his property. And thus here, unless so earnest a search for a lost drachme was to appear exaggerated, only a small number of such pieces could be represented as in the woman's possession. If, then, we have hitherto found the second parable different from the first only in so far as was involved in the difference of the figure used, so now we do not find it otherwise with the conclusion, ver. 9. In keeping with the first parable, the Lord passes on from the question, whether the woman will not seek the lost piece of money till she find it, to describe what she will do when she has found it, namely, she will call together her neighbours and friends, and summon them to rejoice with her over the recovery of the lost money. It is to be noticed that the personal joy of the owner, which we found mentioned, at least cursorily, in the first parable, by the $\chi\alpha i\rho\omega\nu$ added at the close of ver. 5, is here merely assumed in silence. Nothing but the summons to rejoice in common is spoken of, a proof that we must seek an essential element of the purpose of the two parables in this summons to rejoice in common.

After all that has been said, we shall not go astray in finding exactly the same purpose in the present parable as in the parable of the Lost Sheep, and in interpreting it in the same way: If a woman, possessing ten drachmæ, uses all possible care in finding

[1] Stier.   [2] Worth about 8d.

one that is lost, how should not Jesus take all care and trouble in winning back to Himself lost sinners? And if such a woman call on her neighbours and friends to rejoice with her over the drachme found again, how should not Jesus require that we rejoice with Him over sinners won back to Him in their conversion?

Thus we have certainly found in the second parable merely a recurrence of the thoughts of the first, without essentially new features. To those who call this a mere repetition, and think themselves bound to repudiate the very notion of such a thing in the language of the Lord,[1] it is to be replied that a mere repetition, such as might justly be called superfluous, is not found here. For what we have before us is indeed a recurrence of the same thoughts, but under another figure. And the force of this second parable, and the motive for adding it to the first, lie precisely in the fact of the same thoughts recurring in exactly similar fashion under another figurative form, and thus being, so to speak, attested and confirmed anew in the second figure.

In ver. 10, again, the same application meets us as in ver. 7. Again the Lord reminds the Pharisees at the close that His desire for sharers in His joy, expressed in ver. 9, is fulfilled in the joy of the angels of God over the conversion of the sinner. It has certainly been said, in allusion to the fundamental meaning of the preposition ἐνώπιον, that the angels are not here thought of as the rejoicing persons, but God Himself, who makes known His joy *in presence of the angels*.[2] Such passages, however, as Acts vi. 5, and the corresponding Hebrew phrase לִפְנֵי, in Ex. xxviii. 38, Dan. i. 9, *et al.*, show that the use of ἐνώπιον is diversified enough to do away with the basis of this certainly forced exposition. In such cases the preposition ἐνώπιον is not used differently from the German preposition " bei," originally denoting a local relation.[3] Therefore here: "*There is* (γίνεται, springs up, arises) *joy with the angels of God*," *i.e.* the angels of God rejoice. That God's joy is certainly not excluded, but included, was already remarked in ver. 7. " Over one sinner that repenteth," is this time said without adducing any further comparison, such as we found in ver. 7. With a different numerical relation in the second parable, the former comparison could only have recurred here in a flat, insipid form. Instead of this, the thought here comes out all the more clearly, that the conversion

---

[1] Stier, and similarly Olshausen.   [2] Meyer, van Oosterzee.
[3] [The same is perhaps true of the corresponding English preposition "with."]

of but one sinner is enough to move the angels of God to joy, which thought in ver. 7 was thrown into the shade by the other, that one repenting sinner is an object of joy to the angels more than ninety and nine righteous persons.

The Lost Son.

(Luke xv. 11-32.)

With the words εἶπεν δέ, ver. 11, the evangelist makes the transition to a third parable; and this transition is characteristic of the relation of the parable which now follows to the two preceding ones. Whereas we saw the latter, in keeping with their mutual resemblance in form and substance, following directly one on the other in continuous flow, the εἶπεν δέ now interposed intimates that the discourse has here come to a provisional conclusion, and takes a fresh start. Transition is made to the narration of a new parable, independent of the two previous ones in its plan. But, at the same time, the fact of the transition being made simply with the brief εἶπεν δέ, intimates that the following parable, different as it is from the two previous ones, is spoken to the same persons and on the same occasion as the former ones, leading us to expect that it will be allied to them in contents and purpose.

The parable opens, not in an interrogative, but in a positively narrative form: "*A man had two sons, and the younger of them said to his father, Father, give me the portion of the property falling to me*" (belonging to me). The younger son, therefore, asks the father to hand over at once to his free disposal the portion of the property that would fall to him in due time by the existing law of inheritance. According to the Hebrew law of inheritance,[1] twice as large a portion is due in the distribution to the firstborn as to the later-born sons. In this case, therefore, the firstborn son was the chief heir, to whom two-thirds of the entire property fell, whilst the younger son must be content with the last third only. Thus the context explains to us why the *younger* of the two is described as the one making such a request. It is evident how easily one who only took the third place in the household, after the father and after the chief heir, might conceive the desire to be allowed at least the free disposal

[1] Deut. xxi. 17.

of the fragment of property falling to him. His position, simply as a later-born son, must needs have stimulated and strengthened the impulse of false independence to which he yielded. But the older and modern exegetes are mistaken who explain the designation of the first-mentioned son as the younger by a reference to the frivolity of youth, and its liability to be led astray. For it is not even said that the one son is youthful and the other more advanced in age, but merely that it was the younger of the two who made the request, which leaves it quite undecided how old we are to think him. The conception of the younger brother as a frivolous youth has been taken only from what is further related of him.

The father complies with his request, as is said in the words: ὁ δὲ διεῖλεν αὐτοῖς τὸν βίον, i.e. "*he divided unto them his living*," paying over to the younger brother his share, whilst the bulk of the property was reserved for the older son abiding in the father's house as the chief heir. What use the younger one made of the property assigned him is stated in ver. 13 : καὶ μετ' οὐ πολλὰς ἡμέρας κ.τ.λ. Within a brief period it came out what prompted him to make the request to his father, namely, not so much the abstract right of disposal over his property, as rather the power to employ it without hindrance for a definite end—the unlimited indulgence of his sensual lusts. But to such a course the presence of the father and the morals of the household must always be an obstacle. Therefore: "*After a few days he gathered everything together, and took his journey into a far country.*" There he thought he could indulge his lusts in full liberty. Hence we read further: "*And there he wasted*[1] *his substance with riotous living*" (ζῶν ἀσώτως).

But what wretchedness awaited him in the strange country after brief sensual enjoyment is described to us in vv. 14–16: "*After he had spent all*" (his whole property), it is said, "*a great famine came over that country.*" The careful emphasizing of the fact that the famine extended *over that country* should not be overlooked. Only by observing this do we solve the difficulty, that it is the mention of the famine, as an event not due, however, to the lost son, which breaks the connection between his evil conduct and its evil fruits. The design is to point out how he found himself bitterly betrayed in the far country, where he thought he could enjoy his life in unfettered freedom. He might,

[1] διεσκόρπισεν, he scattered; observe the antithesis to the preceding συναγαγών.

indeed, there squander his property in brief sensual enjoyment; but when he has made an end of his property, he is compelled to find that that country has nothing further to give him but hunger and want. In the famine stretching over the country he comes to taste the bitter fruit of his thoughtless forsaking of his father's house. In what circumstances *he* is placed by the famine in the country is told us in the following words: καὶ αὐτὸς ἤρξατο ὑστερεῖσθαι. The αὐτός is not to be overlooked. For him, the stranger in that country, who, after squandering his property, had no means of help there, the consequence of the famine was, that he began to starve. Nothing was left to the stranger but to seek help from the natives of the country. Hence it follows in ver. 15 : "*and he went and attached himself to one of the citizens of that country.*" We ought not (as *e.g.* Stier does) to make this step a new reproach to him, interpreting it to mean that, instead of at once returning to his father's house, he seeks false self-helps in blind, settled apostasy. For in the connection of the narrative at least he is forced to this step by his circumstances; and the resolve to return home in the very beginning of his want, before making the attempt to help himself in that country, would appear to be without motive psychologically. The general emphasis of the narrative here lies, not on what the lost son did, but on what he had to suffer in that far country. Accordingly also the words : καὶ πορευθεὶς ἐκολλήθη κ.τ.λ., stand merely in the sense of a protasis, to which the words : καὶ ἔπεμψεν αὐτὸν κ.τ.λ., form the apodosis having the emphasis. That it is so is proved by the sudden change in the subject in the last clause.

When in his need he seeks help from the inhabitants of that country, he encounters at their hands only insulting harshness and a want of pity which, instead of alleviating his need, aggravates it in the highest degree. This is the general import of vv. 15, 16. The very word ἐκολλήθη intimates that the citizen of that country to whom he applied at first would fain have repelled him, and that he was only induced to take him into his service by persevering and urgent entreaty, and then only to aggravate his wretchedness in the highest degree. For, on the one hand, the service to which he appoints him is the meanest possible, and one most dishonourable to a Jew : "*He sent him into his fields to keep swine,*" ver. 15 ; and, on the other hand, what he gives him by way of recompense so little suffices to appease his hunger, that his hunger grows till he desires to be allowed to satisfy himself with the fodder of the swine: καὶ ἐπεθύμει γεμίσαι τὴν κοιλίαν αὐτοῦ ἀπὸ τῶν κερατίων, ὧν ἤσθιον οἱ χοῖροι, ver. 16. He desired to fill his belly with the pods of the St. John's bread-tree.[1] The former low expression for "satisfy himself" specially signalizes the dishonour implied in appeasing his hunger with such food. When it is added: "*and no one gave to him*," we can scarcely supply anything but κεράτια, although no stress is to be laid on it. For the thought expressed in these words is not that he could not even obtain κεράτια, but that no one—not one even—commiserated and appeased his gnawing hunger. The same pitiless cruelty which he had found in one of the inhabitants of that country he found in all.

Such bitter misery has his forsaking of his father's house and journeying into the far country brought him. The enjoyment of the blessings of his father's house was not enough for him, he had sought unbridled enjoyment of life in the far country; instead of this he has found destitution and hunger in that country, ver. 14. The father's love was a galling yoke to him; he had sought limitless freedom in the far country; instead of this he sees himself enslaved by the inhabitants of that country under a disgraceful yoke, with no sympathy for his bitter need, vv. 15, 16.

In this state of extremest wretchedness he comes to himself, and it is precisely the glaring contrast between his state of need and the comfort of his forsaken home which flashes on his mind and exercises overwhelming influence over him when he now comes to himself. Εἰς ἑαυτὸν δὲ ἐλθὼν ἔφη, so continues the narrative, ver. 17: *i.e.* "*When he had come to himself*," when he who had hitherto blindly followed his impulses without self-reflection now reflected on himself and his position, "*he said*," expressing the result of his self-reflection: Πόσοι μίσθιοι τοῦ πατρός μου περισσεύονται ἄρτων· ἐγὼ δὲ ὧδε λιμῷ ἀπόλλυμαι. He recalls how well off are his father's hired servants, not, as is usually understood, because he desires to compare his (the son's) wretchedness with the circumstances of the meanest servants of his father, but because to him as μίσθιος in his present wretchedness in this far country the condition of those found in like position with his father presents itself for purposes of comparison. He compares the lot of the hired servants there with his lot as μίσθιος here; the former, many as they are

[1] Translated by Luther aptly, but perhaps too strongly, *Träber*, grains. Cf. Winer, *Handwörterbuch*, art. "Johannisbrodbaum."

(πόσοι μίσθιοι), have superfluity of bread, "*while I here* (ἐγὼ δὲ ὧδε) *perish with hunger.*" We thus assume the genuineness of ὧδε and its emphatic position before λιμῷ, and therefore after the ἐγὼ δέ ending in similar letters, which position led to its omission in some manuscripts. And this thought of the superfluity enjoyed by his father's hired servants, in contrast with the need in which he is pining here, works so powerfully upon him that he comes to the determination to go to his father, and ask from him the favour of the like position as his hired servants possess. He expresses this determination without hiding from himself that in order to carry it out he will need to bestir himself. Hence in ver. 18 the ἀναστάς comes before πορεύσομαι πρὸς τὸν πατέρα μου. But that his father may not misunderstand his coming, as if he hoped for reception into the position of son again, he resolves to preface the utterance of the intended request by a confession of the guilt by which he has rendered himself unworthy of such a blessing. Before he ventures on his request, he will say: πάτερ, ἥμαρτον εἰς τὸν οὐρανὸν καὶ ἐνώπιον σοῦ κ.τ.λ. He resolves to characterize his sin as directed against heaven, and done in presence of his father,—the former, because he is conscious of having by his sin violated the ordinances of Him who is throned in heaven; the latter, because he specially reproaches himself with having plunged into sin before the eyes of his father. Heaven can only be meant here as the abode of the heavenly Being, to whose ordinances man owes obedience, not as the dwelling-place of angels, as in ver. 7. For although the angels, according to vv. 7, 10, rejoice over the conversion of sinners, and may therefore be analogously represented as sorrowing over the sin of men, sin cannot for this reason be described as directed against them, as a sinning against them, as would be the case on this interpretation of "against heaven." The avoidance of the definitely personal "against God," and the choice of the impersonal expression "against heaven," have their ground in this, that the relation between the sinner and God, symbolized by the relation between father and son, could not appear definitely in the figurative story alongside the human relation. He intends to prefix this confession in order, on its basis, to say of himself further, ver. 19: οὐκέτι εἰμὶ ἄξιος κληθῆναι υἱός σου. He will humbly acknowledge that by his guilt he has rendered himself unworthy of the name of son, and of the filial position expressed in the name. And after he has thus paved the way for his intended request, he will venture on the request itself: ποίησόν με ὡς ἕνα τῶν μισθίων σου, *i.c.* make me like one of thy hired servants, who are so well situated; cf. ver. 17. Thus the meaning of the ὡς is not: Make me, although a son, as low as one of thy hired servants, but on the correct reference of the request to ver. 17: Make me, who am perishing of hunger, as well off as one of thy hired servants.

Close on the resolve follows the execution, ver. 20 : καὶ ἀναστὰς ἦλθεν πρὸς τὸν πατέρα ἑαυτοῦ. But before he reaches his father's house everything is changed from what he had pictured to himself: ἔτι δὲ αὐτοῦ μακρὰν ἀπέχοντος, εἶδεν αὐτὸν ὁ πατὴρ αὐτοῦ. Of course we are not to take this as a remarkable coincidence, but the circumstance is to be regarded as a proof of the father's unextinguished love for his lost son. In yearning expectation of his son's return the father daily looks out along the road, and when he is now coming, the father, with the keen glance of love, discerns him from afar. "*And he had compassion,*" his heart beats with outgushing pity in response to the child returning in so sorrowful a plight, "*and he ran* (to meet him), *and fell on his neck, and covered him with kisses*" (κατεφίλησεν αὐτόν). With such unrestrained, overflowing manifestation of tender fatherly love does he receive the returning son, as if the latter's filial relation to the father had suffered no interruption—a reception which puts the son into a quite unexpected position. For he sees the request for the place of a hired servant, which he had come to prefer to the father, at once cut short by this reception. Infinitely more and better is given him than he had come to ask. And if he now utters the same words, excepting that request, with which he had resolved to approach his father according to vv. 18, 19, yet these words in the present circumstances have an essentially different reference from the one in which he had meant to utter them. There they were meant to be a penitent confession of his guilt and unworthiness in presence of a justly angry father, and were designed to dispose the father favourably, simply to move him not to refuse the request. Now, coming as they do from the lips of the child, whom the father has taken to his arms and heart, they are meant to tell the father how utterly unworthy he feels himself of this never-expected reception as a child to the father's heart; but they have no longer any reference to the request. We ought not therefore to say, as is often done, that the request is absent here, because the father did not allow the son to finish speaking, all the more that all intimation of such an interruption is wanting in the text. For the words of the father which follow cannot be taken in the light of an interruption, because they are directed to servants, who could not even have been present on the first meeting between father and son, which took place on the road outside. These words are rather to be viewed as spoken when the father brings the son from the road into the house. But certainly in them lies the father's actual answer to the confession of his son, on which account they are joined so directly to that confession. According to the father's command, ver. 22, the servants are to present three objects to the son, not merely to relieve his destitution, but each one of them a mark of honour, a threefold evidence to the son of his reinstatement in the filial position. Hence, too, the servants are not merely commanded to present these objects to him, but to put them on him, in this way ministering to him as the son of the house. We must read, with Lachmann and Meyer: ταχὺ ἐξενέγκατε στολὴν τὴν πρώτην. The stola is the upper dress of the respectable classes, a garment of honour to the wearer.[1] Such a stola the servants are to bring out quickly, *scil.* from its receptacle; and they are to bring out "the first," in order to enhance the honour shown (*i.e.* in this connection the best of those in the house), and they are to put it on the son. Further, they are to put a signet-ring on his hand, and sandals on his feet, both in like manner intended as marks of respect. For even the sandals are not to the Oriental a matter of pressing necessity. They belong to respectability, and are a necessary part of the treatment due to a man of rank.

After the father by this order has replied to his son's confession of guilt and unworthiness, and sealed to him his complete restoration, he gives expression to his great joy by the further commission to the servants, ver. 32: "*And bring the calf, the fatted one,*" *scil.* which, you know well, is quite ready, "*and slay it,*" to which commission the summons is joined: "*and let us feast and be merry.*" The father orders a joyous banquet of all the household, and the best to be provided which the house furnishes, and justifies the order by stating the event to be celebrated in tones of overflowing joy, ver. 24: ὅτι οὗτος ὁ υἱός μου νεκρὸς ἦν καὶ ἀνέζησεν, ἦν ἀπολωλὼς καὶ εὑρέθη. The two parallel clauses, placed side by side without connecting particle, are meant

---

[1] Cf. Mark xii. 38; Luke xx. 46.

in any case to affirm one and the same thing. The first therefore, just like the second, affirms that this his son was lost and has been found. Of necessity the father is to be thought of as the one who had lost, and has again come into possession of him. When the son left the father of his own choice and went into the far country, the father no longer had this his son,—outwardly not, for he had disappeared; inwardly not, for his filial relation to the father was severed; and this state of privation the father expresses when he says once: "*This my son was dead*," and again: "*He was lost.*" But now that he has returned in penitence to the father, he has his son again, and he gives vivid expression to the joy of recovery when he says once: "*He has become alive again*," and again: "*He has been found.*" Therefore neither are the two statements,[1] nor even the first only,[2] meant in an ethical sense, as if they were meant to state in what moral condition the son was formerly, and what change has taken place in him,—a view of the words refuted by a series of other considerations. First, let us observe that these words are spoken to the servants to give a reason for the joyous banquet ordered. Could the father really speak to the servants of the moral change in the son, instead of the fact that the son was restored to the father, and thus, of course, also to the entire household? Let us further compare ver. 27, where one of the servants repeats in prosaic simple style the thought uttered here in the higher tone of overflowing joy, quoting as the reason of the banquet: ὅτι ὑγιαίνοντα αὐτὸν ἀπέλαβεν. Compare, finally, the analogous passages in the two preceding parables, vv. 6, 9, respecting the sheep and the coin found again. It is impossible to understand the expressions "to be lost" and "to be found" here in a quite different sense from the one in those two passages. Certainly in all three parables a moral state is *symbolized* by the being lost, and a moral conversion by the being found; and this is specially conspicuous in the third parable, where the being lost is identical with the departure from the father into the strange country by the son's own choice, and the being found with the return to the father by his own resolve. But on this very account it is an encroaching on the province of interpretation to describe the words as meant in an ethical sense by the father in the parable. What the father ordered is now done: καὶ ἤρξαντο εὐφραίνεσθαι.

The narrative of the younger son has now reached its

---
[1] Meyer *et al.* [2] van Oosterzee, von Hofmann.

conclusion, but not the entire parable. Two sons of the father were mentioned in the beginning, ver. 11. We therefore expect to hear of the elder son, and to him the narrative proceeds. Not, however, to place a separate history of the elder son beside that of the younger one, but merely, in close connection with what has preceded, to say what attitude the elder son took to the reception of the younger one just related. "*But his elder son was in the field,*" it is first said, ver. 25. Thus, the elder son is thought of as absent from the house during the return of the younger, and accordingly what is to be told about him is laid in a later period, when he comes home. In this way both what has been related of the reception of the younger son and what is still to be told of the elder one are entirely distinct from each other, and a simple advance in the narrative from one to another is made possible. Nothing else is to be sought behind the absence of the elder son in the field. As he is returning home he observes that something extraordinary has happened, for on approaching the house he hears music and dancing ($\sigma\upsilon\mu\phi\omega\nu\iota\alpha\varsigma$ $\kappa\alpha\grave{\iota}\ \chi\omicron\rho\tilde{\omega}\nu$). Inside the house the joyous banquet is in full swing with music and dancing, as was usual on festive occasions. When he hears these sounds of feasting, he calls one of the servants, and asks what is going on, ver. 26. The latter replies, ver. 27: "*Thy brother is come, and thy father hath slain the fatted calf, because he has received him sound,*"—a simple answer in which he gives the inquirer information about the occasion and character of the festive meal, whose sounds are heard by the latter, so that we mark in his words how natural and justifiable the festivities in progress seem to his simple vision. That he speaks in heartless mockery of the father, and with a desire to provoke jealousy,[1] is imported without any support in the text. The son, however, is full of wrath at what the servant says, ver. 28: "*and would not go in;*" and when the father, who meantime has heard of his return, himself leaves the festive chamber and with friendly greeting exhorts[2] him to enter and participate in the festive joy, he will not be moved, but gives expression to his wrath in harsh words (ver. 29), expressing plainly enough the feelings of his heart. "*Lo, so many years do I serve thee, and never transgressed a commandment of thine.*" Thus he first upbraids his father with the long blameless service he has rendered to him. "*And to me,*" he continues, putting

[1] von Hofmann. [2] $\pi\alpha\rho\alpha\kappa\alpha\lambda\epsilon\tilde{\iota}\nu$, as in Acts xvi. 39; 1 Cor. iv. 13.

the ἐμοί first emphatically, "*thou never gavest a young goat* (ἔριφον), *that I might be merry with my friends.*" The emphatic position of the ἐμοί shows that he speaks thus in allusion to the calf now slain for his brother, and therefore to the festive banquet prepared with such great array for the latter. The meaning is: *For me* thou didst never prepare such a banquet, even with slight array, that I might even once relieve my toilsome service by making merry with my friends. And then (ver. 30) he contrasts the life which his brother has led, and what has been done for him, with his own long and blameless service without reward. He describes him simply as "*this thy son*," scornfully omitting the name of brother, and also bitterly reproaching the father for acknowledging him as his son. He characterizes the life he has led in the participial clause: ὁ καταφαγών σου τὸν βίον μετὰ τῶν πορνῶν. Whilst *he* has done the father such toilsome service, the *other* has consumed the father's goods in a life of reckless enjoyment. The μετὰ τῶν πορνῶν is said in bitter contrast to the honourable εὐφραίνεσθαι μετὰ τῶν φίλων μου, ver. 29. But the making of this very contrast reveals that he secretly envies his brother's past sinful life as a life of enjoyment and pleasure that has been permitted to him. All the more glaring seems to him the injustice in the father's conduct to the returning one: ὅτε δὲ . . . ἦλθεν, ἔθυσας αὐτῷ τὸν σιτευτὸν μόσχον. Thus, for the latter, over and above the delights of sin, the joyous banquet in the father's house with the best provision the house can offer! To these angry reproaches the father then replies in the most loving way, vv. 31, 32. The same forbearing love which he had shown to the younger son is now shown to the elder. He addresses his son with the tender τέκνον, and condescends to justify himself; and this first against the reproach raised in ver. 29, that he has not rewarded his son's long and blameless service, reminding him that this service carries its reward in itself, namely in uninterrupted fellowship with the father: σὺ πάντοτε μετ' ἐμοῦ εἶ, and in unbroken possession of all the father's goods: καὶ πάντα τὰ ἐμὰ σά ἐστιν. The σύ is put first with emphasis, answering to the ἐμοί, ver. 29. To the complaint respecting the supposed disparagement implied in the emphatic ἐμοί, the emphatic σύ opposes the actual privilege which the elder son had over the younger. In the words: πάντα τὰ ἐμὰ σά ἐστιν, we are not to think, in allusion to ver. 12, of a future legal claim to the whole of the paternal inheritance accruing to the elder son on the father's death to the exclusion of the younger son, but of the circumstance that, as the son who had always been with the father, he stands as matter of fact and always has stood in joint possession and enjoyment of all the paternal property. The presents εἶ and ἐστίν in the two clauses combine the past with the present as one permanent, uninterrupted state.

After the father has thus defended himself against the reproach, ver. 29, that he has not rewarded the elder son for his service, in ver. 32 he refutes the reproach, ver. 30, that he has done too much for the younger son in the feast he had prepared for him. For when he proceeds, ver. 32: εὐφρανθῆναι δὲ καὶ χαρῆναι ἔδει, ὅτι ὁ ἀδελφός σου οὗτος νεκρὸς ἦν καὶ ἔζησεν, καὶ ἀπολωλὼς καὶ εὑρέθη, this is certainly said first of all in reference to the feast prepared by the father. An event so joyous as the living again of one who was dead, and the finding again of one who was lost,[1] ought to be celebrated by a joyous feast. We must not, however, exclude from these words the reference given in Luther's translation, namely, the disapproval of the elder brother's wrath and murmuring. Whether the ἔδει is to be referred to something done as it ought to be done, or to something omitted which ought to have been done, can only be shown by the actual context. But where, as here, the context gives both references at once, the ἔδει also may be meant in *both* references. And that in fact in the present case the latter reference also is included in the meaning of the language, is proved first by the emphatic prefixing of the εὐφρανθῆναι, by which the " to be merry " is contrasted with the indignation of the person addressed, and again especially in the verifying clause by the designation of the one who lives and is found again as *" this thy brother."* This designation, in reponse to the scornful and bitter " this thy son," ver. 30, suggests to the indignant one, that as the father has recovered a son in the returning one, so also he has recovered a brother, and therefore, instead of being angry, he ought to have taken part in the joy of the household.

The parable then at last finishes in almost the same words that we found, ver. 24, at the close of the history of the younger son. That joyous utterance of the father over the return of the lost son recurs here as an assertion of his right against the anger of the brother, and a condemnation of that anger.

Let us now glance back at the entire parable and compare it

[1] Cf. on ver. 24.

with the two preceding ones, and further with vv. 1, 2, in order to see its distinctive purpose alongside those, and interpret it accordingly. After Jesus, to justify His own action towards sinners and to shame the murmuring of the Pharisees, has held up before the latter the image of a man who seeks and finds his lost sheep, and of a woman who seeks and finds her lost piece of money, He begins to tell of a *father* who lost his *son*, and describes the father's conduct to the lost one on his penitent return. The relation between father and son can only be a figure for the relation between God as the heavenly Father and man. Therefore, after justifying His own attitude to sinners in the first parables, He now goes a step farther and deeper, striking back to the attitude of God to the returning sinner, which is the ultimate ground and also the ultimate justification of His own action.[1] This advance in the thought is prepared for by the declarations at the close of the first two parables, in which the joy of the angels of God in heaven over the repenting sinner was spoken of, vv. 7, 10. The purpose of the parable accordingly is this, in contrast with the uncharitable murmuring of human ill-will, *to picture the joy with which God Himself accepts and receives back the sinner returning to Him.* But the central section of the narrative (vv. 20-24), in which the real purpose of the parable finds expression, is preceded on the one hand by an *introductory history*, vv. 11-19, and followed on the other by a *concluding episode*, vv. 25, 26.

Since in this instance it is not an irrational animal or dead coin, but a self-determining person, that serves to represent the sinner, the mere statement of something lost in the first two parables extends here to a figurative history, which spreads before our view the inner history of the sinner who repents. It does this in its three chief elements, characterizing first his sin in its beginning and progress, then the misery into which it leads him, and then the repentance to which in his misery he allows himself to be moved. But the narrative receives its distinctive shape from the reference to the special classes of sinners and publicans who streamed towards the Lord according to ver. 1. It is the past of such sinners as Jesus saw around Him then which is first described in the history of the younger son, and only in the second place, so far as the two coincide in their main features, the history of the sinner generally. The reference to the "publicans and sinners" at once gives

[1] Cf. John v. 19.

us the right interpretation for solving the initial relation between father and son as described in vv. 11, 12. The sinners whom the Lord has in view in the first instance were Jews, sons by birth of the theocratic economy as much as the Pharisees. But the divine law seemed a hard yoke to them, and, longing after unlimited freedom, they cast from them the limits of the law, living an independent life outside the divine economy and its ordinances. And God permitted them to do so, for He does not use outward means of compulsion towards the man who desires to emancipate himself from Him, ver. 12. The portion of property handed over to the son is not to receive a special interpretation; but, the desire for the inheritance simply representing the desire for unlimited freedom of action, the actual handing over of the inheritance is merely the typical form for the granting of such unlimited freedom on the part of God. Of the liberty granted them they then made the use they longed for. Renouncing all fellowship with God and all relation to Him, they lost themselves in the heathen world of alienation from God (the departure into the far country), in order to be able there in utter forgetfulness of God to indulge the sinful lusts of their hearts without restraint, ver. 13.

Thus did they; but how bitterly they found themselves betrayed! They were forced to experience what is described in vv. 14-16. The world in a state of alienation from God can only supply a brief sensuous intoxication to the man who has lost himself in it, and afterwards has nothing to give, nothing that can appease the hunger of man's soul (the famine in that country). And thus, instead of the unlimited enjoyment which he seeks in the world of alienation from God, the sinner finds himself plunged into a state of starvation, ver. 14, and instead of the freedom he longs after, he finds himself plunged into bondage to the children of that world—a shameful bondage without reward, a bondage harsh to the point of barbarity, in which the inner pain of starvation rises to its highest climax, without the sympathy and pity of others to alleviate the pain consuming him, vv. 15, 16. The keeping of the swine serves to represent the shamefulness of the bondage; the longing for husks is meant to picture the aggravation of the pain of starvation to the highest point. Whether in the description of the bondage any allusion is intended to the services rendered by the publicans to the heathen power, can scarcely be decided.

But in this misery the sinner allows himself to be moved to repentance. For so the publicans and sinners who come to the Lord had done. In their wretchedness they came to themselves, and then they became conscious how blessed it is to be permitted to serve God, and how miserable is the service of this world, ver. 17. And the resolve was awakened in them to return back to God, not as if they had any sort of right to recover their lost prerogatives as sons of the theocratic economy,—of this they frankly confess they have made themselves unworthy by their sin,—but they come simply with the humble request to be allowed to serve God like poor servants, vv. 18, 19.

And what then is the attitude of God to sinners, who penitently and humbly return to Him? Jesus describes it in the section forming the centre of the parable, vv. 20-24. First let us observe that nothing is said in this parable of a seeking of the lost one on the part of him who had suffered the loss. But this is at once explained to us by the difference of the figure used here from that used in the first two parables. As the son's being lost is a matter of his own choice, the father cannot seek him as the man sought his lost sheep and the woman her lost piece of money. The necessary postulate for the display of love on the father's part is here the return of the lost one by his own resolve. Nevertheless, even here the circumstance that the father is looking out for the lost one and discerns him from afar, indicates that the divine love is turned to the sinner even during his sinful life and before his conversion, anxiously awaiting and looking for his conversion. And therefore, scarcely has the sinner turned again to God in sincere repentance, when God even anticipates him with heartfelt compassion, overwhelms him with proofs of His fatherly love, receives him as a beloved child to His father-heart, ver. 20, and reinstates him, unworthy as he knows himself to be, in all the privileges of a child, vv. 21, 22. And there is then joy with God and His angels over the converted sinner, who was lost to God by his sin, but by his repentance is given back to the life of divine fellowship and won back to God and the kingdom of heaven, vv. 23, 24. That the putting on of the stola, the ring, and the sandals is not to be interpreted separately in each case, but is simply meant to denote the reinstatement in the filial state in three distinct features, scarcely needs mention. In the story of the preparation of the banquet, vv. 23, 24, the truth expressed in vv. 7, 10 without figure at the close of the first two parables is now resumed and worked out in the figurative form supplied by the context of the parable, on which account we also refer the feast to the joy of God and His angels, without thereby meaning to affirm that the servants in the parable are meant to signify the angels generally.

There follows now the section concluding the parable, in which the attitude of the elder brother on the return of the younger one is described. A glance back at vv. 1, 2 puts it beyond doubt that in the elder brother Jesus sketches an image of the murmuring Pharisees and scribes. In speaking at first of *two* sons of one father, it was His intention from the outset, under the image of the elder brother, to contrast the unbrotherly, unloving murmuring of the Pharisees with the fatherly, loving attitude of God to the returning sinner, which contrast carries in itself a condemnation of their attitude. This definite reference to the Pharisees has been objected to because of the saying of the father in ver. 31, which does not suit the Pharisees,[1] but wrongly. For, of course, the point treated of here is not Pharisaism in itself, but simply that trait of the Pharisaic nature which had shown itself in the murmuring mentioned in ver. 2. First, the purpose is to characterize the mode of thought revealed in the murmuring, and secondly, to give a convincing refutation of that murmuring. This is done in vv. 25-32. In the wrath of the elder brother when he becomes aware of the joy in the household and its occasion, and in his refusal to take part in this joy over his brother's return, Jesus first of all reproduces in figurative form the murmuring of the Pharisees at the reception accorded to the returning sinners, vv. 25-28. But He not only heard their murmuring, but saw through the thoughts of their heart, from which the murmuring arose. And in bringing the parabolic story to such a conclusion as to introduce a conversation between the father and the elder son respecting the reception of the younger one, He lays bare on one hand, in the language of the elder son, the thoughts of the Pharisees which are the ground of their murmuring, and, on the other, in the reply of the father discovers the injustice of these thoughts. They think they are justified in finding in the reception given to sinners a grievous injustice to themselves. To them, who have rendered to God so long and unbroken a service, never transgressing one of His commandments, no special enjoyment has ever been granted, ver. 29,

[1] von Hofmann, also Weiss.

whilst for these sinners, after they have been permitted to partake of the joys of life in the most extravagant way, a reception of such joyous character is prepared by God over and above, ver. 30. So they think, so they reckon, to serve God is to them hard labour without reward; sin seems to them to be enjoyment. In the next place, the answer of the father serves to expose the utter perverseness of these thoughts, and the injustice of the accusation raised against God's justice. This is done most gently, and yet most strikingly. Here, just as much as in the first two parables, Jesus for a moment admits, for the sake of argument, the claim of His opponents to blamelessness of walk before God's law. What He thinks of this claim He tells them plainly enough elsewhere. Precisely because they raise this claim, what the father in the parable says to the son who boasts of his obedience must be said to them. In the words of the father, ver. 31, Jesus reminds them that walking in obedience to God and His commandments carries its incomparable reward in itself, in uninterrupted fellowship with God, and the unbroken possession and enjoyment of all His blessing and grace, ver. 31. How perverse, therefore, to complain of the withholding of other special joys as a reward for this walk! But the special joy with which returning sinners are received rests on essential grounds, for by their conversion these sinners are given back to the life of divine fellowship, are won back to God and His heavenly kingdom, ver. 32. Therefore the joy of God and His angels over them is right, the wrath and murmuring of the Pharisees wrong. They ought, instead of murmuring, to participate in the joy of God and His angels.

The Unjust Steward.

(Luke xvi. 1–9.)

With Luke xv. 31, 32 the discourse of Jesus, which commenced in ver. 4, and reached a provisional conclusion in ver. 10 (only, however, to be at once resumed and continued in ver. 11), has come to an end. When in xvi. 1 it is further said: "and He said also unto the disciples," the narrative goes back beyond the discourse just concluded to the situation described in xv. 1–3, again joining on to what is there related. These words are therefore to be explained by what is said there. As we read there how the publicans and sinners drew near to Jesus to hear Him, and how Jesus, influenced by the murmuring of the Pharisees, directed His discourse to the latter, and, as we hear now that He spoke "*also to the disciples*," we must take the word "disciples" here in the broader sense, and understand not the Twelve alone, but the multitude of earnest hearers in general, consisting principally of publicans and sinners. Hitherto their interest as hearers of the discourse addressed and applying to the Pharisees had only been indirect, but now Jesus speaks *also to them.* Accordingly, in the following discourse, xvi. 1–13, the previous relation is reversed. The disciples are the persons addressed, while the Pharisees are those who "also listen," as is expressly said in ver. 14.

Thus introduced, there begins another parabolic narrative, the purport of which, we expect, will be of especial importance for the multitude of disciples consisting of publicans and sinners.

"*There was a rich man,*" so the narrative begins, "*who had a steward.*" Consequently the latter had a large property to administer. He is not described, like the steward in xii. 42–46, as a slave, but, as vv. 2, 3 will show, as an officer employed subject to notice. Moreover, he is entrusted with the most extensive authority over his master's property, as is shown by the accusation made against him, of which we hear at once: καὶ οὗτος διεβλήθη αὐτῷ ὡς διασκορπίζων τὰ ὑπάρχοντα αὐτοῦ. The accusation does not refer to definite acts of embezzlement in the proper sense, but says generally that he wasted his master's property, as may be most naturally supplied in thought, by an extravagant, luxurious life.[1] Whether the accusation really held good or not cannot be learnt from ver. 1, for διαβάλλειν is indeed a malevolent, but not necessarily a false accusing. And just so the ὡς διασκορπίζων says nothing about the guilt or innocence of the accused. It only says that he was described by his accusers *as wasting* the property, without our seeing whether with or without reason. From ver. 2, however, we see that the master at least is convinced of the steward's guilt, for "*he called him, and said to him, What is this that I hear of thee?*[2] *give the account of thy stewardship; for thou canst be no longer steward.*" Whether we read δυνήσῃ or δύνῃ is immaterial to the meaning, since the latter also can only have the future sense.[3] According to these

---

[1] Cf. xv. 13. [2] Τί τοῦτο ἀκούω = quid est quod audio?
[3] Cf. the present ἀφαιρεῖται in ver. 3.

words, the reason of the master requiring from the steward the account of his stewardship is that he can no longer be steward. Thus the master by no means makes the deposition depend on the account to be given, as if the guilt of the accused were first to be ascertained from the account. But because the steward as a squanderer is to lay down his office, the master requires from him the λόγος τῆς οἰκονομίας requisite on account of the transfer. In view of the union of the two clauses by γάρ, this is the only possible meaning of the words. Against this notice so definitely expressed there is no remonstrance, the matter is at an end, from which we may learn that the truth of the accusation made against the steward is presupposed in the narrative.[1]

In ver. 3 we find the steward considering what he shall do in his present position. It is self-evident that we must no longer think of him as in the presence of his master. The opposite opinion is refuted by the character of calm, mature deliberation worn by the following narrative, for which time and recollection were requisite. "*And the steward said within himself, What shall I do, seeing that my lord taketh away the stewardship from me?*" By the present ἀφαιρεῖται he designates his still impending deposition from office, in accordance with the notice given him in ver. 2, as an already certain fact. Directly he takes his critical position into consideration, he does not deceive himself as to the fact that he is on the point of being left without means of living. Then two ways seem possible in which he may hereafter gain a livelihood, namely, either by earning his bread, and that by severe bodily toil, as no other means would be open to a dismissed official, or by begging. He weighs both alternatives, but only to reject them at once: "*To dig I am not able; to beg I am ashamed.*" Of the one the effeminate man sees himself physically incapable, from the other he is deterred by shame. But is there no other expedient? This is now the object of his further reflection, which really arrives at a result, ver. 4: "*I know what I will do, that, when I am put out of the stewardship, they may receive me into their houses.*" The ἔγνων, prefixed asyndetically, expresses not so much the sudden occurrence of the thought as rather the satisfaction of the speaker at having reached a practical favourable result in his reflections. He has thought of a course of proceeding—so the words say—by which he intends to bring

---

[1] Cf. also the appellation ὁ οἰκονόμος τῆς ἀδικίας in ver. 8, and what is said there.

about, that (ἵνα) they, with whom he thus deals,[1] will receive him into their houses, when he shall be put out of the stewardship, and thus dismissed from the house which had hitherto given him support. What kind of a proceeding it is, and on whom he intends to practise it, he does not say. We learn both first on hearing how he proceeds without delay to execute his plan, ver. 5: "*And he called to him each one of his lord's debtors.*" These debtors, accordingly, are the persons whom he had in view in the proceeding resolved on in ver. 4. According to vv. 6, 7, they are persons who have borrowed natural products from the estate managed by the steward, executing and handing over to the latter a written bond for the amount of stuff borrowed. They are therefore dealers who obtain their wares from the producer. That they are to be viewed as contractors, and τὰ γράμματα, ver. 6, as the contract, there is nothing in the text to intimate. It corresponds neither with the word χρεωφειλέτης nor with the question πόσον ὀφείλεις (vv. 5, 6), on which the impossible meaning must be foisted, at what amount was the interest fixed in the contract?

How the steward proceeds with these debtors of his master, when he has gathered them together, is shown in the sequel, vv. 5b–7. Turning to the first of them, by the question: "*How much owest thou to my lord?*" he gets him first of all to acknowledge the amount of his debt: "*A hundred baths of oil.*" And having thus first made him feel his position as a debtor, and aroused in him the sense of the amount of his debt, he says to him, at the same time handing him his bond: "*Take thy writing,*[2] *sit down, and write quickly fifty.*" Consequently the direction is literally that the debtor shall endorse the bond handed back again, reducing the amount from 100 to 50 baths of oil. But this must not be understood to mean that the steward wished to lead the debtors to falsify the bond, a view with which the publicity of the transaction does not agree. But he acts towards the assembled debtors as the fully authorized steward of the property, and on the ground of the authority of his position he here permits the first of the debtors to reduce the amount of debt specified on his bond by a definite sum. Therefore the injustice done here is not a falsifying of the bond on the part of the debtor, but an abuse of his powers on the part of the steward,

---

[1] Thus must the subject of δέξωνται be supplied from the context.
[2] τὰ γράμματα = litterae, in this connection the bond.

and, moreover, a wasting of his master's property, only in a different way from the one alleged in ver. 1. He has need to make haste, as indicated in the ταχέως γράψον, knowing as he does how soon he will be deprived of his authority. Forthwith he does just the same with the second debtor as with the first. By the question: *"But thou, how much owest thou?"* he compels the former, like the latter, to acknowledge the amount of his debt: *"A hundred cors of wheat,"* in order then to grant him also a remission of a portion of his debt: *"Take thy writing, and write eighty."* So in ver. 7. The σὺ δέ prefixed shows that directly after dealing with the first debtor he turns to the second standing alongside; and consequently puts beyond doubt that he does not deal, as has been said, with each individual privately, but with one after another, and with each one in presence of the rest. It is to be observed, further, that the number one hundred recurs also in the case of the second debtor in specifying the amount of debt, but that the steward orders him to change the 100, not into 50, but into 80. Since the amount of the original debt is both times the same, while that of the reduced debt is different, the difference in the remission is too conspicuous to allow us to explain it as a mere change in the concrete description to avoid monotony. The steward rather gives himself the air—so we are to understand this feature—of acting simply by favour and personal preference, seeking in this way to strengthen the feeling of obligation to his person in the debtors. That he acts with each one of his master's debtors in the same way as with the first and second, is to be supplied in thought from the opening words of ver. 5. From his dealings with the first and second we are to learn his dealings with all. Thus in the eleventh hour, according to vv. 5–7, he has so used the authority of his position, which gave him the formal right to dispose of his master's property, as to grant to all his master's debtors a reduction of their debt, by which means he aimed, as we know from ver. 4, at gaining them to his side, that after his deposition they might receive him into their houses.

But now this entire proceeding is by no means arranged with a view to keeping it concealed from the knowledge of the master, which, moreover, would have contributed nothing to the end to be accomplished. On the contrary, it must necessarily have been noticed and remarked when the office was laid down and the account given in according to ver. 2, since it would be at once known from the bond, which was not artificially falsified, but simply altered. On the assumption of this state of the case the narrative at once continues, ver. 8 : καὶ ἐπῄνεσεν ὁ κύριος τὸν οἰκονόμον τῆς ἀδικίας, *i.e.* when the general reduction of debt came to light on the account being given in, "*the lord praised the steward of unrighteousness.*" The parallels, ver. 9 and xviii. 6, forbid us to connect the genitive τῆς ἀδικίας with ἐπῄνεσεν, as well as the following clause beginning with ὅτι, which first indicates the actual object of the commendation, placing it in something quite different from the ἀδικία. The genitive accordingly is the *gen. qual.*, describing the steward as unrighteous, *i.e.* according to the context here as dishonest, the dishonesty being represented as a quality characterizing him. For this reason the designation cannot be based only upon the solitary dishonest action last told of him, vv. 5-7, but refers to the dishonesty of his stewardship in general,[1] upon which he has only, so to speak, put the crown by the proceeding last related of him and now revealed. All the more strange certainly it is to hear that the master commended this steward of unrighteousness. The language contains an intended antithesis meant to draw the hearer's attention to the solution of the antithesis immediately following in the clause: ὅτι φρονίμως ἐποίησεν. Therefore: the lord could not help admiring and praising the steward of unrighteousness, "*because he acted wisely.*" And here we suddenly find ourselves at the conclusion of the narrative, a conclusion sufficient of itself to indicate that the central point of the entire narrative must lie in this commended wisdom of the course devised and carried out by the steward. But this is made still plainer by the declaration of Jesus, lying outside the figurative history, which He adds by way of verification. In this sense Jesus continues: ὅτι οἱ υἱοὶ τοῦ αἰῶνος τούτου φρονιμώτεροι ὑπὲρ τοὺς υἱοὺς τοῦ φωτὸς εἰς τὴν γενεὰν τὴν ἑαυτῶν εἰσίν. Υἱός with the genitive denotes in both cases the relation of belonging to. Οἱ υἱοὶ τοῦ αἰῶνος τούτου are the men belonging to this age, *i.e.* men whose thoughts and acts move within the limits of this present world, not stretching beyond it. Such an one the steward has shown himself everywhere in the parable. To men of this class generally Jesus ascribes the praise of wisdom, and indeed they are "*wiser than the children of light.*" Οἱ υἱοὶ τοῦ φωτός are the men belonging to the light, *i.e.* those who are enlightened in their thinking and

---

[1] Cf. on vv. 1, 2.

guided in their doing by the light of divine truth. By the choice of such a designation an apparent contradiction again arises in the statement of Jesus. For how can the children of this world be wiser than those whose privilege above the former it is to be children of the light? This seeming contradiction finds its solution in the limiting phrase: εἰς τὴν γενεὰν τὴν ἑαυτῶν. The *pron. refl.* ἑαυτῶν, as the words run, can only be referred back to the subject of the clause: οἱ υἱοὶ τοῦ αἰῶνος τούτου, not also to the children of the light.[1] Nor are the words placed after ὑπὲρ τοὺς υἱοὺς τοῦ φωτός on account of this supposed double reference,[2] but because to the paradoxical statement intentionally put first they add the limitation in which it holds good. When a γενεά of the υἱοὶ τοῦ αἰῶνος τούτου is spoken of, the γενεά can signify nothing but the generation or family formed by these υἱοί as such. "*In reference to their own generation*" is therefore the same as: In reference to those who like them are children of this world, and as such in affinity with them. Their wisdom is limited to their relation to the latter, and therefore to the sphere of the present natural life, which embraces their mutual relations; but taken in this limitation, their wisdom is in fact so great that they far excel the children of light.

Comparing, then, this peculiar conclusion of the parabolic narrative with the words introducing it, ver. 1, according to which it was designed specially for the disciples, we find the following to be the distinctive purpose underlying the parable: The Lord desires in the narrative of the steward of unrighteousness to hold up before His disciples an example of the wisdom exercised among themselves by the children of this world, that they who are and profess to be children of light may be shamed by the wisdom of the former, and may also learn true wisdom. And when, glancing back at the course of the narrative, we observe further that the steward's wisdom was shown in the prudent use of his authority over the property under his management, and bear in mind the circumstance noted in ver. 1, that many publicans were found among the disciples surrounding the Lord, and therefore people who had stained themselves with sin for the sake of earthly wealth, and consequently needed special admonition in their relation to earthly wealth, since in this matter above all the sincerity of their change of heart must be shown,—from all this we learn with what special reference the Lord holds up before

---

[1] De Wette, Olshausen, Godet, *et al.*   [2] von Hofmann.

the disciples the wisdom of a child of the world like this steward. From his example they are to gather the right, because truly wise employment of earthly wealth. This result is expressly confirmed to us by the interpreting utterance of Jesus, ver. 9, in which He now Himself tells the disciples in what the truly wise employment of earthly wealth consists by the example of the steward. By the prefatory "*and I also say to you*," Jesus describes what He has now to say to His disciples on the basis of the parable as something akin to the praise which the master in the parable bestowed on the wise course of the steward, ver. 8. He agrees with the praise, inasmuch as He also commends the wise course of the man to the imitation of His disciples, certainly, as is evident of itself, according to the words in ver. 8, only from their standpoint as children of light. How they are to make a wise use of mammon, in analogy with the conduct of the steward, He tells them in the words: Ἑαυτοῖς ποιήσατε φίλους ἐκ τοῦ μαμωνᾶ τῆς ἀδικίας. The Lord does not mention mammon without characterizing it by the genitive τῆς ἀδικίας, which at once recalls the designation τὸν οἰκονόμον τῆς ἀδικίας, ver. 8. Hence we must not give the word here a different signification from the one there, and attempt to refer it to the unjust distribution of mammon or its treacherous inconstancy, but here as there it is injustice in the sense of unrighteousness or dishonesty. Mammon is named after unrighteousness as a property *essential* to it, and therefore not merely because according to general experience it serves as an instrument of unrighteous dealing,[1] which would be nothing essentially peculiar to it, nor yet merely because there is no possession to which injustice in acquisition does not attach, either of the present or a former possessor,[2] which again must have a deeper reason lying in the nature of the case, but because unrighteousness is really the principle corresponding to the nature of wealth, coming into action spontaneously, directly wealth is regarded as an end in itself, and sought after or managed for its own sake. Accordingly mammon is but a doubtful, nay, dangerous good for the children of light. All the more therefore does it seem enjoined on them to deal wisely with this ambiguous and perilous good in accordance with the admonition: ἑαυτοῖς ποιήσατε φίλους ἐκ τοῦ μαμωνᾶ τῆς ἀδικίας. The ἑαυτοῖς put first emphasizes the truth, that the employment of mammon recommended by the Lord to His disciples is one tending to

---

[1] Meyer.   [2] von Hofmann.

their own advantage, and therefore useful in the highest and best sense. They are to make friends to themselves with mammon,[1] in order to obtain from those friends, when necessary, a proof of their friendship: ἵνα ὅταν ἐκλίπῃ δέξωνται ὑμᾶς εἰς τὰς αἰωνίους σκηνάς. "Ὅταν ἐκλίπῃ (perhaps also ἐκλείπῃ), i.e. "when it shall have come to an end, ceased," is to be read, with Lachmann and Tischendorf, both according to external attestation and also on grounds of internal probability, since the reading ἐκλίπητε (or ἐκλείπητε), i.e. "when ye shall have died," offers itself as a simplifying correction. As to meaning, however, the correction does not differ materially from the original reading. For when Jesus speaks to the disciples of a future ceasing of the mammon, with which they are now to make friends to themselves, plainly mammon only comes into view here as a possession of its present owners. Therefore the ceasing of mammon is its loss as a possession, not a future ceasing of mammon in its essential subsistence, such as enters with the Parousia,[2] a thought altogether foreign to the context.[3] If we inquire the point of time when the ceasing of mammon in this sense befalls every one, this is of course the death of the owner (cf. ver. 22 and xii. 20), and only in the second place the Parousia (if this is to be included) for those who live to see it.[4] With a view therefore to the time when their earthly property will vanish from them, and they in and with it will lose their earthly temporal dwelling-place, they are to make friends to themselves, that these may then afford to them an abiding dwelling-place, "*may receive them into the eternal tabernacles.*" Σκηνή (in Hebrew אֹהֶל) is a poetic expression, current in the language of the Old Testament, for "dwelling" generally. We need not therefore supply to this expression a definite allusion, such as to *the tents of the patriarchs*,[5] or *the tents of Israel*

---

[1] ἐκ here allied to διά; cf. Winer, *Gram.* p. 460.   [2] Meyer.
[3] Cf. the ὅταν μετασταθῶ τῆς οἰκονομίας, ver. 4, to which, as we shall see, the ὅταν ἐκλίπῃ necessarily corresponds.
[4] In opposition to the objection that, according to the Synoptics, Jesus places His Parousia in the lifetime of the present generation, and therefore cannot remit His disciples to a future after their *death* (Meyer), it is sufficient simply to compare the passage in which Jesus seems most definitely to place His Parousia in a time so near, chap. ix. 27; Matt. xvi. 28. Supposing that the coming of the Son of man there is really to be understood of Christ's visible, personal Second Coming, still that passage would only predict as something special, that some of those standing around shall not taste death before, which would expressly imply that, apart from certain exceptions, death is the generally to be expected lot. Cf. also passages like Matt. x. 21, 39, xxiv. 9.   [5] Godet.

in the desert.[1] It rather offered itself naturally as a higher analogon for the "houses" in the parable, ver. 4. What is to be understood by the eternal tabernacles is given in the context. They must be those dwellings, reception into which, beyond their earthly term of life, is to the disciples of Jesus the aim of their care and effort, in opposition to the children of this world, ver. 8, whose care and effort do not extend beyond the limits of this present æon,—thus the dwellings of the world to come, opening there to the heirs of eternal life.[2] When they are expressly denominated *eternal* dwellings, they form an antithesis both to the ceasing of mammon, and also to the merely perishable support which the houses in the parable were able to furnish, ver. 4. And when Jesus so directly annexes the reception into the eternal dwellings to the ceasing of earthly possession which occurs at death, this of course implies that the dying believer is warranted in expecting to be made partaker of that promise at once and immediately, although as yet incompletely.[3] But we must not on this account understand the eternal dwellings themselves simply of the dwellings of departed souls, with which the adjective "eternal" will not accord, but here as everywhere else Jesus directs the glance of His disciples' hope away from their temporal life within the present æon to the eternal life of the world to come.

Whatever is obscure in this utterance of Jesus must be cleared up by reference to the parable on which it is based, as conversely the interpretation of the parable must be worked out from the basis of this utterance, in connection with the words of Jesus in ver. 8. But we cannot obtain workable points of view for interpreting the present parable from what follows in vv. 10-13. For although what follows stands in close connection with the admonition uttered in ver. 9 as regards its intrinsic meaning, as will be shown in the proper place, still the language there no longer proceeds entirely, as in ver. 9, on the basis of the parable. Rather, by advancing first of all a general proposition without connection with what precedes, the truth of which may be assumed to be acknowledged, ver. 10, the Lord lays a quite new and independent basis for His further monitions. And now only, recurring to His theme, He makes the application resulting from that proposition for His theme, vv. 11, 12; an application having its independent basis in ver. 10, as ver. 9 has in vv. 1-8.

[1] Meyer.   [2] Cf. xviii. 30, xx. 35.   [3] Cf. xxiii. 42, 43.

And when again, in ver. 13, a new general proposition is advanced, and in applying it a final warning is given to the disciples in reference to mammon, we must least of all take what is said here as deciding the interpretation of the parable, especially after the independent series of thoughts has intervened, vv. 10–12.

We proceed, then, to the interpretation on the basis of the words of Jesus, vv. 8, 9. From these words we learn the plan underlying the parable. Jesus desires to teach His disciples the really wise employment of mammon. For this end He holds up before them an example of wisdom, such as the children of this world are wont to practise among themselves. From the example of such a man of the world, showing worldly wisdom in his dealings with mammon, they are to gather what employment of mammon true wisdom enjoins on *them*. In order to carry out this plan, the narrative must, above all, be so arranged that the man of the world, whose wisdom is to be an example to the disciples, shall stand in a similar position within the present world as regards mammon to that in which the disciples of Jesus find themselves as regards riches in relation to the future world, so that the disciples may recognise in the position of the man of the world an image of their own position. To this postulate corresponds the first part of the parable, vv. 1, 2, which then forms the groundwork for the main part which follows. Striking into the heart of worldly life and pursuits, the Lord there told of the unprincipled steward of a large property, to whom his master had given notice of dismissal on hearing that the steward was wasting his property. As matter of fact, within the relations of worldly life, the position of this man of the world in reference to the property at his disposal is an image of the position in which the children of light find themselves as regards the mammon in their possession in relation to the future world, lying beyond their earthly life. For, as the former now definitely foresees that the property under his management and at his disposal will within a short time be taken from him, and he will in consequence be stripped of his previous means of support, so the children of light cannot hide from themselves that the mammon, whose use is now in their hand, will within a short time (*i.e.* for *them*, at the end of their earthly life) be taken from them, and beyond this life they will be deprived of that which was the ground and means of their earthly existence.

Thus, in the interpretation, we must lay the emphasis simply and solely on the impending dismissal from the command of the property, and every interpretation at variance with this chief point and wandering into detail must, in view of the peculiar nature of the parable, be excluded. Thus, we must not interpret the rich man of God, and find in the responsible position of the steward in relation to his master the moral responsibility of the disciples, as mere stewards of mammon, to God as the true owner, which would then compel us to find also an interpretation for the complaint brought against the steward. Both the position as steward of a rich man, assigned to the man in the narrative, and the complaint made against him,—viewed, as we saw, as well founded,—serve merely to obtain the necessary postulates, within the worldly relations of an unprincipled man of the world, for the central fact in the interpretation, namely, the impending loss of the property hitherto at command.

In what has been said the necessary groundwork is gained for the second main part of the parable. For after the man of the world is found in a position, in respect to the property under his command, which is an image of the position in which the disciples of Jesus stand as regards mammon, the wise course of conduct which he adopts with the property of his master can become a pattern of a similar course to the disciples. The conduct of the man of the world we found described in vv. 3–7. The wisdom of this conduct, as we saw, consisted in this, that, after recognising the impossibility of obtaining support hereafter by his own labour, ver. 3, he hastened to use the time during which he still retained authority over his master's property to secure beforehand through it other means of support for the future. And he carried out this plan by seeking with his master's property, while in his power, to gain friends, with whom he expected to find a reception hereafter. With what skill and cunning, under favour of his position in worldly life, he pursued this course towards other children of this world, directing his attention to the debtors of his master dependent on him, and presenting himself to them as their friend and benefactor by an abuse of his authority as artful as it was shameful, was described in detail in vv. 5–7. To this wise course the course of the disciples must correspond, in the way Jesus says in ver. 9. For as their position is analogous to that of the steward, wisdom enjoins on them an analogous mode of action. Like the steward, they must use the time during which mammon remains at their disposal (*i.e.* for *them*, the period of earthly life) to secure beforehand through it support for the future lying beyond the present life, when mammon will be taken from them. And indeed they must do this in the same way as the steward, namely, by making friends to themselves with mammon, that, when it shall depart from them, these may afford them a place of refuge; that place of refuge for which they hope as those who are not children of this world—admission into the eternal habitations of the world to come. So far the Lord goes in the comparison, and farther we cannot go. The course of action pursued by the steward, by which "the making to himself friends with mammon" was carried out, must necessarily remain outside the comparison. For, as it depended simply upon his worldly position as steward, so also its description merely serves to characterize the nature of the worldly prudence, artfully calculating every detail, which the children of this world practise among themselves.

Accordingly, from vv. 5–7 we can obtain no material for answering the still remaining question: *What kind of friends is Jesus thinking of in recommending the disciples to make to themselves friends with mammon?* The demand that the relation of these friends to the disciples, and therefore the manner in which they are to be gained, must be analogous to the relation of the debtors to the steward, and the manner in which the steward seeks to bind the debtors to himself, ought not to be made at all, even as no explanation is really true to such a demand, however the "making to themselves friends" may be explained. On the other hand, we must certainly adhere to the principle that only such friends can be thought of as have power to grant or refuse admission into the eternal habitations. To evade this principle, indeed, it has been said that $\delta\acute{\epsilon}\chi\epsilon\sigma\theta\alpha\acute{\iota}$ $\tau\iota\nu\alpha$ simply means to "receive any one" generally, and it has been understood here accordingly as a bare welcoming.[1] And, certainly, it need not perforce always have the sense "to grant reception to any one." It may denote merely: to prepare a reception for any one, whether in a friendly or unfriendly sense. But in this case the emphasis no longer lies in the idea of the $\delta\acute{\epsilon}\chi\epsilon\sigma\theta\alpha\iota$, but in the manner of receiving, which must be more exactly defined.[2] But where $\delta\acute{\epsilon}\chi\epsilon\sigma\theta\alpha\acute{\iota}$ $\tau\iota\nu\alpha$ stands without more precise definition of this kind, it has everywhere the pregnant significance, to which οὐ

---

[1] van Oosterzee.   [2] Cf. Gal. iv. 14: ὡς ἄγγελον Θεοῦ ἐδέξασθέ με.

δέχεσθαι = "to refuse to receive," forms the antithesis.[1] Moreover, in the present passage this signification of δέχεσθαι is rendered certain, first, by the association with εἰς τὰς σκηνάς,—only ἐν ταῖς σκηναῖς could be said of a mere welcoming,—and secondly, by the consideration that it cannot here have a different meaning from the one in ver. 4, where not merely the conjunction with εἰς τοὺς οἴκους, but the entire context, admits only the pregnant significance. Nay, to attempt to understand the δέχεσθαι here differently from there, and to make the Lord here say nothing else and nothing more than that the disciples are to assure themselves of a friendly, grateful welcome in the eternal habitations by the friends they are to gain, would be to abolish the analogy between the parable and the application made of it in ver. 9 precisely in the decisive point, and to resolve it into a futile play of words. The same applies to all attempts to dilute the meaning of δέχεσθαι in ver. 9 in any way, or even to ascribe it to the "friends" in an indirect sense only.[2] They dissolve the analogy between parable and application precisely in the point in which Jesus ratifies it. For this reason the exhortation: "Make to yourselves friends with mammon," cannot certainly be meant in the sense (as the majority, however, explain) that with mammon we are to gain for ourselves friends among *men*, because it cannot be said of such friends that they receive into the eternal habitations. Moreover, so understood, the exhortation would stand in insoluble contradiction with other admonitions of Jesus,[3] according to which the charity to be practised by the disciples of Jesus, whatever other kind of value it may have, must on no account take as its aim to ingratiate itself with the recipients of the benefits and earn their thanks, but only to secure reward *with God*. But rightly understood, the exhortation of Jesus in the present passage harmonizes with these directions. For we cannot here even think of the friendship of *the angels*,[4] because even to them only a ministerial service can be ascribed in the reception to the eternal habitations, not the receiving itself, which includes decision upon the reception. Consequently, nothing else can be meant in the present passage than that, by a charitable employment of mammon, we are to gain for ourselves the friendship of Him to whom alone that reception pertains, and who reserves it to Himself one day openly to reward those

---

[1] Cf. ix. 5, 48, 53, x. 8, 10.   [2] Stier, Nebe, von Hofmann, Weiss, *et al.*
[3] *E.g.* vi. 27, 32-35; Matt. v. 44, 46, 47.   [4] Ewald, Meyer.

good deeds of His people, which they did to their brethren here in secret for His sake alone (Matt. vi. 3, 4), therefore the friendship *of God*. There is nothing in the parable to oppose this view, since the details of the description, vv. 5–7, as we have seen, lie outside the thing to be compared. And just as little is the plural form in opposition to this view. For, in the general exhortation: " make to yourselves friends," the " friends," in any case, is merely a plural of species, where one may be thought of just as readily as several.[1] The general nature of the language is conditioned by the close connection with the parable. In the first instance, the exhortation is purposely left quite general, as the parable requires, to the effect, namely, that "the making to themselves friends with mammon" must be the care of the disciples also. But with the concluding words: " into the eternal tabernacles," definite allusion is made to the question, whose friendship it is that can alone concern the disciples in *their* " making to themselves friends," namely, not, as with the children of this world, the friendship of men, but the friendship of Him who receives into the eternal habitations.

It is therefore—such is the result of the parable—a precept of wisdom to the disciples of Jesus, first to regard the ambiguous good of mammon merely as a means of securing for themselves God's approbation, and again to be guided in its use only by His approbation, that after this perishable possession has ceased they may obtain admission into the eternal habitations. Let us now glance at the further statements up to the conclusion of the discourse commenced in ver. 1, statements which, although no longer resting, like the utterance of Jesus in ver. 9, on the ground of the parable, nevertheless stand as regards their intrinsic purport in such close connection with that utterance that they are not without importance for its interpretation. In that utterance, whilst on one hand mammon was described as an ambiguous (" mammon of unrighteousness ") and perishable (" when it shall fail ") good, such value was attributed to it in reference to the disciples, that admission into the eternal habitations seemed to depend on the manner of its use. The enigma which His hearers might see in this depreciation of mammon on the one side, and appreciation on the other, the two being plainly opposed to each other in ver. 9, Jesus undertakes to solve in what follows. He there explains, that as matter of fact no one can expect to be

[1] Cf. Matt. ii. 20.

one day received into the eternal habitations who does not use the earthly good of mammon here below in accordance with God's will. On this account He first of all advances the proposition, that he that is faithful in the least is so also in much; and again, he that is unjust in the least is unjust also in much (ver. 10), a proposition which, as it commends itself to every one by its intrinsic truth, is also confirmed by universal experience. And He now applies this proposition to the "unrighteous mammon," of which He spoke in ver. 9. Mammon certainly is but an ἐλάχιστον, a mere trifle, because it is nothing "true" (ἀληθινόν), *i.e.* its possession is only of seeming, not real worth. All the less is it something true, seeing that the attribute of unrighteousness is inherent in it, and for this reason it is more a danger than a gain to its possessor. But on this very account he who has not been faithful in the unrighteous mammon cannot expect that the true riches, having real value for man, will be entrusted to him, namely, the inheritance of the kingdom of God—the dwelling in the eternal tabernacles. So ver. 11. And again, mammon is "a mere trifle," because it is and remains a mere ἀλλότριον to its possessor, *i.e.* something foreign to him, having no intrinsic affinity with him, but standing merely in an external, loose, and every moment dissoluble relation to him. But on this very account he who has not been faithful even in that which is "foreign," cannot expect that that which is a real possession to its owner—in the closest affinity with and inseparable from him—will be bestowed on him, namely, the inheritance of God's kingdom (ver. 12). It is now evident how the teaching of vv. 10–12 serves on the one hand to give more urgent intensity to the exhortation uttered in ver. 9, and on the other to explain it in material respects, and guard it against all misapprehension. For, according to the teaching of vv. 10–12, there can be no doubt as to how the exhortation was meant, namely, not in the sense that with mammon we can simply purchase God's approbation, and secure reception into the eternal habitations, but in the sense that the conscientious use of mammon in accordance with God's will is a natural and indispensable condition of reception into the eternal habitations. Hence it must be the prudent care of the disciples to fulfil that indispensable condition so as to obtain this reception. And now Jesus concludes His admonitions to the disciples in reference to mammon with a brief, solemn word of warning. Those of His hearers who fancy they can serve

God without also putting their mammon, as He required (vv. 9–12), altogether at God's service, He again confronts with the universal truth, that no servant can serve two masters, for either he will hate the one and love the other, or (conversely) will cleave to the one and despise the other,—in order, then, in applying this truth, to conclude with the warning: " Ye cannot serve God and mammon " (ver. 13).

When we compare the contents of the entire discourse of Jesus (chap. xvi. 1–13) with the one immediately preceding it (chap. xv.), this fourth parable, and the admonitions attached to it, present themselves to us as a necessary counterpart to those first three parables. The multitude of disciples to whom the Lord here speaks had indeed been among the listeners to the preceding parables; and although the parables were addressed primarily to the Pharisees, still it is certain that Jesus did not give them the form they have without reference to the listening publicans and sinners. In particular, this cannot be mistaken in the third parable, in which Jesus took as the formal theme of His figurative story the joyous, loving reception which the returning sinner finds with God. All this the publicans and sinners also heard, and might apply to themselves. But now they are to know and ponder that they must not make light of the repenting, which, according to the former parables, is the presupposition of God's joy over sinners; that, on the contrary, it requires from them a change of mind thoroughly transforming their previous life and conduct, which must show itself most of all in those matters in which they had most sinned. In this sense Jesus directs His discourse now (xvi. 1–13) to His disciples. It is enjoined on them to prove the sincerity and earnestness of their change of mind by placing the mammon of unrighteousness, whose servants they had hitherto been in sin, from this time without reserve at God's service. Mammon must henceforth be nothing to them but a means, to be used with prudent care for gaining for themselves God's friendship, and securing admission into the eternal habitations (vv. 1–9). For on the employment in a way pleasing to God of this, in itself insignificant and ambiguous good, depends, in fact, the bestowal of the eternal inheritance (vv. 10–12); whereas, to desire to serve God and mammon at the same time, as heretofore, would be to attempt the impossible (ver. 13).

The Rich Man.

(Luke xvi. 19–31.)

The section (vv. 14–18) leads over to a new parable (ver. 19 ff.). In the first place, ver. 14 says: "*And the Pharisees also heard all these things,*" namely, the Pharisees mentioned in xv. 2, to whom Jesus spoke in chap. xv. They had remained when Jesus turned to the disciples (chap. xvi. 1), and heard the discourse addressed to the latter (vv. 1–13). But the phrase: "who were lovers of money," intimates that their listening was by no means uninterested, but, on the contrary, was accompanied with considerable emotion. Although the discourse, in which Jesus condemned love of the mammon of unrighteousness as incompatible with the service of God, was not primarily addressed to them, they still felt that their love of money was struck at and exposed to public gaze. This feeling they seek to hide from themselves and those present by beginning to throw ridicule on Jesus: καὶ ἐξεμυκτήριζον αὐτόν, "*and they scoffed at Him.*" Certainly we are not to understand by this merely the derisive gesture—turning up the nose—which is the original meaning of the verb; but, in keeping with the usual further meaning of the word,[1] a deriding in words. In what words they uttered their mockery is not said. Enough that they try, by deriding the words of Jesus, in a lofty way to make it appear as if they were far above the admonitions, by which they yet feel themselves inwardly smitten. That we have rightly understood the motive of their mockery is shown by the rebuke of Jesus, which they draw upon themselves, ver. 15: "*Ye are they that justify yourselves in the sight of men,*" scil. while in reality and before God they are unjust. The antithesis, therefore, to the "they that justify themselves in the sight of men" is not the Pauline δικαίωσις of God,[2] the being justified by God, in which case it must have run: "they that justify themselves;" but the *making* themselves just *before men* is opposed to a *being* really just, attested as such before *God*, who knows the heart. Hence the contrast follows: "*but God knoweth your hearts;*" i.e., despite the semblance of righteousness with which you surround yourselves before men, God knows your hearts in their secret unrighteousness. That this in fact is

[1] Cf. chap. xxiii. 35.   [2] Meyer.

the case is then confirmed by the clause joined on by "for," declaring how little the divine knowledge can be baulked and bribed by the semblance which deceives men. Only by assigning to the ἐν ἀνθρώποις, "among men," its pregnant emphasis is the generally expressed clause: ὅτι τὸ ἐν ἀνθρώποις ὑψηλὸν βδέλυγμα ἐνώπιον τοῦ Θεοῦ, rightly limited. "That which is exalted among *men*" is that whose value and essence consists in being highly esteemed and lauded among *men*. But such an exalting,—this is the meaning,—so far from deceiving the divine knowledge, is rather an abomination before God, because allied by its very nature with mere hypocritical semblance.

This rebuke administered to the Pharisees (ver. 15) is then separated from the parable following in vv. 19-31 by vv. 16-18, the examination of which in detail is of no importance for the exposition of the parable. It is sufficient to ask, in what sense these declarations are inserted just here.[1] Their purport may be summed up thus: Jesus maintains an inviolable authority in the law (ver. 17), even during the new period opening with John the Baptist, when the law and the prophets have made way for the preaching of the kingdom of God (ver. 16); this authority He then illustrates in a single point (ver. 18), declaring (and as a comparison with Matt. xix. 3-9 shows, on the basis of Gen. i. 27 and ii. 24) that both the man who dismisses his wife and marries another, and the man who marries her that is dismissed, are adulterers. And this individual application of the law declared inviolable, isolated as it may seem at first sight in the context of the present passage, shows us in what sense the insertion of the whole paragraph (vv. 16-18) is here meant. For it is precisely with this individual precept, in the strict form which Jesus declares to be the original, divine meaning of the law, that the Pharisaic laxity stood in flagrant antagonism; and thus the Pharisees, who delight to pose before men as blameless observers of the law, are convicted of standing in antagonism with it really and before God, and of being under its condemnation. Thus Jesus alleges against them (ver. 18) the very law which they were accustomed elsewhere to allege against Him, and to which He certainly assumes a different attitude from theirs (ver. 16), while acknowledging its inviolable authority (ver. 17). He makes even the law bear witness against their unrighteous-

---

[1] This question requires an answer in any case, whether Jesus really spoke the words in this connection, or whether Luke or his authority inserted them here.

ness, which they may succeed in concealing from men, but not from God, who knows their hearts.

And now, in ver. 19, the narrative passes immediately to a new and fifth parable, without any mention of a change in the subject of discourse; for the δέ with which (ver. 19) the parable is introduced simply expresses the formal turn in the discourse at the beginning of a narrative. We accordingly expect to find in the parable a continuation of the rebuke administered to the Pharisees (vv. 15–18) on the occasion related in ver. 14.

The words: "*Now there was a certain rich man,*"[1] in the first place prefix to the narrative the person of whom it is to treat, whereupon the sentence, subjoined independently with καί, opens the narrative itself with a description of what the rich man wasted his riches upon: "*and he was clothed in purple and byssus.*" The first denotes a dark-red material (mostly woollen) dyed with the juice of the purple-shell, which stood in exceedingly high repute for its costly dye, the latter a no less costly cotton or linen material of brilliant white.[2] Hence purple garments were a sign of princely rank, and the garments of the priests were of byssus, according to Ex. xxviii. 39, xxxix. 27, 28. This, however, was not so exclusively the case[3] as to warrant us in finding here an intimation of the rich man's superior rank in the proper sense.[4] It is only said that nothing could satisfy his boundless love of show but garments of the grandest and costliest kind. And the additional participial clause: εὐφραινόμενος καθ' ἡμέραν λαμπρῶς, says that this showing off in costly apparel was not a solitary passion, but was rather in keeping with and conditioned by his whole sensuous, luxurious mode of life. The εὐφραίνεσθαι here, as often (xv. 23, 24, 29), has the special meaning of self-enjoyment in the social pleasures of the table. He enjoyed himself in gay carousing, and that not merely now and then, but καθ' ἡμέραν (day by day), with insatiable craving. In these enjoyments, as the adverb λαμπρῶς shows, he everywhere paraded the same pomp and grandeur as was shown in the sumptuousness of his apparel.

When we read further, in ver. 20, according to the reading of the Recepta: πτωχὸς δέ τις ἦν ὀνόματι Λάζαρος ὃς κ.τ.λ.,

---

[1] Not "A man was rich," Ewald, Bleek, Nebe; cf. ver. 1.
[2] Cf. Winer, art. "Purpur," and "Baumwolle."
[3] Cf. Prov. xxxi. 22.   [4] *E.g.* Starke's *Bibelwerk*.

it seems as if the narrative meant here to break off the previous description of the rich man, and, beginning as it were anew, to pass on to the description of another person, in order to place his character in independent contrast with that of the rich man sketched in ver. 19. But alongside this reading is found another, just as well attested outwardly,[1] according to which the narrative, instead of making a new beginning with πτωχὸς δέ τις ἦν ... ὅς, parallel with the first words of ver. 19, simply continues in unbroken and close connection with what precedes: πτωχὸς δέ τις ὀνόματι Λάζαρος ἐβέβλητο πρὸς τὸν πυλῶνα αὐτοῦ. In comparing the two readings, it deserves notice, first of all, that the reference to the rich man (common to the two) by means of the simple pronoun "his," speaks in favour of the uninterrupted, and against the newly commencing, form of the narrative. In the latter case we should rather have expected "the rich man's" instead of "his," *i.e.* a second independent mention of the rich man instead of a direct reference to what precedes by the pronoun. But the point can only be decided when we see the answer to the question, whether the sequel really presents a new character in independent contrast with that of the rich man as regards its *contents*, or whether what is said of the beggar does not merely serve to continue and complete the description of the rich man begun in ver. 19. If the investigation of vv. 20, 21 should yield the latter result, the reading of the Recepta would thereby be proved spurious, because arising from a plausible but really erroneous conception of the tenor of the narrative.

"*And a beggar named Lazarus was cast at his gateway,*" so it is said first, ver. 20. "Was cast" expresses the helplessness and also the forsaken condition of the beggar. For it implies, first, that he had no power of free movement, and again, that those who brought him there got rid of him like a troublesome burden which one throws down. Thus he was cast down "*at his* (the rich man's) *gateway,*" lying therefore immediately before the entrance to the interior of the house, where he must have been seen by the owner of the house as often as he went in and out. The two participles subjoined intimate how much the state in which the beggar presented himself to him there was adapted to claim his sympathy. He lay at the door εἱλκωμένος,[2] *i.e.* "covered

---

[1] Confirmed by Sinait. and accepted by Tischendorf.

[2] In the Recepta ἡλκωμένος; the usual, but for this very reason suspicious form, and also less attested.

with sores,"—afflicted, therefore, with a malignant disease obvious to every one who saw him, and on this account all the more urgently demanding compassion and care,—"*and desiring to be satisfied with what fell from the rich man's table.*" The words τῶν ψιχίων should perhaps be erased, on weighty evidence, as a spurious addition taken from Matt. xv. 27. Thus, in addition to his uncared-for disease, his unsatisfied hunger appealed to sympathy,—*unsatisfied*, for the words ἐπιθυμῶν χορτασθῆναι κ.τ.λ., as a more exact definition, like εἱλκωμένος, οἵ ἐβέβλητο πρὸς τὸν πυλῶνα αὐτοῦ, describe in any case a permanent state of suffering, a state consequently which, while not precluding a wretched prolongation of life, does preclude the gratifying of the desire for *sufficiency*.

The question, indeed, whether he remained lying at the rich man's door, so helpless and forsaken, sick and hungry, without finding the compassion which his state urgently demanded, is not expressly answered in what has preceded. Hitherto his state has only been described as *deserving compassion*. But the answer to this question is already intimated plainly enough in so far as his lying outside, with sickness uncared for and hunger unsatisfied, could not have become a permanent state if those within had been willing to help. Hence the statement now following, that in fact he found no compassion, instead of being given in a simple form,[1] is given at once with ἀλλὰ καί (*but even*) in a form of drastic severity: "*But* (instead of his finding compassion) *even the dogs came and licked his sores.*" Thus, so far from the care and attention being shown to the poor man which his state required, so little heed was given to him that he was even handed over to the dogs, which came without hindrance to lick his sores in doggish fashion. Certainly this does not mean that the licking of his sores as such caused him special bodily pain.[2] The words simply express the want of compassion, amounting to utter neglect, which handed him over to the dogs and their doggish ways. On the other hand, it is an entire mistake to wish to find a sympathizing alleviation of his pain in the action of the dogs,— a view underlying even the translation of Luther.[3] For apart from the circumstance that elsewhere in Holy Scripture dogs occur only as evil animals, and are used as an image of evil, it is impossible on this exposition correctly to interpret ἀλλὰ καί

---

[1] In similar language to that in xv. 16: "and no one had compassion on him."
[2] Meyer. [3] De Wette, Bleek, Stier, *et al.*

(which supposes an antithesis and at the same time heightens it) without importing very strange ideas.[1]

If we now look back at what has been said of the beggar, it is clear that everything serves in fact to continue and complete the description of the *Rich Man* begun in ver. 19. For when, in the first place, the condition in which a beggar lay before his door was described,—so helpless, forsaken, and appealing to pity in so unusual a degree,—and then it was said, in contrast, that instead of compassionate care he even met with complete indifference, obviously the purpose of the whole account is to give a description of the rich man, who was pictured first (ver. 19) in his love of pomp and enjoyment, and then in his pitiless cruelty and selfish indifference to another's woe; whereas, on the other hand, there is no feature in the story calculated to throw light on the beggar's own inner disposition. For what is said of his humble silence,[2] or of his quiet patience,[3]—"which certainly is the more to be surmised because he did not himself parade it,"— is, as the latter clause itself concedes, without support in the text.

There still remains the question whether the proper name "*Lazarus*," assigned to the beggar, is meant to give an intimation at least respecting his inner disposition, to which no reference is made elsewhere. A definite intention must in any case underlie this strange giving of a name, the only instance of the kind in all the parables of Jesus. Accordingly, it has been conjectured that Jesus meant to refer to a definite person living at the time and known to the hearers,—perhaps to a beggar of this name living in Jerusalem in those days, whose existence, however, is only mentioned in a very uncertain tradition,—or to Lazarus of Bethany. The description of the beggar would certainly remind no one of that Lazarus, because, in complete contrast with the beggar, he rejoiced in a regular household and the care of two living sisters. Moreover, it is quite impossible to see what value such a reference to a contemporary person could have in the tenor of the narrative. Just as little can the name assigned to

---

[1] Hofmann revives this interpretation, alleging against the one advanced above, that then a negative sentence must have come first, to the effect that the poor man had not obtained what he desired. But that this may easily be supplied from what precedes has been shown above. Or is it easier to supply what Hofmann as well as Stier imports: "*The servants gave him something by stealth,*—however, the dogs showed interest in him"?

[2] van Oosterzee. [3] Stier.

the beggar be explained by the conjecture, that the narrative this time is not imaginary, but really historical, and therefore the persons of whom it treats are not fictitious, but historical. For since the chief person in the whole parable—the Rich Man—is not mentioned by name, we must again ask, why the proper name passed over there in silence is here given. In addition, the conjecture will be shown, in the proper place, on weighty grounds to be altogether inapt. The only thing therefore left is to seek the reason of the name being given in its significance, which seems the most obvious way of explanation, considering the symbolism of names usual from early times among the Jews, and employed also in the New Testament, and even by Jesus Himself (Matt. xvi. 18). The name Λάζαρος, then, is either derived from לֹא עֲזָר, "without help," in which case the one so named would be described as one destitute of help, or from אֶלְעָזָר, "God is the help," in this case "one who makes God his help." Decisive for the latter derivation is the fact that אֶלְעָזָר is a name occurring already in the Old Testament, and appearing in the Talmud in the shortened form לְעָזָר, after which analogy the Graecized form Ἐλεάζαρος (LXX.), shortened Λάζαρος, is framed. But internal reasons also decide for this meaning of the name. For in the signification "destitute of help," the name would say precisely the same that is made strongly prominent in the entire description of the beggar, and would therefore merely contain a worthless pleonasm for the tenor of the narrative,—certainly an inadequate explanation of so strange an insertion of a proper name. But if, on the other hand, Λάζαρος is synonymous with the common Eleazar, the insertion serves to intimate to the hearers something which it did not lie in the plan of the narrative to make prominent in the story itself, namely, the God-trusting disposition with which the beggar bore his suffering.

For what reason an intimation at least in this direction is given, is at once shown in the further course of the narrative. By this means the way seems adequately prepared for what is at once said of the happy state into which Lazarus was translated by death. With the ἐγένετο δέ, marking the beginning of a new section of the narrative, ver. 22, the account of the beggar's dying is introduced, and only then is the rich man's dying spoken of. The narrative therefore dwells exclusively (ver. 23 ff.) on the person of the rich man,—what is said of the beggar's dying (ver. 22), and the state on which he entered at death, being only mentioned in reference to the rich man. Hence it is clear that the preceding account of the dying of the poor man simply forms the groundwork for continuing the history of the rich man as intended.

"*And it came to pass that the beggar died,*" ver. 22. The ἀποθανεῖν here can signify nothing but what it signifies everywhere: the separation of the soul from the body, which becomes a corpse, and its descent to the place of the dead. When, therefore, to ἀποθανεῖν the words: καὶ ἀπενεχθῆναι αὐτὸν ὑπὸ τῶν ἀγγέλων εἰς τὸν κόλπον Ἀβραάμ, are added, it is not a special event that is related in these words, distinct from that of dying and following it; as, for example, that the dead man, instead of being buried, was carried away by angels,[1] a view not having even a plausible support in the circumstance that no mention is made of the burial. For we so little miss the mention of the burial here, that, on the contrary, if it occurred, we should have to ask in vain what it could signify. Rather these words simply define more precisely the event contained in the idea of the ἀποθανεῖν, showing how death was to him the end of his suffering and the entrance into blessedness. From the earth, which had been the scene of his suffering, angels bore him away (ἀπενεχθῆναι) into the κόλπος Ἀβραάμ. Ὁ κόλπος is literally "the bosom," hence synonymous with the plural ἐν τοῖς κόλποις αὐτοῦ, ver. 23. "To be in Abraham's bosom" is a designation, common elsewhere in Jewish theology, for the fellowship of dead believers with Abraham in Paradise. To the Israelite, Abraham seems the personal centre and meeting-point of Paradise. Hence his hope is to be gathered to Abraham, and to be permitted, in fellowship with him, to enjoy paradisaic bliss. The idea of *table*-fellowship[2] is not necessarily implied in the expression (cf. John i. 18), and must here be renounced, because occurring elsewhere only of the enjoyment in common of the blessings of the future kingdom of God. The function of the angels is to bring dying believers into Abraham's bosom. Hence also Lazarus, the truster in God, is translated thither by the ministry of angels, without anything being affirmed of him different from what holds good of every dying believer.

After, in this way, everything has been said of the beggar that was necessary to prepare for what follows, the history of the rich man is continued, his death being first of all related: "*the rich*

---

[1] Meyer. [2] Bengel *et al.*

man also died;" therefore he also—this again is implied in the ἀπέθανεν—descended into Hades. But before the condition in which he there found himself is further described, καὶ ἐτάφη is added to the ἀπέθανεν. And little as we missed any mention of the burial in the case of the beggar, where it would have been quite useless, it seems full of significance in the rich man's case. But not because, as is usually understood, we are reminded of the last glimmer of earthly glory vouchsafed to the rich man in a *brilliant* funeral, in which case the brilliance of the funeral must have been emphasized by some more precise definition, as, for example, by a λαμπρῶς, as in ver. 19. On the contrary, the two words καὶ ἐτάφη express with startling brevity the *loss* of all earthly glory that befell the rich man on his death. Precisely in the fact of being buried, the loss of all earthly possession occurring at death presents itself to the gaze with terrible effect. When a man is buried, it is obvious to sense that nothing is left him of all this world's goods but the grave, to the corruption of which the body is consigned. Accordingly, these words involve, of course, a preliminary, but not as yet complete antithesis to the carrying of the beggar into Abraham's bosom, for they signalize the fact that, as death brought to the one the end of his earthly suffering, so it brought to the other the end of his earthly felicity. On the other hand, the notion is quite impracticable, which Meyer would find here, namely, that the rich man, instead of being borne away by the angels like the poor man, was buried, and first came down into Hades from the grave "as to his whole person,"—so impracticable that even the appeal to the alleged poetic character of the narrative cannot justify it, since even in a poetic narrative the incidents ought in some way to be capable of conception.

Upon the impressive conclusion which the earthly history of the rich man has thus found, follows now the resumption of his history in Hades. His coming thither was implied, as we saw, not indeed in the ἐτάφη, but in the ἀπέθανεν. Hence, assuming his having come down there, the narrative can immediately continue, ver. 23 : καὶ ἐν τῷ ᾅδῃ ἐπάρας τοὺς ὀφθαλμοὺς αὐτοῦ κ.τ.λ. Hades, the word in the LXX. for שְׁאוֹל, is the general tarrying-place of departed souls.[1] It is divided into two parts,—a place of felicity for the good, where they sojourn until the resurrection (called Paradise by Jesus, xxiii. 43 ; and also in the Rabbins,

[1] Gen. xxxvii. 35 ; Acts ii. 27, 31.

פַּרְדֵּס); and a place of torment, represented as a burning in flames of fire, for the godless, called Gehenna (גֵּי הִנֹּם) in the Rabbins. It is to be observed, however, that the latter designation only occurs in the discourses of Jesus of the place of *eternal* damnation,[1] to which, after the final judgment,[2] not merely the soul, but both body and soul, are consigned (Matt. x. 28). That the rich man found himself in the place of torment, accordingly follows not from the words καὶ ἐν τῷ ᾅδῃ . . ., but only from the words ὑπάρχων ἐν βασάνοις. The sentence is to be construed: "*And in Hades, when he lifted up his eyes, finding himself in torments, he saw*," etc. The second present participial clause explains the first aorist clause, pointing out the torment in which he found himself as the occasion of the ἐπαίρειν. Consequently the opening of his eyes is to be regarded as a looking up and looking out for help on the sufferer's part. But when mention is made here of a lifting up of the *eyes*, and, further, of the *tongue* of the rich man, and the *finger* of Lazarus, as well as of suffering pain in the *flame* and being refreshed by *water*,—when, therefore, to sum up everything in a word, departed souls are spoken of as if they were in the state of bodily life, this mode of representation is not so much the product of poetic fancy as rather a simple necessity when once the narrative has to be continued in Hades and find its conclusion there, since without such fiction no sensations and outward phenomena of departed souls can either be conceived or expressed in language. On lifting up his eyes in search of help, "*he saw Abraham afar off*,"—namely, in the place of blessedness, far from the place of torment in which he found himself,—"*and Lazarus in his bosom.*" In this sentence the retribution that befell the rich man beyond death for his conduct in life is definitely emphasized as such. For when it is said of him that he finds himself in torment, and beholds Lazarus in the enjoyment of paradisaic felicity, the condition in which he now finds himself, in contrast with Lazarus, appears as the retribution for his having previously allowed Lazarus to pine away in a similar condition in contrast with himself.

When, then, in ver. 24 it is continued: καὶ αὐτὸς φωνήσας εἶπεν, the significance of the αὐτός ought the less to be overlooked, the more superfluous at first sight this special resumption of the subject of the discourse appears to be. In giving to the sentence, ver. 24, its own special subject, the αὐτός preserves

---

[1] Matt. xviii. 8, 9; Mark ix. 43 ff.   [2] Matt. xiii. 40-42, 49, 50.

the independence of the preceding one, ver. 23, which should be marked by a period between the two sentences. Were it wanting, the sentence, ver. 23, would take the position of an introductory protasis to the conversation now opening between the rich man and Abraham, whereas at present the contents of ver. 23 have to be considered independently, and the conversation following is simply added still further to work out and verify what is there said. In his present condition there awakens in the rich man the thought, to which before he gave no place in his selfish, harsh state of mind, how easily one living in abundance may help one pining in misery. The sight of Lazarus in Abraham's bosom excites in him the hope of obtaining help from him—the happy one—in his pain. Hence: καὶ αὐτὸς φωνήσας εἶπεν· πάτερ ᾿Αβραάμ, ἐλέησόν με καὶ πέμψον Λάζαρον, ἵνα κ.τ.λ. The φωνεῖν is not a call meant to reach across the distance,[1] as the free interchange of talk between the two sides proves, but simply an address to draw attention to himself. "*Father* Abraham," runs his cry. But it is importing too much into the address to Abraham as *father* to see in it an appeal of the rich man to his descent from Abraham,[2] giving him a legal claim to the granting of his request.[3] For this appellation regularly recurs even where it is impossible for it to have such a meaning according to the sense of the language (vv. 27, 30). It is therefore simply the address natural and seemly in the lips of a Jew speaking to Abraham. But he turns to *Abraham* with his request to *send* Lazarus, instead of appealing directly to Lazarus, because he feels that in the order of things lying before his eyes Lazarus could not come over to relieve him unless authorized by a command of Abraham. In this consciousness he cries pathetically: "*Father Abraham, have mercy on me, and send Lazarus;*" and in the same consciousness of the unusual and bold character of his prayer, he reduces his request itself to the most modest limits, asking but the least conceivable relief: "*Send Lazarus, that he may dip the tip of his finger in water*[4] *and cool my tongue,*" *scil.* by touching with the moistened finger,—finally, in the same consciousness he feels constrained to assign a reason for the boldness even of this slight request in the torment of his condition: "*for I am in anguish in this flame.*" It is therefore

---

[1] Godet.   [2] Bengel: *gloriatio carnis*.   [3] Stier, Godet.
[4] Βάψῃ ὕδατος, the genitive with verbs of touching; cf. Winer, *Gram. of N. T.* p. 252.

erroneous to suppose that the request, "send Lazarus," implies a disparaging of the person of Lazarus continued even in Hades,[1] leading him to think Lazarus at his beck and call,[2] or to suppose that he makes him his errand-boy,[3] or even assigns as the reason of the request for a touch with the tip of his finger the remembrance of the sores of Lazarus![4] His hoping for help from *Lazarus* arises from the sight of his happiness in Abraham's bosom; and his asking *Abraham* to *send* him merely to give such slight relief, arises from the consciousness that he is asking something unusual and bold.

With εἶπεν δὲ Ἀβραάμ ver. 25 now introduces Abraham's answer to the request. The answer is not one simply declining; but with a certain sympathy, as expressed in the address by "child," he seeks to awaken in the suppliant himself the consciousness that the granting of his request would involve an injustice. For this reason he first of all calls on him to remember what he has already received in his life, and what, on the other hand, Lazarus received: μνήσθητι ὅτι ἀπέλαβες τὰ ἀγαθά σου ἐν τῇ ζωῇ σου, καὶ Λάζαρος ὁμοίως τὰ κακά.[5] The ὁμοίως in the latter incomplete clause indicates that the clause must be completed in entire analogy with the first, so that in its complete form it runs: καὶ Λάζαρος ἀπέλαβεν ἐν τῇ ζωῇ αὐτοῦ τὰ κακὰ αὐτοῦ. Some erroneously think it necessary to lay stress on the fact, that in the second clause only τὰ κακά stands in contrast with τὰ ἀγαθά σου without the corresponding pronoun αὐτοῦ being added. Erroneously, because on account of the equally recurring article the αὐτοῦ is just as naturally suggested to the reader as the remaining completion of the clause; and this all the more that its omission is not only compensated by the ὁμοίως, but seems also to be occasioned by the expressive emphasis falling on the κακά, both as the final word of the sentence, and implying contrast. Accordingly, the words: ἀπέλαβες τὰ ἀγαθά σου, can only be understood of the rich man in a sense in which ἀπέλαβεν τὰ κακὰ αὐτοῦ can also be said of Lazarus. For this reason the idea of a selfish receiving,[6] which the word nowhere signifies, cannot lie in the ἀπέλαβες. Nor does the meaning: "to receive beforehand,"[7] in itself lie in the word. But ἀπολαμβάνειν means simply "to receive," only differing from λαμβάνειν

---

[1] Bengel: *adhuc vilipendit Lazarum.*   [2] van Oosterzee.   [3] Lange.
[4] Lange.   [5] σύ after ἀπέλαβες is to be expunged on preponderant evidence.
[6] Godet.   [7] van Oosterzee.

in this way, that it is specially chosen where the object of the receiving appears in some way as a due.[1] So the compound is chosen here, because the amount of what is received is viewed as a complete due, beyond which nothing remains to be received. In this sense it is said, with the verb emphatically prefixed: "*Remember that thou* (already) *hast received*"—τὰ ἀγαθά σου ἐν τῇ ζωῇ σου. After the emphatic ἀπέλαβες the second (and as the contrast: καὶ Λάζαρος τὰ κακά, proves), the chief emphasis of the sentence rests on ἀγαθά, the σου, on the other hand, remaining unemphasized. It is not said "*thy* good things," the things good in *thy* eyes,[2] which, moreover, applied to the corresponding τὰ κακά, would lead to an absurdity, but "thy *good* things," *i.e.* thy *good* part, the *good* part of thy lot. Finally, the third emphasis in the sentence rests on ζωῇ: "Remember that thou *hast received* thy *good* in thy *life*,"—and we can now complete the words: καὶ Λάζαρος τὰ κακά, with the analogy required by ὁμοίως, without forcing on them any other meaning than what they have in the first clause: "and that Lazarus *received* the *evil* part of his lot in his *life*." With the previous diversity of their lot in their earthly life, now brought to remembrance, is contrasted, by νῦν δὲ ὧδε,[3] the *present* diversity of their condition *here in Hades;* and this time Lazarus is put first in immediate sequence to what precedes: "*But now here he* (after receiving his evil things in life) *is comforted, and thou* (after receiving thy good things in life) *art in anguish.*" ’Οδυνᾶσθαι is to be left in this passage in the middle signification, which it has in ver. 24 and everywhere else, and not to be converted into the passive for the sake of parallelism with παρακαλεῖται.

Accordingly, the present diversity of their condition here in Hades corresponds thoroughly to the diversity of their lot in life, only reversed. Hence the rich man himself must confess that the granting of the request, in which he hopes for alleviation of his present pain from the present happiness of Lazarus, would be an injustice. But it is also now clear that the entire explanation of ver. 25, considered as a negative answer to the rich man's request, would be deprived of all pertinent and convincing force if the latter, during his life, had laid himself out to relieve the beggar's misery out of his own then abundance. For in this case the rich man would have implored nothing from Lazarus in his

---

[1] Cf. *e.g.* vi. 34, xviii. 30, xxiii. 41.   [2] Stier, van Oosterzee, von Hofmann.
[3] According to far preponderant testimony, instead of ὧν δὲ ἰδε.

present condition which he had not himself done to Lazarus in their formerly reversed circumstances. Accordingly, as a declining of the request made in ver. 24, which the explanation of ver. 25 professes simply to be, it is based on what is said in vv. 19–21, according to which the rich man, instead of sharing his abundance with the beggar, applied it simply to his own enjoyment. At that time, during life, when he received his good and Lazarus his evil things, he had let it remain so. And now in Hades, when Lazarus receives his good and he his evil things, it must justly remain so. This is the inference lying in the words according to the connection in which they stand. But no general law of divine justice is here laid down, according to which the circumstances of men, in this life outwardly so different, must needs after death *always* find a corresponding adjustment. But it is simply brought home to the rich man, who, after using his earthly wealth selfishly, and closing his heart against the misery of Lazarus, now in his suffering desires to make use of the happiness of Lazarus, how unreasonable this demand is as far as he is concerned, since the actual distribution of good and evil between him and Lazarus, in the present case, is thoroughly equitable. Hence things must remain as they are in Hades, just as was the case conversely in life.

However, Abraham is not content with proving the impracticableness of the rich man's request, but adds a second reason (ver. 26) : " *And beside all this* (explained in ver. 25), *between us and you, there is a great gulf fixed.*" For what purpose this gulf was fixed between the saved here and the lost there is stated in the telic sentence subjoined with ὅπως: "*that they which would pass from hence to you may not be able, and that none may cross over from thence to us.*" Οἱ ἐκεῖθεν in the latter clause is not to be supplemented by θέλοντες διαβῆναι from the first clause, because while the μὴ δύνωνται there harmonizes with this, the μὴ διαπερῶσιν here does not; but οἱ ἐκεῖθεν is a brachylogy for οἱ ἐκεῖ (ὄντες) ἐκεῖθεν—" those found there from thence." Even if the οἱ before ἐκεῖθεν ought to be omitted, according to some evidence, the meaning remains exactly the same, for even on this reading οἱ ἐκεῖ ὄντες would have to be borrowed from ἐκεῖθεν as the self-understood subject of the clause. The subject of the second clause must not be identified with that of the first,[1] as this would yield the inapposite notion that the fixing of the gulf

---

[1] Godet.

prevented the passing and re-passing of the saved only. It is to be observed that the impossibility of passing to and fro is not viewed merely as a consequence of the gulf existing independently between the place of happiness and misery, but the prevention is stated to be the premeditated end (ὅπως) for which the gulf was established. Accordingly, it does not exhaust the truth to say, as is usually done after Bengel's example, the *argumentum ab impossibili* (ver. 26) is added to the *argumentum ab æquo* (ver. 25), for what is insisted on by Abraham is not simply an accidental, so to speak, physical impossibility, but an order of things unconditionally forbidding the passing to and fro, and to secure this order a great gulf is fixed between here and there. After showing the rich man that compliance with his request would, in the state of the case between him and Lazarus, be opposed to justice (ver. 25), Abraham adds that it would run counter to the inviolable order of things in Hades, an order secured in its inviolability by the gulf. The right observation of the logical position belonging to the "great gulf" in the strain of thought removes the appearance of strangeness to a certain degree, which some have found in this conception, because of its only occurring here, without analogy in the Rabbins, who speak only of a wall dividing the two portions of Hades. The chief point here was not to represent the two parts of Hades as spatially separated by a boundary of some kind,—which led most naturally to the conception of a wall,—but to characterize the boundary assumed to exist between the two parts on that side of its nature, on which it serves to exclude every attempt to pass from one side to the other; and for this purpose the conception of a great gulf, taken from earthly relations of space, offered itself as the most striking.

By the answer of Abraham the impracticableness of the rich man's request has been twice irrefutably proved. This the suppliant himself acknowledges in a certain sense, when, dropping the first prayer, he turns to a second and different one, in the words, ver. 27: ἐρωτῶ σε οὖν, πάτερ, ἵνα πέμψῃς αὐτὸν εἰς τὸν οἶκον τοῦ πατρός μου, i.e., "If, *therefore* (οὖν), as thou sayest, Lazarus cannot be sent to *me*, *I pray thee that thou wouldest send him to my father's house.*" Of what persons in his father's house he is thinking, is then explained in an independent parenthesis graphically thrust in: "*I have five brethren.*" We observe here how thoroughly natural it is for the rich man, in naming to

Abraham those in whom he takes such interest, not merely to speak of brethren in general, but to mention his brethren definitely by number. Therefore, a specification of number is so natural here in the mouth of the suppliant, that there is no need to seek special reasons for its occurrence. Only after the interpolation of this parenthesis is it stated for what purpose Abraham is to send Lazarus to the brethren: ὅπως διαμαρτύρηται αὐτοῖς. The purport of the testifying is not added expressly. For we cannot take it, as in Acts ii. 40, and often outside the New Testament, as an urgent *exhorting*, and find the purport in the following clause: ἵνα μὴ καὶ αὐτοὶ ἔλθωσιν κ.τ.λ., because the clause does not speak of a doing or non-doing, to which one might be exhorted, but of the suffering or non-suffering of a fate which cannot be the object of an exhortation. If, accordingly, the purport must be supplied to διαμαρτύρηται from the context, we must understand it, not as an urgent exhorting, but (as in Acts viii. 25, x. 42, *et al.*) as an intensely solemn testifying, since it is only in this way that the object of the verb can easily be deduced from the previous contents of the narrative. That the rich man finds himself in Hades in the place of torment,—this is what Lazarus, coming thence, is solemnly to testify to his brethren, who are regarded as like him in disposition. That it is this which the suppliant would have testified to his brethren, is confirmed by the final telic clause at once added by him: "*lest they also come into this place of torment*," which clause, however, does not depend grammatically on διαμαρτύρηται, as if it indicated the purpose of the testifying on the part of the testifier; but, depending also on πέμψῃς, it expresses the final aim of the mission implored. By the witness borne to his torment—so the rich man thinks he is justified in expecting—his like-minded brethren will be led to a change of disposition, and will thus escape the like torment.

According to the words, then, the line of thought that led the rich man to the prayer is this: that if Lazarus, according to Abraham's statement, can no longer be useful to him, already found in the place of torment, yet he may perhaps be helpful to his still living brethren, that they also come not to this place. As the inner motive of the request, the words indicate, not a feeling of compassion, such as did not belong to him in life,[1] but the natural love of kinship to his brethren. Nevertheless, the

[1] Bengel *et al.*

conjecture may not be unwarranted, that behind the prayer for his brethren lurks also a self-justifying complaint, that the threatening punishment had not been testified to himself during life with sufficient force. For although the words of the request, taken by themselves, furnish no support for the opinion that they are put into the mouth of the rich man in this sense also, yet the way in which Abraham now replies favours the opinion. Whereas to the first request for a mitigation of the rich man's own suffering he gave a detailed reply, introduced by the friendly "child," for this second request, which yet seems an outflow of fraternal love, he has only a brief, almost sharp refusal (ver. 29): λέγει δὲ Ἀβραάμ, Ἔχουσιν Μωυσέα καὶ τοὺς προφήτας· ἀκουσάτωσαν αὐτῶν. Thus, to the request of the rich man to send Lazarus as a witness to his brethren, Abraham opposes the witnesses they have already: Moses and the prophets. It is true, the Scriptures of the Old Testament, comprised under this appellation, give no express information respecting the pain awaiting the godless in Hades. But they everywhere bear admonitory witness against the rich, who, without feeling for the poor and wretched, squander their wealth in luxurious enjoyment, and testify to them the judgment of God that will inevitably burst upon them. Hence, all further witness being refused, the simple demand must stand: ἀκουσάτωσαν αὐτῶν, i.e. let them hear and obey the witnesses they have. But this refusal provokes the rich man to reply once again, and this all the more that he sees himself not merely deprived of hope for his brethren, but also reminded of his own disobedience to the testimony of Scripture. Now, therefore, he casts a vivid "nay, father Abraham" back at Abraham (ver. 30). In what way the "nay" is to be supplemented from the words against which it raises objection, is shown by the following antithesis: ἀλλ' ἐάν τις ἀπὸ νεκρῶν πορευθῇ πρὸς αὐτούς, μετανοήσουσιν. Therefore: "*Nay, father Abraham, Moses and the prophets they will not obey; but if one go to them from the dead, they will repent.*" He assumes that they will persist in their impenitent disobedience, despite Moses and the prophets, inferring the unreceptiveness of his brethren to the testimony of Scripture from his own unreceptiveness manifested during his life. On the other hand, he thinks he may promise success to the testimony of one coming to them from the dead, because of the effect on the senses of such a miraculous appearance of the dead. But this expectation, ascribing to the testimony of one coming from the dead an effect in awakening to repentance which does not belong to the testimony of Scripture, is wrong, as Abraham is now obliged finally to tell him (ver. 31). Really the case stands thus: "*If they*—as thou assumest of them —*obey not Moses and the prophets*," οὐδ' ἐάν τις ἐκ νεκρῶν ἀναστῇ πεισθήσονται. The οὐδέ here simply adds one negation to another = "neither," and is not ascensive = "not even." For the words: ἐάν τις ἐκ νεκ. ἀν., simply resume the case put in the words of the rich man (ver. 30): ἐάν τις ἐκ νεκ. πορ. πρὸς αὐτούς, with a slight change of expression, and are not meant, as Stier understands, and others seem to take them, to put a second still more wonderful case than the one there, as if the sense were: "If they obey not Moses and the prophets, they will not be moved even in case a dead man (really) came to life again." Ἀνιστάναι ἐκ νεκρῶν merely denotes a rising from the dead quite generally. Whether it takes place on the entrance into eternal life, or merely as a continuation of the former earthly life, or even merely for the purpose of a visit to the still living, the context in each case must decide. A rising from the dead in the last sense is described in quite similar terms (1 Sam. xxviii. 13), only still more strongly, by עֹלֶה מִן־הָאָרֶץ. The expression ἀνιστ. ἐκ νεκ. in the present passage, therefore, does not justify us in understanding something different from what the context supplies, the rising of one from the dead to bear witness to the still living. Just so the expression πεισθήσονται is synonymous with the μετανοήσουσιν corresponding to it in ver. 30. The passive πείθεσθαι means "to be moved, won," either in reference *ad intellectum:* "to hold something true," or *ad voluntatem:* "to do something." Here the latter signification holds good. For the subject of πεισθήσονται, according to the hypothetical protasis, is those who oppose to the witness of Scripture not so much critical unbelief as practical disobedience. If they *do this* despite the witness of Scripture,—such is the meaning,—neither will they *be moved* by the witness of one rising from the dead, *scil.* to the repentance expected by the rich man in this case. Therefore this final reply of Abraham consists simply in a decisive denial of the assertion advanced by the rich man (ver. 30), according to which, not the testimony of Scripture, but that of one coming from the dead, will have the power to produce repentance. To this Abraham rejoins: The testimony of Scripture is so weighty and powerful, that they who harden themselves in disobedience against it cannot be moved to repentance even by an extraordinary testimony acting more on the senses.

Having arrived at the close of the narrative, let us now, in order to ascertain its moral, compare its contents with the preceding discourse of Jesus (vv. 15–18), and its occasion (ver. 14). Before the Pharisees, who, touched by His words (vv. 1–13), in their avarice, tried to conceal their feeling by ridicule (ver. 14), Jesus had there held up this hypocritical concealing of their inner disposition (vv. 15–18), testifying to them that, despite their posing as righteous before men, God knows their hearts; nay, that despite their seeming holy legality, the law itself condemns them. When, then, in immediate sequence to this He tells of a rich man who made such a selfish use of his wealth as we have read in vv. 19–21, the inner connection of such a narrative with the preceding discourse is clearly this, that, after first rebuking the hypocritical *concealment* of the Pharisees, Jesus now in the narrative (ver. 19 ff.) drags to the light, and holds up before them, the *concealed* thing itself, namely, their love of money; because of which the admonitions to the disciples (vv. 1–13) as to how wealth is to be regarded, and what use is to be made of it, became an offence to them. *To disclose to them the selfish use which they make of wealth, in their love of money, and to show them the retribution which they have to expect for it beyond death, unless they repent,*—this is the purpose of the narrative. This purpose Jesus carries out in three sections: in the first (vv. 19–21), depicting the selfish use of wealth by the example of a rich man; in the second (vv. 22–26), pointing out by the same example the retribution falling on such a disposition and course of conduct in the next world; whereas in the third part (vv. 27–31) He exhorts those of the same disposition as the rich man still in the world to avoid the like fate by repentance.

If we have rightly defined the purpose and plan of our narrative, it follows that, just like the narratives of the Merciful Samaritan in chap. x. and the Rich Fool in chap. xii., it is not a symbolic, but a typical narrative, picturing its object not by means of symbol, but merely of concrete example. On the other hand, the notion that our narrative is not fictitious, but the account of a historically real event, is just as untenable as the like conjecture in the case of the story of the Merciful Samaritan.

That this notion is neither necessary nor adequate to explain the proper name occurring in the narrative, we have seen in examining this name. And that it is not needed to explain the specification of number occurring in ver. 28, the examination of the passage has shown. But apart from these merely apparent points of support, the notion has everything against it. Against it is, first, the consideration that the narrative joins on to a series of other imaginary narratives in one and the same connection, without being introduced differently from them. In the second place, the directly productive hand of the narrator betrays itself everywhere in its entire structure, following as that structure does a definite plan that governs all particulars, just as much as in all the other parables of Jesus. Again, the first part of the narrative, falling within the earthly life, contains nothing whose obvious aim is not the laying a basis for what follows. And finally, in the second part, extending into Hades, any historical character is out of the question altogether.

In now proceeding to set forth in detail the didactic import of the narrative, we do not need, in order to do this, an interpretation in the proper sense, *i.e.* a translation of the figure into the thing symbolized, but, as in the previous typical parables, have merely to carry out the application which the example proposed has to the hearers of Jesus. In the rich man's disposition and conduct, described vv. 19–21, Jesus characterizes the Pharisaic disposition and conduct in regard to earthly goods. Therefore, in the person of the rich man He does not represent Pharisaism as such in its distinguishing peculiarities, but a particular aspect of Pharisaic thought and action, with the qualification, however, that in the bearing of the rich man he brings out to view in undisguised distinctness what the Pharisees strive to hide by the veil of their seeming holiness before men.[1] Really they think and act like the rich man. In their avarice they use their wealth to satisfy their passion for parade and enjoyment, ver. 19, whereas they close their hearts in inhuman coldness against the pitiable misery of the poor and sick lying before their eyes, without alleviating it from their abundance, vv. 20, 21. This explanation of the description in vv. 19–21 alone corresponds equally to the wording of the same and the connection in which the narrative stands. On the other hand, both wording and connection are contradicted by the explanation, which finds in

[1] Matt. vi. 2; Luke xx. 47.

vv. 19–21 merely a contrasting of great wealth on one side and great poverty on the other, and sees in the description of the rich man and the poor man a religious and moral basis for the retribution following, asserting that the narrative is meant in its first half (up to ver. 26) to condemn wealth in itself and extol poverty,[1] or at least owes its present form to the (condemnatory) "view of Luke respecting wealth."[2] On this explanation of the narrative any connection with the preceding discourse of Jesus must be renounced altogether. It is also refuted by the wording of the narrative. For in his character as rich, the rich man is merely the subject of discourse. In the description given of him, on the other hand, the being rich is no longer treated of in itself, but simply and solely the wrong use made of his riches: positively, in boundless show and luxury; negatively, in unmerciful hardness against poverty. And as concerns the beggar, he comes into view, as the consideration of the course of the narrative has shown us, in the first instance merely as the object of the rich man's unmerciful hardness; and accordingly, in the description given of him, merely the pitiful greatness of his suffering is treated of, where, however, on account of what follows, an intimation at least of his inner state of heart by the name Lazarus is not omitted.

Vv. 22–26 then discuss the retribution which such disposition and conduct have to expect beyond death. After an admonitory allusion in ver. 22, by the καὶ ἐτάφη, to the inevitable end of all earthly show and indulgence, the description of the condition in which the rich man found himself in Hades, ver. 23, shows the retribution to consist in this, that they who, caring only for their own felicity, are indifferent to the misery of others, now on their part suffer pain and exclusion from the enjoyment of paradisaic felicity in Abraham's bosom; and, accordingly, there they are in a similar position, with regard to the saved in Abraham's bosom, to that in which they allowed others to pine with regard to themselves below. This retribution is pictured in the narrative with special force, by the beggar being translated into Hades before the rich man, and that as a Lazarus into Abraham's bosom, so that the rich man finds the very same beggar, whom he in his happiness before left to the dogs, now sharing in felicity from which he in his suffering is excluded. Further, by this translation

---

[1] De Wette, Strauss, Tübingen school.
[2] Weiss on ver. 19 ff., and *Bibl. Theologie*, p. 580.

of Lazarus into Hades, the basis is gained for the explanations in vv. 24–26. To those overtaken by this retribution—this lies in ver. 24—the thought may then occur, against which below they obstinately closed their hearts, how easily the suffering of the unfortunate may be mitigated by the happy imparting of their abundance, but then too late! For such an equalizing mitigation of the misery of the one by the felicity of the other is there forbidden them for a twofold reason. In the first place, as ver. 25 explains, because it would involve an injustice. When the request of the rich man in reference to this point is rejected by a simple contrasting of the diverse lot of the rich man and Lazarus in life with their diverse lot in Hades, only reversed, it is thereby declared that they who, like the rich man, rest content with the contrast of happiness and misery in life to their own advantage without attempt at mitigation, must in all fairness accept the reversal of this contrast to their disadvantage, without being permitted to hope for any equalizing mitigation. No other and farther-reaching application than this can be given to the address to the rich man in ver. 25, according to the fixed sense which the words have in the connection of the conversation. In particular, the assertion that the narrative condemns wealth in itself, after having been shown to contradict vv. 19–21, can no longer find support in these words of Abraham which rest essentially on what is said there. In the second place, any such equalizing mitigation of the suffering of one class by the felicity of the other is forbidden, as is now added in ver. 26, by the inviolable order of things obtaining in Hades, in virtue of which the saved in their place and the lost in their place are severed from each other by an impassable barrier, the exclusion of the one from the blessedness of the other being thus unconditional and irremoveable.

The narrative might end here, without seeming incomplete. But even in this case the result of the whole to the Pharisaic hearers resembling the rich man, whether expressed or unexpressed, would be an impressive exhortation to a change of mind, "lest they also come to this place of torment." But when we find this exhortation, resulting in any case from the parable, actually expressed within the narrative itself in a third supplementary part, no one has the right to affirm that this part of the narrative is in essential contradiction with what precedes, and to base hereupon the assertion that the previous narrative no longer exists in its original shape, but must have undergone a remodelling that changes the sense,[1] or is at least a one-sided version,[2] or to explain this last part itself as a mere spinning out of the parable for a purpose.[3] These assertions spring simply from the erroneous explanation and application of the narrative refuted above. On the other hand, on the right explanation and application, this last section furnishes a thoroughly appropriate and effective conclusion of the whole; and this all the more that the exhortation to a change of mind in those of the rich man's character is expressed in a form specially adapted to the Pharisaic hearers. For in making Abraham answer the rich man's prayer on behalf of his like-minded brethren for a miraculous testimony to the retribution awaiting them beyond death by a reference to Moses and the prophets as the witnesses whom they are to hear (vv. 27–29), Jesus appeals, against the Pharisees who despise His words (ver. 14) and usually demand confirming signs,[4] to the testimony of Scripture respecting the retribution threatened to them because like the rich man in character, and demands of them the obedience to Scripture which really they do not render, despite their apparent regard for it, as He has already convinced them (vv. 16–18). And He further justifies this appeal and strengthens this demand by the final decision of Abraham (ver. 31) in reply to the rich man (ver. 30), in which He tells them that all further testimony will be superfluous to them if they harden themselves in disobedience against the witness of Scripture, since even a testifying of future retribution by one coming from the dead would not move to a change of mind those who refuse the weighty and powerful testimony of Scripture.

A remark or two is necessary on the details of this concluding section. As regards the number of the rich man's brethren, we have seen, on ver. 28, that a specification of number was required in this place by the need of concrete, vivid narrative; and accordingly we may be content to regard the number as chosen at random,[5] all the more so that all attempts to ascribe a special purpose to the number five as such, or to find a special meaning, prove impracticable. For we cannot suppose a personal allusion to five of the Pharisees present, whom the Lord had specially in view in His description,[6] or to the sons of Annas, who are said by Josephus to have been five in number, because such a personal attack in the disguised form of a play of numbers is out of

---

[1] De Wette.   [2] Weiss.   [3] Tübingen school.
[4] Matt. xii. 38, 39, xvi. 1; Mark viii. 11.   [5] Cf. xiv. 19.   [6] Bengel.

harmony with the accustomed dignity of the language of Jesus. To attempt to find a symbolic significance for the number, by extracting the symbolic number seven,[1] adding not only the rich man as the sixth brother, but also Lazarus (and why not Abraham ?), is altogether too far-fetched. The attempt, again, to find in the words: ἐάν τις ἐκ νεκρῶν ἀναστῇ (ver. 31), a premonitory allusion either to the raising of Lazarus of Bethany or to the resurrection of Jesus Himself,[2] is opposed by the consideration that, according to the tenor of the conversation, the revivifying of a dead man in general is not spoken of, but merely the visit of a dead man to the living to testify to them the retribution awaiting them in Hades. And even if the ἀνιστάναι ἐκ νεκρῶν might rightly be understood in a different sense from this, it must still be borne in mind that in the decision of Abraham on the subject the rising of one from the dead is by no means really purposed, but, on the contrary, is refused as ineffectual, and therefore superfluous.

We cannot avoid saying another word in this place on the dogmatic use to which, in different ways, the part of the narrative extending into Hades has been put. In the first place, various inferences have been drawn from it respecting the states of departed souls in Hades. But certainly it does not lie in the purpose of the narrative to give information on this point. If it did, we must suppose that, in a discourse not even addressed to the disciples, but to the Pharisees, Jesus meant to lift the veil that rests elsewhere throughout Scripture on this mysterious region. As matter of fact, even the fundamental conception, within which the entire portion of the narrative relating to Hades moves, is by no means a new, but simply the current Jewish conception of the twofold division of Sheol into a place of felicity for the pious in Abraham's bosom, and a place of fiery anguish for the godless. And even what is said (ver. 27) of the strict separation of the two places is not so much something new, as rather merely the emphatic mention of a circumstance, without which the entire conception would lack consistency, and again nullify itself. Accordingly, what is said of Hades may certainly be used dogmatically, in so far as the Jewish conception of the twofold partition of the kingdom of the dead is confirmed to us here by the mouth of Jesus, and seems consistently worked out in one relation. But everything else said by Jesus respecting

[1] Bengel, Stier. [2] Olshausen, Stier.

the departed, within the setting of this fundamental conception, is simply transferred with perfect naturalness from the analogy of earthly relations in order vividly to picture the subject in hand, and is therefore unsuited to decide such questions as whether the departed see and know each other, and whether they have means of communication.

It has been thought right to use the contents of our narrative, under another aspect, to decide the question whether the sentence passed on the godless beyond death includes eternal damnation, or whether a purifying, and therefore a deliverance of those under punishment, is to be deemed possible beyond death. Ver. 26 has been quoted in favour of the former opinion,[1] whereas what is said there refers in the first instance merely to the order of things in *Hades*, therefore before the future resurrection and final judgment, and does not necessarily extend farther. In favour of the latter, the observation of a feeling of pity in the rich man, formerly so unmerciful, has been alleged from vv. 27, 28,[2] whereas, at the best, we have there merely an expression of the feeling of natural fraternal love, which is by no means incompatible with the unmercifulness towards poverty described in vv. 20, 21. Thus nothing decisive can be gathered from the narrative either for the one or the other opinion, this controversial question lying outside its circle of thought.

Comparing the contents of this narrative with the parable preceding it, xvi. 1 ff., we see at once that the theme here and there is essentially one and the same, only that the utterly different character of the persons to whom the teaching is addressed leads to a completely different mode of teaching. There it is the disciples, believing in Jesus as the Messiah, and expecting Him to set up the kingdom of God. Hence the teaching of the parable addressed to them is, *in the tone of exhortation*, to this effect, that perishable earthly good must henceforth be nothing more to them than a means of securing for themselves admission into the eternal habitations of that kingdom of God on which their hope is set. Here, on the other hand, it is the Pharisees, sunk in love of money, and hardening themselves against Jesus in hostile unbelief. Hence the teaching of the parable addressed to them is, *in the tone of warning*, to the effect that such a mode

[1] van Oosterzee. [2] Stier, Olshausen.

of thought in regard to earthly goods as they really cherish, although artfully veiled, will exclude them unconditionally from the felicity for which *they* hope, namely, the joys of Paradise in Abraham's bosom. And whereas there, in relation to the disciples, who are receptive to the word and witness of His mouth, Jesus so draws out the doctrine lying in the parable as to pledge His own word for it with the ratifying, "And I say unto you," ver. 9, here, in relation to the Pharisees, who despise His word and accept only law and prophets as authorities, He makes the exhortation to repentance implied in the narrative find expression within the narrative itself by the mouth of Abraham in such a way that Moses and the prophets appear as witnesses to it, demanding from them the obedience of repentance.

The Unjust Judge.

(Luke xviii. 1–8.)

The words introducing this parable, ver. 1: Ἔλεγεν δὲ καὶ παραβολὴν αὐτοῖς πρὸς τὸ δεῖν, join it on as a continuation to the chain of discourse begun in xvii. 20, a continuation as regards contents, but not necessarily immediate in time. It is said that He also spoke a parable to them (*i.e.* the disciples, xvii. 22, 37) in reference to the subject indicated in the words: πρὸς τὸ δεῖν κ.τ.λ. But this can only mean either that besides parables with *other* contents He also spoke a parable with *these* contents, which is out of place here, because no other parables come before, or that besides a *non-parabolic* discourse He also spoke a *parable*, in which case we should expect the subject of this parable, which is indicated, to stand in intrinsic connection with the subject spoken of previously in a non-parabolic form. And this expectation is borne out by the facts of the case. We have for the present sufficient provisional security for this conclusion in the circumstance that as the coming of the Son of man and what precedes it were treated of in the section xvii. 22–37, so also the parable, xviii. 8, runs out into an utterance referring to the coming of the Son of man. Accordingly the first thing necessary to an understanding of the parable is a review of the preceding discourse.

To the question of the Pharisees, when the kingdom of God

will come, Jesus had replied merely by pointing *them* to the fact that the kingdom of God is in their midst, xvii. 20, 21. But to the *disciples* He really discoursed of the future coming of God's kingdom (*i.e.* of His, the Son of man's, Parousia). There will come times, He foretells, when they will long with ardent expectation for "the days of the Son of man," *i.e.* for the days of felicity that will dawn on them with His coming to save and deliver, and yet they shall not see them, ver. 22. The words "one of the days" express the intensity of longing, to which but a little of the thing longed for seems a comfort. It is the times of tribulation and persecution preceding the Lord's coming [1] which will awaken in them a desire so ardent, yet so long unfulfilled. In these times of tribulation and unfulfilled longing, Jesus exhorts further, they are not to be misled by the latter into running after false Messiahs,[2] such as will be pointed out to them now in this, now in that place (ἰδοὺ ἐκεῖ, ἰδοὺ ὧδε), ver. 23. For not in this or that particular place will the Son of man appear, but like the flashing lightning His coming will shine from one part of heaven to the other, and therefore visibly and unmistakeably in every place, ver. 24. And how in the day of this lightning-like revelation of the Son of man judgment also will burst upon the godless with lightning-like suddenness amid their fancied security, finding and surprising them everywhere, as the eagle the carcase, and what course of conduct is therefore incumbent on the disciples of Jesus on that day of judgment,— this forms the subject of the further explanations up to the close of the chapter, ver. 37.

When then, in xviii. 1 ff., the historian makes the parable follow as a continuation of this line of discourse, and says at the outset that in it Jesus referred πρὸς τὸ δεῖν πάντοτε προσεύχεσθαι αὐτοὺς καὶ μὴ ἐγκακεῖν, it is evident that these latter words cannot be meant by him in the sense of a general, abstract principle, which Jesus wished to advance in the parable,—a misunderstanding that has led to the dropping out of the concrete αὐτούς after προσεύχεσθαι (Rec.),—but that he means it as a definite piece of counsel which Jesus wished to give the disciples in the parable with regard to their conduct in the last times treated of from xvii. 22 on. Certainly not on the day of the revelation of the Son of man itself, like the advice in

---

[1] Cf. Matt. xxiv. 21 ff.; Mark xiii. 19 ff.
[2] Cf. Matt. xxiv. 23 ff.; Mark xiii. 21 ff.

xvii. 31, but with regard to their conduct in the preceding times of unfulfilled longing, and therefore just like the admonition in xvii. 23. Accordingly the supposition of parenthetic conversations between chaps. xvii. and xviii.[1] would be needless, even on the assumption of a chronological continuity between the two parts of the discourse. A parable with such contents as are here indicated at the outset, simply goes back beyond the parenthetic description of the mode in which the day of Christ's coming will appear to the beginning of the discourse addressed to the disciples, to the days of unfulfilled longing there dwelt on, ver. 22. The way in which this is done is, that side by side with the warning in ver. 23 not to be misled in those days, appears an admonition rather to persevere unceasingly in prayer. For this is the meaning of the words: πρὸς τὸ δεῖν πάντοτε προσεύχεσθαι αὐτοὺς καὶ μὴ ἐγκακεῖν. How the πάντοτε προσεύχεσθαι is to be understood is stated by the epexegetical clause: καὶ μὴ ἐγκακεῖν, namely, not as a continuous praying in the sense that the suppliant is never to intermit a moment, as if the uninterrupted inner direction of the spirit to God, the breathing of the inner man, were here spoken of,[2] but as a continuous praying in the sense that the suppliant "weary not"[3] in the exercise of prayer, and therefore as he has exercised it hitherto, continue to do so always, without letting himself be robbed of the joyousness and confidence of prayer. The expression contains nothing hyperbolical.[4] It is also clear from xvii. 22 what kind of prayer and what danger of wearying in prayer are thought of, namely, the prayer of longing for the coming of the Son of man, and the danger of growing weary in this prayer when, despite their ardent longing, nothing shall be seen of His coming. Thus, according to the evangelist's prefatory statement, Jesus is said to have spoken the parable with reference to the necessity (πρὸς τὸ δεῖν) of persevering unweariedly in prayer in these circumstances. Let us consider the wording of the parable.

"*There was a judge in a certain city,*" thus the narrative begins, ver. 2. According to Deut. xvi. 18, judges were to be placed in all the cities of Israel, and by the addition " in a certain city " the judge in the parable is described as such a local judge. There follows the description of his moral character in the words: τὸν

---

[1] *E.g.* Kuinoel, Olshausen.   [2] Olshausen.
[3] ἐγκακεῖν wherever it occurs = *defatigari;* cf. 2 Cor. iv. 1, 16; Gal. vi. 9; Eph. iii. 13; 2 Thess. iii. 13.
[4] Meyer.

Θεὸν μὴ φοβούμενος, καὶ ἄνθρωπον μὴ ἐντρεπόμενος. The daring unscrupulousness of his disposition both towards God and man is aptly characterized by these words, as is often done in similar terms in profane authors,[1] here, however, with special reference to judicial capacity. What ought to restrain a judge from violating his official duty by injustice is the fear of God; and whoever lacks this should be kept at least from gross, open injustice by regard for men and their moral judgment. From a judge who lacks both at once, like the one in the parable: "*who feared not God, and regarded not man,*" no justice can be expected. Over against a judge of this character the narrative then places a person seeking justice from him, ver. 3: χήρα δὲ ἦν ἐν τῇ πόλει ἐκείνῃ καὶ ἤρχετο πρὸς αὐτὸν λέγουσα κ.τ.λ. It was a widow that came to him, therefore a defenceless woman, deprived of her natural protector; and a widow in that city, to whom therefore this judge was the magistrate to apply to. The imperfect ἤρχετο is used, because not a single, but a repeated, continual coming is meant. And the prayer with which she comes to the judge again and again runs: ἐκδίκησόν με ἀπὸ τοῦ ἀντιδίκου μου. Ἐκδικεῖν τινα means: "to do justice to one" (suffering injustice). This already implies the notion of delivering. Hence joined here with ἀπὸ τοῦ ἀντιδίκου μου: "*Deliver me* (suffering injustice) *from my adversary* (doing me injustice), by granting legal relief." The defenceless woman is thus illegally oppressed by an adversary, and the aim of her coming and praying is that the judge may do her justice against this adversary, and deliver her. But pressing and reasonable as is her petition, it has no likelihood of gaining an answer. For so it is said, ver. 4: καὶ οὐκ ἤθελεν ἐπὶ χρόνον, "*and he would not for a while.*" How, then, is he to be made willing? The motive of justice does not exist for him, the utterly unprincipled judge; and he has just as little any other motive to render help, because the fate of the defenceless woman has no interest for his selfishness. Nevertheless, the phrase ἐπὶ χρόνον (which, of course, means not "a long time,"[2] but simply, according to the wording, "for a while") already presages the impending change in the will of the judge, preparing the way for the antithesis introduced by μετὰ δὲ ταῦτα, vv. 4, 5: "*but afterwards he said within himself, Though I fear not God nor regard man*,"—διά γε τὸ παρέχειν μοι κόπον τὴν χήραν ταύτην, ἐκδικήσω αὐτήν, i.e. "*for this reason at least,*[3] *because this*

---

[1] Cf. Kuinoel here.   [2] Vulgate, Luther.   [3] On διά γι, cf. xi. 8.

widow troubleth me, I will do her justice." The form of the soliloquy used makes the motives of the judge's change of will stand out clearly and sharply, giving them a conscious character. And first, the absence of every moral motive is emphasized. Even now, so far is he from being influenced by any feeling of fear for God or regard for man, that in cynical fashion he expressly rejects this possibility. In deciding to help the woman to her rights, he confesses to having but one motive, that this woman troubles him, *scil.* with her coming and praying. And in what sense this motive alone has become decisive and conclusive to him is stated in the telic clause: ἵνα μὴ εἰς τέλος ἐρχομένη, ὑπωπιάζῃ με. It is implied in the very nature of the case that the longer the troubling lasts the greater it becomes, because a request persisted in despite the refusal of the one petitioned naturally grows more and more urgent; and this in a twofold degree when, as here, a *woman* has once resolved to pester and besiege one with a request. To put an end to this ever-growing persistency of the suppliant, and thus prevent the annoyance rising to an extreme point,—this according to the telic clause is the aim governing the decision, provided we rightly translate the words thus: "*lest at last she come and assault me.*" The word ὑπωπιάζειν, from ὑπώπιον = " to beat one black and blue under the eyes," cannot be diluted to the general meaning of " harass, pester," as is done by most expositors, translating "lest coming without ceasing she harass me."[1] The two passages quoted in favour of this weakened meaning do not prove the case. In the passage quoted from the New Testament (1 Cor. ix. 27: ὑπωπιάζω μου τὸ σῶμα [2]), although not the literal signification, in any case the element of *bodily* ill-treatment is to be retained; and in the passage brought from profane literature (Aristoph. *Pax.* 541) the πόλεις ὑπωπιασμέναι are cities which, badly used in the war, and therefore *actually* attacked, bear the traces of the blows of misfortune. Therefore, underlying the metaphorical use of the word found here is the element of actual assault and infliction of blows. The two passages quoted show, indeed, that we need not adhere quite literally to the meaning: "to beat the visage black and blue,"[3] but they do not on this account justify us in reducing it to a mere " harassing," in which case it would also be

---

[1] *E.g.* De Wette, Kuinoel, Baumgarten-Crusius, van Oosterzee.
[2] Unless ὑποπιάζω is to be read there; cf. von Hofmann here.
[3] In opposition to Meyer.

impossible to see why so strange and special a word was chosen for so common a notion. It must rather be taken here also as an actual assault; and this all the more since we are not then compelled to translate the adverbial εἰς τέλος "incessantly" by a Hebraism only proveable in the Septuagint (לָנֶצַח), but can leave the words the meaning usual elsewhere: "at last."[1] Nor, if the cynical style of the entire soliloquy be kept in view, can it be said that the meaning now given: "lest she come at last and assault me," is at all unsuitable and out of place in this connection. The woman is not set down as a fury by the narrator of the parable.[2] Only the judge gives an intentionally exaggerated plastic expression to his fear of a still further aggravation of her persistency.

With the announcing of this decision on the part of the judge the parabolic narrative has reached its end, and the Lord now passes on to tell the disciples what doctrine they are to draw from the parable, a transition marked in the text by the interpolated words "And the Lord said." He first directs their attention to the words of the judge at the end of the narrative, as the words giving the decisive solution of the conflict previously stated, ver. 6: Ἀκούσατε τί ὁ κριτὴς τῆς ἀδικίας λέγει. Respecting the *gen. qualitatis* τῆς ἀδικίας, cf. on xvi. 8. Here, as there, by the use of the *gen. qual.* instead of the simple adjective, injustice is described as permanently inhering in him, characterizing him. In this sense it is said: "*Hear what the judge of injustice says*," scil. respecting his decision to deliver the widow from no other motive than because of her continuous, increasing pressure. With this judge of injustice Jesus then, by ὁ δὲ Θεός, contrasts the God of justice, in order to ask whether what even the former decides to do may not much more be expected from the latter, ver. 7: ὁ δὲ Θεὸς οὐ μὴ ποιήσῃ[3] τὴν ἐκδίκησιν τῶν ἐκλεκτῶν αὐτοῦ τῶν βοώντων αὐτῷ[4] ἡμέρας καὶ νυκτός κ.τ.λ. The οὐ of the negative question requiring an affirmative answer is intensified into οὐ μή ("not indeed?"), because, according to what precedes, the event in question must take place beyond doubt.[5] It is self-evident that the fuller periphrastic form ἐκδίκησίν τινος ποιεῖν must have just the same meaning as ἐκδικεῖν previously,

---

[1] Cf. *e.g.* John xiii. 1. See passages from classical Greek in Grimm, *Lexicon of N. T.*

[2] In opposition to van Oosterzee.   [3] Instead of ποιήσει, Rec.

[4] Instead of πρὸς αὐτόν, Rec.

[5] Cf. John xviii. 11, also Winer, *Gram.* p. 620, and on the subjunctive aorist joined with οὐ μή, p. 635.

vv. 3, 5, therefore = "to effect the deliverance of one suffering injustice." But the article before ἐκδίκησις, recurring also in ver. 8, must not be overlooked, the less so that the periphrastic form is chosen for its sake. The article is used because a definite act of deliverance at Christ's Parousia is thought of, not merely an ἐκδικεῖν generally, but the divine bringing about of this definite ἐκδίκησις. Further, they who are promised deliverance on the part of God are designedly named after the relation in which they stand to Him as His "elect ones," they who in a special sense are the object of His divine purpose and providence. Herewith a new element is made prominent, putting the bringing about of the ἐκδίκησις if possible still further beyond doubt, i.e. provided these elect ones do as the participial clause says: τῶν βοώντων αὐτῷ ἡμέρας καὶ νυκτός. Formally the participle cannot be resolved conditionally because of the article, but must be resolved relatively, "such as (*quippe qui*) call day and night to Him"—thereby attesting their election. The meaning, however, remains conditional, for as to the fact it is clear that this attesting of themselves in the state of election by crying day and night is viewed as the *precondition* of deliverance. The crying day and night, just like the praying always, ver. 1, is to be understood, not so much of a praying never interrupted day or night, as rather of the cry for deliverance raised ever anew with unwearied persistency day and night, the strong expression βοᾶν again corresponding to increased urgency in prayer, continued despite long delay in the answer. That delay will take place in regard to the ἐκδίκησις of the elect, forms accordingly the tacit presupposition of the words: τῶν βοώντων ... νυκτός. This gives rise to the expectation, which is supported, moreover, by the emphatic prediction at the beginning of the entire discourse (xvii. 22), and by the parabolic narrative (ver. 4), that the participial clause now to be added: καὶ μακροθυμῶν ἐπ' αὐτοῖς, will refer to this delay of God in delivering His elect, as to a circumstance that cannot interfere with the already proved security of the final occurrence of the ἐκδίκησις. But here a difficulty seems to present itself. Elsewhere μακροθυμεῖν ἐπί τινι signifies usually "to have patience with one, exercise forbearance to one," as in delaying *punishment*.[1] It is therefore generally used, not of the postponement of deliverance, but of the postponement of punishment. But this signification is by no means so necessarily

---

[1] Matt. xviii. 26, 29; Ecclus. xviii. 11, xxix. 8, xxxv. 18.

inherent in the word as to compel us to retain it here at any price, even by making ἐπ' αὐτοῖς refer to the unmentioned persecutors of the elect instead of to the elect themselves,[1] a grammatical impossibility, made no whit more acceptable by the hypothesis of a borrowing from Ecclus. xxxv. 18,[2] especially when we take into view the αὐτῶν (ver. 8), referred offhand to the ἐκλεκτοί. The general root-meaning of μακροθυμεῖν is determined by that of θυμός. In itself this is simply a vivid, strong emotion, hence, of course, with special frequency anger, but also not seldom sympathy.[3] Μακροθυμεῖν in this case is a long restraining of the emotion in question, a postponing its outbreak, hence with special frequency restraining anger or delaying punishment, but if the context requires, just as well also the restraining of sympathy or delaying help. So, not μακροθυμεῖν indeed, but μακροθυμία, is used in Jer. xv. 15, LXX. Thus, the general idea of delaying is not extracted here from the meaning: "to exercise forbearance;"[4] but the original meaning of the word— the long restraining of an emotion—is applied, as often elsewhere to an unfriendly, so here with the same right to a friendly feeling. On this correct interpretation also the combination with ἐπ' αὐτοῖς assumes the easiest and most unforced form. We need not then render ἐπ' αὐτοῖς by "on their account," on the assumption that the unmentioned persecutors of the ἐκλεκτοί must be supplied as the proper object of the μακροθυμεῖν;[5] but as on one side ὀργίζεσθαι ἐπί τινι means, "to be angry at one,"[6] and on the other, σπλαγχνίζεσθαι ἐπί τινι, "to have mercy on one,"[7] so also μακροθυμεῖν ἐπί τινι, "to defer anger at one, i.e. to defer punishing him," or also, if the context requires, "to defer sympathy with one, i.e. to defer delivering him." Accordingly the entire sentence is to be translated: "*And should not God effect the deliverance of His elect, who cry day and night to Him, although*[8] *He long - defer His sympathy with them?*" The other reading: καὶ μακροθυμεῖ,[9] which, since καί here could then no longer be taken in the sense of "although" without great harshness,[10] has led to the translation: "and does he tarry on their account,"[11] must be

---

[1] Grimm, *Lexicon of N. T.*
[2] ποιήσει κρίσιν, καὶ ὁ κύριος οὐ μὴ βραδύνῃ, οὐδὲ μὴ μακροθυμήσει ἐπ' αὐτοῖς.
[3] Cf. *e.g.* the phrase θυμὸν ὀρίνειν in Homer for "to excite sympathy," *Odyss.* iv. 366, xiv. 361, xv. 486; *Il.* iv. 208, *et al.*
[4] Olshausen *et al.*   [5] De Wette, Godet.   [6] *E.g.* Rev. xii. 17.
[7] *E.g.* vii. 13.   [8] καί, like καίπερ, in the limitive sense before the participle.
[9] Tischendorf *et al.*   [10] In opposition to Stier.   [11] Meyer, van Oosterzee.

renounced, if not on external, still on internal grounds. For this second question in the *present* tense,[1] requiring now a negative answer, would unconditionally exclude *all* delay in the ἐκδίκησις by God of His people, and would thus not merely put itself in insoluble contradiction with xvii. 22, but also forthwith abolish the postulate of the crying day and night.[2] The reading arose out of an assimilation to the preceding ποιήσει; hence also the further change into μακροθυμήσει in a like direction. To the rhetorical question proposed on the basis of the parable Jesus then expressly appends the answer (ver. 8), confirming the inference drawn in the question from the parable by positively pledging His own word (" I say to you "), and at the same adding that God will effect the deliverance *within a short time*. For nothing else can be the meaning of the ἐν τάχει here : " *I say to you, He will effect their deliverance quickly*," i.e. " within a brief time." The words can on no account mean the *sudden* occurrence of an event in opposition to one expected and prepared for,[3] but only either the rapid course [4] or the speedy occurrence of an event.[5] The first signification is inapplicable in the present context. As certainly as the βοῶντες do not think how rapid or slow will be the process of the ἐκδίκησις, but pray simply for its speedy occurrence, so certainly the ἐν τάχει, meant to certify the hearing of the prayer, cannot be intended to promise the rapid course, but only the speedy occurrence of the ἐκδίκησις. This promise is not in conflict with the postponement of the deliverance declared before, because that delay was already the postulate of the elect crying day and night, whereas this speedy entry of the deliverance is only promised them as the effect of their persevering prayer during the times of delay, and consequently merely as a final cutting short of those times of tribulation.[6] Hence also this promise has nothing at all to do with the question how soon, reckoned from the time of the speaker, the Parousia will occur.[7]

Upon what has now been said follows a final question,

---

[1] Only few codices read μακροθυμήσει.

[2] Hence Hofmann, who adheres to this reading, attempts to take the clause: καὶ μακροθυμεῖ ἐπ' αὐτοῖς, as an answer to the question. "He also exercises forbearance towards them" (the elect), meaning that the forbearance which he exercises is also forbearance towards *them*. But few will follow him in this view, especially when the following λέγω ὑμῖν, which plainly introduces the answer, is taken into account.

[3] *Repente, inopinato*, Kuinoel *et al.*   [4] So perhaps Rom. xvi. 20.

[5] So Rev. i. 1, xxii. 6. Both combined, Acts xii. 7, xxii. 18.

[6] Cf. Matt. xxiv. 22 and parallels.   [7] In opposition to Meyer.

proposed, however, not on the basis of the parabolic story, but merely in allusion to it, ver. 8b: "*But will the Son of man, where He shall have come, indeed*[1] *find the faith on the earth?*" The article before "faith" intimates that this word is to be taken in the specific sense given in what goes before, not as faith in the Messiah generally,[2] but as the faith that does not let itself be deceived as to the certainty of the final redemption by the times of tribulation, and therefore perseveres unweariedly in the prayer of faith for that redemption. In exhorting His disciples to such persevering prayer, the thought comes to the soul of Jesus, which in another place He expresses in definite prediction,[3] that in the last times of tribulation many will be deceived. Hence the foreboding question. It is only of importance for the exposition of the parable in so far as it puts beyond doubt the pervading reference of the parable to the Parousia of Christ and the last times preceding it.

After following to the end the parabolic narrative, along with the additional declarations of Jesus, it is not hard for us to define the general moral of the parable. According to the inference added by Jesus Himself, it consists in the *exhortation to the disciples to constant prayer in the approaching days of tribulation and of delay in the coming of the Son of man, as the means by which they will infallibly bring in the longed-for deliverance at the end.* It is evident how completely this harmonizes with the evangelist's prefatory remark, that in addition to the previous non-parabolic discourse to the disciples respecting the last times and things, Jesus also spoke a parable "to the end that they ought always to pray, and not to faint," ver. 1.

Let us now see how this purpose is carried out in the parable. First of all a description was given of the critical position of an oppressed widow before an unjust judge, who refused her prayer for deliverance from her adversary. According to the context this can only be meant to describe the position in which the disciples of Jesus find themselves in the times preceding the advent of Christ.[4] Like the widow in the parable, who as such is exposed without defence to her adversary's ill-will, they will then be exposed without defence to the persecution of their adversaries oppressing them with unjust violence. And like as the widow in this position turns with her prayer for deliverance

---

[1] To be accentuated ἄρα.   [2] Meyer.
[3] Matt. xxiv. 24 and parallels.   [4] Cf. xvii. 22.

to the judge as the one whose duty it is to guard her rights, so will they then bring the like prayer to God, the guardian of their rights and judge of their foes. But they will experience the same fate with their request as the widow. As the latter is at first refused the implored deliverance by the judge, so the salvation longed for and implored will not at once be granted them by God, but, contrary to hope and expectation, will be refused for a time. According to this view, therefore, the point of comparison between the position of the disciples and that of a *widow* consists simply in defencelessness against hostile oppression, not in the widowed condition itself, as though (as in several passages of the Old Testament inaptly quoted here [1]) the relation of the Church to God were here represented under the image of a wife forsaken of her wedded lord, whereas the disciples here stand to God in a quite different relation, namely, in that of complainants to a judge. In this case the introduction of the widow as an individual person contains no definite allusion to the single idea of the Church, just as little as the singular " from my adversary" points to a single definite adversary, such as the prince of this world.[2] Thereby the *position* of the disciples, or as one may even say, of the body of disciples in those days of severe, long-continued persecution, is compared on one side (in relation to the persecuting foes) with that of a widow defenceless against her adversary, and on the other side (in relation to God) with that of a complainant, to whom the relief implored against unjust oppression is for a time refused by the judge.

Certainly, similar as is the widow's position to that of the disciples, which it serves figuratively to represent, there is an essential distinction in one point. The widow finds herself in presence of an unjust judge, who refuses legal relief, because there is no motive to give it in his audacious, unprincipled character, while the disciples are in presence of a God of justice, who, whatever motives in the hidden counsel of His wisdom cause the temporary refusal of help, really in virtue of His unchangeable justice can never permit the power of their enemies to prevail over them—the unjustly persecuted. But the reason of this distinction is not that the parable is imperfect and limping in this point. Rather the emphatic prefixing of the characteristic of the judge, as one utterly without principle before God and man, at the head of the entire narrative, shows that this

[1] *E.g.* Stier *et al.* [2] *E.g.* Stier.

distinction is introduced into the parable of set purpose as an essential point of contrast, and is consequently of importance as such for its moral. And, in fact, this contrasted distinction forms the starting-point from which the interpretation of the final part of the parable giving the solution of the widow's critical position must be carried out. For when the close of the narrative shows how the unjust judge, despite his want of principle, nay, expressly renouncing all motive implied in a remnant of conscientiousness, nevertheless finds himself compelled to deliver the widow, simply because she threatens to make her coming and praying intolerable, it is clear that here the interpretation is not to be worked out in the way of simple comparison, but, as already more or less similarly,[1] in the way of an inference *a minori ad majus* starting from that very distinction. Accordingly the interpretation is as follows. If the widow does not let herself be misled by the refusal of the *unjust* judge, but, in presence of this man of *injustice*, whose moral character gives her not the least pledge of success, proceeds unweariedly with her prayer, relying on the power inherent in such prayer, how much less ought the disciples, when they find themselves in a similar position with respect to the God of *justice*, to be led astray by the temporary delay of His help, — how much more is it then incumbent on them to persevere in their prayer for help, since they know that in imploring with their deliverance the triumph of justice over violence and wrong they are only praying in His mind! And if even the *unjust* judge, indifferent to him as are both the rights of the petition and the person of the petitioner, cannot at last resist the persistent prayer simply on account of the trouble it gives him, but decides to deliver the widow, how much less—such is the force of the inference added by Jesus Himself—will and can the God of *justice* resist the prayer of His people, and how much more will He grant the salvation sought— He who really needs no mechanical constraint to grant a prayer that seeks the intervention of justice against unjust persecution, and is presented to Him by His elect who are the object of His innermost love and care! What Jesus says at the close thus becomes a certainty raised above all doubt, namely, that although God delay long, He will yet shorten the days of tribulation for His elect that cry day and night to Him, and hasten the longed-for day of their deliverance.

---

[1] xi. 5 ff., xv. 4 ff., 8 ff., xvi. 1 ff.

We have thus seen the eschatological character of the parable, referring as it does everywhere definitely to the Coming of Christ and the times preceding it. And herein lies its essential distinction from the other parable of the Importunate Friend, apparently so like it, xi. 5 ff. The affinity in the teaching of the two is indeed unmistakeable, for both exhort to persevering prayer in the assurance that in this case the answer will infallibly come. Nevertheless the essential distinction remains, that the parable of the Importunate Friend commends persevering prayer generally as the right kind of prayer, whereas the present parable recommends it as the right course in a concrete necessity of the future, in the times of tribulation preceding the Parousia of Christ, the object of the prayer being here definite, namely, the final appearing of deliverance at the Parousia. On the other hand, it is certainly implied in the nature of the case that the exhortation in the latter parable, like the promise connected with it, although not proposed in the first instance as a permanent rule,[1] still finds a *justifiable application* to the disciples of Jesus, not merely in the final days of tribulation primarily considered here, but also in all similar times, because the presuppositions, on which the parable proceeds, are of a general nature and always seasonable, namely, the power inherent in persevering, earnest prayer on the one hand, and the divine justice and love irrevocably pledging its answer on the other.

The Pharisee and the Publican.

(Luke xviii. 9-14.)

With chap. xviii. 8 the line of discourse begun in chap. xvii. 20 has reached its end; and with chap. xviii. 9 a new example of the teaching of Jesus is added, without anything being affirmed or intimated respecting a connection of this section with the preceding eschatological teaching and the parable of the same import, xviii. 1 ff. For when it is said, ver. 9: "And He spake also this parable to certain" . . ., the hearers to whom the following discourse is addressed are neither the Pharisees, to whom chap. xvii. 20, 21 was spoken, nor the disciples, to whom chap. xvii. 22 up to xviii. 8 was spoken, but "certain" persons,

---
[1] In opposition to Düsterdieck on Rev. i. 1.

who are merely described by a type of thought peculiar to them, without reference to what precedes, and without defining their outward position. "And He said also" therefore simply attaches one utterance of Jesus to another in a general sense. In this way the question becomes superfluous, whether the following parable is or is not related in its contents to the preceding discourse. For, since no such reference is intimated by the historian himself, this question is only asked in the interest of the attempt to discover substantive points of view, under which Luke has combined the single examples of the teaching of Jesus,[1] a point lying outside our province. By way of preparation for understanding the parable, we are remitted to the characterization of those to whom it was spoken, namely: πρός τινας τοὺς πεποιθότας ἐφ' ἑαυτοῖς ὅτι εἰσὶν δίκαιοι καὶ ἐξουθενοῦντας τοὺς λοιπούς. It is self-evident that λέγειν πρός τινα here as elsewhere means "to speak to one," there being no necessity to give up this obvious meaning and choose the far-fetched one, "in reference to one."[2] They *to* whom the parable was spoken are accordingly more exactly defined as those "who trust *in themselves*," namely, in the particular respect "that they are righteous," *i.e.* in a state of blameless moral rectitude. Since, then, the special mention, that they put this confidence *in themselves*, is quite superfluous in the first clause, except to prepare for an antithesis, the second clause gives the antithesis: καὶ ἐξουθενοῦντας τοὺς λοιπούς. These people trusted *in themselves* that they were righteous, but *the others*—not merely some others, but the totality of the others (τοὺς λοιπούς)—they despised, *scil.* as unrighteous. Hence they are not simply described as those who thought themselves righteous, but as those who ascribed righteousness *to themselves*, whilst looking down on *the mass of other men* with scorn as unrighteous. The question has been asked, whether these people were Pharisees or disciples of Jesus. Against the former view it has been rightly observed,[3] that Jesus would not have held up a Pharisee before Pharisees as a parabolic example. The latter view is discountenanced by the characterization itself, which in such sharp outline certainly does not fit the declared disciples of Jesus. Against both views is the fact that, when the language of Jesus was specially addressed to one or the other class, Luke never elsewhere omits to mention it expressly. The persons to whom Jesus here speaks are consequently hearers of

[1] Cf. Introductory, p. 124. [2] De Wette, Stier. [3] Schleiermacher.

Jesus, without being declared disciples, and on the other hand resemble the Pharisees in their style of thought, without being declared Pharisees. How they gave expression to their style of thought is not more precisely stated. Enough that in some way they made it known, and the answer of Jesus is given in the following parable, whose purpose is directed against the line of thought ascribed to them; and indeed not simply against self-righteousness, but more definitely against the self-exaltation by reason of which any one fancies himself raised by the righteousness he thinks himself to possess above the rest of men in their unrighteousness.

The parable begins, ver. 10: "*Two men went up into the*[1] *temple*[2] *to pray.*" The Jews of Jerusalem were accustomed to perform their prayers in the forecourt of the temple at the usual hours of prayer. For this end the two men go up there,—and at the same time, because, as is tacitly assumed, of the arrangement of fixed hours of prayer. But, although they go up into the same temple, for the same end and at the same time, they are quite different, "*one a Pharisee and the other a publican.*" They are separated from each other by the farthest conceivable distance existing in a moral and religious respect between the different classes of the Judaism of the day,—the one as a Pharisee, a man of strict and blameless legal observance; the other as a publican, in public opinion not without actual contact with sinners living in open shame and vice, and even standing on a level with the heathen.

The narrative then first dwells on the Pharisee, stating how he went through his prayer, ver. 11: Ὁ Φαρισαῖος σταθεὶς πρὸς ἑαυτὸν ταῦτα προσηύχετο κ.τ.λ., *i.e.* "*The Pharisee took his stand apart, and prayed thus.*" The conjunction of πρὸς ἑαυτόν with σταθείς is not merely necessary because of the isolation of σταθείς in the other case, but is also required by the connection with ver. 10. After the publican, as was unavoidable, has gone up with him by the same road, the Pharisee hastens, when he has reached the temple, to assume a distinctly separate position. And finally, the correctness of this conjunction is ratified by the manifest correlate μακρόθεν ἑστώς in the description of the publican's prayer, ver. 13. It is said indeed that "he took his

---

[1] The temple of Jerusalem, situated on a hill.

[2] Τὸ ἱερόν, in distinction from τὸ ἅγιον, the temple generally, inclusive of its forecourts, halls, etc.

stand apart" could only be expressed in Greek by σταθεὶς καθ' ἑαυτόν (Acts xxviii. 16; Jas. ii. 17), but wrongly. In a verb of movement like "to take his stand, come there," it was much more natural to say πρὸς ἑαυτόν. As ἀπέρχεσθαι πρὸς ἑαυτόν means "to go where one is alone" (Luke xxiv. 12; John xx. 10), so σταθεὶς πρὸς ἑαυτόν here means: "he took his stand where he was alone." To whom the separation expressed in πρὸς ἑαυτόν refers is then stated in the context, in the other passages quoted above to the outer world generally ("to go home"), here to the other worshippers, and in particular to the publican. Whilst the conjunction with σταθείς is thus free from difficulty, the conjunction, on the other hand, with προσηύχετο, generally preferred, must be held to be impossible. For even if πρὸς ἑαυτὸν ταῦτα προσηύχετο could mean "*with* himself he prayed thus," it is impossible to see what could be meant to be said characteristic of the Pharisee by the "with himself" so strangely put first. But προσεύχεσθαι πρὸς ἑαυτόν would not mean "to pray *with* himself," but "to pray *to* himself."[1] Even in the combination with λέγειν (in the classics), πρὸς ἑαυτόν means "to speak *to* himself," and in 2 Macc. xi. 13,[2] ἀντιβάλλων πρὸς ἑαυτόν does not mean offhand, "taking counsel *with* himself," but "*to*" or "*towards* himself," *i.e.* "taking counsel with himself."[3] That in such combinations πρὸς ἑαυτόν is the same as to meaning as ἐν ἑαυτῷ, is immaterial to the present passage, because in the combination with προσεύχεσθαι, by reason of the special meaning of the verb, this is by no means the case. Here the combination with πρὸς ἑαυτόν would only yield the notion of praying to oneself, a notion absurd in itself, and doubly so alongside the apostrophe ὁ Θεός.[4]

To the *attitude in prayer* assumed by the Pharisee—apart from the rest of the worshippers—the *words of prayer* exactly correspond: Ὁ Θεός, εὐχαριστῶ σοι, ὅτι οὐκ εἰμὶ ὥσπερ οἱ λοιποὶ τῶν ἀνθρώπων κ.τ.λ. He begins with "*God, I thank Thee.*" But we must not conclude from this language that the Pharisee is actuated by the lowly feeling that he owes what he is to God. That, on the contrary, the thanksgiving is merely the form of self-glorying

---

[1] Cf. 2 Cor. xiii. 7; Rom. xv. 30.   [2] Quoted by Meyer.

[3] The passage, Mark xiv. 4, quoted by Bleek, is quite dissimilar, for καὶ λέγοντες there is spurious, and πρὸς ἑαυτούς, as often, is equivalent to πρὸς ἀλλήλους. Ἀγανακτοῦντες πρὸς ἑαυτούς therefore means "expressing themselves indignantly to each other."

[4] Nor can the meaning be "he prayed *in reference to himself*" (Hofmann), because in this way again nothing characteristic would be said. The publican does the same.

seemly in prayer to God, is shown by this, that in setting forth the object of his thanksgiving he says not a word of what God has done or given to him, and what he owes to God, but speaks only, on the one hand, of the sins and vices of others degrading them beneath him, and, on the other, of his own meritorious conduct raising him above them, ver. 12,—both, it is plain, equally little adapted to be the object of sincere thanks. In the form of thanksgiving he first of all boasts that he is not as the rest of men (οἱ λοιποὶ τῶν ἀνθρώπων, the remaining totality of men; cf. on ver. 9). It is a strong but characteristic expression of his disposition, that he thus contrasts the rest of men in a mass as corrupt with himself,—they stained with sin and vice,—he the spotless one. For by appositional predicates he describes them as ἅρπαγες, ἄδικοι, μοιχοί. He emphasizes the offence against another's property, whether by open violence (ἅρπαγες) or dishonest overreaching,[1] and along with this the crime of adultery, as sins generally current among the corrupt mass of the rest of men,—the first two sins, because the sin against property seems the sin of sins to the money-loving Pharisee,[2] and also because the irritating spectacle of the publican especially suggested the mention of this species of sin, and then the sin of adultery as the sin associated above others with shame, without the mention of which the shamefulness of the behaviour " of the rest of men" would not be duly characterized. But as he lets us see even in this general enumeration that he is thinking of the publican, so afterwards he does not omit directly to mention him, adding to the general boast the personal comparison, "*or even as this publican.*" The ἢ καί here by an easy logical inexactness passes, not to another and different one, but simply from the general species (οἱ λοιποὶ τῶν ἀνθρώπων) to the special example, οὗτος ὁ τελώνης. The pronoun οὗτος is used scornfully = "this one here." On this publican, who is to him an extortioner and unjust in an eminent sense, the Pharisee looks down with special contempt.

To the guilt of other men degrading them beneath him, is now added his own meritorious conduct raising him above them and doubling the distance. He not merely stands clear of such transgressions of the law, of which others are guilty, but he even outdistances the law's demands in his pious zeal. He thus heightens his boasting; and as he does so, the dependence of his

---

[1] ἄδικοι is to be taken here in this stricter sense. [2] Cf. xvi. 14.

language on ὁ Θεός, εὐχαριστῶ σοι even in a formal respect is lost, and therewith even the *semblance* of gratitude. He continues his boasting in an independent sentence, ver. 12 : νηστεύω δὶς τοῦ σαββάτου, ἀποδεκατῶ πάντα ὅσα κτῶμαι, i.e. "*I fast twice in the week*,[1] *and give tithes of whatever* (ὅσα) *I acquire.*"[2] The legally prescribed fasting once a year[3] he surpasses by fasting twice a week,[4] and the legally prescribed tribute of the tenth of the produce of the field and herd for the support of the Levites[5] he surpasses by tithing his entire income, from whatever source derived. Such is the force of the words: πάντα ὅσα κτῶμαι, which are not, with Meyer, Godet, *et al.*, to be limited to the strict tithing of all, even the least produce of the field, down to the anise and cumin,[6] which the Pharisees exacted and rendered as a legal duty.

The narrative then passes (ver. 13) from the prayer of the Pharisee to that of the publican: καὶ ὁ τελώνης μακρόθεν ἑστὼς οὐκ ἤθελεν κ.τ.λ. The words μακρόθεν ἑστώς again define, in correspondence with the σταθεὶς πρὸς ἑαυτόν in the account of the Pharisee, the *attitude in prayer* assumed by the publican. In consideration of this plain correlative relation, the same reference must be left to the μακρόθεν ἑστώς as the σταθεὶς πρὸς ἑαυτόν had. If the latter words pictured the Pharisee standing apart from the crowd of worshippers in a place by himself, the former words picture a standing aloof from the other worshippers in the solitary background. There, it was a proud keeping apart and away, the Pharisee thinking himself too good ; here, it is a timid remaining behind, the publican feeling himself too unworthy to unite with the rest of the worshippers. Thus standing afar: οὐκ ἤθελεν οὐδὲ τοὺς ὀφθαλμοὺς ἐπᾶραι εἰς τὸν οὐρανόν. Instead of referring the climactic οὐδέ to the entire connected idea of lifting up the eyes or looking up to heaven, expositors strangely refer it merely to τοὺς ὀφθαλμούς, thus getting the sense: " he would not lift up even the *eyes*" (to say nothing of the *hands* or *arms*).[7] But, apart from the arbitrariness of such a supplement, it is impossible thus to separate the lifting up of the eyes and

---

[1] τὸ σάββατον, here "the week," cf. Mark xvi. 9 ; τοῦ σαββάτου, genitive of time.

[2] κτῶμαι, not "possess," which would be κέκτημαι, but "acquire."

[3] Lev. xvi. 29 ff. *et al.*

[4] According to Pharisaic custom, on the second and fifth day of the week ; cf. Riehm, *Bibl. Handwörterbuch*, p. 425 f.

[5] Lev. xxvii. 30, 32 ; Num. xviii. 21, 24.   [6] Chap. xi. 42 ; Matt. xxiii. 23.

[7] Meyer, Nebe, van Oosterzee.

that of the hands, so naturally bound together in the attitude of prayer, as if the latter expressed a higher degree of confidence than the former. Really there is no need to supply the starting-point for the climax implied in οὐδέ, since it is given in μακρόθεν ἑστώς. The statement that he did not dare to unite with the other worshippers, is enhanced to the effect that he did not even dare to use the gesture otherwise natural to every worshipper to express the raising of the soul to God, "*he would not even lift up his eyes to heaven.*" Why not is shown in the antithesis following: "*but smote his breast.*"[1] Whereas the usual κόπτεσθαι is the gesture of great sorrow in general,[2] τύπτειν τὸ στῆθος here and in xxiii. 48 seems more strongly and definitely to be the gesture of sorrowful, penitent contrition. In such contrition, instead of lifting up his eyes to heaven like other worshippers, with bowed look and head he smites his breast ("ubi dolor ibi manus"), whilst saying (λέγων): Ὁ Θεός, ἱλάσθητί μοι τῷ ἁμαρτωλῷ, i.e. "*God, be gracious to me the sinner.*" In this brief but weighty prayer the emphasis falls on the two last words: τῷ ἁμαρτωλῷ, and in keeping with this emphasis they are to be understood in the pregnant sense. Not merely for himself as one sinner is like another does he pray, but for himself as *the* sinner, distinguishing himself by the article as "sinner" from those who are not such, *i.e.* not in the sense and degree in which he is such. Only thus understood does this brief, pregnant confession of the suppliant correspond exactly to the special attitude he assumed in prayer,—in ashamed self-isolation from the other worshippers,—and to the special gesture with which he accompanies it, the smiting on the breast instead of the usual looking up to heaven. Only thus understood is the type of thought opposed to that of the Pharisee really expressed. For as, according to the Pharisee's words, other men were all sinners to him and he only righteous, so conversely to the publican, according to his confession, all were (relatively) righteous, and he only the sinner. Hence follows the other distinction, that whereas the prayer of the Pharisee was simply a long self-glorying, but poorly veiled by the form of thanks without a word of petition,—with the brief, expressive confession of the publican is joined the just as brief prayer, groaned from the depths of a sorrow-riven heart, "*God, be gracious to me,*" in which he implores from God, as a free gift of His mercy, the

---

[1] τὶς before τὸ στῆθος (Rec.) is perhaps to be erased, with Tischendorf.
[2] Cf. viii. 52, xxiii. 27; Matt. xi. 17, xxiv. 30; Rev. i. 7, xviii. 9.

experience of the favour of which he—the sinner—knows himself to be destitute, and to which he has no claim.

Herewith the narrative is at an end, so far as it relates outwardly cognizable events. For the going down to the house after the prayer is done is understood of itself, and does not need mention for its own sake. But the final decisive act here is a non-earthly, divine act, one removed from sight, such as can only occur in the typical parable, the narrative of which is itself directly religious.[1] For ver. 14 gives an asseveration of Jesus, having the previous narrative as its basis, respecting the success attending the publican's prayer in regard to his relation to God, and respecting the position he thus gained before God in comparison with the Pharisee. In the former respect the asseveration (λέγω ὑμῖν, κατέβη οὗτος δεδικαιωμένος εἰς τὸν οἶκον αὐτοῦ) affirms that the publican went down to his house "justified," *i.e.* according to the obvious sense belonging to the word in this context, he went down with his prayer for grace to the sinner heard, and therefore made or declared just by pardoning grace. But, at the same time, the righteousness imparted to the publican is put into comparison with that of the Pharisee, παρ' ἐκεῖνον at the close of the sentence being set over against κατέβη οὗτος δεδικαιωμένος. So we must read with Lachmann, according to the best witnesses, instead of the unattested reading of the Recepta, ἢ ἐκεῖνος, and the certainly well attested but meaningless ἢ γὰρ ἐκεῖνος, which may have arisen from the clerical error γάρ for παρ being blended with the gloss ἢ ἐκεῖνος. Those who maintain the genuineness of the last reading, in order to give the γάρ any meaning are driven to take the words: ἢ γὰρ ἐκεῖνος, with intolerable harshness, as an independent supplementary sentence: "Or did then the other one go down justified?" the γάρ being added to strengthen the question.[2] On the contrary, we adhere to the reading: παρ' ἐκεῖνον, the sentence running completely: "*This man went down to his house justified beyond the other.*"[3] But this cannot mean either that justification came to the publican in a higher and to the Pharisee in a lower degree, or that in the sense of an absolute preference justification was granted to one and refused to the other.[4] Not the first, because justification on God's part, in the sense in which it came

---

[1] Cf. Introduction, p. 6 f. [2] Winer, *Gram.* p. 302.
[3] παρά with the accusative = supra, ultra, as in xiii. 2, 4; Heb. i. 9, *et al.*
[4] Luther and most moderns.

to the publican, by its very idea cannot come to one in a higher and to another in a lower degree, but can only either take place or not take place. Nor, again, the second, because a granting or refusing of justification could only come into question in regard to the publican's prayer, not in regard to the Pharisee's, which so little sought a bestowal of righteousness that, on the contrary, it consisted merely in a boasting of the supposed possession already of a blameless righteousness. The comparison therefore cannot refer to the act of justification which does not come into question in the Pharisee's case, but simply to the idea "just" lying in the word "justified." The meaning of the comparison is, that the righteousness obtained by the publican through pardoning grace is better[1] than that of which the Pharisee boasted on the ground of his works. In free translation, therefore: "*This man went down endowed with a righteousness better than that of the Pharisee.*" Thus the judgment indirectly passed on the righteousness of the Pharisee is one not of absolute, but merely of relative condemnation. The inference at once suggested, that a righteousness which is exceeded by that of a forgiven publican and sinner is no righteousness at all, is left to the hearers themselves to draw. In order still further to confirm His asseveration, that the relation of mutual superiority and inferiority, which the two suppliants ascribe to themselves, was reversed by God, Jesus then appeals to the general maxim elsewhere quoted by Him,[2] which is also a law of the kingdom of God.[3] "For every one that exalteth himself shall be humbled, but he that humbleth himself shall be exalted."

The comparison of this issue of the parable with the prefatory description of the type of thought of its hearers (ver. 9) at once reveals its purpose. *It is meant to show how perverse is the type of thought of those who claim to be righteous themselves, while despising the rest as unrighteous, since the precisely opposite line of thought, leading one to seek sin not in others, but in himself, is well-pleasing to God, and therefore the way to the true righteousness which God accepts.* And this truth is pictured to view, as we have already found in a series of other parables, not by means of a figurative representation proper, but simply by describing a particular example, so that here again what is needed in order to ascertain the purport of the parable is not an interpretation proper, but merely a correct generalizing application.

[1] Matt. v. 20.   [2] Luke xiv. 11.   [3] Matt. xxiii. 12.

Jesus pictures this truth to His hearers in the example of two men, proposing as the representative of the type of thought which He designs to oppose in His hearers, a Pharisee, a man of apparently exemplary righteousness, and as the representative of the opposite line of thought, a publican, according to the evil repute of his order a man of exemplary unrighteousness, the two therefore separated from each other in this respect by the widest conceivable distance. The historical fact that the proud disposition condemned was usual among the Pharisees, whilst many of the publicans came humbly and penitently to Jesus, merely supplied the outward occasion for the choice of these examples. The inner reason why Jesus chose just these examples is, that such a contrast was of necessity specially effective for the moral of the parable. For if the result in the present case was to show that the *publican*, as representing the second mode of thought, was preferred by God above the *Pharisee*, as representing the first, then God's approval of the second and disapproval of the first were certainly established for all cases.

Jesus makes both men go up to the Temple to *pray*, and the point of His parable consists essentially in His making them speak *in prayer before God*. The question must be asked, for what end did Jesus give this special form to the description? It is obvious, first, that in this way He wishes to bring out into clear expression what is characteristic of the inner mode of thought of the two men. But for this purpose merely the form of soliloquy used in other parables would have sufficed.[1] The intention of Jesus here consequently must have been something further. In making the two not merely speak *to themselves*, but speak *in prayer to God*, His intention is to show in what relation a man of the one and a man of the other disposition places himself *to God*. He makes the rightness or wrongness of their type of thought to be tested by the attitude in which it places them *to God*.

This first of all in the Pharisee's case. In the separate position which he takes, and in the words with which he exalts himself as a model of righteousness above the mass of other men sunk in sin and vice, Jesus holds up to His hearers a true picture of their own mode of thought, ver. 9. When they see and hear this Pharisee *pray*,—the unmistakeable representative of their own type of thought,—they cannot help seeing in what

[1] Cf. *e.g.* xii. 17 ff., xvi. 3 ff., xviii. 4 f.

a perverse attitude *to God* they put themselves by such a course. For as the entire prayer of the Pharisee is summed up in enumerating the sins and vices of other men, and his own pious deeds, and boasting of the distance put between him and others by their guilt and his merit, so every one of like disposition stands before God as one who is self-sufficient in his fancied superior righteousness, and neither desires God nor needs Him, save as a spectator of his meritorious conduct, and a listener to his boasting.

And when Jesus alongside the praying Pharisee also depicts the publican praying, — his standing-place the solitary background from timid shame, his bearing that of self-condemning contrition, his language the language of confession, calling himself the sinner in a distinctive sense,—Jesus here paints before His hearers in sharp lines the image of the mode of thought precisely the opposite of theirs; the image of a man who, instead of trusting in himself that he is righteous, and despising the rest as sinners, ver. 9, knows and feels himself a sinner, whilst ascribing righteousness to all the rest. When they see and hear this publican *pray,*—the unmistakeable representative of the type of thought opposed to theirs,—they cannot help seeing how different such an one's attitude *to God* is from theirs, and how much better. For as the publican pours out his whole heart before God in the supplication: "God, be gracious to me the sinner," so every one who, like him, seeks sin in himself, and not in others, stands before God as one who knows himself lost without God, whose sole hope is God's free grace, and whose sole prayer is a beseeching of that grace. That this latter attitude of heart to God, such as a disposition like that of the publican gives man, corresponds to the true relation of man to God, just as the attitude taken by the Pharisee in prayer to God is a perversion of that relation, is so plainly implied in the entire representation, without being positively expressed, that even the hearers of Jesus could not avoid receiving the impression.

Accordingly the asseveration with which Jesus concludes the parable, ver. 14, is by no means unrelated to what has gone before, as if the narrative were merely an objective psychological description, to which the decisive judgment is now added in abrupt contrast. But this concluding asseveration respecting a divine act removed from sight merely deduces from the previous narrative the inference with which every one must agree who has listened and understood rightly.[1] As an inference, therefore, from the previous narrative, Jesus declares that the publican in the answer to the prayer, in which he committed himself entirely to divine grace, received a righteousness better than the righteousness in which the Pharisee presented himself before God as a worshipper unwarrantably condemning others' sin and proudly boasting of his own merits, but neither desiring nor susceptible to divine grace. As certainly, therefore, as the publican's type of thought makes him partaker of a righteousness better than that of the Pharisee, so certainly—thus is the meaning of the concluding asseveration to be generalized—will a similar mode of thought, because alone giving man the right, trustful attitude of heart to God, obtain the righteousness which is accepted by God as such, because the gift of divine grace; whereas a mode of thought like the Pharisee's, whatever brilliant show of righteousness he may borrow from a spotless outward walk and the heaping up of good works, will pollute him in God's sight with the guilt of uncharitable judgment and arrogant self-exaltation, so that his righteousness cannot stand beside the righteousness that is the gift of divine grace.

[1] Cf. x. 36, 37.

PART III.

THE PARABLES OF THE LAST PERIOD.

GENERAL VIEW.

A THIRD series of parables meets us in the section of Matthew's Gospel that embraces the period of the last journey of Jesus from Galilee to Jerusalem, and the last days in Jerusalem. According to Matthew, Jesus spoke the first of these (xviii. 21–35)—that of the *Unmerciful Servant*—during His last sojourn in Capernaum, before leaving Galilee for ever, and entering on the last journey to Jerusalem. The second—that of the *Labourers in the Vineyard*—was delivered on the journey to Jerusalem through Peræa (xx. 1–16). That of the *Wicked Vinedressers* (xxi. 33–44), with parallels in Mark and Luke, and that of the *Royal Marriage-Feast* (xxii. 1–14), belong to the teaching of Jesus in the temple at Jerusalem during the Passion week itself. And the two last—*The Ten Virgins* and *The Talents*—belong to the eschatological discourse on the Mount of Olives after Jesus left the temple (xxv. 1–13, 14–30).

Beside the parable last mentioned we shall finally place, for the reasons stated in the Introduction (p. 19), the exposition of the similar parable of Luke—*The Pounds*—which, according to this evangelist, was spoken shortly before the entry of Jesus into Jerusalem, and therefore also belongs, according to him, to the parables of the last journey.

The Unmerciful Servant.
(Matt. xviii. 21–35.)

During His last sojourn in Capernaum, before finally leaving Galilee for Jerusalem,[1] Jesus had a conversation with the

---
[1] Cf. xvii. 24, xviii. 1, xix. 1.

disciples who constantly accompanied Him in His wanderings (xvii. 22), and therefore with the Twelve. In this conversation He gives them instruction in regard to His approaching departure, then ever before His mind (xvii. 22, 23), as to the lowly, tender love they are to show to one another as His disciples. On occasion of the question proposed by them, who is great in the kingdom of heaven [1] (xviii. 1), Jesus told them, first, that he is great in the kingdom of heaven who, like a child, renounces all claim to greatness above others, and humbly shows love to the little ones (vv. 2–5). Hence He further adjured them, with threatening solemnity, not to give offence to the little ones,[2] vv. 6–9, and warned them not to despise these little ones, who are in high esteem before God, ver. 10,—so high, that each one of them is an object of God's special care, the only purpose of which is to restore and save the erring.[3] Instead, then, of despising the little and weak, the disciples of Jesus are to imitate this divine care for the erring. In this sense the exhortation, vv. 15–17, joins on to what precedes. He that is in the position of one sinned against by a brother,[4] is to direct his whole effort towards restoring and regaining the erring one. For this end he—the wronged one—must go to the wrong-doer himself, and offer him the hand of reconciliation, telling him his wrong alone. And if the erring one refuse to listen, he is to repeat the attempt in the presence of one or two witnesses, nay, even if the brother will not hear these, he is not to give him up, but to make a last attempt by invoking the aid of the Church. Only when the wrong-doer refuses to hear the Church summoning him to acknowledge his wrong and renounce his hostile disposition, may a disciple regard brotherly fellowship as at an end.

We may leave the sayings of Jesus in vv. 18–20 out of sight, because the question of Peter, to which Jesus replies with the parable, goes back beyond them to vv. 15–17. In ver. 21 it is said: "Then came Peter (out of the circle of the remaining disciples, and to the Lord) and said: Κύριε, ποσάκις ἁμαρτήσει

---

[1] Comparatively great, hence μείζων.
[2] According to the context, those who had nothing to distinguish them above others but their perhaps weak faith in Jesus.
[3] See p. 196.
[4] The reading of the Recepta: ἐὰν δὲ ἁμαρτήσῃ εἰς σὲ ὁ ἀδελφός σου, is to be adhered to (cf. Meyer), against Lachmann et al., who expunged εἰς σέ, according to some authorities.

εἰς ἐμὲ ὁ ἀδελφός μου καὶ ἀφήσω αὐτῷ; ἕως ἑπτάκις;" The construction: ποσάκις ἁμαρτήσει . . . καὶ ἀφήσω αὐτῷ, is a Hebraism for: ποσάκις τῷ ἀδελφῷ ἁμαρτήσαντι ἀφήσω. The future ἀφήσω here is used of what is to be taken as morally enjoined. Therefore: "*How often ought I to forgive my brother who sins against me? Until seven times?*" Such a course towards the wrong-doer as Jesus has enjoined on His disciples (vv. 15–17), requiring the injured one spontaneously to seek to restore brotherly fellowship, and to go to the utmost limit of possibility in the attempt, necessarily has for its postulate that he on his part has not allowed brotherly feeling for the wrong-doer to be disturbed by the wrong suffered, and that as soon as the other acknowledges his sin, and desires forgiveness, he is willing from the heart to accord it. While considering the duty of forgiving a brother implicitly uttered in vv. 15–17, the question forces itself on Peter, how often the duty of forgiveness is to be exercised in regard to repeated offences. And indeed he puts the question more definitely, whether the obligation extends to seven times. The words ἕως ἑπτάκις do not ask whether seven is enough, or whether it in turn is to be exceeded,[1] but (which ἕως ἑπτάκις can alone mean) whether the seven times must be observed, *i.e.* whether he must forgive but once, or at most twice, or whether oftener, as far as seven times. The number seven is chosen as the limit of frequent repetition.[2] Jesus then said to him, ver. 22: "*In no wise, say I, seven times,*" a negative answer, to which, however, He does not oppose as an antithesis in the sense of the question: "Once or twice is enough," but in surprising fashion gives an unlooked-for antithesis in the words: ἀλλὰ ἕως ἑβδομηκοντάκις ἑπτά, *i.e.*, adhering to the literal wording: "*but until seventy times seven,*" therefore not merely until seven times, but up to the limit of seven multiplied by seventy. As to meaning, then, this is equivalent to ἑβδομηκοντάκις ἑπτάκις, only the second κις[3] is omitted as awkward, and thus the number seven multiplied by seventy stands alone with all the greater emphasis. There is consequently no reason, to say nothing of right, to change the seventy times seven, contrary to Greek idiom, into seven and

---

[1] Luther: "Is seven times enough?"
[2] *E.g.* Gen. xxxiii. 3; Ps. cxix. 164; Prov. xxiv. 16; also Luke xvii. 4.
[3] The second κις in distinction from the first, which multiplies the first number by the second, would point to each act of forgiveness being a repetition of the other.

seventy times,[1] which would be ἑβδομήκοντα ἑπτάκις. Nor can the appeal to the similar passage, Gen. iv. 24, make any difference here. For that the latter passage is referred to here, is but a very uncertain conjecture, which would only gain probability in case of the agreement of the number in both passages. But when Jesus thus tells Peter to multiply the number seven, which seemed to him the limit of an often-repeated forgiveness, not merely with itself, but with its decuple, if he would reach the limit of the duty of forgiving, it is laid down that a disciple of Jesus must exercise this duty to a brother oftener than the latter will give him occasion for, or he himself can recount, and that consequently there is no limit in the number of a brother's offences beyond which forgiveness would not be a duty.

With the words: διὰ τοῦτο ὡμοιώθη ἡ βασιλεία τῶν οὐρανῶν κ.τ.λ., Jesus then introduces the figurative history, ver. 23. But this can only mean: Because the case is as was just stated, that to a disciple of Jesus and member of the heavenly kingdom the duty of forgiving a brother is unlimited, "therefore the kingdom of heaven has become like," etc. Jesus thus deduces the resemblance of the kingdom of heaven to the incident to be related, not simply from the duty of placableness in general, but from the unlimited character this duty has for a disciple of Jesus. Accordingly, we expect to find that the narrative will exhibit in figure the unlimited nature of this obligation for one belonging to the kingdom of heaven. Respecting the preterite ὡμοιώθη, see on chap. xiii. 24. See also there respecting the form usual in Matthew of introducing the figurative story by putting first the particular idea, to which the story is attached by a relative. So here: ὁμ. ἡ βασ. τ. οὐρ. ἀνθρώπῳ βασιλεῖ. But the ἀνθρώπῳ put first does not stand in contrast with the τῶν οὐρανῶν, in order to distinguish, as would otherwise be natural to suppose, the βασιλεύς, used for comparison, as human and earthly from the heavenly king of the βασιλεία compared, but, as xiii. 45, 52, and xx. 1 prove, in order to set over against the *heavenly kingdom* the sphere of *man's* natural life as a means of figurative representation. Therefore: "*The kingdom of heaven has become like a man* (namely), *a king*,"—and now begins the narrative itself joined on by a relative,—"*who wished to reckon with his slaves.*" Συναίρειν λόγον μετά τινος, unusual elsewhere, here and xxv. 19 = "to make a reckoning with one." The "slaves" here

---

[1] *E.g.* Bengel, Meyer, Lange, *et al.*

are not slaves in opposition to the free, but simply slaves in relation to the king, therefore royal servants, officials of the royal house and court.¹ And since they appear as those bound to give account to the king, they are to be regarded more definitely as managers of the royal treasure or property. The king has decided to hold a general reckoning with them, and to settle and call in the arrears of payments and contributions due. And forthwith we see him engaged in the execution of his purpose, when it is said further, ver. 24: ἀρξαμένου δὲ αὐτοῦ συναίρειν, i.e. "*and when he had begun to reckon.*" This does not mean that the following occurrence took place directly the reckoning began,² but merely that, when the reckoning was going on, προσήχθη³ αὐτῷ εἷς ὀφειλέτης μυρίων ταλάντων, i.e. "*there was brought one, a debtor of ten thousand talents.*" The εἷς does not emphasize that one individual owed so much (Meyer), but merely distinguishes the one to be spoken of from the rest. The words: προσήχθη ... ὀφειλέτης, give the impression that he would fain have evaded the king's notice, but that, when the general reckoning had disclosed a debt of 10,000 talents due from him, he was brought forward as the one burdened with a debt of this magnitude. By τάλαντον, a designation of a sum of money taken from weight, we are not to understand the Jewish talent,⁴ but the usual Attic talent,. since only on this supposition does the comparison in value with the denarii afterwards, essential to the parable, come clearly out. An Attic talent = 60 (Attic) Minæ, 1 Mina = 100 Drachmæ, a drachma being equivalent in trade to the Roman denarius; therefore, 1 talent = 6000 denarii. Of such talents, each one being equal to 6000 denarii, the man owed no less than 10,000 (altogether = 45 million marks, £2,250,000, others reckon somewhat less). It must be observed not merely that a king's (to some extent a kingdom's) administration is in question, but also that the highest possible amount of debt, touching the limit of the conceivable, lies in the purpose of the narrative. Hence there is no ground for taking the considerably smaller Syrian talent (about = 1000 marks, £50) in order to reduce the amount.

To the man who is brought before the king as owing so vast

---

¹ Cf. 1 Kings ix. 22, where the corresponding עָבַד is used both in the first and second sense side by side.

² Lange.

³ So it must be read instead of προσηνέχθη, without difference of meaning.

⁴ Reckoned by Winer (*Handwörterbuch*) at 2618 thalers (about £390).

a sum. the summons is naturally given to pay. And "*since he*," as was to be expected from the vastness of the sum, "*had not to pay*,"[1] the lord[2] commanded "*him*[3] *to be sold, and his wife and children and all that he had*."[4] According to the Mosaic law,[5] and also among other nations of antiquity, the debtor was responsible for his debt not merely with all his property, but also with his person, so that he might be sold to indemnify the creditor, and as he himself, so also his wife and children as the most precious part of his property.[6] The action of the king here[7] therefore aimed not so much at punishing the debtor, to say nothing of his wife and children, as merely at pursuing the legal course usual in recovering money. Hence the conclusion of the command runs: καὶ ἀποδοθῆναι, *i.e.* "*and payment to be made*." We need as little supply anything to this infinitive—such as "the debt" or "the proceeds"—as to the ἀποδοῦναι at the beginning of the sentence. Here as there, the idea "to pay" stands absolutely. The command says that payment shall be neither respited nor reduced, but rendered in the way stated. The question, how far the proceeds of the sale will suffice to cover the debt, is left quite out of account. But the servant had scarcely heard this command of the king, by which he saw himself handed over, with wife and children, to slavery, than he "*therefore*" (οὖν, in consequence thereof) "*fell down and cast himself before him, saying, Have patience with me, and I will pay thee all*," ver. 26. Here, as in chap. ii. 11, iv. 9, the participle πεσών is joined with the finite verb προσεκύνει,—πίπτειν meaning to fall on one's knees from an upright position, and προσκυνεῖν to throw oneself prostrate from a kneeling position. The two expressions do not, as in those passages, denote deferential worship,[8] but imploring entreaty. The contents and form of the petition correspond exactly to the distressed circumstances of the petitioner. That he does not venture to ask for a sudden remission of his debt, but merely for patience, and that he supports this request with the promise to pay all, is only

---

[1] ἔχω with the infinitive = δύναμαι; cf. Luke xii. 4.
[2] αὐτοῦ after κύριος is too weakly attested.
[3] In the first place *himself*, αὐτόν made emphatic in Greek by being put first.
[4] ἔχῃ is to be read, with Tischendorf, instead of εἶχε, the present for the imperfect in dependent sentences; cf. Winer, *Gram.* p. 335.
[5] Ex. xxii. 3; Lev. xxv. 39, 47; Amos ii. 6, viii. 6.
[6] 2 Kings iv. 1 *et al.*   [7] Differently in ver. 34.
[8] Therefore not, with Luther, "he worshipped him."

natural in his circumstances, especially in view of the king's last command: "Payment must be made." Certainly he promises more than he can perform, considering the amount of the debt, but we must not on this account think him a deceiver. He is simply a man in distress, in his anxiety thoughtlessly giving the only promise that can rescue him from the difficulty of the moment, without soberly pondering the limits of the possible. And he does not ask in vain, as ver. 27 tells: "*And the lord of that servant was moved with compassion, and released him,*" i.e. restored to him the freedom, of which he had deprived him by the command, ver. 25. So far, therefore, what the master does corresponds to the prayer of the servant: "Have patience with me," in which the latter implored the non-execution of the command to sell. But the master in his compassion does much more to the servant than he asked. He extended his merciful relief, not merely to the momentary necessity, but also to the debt itself. Hence, the object being put first, the narrative continues: καὶ τὸ δάνειον ἀφῆκεν αὐτῷ, i.e. "*and* (even) *the debt he forgave him.*" Δάνειον is properly "loan." But every payment due, but not made and further delayed, is practically a loan, even without formal borrowing, which is not to be thought of here.

In this way the lord had pity on *that* servant (τοῦ δούλου ἐκείνου), as is circumstantially said instead of the simple αὐτοῦ, not without intention. For this τ. δ. ἐκείνου at the close of the first section is now resumed with ὁ δοῦλος ἐκεῖνος in ver. 28, where the second section of the narrative begins. Lachmann and Weiss would wrongly erase the pronoun ἐκεῖνος (after B) here as well as in ver. 27. It may seem superfluous, hence the omission is explicable, but only when the mutual correspondence of the pronoun in the two sentences, significant in this part of the narrative, is overlooked. We are to bear in mind that it was *that* servant, one and the same servant, that had received such treatment as was told in the first section, who now does as the second section is about to relate. Ver. 28 says: "*But that servant*[1] *went out and found one of his fellow-servants, who owed him a hundred denarii.*" The number hundred is a number of multitude, and considered in itself it makes the amount of the debt not inconsiderable. Only by comparison is it trifling. For here denarii merely are in question, the minor coins of commerce; there, we have to do with talents 6000 times greater. And even

---

[1] Luther: *the same servant*.

the number of the denarii, although not inconsiderable in itself, how trifling against the 10,000 there! Yet we read: καὶ κρατήσας αὐτὸν ἔπνιγεν λέγων κ.τ.λ. The word πνίγειν, like ἀποπνίγειν or ἄγχειν, might indeed in itself stand figuratively for "torment, annoy."[1] But from the circumstance that κρατήσας αὐτόν precedes, which is only used of actual seizing, not figuratively, and from the fact that the next words: λέγων Ἀπόδος κ.τ.λ., expressly distinguish the annoying language from the accompanying gesture, it is clear that here a real seizing by the throat is meant. According to Roman law, it was permitted the creditor, and not unusual, to seize the fraudulent debtor by the neck and drag him before the tribunal. Here the creditor does it with the words: Ἀπόδος εἴ τι ὀφείλεις. This reading, confirmed also by the *Sinaiticus*, decidedly deserves the preference above ὅ,τι ὀφείλεις, the latter a natural but inconsiderate improvement. "*Pay, if thou owest anything*," run the words. But this is by no means to be understood, in opposition to the context, as an expression of uncertainty, whether the one addressed is really in debt,[2] or as a courteous phrase of Hellenic urbanity;[3] but, on the contrary, it is a sharp putting of the demand "Pay," as a demand following directly and inevitably, if anything is owing, from the simple fact, as we might say, "Answer, if thou art asked," and the like. Terrified, then, by the rough bearing of the creditor, the debtor does exactly the same before him that the former himself had done before the king, ver. 29: πεσὼν οὖν ὁ σύνδουλος αὐτοῦ (εἰς τοὺς πόδας αὐτοῦ) παρεκάλει αὐτὸν λέγων, Μακροθύμησον ἐπ' ἐμέ, καὶ (πάντα) ἀποδώσω σοι. Whether the words: εἰς τοὺς πόδας αὐτοῦ,[4] should be erased or retained is doubtful, but immaterial to the sense. But the πάντα before ἀποδώσω is to be erased on weighty evidence, being evidently borrowed from ver. 26 and out of keeping with the insignificant sum. The sentence therefore runs: "*Then his fellow-servant fell down at his feet and besought him saying, Have patience with me and I will pay thee.*" The words which he hears from the mouth of his kneeling fellow-servant are thus the same that he had addressed a short time before to the king in like way. Yet he remains unmoved, ver. 30: "*But he would not*," *scil.* exercise patience, to say nothing of his forgiving his fellow-servant his debt, as had been done to himself, "*but went and cast him into*

---

[1] *Quasi collo constricto* (Kuinoel). [2] Baumgarten-Crusius *et al.*
[3] De Wette, Olshausen. [4] Cf. John xi. 32.

prison." Nothing is said here of *selling* the insolvent debtor, because no servant had such power against his fellow-servant. But he uses to the utmost the power which the law gives him over the person of his debtor, applying violence and throwing him into the debtor's prison, and this, as is now added, "till he should pay that which was due." This sentence also, in stating the term up to which the debtor's imprisonment is to last, according to the will of the creditor who cast him into prison, does not so much indicate the latter's hope of repairing his loss by such means,— this might have been better effected some other way,—but rather the harsh inflexibility with which he determined to exact his rights from the debtor to the last farthing. However long it may last, he shall not be released "*until he has paid the debt.*"

The third section of the narrative tells of the retribution that overtook the servant for his unmerciful conduct, ver. 31: ἰδόντες οὖν οἱ σύνδουλοι αὐτοῦ τὰ γενόμενα ἐλυπήθησαν σφόδρα, καὶ ἐλθόντες διεσάφησαν τῷ κυρίῳ ἑαυτῶν πάντα τὰ γενόμενα. The verb λυπεῖσθαι must retain the signification "to be grieved," and the too little attested signification "to be indignant" must not be fathered upon it.[1] Still the object of the sorrow is not so much the debtor's lamentable fate,[2] as rather the creditor's lamentable conduct, as is clear from the fact that the persons grieved are described as the fellow-servants of the creditor, not of the debtor. Without doubt, αὐτοῦ in ver. 31, like αὐτόν in ver. 32, must be referred back to the subject of ver. 30. When his fellow-servants saw how he, himself just set free, dragged his debtor to prison, as his fellow-servants they were sorely grieved for him and his conduct. That only a being grieved is spoken of, not a being angry, corresponds with their position as fellow-servants; anger with servants is reserved for the lord (see ver. 34). Seeking help in their grief, "*they came and told their lord*[3] *exactly all that was done.*" Διασαφεῖν, properly "to make plain," then also "to tell exactly,"[4] here joined with the corresponding πάντα τὰ γεν.: They recounted at length the entire proceeding, with all its grievous circumstances. And not in vain did they turn in their trouble to their lord, who

---

[1] Kuinoel, Bengel.   [2] Weiss.

[3] τ. κυρ. ἑαυτῶν is to be read on decisive testimony instead of αὐτῶν. As to their lord, they cherish the confidence that he will afford relief to the just sorrow and complaint of his people

[4] Cf. 2 Macc. i. 18.

is also the unmerciful servant's lord. For "*then his lord called him unto him, and saith to him:*" Δοῦλε πονηρὲ κ.τ.λ., ver. 32. The blame expressed in the word "wicked" cannot, of course, refer to the hypocritical guile and wickedness which the servant is supposed to have cherished in his heart even on his request in ver. 26,[1] since we have found nothing of all this, but merely to the conduct to his fellow-servant described in vv. 28–30. But we need not on this account narrow the general idea πονηρός into that of hard-heartedness,[2] but the adjective πονηρός, just as in xxv. 26 and Luke xix. 22, is to be closely joined with the noun which it qualifies. He is called wicked in his position as servant, one who has proved himself *a wicked servant*. In what sense, the next words of rebuke show. The king first reminds him how he, the lord, acted to him in the like case: "*All*[3] *that debt of thine I forgave thee, because thou besoughtest me.*" The last clause: "*because,*" etc., especially recalls the similarity of the case, in which the king then stood to him, to that in which he himself afterwards stood to his fellow-servant. The king was addressed with imploring entreaty by him, as afterwards he himself by the fellow-servant, and on this entreaty of his the king showed such mercy. Hence the inference, addressed to him in convincing interrogative form, ver. 33: "*Shouldest not thou also have had mercy on thy fellow-servant, even*[4] *as I had mercy on thee?*" Had he been not a wicked, but a *righteous* servant, he would have acted after the pattern of his lord; in the spirit shown to himself, he must needs have exercised the same mercy to his fellow-servant that his lord had exercised to him. Close in the wake of the rebuking word follows the punishing act, ver. 34: καὶ ὀργισθεὶς ὁ κύριος αὐτοῦ παρέδωκεν αὐτὸν τοῖς βασανισταῖς ἕως οὗ ἀποδῷ πᾶν τὸ ὀφειλόμενον. Of course, in καὶ ὀργισθείς being put first the meaning is not, that he first became wroth after uttering the words, vv. 32, 33; but here first is there occasion to mention it, because now the punishment is to be spoken of, in which he gave expression to his righteous anger with the unmerciful servant. This is the distinction between the order issued by the king now and the one issued at the reckoning with the servant, ver. 25, and revoked, ver. 27. There, the king's only concern was for the payment of the debt and the use of the requisite means. Here, the king *having*

---

[1] Nebe *et al.*
[2] *E.g.* Kuinoel.
[3] πᾶσαν, immeasurably *vast* as it was.
[4] The double καί *comparativum*.

become angry, the purpose of his order is the infliction of severe punishment. The question is therefore no longer the payment of the debt, but the requital of the unmerciful one for his unmercifulness. For, although it is said here, he delivered him to the tormentors "*until he paid the whole debt*," the reference is far less than in ver. 30 to a payment of the entire debt to be realized in this way; but the same term, and in this case certainly reaching *in infinitum*, which he himself with implacable harshness had assigned to the durance of his fellow-servant, is now assigned in strict retribution to his delivery into the hands of the tormentors. He, too, shall not be released until he has paid the *entire* debt, immeasurably vast as it is. The revocation of the previous remission is presupposed at once, no formal justification being necessary in the case of a king ruling with absolute power. The immeasurableness of the term also decides the acceptation of the chief clause: delivered him to the tormentors. For although βασανισταί signifies primarily "tormentors," the idea is inconceivable in the light of the figurative story, that the βασανισταί are to torment the delinquent with their instruments of torture, until he has paid the whole debt; but the word "delivered" simply implies, that they are to keep him in their custody until the term mentioned, certainly an endless one. Although, therefore, it cannot be said offhand that βασανισταί here signifies δεσμοφύλακες [1] merely, in the present connection the former by the nature of their calling simply come into view as a special class of the latter, and the delivery of the unmerciful one into their hands can according to the context mean nothing but that he was given up to the roughest class of prison-attendants to be kept in hard, painful durance. Consequently, according to the strict law of just retribution, the king simply does to the servant as he himself had done to his fellow-servant, he casts him into prison until he has paid the debt; cf. ver. 30. Because he had not done to his fellow-servant as the lord had done to him, the lord now does to him as he himself had done to his fellow-servant, only that—and herein lies the terror of the retribution—the immeasurably higher amount of his debt renders his durance specially painful, and, moreover, leaves *him* without any prospect of its termination.

The narrative having come to an end, Jesus at once adds the interpreting word, ver. 35: οὕτως καὶ ὁ πατήρ μου ὁ οὐράνιος

[1] Kuinoel, de Wette.

ποιήσει ὑμῖν, ἐὰν μὴ ἀφῆτε ἕκαστος τῷ ἀδελφῷ αὐτοῦ ἀπὸ τῶν καρδιῶν ὑμῶν (τὰ παραπτώματα αὐτῶν). The words in brackets are probably a spurious explanatory addition from chap. vi. 14, 15, so that, according to the original reading, ἀφιέναι here, as in ver. 21 and often, stands absolutely and without object. "My heavenly Father," or "My Father who is in heaven," is a designation of God especially common on the lips of Jesus in Matthew, and apparently convertible at will with the no less frequent "*your* heavenly Father" in addressing the disciples. But then we must neither seek in the phrase "heavenly" a specially designed antithesis to the "certain king," ver. 23, nor in the "*my* Father" for "*your* Father" a special intimation that God cannot be called the father of an implacable man.[1] The passage of like meaning, Matt. vi. 15 (Mark xi. 26), where "*your* Father" is found, tells against the latter view. It can only be said, that here and wherever Jesus gives His disciples teaching or assurances respecting God, calling Him "my Father," the assurance acquires special emphasis, inasmuch as in reference to what He desires to affirm of God He does not fail to assert the unique relation of Son in which He stands to God, a relation including in it mutual knowledge.[2] With such emphasis He gives the assurance: "*So*," i.e. *mutatis mutandis*, just as the king, ver. 34, did to the servant, "*shall also my heavenly Father do to you, if ye do not*," etc. Wherein the analogy, intimated in "so," between the conduct to be expected of God and the conduct of the king, described in ver. 34, consists, the interpretation will show in the right place. But so much is clear at once, that Jesus threatens His disciples with divine punishment, in the case put by Him, namely, "*if ye forgive not every man his brother from your hearts.*" Τὸ ἀδελφῷ αὐτοῦ it is said, not τῷ πλησίον αὐτοῦ. Here therefore it is not, as in the discourse preceding the parable, primarily their conduct to other men generally that is spoken of, but the tender love which the disciples of Jesus, who as such are brethren,[3] are to show one to another. Then "from your hearts" is specially added to "forgive." But this does not mean a forgiving from heartfelt sympathy in opposition to one from stoical apathy,[4] for the latter feels no injury and therefore grants no forgiveness, but forgiving "from your hearts" has its simple contrast in the forgiveness not springing from the heart,[5]

---

[1] Chrysostom, Nebe.   [2] Cf. xi. 27.
[3] Cf. ver. 21 and 15–17.   [4] Meyer.   [5] Similarly ἐκ ψυχῆς, Eph. vi. 6.

which indeed is accorded and promised, but not without inner reluctance, a bitter remnant of ill-will being left in the heart. Only on the supposition of such a remnant of bitterness being found in the heart, despite the forgiveness outwardly accorded, is such a counting of a brother's already-forgiven sins possible as was implied in the question of Peter in ver. 21: "How often shall I forgive?" since the sins forgiven from the heart, and therefore entirely, no longer come into account, even as to their number.

We thus find ourselves remitted by the interpreting word of Jesus to His answer to Peter's question directly preceding the parable (ver. 22). From the comparison of the two declarations with each other, and with the intervening parable, the purpose of the latter is clear. Jesus there said to Peter, that the duty of forgiving a brother is not limited, as Peter thought, to a certain number of sins, but is unlimited and unconditional. When, further, He deduced from this the similarity of the kingdom of heaven to the narrative of a servant who, after special experience of his lord's clemency, inexorably stands on his rights against a fellow-servant in debt to him, and thus inevitably incurs the heavy wrath and sentence of the king, concluding with the interpreting word: "So also shall my heavenly Father do to you, if ye forgive not every one his brother from your hearts,"— the unmistakeable purpose of the parable is to show *that to a member of the kingdom of God, in virtue of the special position in which he stands in relation to God, the implacable refusal to forgive a brother in every case, and without regard to the number of offences to be forgiven, is a sin, by which he will infallibly forfeit his own state of grace, and incur the judgment of the wrath of God*. It is also clear what function belongs in the carrying out of this purpose to each of the three parts of which the narrative is built up. The first part lays a basis for the sequel, sketching in the special position of the servant a picture of the position in which every member of God's kingdom stands to God in reference to his own debt. Next, the second part shows, by describing the hard-hearted conduct of the same servant to his fellow-servant, the contradiction in which a member of God's kingdom puts himself with his own position by implacably refusing to forgive a brother; upon which the third part, with the account of the king's sentence upon that servant, testifies the divine judgment that will be the infallible result of such non-forgiveness.

Within this framework the interpretation of the particula

incidents is to be worked out. In reference to the first part, it is above all to be borne in mind that its purpose is merely to lay a basis for what follows. First of all, the point is to obtain in the sphere of earthly relations the necessary conditions under which the servant in the parable may serve as a warning to the disciples of the wrong and guilt of non-forgiveness. When, therefore, we are told first of a reckoning held by a king with his servants, then of one being produced who was burdened with a debt unmeasurably great; further, of the issue of a royal command for payment to be made by selling the debtor and his whole property; again, of the servant falling down on his face with the prayer for patience; and finally, of his release with his entire debt forgiven,—these incidents are not meant, each one separately and in the same order and dramatic combination, to represent a series of definite corresponding incidents in the sphere of God's kingdom. For however readily the two incidents last mentioned (vv. 26, 27) suggest a reference to the sinner's repentance and the act of absolution following it on God's part, it is impossible in a similar way, as ought necessarily to be done, to interpret the preceding incidents—the king's reckoning with the whole body of his servants, the production of one specially laden with debt, the command to sell him and make payment—of a corresponding series of incidents preceding the act of repentance and the act of absolution in the sphere of God's kingdom. Moreover, the wording of the servant's prayer (ver. 26), however appropriate in the mouth of a distressed debtor before his creditor, is thoroughly unsuited to express figuratively the true nature of the sinner's repentance before God, and not seldom has led to a question so strangely confounding figure and thing as this, whether the penitence of the servant was sincere or merely hypocritical. Rather, the entire series of events in the first part of the parable is freely imagined and combined in the present manner for the purpose of putting the servant, who is to be a warning example to the disciples, in a position in relation to his lord which shall represent in figure the position of the members of God's kingdom in reference to their own indebtedness to their heavenly King. For this purpose he must appear, on the one hand, as laden with an enormous debt to his lord, which he is unable to pay, and which, if legal measures are taken against him, must bring him to ruin with all he has. He is represented in this light by the story of a king reckoning with his servants, one of whom appears laden with an enormous debt, and of a decree being issued in accordance with the law of debt to sell the debtor, with wife and children, and all he had. But, on the other hand, he must appear as one conscious that his lord has remitted this whole vast debt from mere sympathy with his distress. Hence the further narrative of the praying and beseeching on the anxious debtor's part in the words descriptive of his anxiety and distress: "Have patience with me, I will pay thee all," and of the lord's compassion thus awakened moving him freely to release the debtor and remit the debt. Now the servant is seen to be in a position in relation to his lord in which the hearers of the parable must recognise the position in which they stand in reference to their own debt to God. And here, where at the close of the first part of the parable we are able to review its result, the interpretation must be put as follows: Like as the servant is laden with an enormous debt to his master, which he is unable to pay, and therefore must go to ruin with all he has, if the king insists on payment, so the members of God's kingdom are consciously laden with an enormous debt of sin to God, which they will never be in a position to make good, so that they must be lost, with all they are and have, if God exacts satisfaction. But, like as the servant, despite the enormous size of the debt, not merely sees himself spared by his lord, from sympathy with his anxious entreaty, but also sees his entire debt remitted, so the members of God's kingdom as such are certain that, merely on the prayer of their contrite spirit and broken heart, God, in pity, has not merely treated them with forbearance, but also forgiven their whole enormous debt of sin. The correlation of the two ideas of remitting a debt and forgiving a sin, which is the pivot of the entire parable, appears all the more distinctly in the Greek, as the two ideas are expressed by the same word—ἀφιέναι, cf. vv. 21, 25, and 35.

Because of the similarity of the servant's position to that of the disciples, as regards their indebtedness to their Lord, the description in the second part of the narrative of the unmerciful conduct of the former to his fellow-servant in debt to him becomes a warning against like unmerciful conduct on the part of the latter to a brother who has sinned against them. The warning lies first in the exposure of the glaring contradiction of such a course with their own state of grace. Like as the servant was met by a fellow-servant who owed him a hundred denarii (a great number of such coins indeed, but still merely denarii), while talents had been forgiven to him, and only a hundred denarii, while ten thousand talents had been forgiven to him; so everything with which one brother can reproach another, however often the latter may have sinned against him, is still infinitely little in comparison with his own debt, which God has forgiven. For how light the weight of such offences as one brother can commit against another in comparison with the infinite gravity belonging to every offence of man against God—of the creature against the Creator! And how small is an apparently vast number of offences, such as one brother can impute to another, compared with the incalculable number of offences which he himself has committed against God! The interpretation must proceed in this definite way, provided we are right in supposing that the contrast is twofold; first, between talents and denarii; and secondly, between the high number ten thousand and the, although not inconsiderable in itself, yet to the former one insignificantly small number one hundred. Therefore, as glaring as is the contradiction in which the servant puts himself with his own position by roughly demanding payment from his fellow-servant, and also by not remitting his debt when the latter lies suppliant before him, as he himself was forgiven shortly before, but instead, exacting his right to the uttermost,—so glaring is the contradiction in which a disciple of Jesus puts himself with his own state of grace by insisting on satisfaction for the sins of a brother against him, and, instead of granting forgiveness in remembrance of the forgiveness he has himself received, making his brother suffer for his sin until he has made full satisfaction. It is evident how in this way the particular features of the figurative story have received their due within the limits of the interpretation.

Finally, the inevitable consequence which such conduct, precisely because standing in gross contradiction with a believer's own state of grace, must have on this state itself, transforming the divine grace into wrath and punishment for the unmerciful, is shown in the third part of the parable by the account of the punishment inflicted by the king on the servant. We were told first in this part that the fellow-servants, when they saw this, reported it to their lord. This might seem a feature of the narrative merely added by way of transition to what follows, incapable of special interpretation, since God—the All-knowing One—does not need events to be reported to Him by others. But if the narrator merely needed such a means of transition, the simple ἀκούσας οὖν ὁ κύριος τὰ γενόμενα κ.τ.λ. would have sufficed. When, on the other hand, it is expressly mentioned that the fellow-servants, seeing such conduct, *were sorely grieved*, and told *everything* that was done *exactly* to their lord, as the one from whom they confidently expected protection and redress, this element of the narrative is far too strange and emphatic for it not to demand a special interpretation. And this interpretation can only be the following: Similar conduct on the part of a disciple of Jesus must needs awaken great grief, such as the conduct of that servant awakened, in those who are fellow-disciples and fellow-members of God's kingdom. And as his fellow-servants seek help from their lord with a common, earnest complaint[1] against the conduct of that servant, so a complaint must rise with one accord before God from the disciples against such a disciple, with zealous earnestness they must beseech from their Lord divine redress for such a scandal. And all the more infallibly will that happen of which the close of the parable tells. As little as the servant would have justification or defence before the king, so little justification or defence would an unforgiving disciple have before God, in answer to the question: "All that debt of thine I forgave thee, because thou besoughtest me,—shouldest not thou also have had pity on thy fellow-servant as I had pity on thee?" Therefore, like the man in the parable, he would be found a *wicked servant* before God, because he did not act to his brother in the spirit shown by his heavenly Lord and King to him, but sinned against the spirit of divine compassion by his want of mercy. For this reason, as certainly as the inevitable consequence there is that the king, who formerly showed himself so gracious to the servant, now burns with anger against him, so inevitably will God's pardoning grace be changed for the unforgiving into retributive wrath. And as there the angry king inflicts severe retribution on the servant, doing to him as he had done to his fellow-servant, and delivering him to prison until he has paid his whole debt, so will God in anger deal with the unforgiving sinner exactly as he himself dealt with his brother, and visit upon him his sins against God in their vast weight and number, delivering him to the pain of just punishment, and refusing to remove it, unless he

---

[1] The earnestness lies in διεσάφησαν ... πάντα.

render to the holy God the impossible thing which he thought himself justified in demanding from his brother,—full satisfaction for all his sins. "Delivered him to the tormentors" is now exhaustively interpreted in the sense of the parable. The meaning simply is, that strict retribution for his own sins against God, and delivery to pain, corresponding to their greatness and weight, await him who forgives not his brother, a statement which certainly indirectly suggests reference to the pain of Gehenna. But there is no direct allusion to Gehenna, neither in the mention of the "tormentors," as though picturing it without Biblical analogy as a place where the lost are tormented by evil angels,[1] for no tormenting of the delinquent was referred to, but simply a delivery of him into their custody,—nor in the conception of imprisonment, so that the prison as such would be Gehenna, for the prison thought of in ver. 34 appears merely as the correlate to the prison mentioned in ver. 30. The former can as little require a definite interpretation as the latter. In the same way the interpretation has declared, and the examination of the course of the narrative has proved, that the clause: "till he should pay all that was due," contains no intimation of any ceasing of hell-punishment at some term of the future (purgatory); but, on the contrary, is meant to intimate the endless duration of the punishment, to which, by the law of retribution, he who cherishes resentment against his brother is exposed until full satisfaction is rendered.

The Labourers in the Vineyard.

(Matt. xx. 1-16.)

From chap. xix. 1 onwards we find Jesus no longer in Galilee, but journeying on the road through Peræa to the borders of Judæa. It was on this journey[2] that, in reply to a young man, who asked what good thing he must do to have eternal life, and in particular what he still lacked after, as he supposed, keeping the commandments, Jesus said: "If thou wilt be perfect, go and sell what thou hast and give to the poor; and come, follow me," vv. 16–21. The first demand: "Sell what thou hast," stands, of course, in very close connection with the second: "Follow me."

[1] Nebe and the ancients.   [2] Cf. ver. 15 with ver. 16 ff.

The selling of what he has is required as a means to the end; in this way the young man will be able to begin to follow Jesus. But according to the context the entire demand is put forward as the condition of possessing the eternal life, which the young man wished to secure (cf. ver. 16). Nevertheless, before uttering the chief demand: "Come, follow me," on the fulfilment of which the possession of eternal life will depend, Jesus is careful to add to the first demand, referring to the sale of his property, the special promise: "and thou shalt have treasure in heaven." Accordingly this treasure in heaven cannot be identical with eternal life itself, but must be a special compensation reserved for him in heaven in return for the surrender of his earthly treasures, a compensation to be given him in the future kingdom of God, when he enters upon eternal life, along with the latter. But when the young man heard this demand, he went away sorrowful, for he had great possessions (cf. ver. 22).

The question which Peter puts to the Lord in ver. 27, after the parenthetic remarks of Jesus, vv. 23–26, undoubtedly refers to this occurrence. The question runs: "Lo, we ($ἡμεῖς$ in contrast with the young man) have left all and followed Thee; what then ($ἄρα$) shall we have?" From the fact of Jesus promising the youth a special compensation for the sale of his possessions, Peter infers that for them—the Twelve—who have left every earthly possession to follow the Lord, and have thus really done what the youth refused to do, a special compensation is reserved in heaven, and asks in what this compensation consists. That we have rightly understood the meaning of the question is confirmed by the answer of Jesus, ver. 28: "Verily I say unto you, That ye which have followed me (*scil.* giving up every possession), in the regeneration (of the world to be the scene of God's eternal kingdom [1]) when the Son of man shall sit on the throne of His glory, ye also shall sit upon twelve thrones, judging the twelve tribes of Israel." The more precise examination of the import of these words lies outside our province. We have only here to note, that according to this promise the special sacrifices made by the Twelve in leaving all to follow Jesus fully will, as matter of fact, be recompensed by a position of special influence in the Messianic kingdom of the future. The point in question is not participation in the kingdom of God in general, but a reward of special grace and honour reserved for them in

[1] Isa. lxv. 17.

heaven, to be given to them when and if they enter upon the eternal life of God's kingdom, along with that life. And when Jesus immediately proceeds, ver. 29: "And *whosoever* (πᾶς ὅστις) has left houses, or brethren, or sisters, or father, or mother . . . for my name's sake, shall receive a hundredfold, and shall inherit eternal life," this is plainly nothing but a generalization of what has just been said to the Twelve. Not the Twelve alone will receive special compensation for their special sacrifices, but every one who has made special sacrifice in confessing Jesus, will, just like the Twelve, " receive a hundredfold, and inherit eternal life." Thus two things are clear. First, that the promise: πολλαπλασίονα λήμψεται, cannot be understood in the present context of a reward in this life, but only of a recompense for self-denying confessors reserved to the future kingdom of God and bestowed on them there; that therefore the same utterance in the parallel passages in Mark[1] and Luke[2] (where the special promise to the Twelve is wanting, and a distinction is made in the now general and independent promise between a manifold recompense "in this time," and the eternal life "in the world to come") has by no means a contradictory although a different meaning from the one necessarily given by the passage in Matthew with its simpler wording and more complete context. Nor can the appeal to those parallel passages justify an attempt to refer the future λήμψεται in the present passage to a quite different period from the immediately preceding καθίσεσθε and the immediately following κληρονομήσει. But, on the other hand, it is just as clear that by the manifold gift, which self-denying confessors shall receive in the future kingdom of God, must be understood here also a special recompense not identical in itself with the possession of eternal life, a recompense to be given to every one for the special sacrifices he has made for Jesus' sake just as much as to the Twelve; that therefore the two clauses πολλαπλ. λήμψεται and ζ. αἰών. κληρονομήσει mean, not the same,[3] although closely related things, and the καί joining the two clauses is the usual "and," not a καί *epexegeticum*, which, moreover, would be exceedingly harsh here. The promise is to the effect, that in the future kingdom of God every one shall receive manifold recompense for his special sacrifices, and in addition shall inherit the supreme blessing of eternal life.

After Jesus has given this reply to Peter's question, with δέ

[1] x. 29, 30.   [2] xviii. 29, 30.   [3] Meyer, Weiss, *et al.*

He turns to a qualifying utterance intended to guard what was said against a natural misunderstanding, ver. 30: πολλοὶ δὲ ἔσονται πρῶτοι (ὄντες) ἔσχατοι, καὶ (πολλοὶ ἔσονται) ἔσχατοι (ὄντες) πρῶτοι. The words in brackets show how the gnomological brevity of the utterance is to be filled up in the two clauses. There is no reason to depart from this obvious mode of supplementing the sentence, which assigns the preceding words πρῶτοι and ἔσχατοι in each clause to the subject, and the following words ἔσχατοι and πρῶτοι to the predicate, and to invert the relation. Since the future ἔσονται can only be referred to the same period as all the preceding futures in vv. 28 and 29, the sentence affirms that many who were first in the kingdom of God on earth shall be last in that kingdom hereafter, and the converse. Moreover, the twofold reference in which the πρῶτοι or ἔσχατοι εἶναι is meant first in the present and then in the next life, results from the position of the saying in the context as a qualifying addition to the promise given in vv. 28 and 29. The inference which it seems so natural to the ambitious heart of man to draw from what had been said is this, that, if every one shall receive manifold recompense in the future world for special sacrifices for the sake of Jesus, they who take a pre-eminent position in this life by the greatness of their services may reckon on a special reward in the next life. But, denying this apparently logical conclusion, Jesus says it will by no means be the case, many who were first in amount of service will be last as regards amount of reward, and conversely. That this meaning of the utterance naturally follows from the previous tenor of the discourse, can scarcely be denied. If, however, the meaning is otherwise understood, the force of "all" being arbitrarily assigned to "many,"[1] or the difference between first and last in this life being referred to the earlier and later period of entering the kingdom of God, without the inverting of the relation in the next life being also logically referred to a temporal relation of earlier and later,[2] the reason is that it is thought necessary to determine the meaning of the saying prematurely by the following parable instead of by itself and the previous tenor of the discourse. But in so far as the saying is and is meant to be enigmatical, its elucidation must, no doubt, be drawn from the figurative story joined on to it by the explanatory "for," xx. 1 ff., and running out into a similar saying,

[1] Lisco.   [2] So Meyer and many others.

xx. 16, which plainly resumes what is said here, and professes to be a solution of the apparent contradiction between the thesis of xix. 29 and the antithesis of xix. 30. In what sense, therefore, the "many," to whom the prediction applies, are in this life first or last as to their services, and in what way the prediction, that they will be last or first as to reward, will be fulfilled in them, is not to be determined here. We expect to find these questions solved in the parable. At the same time it will also appear whether they are right who deny a strict connection between the parable and this utterance, ascribing the fault to redaction on the part of the evangelist.[1]

The figurative story is introduced in the manner now become familiar to us, xx. 1 : ὁμοία γάρ ἐστιν ἡ βασιλεία τῶν οὐρανῶν ἀνθρώπῳ[2] οἰκοδεσπότῃ, ὅστις ἐξῆλθεν ἅμα πρωὶ μισθώσασθαι ἐργάτας εἰς τὸν ἀμπελῶνα αὐτοῦ. "Ἅμα = una cum,[3] stands as a preposition before πρωί, as in Acts xxviii. 23 the preposition ἀπό. Similarly in the classics : ἅμα ἕῳ, ἅμα τῷ ἡλίῳ, ἅμα τῇ ἡμέρᾳ. The meaning is that he went out directly at early morn, directly at sunrise, *i.e.*, since the Jews divided every natural day from sunrise to sunset into twelve hours,[4] at the beginning of the first hour of day. The purpose to hire labourers includes that of sending them into the scene of labour. Hence μισθώσασθαι εἰς τ. ἀμπ., which must not be translated "*for*," but as in vv. 2, 4, 7, "*into* his vineyard." That the householder, who thus "*went out directly at early morn to hire labourers into his vineyard*" actually found such, is assumed when the narrative continues : "*And when he had agreed with the labourers*" (the labourers met with at the going out mentioned) "*for a denarius a day, he set them into his vineyard.*" In the participial clause: συμφωνήσας δὲ μετὰ τῶν ἐργατῶν ἐκ δηναρίου τὴν ἡμέραν, the preposition ἐκ indicates the starting-point from which the parties came to an agreement; and this starting-point is δηνάριον τὴν ἡμέραν, so that τὴν ἡμέραν belongs as acc. *temporis* directly to δηνάριον, and is not to be referred back as acc. of more precise definition independently to συμφωνήσας, since it belongs not so much to the mode as rather to the contents or starting-point of the agreement. A denarius was the usual amount of a day's pay,[5] and also the day's wage of the Roman soldier.[6]

---

[1] Neander, Bleek, Weiss. [2] Cf. on xviii. 23.
[3] Cf. xiii. 29. [4] Winer, *Handwörterbuch*, "Tag."
[5] Tob. v. 15 in the Greek text. [6] Tac. *Ann.* i. 17 ; Plin. xxxiii. 3.

But the householder is not content with this first going out at early morn, but goes out again and again the whole day till towards evening for the same end,—an unusual proceeding, which shows that his chief thought was not simply the amount of work to be done, but the putting of as great a number as possible of the unemployed to labour in his service, and the doing of everything in his power to prevent any one remaining idle, whilst he has work enough for all.

Of the second going out it is said, ver. 3 : "*And having gone out about the third hour*" (*i.e.* about the third completed hour, or at the beginning of the fourth), "*he saw others standing in the market-place idle.*" "*Others*" is expressly said, therefore not such as were met with the first time and had then refused to obey his call, but such as for any reason whatever had not come in his way the first time. And he lights upon them also "*standing idle*," not because they were deliberately addicted to idle loitering, which would little suit the "in the market-place," but they stand in the market idle, because hitherto they had waited in vain for any one to hire them. The householder at once hires these also, vv. 4, 5a : "*And also to them he said, Go ye also into the vineyard, and whatsoever is right I will give you. And they went their way.*" The ruling thought is, that despite the advanced hour he hired these *also*, like those met with at daybreak. For this reason the double "also" has nothing strange, and, whether we read κἀκείνοις or καὶ ἐκείνοις, we ought not to make a mere "and" of the first καί,[1] in which case, instead of the pronoun κἀκείνοις being chosen and prefixed to the verb, καὶ εἶπεν αὐτοῖς would simply have been said as in ver. 6. The first "also" in the clause κἀκείνοις εἶπεν is not unimportant, precisely because it places the householder's entire address, inclusive of the promise of reward, on an equal footing with the first transaction with the labourers hired in the early morning. The promise of reward also : "and whatsoever is right I will give you," resembles in substance the one made to the labourers in the morning, inasmuch as the later labourers are definitely promised an amount fully corresponding to the laws of justice for their piece of a day's work, just as the former were promised a full day's pay for a full day's work. In comparison with this resemblance the difference is immaterial, that here the amount is not definitely settled in pence and farthings, but instead of this the mere offer "whatever is just I will give you"

[1] Weiss.

is made on one side and accepted on the other. The only reason is, that in this unusual case the basis of an ordinary sum is wanting to fix the amount of wage, and thus a general agreement on the basis of right and justice naturally suggests itself. On the other hand, there is nothing in the narrative to intimate that those hired later were different from and better than those hired earlier, because they had confidence in the spontaneous goodness of the hirer, which the others lacked. A notion of this kind can only be found by previously importing it for the sake of a preconceived interpretation. In the narrative these labourers are just as much *hired* labourers as those hired in the morning, and just like them expect their hire not from the spontaneous goodness, but from the justice ("whatsoever is *just*") of the hirer.

The same occurrence is repeated about the sixth and the ninth hour, ver. 5b: "*Having gone out again about the sixth and the ninth hour, he did likewise.*" Because the occurrence about the sixth and the ninth hour is exactly the same as that related of the third hour, it is passed by briefly with "did likewise." At both these hours he goes out again, finds other labourers who had not come in his way before, and sends them into the vineyard with the like promise to give them whatever is just.

And about the eleventh hour, told of in ver. 6, exactly the same is the case. But the advanced period of the day, only a single hour before sunset, makes the repetition of the occurrence here specially noteworthy, and leads to a detailed account: "*And about the eleventh,*[1] *having gone out, he found others standing.*"[2] Even now he finds labourers standing unemployed. And it is well worthy of notice that the narrative expressly shows, by a conversation in the form of question and answer, in what the reason of this standing unemployed is to be sought. The householder asks: "*Why stand ye here all the day idle?*" and the labourers reply, ver. 7: "*Because no man hath hired us.*" If this answer were meant as a false subterfuge, as has been arbitrarily supposed,[3] it must in some way have been marked as such, and must at least have called forth a reply from the householder. In its simple terms and independent position it can only be meant to evince that, in the case also of those hired about the eleventh hour, the reason of their long idleness is not to be

---

[1] ὥραν is to be deleted, with Lachmann and Tischendorf.
[2] ἀργούς again is to be deleted, Lachmann and Tischendorf.   [3] Stier, Nebe.

sought in a special inclination to indolence, but simply in the circumstance that no one had hired them. And it must be of value to the understanding of the whole to keep this in view, because a possible misunderstanding on this side is excluded by the insertion of a special conversation. With the words: "*Go ye also into the vineyard,*" these also are set to work. Whether the clause: καὶ ὃ ἐὰν ᾖ δίκαιον λήψεσθε, here is genuine, or is transferred, with a slight change, from ver. 4,[1] may appear doubtful as regards external testimony. Inasmuch as, even in case of its spuriousness, it would be understood, both from the nature of the case and the previous course of the narrative, that work is not required even of these late-hired ones without proportionate payment, the clause may be dispensed with. Whoever thinks it right to infer, from the general offer (ver. 4), a spontaneous trust on the part of the later-hired ones in the householder's goodness, may also in this passage infer, from the absence of such an offer, that these hired labourers did not think of reward at all, and engaged themselves from pure delight in work.

With ver. 8 begins the second part of the narrative, giving an account of the payment of the wages at evening, when the day's work was done: "*And when even was come,*"—when, with sunset, the day was ended and its work over,—"*the lord of the vineyard saith unto his steward, Call the labourers, and pay them their hire, beginning from the last unto the first.*" The "last," of course, are those hired at the eleventh hour; the "first," those hired at early morn. Nevertheless, according to the context, the ideas "the last" and "the first," occurring here for the first time in the narrative, by no means express a bare temporal relation, but a relation of rank within the setting of the temporal relation. The earlier or later period of hiring in the first part of the narrative was not of importance for its own sake, but only in so far as on it depended a more or less amount of service, since, according to the period of hiring, a maximum of work (a full day's work) fell to one class, and a minimum (a single hour's work) to others. What, therefore, makes the one class "first" and the others "last," is not a coming before or after each other in time,—at last all laboured together,—but the great or little quantum of service, measured by the early or late period of their being hired. The overseer is entrusted by the householder with the payment of the different classes of labourers. As it does not appear, from the tenor of

[1] Lachmann, Tischendorf.

the narrative, why this middle person—the overseer—is introduced, and no further mention is made of him, we may expect the interpretation to supply the clue. On the other hand, the purpose of the formal arrangement by which the payment proceeds from the last to the first is clear from the tenor of the narrative itself. No real preference or disparagement of one or the other class is implied in this arrangement, for whether one labourer at evening receives his pay a moment earlier than another is immaterial in itself. The significance of the arrangement rather is, that it prepares the way for the issue of the narrative. Its meaning is, that the payment of the last is to take place publicly in presence of all,[1] and so, further, the payment of the labourers of lesser service always in presence of those of greater service, because the householder's wish is not merely that every labourer may receive the pay due to him, but also that the natural discontent of the first with the pay seemingly out of proportion to the amount of their service may find expression in words, and so occasion may be given him to vindicate the justice of his conduct. Accordingly, we read in ver. 9 the unexpected news of the payment of the last: "*And when those* (*scil.* hired) *about the eleventh hour came,*" *i.e.* came forward to receive their hire, "*they received every man a denarius,*"[2] therefore the pay of a full day's work, although they had laboured but one hour. In accordance with the arrangement of ver. 8, the payment of those hired about the ninth, sixth, and third hours must have taken place in order. But their payment and the amount of their pay are passed by in silence. This gap may be filled up by supposing that they all received a denarius; but it should not be forgotten that nothing is expressly said on the point, as must necessarily have been done if it were of importance to the narrative to assume that all without exception received exactly the same pay. Since the narrative passes at once from the payment of the last to that of the first, it merely emphasizes the point that, in the latter as in the former case, something unexpected happened, only in the reverse direction. And we are told first of all the nature of the expectation of the first labourers, ver. 10: καὶ ἐλθόντες οἱ πρῶτοι ἐνόμισαν, ὅτι πλεῖον λήμψονται. We must not read πλείονα, which seems to have arisen from trans-

---

[1] Cf. the κάλεσον τοὺς ἐργάτας placed first, according to which all the labourers are supposed to be gathered to receive their pay.

[2] ἀνὰ δηνάριον, cf. Winer, *Gram.* pp. 312, 497.

ferring the Α of λήμψονται as A, but πλεῖον on good evidence, since the former reading (Rec.), as an antithesis, would require the *one* denarius to be emphasized, which is not done anywhere. Therefore: "*And when the first came, they supposed that they would receive more,*" cherishing the natural expectation, that for their so much greater service they would receive a greater reward than had been just given to the last. But then the second unexpected thing happened: καὶ ἔλαβον τὸ ἀνὰ δηνάριον καὶ αὐτοί,[1] *i.e.* "*and they also received every man the sum of a denarius.*" The article τό before ἀνὰ δην. points back to the amount of pay already known from the payment of the last, thus emphasizing the fact that the first received the same as the last, and nothing else. Consequently two unexpected things happened in paying the wages. First, the last saw themselves placed, contrary to expectation, in the matter of reward in the same position as the first, who had done a full day's work; and again, the first saw themselves placed, contrary to expectation, in the matter of reward in no different position from the last, who had worked but one hour.

On the part of the first, who are apparently placed at a disadvantage, protest is not wanting, especially when the householder had himself provoked protest by the order of payment fixed, ver. 11: "*And when they received it, they murmured against the householder, saying:* οὗτοι οἱ ἔσχατοι μίαν ὥραν ἐποίησαν, καὶ ἴσους ἡμῖν αὐτοὺς ἐποίησας τοῖς βαστάσασιν τὸ βάρος τῆς ἡμέρας καὶ τὸν καύσωνα." The first clause may be rendered either: "*These last have spent one hour,*"[2] namely, in the vineyard, which definition of place may easily be supplied from what precedes;[3] or: "These last have *wrought* one hour."[4] The former, however, is to be preferred, the signification of ποιεῖν χρόνον = "to spend a time," being current in the classics and also in the New Testament,[5] whereas the intransitive use = "to work, make," is only conceivable by a Hebraism,[6] and is not supported beyond doubt by the single passage of the Septuagint, Ruth ii. 19. Moreover, a sharper and more complete contrast to the following clause follows on the retention of the former signification. For whereas the translation: "they have wrought (but) one hour," placing the

---

[1] So we must read, with Tischendorf, instead of: καὶ ἔλ. καὶ αὐτοὶ ἀνὰ δην., Rec.
[2] Meyer.   [3] In opposition to Weiss.   [4] De Wette, Weiss.
[5] Cf. Acts xv. 33, xviii. 23, xx. 3; 2 Cor. xi. 25; Jas. iv. 13.
[6] After the analogy of עָשָׂה.

emphasis wholly and exclusively on "one hour," leads us to expect the long duration of their own toil to be emphasized in contrast, the murmurers in the second clause really lay less stress on the *duration* of their toil than upon the *hardship* they submitted to. "*And thou hast made them equal to us, who have borne the burden of the day and the heat.*" To the easy spending of one hour in the vineyard, as they describe the minimum of exertion expended by the last, with fresh powers, in the cool of the evening, they oppose the fatigue submitted to by them in bearing the burden of toil and noontide heat. Appealing to this contrast, they remind the householder of the fact in a tone of reproach: "Thou hast made them equal to us." As to the expression of such a feeling, we ought so little to attach importance to the protest, that, on the contrary, it would have been matter of wonder, in the circumstances of the case, if these hired labourers had regarded the householder's strange proceeding in the right light and accepted it without reply, apart from explanation. But assuming that they needed such explanation, the householder intended from the outset to give it, and for this end directed the labourers to be paid in reverse order. And thus the protest on the part of the first is at once followed by the reply on the householder's part, ver. 13: "*But he answered one of them, and said:* ἑταῖρε, οὐκ ἀδικῶ σε· οὐχὶ δηναρίου συνεφώνησάς μοι;" He turns to one of them, his answer to him applying, of course, to all. In the tone not of sharp fault-finding, but of friendly remonstrance, he reminds him that he cannot complain of the reward given him, as if he had been unjustly treated: "*Friend, I do thee no wrong; didst thou not agree with me for a denarius?*"[1] He himself had agreed with the householder for "a denarius a day," ver. 2, and a denarius he has received for the day's work, ver. 10. Consequently there can be no question of an injustice done him. Hence the summons of the householder, ver. 14: ἆρον τὸ σὸν καὶ ὕπαγε, *i.e.* "*take what is thine*,"—what is thine and has been given thee legally,—"*and go thy way*," *i.e.* to thy house. As little as the first imperative ἆρον assumes that the person addressed has hitherto left the denarius lying in scorn[2] (which is excluded by the ἔλαβον in ver. 10), so little does the second imperative ὕπαγε imply that the householder dismisses these first ones as incorrigible people with whom he will have nothing more to do.[3]

---

[1] The simple *gen. pretii*, different from ver. 2.
[2] De Valenti.   [3] Stier, Nebe.

It follows from the natural course of the narrative that the labourers go home at evening after receiving their pay. How, then, can the summons to do so denote an angry dismissal? Rather as the ἆρον in this context can only signify that he is to *accept* what is his *without further objection*, so the ὕπαγε means that he is *to go home with what is his* as one who has received what is legally due to him, and therefore *has no reason for longer tarrying*. That, after receiving the pay due *to himself*, he has no justification for finding fault with what *others* have received, is stated in what follows, ver. 14*b*: θέλω δὲ τούτῳ τῷ ἐσχάτῳ δοῦναι ὡς καὶ σοί, i.e. "But it is my will to give to this last[1] even as to thee." Θέλω stands first with emphasis. As the reason why he gave just as much to this last one as to him, he simply says that it is his will so to do. And that this reason is sufficient, and admits no objection, is confirmed by the question following immediately, ver. 15: οὐκ[2] ἔξεστίν μοι ὃ θέλω ποιῆσαι ἐν τοῖς ἐμοῖς; i.e. "Is it not permitted me to do what I will in matters of my own property?" He is justified in regarding it as conceded by every one—even by the person addressed—that he may act according to his will in matters of his own property, and consequently, as proved, that the latter has just as little right to complain respecting the pay received by the last as respecting the pay received by himself. If, nevertheless, he persisted in his discontent, even after the absence of any justification for it has been made clear to him, it must be supposed that his murmuring springs not so much from a wrong view of the circumstances of the case, as from malicious envy. Whether this supposition is correct is the import of the last question: ἢ ὁ ὀφθαλμός σου πονηρός ἐστιν, ὅτι ἐγὼ ἀγαθός εἰμι; i.e. "Or is thine eye bad, because I am good?" which, as to meaning, is: Or is the reason of thy murmuring not so much, as was supposed before, the belief that I had not acted *justly*, as the wickedness of thy eye, to which I had acted too *kindly*? Ὀφθαλμὸς πονηρός here, as in xv. 19, Mark vii. 22, and oftener in the Old Testament (רַע עַיִן), is an evil-glancing eye,[3]—more precisely, an eye leering enviously at others. To be obliged to assume such πονηρία of the eye in the person addressed would be all the more painful to the householder, that this wickedness found its occasion in his, the

---

[1] Allusion to one of the last, corresponding to the address to one of the first.
[2] ἤ before οὐκ, rendering the connection easy, is to be expunged on good evidence.
[3] Different from vi. 23, where it is an evil eye.

householder's goodness. This is specially intimated by the contrast: ὁ ὀφθ. σου πονηρός ... ἐγὼ ἀγαθός. Instead of ἤ at the beginning, the just as well-attested interrogative particle εἰ may also be read:[1] "Perhaps thine eye," etc. ?[2] The outward connection of the second with the first question by means of "or" would be wanting, while the inner connection remains exactly the same. That such a doubtful question is quite out of place in the present context[3] is so far from being correct, that rather the opposite is true. The householder by no means directly accuses the labourer of an envious disposition, but by asking whether he is to think so of him would fain shame him, assuming that the labourer will be unwilling to have this believed of him, and from fear of such a result will dismiss the last relic of discontent from his heart. Thus the question forms an apt conclusion to the whole narrative, evincing as it does that the unexpected course followed in the payment of the labourers, which plainly formed the centre of the narrative, despite the strange, unusual look it wears, so little implies injustice, that *when candidly considered it could only give offence to one of evil disposition.*

To the narrative now brought to an end Jesus adds the interpreting utterance, ver. 16: οὕτως ἔσονται οἱ ἔσχατοι πρῶτοι καὶ οἱ πρῶτοι ἔσχατοι. The clause following in the Recepta: πολλοὶ γάρ εἰσι κλητοί, ὀλίγοι δὲ ἐκλεκτοί, still retained by Lachmann and de Wette on the ground of preponderant external testimony, now that the counter-testimony of B L Z, *et al.*, is strengthened by the Sinaiticus, must be expunged, with Tischendorf and Weiss. When the evidence is doubtful, it is decisive against the genuineness that this sentence is found on unanimous evidence in exactly the same terms at the close of another parable—the Marriage of the King's Son (xxii. 14). The similar ending of its last word to that of the preceding sentence (ἔσχαΤΟΙ and ἐκλεκΤΟΙ) is not sufficient[4] to make it credible that the sentence originally stood at the close of both parables, but that in the present passage the entire sentence afterwards dropped out by mere oversight. On the other hand, its transference here from xxii. 14 as an elucidatory sentence is easily explained by

---

[1] Tischendorf.

[2] On εἰ, as an interrogative particle, before direct questions in the N. T., see Winer, *Gram.* p. 639.

[3] So Meyer, who would make εἰ ὁ ὀφθ. σου κ.τ.λ. a limping conditional sentence.

[4] In opposition to Meyer.

the ancient misunderstanding of the present parable, making its purpose to be, like that of the Marriage, to announce the final rejection of a certain class belonging to the earthly kingdom of God. Those who wish to retain the sentence, without thus misunderstanding the parable, are compelled to refer the contrast of the "elect" and "called," instead of to the real partakers in God's kingdom in contrast with the merely called, rather to the superiority of some partakers above others, either a superiority in disposition,[1] or an extraordinary degree of reward,[2] but both in opposition to the else unanimous usage of the New Testament.

The interpreting utterance is therefore limited to the first sentence: "So the last shall be first, and the first last." The meaning of this utterance, almost identical with xix. 30, and resuming on the basis of the parable the prediction left unexplained there, is now to be determined entirely by the preceding narrative, to which it is expressly joined by "so." In fact, a review of the course of the narrative lying transparent before us leaves no doubt how the sentence annexed to it in ver. 16 is to be understood. First, it is clear that the categories "the first" and "the last" in ver. 16 must correspond exactly to the categories "the first" and "the last" in the narrative. If, then, "the first" in the narrative were the labourers standing above all the rest as respects the magnitude and weight of the day's work allotted to them, because hired in the early morn for a full day's labour, and "the last" in the narrative the labourers standing below all the rest in the same respect, because hired in the late evening only for one hour,[3] "the first" in ver. 16 can only be the members of God's kingdom standing above the rest as respects the magnitude and weight of the day's work assigned them in the labour of God's kingdom, because charged by the peculiarity of their calling with the most extensive functions, and "the last" those standing below the rest in the same respect, because placed by the peculiarity of their calling in the most limited circle of influence. Moreover, the assertions respecting the last or first in God's kingdom, "shall be first" and "shall be last," by the relation in which they stand to the foregoing narrative, admit but one exposition. For, if the pivot of the whole narrative lay in the doubly unexpected incident related in vv. 9, 10, first, that the last, despite their so much smaller service, are treated as respects amount of reward as if

[1] Olshausen.   [2] Meyer.   [3] Cf. on ver. 8 and ver. 12.

they belonged to the category of the first, ver. 9 ; and, secondly, that the first, despite their so much greater service, are treated as respects reward no better than the last, whilst all that follows is nothing but a justification of these two occurrences from the mouth of the householder,—it is clear that the assertion made first (corresponding to the order of payment in the narrative) respecting the last in God's kingdom, ver. 16 : " shall be first," must be understood in all respects after the analogy of ver. 9 in the narrative, and the corresponding assertion respecting the first : " shall be last," just as precisely after the analogy of ver. 10 in the narrative. Moreover, if the subject treated of in the preliminary section (xix. 27-30) is everywhere the reward of grace in the future kingdom of God, then certainly the distribution of reward spoken of in vv. 9 and 10 of the parable must be referred to the dispensing of reward in God's future kingdom. The meaning, therefore, of the interpreting utterance, ver. 16, is as follows :—First, those labourers in God's kingdom to whom, by the peculiarity of their calling only a relatively insignificant work was assigned on earth, will in God's future kingdom be treated in the matter of reward as if the greatest work had been assigned them ; secondly, they who were above all the rest in respect of the magnitude and weight of the work assigned them on earth by divine calling, will not on that account merely be treated differently in the matter of reward from those standing farthest below them in this respect. This by no means implies that despite great diversity in service all labourers in God's kingdom will, as respects reward, be placed on a level in the next world. On the contrary, the presupposition in the utterance of Jesus is, that in God's kingdom of the future there is a manifoldly diverse reward for service of diverse worth in this life. But, this presupposition being understood, it is affirmed that the standard for determining the difference in the reward will not be the difference among the labourers of God's kingdom first striking the eye in this life, namely, the difference in the magnitude and weight of the different functions, to which individuals are assigned in this life by a different divine calling, and the consequent difference in the outward amount of service. Of those who *in this respect* were the last or first, it is said that in the matter of future reward neither the one will be injured nor the other privileged by their position in this life. The future reward of grace, instead of being adjudged to each according to the difference in the outward amount of service, obvious to human eyes and open to human calculation, will rather, as may here be supplementarily added, be adjudged according to the difference in the inner worth of the service known only to God, *i.e.* according to the different degree of self-sacrificing fidelity with which every one has laboured in the function assigned to him, whether small or great, and has borne corresponding fruit within the sphere of influence, great or small, allotted to him. We may especially compare the parable of the Talents, where, as in the present parable, the servants of different service received the same praise and reward, because the diversity of their service corresponded only to the diversity of their gifts and the functions determined thereby,[1] with the parable of the Pounds, where the servants actually received different rewards even in the same relation for different service, because here with *equal* endowments and functions a different degree of fidelity and zeal showed itself in the different service.[2]

But if the case is as chap. xx. 16 affirms, then the enigma of the almost identical utterance preceding the parable: "But many shall be last that are first, and first that are last," is solved. Apart from the unimportant point that in chap. xx. 16, in conformity with the figurative story, the assertion respecting the last comes first, the two sayings are only different in this respect, that there it is said "*many* first" or "last," whereas here it is merely said "the last" or "first." But this difference in the wording arises simply from the fact that the categories first and last, which are there conceived quite generally, merely in reference to the different amount of services, have here through the corresponding categories in the figurative story acquired a strictly definite sense. There it was foretold generally that in many cases they who were first in this life as to their services will be last there as to their reward, and conversely. But this general prediction has received in the parable its elucidation and its more exact definition on the basis of the parable to this effect, that the prediction holds good of the first or last, whose pre-eminent or secondary services are the effect of a different divine calling, and that it will be fulfilled by the last in this sense not being put below the first, and the first in this sense not being preferred above the last.

And in this way also the general moral of the parable is made

---

[1] Matt. xxv. 15 and 20–23. [2] Luke xix. 13 and 16–19.

plain. It can be nothing else than this, to elucidate the first utterance preceding the parable in the sense of the second utterance with which it concludes. The moral of the parable, consequently, is to show that in the dispensing of reward in the future kingdom of God a quite different rank and dignity will often emerge from what the visible difference of service in this life leads to expect, *because notwithstanding the manifoldly diverse greatness of the functions allotted to individuals in labour in God's kingdom, the last in this respect will not be placed below the first in the assignment of reward hereafter, and the first in this respect will not be preferred above the last.* The parable exhibits this truth thus. In its first part it represents in figure the manifold and great diversity of the day's work assigned to individuals by the special circumstances of their calling in this life, whereas the second part not merely represents the fact of the future, that they who were last or first in this respect shall not on this account be treated differently in the matter of reward from the first or last, but at the same time proves this fact to be in harmony with the postulate of the divine justice.

The way is now indicated and also smoothed for rightly interpreting the figurative history in detail. For from this starting-point the much-debated difficulties of interpretation all find their solution. An owner of a vineyard, who in search of labourers summons the idlers in the market-place to work in his vineyard,—this is the general framework embracing the figurative occurrences of the first part of the narrative. To this corresponds in the sphere of the kingdom of heaven the divine call to labour in God's kingdom, issued to men busy about nothing, or next to nothing, and standing idle in the market-place of worldly life. The call meant is the call to enter upon labour in God's kingdom going forth to men in the preaching of Jesus respecting the kingdom of God, the same call that came to the rich youth from the lips of Jesus in the "Come, follow me" (xix. 21), and to which the Twelve had given willing heed in beginning to follow Jesus (xix. 27), without, however, the conveyance of the divine call through the person and words of Jesus being included in the compass of the figurative representation. In substance, therefore, it is the same call to the kingdom of God that was spoken of in the parable of the Great Banquet (Luke xiv. 16 ff.), save that here it is represented on a quite different side from there. Whereas there it was set forth as an invitation to partake in a banquet all ready, here it appears as a summons to undertake the labour of a vineyard. The vineyard-*labour* is the *tertium comparationis* on which everything depends in comparing the kingdom of God to a vineyard. The figure of a vineyard already used of the Old-Testament theocracy of Israel,[1] and also employed in other parables of Jesus to represent the kingdom of God,[2] is here used to compare the labour in God's service and for God's cause to the labour in a vineyard with which a householder entrusts labourers. Only so far, therefore, in the sense of the parable is the comparison with the vineyard to be more precisely worked out, that as vineyard-labour is exceedingly heavy and irksome, so labour in God's kingdom imposes great sacrifice, denial, and hardship on him who enters upon it. So far we are definitely led in the comparison both by the introductory discourse of Jesus respecting the sacrifices, which following Him in this life entails, and by the further course of the narrative itself, where the hardship connected with the labour is emphasized, ver. 12. Accordingly, in respect to the labour we are not merely to think of official work outside for the extension and organization of God's kingdom on earth; but the idea of labour in the sense of the parable comprises every kind of exertion, hardship, and self-denying surrender of one's own in time, strength, and possession, which the divine call into God's kingdom imposes on man for the sake of God and His cause.

The first part of the parable, therefore, treats in the most general sense of the divine call to men to work in God's kingdom. And it shows, first of all, the special manner in which God proceeds in this call. The presupposition of the householder's entire conduct was, that his chief thought in procuring labourers was not so much the overtaking of as great an amount of work as possible, as rather the persons of the labourers themselves, that they might not stand idle, but find employment. So also God's calling men to labour in His kingdom aims not so much at what they are to do for God, as if He needed their labour for His own sake, as rather at the persons of the called themselves, that they may not miss the design of their existence by idle inactivity, but may fulfil their destiny by labour in His service. For this reason, as the householder goes forth anew unweariedly to secure fresh labourers, so the divine call never

---

[1] Isa. v. 1–7, xxvii. 2; Jer. xii. 10; Joel i. 7.
[2] xxi. 28 and 33 ff.; Luke xiii. 6 ff.

ceases to follow men, seeking as its aim to attract as many idlers as possible, and if possible, all, for their own sake, to labour in the kingdom of God. And as the householder engages every labourer he finds, without distinction, no matter at what hour he finds him, or what the amount of service he is able to render, so the divine call goes forth to all without distinction, irrespective of whether in the circumstances in which the call finds them they are able to render more or less service. In this way, among those who at the divine call enter upon labour in God's kingdom, there arises the same great distinction which exists among the labourers of the vineyard. Like those hired in the early morn, who saw before them work lasting the whole twelve hours, and had to bear all the burden and heat of the day, so some among the labourers in God's kingdom are appointed to labour of the greatest possible extent, and imposing the greatest possible hardship; whereas others, like those hired at eventide, for the comparatively slight work of one hour, are set to work of very limited extent and apparently little hardship. And this distinction between the first and the last has its ground merely in the different calling, *not* in special merit in the first or special fault in the last, as if the latter had obeyed the call to labour less willingly than the former. That this is the case is intimated in the narrative by " he saw *others,* found *others,*" vv. 3 and 6, and is also guarded against all misunderstanding by the special conversation between the householder and the last (vv. 6, 7).

In this way the inquiry as to the meaning of the hours when the householder goes forth, and the particular classes of labourers begin work, is already answered. As certainly as the earlier or later hour of hiring in the narrative has no importance for its own sake, but merely as the initial term conditioning the amount of work, so certainly is this earlier or later merely the temporal form in which are represented in pictorial figure the unwearied and manifold character of the divine call on the one hand, and the consequent great diversity of service to which individuals are called on the other. As matter of fact, every attempt to transfer this temporal succession of the hours of the day into the interpretation proves unworkable. Those who see prefigured in them the different periods in the history of redemption and the Church, whether from the beginning of the Old-Testament period,[1] or from that of the New-Testament period,[2] give a temporal inter-

---

[1] So many older expositors.   [2] Meyer, Lange.

pretation merely to the initial term of labour in the different classes of labourers, not also, which ought of necessity to be done, to the final term, and to the period of labour lying between both, and determined by them in its duration. Thus, in order to be able to expound the temporal form of the narrative on one side, they leave out of account the thing itself on which everything in the narrative turns, namely, the relation of rank among the labourers depending, not upon an earlier or later of *time*, but upon a more or less of *service*. Against Meyer, who takes refuge here in the supposition of the entry of the Parousia in the lifetime of the present generation, what is said on Luke xvi. 9 should be consulted. As to the other theory of older expositors, which refers the different hours in the narrative to the different periods in the life of the individual, from early youth to late age, it is not really true to the temporal form of the narrative, which it seeks likewise to explain. In this way, indeed, the several hours as the initial term of labour are placed in a relation to the twelfth hour, as the final term, corresponding to the narrative, but only by the unity of the day of labour with its termination—the latter in the narrative the same for all—being resolved into a countless multiplicity of life-days. However natural, therefore, in applying the thought of the parable may be an allusion to the empirical fact that some, called in early youth, devote the whole of a long life to the labour of God's kingdom, whilst others, called first in the late eventide of life, are able to do scarcely anything, still such an allusion is only justified as a free adaptation of the far more comprehensive thought of the parable, and ought not to claim to be an interpretation in the proper sense of the periods into which the day of toil is divided.

It remains still to interpret the last essential trait in the first part of the narrative—the promise of reward made when the labourers are hired, which leads, then, to the question of the significance of the denarius, generally esteemed the most difficult. But here, too, the way to the correct interpretation is indicated to us by the previous investigation. As the householder does not send those hired in the early morn into the vineyard without assuring to them the full day's pay agreed upon[1] for the full day's work, nor the other labourers, without promising them full compensation for the amount of work assigned to them; so, too, God calls no one into His kingdom without the promise, that in

---

[1] συμφωνήσας δὲ μετὰ τῶν ἐργ., ver. 2.

the future kingdom of God he shall receive full recompense for every sacrifice and hardship suffered in this life for God's sake. Therefore, to those called to the greatest conceivable labour, a reward is promised ensuring to them without doubt full recompense for the service they have to render; and further, to every one a degree of reward abundantly compensating him for the amount of labour demanded of him. This interpretation exactly corresponds to the figurative story itself, to the Lord's introductory discourse, and in particular to the utterance, chap. xix. 29 : καὶ πᾶς ὅστις ἀφῆκεν ... ἕνεκεν τοῦ ὀνόματός μου, πολλαπλασίονα λήμψεται. The reward in the parable, and especially the denarius, is therefore not a recompense accruing to the labourer in God's kingdom in this life,[1] an interpretation utterly obliterating and confusing the relation of the promise of reward, by which the labourers are procured and for which the labour is done, to the distribution of reward after and for the finished work. Nor can the denarius be merely eternal life in God's future kingdom generally, since this is the same for all true labourers, and is promised alike at the outset to them all without distinction; whereas the denarius represents a particular degree of a reward, which in itself may be of higher or lower value, and which precisely at this amount is only promised to the first in distinction from the rest. Since, then, on the one hand we can only think of a reward belonging to the future kingdom of God, and on the other of a reward which is not from the first the same for all having part in that kingdom, but may be adjudged to individuals in different degrees, the reward in the narrative can only mean the special reward of grace promised to every individual alongside and with the possession of eternal life in the future kingdom of God as a recompense for all sacrifices and hardships endured in this life for God's sake.[2] And the denarius especially is the full measure of the reward of grace, corresponding to the greatest and severest conceivable day's work on the part of a labourer in God's kingdom, just as the denarius is the ordinary full day's pay for a full day's work on a man's part. It is also now made clear why, in the case of the first labourers, express mention is made (συμφων. δ. μετ. τ. ἐργ.) of the self-evident circumstance, that the amount of the pay is settled between the hirer and hired, not by a one-

---

[1] Stier, Nebe.

[2] Cf. the "treasure in heaven" promised to the rich youth by Jesus, and the sitting on twelve thrones promised to the apostles, chap. xxvii. 21, 28.

sided arrangement, but by mutual agreement. The reason is, that it was important for the thought of the parable, by express acknowledgment on the part of the labourers, to certify beyond question the amount promised to the first as the pay of a complete day's labour,—not that the first labourers in God's kingdom are meant to be pictured as specially mercenary, an explanation lacking any kind of support from the narrative, which speaks everywhere of hired labourers only. If, therefore, in the sphere of God's kingdom there can be no question, as in the figurative story, of a legal claim on the basis of mutual agreement between God and man respecting service and counter-service, but only of a reward promised and reserved for man by God's free grace, and only becoming an object of claim to man in so far as he trusts unconditionally in that promise, this is just the all-pervading, because necessary and self-evident, distinction between the thing symbolized and the relation used figuratively to set it forth.

From the earthly present, belonging to labour in God's kingdom, the second part of the narrative passes to that period in the future when, labour being over, the reward of grace promised to all will be given to each one. For when the second part begins with the account of the householder charging his steward at even to call the labourers and pay them their hire, this is a definite allusion to the time when the Messiah, after the completion of the earthly period of labour, shall, in God's name and at God's command, assemble around Him the members of the kingdom, and give each one his special reward in the future kingdom of God. As concerns, first, the *evening*, from the fact that the several hours in the narrative will not bear a temporal interpretation, it does not follow that the evening is merely "the form for God's pronouncing judgment on the labour,"[1] and cannot denote the time for receiving the reward after labour is done. Were it really so, there would be good reason to attempt a temporal interpretation of the hours, or to despair of solving the difficulty there, rather than give up the signification of the evening which plainly forces itself on every unprejudiced hearer and reader in view of the position of the evening as a boundary-line between the two parts of the narrative. But the inference just referred to is by no means necessary. Rather the whole of the day in the narrative, as the time of labour, forms of itself a contrast to the evening as the time for receiving and enjoying

[1] Nebe.

the reward. This contrast is independent of the contrast of the several hours with each other, and consequently remains, even if we are compelled to think that the distinction of the hours, by which the diverse length of labour is determined, cannot represent a different time, but merely the different amount of the labour falling to individuals in the great work-day of God's kingdom. Again, as concerns the steward ($\dot{\epsilon}\pi\dot{\iota}\tau\rho\sigma\pi\sigma\varsigma$) in the parable, the course of the narrative itself has thrown no light on the introduction of this person. Unless, therefore, his introduction in this passage is to be explained as mere by-play, we must here recognise an express allusion to the person of the Messiah, as He who, in God's name, will give every one his reward,—a far-fetched allusion indeed, if the evening has really no signification, but very natural if the evening coincides in the interpretation with the setting up of the future kingdom of the Messiah. If, then, we add the interpreting utterance of Jesus Himself (ver. 16), referring back directly to vv. 9 and 10, the central teaching of the parable, founding on the presuppositions given in what precedes, fits into the course of the interpretation thus: When one day the Messiah, after the present dispensation has come to an end, shall do as the steward in the parable did in the evening, when in the name, and at the command of God, He shall assemble the members of the kingdom round Him, and give every one his special reward, then (like the last labourers in the parable, who received the full day's pay) they to whom the least amount of labour was assigned in God's earthly kingdom shall not on this account lose any of the reward of grace; but, despite the seeming insignificance of their services, shall receive a reward as rich and great as if the greatest amount of labour had been assigned them in this life. And, on the other hand (like the first labourers in the parable, who also received the same pay), they to whom the greatest amount of labour was really assigned in this life shall not on this account be privileged in the matter of reward, but will find themselves on an equality with those whose services on earth stood at the farthest distance below theirs.

So far the interpretation has given no explanation of the circumstance that the householder causes the distribution of the pay to proceed from the last to the first. As little as on the ground of the narrative a real preference of one class and disparagement of another can be found in the mere succession of the order of payment, so little ought the interpretation to use

this arrangement of the householder to show that one class of
labourers in God's kingdom will be privileged and another suffer
loss at the future dispensing of reward. The real value of this
trait for the import of the parable corresponds exactly to the
significance it had within the figurative story,—it serves to prepare for and introduce the discussion concluding the whole. To
the purpose of the householder—by the peculiar order of succession to bring sharply out what was strange and unusual in
the amount of the pay, in order next to vindicate the justice of
his course against the natural objection of the first—corresponds
the purpose of Jesus Himself, as the author of the parable, to
direct the attention of His hearers,—the Twelve,—who might
justly class themselves with the first, to what was unusual in the
amount of the reward. By what is told of the reward of the
last, ver. 9, the same expectation is awakened in them that is
mentioned in ver. 10, namely, that they would receive more.
Then by what is told in ver. 10b they see that they are mistaken in the impression that in the future rewards of God's
kingdom an injustice would be done to the first by a like course.
From this point of view it is unmistakeably clear what significance the conversation at the close of the parable between the
first labourers and the householder has for the import of the
parable. The meaning cannot be, that at the future dispensing
of rewards in the Messiah's kingdom a transaction corresponding
to this conversation will really take place between the members
of the kingdom belonging to the category of the first on one side,
and God on the other. As little as in the parable of the Rich
Man the lengthy conversation at the close between Abraham and
the rich man [1] can mean, that a like conversation will really
take place in Hades between Abraham on one side, and the dead
represented by the rich man on the other; or in the parable of
the Lost Son the closing conversation between the father and the
elder brother [2] can mean, that a like transaction will take place
between the Pharisaically righteous, after the pattern of the elder
brother, on one side, and God on the other; so little does the
conversation at the close of the present parable mean, that at the
future dispensing of the rewards of grace a transaction of this
kind will take place between God and the first. Rather, as the
conversations in those two parables are merely intended to point
out to the hearers the justice of the divine dealings with men in

[1] Luke xvi. 24 ff.   [2] Luke xv. 29 ff.

the pictorial form of a fictitious discussion incorporated with the narrative itself and clad in its figurative form, just so is it with the concluding conversation here. After Jesus has in the narrative first depicted the strange divine proceeding in reference to the amount of the reward, in the discussion appended He gives a justification of the proceeding that strikingly refutes the suspicions awakened. As concerns the protest of the first, vv. 11 and 12, it is not the figurative representation of a protest that will be raised by the first labourers of God's kingdom at the time of the future reward,—a point overlooked by all expositors, who insist against the correct reference of the reward in the parable to the reward of grace in the future world, that such a protest on the part of the beatified is inconceivable,—but, in making the apparently injured labourers bring forward the objection naturally called forth by the preceding distribution of pay, Jesus merely brings out in expression, in the figurative form supplied by the narrative, the suspicion awakened by the divine proceeding. To this suspicion He Himself purposely directed the attention of His hearers by the mode of the foregoing description, and He now hears it issue from their lips. As the first labourers appeal to the great distinction existing between the last and themselves as respects labour,—there, the mere spending of one hour; here, bearing the burden and heat of the day,—and think they are justified in concluding from this that an injustice would be done them by placing the last on a level with them as respects reward; so it seems to follow, from the great distinction existing between the different labourers in God's kingdom, the greatest conceivable amount of labour being assigned to the one, and a quite trifling amount to the other, that an injustice will be done the first if the last were made equal to them in the matter of reward. But it is not so, the divine proceeding set forth in vv. 8–28 is thoroughly consistent with the divine justice. This it is that Jesus states to His hearers in the answer with which He makes the householder reply to the protest of the first; and solely in this statement to the hearers of the parable consists the significance of the answer. The expositors who, persistently mistaking the purpose of the final conversation, which has in view simply the instruction of the hearers, find in the answer of the householder an announcement to men of mercenary disposition of their final condemnation and exclusion from the kingdom of God, have against them also, apart from the groundlessness of the notion of a mercenary disposition distinguishing the first from the last labourers, the entire wording of the householder's reply. That reply, while repelling the objection brought forward as unfounded, by no means rejects the persons as of evil disposition, but only at the close presses on their conscience the question, whether, perhaps, the objection springs, not so much from deficiency in understanding as from an envious (not *mercenary*) disposition. And to this reply of the householder corresponds exactly what Jesus wishes by it to suggest to the hearers of the parable, from the meaning of which the objection (ver. 12) arose. He shows them first, that in such an apportionment of the future reward as was promised, vv. 9 and 10, as little injustice is done to the first labourers in God's kingdom as to the first labourers in the parable. Not to the latter, because they had received without curtailment the day's pay for which they had been hired with their own consent, ver. 13; not to the former, because the amount of the reward, giving them full compensation for all the toil and labour of their earthly work, is in no wise diminished to them; but the promise of such recompense, with which so to speak they were hired for labour in God's kingdom, and in prospect of which they toiled, shall be fulfilled to them in every case without curtailment. But if no injustice is done them, there is no sort of justification for objecting to what others receive. So Jesus shows His hearers in the second place. In the summons to the first, put into the householder's mouth, to be content with the pay due to them by law, ver. 14*a*, lies the summons of the Lord to His hearers, belonging to the category of the first, to be content with the righteous divine order set forth in the parable, whatever others may receive. For—thus speak the householder's further words, with which he appeals to his free right of disposal in matters of his own property, vv. 14*b* and 15—even if the will of God be so, to give to the last a like reward as the first, every one must acquiesce in the divine will, provided God, the Lord of all things, possesses the same right as a human householder to deal with His own in sovereign freedom, and to dispose of it according to His own will. If we only bear in mind these two truths,—first, that at the dispensing of the future reward of grace no one will really lose anything of what is assured to him by God's promise as a recompense for his labour in this life; and secondly, that if by God's will others are rewarded far beyond what seems due to them, according to their position in this life, still no protest against this free gracious will is admissible,—we shall willingly acquiesce in the law of reward in God's kingdom set forth in the parable, even though we belong to the class of the first. An unwillingness to acquiesce would, after all that has been said, only be conceivable if our discontent were directed, not so much against the divine justice from lack of knowledge, as rather against the goodness of God from defect of disposition, looking at that goodness with envious eyes, because grudging it to a brother. This it is that Jesus suggests to His disciples in the householder's concluding question: "Is thine eye evil, because I am good?" ver. 15b. Whoever among them, after the objection against the supposed injustice has been so strikingly refuted, should not feel content with the divine proceeding set forth, would betray an envious disposition against the manifestation of divine goodness to a brother, a disposition that ought never to appear among the members of God's kingdom. His business would then be, above all, to correct himself in this point, and to take the path of repentance.

The Wicked Vinedressers.

(Matt. xxi. 33-44.)

In ver. 23 of the twenty-first chapter of Matthew we find Jesus in the temple at Jerusalem, teaching the people gathered round Him there. As the more precise statement of Mark[1] shows, two days had passed since His triumphal entry into Jerusalem. On the previous day—the first after the entry—when Jesus purified the temple, and healed the blind and lame brought to Him there, the members of the Great Council present had taken offence at His prophetic bearing and action, and especially at the "Hosanna to the Son of David" of the children, who children-like imitated the cry of the people the day before (xxi. 12-17). And when Jesus on the following day teaches and continues His prophetic work in the temple, according to ver. 23, the members of the Sanhedrim[2] come to Him with the question: "By what authority

---

[1] Cf. Mark xi. 11, 15, 19, 27, according to which a night intervenes between ver. 11 and ver. 12 of Matt. xxi.

[2] "The high priests and elders of the people," namely, in official deputation.

doest thou these things,[1] and who gave thee this authority?" To this question Jesus replies with the counter-question, whether the baptism of John was from heaven or of men, vv. 24, 25. For by their answer to this counter-question, by their believing acknowledgment or unbelieving rejection of the divine mission of His forerunner, they must needs show whether they are or are not receptive to the testimony respecting His own divine mission. And since the Sanhedrists, as they say to themselves, cannot acknowledge the divine mission of the Baptist without contradicting their virtually unbelieving attitude to his person, and on the other hand dare not deny it for fear of the people, ver. 26, and prefer in this dilemma answering the Lord's preliminary question with a "We know not," He also declines to answer their question as to His own authority, ver. 27. And now, after silencing those who wished to find fault with Him, Jesus proceeds to find fault with them in such a way as to compel them to pronounce judgment on themselves. He does this first by means of the short parable, prefixed to the greater one, of the two unlike sons of a father. To the summons of the father to go to work in the vineyard, so Jesus tells them, the one son answered: "I will not," but afterwards changed his mind, and went; whereas the other answered with an eager "I, I, Lord" (ἐγὼ κύριε), but really went not, vv. 28–30. To the question of Jesus: "Which of these two did the will of his father?" the Sanhedrists are compelled to reply: "The first." But thus they have pronounced judgment on themselves. They have thus themselves said what Jesus now ratifies with "Verily I say unto you," that the publicans and harlots, because really obedient, go before them into the vineyard of God's kingdom, whilst they, because really disobedient, remain outside, ver. 31. For they hitherto had said "I, I," and put on an appearance of zeal in obeying God's commands, whilst the publicans and harlots had openly disclaimed obedience to God's law. But when with the appearance of John the time came really to render obedience and to meet the approaching kingdom of God in the way of righteousness pointed out by the Baptist (ἦλθ. Ἰω. ἐν ὁδῷ δικαιοσύνης), they then hardened themselves in unbelief against his divine mission, and actually refused obedience, nor were they moved to repentance by the example of the publicans and harlots, who

---

[1] ταῦτα, the plural, combines the present teaching with the purification and healings of yesterday.

believed in the Baptist, and believing obeyed his call to repentance, ver. 32.

With the words: "Hear another parable," Jesus at once adds a second parable, ver. 33 ff., found also in Mark (xii. 1 ff.) and in Luke (xx. 9 ff.); in the two latter evangelists, however, in immediate connection with the dialogue between Jesus and the Sanhedrists having reference to the authority of Jesus and the origin of John's baptism, without the short parable of the dissimilar sons intervening. Still it is observable that Luke also separates the parable of the Vinedressers from the dialogue by the remark peculiar to him: "And He began to speak *unto the people* (πρὸς τὸν λαόν) this parable," ver. 9. Here it is assumed that the Sanhedrists also were present and were even primarily addressed,[1] as, on the other hand, in Matthew the presence of a number of people also is assumed, in teaching whom Jesus was interrupted by the deputation of the Great Council, and who certainly had not become fewer during the transaction with the latter.[2] Still Luke's introductory remark gives us the important intimation, that in beginning to relate this parable Jesus exchanged the tone of the special dialogue with the Sanhedrists for that of a public address to the entire company of assembled people. In expounding the text of the narrative we follow primarily the account of Matthew, while constantly comparing the other two evangelists.

The narrative begins: "*There was a man,*[3] *a householder, who planted a vineyard, and set a hedge about it*" (for protection against the beasts of the field), "*and dug a winepress in it, and built a tower*" (πύργον, a watch-house, with tower for a look-out, perhaps also for the vinedressers to live in), thus carefully furnishing it with every requisite. This description of the householder's thoughtfulness in providing hedge, winepress, and tower, closely resembling Isa. v. 2,[4] is wanting in Luke. Mark, on the other hand, has it in the same form, save that instead of ληνός, which is the entire winepress-apparatus, he says ὑπολήνιον (Sept.: προλήνιον), in more exact keeping with the ὤρυξεν, i.e. specially the winepress-trough dug in the ground, into which the expressed juice runs from above. The relative sentence then proceeds: καὶ ἐξέδοτο[5] αὐτὸν γεωργοῖς, καὶ ἀπεδήμησεν, i.e. "*and handed it over*

---

[1] Cf. ver. 19. [2] Cf. vv. 23, 26, 46. [3] Cf. on xviii. 23.
[4] Sept., only the order is there somewhat different: φραγμός, πύργος, προλήνιον.
[5] Tischendorf reads ἐξέδιτο; cf. Buttmann, *N. T. Gr.* p. 41.

to vinedressers, and took a journey." To the ἀπεδήμησεν Luke adds χρόνους ἱκανούς, which, however, does not mean "a sufficient time" in reference to the period necessary after establishing the vineyard for bearing fruit,[1] for the absence of the householder extends beyond the time of fruit-bearing; but, according to the more general meaning of the word, "a considerable time."[2] The choice of the verb ἐκδίδωμι, i.e. "to give something out of one's power, out of one's hand," along with the contemporaneous departure of the householder, shows us the independent position assigned to the vinedressers as regards the vineyard. They are not sent into the vineyard as mere hired labourers to do this or that work, but the vineyard with all belonging to it is given up to them to cultivate and manage independently, of course with the obligation to deliver to the owner in due time the fruits belonging to him. Everything in the narrative turns on this position of the vinedressers, in virtue of which they acquire independent possession of the vineyard with all its appliances, and are responsible to the master for its produce. On the other hand, it is idle to ask in what way they are to be paid by the master, whether in money or in a portion of the fruits, or in what other way, since this side of the relation between the householder and the vinedressers remains quite out of sight.

From the time of the handing over of the vineyard, ver. 34 passes at once to the time of the vine harvest, when the fruits should be delivered: ὅτε δὲ ἤγγισεν ὁ καιρὸς τῶν καρπῶν, ἀπέστειλεν τοὺς δούλους αὐτοῦ πρὸς τοὺς γεωργοὺς λαβεῖν τοὺς καρποὺς αὐτοῦ. Instead of the protasis: *"and when the season of the fruits drew near,"* Mark (ver. 2) merely adds τῷ καιρῷ, Luke (ver. 10) merely καιρῷ, to the verb ἀπέστειλεν, i.e. "at the right season," here the season of the vine harvest. In the apodosis the second αὐτοῦ can only refer to the same as the first, namely, to the householder as the subject of the sentence, not back to the vineyard, which is not even mentioned in the protasis, therefore: "*he sent his servants to the vinedressers to receive the fruits belonging to him.*" Instead of τοὺς κ. αὐτοῦ, Mark has: ἀπὸ τῶν καρπῶν τοῦ ἀμπ., and Luke similarly: ἀπὸ τοῦ καρποῦ τοῦ ἀμπ. To explain the preposition ἀπό used here we do not need the artificial supposition of a contract, according to which the vinedressers had merely to deliver a portion of the fruits as rent, the rest remaining theirs;[3] but, since the fruit of a vineyard is neither exhausted

---
[1] Stier. [2] Cf. Luke viii. 27, xxiii. 8; Acts viii. 11, xiv. 3. [3] Meyer, Weiss.

in one year, nor the fruit of the same year comes to maturity at one time, ἀπὸ τῶν κ. or τοῦ κ. means simply: They are to receive the fruit of the vineyard due at the time.

But the servants sent in this way for the fruits found an ill reception at the hands of the vinedressers. Of this ver. 35 (in Matthew) says further: "*And the vinedressers took his servants, and beat one, and killed another, and stoned another.*" Thus, so far from giving them the fruits they came to demand in their master's name, they replied to their demand with hostile violence, which rose from beating to killing, and from killing to brutal stoning. It is here made plain, what ver. 34 did not put beyond doubt, that ἀπεστ. τοὺς δούλ. αὐτ. there did not mean so much the sending of a body of servants who came to the vinedressers together, as rather the sending of a series of servants coming one after another to the vinedressers with the same orders. For it is impossible to conceive that a body of servants who came together were subjected by the vinedressers individually to different treatment, but only that in face of the servants coming one after another, and naturally becoming more and more urgent in their demands, their hostility grew in passionateness and stirred them to greater violence, such as is exhibited in the three cases cited by way of example (not as if these were the only ones).

What will the householder do now, the mission of his servants having had no other effect than to reveal the hostility of the vinedressers, hostility rising in aggravation, and not shrinking from the worst outrages on the person of the servants? This is the question suggested at this point of the narrative to the hearers, who expect the householder to inflict punishment on the vinedressers. But, instead of doing this, with wonderful forbearance he makes another attempt to recall the malcontents to their duty by kindness, ver. 36: "*Again he sent other servants.*" And to give greater emphasis to his demand on this second mission, he sends this time πλείονας τῶν πρώτων. These words are usually referred without more ado to a *greater number* of servants, but without explaining how this is to be viewed. That he this time sent a more numerous body of servants together than the first time cannot be the meaning, because in ver. 34 not a body, but a series of servants was spoken of. But even if a body of servants were understood there and here, one does not see how the householder could promise himself greater success from sending a more numerous body, since, according to the context, there is no thought of wresting the fruits from the vinedressers by superior force, but only of demanding them through messengers. All that is left, if πλείονας is to be understood of a "greater number," is to suppose the sending of a second series of servants longer than the first. But this is absurd. For if the result of the first sending was no other than this, the longer the series of servants the greater the defiance and the worse the violence of the vinedressers, how could the householder expect to make an impression by sending a second and longer series? The case is quite different as soon as the words: πλείονας τῶν πρώτων, are understood, not so much of the greater number, as of the higher rank of those sent. That πλείων expresses in New-Testament language not merely the greater number, but just as much also the higher worth, grade, or rank (just so in Homer), is proved by comparing passages like vi. 25, xii. 41 f.; Mark xii. 33; Luke xi. 31 f., xii. 23; Heb. iii. 3, xi. 4. The translation then is: "He sent other servants higher than the first." In this way, and in this way only, could the householder really hope to receive the fruits of the vineyard from the vinedressers, in the expectation that they would not dare to show hostility to these messengers as to the first. It is at once apparent how this second mission in ver. 36 forms a fitting transition from the first to the third and last one in ver. 37. The gradation ascends from lower to higher servants, and then from the latter to the son of the house. Finally, the following statement: "And they did unto them in like manner," now receives its true significance. For it is no longer a mere quantitative, but a qualitative aggravation of the crime of the vinedressers, that they attack these higher messengers with like violence as the first. They thus do what the householder himself had been unwilling to give them credit for.

In the two other evangelists the entire account of the sending of the servants differs in not unimportant respects. Whereas the second mission of higher servants mentioned by Matthew is altogether wanting in them, the first mission in Matthew (ver. 34), summed up in the generalizing: ἀπέστ. τοὺς δούλους αὐτοῦ, is divided in Mark and Luke into a thrice sending, a single servant each time. So Mark: καὶ ἀπέστ. δοῦλον ... καὶ πάλιν ἀπέστ. ἄλλον δοῦλον ... καὶ ἄλλον ἀπέστ., vv. 2, 4, 5, and Luke: καὶ ἀπέστ. δοῦλον ... καὶ προσέθετο ἕτερον πέμψαι ... καὶ προσέθετο τρίτον πέμψαι, vv. 10, 11, 12. Thus the aggravation in the outrageous conduct of the vinedressers, which Matthew only exhibits in three servants singled out by way of example from the entire series, takes place in Mark and Luke in relation to three particular servants distinguished throughout. Mark advances from mere dismissal with blows, which he has at the first stage in common with Matthew,[1] not at once like Matthew to killing, but first merely to ill-treatment joined with special insult,[2] and first reaches simple killing (ἀπέκτειναν, ver. 5) at the third stage; whereas Luke, in essential agreement with Mark in the first two stages,[3] after the ill-treatment joined with special insult, advances merely to wounding even at the third stage (τραυματίσαντες ἐξέβαλον, ver. 12). In the last-mentioned evangelist the entire account of the sending of the servants finishes here, so that only three servants sent one after another are spoken of, the generalizing being left to the interpretation. Mark, on the other hand, in adding to the account of the third servant,[4] ver. 5, the words: καὶ πολλοὺς ἄλλους οὓς μὲν δέροντες οὓς δὲ ἀποκτέννοντες,[5] "and many others (they ill-treated likewise), beating some, killing others," generalizes within the figurative story itself. By this generalizing clause what was said before of three individual servants acquires the character of three examples merely, taken out of a multitude of like occurrences, to give a vivid picture of the growing criminality of the vinedressers. Thus the entire account in Mark finally yields exactly the same meaning in this respect as that of Matthew respecting the first sending.

We return to the passage in Matthew, where the failure of the second mission was spoken of. What will the householder do after the vinedressers have done like violence to the higher servants of the second mission? This question, forcing itself on the hearer before, recurs here with heightened intensity, so that one scarcely expects to hear of anything but the punishment of the vinedressers. But so far does the householder's forbearance go, that even now he ventures on a third attempt, but of such a kind that by its very nature it must be the last. The messenger whom he now sends is of such dignity that the sending of a greater one after him is inconceivable, ver. 37: "*But afterward*

---

[1] ἔδειραν καὶ ἀπέστειλαν κενόν, ver. 3.
[2] According to the correct reading, ver. 4: ἐκεφαλαίωσαν καὶ ἠτίμησαν, i.e. since κεφαλαιόω in this connection can only be a secondary form of κεφαλίζω, "they beat him on the head, and used him shamefully."
[3] δείραντες ἐξαπέστ. κενόν, ver. 10; δείραντες καὶ ἀτιμάσαντες ἐξαπ. κεν., ver. 11.
[4] κἀκεῖνον ἀπέκτειναν. [5] So according to the correct reading.

he sent unto them his son, saying" (with himself), *"They will reverence my son."* He hopes that reverence for him as the householder's own son will prevent their refusing the fruits to him, and still more laying hands on him. Mark specially emphasizes the personal sacrifice made by the householder in sending his son, putting first the independent statement, ver. 6 : ἔτι ἕνα εἶχεν υἱὸν ἀγαπητόν,[1] *i.e.* either : " he yet had one only (whom he could send), a beloved son,"[2] or : *" he yet had an only son, a beloved one."* The latter usual acceptation is to be preferred, because the prefixing and isolation of the ἕνα are explained by the importance this idea of quality has for the following statement, without our needing actually to separate it from the υἱόν. And now Mark relates the mission itself : *" he sent him last unto them, saying,"* etc. Thus him, his only son, to whom his heart's love clings, he tears so to speak from his heart, and sends into the danger only too probable despite the hope of the success of his mission. Finally Luke, instead of the fact of his being sent, relates merely the soliloquy, in which the householder takes counsel with himself and decides to send his son, ver. 13 : *"And the lord of the vineyard said, What shall I do? I will send my son, my beloved one ; it may be they will reverence him when they see him"* (ἴσως τοῦτον ἰδόντες).

But instead of the impression hoped for, even the sending of the son had no better success than that of the servants, ver. 38 : *" But the vinedressers, when they saw the son, said among themselves,*[3] *This is the heir, come, let us kill him and possess* (σχῶμεν) *his inheritance !"* The reading of the Rec. κατάσχωμεν, " let us take into possession," is a probable simplifying of the σχῶμεν, which means in this connection : " After the heir is removed out of the way, let us further possess his inheritance unhindered." Thus they do not speak of obtaining something not already in their possession, but, after getting rid of the heir and his threatening claims, they hope to possess as undisputed owners, and so far for the first time really, the vineyard, which they had already unjustly seized, but the possession of which is now seriously threatened by the appearance of the heir. The same meaning is to be accepted when in Mark (ver. 7), after ἀποκτείνωμεν αὐτόν, it is said : καὶ ἡμῶν ἔσται ἡ κληρονομία, and in Luke, ver. 14 :

---

[1] So according to Tischendorf.   [2] So Weiss.
[3] ἐν ἑαυτοῖς, here not "with themselves," but "among themselves." Cf. in Mark πρὸς ἑαυτούς, ver. 7, and in Luke : πρὸς ἀλλήλους, ver. 14.

ἵνα ἡμῶν γένηται ἡ κλ., referring to the hope of the undisputed, and so far then for the first time real, possession of the vineyard in the future. Instead, therefore, of reverencing the son of their lord in this last messenger, his character as the rightful heir of the property usurped by them the more excites their hostile passion; and for this reason, instead of giving him the fruits of the vineyard which they refused to the servants, they enter into a formal murderous plot against him, with the premeditated purpose by killing the heir to secure the unopposed possession of his inheritance. The assumption in this scheme, of course, is, that the absent householder, who has been unseen so long, and who let the whole series of his servants be abused and murdered with impunity, will also leave this last deed unpunished, and will not show himself. The way in which a long absent master, who apparently leaves everything unpunished, is entirely ignored, is really so much in keeping with the character of dishonest, refractory servants, that even such a course supplies no ground for the assertion made by Weiss, that in the circumstances of the parable the vinedressers could not have hit upon the thought of getting possession of the vineyard by murdering the heir. The actual execution of the plot is then told in ver. 39 : "*And they took him, and cast him forth out of the vineyard, and killed him.*" The mention of the casting forth must not be taken here as a mere graphic description of the act of killing, the casting forth having no independent significance.[1] One might perhaps say so, if it were merely said: καὶ ἐκβαλόντες αὐτὸν ἀπέκτειναν. But the formal way in which the ἐξέβαλον, introduced by λαβόντες, and intensified by ἔξω τοῦ ἀμπελῶνος, appears independently before and alongside the ἀπέκτειναν, emphasizes it as a special aggravating element in the conduct of the vinedressers, that they, the usurpers, cast him, the heir, out of the vineyard, which was his rightful property, so that he had to endure at their hands both the violence of ejection from his property, and the atrocity of murder. The same is to be understood in Luke, as the phrase: ἔξω τοῦ ἀμπ., there also proves, ver. 15. Nor is it otherwise in Mark, where ἀπέκτειναν αὐτόν comes first, and then follows: καὶ ἐξέβαλον αὐτὸν ἔξω τοῦ ἀμπ., ver. 8. These words can indeed only be understood of the casting forth of the man previously killed. For that a Hysteronproteron occurs here,[2] and ἀπέκτειναν ἐκβληθέντα is to be understood,[3] is merely a violent inference

[1] Meyer. [2] De Wette. [3] Stier.

from the parallel passages, whereas no ground for or intimation of such a thing is found in the passage itself. But it is not on this account the casting forth of the *corpse* which the words emphasize as a special aggravating element, in which case a corresponding object would not be wanting to the ἐξέβαλον; but by the action of casting out itself alongside, and this time after the killing, the usurpers would notify that the heir has lost his inheritance, and that henceforth they alone are masters in the vineyard.

And here, where the conflict between the householder and the vinedressers has reached its climax, Jesus himself proposes the question, to which the narrative has again and again led the hearers, and which it has now raised to the highest pitch of intensity, ver. 40: ὅταν οὖν ἔλθῃ ὁ κύριος τοῦ ἀμπελῶνος, τί ποιήσει τοῖς γεωργοῖς ἐκείνοις; When the householder comes (contrary to the expectation of the vinedressers, who altogether ignored him), what will he do to the vinedressers, who had even killed his son? This question Jesus expressly proposes to the deputies of the Great Council, that they may answer it for themselves, and by the only possible answer pronounce judgment on themselves. And this answer they hasten to give, for the very purpose of appearing like persons unconcerned, although, considering the transparent connection of the parable with Isa. v. 1–6, its polemical reference to themselves could not altogether escape them, ver. 41: κακοὺς κακῶς ἀπολέσει αὐτούς, καὶ τὸν ἀμπελῶνα ἐκδώσεται ἄλλοις γεωργοῖς, οἵτινες ἀποδώσουσιν αὐτῷ τοὺς καρποὺς ἐν τοῖς καιροῖς αὐτῶν. Two things, they say, are certain. "*As wicked people he will wickedly destroy them,*" or as Meyer translates: "As wretched people he will wretchedly destroy them." Thus, no mere chastisement, but a sentence of destruction will the householder inflict on these vinedressers, after they have replied to the extremest proof of forbearance with the extremest outrage. And for the special κακία of their conduct he will inflict a sentence of special κακία, of a specially bad, terrible kind. And as concerns the vineyard, which they have had in possession, what the second sentence says is certain: "*And he will hand over*[1] *the vineyard to other vinedressers, who*[2] *will deliver to him the fruits in their*[3] *seasons,*" at the yearly

---

[1] ἐκδώσεται, corresponding to the ἐξέδοτο, ver. 33.

[2] οἵτινες, quippe qui, *i.e.* here, they of whom it is to be expected, that they.

[3] The seasons of the fruits; cf. ver. 34: ὁ καιρὸς τῶν καρπῶν.

recurring seasons of fruit-ripening. For the householder's position is not such that those vinedressers are indispensable to him to the obtaining of fruit from his vineyard, but conversely such that their supersession by other vinedressers has become necessary for this end.

In the other two evangelists, also, the parable concludes here in a manner not quite the same, but still similar. There also on the basis of the parable, Jesus at this point proposes the question: "*What then will the Lord of the vineyard do?*"—upon which in reply to this question the prediction follows: "*He will come and destroy the vinedressers, and give the vineyard to others.*"[1] On the other hand, the more precise characterization of the "other vine-dressers," as those who will render the fruits, is wanting in the answer here. The question and answer also differ from the form of the text in Matthew, in so far as there the householder's coming is adopted into the question itself (ὅταν οὖν ἔλθῃ ... τί ποιήσει), whereas here it is simply asked τί ποιήσει, and the coming then forms the first part of the answer: ἐλεύσεται καὶ ἀπολέσει. But the strangest difference is this, that the question proposed in Matthew to the Sanhedrists, and answered by them, is here only put rhetorically, the answer also being given by Jesus Himself. But even this is merely a formal difference, inasmuch as on one side the rhetorical question (in Mark and Luke) is still an appeal to the assent of the hearers to the statement introduced by the question; and, on the other, the acceptance of the answer of the Sanhedrists by the Lord (in Matthew) is equivalent in substance to a statement of His own of the same purport. When, finally, Luke tells of a deprecatory exclamation uttered by the hearers of the parable after the concluding prediction of the Lord, ver. 16: "*And when they heard it, they said, Far be it*" (μὴ γένοιτο), these words cannot be conceived as spoken by the same persons who, according to Matthew, put on an appearance of unconcern, and themselves uttered the prediction. Which of these two accounts corresponds more exactly to the actual occurrence, or whether (for which Luke, ver. 9: πρὸς τὸν λαόν, might be quoted) the speakers in Luke are different persons, *i.e.* not the deputies of the Great Council, but some of the people, must remain uncertain, there being no sufficient means for deciding the question. In any case, the common element in the two accounts is, that the listeners gave

[1] Cf. Mark xii. 9, and almost in quite similar terms Luke xx. 15, 16.

some audible expression to their reluctance to apply the parable to themselves. For the specious simplicity with which the Sanhedrists in Matthew take it upon them to utter the prediction naturally resulting from the narrative is just as characteristic an expression of such reluctance as the special deprecation "Far be it" in Luke.

Jesus, then, on His part replies again with the citation of a passage of Scripture appended to the parable in all three evangelists. Only in Matthew, however, does it lead on to an utterance interpreting the foregoing parable, whereas in Mark and Luke no further reference to the parabolic narrative is found. Here, therefore, the parallels fail us. To the Sanhedrists, who bear themselves as if they had nothing in common with the vinedressers of the parable, Jesus replies with the question, ver. 42: "*Did ye never read in the Scriptures, The stone which the builders rejected, the same was made the head of the corner?* (εἰς κεφαλὴν γωνίας). This[1] *was from Jehovah, and is marvellous in our eyes.*" The passage[2] is cited literally from the Septuagint. Even the αὕτη, which does not stand Hebraistically for τοῦτο, but is referred in the Septuagint to κεφ. γων., from an erroneous conception of the זֹאת used neutrally in the Hebrew, is taken from there. The pith of the statement in the Psalms plainly is, that the same stone, which *the builders rejected* as useless for the building (therefore not a despicable stone in general, which is an indefinite, inappropriate idea), has been made the corner-stone (of the theocracy). And the enigma contained in this statement, since the question at once arises, by whom the stone rejected by the builders has been made the corner-stone, is then solved by the sentence: מֵאֵת יְהֹוָה הָיְתָה זֹּאת, etc. But if so, then the builders cannot be explained as secondary persons without definite reference, and can just as little be referred to the heathen, since they cannot possibly be called "the builders" in the theocratic sense; but the builders can only be Israel as the people of the theocracy, called to be the builders of the theocracy, or the leaders of Israel, having this office in an eminent sense. Consequently, the stone itself cannot be the people of Israel, so that, as often explained, the original meaning of the saying would merely be, that from being a people rejected by the heathen, or a despicable people generally, Israel was raised by God into being the depository of the theocracy. But, as the builders are the

---

[1] αὕτη, scil. ἡ κεφ. γων.   [2] Ps. cxviii. 22, 23.

people and its leaders, so the stone is an individual historic person, an elect one of Jehovah, who, despite the contradiction and resistance he encountered among the people of the theocracy or from its leaders, has, nevertheless, by Jehovah's wonderful guidance, come to a position in which the theocratic commonwealth rests essentially on his shoulders. Only this explanation yields a clear meaning in exact correspondence with the words, a meaning also which, since the person spoken of need not of necessity be an Israelitish *king*, leaves sufficiently wide scope to the difficult question of the time of composition and historical circumstances of the Psalm. Just as clear also is the meaning in which Jesus cites the passage. What is said in the Psalm of the builders who rejected the stone made by Jehovah the cornerstone, this Jesus sees now coming into antitypical realization in the hostile plots of the leaders of Israel against the person of Him who, as the Messiah of God, is the true corner-stone, the new founder of God's kingdom upon earth. When Jesus, therefore, in direct allusion to the parable with the question: "Did ye never read in the Scriptures?" etc., points the Sanhedrists to this passage, the meaning of the question is this: Are they,—students of Scripture,—just as if they had never read this well-known passage in a Psalm acknowledged as Messianic among them, blind to the obvious fact, that by their hostile plots against Him, the Anointed of God, they themselves are about to initiate the final fulfilment of that Scripture saying, seeing that they, the called builders of the theocracy, reject the stone that is to be made the corner-stone, or *mutatis mutandis*, seeing that they, the vinedressers of the theocratic vineyard, lay hands on Him who is the heir of the vineyard?

We now see clearly the reference of the διὰ τοῦτο, with which Jesus continues, ver. 43: "*Therefore*,"—namely, because you, just as if you had never read this Scripture saying, are about to do to me as the builders to the corner-stone, or the vinedressers to the heir—"*therefore say I to you:*" ὅτι ἀρθήσεται ἀφ' ὑμῶν ἡ βασιλεία τοῦ Θεοῦ καὶ δοθήσεται ἔθνει ποιοῦντι τοὺς καρποὺς αὐτῆς. From the fact of "a *nation* bringing," etc., being opposed to the "from you" here, it is evident that the address directed primarily to the Sanhedrists includes also the Jewish *nation* legally under their direction, and actually following their example, a circumstance which would present no difficulty even if we did not know that before the Lord there was a multitude of people surrounding the deputies of the Great Council, and that He had already given the whole parable the character of a public address designed for all present (Luke xx. 9). The meaning therefore is: Ye heads and representatives of the Jewish nation, *the kingdom of God shall be taken from you, and given* ἔθνει ποιοῦντι κ.τ.λ. The singular "nation" is only explained when the emphasis is laid, not on this noun, but entirely on the participial clause more precisely defining it. The reason of the singular being used cannot be, that here the whole of heathendom is combined as a single nation in contrast with Israel,[1] whereas the plural form "nations" elsewhere expresses the contrast with Israel,—or that here all future participants in God's kingdom in a spiritual sense are viewed as one nation,[2] since the future community of the kingdom of God is not in question, but a nation already existing outside God's kingdom, to which hereafter the kingdom of God will be given. The contrast then is not between the Israel "after the flesh" and that "after the spirit," but simply between the Israelitish and another nation. The statement made is quite general, to the effect that they to whom the kingdom of God will be handed over will be *a nation bringing forth its*[3] *fruits.* It is thus self-evident that after the rejection of the unfruitful nation of Israel such a nation must be sought in the sphere of the heathen world, and in so far they are right who explain "nation" of the heathen. But the characterizing clause: ποιοῦντι τοὺς καρποὺς αὐτῆς, upon which the entire emphasis lies, corresponds too plainly to the relative clause in ver. 41: οἵτινες ἀποδώσουσιν αὐτῷ τοὺς καρποὺς (*scil.* τοῦ ἀμπ.), to allow it to be understood otherwise than in agreement with the latter. The participle ποιοῦντι, which simply characterizes, and is therefore in the present tense, must be resolved as a future in correspondence with the ἀποδώσουσιν. And the fruits of God's kingdom can here mean nothing else than the fruits of the vineyard in the parable. The reference cannot be to the fruits requisite for entering God's kingdom,[4] or worthy of it,[5] but only to those aimed at in the planting of God's kingdom. Whilst in this way the figurative idea of the fruits is preserved, the only difference is that the *delivering* of the fruits, which is the primary question in the narrative, is transformed in the interpreting utterance into the *bringing forth* or *obtaining* of the fruits, from which it is

---

[1] Weiss *et al.* [2] Ἰσραὴλ κατὰ πνεῦμα, Meyer.
[3] The fruits of the kingdom of God. [4] Meyer. [5] Bleek.

evident that in the sense of the author the delivery or non-delivery of the fruits spoken of in the parable coincides in reference to the thing symbolized with the bringing forth or non-bringing forth of the fruits themselves. Thus, the entire utterance alludes directly to the prediction uttered perforce by the Sanhedrists at the close of the narrative, Jesus telling them that they have now for the second time (ver. 31) pronounced judgment on themselves. What you yourselves foretold of the vinedressers —so He announces to them—will happen to *you*. The kingdom of God will be taken from you as the vinedressers hitherto, and handed over, as you have said, to other vinedressers, who will render the fruits, therefore to a people that will bring forth the fruits of God's kingdom.

So far the Lord has only confirmed the removal of the vinedressers from their position in the vineyard, not the ensuing sentence of destruction which the Sanhedrists also rightly foretold. Jesus now confirms their own prediction on this point in the utterance [1] alluding in its figurative form to the passage in the Psalms quoted (Ps. cxviii. 22, 23), and coupling the latter with other passages like Isa. viii. 14, 15; Dan. ii. 34, 35: "*And he that falls on*[2] *this stone*[3] *shall be dashed to pieces*[4] (on it); *but on whomsoever it shall fall, it will scatter him as dust,*"[5] ver. 44. Therefore a hostile collision with this stone—either by stumbling against and falling on it as it lies in the way, or by putting oneself in the way of its descent and the stone thus falling on him—must in every case prove fatal to him who engages in such a conflict. Or apart from figure: Hostility to the Messiah, who is the corner-stone of God's kingdom, brings certain destruction. He that runs hostilely against Him, because anxious to have Him out of the way, will be dashed to pieces on Him, as on a stone lying in the way which one stumbles and falls against; and him that places himself hostilely in His way to delay His victorious Messianic march, He will scatter as dust, like a stone rolling down from a height, and crushing everything in its way. This is the only natural sense of the twofold utterance, compared with which the exposition, that would find in the two quite parallel future clauses the distinction between a pre-

---

[1] Its genuineness in Matthew is certified by the weight of the external testimonies.
[2] Not "over;" cf. the ἐφ' ὅν in the second clause.
[3] The one made the corner-stone by Jehovah, according to ver. 42.
[4] συνθλασθήσεται. [5] λικμήσει, properly "to winnow."

liminary and the final judgment, seems an artificial importation. But the very obvious application of the general figurative utterance to themselves, the builders rejecting the stone, is left to the hearers.

Consequently the words of Jesus subjoined to the parable refer exclusively, partly by way of confirmation, partly also by way of interpretation, to the prediction of ver. 41 that formed the conclusion of the parabolic story in reply to the question of ver. 40. But everything in the parable was arranged from the first with a view to this question (what the householder will do to the vinedressers), and the prediction replying to it. Even in the account of the first revolt of the vinedressers against the messengers the question forced itself on the hearers. And when in the further course of the narrative it found its preliminary answer in the account of the forbearance of the householder, who, instead of proceeding to the well-merited punishment, made new attempts to recall the rebels to their duty by kindness, it must have recurred with heightened intensity at every stage, until, where the last and greatest attempt is made by the householder sending his son, and the last and greatest outrage is committed by the vinedressers killing the son, it was expressly proposed, and now, as the Sanhedrists themselves were forced to confess, could find but one answer, the one given in the concluding prediction of ver. 41. Accordingly, the single purpose of the whole narrative is to foreannounce to the hearers the same fact of the future that is figuratively expressed in this prediction, and is then repeated in vv. 43, 44, without figure, or under another figure, and to foreannounce it as the only possible conclusion of the history of Israel figuratively set forth in the narrative. What Jesus says in the parable fits into the preceding context of His discourse thus: After reducing to silence the deputies of the Great Council, who came to ask Him as to His authority, by proposing the question as to the mission of the Baptist, which they could not answer because of their unbelief in the Baptist, He proceeded to find fault with them. He does this first in reference to their unbelief in the Baptist. The parable of the two unlike sons and its application, convicted them of making in John's days an outward show of zeal in fulfilling the divine will, while really resisting that will in unbelief. And when He then passes from the tone of the special dialogue to that of a public address to them as the representatives of Israel, and tells the parable of the Wicked Vinedressers with the final question, in which it terminates, and the prediction that is its only possible conclusion according to their own confession, His intention is to show, *what must needs be the inevitable issue of their present confirmed obduracy in unbelief and enmity against the person of the Messiah after a history in the past marked by constantly repeated rebellion against earlier divine messengers. The issue can only be that the long-merited divine judgment will actually burst upon them, and the kingdom of God will pass from them to other nations.* In this behalf He first characterizes in the course of the narrative the crime which they are about to perpetrate, in its connection with what they and their fathers did to earlier messengers of God, as a work of such obduracy in hatred to God as to cut off the last hope of repentance, in order on this basis to announce to them what, as they themselves concede, must follow hereupon, namely, the judgment of God bringing rejection and destruction upon them.

In proceeding to interpret the course of the narrative in detail, there meets us again the image of the vineyard for the kingdom of God, here in definite allusion to the Old Testament passage, Isa. v. 1 ff., as is clearly shown by the enumeration of the several appliances reminding of that passage, with the difference, however, that there the theocracy is depicted merely in its then concrete historical form, in which it was one with the theocratically constituted nation, and so the vineyard is Israel itself, whereas here a distinction is drawn between the theocracy as a divine institution and those to whom it is entrusted, so that they are its temporary incumbents. Thus the vineyard is simply the theocracy as an institution, not the theocratic nation itself.[1] As, then, a householder planted a vineyard and furnished it with everything necessary to its bearing produce, with hedge, winepress, and tower, so God founded a divine state upon earth, and endowed it with all the particular institutions adapted to subserve the realization of the end of such a theocratic institution. Thus, hedge, winepress, and tower, as the things necessary to the perfect equipment of a vineyard, represent pictorially the particular theocratic institutions of the Old Covenant, which make the entire system of the theocracy correspond in every respect to its end. But it is arbitrary to explain hedge, winepress, and

---

[1] Cf. the interpretation of the parable of the Fig-Tree, p. 165.

tower independently, *e.g.* the hedge = the law or circumcision, the winepress = the altar or the teaching office, the tower = the temple or royalty.[1] And as the householder entrusted the vineyard, to which he had done all he could, to vinedressers, the latter as the authorized managers of his vineyard being responsible to him for its produce, so God entrusted the institution of the theocracy to the Israelites, so that as its divinely chosen incumbents and administrators they are responsible to God for realizing its design in historical life. The usual but erroneous reference of the vinedressers merely to the heads and leaders of the Jewish nation in distinction from the nation itself is based on the circumstance, that according to Matthew and Mark the parable seems addressed exclusively to the deputies of the Great Council. But we know already from ver. 43 compared with Luke xx. 9 that the latter are addressed by the Lord in a public discourse designed also for the multitude present, and addressed as the representatives standing before Him of the entire Jewish nation. Moreover, if the vinedressers were exclusively the leaders of the nation, the vineyard itself must necessarily be the nation under their guidance,[2] in plain opposition to ver. 43, where the vineyard is referred by Jesus Himself to the kingdom of God passing from one nation to another, and in opposition to the application elsewhere of the image of the vineyard on the lips of Jesus, which is always the kingdom of God in itself, and nowhere the theocratic nation of the Old Covenant.[3] Nor would it be at all possible to refer merely to the leaders of the nation addressed. We should have to obtain the counterpart of the vinedressers by combining the then leaders with all former leaders of the nation in every past century into the unity of a moral person, which is impracticable, because there is no such continuity between the present members of the Sanhedrim and all former spiritual or secular leaders of Israel as would allow whatever was done by the latter to be represented as done by the former. Only Israel in its national unity, with its national guilt growing from one epoch to another, furnishes a suitable counterpart to the vinedressers of the parable adding guilt to guilt. When it is said further that the householder took a journey, and that a considerable time (Luke), this also is a feature influencing the sequel, and

---

[1] So older expositors. Recently also Lange.
[2] So Godet, Klostermann logically.
[3] Cf. vv. 28-31, xx. 1 ff.; Luke xiii. 6.

requiring at all events a definite interpretation. This can only be meant to symbolize that after God on the institution of Israel had made known His presence to the people of the theocracy by extraordinary revelations of power (the miracles of the exodus, the law-giving, and the bringing into Canaan), He withdrew into expectant passivity, leaving room for the spontaneous moral development of the nation on the soil of the theocracy and under the influence of its institutions. This period of the divine passivity, whose long duration is specially marked in Luke, reaches not merely to the sending of the first prophets,[1] nor describes merely the period of the Old Covenant,[2] but must just as certainly embrace also the period of Christ's appearance in Israel as the period of the householder's absence in the parable includes the period of the sending of the son. This period is brought to an end, not by a revelation of *grace*, but by a revelation of divine *power*, which forms such a crisis in the national history of Israel, that it answers as a counterpart to the deeds of divine power constituting the beginning of its history.

Within this period God has done as the householder did within the period of his absence. As the latter, when the time of fruit came, sent his servants one after another to require the fruit from the vinedressers, so at the times when it might justly have been expected that, by faithfully using the theocratic institutions committed to it, Israel would have succeeded in bringing its life into harmony with these institutions and the divine will expressed in them, God sent His servants, the prophets, to them one after another to demand from them the fruit of penitence and righteousness, ver. 34. But it then fared with the prophets of God at the hands of the children of Israel as with the servants of the householder at the hands of the vine-dressers. Not only did they harden themselves in impenitence against their prophetic monitions and demands, and refuse the fruits of righteousness demanded, but rose in hostility against the troublesome monitors, and attacked them, ill-treating them, even killing and barbarously murdering them, ver. 35. The figurative story made no allusion to the question, whether the vinedressers refused the fruit because they had not obtained it, or because they wished to keep it for themselves. As much was said as served for a point of comparison, namely, that instead of rendering to the servants of their lord what the latter had a

[1] Stier.   [2] Keil.

right to demand, they attacked them. It is a separate matter, merely involved in the nature of the relation symbolized, that *here* disobedience to the prophetic monitions and demands is synonymous with the absence of the fruits themselves. For the bodily ill-treatment of the prophets, the example of Jeremiah may be compared,[1] and of Micah;[2] for the killing, the murder of the prophets in the time of Elijah,[3] and of Urijah by Jehoiakim;[4] and for the stoning, the example of Zechariah.[5] Certainly these definitely attested examples of killing are but few, but at the same time the killing of the prophets collectively is mentioned in the Old Testament as a fact,[6] and is confirmed by Jewish tradition as a frequently repeated fact; for example, Isaiah is said to have been sawn with a sword, Jeremiah stoned, Amos beaten to death with a club, the exactness, however, of these details being uncertain. Jesus refers to this fact in general terms also in xxiii. 31, 35, 37; cf. Acts vii. 52; Heb. xi. 35, 37. It is obvious that the accounts of Mark and Luke, in relating differently from Matthew a threefold sending of single servants, do not require a definite reference to individual prophets. In Mark this is evident from the generalizing clause: "and many others," etc., within the figurative story itself, and in Luke from the circumstance that the three single servants are not distinguished from each other by any marks. The individual cases are merely distinguished by the aggravation in the revolt from case to case, which suggests in the interpretation the same general thought as in Matthew.

But more than a general interpretation is required in the latter evangelist, when before passing to relate the mission of the son he places a second mission of servants beside the one first mentioned, ver. 36. For here these servants of the second mission are definitely distinguished from those of the first by the phrase: πλείονας τῶν πρώτων, whereas, on the other hand, the conduct of the vinedressers in this case is emphatically described as the same as in the first case: καὶ ἐποίησαν αὐτοῖς ὡσαύτως, the aggravation of guilt consisting in the fact that their conduct remains the same also to πλείονας τῶν πρώτων. The latter words, distinguishing the second mission from the first, require therefore a definite interpretation, so that

---

[1] Jer. xx. 1, 2, xxxvii. 15, xxxviii. 6.
[2] 1 Kings xxii. 24.
[3] 1 Kings xviii. 4, xix. 10.
[4] Jer. xxvi. 20-23.
[5] 2 Chron. xxiv. 21, 22.
[6] Jer. ii. 30; Neh. ix. 26.

according to Matthew two periods of prophetic mission must in the interpretation be placed before the mission of the son. If πλείονας be erroneously understood of a greater number, this twofold prophetic period fails to present itself in the sphere of sacred history. For to distinguish between Elijah, Elisha, and their contemporaries as the first body, and Isaiah, Jeremiah, and the other prophets under the later kings as the second,[1] is an inadequate makeshift, since these two periods are neither distinguished in the Old Testament history by specific characteristics, nor in particular by a surprisingly large number of prophets in the second period,[2] nor, finally, do the two together comprise the entire history of prophecy. If, on the other hand, the πλείονας τῶν πρώτων be rightly understood of higher rank, the mission of John the Baptist at once presents itself as the one standing midway between the mission of the prophets and that of the Son in exact correspondence with the course of the figurative story. The characteristic of the period including the appearance of the Baptist would then be the higher rank distinguishing the messenger of his period. It is evident what a weighty argument for this view is found in the circumstance that in another passage, where Jesus had occasion to speak at length of the person of the Baptist,[3] He not merely sets his appearance as that of Elijah, who was to come, over against the whole prophecy of the Old Covenant,[4] but also describes him emphatically as he who is "much more than a prophet,"[5] so that among those born of women a greater than he has not arisen."[6] Moreover, in the conversation of Jesus with the deputies of the Great Council preceding the parable, express mention was made of the Baptist; and in the smaller parable immediately preceding this one and its application, Jesus directly rebuked them for their unbelieving conduct to John. In the second parable, then, meant to set forth what they are about to do to the Messiah in its connection with all that they and their fathers did to earlier messengers of God, how could another allusion be wanting to the Baptist and to the reception which he met with from them? Over against all this stands merely the difficulty which the plural "other servants" seems to present in the narrative. But this difficulty is only apparent. For in the figurative history this plural was

---

[1] Stier, Thiersch.
[2] The prophetic schools in the time of Elijah should be remembered.
[3] xi. 7–14. [4] xi. 13, 14. [5] xi. 9. [6] xi. 11.

suggested by the relation chosen as a means of representation. The relation there could only be from lower to higher servants, and thence to the son of the house, who as such stands alone in his kind over against all servants, whether lower or higher. The circumstance, therefore, that in the actual history the second stage is only represented by one person can so little diminish the appropriateness of the representation, that, on the contrary, the interposing of a singular at the second stage would have awkwardly lessened the gulf actually existing in the history symbolized between the second stage, which, because still a mission of *servants*, coincides with the first, and the third, which, as the mission of the only son, stands in contrast with both. But as the vinedressers treated the higher servants no better than they treated those first sent, so the people of the theocracy treated him, who represented the higher servants on the soil of sacred history, although a prophet and more than a prophet, no better than they treated the earlier prophets. This is the statement of ver. 36. And Jesus is able to say this, because not merely the essentially unbelieving attitude which the leaders took to John, but also the impenitent attitude taken by the people under the dominion of Pharisaism, while outwardly acknowledging his prophetic dignity (ver. 26), made it possible for the worldly ruler in Israel to bring the Baptist to a cruel end, whereas the really more profound movement called forth by his appearance remained limited to the classes of people shut out of the theocratic community (ver. 32).

But even this fate, inflicted by the hardened impenitence of Israel on the greatest of the prophets, was unable to exhaust the riches of God's patience with His people. As the householder, in order to recall the rebellious vinedressers to their duty, makes the last conceivable attempt in sending his son, only and beloved,[1] saying, They will reverence my son, ver. 37, so God did to His people. His Son, standing to Him not, like all the prophets inclusive of John, in a servant-relation, but in that of son to father, the only one, beside whom He has none like Him, beloved, incomparably dear to His divine father-heart,—Him He tore from His bosom and sent among the disobedient children of His people, in the expectation that they will reverence His Son, and yield Him the obedience of penitence, which they refused to the servants of God preceding Him. That the self-designation of

[1] Mark xii. 6.

Jesus as Son of God here expresses more than merely the unique relation to God belonging to Him in virtue of His Messianic calling, appears less plainly from the text of Matthew and Luke, but unmistakeably from that of Mark. For whereas in Matthew and Luke the character of son is only mentioned in immediate connection with the mission itself, so that in the interpretation it might be referred merely to a position as son given him in and with the mission, just as must necessarily be done at the second stage in Matthew with the higher rank of the servants, in Mark the relation between father and son is expressly referred to as existing by itself independently of the mission, with unmistakeable allusion to the sacrifice made by the householder in parting with his only beloved son and exposing him to the violence of the rebellious vinedressers. The interpretation therefore must trace back the designation of Son to a relation between Father and Son independent of the Messianic mission, and describe the sending of the Son as a self-sacrificing act of the Father in parting with the Beloved, and giving Him up to the violence of a disobedient people.

The representation of the parable has now reached a point where it causes the figure to mirror, no longer past, but present events. For, in describing the plotting of the vinedressers on the appearance of the heir, ver. 38, Jesus discloses the plots against His person with which the rulers of Israel have long been busy, and are especially busy now, describing both their contents and motive. As the vinedressers feel themselves seriously threatened by the appearance of the heir in the usurped possession of the vineyard, so they by the appearance of the Messiah, as the Lord and heir of the theocracy, in their selfish employment of the theocratic commonwealth as if it were a possession of their own, meant only to serve their own selfish ends. And therefore like the vinedressers, who plan the murder of the heir in order to possess his inheritance without hindrance, so they are busy with the plan of killing the heir of the theocracy, in order to be able to lord it as they please in the theocratic commonwealth as its undisputed lords and possessors. As in the case of the vinedressers the ground of this calculation is the ignoring of the householder encouraged by his long absence, so in the case of the leaders of Israel it is the disbelief in God's intervention fostered by His long withdrawal. But while certainly it is merely the *leaders* whose plans are figuratively represented by the plot of the vinedressers against the heir, this by no means involves a contradiction with the reference of the vinedressers to the whole of Israel as the people of the theocracy. The thoughts and plans guiding a nation in its action proceed, of course, from its heads and rulers. The national soul, where it is pictured as consciously thinking and scheming, is one and the same with the guiding personages, whose plans control the action of the nation. Only in case of an intestine conflict between the rulers whose are the guiding thoughts, and the people whose is the physical power, the latter opposing instead of following their plans, could it be inadmissible to identify, as is done here, the persons of the present rulers with the nation. But it is not so in the present case, as Jesus sees and knows only too well despite the fleeting enthusiasm of the crowd on the day of His entry.[1] He knows that as the vinedressers at once translated their plans into act, casting forth the heir from the vineyard and killing him (ver. 39), so the people will convert the plans and decisions of its leaders into fact, and cast Him out of the theocratic commonwealth, of which He is Lord by divine and human right, and will kill Him. That the act of casting forth out of the vineyard and that of killing are meant to be specially indicated, the exposition of the narrative has shown, and also that the inversion of these acts in Mark yields the same meaning. The prediction here implied of the exclusion of Jesus from the theocratic community, with His handing over to the heathen as an outcast, was fulfilled in fact. And symbolical of this fact again was the external occurrence of His being led out of Jerusalem the city of God, and His suffering and dying "without the gate" (Heb. xiii. 12). But it does not follow from this that there is an intentional allusion to this latter external occurrence in the words of the present passage,[2] a view with which the inversion of the two acts in Mark would not agree.

What, then, will God do to the children of Israel, when to all the guilt they have incurred by rebellion against former divine messengers they have added the guilt of murdering the Son of God, thus rendering futile the last conceivable attempt to recall them to obedience? This is the meaning, clad in figurative form, of the question of Jesus in all three evangelists as to the course the householder will take against the vinedressers. If to this question, as the leaders present are obliged themselves to

[1] Cf. Luke xix. 41, 42. [2] Stier, Olshausen.

allow, either explicitly (Matthew) or implicitly (Mark and Luke), there is but one answer, namely, that the householder will come and destroy the vinedressers, and give the vineyard to others who will render its fruits, the fate that must inevitably overtake Israel after the murder of the Son of God is given in the same answer. The God, who in His infinite long-suffering has hitherto spared the disobedient people, will and must come forth from His retirement, visit the nation with outstretched hand, and destroy it, *i.e.* destroy the people in their national existence. But the kingdom of God, whose possessor Israel has hitherto been upon earth, He will hand over to another people, namely, to one as to which He may expect that it will render what it is able and bound to do as possessor of God's kingdom — the obedience of penitence and the works of righteousness. On this interpretation the figurative "other vinedressers" (ver. 41) is left in its generality. If the vinedressers are the people of Israel, the "other vinedressers" are any other people, and therefore the heathen, but not the heathen in their entirety. Thus the correct interpretation agrees in all points exactly with the utterance of Jesus Himself correctly interpreted: "and shall be given to a nation," etc.[1] Here, then, is a prophecy of a new period of development, opening with the judgment upon Israel, in which in place of rejected Israel the heathen shall be the possessors of God's kingdom, a prophecy as definite as the one in the parable of the Great Banquet, Luke xiv. 16 ff.[2] But then it is self-evident that the divine coming, which puts an end to the previous withdrawal of God, as the householder's coming in the parable does to his previous absence, is not His coming to judgment at the end of the present dispensation, but merely a coming of God to Israel within the present course of history, and indeed in the immediate future, an intervention of God's mighty hand destroying the national existence of the people, such as was realized in history at the destruction of Jerusalem.

The entire section, beginning in ver. 23 with the question put by the deputies of the Great Council, and relating the transactions following upon the question, is now concluded by

[1] Cf. on ver. 43.
[2] On this point and on the relation to the parable of the Fig-Tree, see the interpretation of the parable of the Banquet, p. 189.

the observation in vv. 45, 46. These two verses rightly understood state : "*And when the chief priests and Pharisees heard His parables, they perceived that He spake of them.*[1] *And although intending to arrest Jesus*"—i.e. they had come and put the question with this intention—"*they feared the people,*[2] *because they took Him for a prophet,*" so that out of fear they desisted at present from their real intention to arrest Jesus. After Jesus had so plainly described (ver. 38) to the people the plot they had in their mind, they thought it better not to make the attempt to put the plot into execution just then, from fear of seeming to the people to be murderers of a prophet. Thus the entire construction points from the first to the " feared the multitudes " as the chief statement, even the clauses of ver. 45 having logically the position merely of protases to this last statement. The meaning is not, that they had wished to seize Jesus from disgust at what they heard, but refrained from fear of the people; but, that under the impression of what they had heard they who really desired to arrest Jesus were afraid to carry their plot into effect at present on account of the people. Consequently, when Mark and Luke prefix [3] the statement that the Sanhedrists had wished to seize Him, but feared the people, and then assign a reason for their fear: "For they perceived that He had spoken the parable in reference to them," they do not give a different meaning from Matthew, but only express the same meaning more plainly.

The Royal Marriage-Feast.

(Matt. xxii. 1–14.)

The statement made in xxi. 45, 46 respecting the effect of the parable uttered by Jesus on the hearers, seems to imply that the conversation with the deputies of the Great Council begun in ver. 23 has come to an end. The two other evangelists also in the parallel passages proceed at once to describe a new conversation arising from a different occasion.[4] On the other hand, Matthew, before commencing the account of this new conversation and its special occasion, inserts here a further parable with the

---

[1] In ver. 30, and especially in ver. 38.
[2] With the fear of an evil conscience especially aroused by ver. 38.
[3] Mark xii. 12 ; Luke xx. 19.   [4] Mark xii. 13 ff.; Luke xx. 20 ff.

words, xxii. 1: καὶ ἀποκριθεὶς ὁ Ἰησοῦς πάλιν εἶπεν ἐν παραβολαῖς αὐτοῖς λέγων. In these words two things are clear: first, that πάλιν can only be referred to the foregoing parables, chap. xxi., and αὐτοῖς only to οἱ ἀρχιερεῖς καὶ οἱ Φαρισαῖοι in xxi. 45; and secondly, that nevertheless ἀποκριθείς here cannot mean an answer in immediate continuation of the foregoing conversation, since in xxi. 45, 46 there is no mention of any words of an opposite party to which what follows could be an answer. Only their conduct was described. Consequently ἀποκριθείς here, as *e.g.* xi. 25,[1] is used in a broader sense: To begin to speak on occasion given, the following discourse being like an answer to the occasion in question. But then nothing compels us to suppose that the evangelist regards the following parable as delivered immediately after the preceding one,[2] a supposition inconsistent with the concluding formula in xxi. 45, 46. It is only said that on occasion of the plots of the rulers against His person Jesus once more (πάλιν) spoke to them parabolically,[3] the parable being thus placed in the same time as the preceding one in a general sense, namely, in the first days of the Passion week, when the rulers assailed the person of Jesus without venturing actually to lay hands on Him—but not exactly in the same hour. Thus the evangelist's introductory words respecting the situation of the following parable give only the general intimation, that it was similar to the one described in the second part of chap. xxi.: Jesus in the first days of the Passion week in presence of the rulers planning His arrest, a group of listeners which can just as little be wanting here as in the conversation related in chap. xxi., and again as a standing circle of hearers the Twelve, whom we always find accompanying Jesus at this time. In any case, if it should turn out that the contents of the parable are not directed exclusively against the hostile disposition of the rulers, but apply also to the listening of the adherents of Jesus, there would be nothing in this incompatible with the introductory words expressed in such general terms, and saying nothing about the special nature of the occasion of this parable.

The narrative begins, ver. 2: "*The kingdom of heaven has become like*[4] *a man,*[5] *a king, who made a marriage for his son.*"

---

[1] Cf. Meyer here.   [2] So still Meyer, Nebe.   [3] ἐν παραβολαῖς, plural of category.

[4] ὡμοιώθη, the epoch has already begun its course, which the following parable exhibits and describes in its consequences. Cf. on xiii. 24.

[5] Cf. on xviii. 23.

When it is here said of a king: ἐποίησεν γάμους τῷ υἱῷ αὐτοῦ, we can only understand γάμοι[1] in the original and ordinary signification "marriage," the king's son being regarded as the bridegroom, in whose honour the feast is prepared—not in the supposed more general signification "banquet." For if merely a banquet in general were meant, why mention the king's son, for whom the royal father makes the banquet? We shall then arrive at a banquet to celebrate the handing over of the kingdom (Kuinoel), and substitute for the marriage-feast another feast just as special, but altogether foreign to the original signification of the word γάμος. Therefore, even if the circumstance of the Septuagint often translating מִשְׁתֶּה (epulum) by γάμος[2] supplied proof of the more general signification alleged, this meaning would not be applicable in the present passage. The words "made a marriage" here include already the first invitation of the marriage-guests. For this is presupposed when it is at once said, ver. 3: "*And he sent his servants to call them that were bidden* (καλέσαι τοὺς κεκλημένους) *to the marriage.*" Thus the same Eastern custom is implied here as in Luke xiv. 16, 17,[3] according to which the guests are first invited beforehand, and then, when the feast is prepared, are specially summoned to come. But when the guests were summoned to come to the festive board prepared, an unexpected thing happened: "*and they would not come.*" Why not, is not said, nor are any particulars stated respecting the answer they gave to the king's messengers, or the conduct they pursued towards them. Merely the fact of their unwillingness to come is mentioned, the narrative passing at once to a specially detailed[4] account of a second mission to the guests, ver. 4: "*Again he sent other servants, saying,*" etc. Thus the king does not give up the unwilling ones, he desires once more to try whether they only mean to delay, or whether they will really persist in declining the summons. For this reason he again sends messengers to

---

[1] The plural, as frequently, synonymous with the singular γάμος, with reference to the series of marriage festivities.

[2] Gen. xxix. 22; Esth. ii. 18, i. 5, cf. ver. 3, ix. 22. But in the first two passages a *marriage*-feast is in fact spoken of, and in the two last ἡμέραι τοῦ γάμου or γάμων are in the sense of the translators proverbially "days of marriage joy." Also Luke xii. 36, xiv. 8, give no occasion for departing from the original meaning "marriage."

[3] Where also the first καλεῖν constituting the idea οἱ κεκλημένοι was expressly mentioned. Cf. there.

[4] In contrast with ver. 3.

them, not the same, but others, in the hope that the guests who disobeyed the call of the first servants may perhaps be moved by these others. And he now gives the servants the instruction: εἴπατε τοῖς κεκλημένοις, Ἰδοὺ τὸ ἄριστόν μου ἡτοίμακα,[1] οἱ ταῦροί μου καὶ τὰ σιτιστὰ τεθυμένα, καὶ πάντα ἕτοιμα· δεῦτε εἰς τοὺς γάμους, i.e. "*Say to them that are bidden, Behold, my luncheon* (ἄριστον) *I have in readiness,*" etc.[2] Ἄριστον, originally the first breakfast (jentaculum), among the later Greeks and in the New Testament is the luncheon (prandium) taken in the course of the day before the chief meal. In the present passage there is all the less reason to identify ἄριστον completely with δεῖπνον,[3] that the idea of luncheon is quite in place in the connection of the passage. The luncheon as such denotes the *beginning* of the marriage festivities; the statement therefore that it is ready simply emphasizes that there is nothing in the way of *the feast beginning.* But this by no means implies that the marriage-feast proper is not yet ready. For the following words: "*my oxen and the* (other) *fatlings are killed, and* (in general) *all things are ready,*" in their connection with the summons immediately based upon them, "*come to the marriage,*" can on no account refer merely to the preparations for the luncheon in distinction from the dinner proper, but plainly comprise the preparations for the entire festivities, *all* of which are ready, so that as soon as the guests are assembled the feast, beginning with the ἄριστον, may take its course without interruption.

The entire instruction is not one different in substance from the charge given to the first servants, as if the business of the latter previously was not to summon to the marriage-board already prepared. The occasion of the second mission was not to announce something new to the guests in reference to the feast, but solely the failure of the first one. Consequently the instruction given to the servants of the second mission simply impresses on them that they are once more to set before the guests plainly and urgently the same position of things which existed on the first mission. They are to tell (εἴπατε) them, expressly and circumstantially, that everything is ready, and thus put an end to all notion that there is time for delay and reflection, and insist upon immediate compliance. The guests are to know: Still to delay in the present state of things is to

---

[1] On preponderant evidence instead of ἡτοίμασα.
[2] Observe the perfect ἡτοίμακα.   [3] Kuinoel, Olshausen, Stier.

despise the marriage-feast of the royal host in the most shameful manner. But on the servants of the second mission executing the commission given there happens what is related in vv. 5, 6 : οἱ δὲ ἀμελήσαντες ἀπῆλθον ὃς μὲν¹ εἰς τὸν ἴδιον ἀγρόν, ὃς δὲ ἐπὶ τὴν ἐμπορίαν αὐτοῦ, οἱ δὲ λοιποὶ κρατήσαντες τοὺς δούλους αὐτοῦ ὕβρισαν καὶ ἀπέκτειναν. The two participles put first, ἀμελήσαντες in ver. 5 and κρατήσαντες in ver. 6, plainly stand in mutual contrast,—there, listless disregard; here, active ill-treatment of the king's messengers. This contrast presents itself too plainly to be overlooked in the exposition. Accordingly we must not solve the difficulty in the construction of the sentences by referring the ἀμελήσαντες to all the guests, and saying that the exact statement would have run : οἱ δὲ ἀμελήσαντες, οἱ μὲν ἀπῆλθον . . . οἱ δὲ λοιποὶ κρατήσαντες κ.τ.λ.² And still less by saying, that in the first words : οἱ δὲ ἀμελήσαντες, the narrator had not yet the subsequent οἱ δὲ λοιποὶ κρατήσαντες in mind.³ For the statement of ver. 6 by no means forms a mere appendage to that of ver. 5, perhaps occurring subsequently to the narrator; but, on the contrary, the statement in ver. 5 is merely the introduction to that of ver. 6, which with its οἱ δὲ λοιποί comprises the entire body of the guests apart from the first. Hence, too, the account of the punishment of the guests (ver. 7) refers only to the chief statement in ver. 6, not to ver. 5. We must agree with the first solution just mentioned so far as to admit that, in order to get at the speaker's meaning, we must supply an οἱ μέν in the introduction of the first sentence, not however after, but before the participle ἀμελήσαντες, where it was naturally omitted by the speaker himself just because of the obvious harshness with which it would stand immediately after οἱ δέ,⁴ so that it is now embodied in the οἱ δέ, and the οἱ δέ itself acquires a particular sense which only becomes evident to the reader afterwards by the contrasting of οἱ δὲ λοιποί. It is just the same, *e.g.*, in Luke ix. 19 : οἱ δὲ ἀποκριθέντες εἶπον . . . ἄλλοι δὲ κ.τ.λ. Thus in the speaker's meaning οἱ δὲ ἀμελήσαντες is to be translated at once in the particular sense : "*And some making light of it went their ways, one to his own field, another to his merchandise; and the rest seizing his servants,*" etc. Of the first-mentioned therefore it is said, they went away (instead of coming to the marriage) without paying any heed to the king's

---

[1] ὃς μὲν . . . ὃς δέ is better attested than ὁ μὲν . . . ὁ δί.   [2] Fritzsche, Lange.
[3] Meyer.   [4] οἱ δὲ οἱ μὲν ἀμελήσαντες.

messengers and their summons, one to his own field, another to his merchandise. The ἴδιον standing before ἀγρόν in this connection is far too pertinent to be treated as a mere possessive pronoun,[1] which, moreover, is not the case anywhere else in the New Testament.[2] Just because the field is his own, he prefers going there to going to the marriage-feast of the king. The characteristic therefore of this class of guests is indifference to the call to the royal marriage, having its root in the selfish interest in *one's own possession* which fastens the possessor here to the clod that is his own, and the earner there to the business that is to bring gain. And this disregard of theirs is doubly guilty, because retained in presence of what the rest do, ver. 6: "*And the rest, seizing his servants, shamefully entreated[3] and killed them,*" not in the sense that none was left, but generally: they perpetrated outrage and even murder upon them. How many of the messengers were so treated, or how many were ill treated and how many killed, is left uncertain. Such terms might be used, even if one only were actually murdered. Whilst, then, the first, ruled by their selfish interest, are indifferent to the king, the rest are inspired with rebellious feelings against him. For this reason the urgent summons: "Come to the marriage," that met with listless indifference in the first, becomes to the rest an occasion for open revolt and murderous violence on the servants urging them to decision. That this is quite inconceivable in the circumstances of the figurative story,[4] can only be maintained in the interest of a critical hypothesis. If from the first it is a *king* that is in question, whose guests are also his subjects, why should it be inconceivable that rebellious-minded subjects reply with open violence to the message urgently requiring their presence at the royal feast without further delay? But of course it is certain that by abusing and killing the king's messengers they commit the grossest outrage against the king. And this is the reason why the hitherto peaceful image of an invitation to a marriage-feast is now changed into the warlike image of a military raid with fire and sword against murderous rebels, ver. 7: "*But the king was wroth,[5] and sending his armies, destroyed those murderers, and burned their city.*" Only the

---

[1] Kuinoel, Grimm.   [2] Not even in xxv. 14, or John i. 42, cf. Meyer there.
[3] ὕβρισαν in conjunction with κρατήσαντες an active insulting.   [4] Weiss.
[5] The reading ὁ δὲ βασιλεὺς ὠργίσθη is to be regarded as genuine; the reading of the Recepta: ἀκούσας δὲ ὁ β. ὠργ., is a supplementary gloss, right in substance.

murderers, "the rest," in ver. 6 are here named as the object of the punishment, whereas the guests characterized in ver. 5, who did not directly participate in the violent deeds, are no longer specially mentioned in regard to the punishment. But not because they were excepted from the punishment of the rest, in which case rather they must have been specially mentioned, but because in the punishment no special notice is taken of them and their only apparently less guilty conduct. Although not comprehended in the expression "those murderers," they still actually suffered the punishment of murderers. It is impossible to think that the mention of a *city* as the object of chastisement, and this city being called "their (the murderers') city," necessarily involves the notion, that only the hostile guests of ver. 6 were the inhabitants of a special city apart, whereas those merely disobedient from selfishness (ver. 5) did not dwell in a city, or dwelt in another city. In this case the guests, hitherto distinguished only in inward disposition and conduct, would now be suddenly placed in a state of local separation, having no connection with the distinction of disposition. The guests generally are pictured as citizens of a city, just as was the case in the parable of the Banquet,[1] only that this idea is still more appropriate to the circumstances of the present narrative, which treats of a feast in a royal court, than to the other parable treating of the banquet of a rich man. This city, the city of the guests generally, after its citizens have become murderers of the king's messengers, is treated and chastised as "their (the murderers') city," because regard for the portion of the citizens who had not directly participated in the murder can just as little divert the penalty from the citizens and their city, as that portion of the citizens in their thoughtless selfishness had taken any trouble to divert the guilt of blood from the whole body. But if the murderers are not individual marriage-guests, but the unopposed ruling party in the city, whose citizens are the royal guests, it is not strange that the penalty on the marriage-guests should be represented as a military raid, the king sending now, instead of messengers of royal grace as hitherto, his armies, the organs of his royal might, against the citizens in open revolt and their city, cutting down the murderous citizens and burning their city. Consequently it cannot be said that here the limits of the parabolic figure are utterly violated by a foreign

[1] Cf. on Luke xiv. 21.

importation.[1] Only, of course, we ought not to ask further, what position the city takes in the king's *empire*, whether it is viewed as its capital or otherwise, the parable giving no answer to such questions. We have to do with a figurative narrative developing its circle of figures no farther than is necessary to the figurative presentation of its subject. And as the central idea placed at the head was not so much the empire, whose ruler is a king, as rather the marriage-feast of the king's son, whose host is a king, so the city only comes into view in reference to this royal marriage as the city whose citizens have this privilege above those outside, that they are the king's invited guests.

The narrative then continues with the words: τότε λέγει τοῖς δούλοις αὐτοῦ. The question is, to what in the preceding narrative the τότε alludes. In the midst of a continuous narrative it cannot mean "then," as often elsewhere, but only "thereupon." But to assert that the narrator thinks of the following words as first spoken after the penalty on the murderers and their city has been carried out,[2] is again quite needlessly to suppose a complete violation of the circumstances possible in the story. The first words spoken by the king to the servants: "The marriage is ready," show at once that the feast has not meantime been postponed until further notice, but that it is just as ready and just as urgently awaits the lacking guests as in ver. 4. How then is the history of a military expedition to come between? The words: τότε λέγει τοῖς δούλοις αὐτοῦ, exhibiting the king still *in conversation with his servants*, join on without violence to the initial words of ver. 7, ὁ δὲ βασ. ὠργίσθη, there governing the entire statement. "But the king," hearing through his servants of this outrage of the guests,[3] "was wroth," so it was just said; and then the order is related, issued by the king in his wrath to his armies. For although what the armies are to do is not stated in the form of a mere injunction, but is pictured more drastically as an act issuing from the king, still the king himself is represented as the agent (ἀπώλεσεν . . . ἐνέπρησεν), and the action, so far as it issues from him, is just the angry order. But then (τότε), after the king, burning with wrath against the criminals, has first inflicted just punishment on them, he again turns to the messengers, awaiting his further orders, to tell them what is to be

---

[1] Weiss.   [2] Weiss, Meyer, Nebe, *et al.*
[3] Cf. the correct supplementary gloss of the Recepta: ἀκούσας δὲ ὁ βασ.

done in reference to the feast standing ready. That τοῖς δούλοις αὐτοῦ here is not to be understood of the king's servants generally, but of the same particular servants now returned, who are spoken of in vv. 4–6, is a supposition not merely without difficulty on the right understanding of ver. 6, but also further confirmed by ver. 10, where the words "*those* servants" show that there the particular servants are meant who were distinguished in ver. 4 as "other servants" from the servants of the first mission in ver. 3.

The king then begins to the servants: "*The marriage indeed is ready*,[1] *but they that were invited were not worthy*," scil. to be invited. So οὐκ ἦσαν ἄξιοι must be translated, with Luther. For ἄξιοι must not be supplemented from the ὁ γάμος found already in the first clause, "they were not worthy of it"[2] (in which case one does not see why αὐτοῦ should be wanting), but simply from its own subject οἱ κεκλημένοι. And the entire statement is not meant to justify the exclusion of those first invited, as if the king wished to insist that their not coming to the marriage was not his fault, but the fault of their own unworthiness,—such a justification of mere exclusion is no longer in place after the passing on the guests of a sentence justified as matter of course by their own evil deeds,—but the statement is simply made to assign the reason of the commission introduced by οὖν. Because the feast indeed is ready, but is left without guests through the unworthiness of those invited, the servants are to do as ver. 9 states: πορεύεσθε οὖν ἐπὶ τὰς διεξόδους τῶν ὁδῶν, καὶ ὅσους ἐὰν εὕρητε καλέσατε εἰς τοὺς γάμους. The διέξοδοι τῶν ὁδῶν are not merely the outlets and inlets of the streets [3] (which does not explain the use of the rare double compound, and in particular the preposition διά failing to receive its due force), but the *thoroughfares* of the roads which, crossing other roads, furnish also various *outlets*, therefore *crossing-points of the roads*. The disputed point, whether city streets [4] or country roads [5] are meant, is no longer a question after the right interpretation of the city mentioned in ver. 7. If the first invited were identical with the citizens of the city now fallen a prey to destruction, the ὁδοί mentioned here must be meant in contrast with the city,

---

[1] *Scil.* the wedding-feast, ver. 4.   [2] Lange, Weiss.
[3] Stier, Grimm's *Lexicon*, the latter with reference to the boundaries of the heathen world.
[4] Kuinoel, Weiss.   [5] So the majority.

and therefore country roads outside.[1] The servants therefore are to go to the highways, and to their crossing-points as special gathering-places, and as many as they find there they are to invite as guests to the marriage in place of the first invited: *"And as many as ye shall find, summon to the marriage."*

The first part of the parabolic narrative is now at an end, a new section commencing with ver. 10, not, as is usually supposed in error, with ver. 11. At this point the previous line of narrative has in substance reached a complete conclusion. The obstinate wickedness of those first bidden having been first described, the just and inevitable consequences of this wickedness were completely characterized on one hand by the despatch of armies to punish the rebels, ver. 7, and on the other by the despatch of the servants to fetch in other guests in place of the first, vv. 8, 9. Thus, just as the parable of the Great Banquet concluded with the command to the servant to go into the highways and compel men to come in,[2] the execution of the command being understood of itself, so the present narrative would be at an end here without needing a special account of the execution of the command, unless the narrator had intended to add to the first part of the narrative a second one of independent meaning. And thus even the wording of ver. 10 itself shows that it is not a conclusion of what precedes, but a preparation for what follows. It is said: καὶ ἐξελθόντες οἱ δοῦλοι ἐκεῖνοι εἰς τὰς ὁδοὺς συνήγαγον πάντας οὓς[3] εὗρον, πονηρούς τε καὶ ἀγαθούς. In the first place, the pronoun ἐκεῖνοι after δοῦλοι intimates that the speaker, after making a preliminary conclusion, here begins a new narrative. This makes it necessary for him to go back beyond the break, and join on to what precedes by the pronoun ἐκεῖνοι. But even the statement itself: *"And those[4] servants went forth into the highways, and gathered together all, as many as they found, both bad and good,"* contains more than a mere account of the actual execution of the command given to the servants in ver. 9. More precisely defining the πάντας οὓς εὗρον by the special clause: πονηρούς τε καὶ ἀγαθούς, it signalizes an element in the proceedings of the servants just as meaningless in a mere conclusion of the previous section as it is significant in prospect

---

[1] Cf. the ὁδοί in Luke xiv. 23, in their contrast with αἱ πλατεῖαι καὶ ῥῦμαι τῆς πόλεως, ver. 21.   [2] Luke xiv. 23.

[3] The reading of the Recepta, ὅσους, seems transferred from ver. 9.

[4] Those mentioned ver. 8, or vv. 4–6.

of what follows. We have no right to weaken the force of these words by designating them without proof a kind of proverbial phrase,[1] but they must be understood as they run. That the servants were subject to no sort of outward limit in gathering guests to the marriage, was involved in the nature of the commission sending them into the highways. But the special element signalized in these words is, that in this gathering of guests they did not even make any moral distinction, that they took bad[2] (*i.e.* people with an evil past, of ill report, such as must needs be met with among the crowds of the highway) just as well as good, without inquiry into antecedents. Respecting συνήγαγον, see what was said on Luke xiv. 21, 23 (εἰσάγαγε ... ἀνάγκασον εἰσελθεῖν). They gathered the guests together, not with outward force,[3] but with friendly urgent call, which found ready hearing with the people of the highways in contrast with the citizens of the city. And by means of this absolutely indiscriminate gathering the marriage-feast was filled with guests: καὶ ἐπλήσθη ὁ γάμος ἀνακειμένων, *i.e.* "*And the marriage-board was filled with those reclining at table.*" Through the predicate ἐπλήσθη ἀνακειμένων the subject-notion ὁ γάμος acquires, of course, the limited meaning of marriage-*board*. The likewise well-attested reading ὁ νυμφών instead of ὁ γάμος seems a needlessly simplifying correction.

After the marriage-board in this way has been filled, there is nothing, as one might think, to prevent the festivity beginning, and the assembled guests, as they were collected without distinction of worthy and unworthy, actually joining without distinction in the festive joys. But just when the host appeared to begin the festivity, there enters once more a sifting judicial process for the multitude of guests. Contrasting by the particle δέ the following events with the indiscriminate invitation in ver. 10, the narrative proceeds, ver. 11 : εἰσελθὼν δὲ ὁ βασιλεὺς θεάσασθαι τοὺς ἀνακειμένους εἶδεν ἐκεῖ ἄνθρωπον οὐκ ἐνδεδυμένον ἔνδυμα γάμου. While the guests were assembling, the king himself was not present; but when all are assembled, and the tables are full, he enters the banqueting-hall to behold (θεάσασθαι) the guests (τοὺς ἀνακειμένους). But this beholding cannot be meant from the first as an inspection with the premeditated aim of excluding those who cannot stand the test, which would ill accord with the

---

[1] Bengel: "locutio quasi proverbialis." [2] πονηρούς τι, standing first with emphasis.
[3] Bengel: "interdum adhibita vi non optima."

figurative notion of a host entering to his guests to begin the feast. Here, according to the context, we should really have a specially purposed inspection of the *attire* of the guests. Consequently all that is meant is a viewing of the guests by the royal host in the general sense, such as is implied in the nature of the situation, the guests being strangers gathered by chance from all quarters. Not as the anticipated result of an inspection, but as the occurrence of an event unexpected and disturbing the harmony of the feast, we are told: "*But when the king came in to behold the guests, he saw there a man which had not on a wedding garment.*" Ἔνδυμα γάμου is a garment suited to a wedding, thus a clean, neat, festive garment, in opposition to a dirty or ragged everyday garment, standing in ill contrast with the festal array of a wedding. For this contrast we must not substitute the quite different one between a garment given by the king and one brought by the guest himself. That one bidden to a wedding appear not in soiled everyday dress, but in neat festal attire, is a general precept of decorum, the violation of which involves a gross affront to the host, and in this case a criminal disregard of the majesty of the king. Certainly the question, how the appearance of a guest without wedding garment could seem so strange to the king who had gathered the people from the highways, can only be answered to this effect, that those invited so unexpectedly to the royal feast must with the invitation itself have had the opportunity of obtaining a suitable dress, so far as from seemly reverence for the king they troubled themselves about one. Thus we should be obliged to affirm, even if it were not established by modern observation as an Oriental custom for royal hosts to supply festal dresses to their guests,[1] a custom whose disputed antiquity[2] seems at least so far attested in the Old Testament as festal dresses appear there as objects of princely generosity.[3] But at the same time it is quite certain that what surprised the king was, not that the guest had on a garment of his own instead of one given, but that he had not on a wedding garment at all. With this agrees the question of blank astonishment, which the king at once addresses to him, ver. 12: καὶ λέγει αὐτῷ, Ἑταῖρε, πῶς εἰσῆλθες ὧδε μὴ ἔχων ἔνδυμα γάμου; For the point of the question is not, how he could have despised the king's festal garb and pre-

---

[1] Harmar, *Beobacht*, ii. p. 117; Rosenmüller, *Morgenl.* v. p. 75 ff.
[2] Keil, Meyer, Weiss.
[3] Gen. xlv. 22; Judg. xiv. 19; 2 Kings v. 22, x. 22; Esth. vi. 8, viii. 15.

ferred his own, but how he could have come in without a wedding garment at all. And εἰσέρχεσθαι does not mean a passive getting in, in which case the question of surprise must rather have been addressed to the servants who admitted him, but it is an active entering, which the subjective negation μὴ ἔχων also shows. Therefore: "Friend, how couldst thou enter here with the consciousness of not having a wedding garb?" The question, asked not in the tone of anger, but at first merely in that of just surprise,[1] expects from the man questioned an explanation of his incomprehensible beginning. But he has none to give. For it is said: "*and he was speechless.*" This silence is a confession that he has no excuse, because in fact nothing but criminal disrespect for the king led him to neglect providing himself with a suitable dress. Thus the wrath of the king is kindled, and he punishes the speechless one, ver. 13: "*Then the king said to the servants*" (τοῖς διακόνοις), therefore not to the menials who acted as messengers in inviting, but to the house-servants waiting at the feast: Δήσαντες αὐτοῦ πόδας καὶ χεῖρας ἄρατε αὐτὸν καὶ ἐκβάλετε[2] εἰς τὸ σκότος τὸ ἐξώτερον. The binding of the feet and hands, prefixed in participial form to the ἐκβάλετε as the chief idea, has no independent significance, but simply comes into view as the method of the ἐκβάλλειν, cutting off beforehand from the one expelled all possibility of resistance, and all hope of delivering himself from the darkness into which he is cast. The comparative ἐξώτερον does not compare the darkness, into which they are to cast him, with another darkness less remote,[3] but simply calls the darkness the outer space in relation to the inner space of the marriage-hall or house (therefore: "into the darkness outside"). Whilst within everything shines with festive radiance, outside is blank darkness. Thus the lot to which the king condemns the guest without a wedding garment is to be cast out of the joy of the marriage-feast and the radiance of the marriage-hall into the blank darkness without. The figurative expression: "the outer darkness," is found also in viii. 12 and xxv. 30, and in both passages just as here is the joyless, gloomy space without in contrast with the place of festive joy within. But in all three passages the place figuratively described by "the outer dark-

---

[1] The apostrophe ἑταῖρε is not one of friendship, like φίλε, but still not unfriendly.
[2] Lachmann and Weiss read only ἐκβάλετε αὐτόν after χεῖρας; the external evidence is vacillating, the sense remains the same.
[3] Luther: "into the outermost darkness."

ness" is still more precisely defined by the clause: ἐκεῖ ἔσται ὁ κλαυθμὸς καὶ ὁ βρυγμὸς τῶν ὀδόντων, i.e. "there shall be the (well-known) wailing and gnashing of teeth," a saying which Jesus also adds or inserts elsewhere, where He is speaking of the place of damnation.[1] The article before κλαυθμός and βρυγμός puts beyond doubt that the saying is not so much a special prediction that those found in that place will suffer great pain, as rather an admonition on the part of the speaker to the hearers, that the well-known wailing and teeth-gnashing (from pain) of the condemned will happen in the place in question, that they therefore are to think of no other than the place of eternal pain (xxv. 46). And in this case it is self-evident that here, as everywhere else, the saying is a direct admonition of Jesus to His hearers, by which He solemnly interprets to them the expression "the outer darkness," employing for this purpose another image familiar to them,—and that the words ought not to be incorporated with the address of the king,[2] merely because the figurative story here accidentally ends in the direct address of a figurative person, where as an addition to the king's command to the servants they would be least of all suitable.

To ver. 13, containing the king's final sentence and the emphatic addition, there is added the general proposition introduced in explanation by γάρ, ver. 14: πολλοὶ γάρ εἰσιν κλητοί, ὀλίγοι δὲ ἐκλεκτοί. The mutually opposed ideas "called" and "chosen" are definitely explained by the reference of the two in the context to the kingdom of God. Therefore: Many are called of God to His kingdom, the call to enter God's kingdom coming to them by God's will; but few are chosen by Him to His kingdom, so that they are separated from mankind to be partakers of His kingdom by God's choice. From mankind, we say advisedly, not from the number of the called,[3] for the predicates "called" and "chosen" are absolutely opposed to each other. Therefore the second must be understood just as absolutely as the first, and does not receive its meaning through relation to the first. But the statement itself, that the first holds true of many, the second only of few, is, of course, meant in mutual relation. The affirmation is, that *in relation* to the great number of those who are the object of the divine call, only few are the object of the divine choice. The exegetical discussion of the passage

---

[1] xiii. 42, 50 (see there), xxiv. 51; Luke xiii. 28.
[2] Lange, Nebe, Weiss.   [3] Weiss.

(without prejudice to the dogmatic) has simply to keep to this meaning, without carrying back the predicate "chosen" in this connection to anything but the divine choice. The word "chosen" must not, in the light of the parable, be explained to mean: Separated from the number of the unworthy on the ground of proved worthiness.[1] Were this the meaning of the utterance, it would simply draw out the result of the parable, and instead of being introduced by γάρ, as is done in xx. 16, must be introduced by οὕτως. Moreover, in that case we should at least in the second clause expect the future ἔσονται instead of the present εἰσίν, since the predicate "chosen" would then be viewed as the eventual consequence of a future line of conduct, so that the saying would run: οὕτως πολλ. εἰσι κλητ., ὀλ. δὲ ἔσονται ἐκλεκτοί. But as it stands, and joined to the parable by γάρ, it must not be explained from the parable, but, conversely, what is said in the parable must be explained from it. And, indeed, the explanatory γάρ refers primarily to what immediately precedes (ver. 13), therefore to the issue of the parable, although certainly the indissoluble, inner connection of this appendix with the entire course of the narrative involves substantially a reference to the whole of the parable. What might seem strange in the issue of the narrative was this, that not merely the first invited, who set themselves in opposition to the invitation, but even such as obeyed the invitation, were cast out of the feast into darkness (i.e., according to ver. 13b, from the kingdom of God into the place of the lost, and therefore the being invited or called gave no certain security of participating in God's kingdom); that not even they who obey the call are secure against exclusion. And the strangeness is now explained by an allusion to the general truth: πολλοὶ γάρ κ.τ.λ. It is not the same, but something essentially different, to be called by God to His kingdom, and to be chosen by God for His kingdom. So little do the two coincide, that the first applies to a very *great* number of men, whereas the second can only be affirmed of a comparatively *small* number. This is the truth uttered by way of explanation. And it is clear that whoever keeps it in view cannot be surprised at the exclusion of the called from participation in God's kingdom, such as the parable teaches; and least of all will he be inclined himself to rely on the calling he has received, and to make it a pillow for indolence.

[1] So most moderns.

Thus this general utterance of Jesus, although referring primarily to the issue of the parable, furnishes also an explanation of the fundamental thought governing the parable in its entire course and binding it into unity. Looking back from this point on the whole of the narrative, we see at once that it consists of two sections, each one having an independent import. For after the part begun with ver. 2 had reached a complete conclusion with ver. 9, ver. 10 commenced a new, independent section, so that each of the two parts might fitly be regarded as a complete parable by itself. And yet the two sections, as they are here joined together, form but one narrative, not only outwardly, but also intrinsically, the second section presenting itself, because of the resemblance in its incidents to those of the other, not merely as an appendix outwardly connected, but also as a real intrinsic continuation of what precedes. If the essential import of the first part was this, that the guests first invited, nevertheless, did not actually partake in the feast, but drew on themselves the wrath of the king by their disobedience to the call at the decisive hour, and were the cause of strangers being invited in their place, this result is now extended in the second part to the effect, that even among the guests gathered by indiscriminate invitation, some were found who must be excluded from sharing in the feast, because appearing without the right dress. If, then, we remember that, according to ver. 1, Jesus spoke the parable primarily to the hostile leaders of the Jewish people, and also (seeing that the parable belongs to the time of His last public teaching in the temple) before a listening group of people, among whom individuals receptive to His word were not wanting, and again before His disciples, who always accompanied Him in those days, it is clear that each of the two parts of the parable is adapted to a different class of hearers, while, at the same time, they contain common truth which Jesus desires to speak to hearers of both kinds in one connected narrative. The first part is addressed to hearers of the first class as the leading representatives of the Israelitish people, since the first invited, just like the similar category in the parable of the Great Banquet, and the Wicked Vinedressers in the preceding parable, are meant to symbolize the people of Israel as the people of the theocracy. The second part, on the other hand, is addressed to hearers of the second class, of whom Jesus may hope that individually they are free from the decided enmity of their nation to Jesus, and will willingly be gathered with the heathen into God's kingdom. The common teaching, in which the entire import of the parable is summed up, is this: *The grace of the divine calling by no means gives security of participating in the kingdom of God; on the contrary, to all who abuse it the grace will turn into the condemnation of God's wrath.* And the special purpose of the first part is to tell the leaders of Israel that this principle will be proved first in the Israelitish people, who first received the grace of God's call. The members of this nation by continued resistance to the call to enter God's kingdom will cause God's sentence of destruction to burst upon them, and strangers will be called to God's kingdom in their stead. But to the individuals among His hearers who are not unwilling for themselves to obey the call, He says in the second part, that even in the new period now opening, the same principle will retain its validity. He shows them that, despite the indiscriminate gathering of all classes of men into God's kingdom, at last every one not found with the character alone qualifying for participation in God's kingdom, will be again cast out by God into damnation.

Returning to the beginning of the parable in order to interpret the entire course of the narrative, we see first of all, just as in the parable of the Great Banquet, a festive meal to be the fundamental idea, vv. 2, 4. As to the interpretation of this figure and its Old Testament basis, what was said on Luke xiv. 16 may be consulted. Under the image of a rich, costly meal is represented the sum of the blessings prepared by God in His kingdom for the perfect satisfaction of man's soul pining in estrangement from Him. But whereas Luke's parable stopped at the simple figure of a banquet, we find here at the head of the narrative another figure coupled with this one, the banquet being more precisely defined as a marriage-feast prepared by a king for his son. Already in the Old Testament the covenant-relation between God and His people is represented under the figure of a marriage-covenant.[1] In keeping with this, Christ is called in the New Testament the Bridegroom,[2] and the joining of Christ and the New-Testament people of God into intimate and blessed fellowship in His kingdom is designated the marriage of the Bridegroom with the Bride.[3] The present passage as certainly

---

[1] Jer. liv. 5; Hos. ii. 19, 20, *et al.*   [2] ix. 15, xxv. 1 ff.; John iii. 29.
[3] Rev. xxi. 2, 9.

alludes to this figurative idea as γάμοι in ver. 2 can signify nothing but a marriage-feast. But here, certainly, where the bride is not even mentioned, the idea of the union between bridegroom and bride does not come into use, but only so much is borrowed from the figurative idea as serves to enrich the all-dominant image of the banquet. Since in allusion to this other circle of ideas the banquet is pictured as a marriage-feast prepared by a king for his son (the king being the host, the king's son, as bridegroom, the centre of the feast, and all the festal joy participation in his joy), the kingdom of God is described as the highest conceivable joy prepared by God for His Son, and participation in the blessedness of the kingdom is participation in this perfect joy of the Son of God, prepared by the Father for Him, so that to members of the kingdom Christ's person is the object and centre of their joy. The difficulty, therefore, lying in the fact that only the Church of Christ can be viewed as the bride of the King's Son, which Church in the further course of the narrative is the whole body of guests, is to be solved thus: As in the narrative the person of the bride is left unmentioned in the background, so in the interpretation she is to be left in the background, and not to be brought into the comparison. When again, in ver. 3, the same category of the first invited appears, that we already know from the parable of the Great Banquet; and when, moreover, they are viewed, not as scattered individuals, but as the citizens of a city, just as in Luke's parable,[1] their interpretation must be the same here as there. The members of the Israelitish theocracy, as such, received first from God the promise of the blessedness of His kingdom. That in Luke's parable special mention was made of the previous act of invitation, by which they became "invited," whilst here they appear at once as κεκλημένοι on the supposition of that act, makes, of course, no difference. And in this case nothing more is meant by the sending of the servants, ver. 3, "to call those bidden to the marriage," than is meant there by sending the servant, "at the hour of the feast, to say to those bidden: Come, for all is now ready" (Luke xiv. 17). Just as little as there is any room, in the figurative circumstances of the narrative, for a second call pointing to the future between the first invitation to the feast in prospect, and the calling of those so bidden to the feast now ready, so little can the interpretation put a further

---

[1] Cf. on ver. 7.

call, pointing only to the future between the Old-Testament calling of Israel, by which it became the possessor of the promise of God's kingdom, and the New-Testament call, by which the fulfilment of the promise was announced to it, and it was summoned to enter God's kingdom now manifested, as is done by those who refer the sending of the servants in ver. 3, "to call those bidden to the marriage," to the prophets of the Old Covenant.[1] It is true, in the present parable, differently from that of the Great Banquet, a twofold calling of those already invited is distinguished after the first invitation. But as certainly as in the narrative the second calling of those bidden in ver. 4 is simply presented as a repetition of the first in ver. 3, occasioned not by any alteration in the feast, but merely by the failure of the first calling, so certainly this twofold calling in vv. 3, 4 can only symbolize the repetition of the same New-Testament message of God to Israel respecting the kingdom having appeared, and of the same divine call to enter into it, a repetition occasioned by the nation's disobedience. And when the narrative makes the second calling (ver. 4) to be carried out by *different* servants from the first, this can only symbolize the fact that the same New-Testament message of God to Israel, after its first bearers have found no response in Israel, will be brought to Israel by other messengers. And this interpretation given by the wording of the narrative, directly that we compare the facts of the history with it, finds in those facts at once its evident confirmation. For the two periods of the New-Testament preaching of God's kingdom brought to Israel by different messengers are as distinctly marked off from each other in the history as in the figurative narrative,—once by the Baptist and Jesus, and afterwards, when these messengers found no response, again by the apostles and their fellow-labourers. It is true, several expositors have found an insuperable difficulty in the person of Christ, represented in ver. 2 under the image of the king's son and bridegroom, appearing again as a servant inviting to the marriage. On this account, in the first servants mentioned in ver. 3, excluding Jesus, they would see along with the Baptist, the Twelve and the Seventy sent forth in the lifetime of Jesus,[2] or, since the apostles, who are expressly described, ver. 4, as "other servants" cannot also be the messengers of the first mission, those persons who, according to the oft-repeated state-

---

[1] Luther, de Valenti, Thiersch, Weiss, and most of the ancients.   [2] Stier.

ment of the Gospels, spread abroad the fame of Jesus through the whole land.[1] But what necessity is there in a figurative picture of the twofold call to Israel in New-Testament days to pass by entirely the prophetic work of Jesus, and fill up the great gap thus arising by some artificial means? It would be better simply to assume an incongruity in the figurative representation on this point. But really there is no such incongruity. There would only be one, provided the same Christ, who once appeared as the king's son and bridegroom, were further distinguished as a particular servant of the king from the son and other servants. But such is by no means the case: the parable merely says generally that God, by His servants, called the people of promise to the manifested blessedness of God's kingdom, whose centre is the Son of God, and this not once only, but again, by other servants, after the rejection of those first sent. Certainly there is no inconsistency here. The parable says nothing specific, and in particular there is no allusion to the individuality of any of the messengers. Only when seeking the confirmation of this statement of the parable in the concrete history do we encounter the strange fact, that the Son of God, who is the centre of the joy of God's kingdom, also appears as a servant of God like others in Israel, calling Israel to the kingdom. But there is no need in the parable, which simply knows the servants as a category, and only says that after the rejection of the first messengers others will be sent, to include this identity of the Son with one of the servants in the circle of the figurative representation. This explains how it happens that in the case of the first mission of the servants, although this really includes the mission of Christ Himself, the narrative simply notices the unwillingness of the guests to come, without mentioning the violence to the persons of the servants, so that the killing of Christ, which, in the preceding parable stood at the close as the critical element, is here passed over in silence. But the former parable, in contrast with the wide field of the Old-Testament history of Israel, with its long series of messengers, summed up the New-Testament gracious visitation of the people merely in its focus—the mission of the Son. When, on the other hand, the gist of the present parable, whose standpoint from the first is in the New-Testament age, is that the message of the manifested kingdom of God will be brought again by

[1] Nebe.

other messengers after the failure of the first, in a detailed account of the *New-Testament* history of Israel, Israel's conduct to the first messengers only appears as the occasion of the second mission, its conduct to the other messengers of the second period appearing as the decisive factor. Hence, the former is merely mentioned briefly as a transition to the sequel, and the latter only is made the object of particular description. Accordingly, vv. 3 and 4 of the narrative are to be interpreted thus: As the king in the parable called the invited guests to come to the feast prepared, and on their refusing to come sent other servants, representing to them the readiness of the feast, which forbade further delay, and urging them to come at once, so God does to Israel. In the period beginning with the appearance of the Baptist and reaching to the present moment, He called them— the children of the people of the promise—to God's kingdom by His messengers, but the people refused obedience to the call. Then God again sends other messengers to tell them once more, with the emphasis demanded by the decisive importance of the last attempt, that all the blessings of God's kingdom are made ready for their enjoyment by divine grace, and therefore no further delay is possible, but an instant coming with the obedience of penitence and faith is earnestly enjoined on them. That the allusion to the readiness of the luncheon does not exclude, but includes the readiness of the entire feast, was shown by the exposition. And in this case the word $\mathring{\alpha}\rho\iota\sigma\tau\text{ο}\nu$ cannot be chosen for the purpose of distinguishing the blessings already prepared in the present period from a more perfect stage of glory and blessedness to be realized later. But God's messengers are to proclaim to Israel, that on God's side *all* is ready for giving men perfect blessedness in His kingdom, and He only waits for them to come and enter into the kingdom of God.

But the citizens of the theocracy of Israel acted towards this last urgent summons like the citizens invited to the feast in the parable. As there—so we proceed in interpreting vv. 5, 6 on the ground of the exposition given—the one class, taken up with selfish interest in enjoying or increasing their possessions, meet the pressing summons of the king's messengers with indifference, while the rest, rather encouraged than hindered by the stupidity of the former, in their hostile hate perpetrate shameful violence, and even murder, on the messengers, so the hostile hate of the ruling parties in Israel, in league with the indifference of the classes of the people sunk in selfish gain and enjoyment, rise in rebellion against God's last messengers to them. And while the one class, persisting in stupid indifference to God's message and its bearers, only run after enjoyment or the getting of the earthly possessions, to which their whole heart cleaves, the rest, full of hostility and hate to God, fall upon God's messengers with shameful violence and murder. All this Jesus foresees and foretells in figurative form as definitely as without figure in xxiii. 34; Luke xi. 49. He knows that in the present obduracy of the people against His person and mission Israel's inner decision against God is present, and that this obduracy will remain the same even in presence of the later and last messengers sent to it. The prediction was fulfilled historically in the persecutions suffered afterwards by the apostles and their fellow-workers and fellow-confessors at the hands of the Jews.[1]

But, then, God's long-suffering with His people will be exhausted, and the period in the history of God's kingdom will begin that is characterized on the one side by the rejection of Israel, and on the other by the calling of others in their stead to the blessedness of God's kingdom. So Jesus predicts in the words concluding the first section, vv. 7–9. As the king, on the news of the treatment of his servants, was wroth with the rebels, and in his wrath sent his armies instead of messengers against them, destroying them and burning their city, so will God's wrath be kindled against the children of Israel, and in His wrath He will send, instead of messengers of salvation, the instruments of His judgment against them, and through these will annihilate the people stained with the blood of God's servants, and overthrow their commonwealth. Such is the correct interpretation of the three particular features in ver. 7. *The sending of the armies* must just as certainly receive a special interpretation as the sending of the servants, and, like the latter, must be referred to the bearers of a divine mission within history, therefore not to the heavenly hosts, as older expositors suppose, but to the earthly instruments which God uses, like a king his military power, to carry out the judgments of His wrath by a display of authority. This certainly suggests the worldly powers and kingdoms standing at God's command, and executing His judgments with fire and sword; but not specifically the *Roman armies*,[2] which are not definitely referred to. *The destroying of the murderers*, just like

---

[1] Acts v. 40, vii. 58, viii. 1, xii. 2, 3, *et al.*   [2] Stier, Nebe, *et al.*

the destroying of the wicked vinedressers,[1] and the cutting down of the fig-tree,[2] signifies not the killing of individual persons merely, nor the extirpation of every individual member of the nation, but the annihilating of the nation that had shed the blood of God's servants in its national existence; the portion of the nation not directly concerned in the violent deeds also falling under the punishment of murderers, because the selfish indolence of its indifference made it a partner in guilt. And finally, *the burning of the city*, according to the meaning belonging to the *city*,[3] in contrast with the highways, whose citizens are the invited guests, symbolizes the overthrow of the theocratic commonwealth of Israel. It does not predict, as nearly all expositors arbitrarily suppose *ex posteriore*, the specific fact of the burning of Jerusalem, in which case the prophecy would no longer be figurative, but directly literal, although inserted in a figurative history, and would form an altogether alien element. Certainly in the siege and overthrow of Jerusalem by the Romans the prediction of the present passage was fulfilled in a pre-eminent sense, even its figurative form receiving a literal fulfilment in the conflagration of the city, and this is certainly a divine sign worthy of note. Still the prediction as such remains figurative, and as a prediction must be understood and interpreted in accordance with the figurative form of the narrative, in the line of which it stands.

And as the king in the parable, with the command to his armies to execute the judgment on the rebels, links the command to the servants rejected by the latter, after the guests invited have proved themselves unworthy, to go to the highway-crossings and bring to the marriage as many as they find; so, when God calls forth the instruments of His judgment against Israel, He will command the messengers rejected by Israel to go to the thoroughfares of the world, hitherto alien to God's kingdom and its promises, and there invite as many as they find, in place of unworthy, rejected Israel.[4] In the narrative the recipients of this commission were the same servants who were already mentioned in vv. 4, 6; in the interpretation, therefore, the same messengers of God, who at God's command made the last attempt in Israel, and were rejected with murderous violence. Since the

---

[1] Cf. on xxi. 41.
[2] Luke xiii. 6 ff.
[3] Both in the present parable and in that of the Great Banquet.
[4] On the interpretation of the highways, see on Luke xiv. 23.

τότε, ver. 8, in the connection of the narrative could not be meant to place the sending of the servants to the highways after the burning of the city in time, but only made one command follow the other, so also it cannot be meant to place the epoch of the calling of the Gentiles after the execution of the judgment on Israel in time, or after the destruction of Jerusalem.[1] It merely says that on the one decree, by which the sentence of doom is inflicted on Israel, the other will follow, supplementing the first, and commanding the Gentiles to be called in place of rejected Israel. This only implies the obvious truth, that the second depends on the first in the divine arrangement, but not a chronology of future historical events.

Here the interpretation of the first section, resembling the parable of the Banquet,[2] is at an end. Like that similar parable, the section ends with the prediction of the divine decree that will command the calling of the heathen in place of Israel. But the present parable is not satisfied with showing in the future the decision to call the heathen as the other side of the doom of rejection passed on Israel, but in the second section of the narrative it enters with its prediction upon the new epoch now opening for the purpose of showing how the same law at work in the rejection of Israel, in virtue of which the grace of God's calling turned to those who abused it into the judgment of God's wrath, will also be active in the new order of things in the case of those who by God's will enter into the gap caused by Israel's rejection. The calling of men to God's kingdom will be absolutely general and indiscriminate. As the servants sent into the highways, in executing their commission, gathered to the marriage all they found, making no distinction outward or inward, collecting bad just as well as good, so God's messengers sent into the heathen world will address themselves with the call to God's kingdom to all without distinction, and will go so far in this, that they will take as little notice of the distinction of good and evil as of any outer distinction, gathering into God's kingdom men of evil history just as well as those of moral integrity. The ideas bad and good, which could only have a moral sense in the narrative, are to be simply taken over into the interpretation in the mode indicated. But there is not on this account any violation of the figurative form of the narrative, as has here again been assumed offhand. The fact in the figurative story,

---

[1] Meyer, Weiss.   [2] Luke xiv. 16 ff.

that disreputable as well as reputable persons were brought to the king's wedding, teaches that not merely those who bear a good character, but those whose past history makes them seem to the human judgment of God's messengers men of evil character, will be gathered into God's kingdom. While thus the existence to human judgment of an outwardly cognisable distinction of good and evil is acknowledged in the portion of mankind still far from God's kingdom, all decisive importance is at the same time refused to it as regards participation in God's kingdom. The assumption in this statement is that the messengers who summon to the kingdom will not meet with rejection in this course, such as was their lot at the hands of the people of Israel, but will find willing obedience. Hence, as the marriage-board was full of guests, so it will come to pass in the way described, that the complement of men [1] will be gathered into God's kingdom to participate in its blessedness and glory. The accomplishment of this end seems joined — the circumstances of the figurative story permitting no other view — immediately to the labour of the servants of God rejected by Israel and then turning to the heathen, and therefore to the labour of the apostles and their fellow-workers. The prediction thus beholds the beginning of the period of Gentile-calling in immediate connection with its end, and overlooks the intermediate period separating the beginning from the end in the historical fulfilment. But this intermediate period contains nothing but the homogeneous continuation and completion of the work begun by those servants of God in calling men to God's kingdom without distinction, and thus does not disturb, however long it may last according to human reckoning, the relation of cause and effect established in the parable between the beginning and the end.

But when the universality of the calling implied that none of the distinctions prevailing in the whole sphere of man's natural life—not even that of good and evil—is able to exclude from God's kingdom, it seems as if upon the calling now concluded there must follow just as universal and indiscriminate an admission of those so gathered to participation in the blessedness of God's kingdom. But it is not so. When the calling has come to a conclusion, a judicial process is again applied, sifting the number of those gathered into the kingdom, and for ever excluding a portion of them from its blessedness.

[1] Cf. on xiii. 48, and on Luke xiv. 23.

How this is done is stated in vv. 11–13, in contrast with ver. 10. The ground of the exclusion in the narrative was the not having on a wedding garment. For in its figurative circumstances it was evident that the indiscriminate gathering of the guests changed nothing in the indispensable requirement, that every one desirous of actually partaking of the feast put on a clean, neat festive dress in keeping with the occasion. And this can symbolize nothing but the requirement, indispensably grounded in the ethical nature of God's kingdom, that every one who would actually have part in its blessedness, acquire the corresponding moral character, and therefore obtain the moral righteousness ($\delta\iota\kappa\alpha\iota\sigma\sigma\acute{\upsilon}\nu\eta$) that corresponds to the holy will supreme in God's kingdom. And this requirement, in fact, is just as little incompatible with the indiscriminate calling of men to the kingdom as the requirement to put on a festive dress is with the indiscriminate gathering of the guests. For just as little as the latter has it anything to do with the previous state of those called. It is a requirement, like that of putting on a festive dress, coming to all with and in the call just as indiscriminately as the call itself, and must be fulfilled by all alike, when they obey the call, by the "good" just as much as by the "bad." For even to the former, who seem to human judgment comparatively righteous, the obtaining of *the* righteousness corresponding to God's holy will, and qualifying for participation in the blessedness of God's kingdom, is a requirement as absolutely new and still to be fulfilled as to all else.[1] Accordingly, the interpreters are all in error who would interpret the wedding garment only of the righteousness of faith coming by gift.[2] For as certainly as the object of rebuke, or ground of exclusion, described in the parable, was not the bringing of a festive dress of the man's own, instead of one given by the king to the guests, but the want of a wedding garment simply, so certainly the ground of future exclusion from God's kingdom described here is not self-righteousness in opposition to the righteousness of faith coming by gift, but simply the want of a moral character and walk corresponding to God's holy will. But, on the other hand, the parable plainly assumes, both in the surprised question of the king and in the silence of the guest, that with the invitation itself not merely is the putting on of a wedding garment required of every one invited, but the obtaining of such a garment must have been made possible to

---

[1] Chap. v. 20.   [2] Stier, Olshausen, Thiersch, Nebe, *et al.*

every one. Thus, the wedding garment is the moral character corresponding to the supremacy of God's holy will in God's kingdom, and in this sense the righteousness of God's kingdom, the obtaining of which, as it is required of every one without distinction with the call to God's kingdom, so it is made possible to every one without distinction by God's grace. So far, and no farther, ought interpretation to go. Any more definite statement respecting the way in which this righteousness is procured did not lie within the purpose of the parable, which places the whole emphasis on the indispensableness of the requirement.

Accordingly, what is said vv. 11-13 must be interpreted as follows:—Like as, when all the guests were assembled and the feast was on the point of commencing, the king comes in and finds one who had not on a wedding garment, so when the period of calling is ended, before mankind gathered into God's kingdom is put in possession and enjoyment of its blessedness and glory, the eye of God will find out every one who is without the righteousness of God's kingdom. So we must interpret, without assigning a special signification to the act of the king's entering to view the guests. Since the entering, in the circumstances of the parable, could not mean a special coming of the king with the premeditated purpose of judging and sifting the guests, but merely served to fix the moment of beginning the feast, so it cannot contain a special allusion to the divine coming for the purpose of holding the final judgment. If such an allusion were really intended, the question must then be raised, Why the King Himself is named as the subject of the coming to the final judgment, not the King's Son, and therefore the Messiah, as everywhere else in the New Testament? In the above putting of the interpretation, the circumstance that in the narrative but one man is mentioned as without the wedding garment has found its corresponding appreciation. Expositors usually say that this circumstance should not be pressed, but without showing why only one is mentioned, since it would seem more in keeping with the purpose of the parable if, instead of one, many were mentioned. This circumstance, therefore, has its significance. In the fact that among the multitude of the guests duly clad one without wedding garment does not escape the king's eye, it is taught that none, not even one, without the righteousness of God's kingdom will be able to hide from God's eye among the rest of the members of the kingdom. And such will have just as little excuse before God as the marriage-guest before the king. As the latter's silence to the question, how he dared to come in without a wedding garment, makes him seem a man who profaned the royal feast and despised the majesty of the king, so will they stand without excuse before God as those who polluted His kingdom and profaned the majesty of His name. And then it will be done to them as to that marriage-guest. As the king commanded the servants to cast him out, bound hand and foot, into the darkness, so that he can neither resist the expulsion nor deliver himself from the darkness to which he is consigned, so, in executing the divine command, God's angels will sever every similar one from the midst of the righteous, and exclude him from the blessedness of God's kingdom, handing him over to the place of punishment, without there being any possibility for those concerned to resist the exclusion or deliver themselves from this place of punishment. The διάκονοι of the king must be just as definitely interpreted as his δοῦλοι, from whom they are plainly distinguished, and his στρατεύματα, ver. 7. In distinction from the former, as the messengers of divine grace, and the latter, as the agents of divine judgment within the present course of history, they are the angels who, as God's ministering spirits, will at the end of the present dispensation, and before the setting up of God's eternal kingdom, execute the divine judgment of exclusion to condemnation on all unworthy members of God's Church on earth.[1]

Only after the exposition and interpretation of the narrative have come to an end can the relation of the present parable to that of the Great Banquet[2] be clearly seen. It has been shown that the two parables are exceedingly similar, not only in figurative form, but also in their fundamental thought, the second also referring to the relation of Israel to God's kingdom. Both times a festive banquet is the image of the blessedness of God's kingdom; both times the citizens of a city invited as guests are the image of the citizens of the Israelitish theocracy, to whom participation in the blessedness of God's kingdom was promised first. Both times, in contrast with the citizens of the city, the populace of the highways are the image of the heathen world, hitherto without contact with God's kingdom. And both times

[1] Cf. in the parable of the Tares on xiii. 30, 41.   [2] Luke xiv. 16 ff.

the purpose of the representation is to announce to the former their exclusion from the kingdom, and the calling of the heathen in their stead, as the consequence of their disobedience to God's call. But this similarity makes the diversity all the more evident. Certainly the intention is not in Luke's parable to picture the infinite goodness and grace of God, whereas in the present one the standpoint of judgment prevails.[1] For the exclusion of Israel, in punishment of its disobedience, was just as much the all-dominant thought in the former as in the first part of the latter.[2] But the great diversity lies in the concrete historical matter, figuratively represented, corresponding to the different periods in which the one and the other parables were uttered. That of the Great Banquet, uttered amid the period of the public teaching and working of Jesus, was essentially a description of the *then present*. It represented in figure the unanimous resistance, already apparent, of the people of the theocracy to the call to God's kingdom which they had received, exposing its motives (vv. 17–20), in order to show next how God's wrath has already pronounced judgment on the unwilling citizens of the theocracy by calling the publicans and sinners in their place (vv. 21, 22). And it only mentioned the divine decree hereafter to call the heathen as the confirmation of the judgment already pronounced on official Israel by calling the publicans and sinners (ver. 23). How entirely different the present parable! Uttered in the last days of the life of Jesus, after a brief preliminary mention of His work now past and finished (ver. 3), it takes its stand at once in the future, and presents itself as a prophetic description, in broad but very definite lines, of *the future* awaiting Israel. What it predicts in figurative form, line by line, is that God's long-suffering will again send other messengers of His grace to Israel, that Israel will also reject them with murderous violence, and that God, in consequence of this, will annihilate this people, overthrow its commonwealth, and command the heathen to be called in their stead. So entirely different are its contents from the former parable even in its first part. And then, ignoring Israel, it enters with its description upon the new period of calling to God's kingdom, pictures the course of the calling in its indiscriminate universality, and concludes with the prediction of the judicial process that will again sift the called, before they become participants in the blessedness of God's eternal kingdom. Thus,

---

[1] So Lange.   [2] Cf. on Luke xiv. 24.

along with the essential similarity of the figurative form, as well as of the fundamental thought in the first parable and the first part of the second, there is still an almost complete diversity in the matter figuratively represented. There a description of the present, merely concluding with a brief glimpse into the future; here, after a brief preliminary touching on the present, a prophetic description of the entire future of God's kingdom in the course of its earthly development up to the end. This is the result arrived at, directly independent exposition gives each of the two parables its rights. We may leave it to the reader's judgment to decide, whether in this relation of the two parables to each other there is any need to suppose that the second one, less original than the first, arose subsequently from the latter by remodelling, or by welding together portions from other parables,[1] or that both are derived from one common and alone original source.[2]

[1] Cf. Strauss, de Wette, Ewald, *et al.*

THE ESCHATOLOGICAL DISCOURSE UP TO THE ESCHATOLOGICAL PARABLES.

(Matt. xxiv. 1-51.)

THE parable of the Ten Virgins, to which that of the Talents immediately joins on, forms part of the eschatological discourse of Jesus recorded in chaps. xxiv. xxv. of the Gospel of Matthew.

It was probably on the third day of the Passion-week that Jesus visited the temple of Jerusalem for the last time, and then, leaving it for ever with His disciples, took the accustomed road over Olivet to Bethany. He sat down on Olivet to rest. Then, as chap. xxiv. 3 relates, His disciples came to Him with the question: "*When shall this be* (namely, the destruction of the temple, of which Jesus had spoken on leaving the temple, ver. 2), *and what is the sign of Thy coming, and the end of the* (present) *dispensation?*" A twofold question, depending on the assumption that the destruction of the temple predicted will be in connection with the occurrence of the Parousia of Christ and the end of the world. To this Jesus gives the answer in the following discourse. Without touching further on the destruction of the temple, or saying anything about the assumed connection between it and His Parousia,[1] He treats in the discourse only of the When, or of the premonitory tokens of His Parousia and the end of the world. In the first part of the discourse (vv. 4-35) He tells them positively what they ought really to know and ponder respecting the time of the end, or respecting its premonitory signs. This first part consists of four sections, clearly enough marked off from each other. The discourse moves, so to speak, in three concentric circles, drawn closer and closer round the centre,—the End,—the third comprising the last period itself, after which the discourse enters upon the centre, which is the coming of Christ. The first section (vv. 4-8) closes with the words: πάντα δὲ ταῦτα ἀρχὴ

---

[1] Also the words in ver. 15: Ὅταν οὖν ἴδητε τὸ βδέλυγμα τῆς ἐρημώσεως κ.τ.λ., are not a sudden recurrence to the destruction of the temple-structure predicted in ver. 2, but a quite independent reference to Daniel's well-known prophecy respecting the last time (Dan. xi. 31, cf. xii. 1 with Matt. xxiv. 21), which speaks of a future desecration of the temple by setting up the βδέλυγμα τῆς ἐρημώσεως in the Holy Place, which in any case is different from a destruction of the temple-structure.

ὠδίνων, i.e. "*But all this is only the beginning of the travail* (of the End)." It treats of the woes foreannouncing the approach of the end from afar, so to speak, before it is directly under way, adding a warning against premature expectation of the end. The second section (vv. 9–14) comes nearer the End; for it closes with the words: "and then shall the end come." It treats of the aggravated woes actually introducing the coming of the end, and connects therewith an exhortation to stedfast perseverance to the end. Finally, the third section (vv. 15–28), beginning with an allusion to Daniel's prophecy of the last period, treats of this period itself, and passes, in ver. 29, directly to the description of Christ's coming. It foretells the last days of extreme tribulation, and advises to flight in those days. Then the fourth section (vv. 29–35) describes the visible advent of the Son of man following close[1] on this last tribulation, and the gathering of the elect unto Him (vv. 29–31). Hence the exhortation, that they are to regard all these baleful occurrences, which presage the approach of the last period, as the buds of the leaves of the fig-tree announcing the approach of summer, and therefore as welcome signs "that it"—namely, the End which brings to the elect the gathering to the Lord—"is nigh, at the door" (vv. 32, 33). And they are to lay this exhortation to heart all the more as it is certain that, before the contemporary generation[2] has died out, all those woes will occur which are to precede the end[3] (vv. 34, 35).

After Jesus has thus positively informed them what they ought to know and ponder respecting the end and its premonitory signs, with ver. 36 the discourse turns into a negative statement respecting what they cannot know, because it is known to none but the Omniscient: "*But of that day and hour knoweth no one, not even the angels of heaven, but the Father only.*" This main proposition, placed at the head, is then expounded in the second portion of the discourse under different aspects, but always so as to bring out the urgent exhortation to constant readiness for the Lord's coming, the day and hour of which no one knows, and therefore for whose occurrence His disciples must be ever pre-

---

[1] εὐθέως δὲ μετὰ τὴν θλῖψιν τῶν ἡμερῶν ἐκείνων, ver. 29.

[2] ἡ γενεὰ αὕτη can mean nothing else in this connection.

[3] πάντα ταῦτα in ver. 34 can mean nothing different from πάντα ταῦτα in ver. 33, therefore the tokens of the end, not the end itself. An examination of the relation in which prophecy and fulfilment here stand to each other would lead us too far.

pared. Thrice does this exhortation find expression in what follows. The first time, xxiv. 42: γρηγορεῖτε οὖν, ὅτι οὐκ οἴδατε, ποίᾳ ἡμέρᾳ ὁ κύριος ὑμῶν ἔρχεται. The second time, ver. 44: διὰ τοῦτο καὶ ὑμεῖς γίνεσθε ἕτοιμοι, ὅτι ᾗ ὥρᾳ οὐ δοκεῖτε ὁ υἱὸς τοῦ ἀνθρώπου ἔρχεται. And the third time, xxv. 13: γρηγορεῖτε οὖν, ὅτι οὐκ οἴδατε τὴν ἡμέραν οὐδὲ τὴν ὥραν. The first time (ver. 42) the exhortation is based on the exposition in vv. 38–41, according to which the Parousia of Christ, as once the Flood, will burst on a world sleeping in careless security, bringing a crisis to every one so suddenly, that of two companions in labour surprised at their common toil, one will be taken, the other not, according as they are found in a state of readiness or not. How necessary then it is: "*Watch, for ye know not on what day your Lord cometh.*" The second time the like exhortation, only clothed in somewhat different words (ver. 44), is based upon the parabolic saying of the householder, who, had he known the time of the thief's coming, would have watched and prevented his breaking in, and who, because he thought he might neglect to watch because of the uncertainty, rendered it possible for the thief to break in (ver. 43). How little, therefore, ought the uncertainty of the hour of the Parousia to lead to remissness in spiritual watchfulness—how much, on the contrary, is a constant preparation requisite, "*because at an hour when you think not the Son of man cometh.*" And again follows another parabolic utterance, intimating the same in a different manner, vv. 45–51. A servant is pictured, whom his lord had appointed to give the servants their food in due season during the time of his absence. If, on his return, the householder finds the servant engaged in the conscientious discharge of the office entrusted to him, he will set him as a proved servant over all his goods (vv. 46, 47). If, on the other hand, the servant allows the delay of his lord to rock him into security, and begins to abuse his fellow-servants, whom he ought to care for, whilst he himself gives way to excess, the householder will come in an hour unexpected, and inflict on him the severest punishment (vv. 48–51). It is clear that the point of this parabolic utterance, also, is the like exhortation to the disciples, but here with special reference to the conscientious discharge of their duty to their fellow-disciples, the exhortation to constant readiness for the Lord's coming, because the time of His coming is uncertain. But in this passage the exhortation is not expressly repeated. But now begins, joining on immediately to that parabolic utterance, a formal parabolic narrative,—that of the Ten Virgins, xxv. 1–12,—and only at its close, and based upon it, the exhortation is uttered for the third time: "*Watch, therefore, for ye know neither the day nor the hour*," ver. 13. Therefore, in accordance with the position which the parable takes in the line of the eschatological discourse, it can have no other purpose than to give a new and special justification of the exhortation, already several times enjoined and twice uttered, to constant readiness for the Lord's coming because of that uncertainty of the day and hour, which was solemnly testified in the declaration standing at the head of this entire section of the discourse, xxiv. 36.

The Ten Virgins.

(Matt. xxv. 1–13.)

After what has been said there can be no question to what the τότε points, with which the parabolic narrative begins : τότε ὁμοιωθήσεται ἡ βασιλεία τῶν οὐρανῶν δέκα παρθένοις κ.τ.λ. For if it is correct that the parable, just like all the preceding sections,[1] alludes to the solemn declaration of the uncertainty of the day of Christ's coming for the purpose of renewing the exhortation to be ready for it, the τότε can only refer to the same as the τότε in ver. 40, namely, to the unknown day of ver. 36, spoken of uninterruptedly with and without figure. Therefore, in the day and hour of Christ's coming, "the kingdom of heaven shall be made like ten virgins," etc. Ὁμοιωθήσεται cannot here mean "shall be compared," since the comparing is done already by the narrator of the parable, but ὁμοιοῦσθαι is "to become like," as in vi. 8, vii. 26,[2] xiii. 24, xviii. 23, xxii. 2. "*The kingdom of heaven shall become like ten virgins*," i.e., according to Matthew's well-known manner of introducing a parabolic narrative : In the hour of Christ's coming, a development shall take place in the sphere of the kingdom of heaven, resembling the occurrences of the following narrative of ten virgins, whereupon the narrative itself begins as usual with a relative sentence : αἵτινες λαβοῦσαι τὰς λαμπάδας ἑαυτῶν ἐξῆλθον εἰς ἀπάντησιν τοῦ νυμφίου. The choice of the composite relative pronoun αἵτινες = *tales quae*, is

[1] Cf. xxiv. 37–42, 43, 44, 45–51.   [2] There also the future ὁμοιωθήσεται.

not accidental here. What the virgins in question did is told with a view to define more precisely the general description as virgins, that it may be seen what kind of virgins are to be spoken of, namely, such as "*took their lamps and went forth to meet the bridegroom*,"[1] therefore *bride*maids who went to meet the bridegroom in a festive procession with lamps. The situation, into which the following narrative introduces, is in the main clear from these words. An evening marriage-feast is to take place, but the bridegroom is still absent; as soon as he comes, the feast will begin. A procession of bridemaids with lamps is to meet him, in order to receive him in festal style, and then to celebrate the marriage-feast with him. Neither is the place more exactly defined from which the procession starts, nor the house in which, after the festive reception of the bridegroom, the feast itself is to take place. The usual Jewish custom seems to have been for the bridegroom, accompanied by his friends, to go on the wedding-day to the home of the bride, and, after the bride has been there delivered to him by her parents, to lead her, accompanied by her friends and the wedding-guest, to his own or his parent's house, where the marriage-feast was held.[2] But this supposes that bridegroom and bride dwell in one place, or near each other, and the procession of the bridegroom to the house of the bride is then itself part of the festive ceremonial. Here in any case it is so far different as that the procession of bridemaids meets the coming bridegroom. Moreover, the long delay in the bridegroom's coming (ver. 5), and the beginning of the feast in the marriage-house directly on his arrival (ver. 10), do not agree with the customs just described. Plainly the conception here is, that the bridegroom not merely proceeds from one house to another, but comes to the marriage *from abroad*, and when he approaches, the bridemaids meet him to conduct him into the house of the bride, where the feast is celebrated.[3] But, of course, no stress must be laid on the circumstance that the marriage takes place in the house of the *bride*, because if this had borne on the narrator's purpose, he would have mentioned instead of tacitly assuming it. To him the bride remains entirely in the

---

[1] Cf. Gen. xiv. 17: יָצָא לִקְרָאתוֹ.

[2] Cf. Riehm, *Bibl. Handwörterbuch*, art. "Ehe" 5, and Winer, *Handwörterbuch*, art. "Hochzeit."

[3] Cf. Judg. xiv. 10; Gen. xxix. 22; Tob. viii. 20 ff.; in each case the marriage takes place in the house of the bride.

background. His theme is exclusively the bridemaids, whose duty it is to receive the bridegroom, and whose hope is then to be permitted to take part in the feast. Moreover, the question as to the place from which the procession starts, whether the bride's house or some other place, is quite irrelevant. This only is clear, that the starting-point for the ἐξῆλθον εἰς ἀπάντησιν τοῦ νυμφίου can only be the place from which they start *in common*, not, as has been supposed, on account of subsequent imagined difficulties, the bridemaids' own houses, from which they first resort to their common meeting-place.[1] The number of the virgins is *ten*, the number of completeness, inasmuch as in it the units are again combined into a single whole. It is a complete virgin-choir that is to receive the bridegroom and take part in the marriage, so that each individual virgin shares in the duty and the hope as belonging to this complete choir. But nevertheless they bring their *own* lamps to receive the bridegroom. For, according to the best witnesses, the reflexive pronoun ἑαυτῶν must be read here,[2] as also in ver. 7 after λαμπάδας, and also in ver. 4 it is questionable whether ἑαυτῶν[3] ought not to be read after μετὰ τῶν λαμπάδων, whereas in ver. 3, where the Recepta has it after λαμπάδας, the weight of the evidence rather favours αὐτῶν. In any case the reflexive pronoun should be noted. It can only be meant to emphasize that the lamps were not hired articles, for whose putting in order the virgins were not themselves responsible, but the personal property of the virgins, so that they were themselves responsible for the due preparation of the lamps, each one for her own.

When further, in ver. 2, according to the best attested reading it is said: πέντε δὲ ἐξ αὐτῶν ἦσαν μωραὶ καὶ πέντε φρόνιμοι,[4] i.e. "*And five of them were foolish, and five wise*," and it is then recited how the foolish acted in their folly and the wise in their wisdom in the taking of the lamps mentioned in ver. 1, it is at once unmistakeable that the narrative does not proceed to tell what took place *in the road* after the departure mentioned in ver. 1, but that it gives the details of the general statement there, making the preparations for the procession its starting-point. The first information is, that an essential distinction existed among the ten virgins. Half of them were foolish, and

---

[1] Stier *et al.* [2] Tischendorf. [3] Weiss.
[4] In the Recepta the position of μωραὶ ... φρόνιμοι is reversed.

half wise. The foolishness of the first half stands first, because this is the characteristic circumstance forming the occasion of the peculiar and unusual course of things to be related; and the second clause: καὶ πέντε φρόνιμοι, then serves to confirm the contrast in which the foolish stood to the rest. The qualities "foolish" and "wise" are, of course, to be understood in the usual sense. The religious and moral meaning of the Hebrew נָבָל must not here be introduced, in order then to discover in the designation "foolish" the want of virgin modesty,[1] a view that would mix quite alien elements in a figurative story treating of a procession of bridemaids.

After this prefatory remark respecting the difference of character existing among the virgins, the narrative refers to the taking of the lamps mentioned in ver. 1, and relates the folly committed by the foolish in this act of preparing for the procession. Ver. 3 does not, as might appear, give reasons for the distinction made in ver. 2;[2] but conversely on the basis of the distinction made it is related: αἵτινες μωραί, λαβοῦσαι τὰς λαμπάδας ἑαυτῶν[3] οὐκ ἔλαβον μεθ' ἑαυτῶν ἔλαιον, i.e. "*They then* (quippe quæ) *who were foolish, when they took their lamps, took no oil with themselves.*" The folly of this course is placed in a clear light by the antithesis formed by intentionally repeating the same verb: λαβοῦσαι τὰς λαμπάδας ... οὐκ ἔλαβον ἔλαιον. To take a lamp and not to take oil also is folly, and just this it is which the foolish virgins did. How they fell into such folly is shown by the very noteworthy reflexive pronoun μεθ' ἑαυτῶν, i.e. they took not oil *with themselves*. We now see in what sense they thought they could dispense with taking oil. It did not seem to them requisite to have it with themselves. Trusting with foolish thoughtlessness to the fact that they belong to the choir of virgins destined to receive the bridegroom and take part in the marriage, they did not consider that each one of them is herself responsible for her own lamp, and has herself to see to its burning.

It is true, the ordinary exposition would find an altogether different meaning in these words. Although it is simply said, "they took no oil with themselves," almost all expositors explain: They had taken oil enough in their lamps for some time, and had

---

[1] Cremer, *Die eschatologische Rede*.
[2] Hence the origin of the divergent reading αἱ γὰρ μωραί in several codices is easily explained.
[3] Or αὐτῶν, see ver. 1.

only neglected to procure a special reserve beyond this. It is conceded that this view finds no support in ver. 3 at least. It has arisen from a retrospective inference from what is said of the wise in ver. 4. But even there it finds no justifiable basis. For when, in opposition to the conduct of the foolish, the conduct of the wise is described to this effect: αἱ δὲ φρόνιμοι ἔλαβον ἔλαιον ἐν τοῖς ἀγγείοις[1] μετὰ τῶν λαμπάδων αὐτῶν,[2] all that is affirmed is that these, as sensible persons, did what the nature of the case required: "*But the wise took oil in the vessels with their lamps.*" It is the words ἐν τοῖς ἀγγείοις, "in the vessels," that have led exposition astray. Instead of the emphasis being laid on the folly of the foolish, who are placed in the foreground by the narrator himself in ver. 2, and again in ver. 3, and so remain the chief persons to the end, the emphasis has been laid on the wisdom of the wise as persons who, in order to be prepared for every event, took with them a special reserve of oil beside the usual amount, and for this purpose brought quite special vessels. But this is to make the wise, with far too conspicuous wisdom, provide for a case altogether inconceivable in the circumstances of the story. For how could the most far-sighted hit on the thought that they might have occasion to burn their lamps many hours before the bridegroom's arrival, and thus let the oil consume uselessly away? Such a procession, simply prepared to receive one coming from abroad, does not journey at random into the night, but only starts when news of his approach comes. This is the natural course, and is expressly confirmed by the further course of the narrative.[3] In this case, so long as there is no news of the approach of the expected one, the lamps of the procession will not be kindled, to say nothing of the fact that if his arrival is delayed, it would be requisite to let the lamps burn uselessly. Nor is the supposition, that the wise virgins had in view the possibility of such an event, made necessary by the mention of the vessels in ver. 4. On the contrary, the article before ἀγγείοις plainly describes the vessels in question as the particular vessels known to every one where lamps are spoken of, or at least lamps to be carried in the open air are spoken of. Consequently, the vessels cannot be vessels carried only by the wise in an unusual manner from simple precaution; but they are either the vessels for the oil in the lamps themselves, or

---

[1] αὐτῶν after ἀγγείοις, according to far preponderant testimony, is to be deleted.
[2] Or ἑαυτῶν, see ver. 1.   [3] Cf. ver. 6.

vessels usually supplied to lamps carried in the open air, and forming part of the outfit of the lamp-bearers, in order perhaps to be able at any time to replenish the lamps which held but a small amount of oil.[1] Either view suits the words: "they took oil in the vessels with their lamps." For even the mention of the vessels in the lamps themselves would be very well explained as an antithesis to the οὐκ ἔλαβον μεθ' ἑαυτῶν in ver. 3. The oil which the foolish did not think it necessary to have *with themselves*, the wise—so it would be said emphatically—have already inside the vessels with their lamps. But whatever the nature of the lamps, in any case the wise sensibly considered that it was their business to see to their lamps burning on the bridegroom's arrival, and accordingly made provision to be for their part ready every moment to receive him with lamps burning.

Thus in vv. 2-4 the λαβοῦσαι τὰς λαμπάδας ἑαυτῶν of ver. 1 was described in detail, and therefore the preparations of the virgins for setting out. It is accordingly to be expected that on the description of the preparations will follow the more detailed description of the setting out itself also mentioned in ver. 1. Yet the setting out does not ensue at once, but a delay intervenes, as told in ver. 5, which gives its peculiar shape to the history of the setting out. Thus ver. 5 simply prepares for the more detailed description of the setting out, just as ver. 2 prepared for the more detailed description of the preparations. In ver. 5 it is said: χρονίζοντος δὲ τοῦ νυμφίου ἐνύσταξαν πᾶσαι καὶ ἐκάθευδον, i.e. "*Now, while the bridegroom tarried, they all slumbered and slept.*" Thus, the virgins await tidings of the bridegroom's approach, in order then to kindle their lamps, arrange themselves in festal procession, and go forth to meet him. But they wait in vain. The time runs away without sound of the bridegroom's coming. Then gently and gradually sleep fell on the waiters; one after another, and at last all, slumbered and slept. How forced, on the other hand, the ordinary view, which would join the statement of ver. 5 again suddenly to ver. 1,

[1] Nothing certain is known respecting the nature of the lamps. Lightfoot, *Hor. Heb.*, quotes on the passage: "A Rabbi Salomone hæc etiam adducuntur: mos est in terra Ismælitica, ut sponsam ducant a domo patris sui in domum sponsi, ante introductionem in thalamum, ferantque ante eam circiter *decem baculos ligneos, in uniuscujusque summitate vasculum instar scutellæ habentes, in quo est segmentum panni cum oleo et pice.*" But nothing definite can be learnt from this in reference to the present parable, because only Ismælitish, not Jewish customs are here in question.

instead of to vv. 3, 4, and thus give to the statements in vv. 2–4, so important for the whole course of the narrative, the position of a mere explanatory parenthesis! And how confused and incongruous the situation emerging, directly a serious attempt is made to picture to oneself the incidents of ver. 5 as taking place on the road after the setting out has taken place! The virgins are supposed to have gone forth into the night at random to meet the bridegroom without having heard of his coming, and then not to have continued their journey till they actually met him, but to have stopped somewhere,—why, but because the journey was too long for them,—and to have preferred to shelter in a house by the way,[1] of which certainly some mention should have been made, or to have sat down to rest on the road outside in some ditch,[2] certainly a strange notion in the case of bridemaids in wedding attire. And there in some house or ditch they are supposed to have slept, and during their sleep their lamps burnt without interruption. But how can any one sleep with a burning lamp in the hand, which yet must have been the case with all? And if this were done, the lamps would not continue burning, but would fall from the sleeper's hand and go out.

To this is to be added, finally, that now in ver. 6 the summons is first really heard to the setting out supposed to have taken place long before: μέσης δὲ νυκτὸς κραυγὴ γέγονεν, Ἰδοὺ ὁ νυμφίος, ἐξέρχεσθε εἰς ἀπάντησιν.[3] Here, therefore, the more detailed description has again arrived at the general statement of ver. 1: ἐξῆλθον εἰς ἀπάντησιν τοῦ νυμφίου. For it is hard to believe that literally the same words denote a second different departure from the one there, as is supposed on the other view of the course of the narrative. "And at midnight a shout arouse, Lo, the bridegroom; go out to the meeting." It is the announcement of the bridegroom, for which they have long waited in vain, only that it is now heard in a way such as they had not conceived. For it does not come to those eagerly awaiting it as a timely notification of his gradual approach from afar, but as a sudden excited *shout*, loud and piercing, "Lo, the bridegroom;" it precedes the bridegroom coming immediately behind. Demanding instant departure, it falls with terror on those who, lying *in midnight sleep*, are

---

[1] Meyer, Weiss, *et al.*   [2] De Wette, Nebe, *et al.*
[3] The ἔρχεται after νυμφίος in the Recepta, and also the αὐτοῦ after ἀπάντησιν, are to be expunged on weighty testimony as glossarial additions to fill up the excited brevity of the summons.

now least expecting him. Now it must needs appear who of the virgins are prepared to receive the bridegroom, and who not. For it is necessary without delay to kindle the lamps, in order to meet him on his unexpected coming. Hence the narrative proceeds, ver. 7 : τότε ἠγέρθησαν πᾶσαι αἱ παρθένοι ἐκεῖναι καὶ ἐκόσμησαν τὰς λαμπάδας ἑαυτῶν, i.e. "Then all those virgins arose, and trimmed their lamps" (every one her own, ἑαυτῶν, cf. ver. 1). Κοσμεῖν means to arrange, set in order, e.g. an army for battle,[1] a table for eating,[2] a lamp, therefore, for burning. Thus the κοσμεῖν of the lamps here is to be understood in this obvious sense of the trimming necessary for the lamps to burn, and includes the kindling, whereas all the expositors who represent the lamps as burning long before are compelled to refer it with far less aptness to some trimming of the burning lamps. It is an exciting situation with correspondent hasty action. Awakened suddenly from midnight sleep, all the virgins hasten to do what will brook no delay in face of the shout: "Lo, the bridegroom," —they kindle each one their lamps. But then the folly of not taking oil with themselves recoils on the foolish. For when they, starting from deep sleep, hastily kindle their lamps, these at once go out, after the manner of a lamp not supplied with new oil for new use, which shows a flame for a moment, but only to expire again forthwith. In their trouble they then try whether it is not possible even yet to borrow the oil, which they have not themselves, from the rest. They turn with their prayer for help to their companions, to whom the sudden appearance of the bridegroom at an unexpected hour causes no perplexity, because they have oil in the vessels (ver. 4) for their lamps, ver. 8 : αἱ δὲ μωραὶ ταῖς φρονίμοις εἶπαν, Δότε ἡμῖν ἐκ τοῦ ἐλαίου ὑμῶν, ὅτι αἱ λαμπάδες ἡμῶν σβέννυνται, i.e. "And the foolish said to the wise, Give us of your oil, for our lamps are going out." That the last statement does not prove that the lamps were burning from the first, and continued so during the sleep,[3] is clear from what has been already said on ver. 7 respecting ἐκόσμησαν. The word σβέννυνται denotes here, not the final extinction of a lamp after burning long, but—what it may just as well signify—the quick going out again of a lamp just kindled, because not supplied with fresh oil. But it is an utterly impracticable prayer which the foolish address to their companions. This is stated in the answer of the latter, ver. 9 : "But the wise answered, saying, Μή ποτε

[1] So often in Homer.   [2] Wisd. xxix. 26 et al.   [3] Weiss.

οὐκ ἀρκέσῃ ἡμῖν καὶ ὑμῖν, i.e. (imitating the elliptical phraseology, which makes the sentence depend on the supposed apprehension of the speaker[1]), "that it be not insufficient (literally, that it may not be not sufficient) for us and you." But this reading of the Recepta is probably a mere simplification of the other just as well attested one: Μήποτε, οὐ μὴ ἀρκέσῃ κ.τ.λ. In this case the μήποτε (scil. τοῦτο γινέσθω) stands first and alone in a deprecating sense, and there follows as an independent sentence the strengthening double negation οὐ μή, with the conjunctive aorist, which in such cases is scarcely distinguishable from the indicative future,[2] therefore: "*Never shall this be done, by no means will it suffice for us and you.*" As regards the meaning also the latter reading is preferable, because it excludes the possibility of the foolish being able to borrow oil from the wise at the decisive moment with still greater emphasis than the former, a feature plainly more in keeping with the purpose of the narrative. Certainly this unconditional refusal would appear strange and motiveless in the circumstances of the narrative, if the view were right which makes the wise bring with them a special reserve of oil. For, after the lamps themselves had been able to burn a long time, such a reserve must have sufficed also for their companions in these last decisive moments. On the other hand, the refusal has motive enough if their wisdom only consisted in their taking with them what each one needed for herself in receiving the bridegroom. Thus the view we took on this point is confirmed here.

But to this refusal the wise add the counsel: πορεύεσθε μᾶλλον πρὸς τοὺς πωλοῦντας καὶ ἀγοράσετε ἑαυταῖς. For this is certainly no mockery, as the ancients called it,[3] but well-meant counsel. Nor can the counsel, from the speaker's standpoint, be even called perverse. In the difficulty in which the foolish found themselves nothing was left but the attempt to repair their former neglect, and do what the wise had done in time, namely, provide *themselves* with the oil necessary to their lamps burning. However improbable it seems that they will now succeed, still it was the only thing the wise could say to them: "*Go rather to them that sell, and buy for yourselves.*" Plainly the emphasis rests on the last word, "for yourselves," and thus on the last clause, to which the former is only an introduction. The antithesis introduced by "rather" is not: instead of turning to *us*, go rather to

---

[1] Winer, *Gram.* p. 632. [2] Cf. xxiv. 2, and Winer, p. 634. [3] Augustine, Luther.

the *sellers*, but: instead of trying to fill your lamps with *borrowed* oil, which is out of the question, go rather where it is sold, and *buy for yourselves*, that you may fill your lamps with your own oil. The introductory prefixing of the first clause, and the mention of the sellers, might be dispensed with, unless it were meant to intimate to the foolish virgins the perilous circumstance, that the essentially necessary buying for themselves could not be done in the moment of need on the spot, but necessitated a going to those who sell.

The participial clause: ἀπερχομένων δὲ αὐτῶν ἀγοράσαι, in ver. 10, informs us that the foolish virgins do as the wise advised. Instead of going direct to meet the bridegroom, they first go away to buy, in the hope of being back in time to receive him with lamps burning. With this the statement made in ver. 1 of all the ten virgins without distinction: ἐξῆλθον εἰς ἀπάντησιν τοῦ νυμφίου, is perfectly consistent. Only in its more precise explanation by the antithesis between the foolish and wise which governs the entire story, it has gained this special form, that, when at the summons, "Go forth to the meeting," all ten set out to receive the bridegroom, only the latter were in a position to go to meet him directly, whereas the former were compelled to take a bypath, exposing them to the danger of coming too late. And such was the fact. This is told in ver. 10: ἀπερχομένων δὲ αὐτῶν ἀγοράσαι ἦλθεν ὁ νυμφίος, καὶ αἱ ἕτοιμοι εἰσῆλθον μετ᾽ αὐτοῦ εἰς τοὺς γάμους, καὶ ἐκλείσθη ἡ θύρα, i.e. "*And while they were going away*[1] *to buy*," therefore while the *five foolish* were absent,[2] the whole series of decisive events took place. First, "*the bridegroom came*," next: "*and they that were ready*[3] *went in with him to the marriage festivities*,"[4] which can only be represented as something following without delay on the bridegroom's arrival during the absence of the foolish, in case the festivities are regarded as beginning *in the house of the bride* directly on the bridegroom's arrival. Moreover, the ἦλθεν ὁ νυμφίος is continued in the εἰσῆλθον μετ᾽ αὐτοῦ with such evident directness, that it is impossible to interpose a fetching of the bride and then a return of the entire procession.[5] And with just as little delay

---

[1] ἀπερχομένων, part. pres.
[2] In opposition to Stier, who finds a "gentle, very concealed" possibility left open that one or other returned in time.
[3] Ready with lamps burning to receive him.
[4] Respecting the plural εἰς τοὺς γάμους, cf. on xxii. 1.   [5] Cf. on ver. 1.

follows the third event: "*and the door* (of the festive hall) *was shut*," not merely to shut out from participation in the festive joy all improper persons in general, but in particular the bridemaids who were not ready. So the latter, on returning from their journey, find the bridegroom already within, their companions with him, and the door shut. And they are forced to learn that the door was shut expressly against them, when they pray for admission, ver. 11: ὕστερον δὲ ἔρχονται καὶ αἱ λοιπαὶ παρθένοι λέγουσαι, Κύριε, Κύριε, ἄνοιξον ἡμῖν. The present ἔρχονται vividly portrays the perilous moment of undeceiving: "*Afterwards come also the other virgins*," seeking admission, to the door through which their companions had previously entered with the bridegroom, but which was closed against them, and repeating the κύριε with anxious entreaty, they cry: "*Lord, Lord, open to us.*" It has been asked whether they obtained oil or not. But instead of seeking an answer to this question, we should rather note that the narrative passes it by in silence. The only importance of the oil in the narrative was to make the lamps of the virgins burn in order to their receiving the bridegroom. When it can no longer serve this purpose it no longer comes into view. Whether they obtained it or not, the attempt to repair the neglect of preparing to receive the bridegroom fails, because his rapid arrival left them no time to do so. Hence, too, the unconditional refusal which their prayer found with the bridegroom, ver. 12: "*But he answered, and said:*" Ἀμὴν λέγω ὑμῖν, οὐκ οἶδα ὑμᾶς. The bridegroom introduces the refusal with the assurance: "*Verily I say to you.*" To make the prefixing of this asseveration explicable, we need not suppose that it was interpolated by the evangelist, who views the words "I know you not" as the words of the returning Messiah,[1] and therefore confounds the figure with the thing prefigured; but the bridegroom speaks so emphatically because he knows what the refusal signifies to those craving admission, namely, their irrevocable exclusion from participation in the festive joy, to which as bridemaids they seem to have a right, and on which they reckoned with certainty so long. With this the wording of the refusal is not inconsistent. For it does not mean: "I know nothing of you," but, according to the well-known use of εἰδέναι with the accusative of the person: "*I know you not*," namely, as bridemaids and sharers in the feast, a statement which does not preclude his knowing well who they are, and what con-

[1] Weiss.

dition they are in. How could the reason of five bridemaids only, instead of ten, receiving him be unknown to the bridegroom? And had he not really known what the condition was of those craving admission, how could he have refused them so curtly, without asking the reason and right of their wish? In this case not merely the emphatic introduction, "Verily I say to you," but also the brief refusal itself, would be unintelligible. But the meaning of the bridegroom's answer, so weighty in its brevity, is rather this: Verily I say to you, although you belonged to the choir of bridemaids, you are unknown and strangers to me, because in the decisive hour you were not ready as bridemaids to receive me. And now the narrative is at an end. Of the hope of a subsequent admission at a later term,[1] the figurative story contains no trace.

When, then, the word οὖν joins to the narrative the exhortation: γρηγορεῖτε οὖν, ὅτι οὐκ οἴδατε τὴν ἡμέραν οὐδὲ τὴν ὥραν, we know already from the examination of the strain of the discourse to which the parable belongs, that in these words we have before us the third repetition of an exhortation, the justification and explanation of which were the exclusive object of the Lord's discourse from xxiv. 36 on. But if this utterance is only the repetition of an otherwise certain dictum, it cannot be meant here to express the special purpose of this parable in distinction from the preceding parabolic sayings; but it only affirms that the special teaching of this parable is again comprehended under the general exhortation: "Watch, therefore, for ye know not the day nor the hour" (scil. of the Son of man's coming).[2] We have accordingly to obtain the special teaching of the present parable by an independent review of the course and contents of the narrative, with the proviso that the teaching must be subordinate to the general exhortation to watchfulness because of the uncertainty of the time of Christ's coming, as a special form of the exhortation.

In thus turning back to the figurative story to ascertain its moral, we shall no longer be tempted, after what has been said, to recur, on account of the exhortation to *watchfulness* (γρηγορεῖτε), annexed to the parable, to the *sleeping* mentioned in the parable as the essential and critical element, as though that figurative expression in the exhortation must necessarily correspond to this figurative trait in the narrative. The metaphorical meaning of

[1] Stier.   [2] xxiv. 42, 44.

unbroken, persistent attentiveness, therefore of constant readiness for everything that may come, inheres so permanently and naturally in the γρηγορεῖν of Biblical Greek,[1] that the use of the word in this sense by no means implies a special reference in the speaker's mind to the antithesis of waking and sleeping in the sensuous life. Moreover, the γρηγορεῖτε here is merely the resumption of the γρηγορεῖτε in xxiv. 42, where also it stood independently without resting on a corresponding figurative trait in the previous exposition, vv. 37-41; whereas in ver. 44, just where the preceding parabolic saying of the sleeping householder and the thief really suggested the choice of the figurative expression, it was replaced by the synonymous γίνεσθε ἕτοιμοι. Accordingly, to ascertain the purpose of the narrative, we shall simply go back to its general essential purport, without being diverted in estimating the essential point by the figurative form of the exhortation. Again, it is at once apparent that in fact the figurative trait of the sleeping of the virgins is but a relatively unimportant circumstance in the construction of the whole, having no immediate connection with the hortatory purpose of the narrative. The chief element in the narrative, upon which alone its hortatory purpose can be based, was plainly the foolish conduct of the one-half of the virgins, having for its consequence their exclusion from the marriage. But this foolish conduct so little consisted in their sleeping, that this was not presented as a characteristic of their conduct, but only as an event happening alike to all the virgins, foolish and wise. Their folly rather lay simply in neglecting their personal preparation to receive the bridegroom. The first fundamental part (vv. 1-4) said, that in a marriage-procession of ten virgins five neglected to provide themselves with the oil necessary for their lamps; whereupon the second part (vv. 5-12) shows how perilous this neglect became to them through the manner of the bridegroom's coming, which, ensuing in an unexpected moment, suddenly revealed their want of preparation without leaving them time to repair it, so that they were excluded from the marriage. And if we are warranted by the strain of the discourse, in which the parable stands, in assuming beforehand as beyond doubt that the waiting of the Church for the coming of its Lord to set up His kingdom corresponds to the waiting of the virgin-choir for the bridegroom's coming to the marriage, then the moral of the parable can only

[1] Cf. Acts xx. 31; 1 Cor. xvi. 13; Col. iv. 2; 1 Pet. v. 8.

be the exhortation, *that no one is to suppose, because he belongs to the Church of Christ, which waits for the Lord and His coming, that he can neglect personal preparation for His Parousia, seeing that on the speedy coming of the Lord in the moment least expected, this want of self-preparation will be revealed, and because then incapable of remedy, will irretrievably exclude from the blessedness of God's kingdom.* The order of the parable is, that the first part (vv. 1–4) exhibits the character of this neglect in the conduct of the foolish virgins, whilst the second (vv. 5–12) sets forth its perilous, irretrievable consequences at the coming of the Son of man by the fate of the virgins at the coming of the bridegroom. Directly one bears in mind that the γρηγορεῖτε, ver. 13, as in xxiv. 42, is nothing but a synonym of the γίνεσθε ἕτοιμοι lying between in xxiv. 44, it is self-evident how aptly this special exhortation of the parable subordinates itself to the general one in ver. 13 : γρηγορεῖτε οὖν, ὅτι οὐκ οἴδατε τὴν ἡμέραν οὐδὲ τὴν ὥραν, for which, indeed, the parable is meant to assign new and special reasons.

Returning, then, to the beginning of the parable, in order on the basis now gained to carry out the interpretation in detail, we see in ver. 1 the general figurative setting, within which the particular occurrences will move, described as a procession of lamp-bearing bridemaids who go forth to meet the bridegroom coming to the marriage. Here, therefore, as in the parable of the Royal Marriage-Feast,[1] a marriage-feast serves figuratively to represent the festive joy of God's kingdom. Moreover, the limits within which the comparison with a marriage-feast keeps are the same in the present parable as those exhibited by us in interpreting the parable of chap. xxii. The union of the bridegroom with the bride is not drawn into the comparison, the bride here again remaining quite in the background. Only the marriage-joy, as the highest, all-satisfying joy, which the guests share with the bridegroom, and the bridegroom with them, becomes the image of the eternal, all-satisfying joy of God's future kingdom, which the members will share with Christ, and Christ with them.[2] But when to this general idea of association in a marriage-feast is added the more definite one of the choir of bridemaids, complete in number, and awaiting the coming of the bridegroom with joyous hope, in order when he comes to go forth to meet him with shining lamps, and enter in with him to the marriage-joy,

[1] xxii. 1 ff.   [2] Cf. p. 366.

what can be symbolized but the Church of the disciples of Jesus, anticipating the coming of its Lord with joyous hope, in order when He comes to carry before Him the light whose brightness will attest it in His eyes as His Church, *i.e.* in order in the hour of His coming to present itself before Him in the glory of its moral purity and holiness? When already in the general statement in ver. 1 the lamps are seen to be the characteristic feature in the marriage-procession, and accordingly the only essential element in the virgin-choir going to receive the bridegroom is that it shine before him with light of festal lamps,—so much so, that the preparation for the procession bears exclusively on this point, and the participation of the individuals in the marriage depends exclusively on their letting their lamps shine before the bridegroom,—the interpretation must above all ask, what condition, required of the Church in receiving the coming Messiah, is meant to be symbolized by this shining of festal lamps before the bridegroom? The first inquiry in the interpretation ought not, as is usually done, to be directed to the oil as the supposed central idea in the narrative, whereas in truth everything said of the oil simply bears on the preparation for fulfilling that condition. But directly the question is thus correctly put, the correct answer follows of itself. The march of the virgins to meet the bridegroom with shining lamps can only be a figurative expression for the solemn self-presentation of the Church before its returning Lord in the glory of the moral purity and holiness that is its characteristic. It is the same thought, only in figurative dress, that is often expressed elsewhere in the New Testament.[1] On the manner in which the self-presentation of the Church in its moral state is pictured as the letting its light shine, chap. v. 16 especially may be consulted. As it is there required of the disciples, that what they are and have morally they are to let shine clearly before men (λαμψάτω τὸ φῶς ὑμῶν), like a light set on the candlestick (ἐπὶ τὴν λυχνίαν, ver. 15), so that men may see it and recognise God's work in them as God's children; so the thought here is, that the Church of Jesus is to let the moral purity and holiness characteristic of it, like a festal light borne in lamps, shine before its Lord in the hour of His coming, that by this light issuing from it He may recognise it as His. But the distinction is self-evident, that the letting its light shine,

---

[1] 1 Cor. i. 8; Eph. v. 27; Phil. i. 10; Col. i. 22; 1 Thess. iii. 13, v. 23; 2 Pet. iii. 12, 14.

as there required of the disciples, is limited to what is cognizable by men, and therefore to manifestation in "good works" (ὅπως ἴδωσιν ὑμῶν τὰ καλὰ ἔργα), whereas here it is a figurative expression for their solemn self-presentation before the Lord in the completeness of their moral being, and therefore in their entire character and walk sanctified by faith in Him, and hallowed by love to Him. If thus the interpretation has to lay the entire stress on the festal shining of the lamps with which the bridemaids are to receive the bridegroom, and if the idea of purity of heart and life has rightly found its place in the interpretation of this central trait, no room is left for a reference of the chastity in the bridemaids to a corresponding inner purity from polluting contact with sin and the world.[1] Nor does the narrative itself permit an independent figurative significance to be given to the designation "virgins" here, since it is only introduced in connection with the notion of a marriage-feast. The ten lamp-bearers nowhere come into notice in the narrative as virgins in opposition to those who are not such, but always simply as *the definite bridemaids,* therefore in distinction from other virgins not having this character.

So far we have only interpreted the general figurative setting of the narrative first given in ver. 1. On this general background the special purport of the parable must now rise to view, just like the special course of the narrative from the general notion of a festal procession of bridemaids to receive the bridegroom.

The first part of the narrative tells of a distinction of foolish and wise among the individual virgins, making a breach in the complete number ten, and showing itself in the different conduct of the one class and the other in preparing for the festal procession. If the whole body of bridemaids, complete in number, was the image of the Church of Jesus waiting for the coming of its Lord and His kingdom, the emphasizing of the above distinction contains a warning allusion to the fact that a common belonging to the Church looking for Christ's Parousia, and therefore a common waiting and hoping for the day of the Lord, does not exclude a perilous distinction of folly and wisdom among individual disciples as regards the manner in which the one class and the other make ready for the Lord's coming. When the foolish virgins take indeed their lamps in hand, and thus set themselves in company with the rest to receive the bridegroom,

[1] Cremer, Lange, Nebe, *et al.*

but in thoughtless reliance on their belonging to the number of bridemaids, and in forgetfulness of their personal responsibility for their own lamps, neglect to provide themselves with the oil that can alone make their lamps shine before the bridegroom, this is plainly meant to describe in figure similar conduct to which false security may lead individual members of Christ's Church. And in keeping with the figure this conduct can only consist in this, that in false reliance on his belonging to Christ's Church, and on the promise given to it of partaking in God's glorious kingdom of the future, the individual neglects earnest care for personal preparation for the Lord's coming; or, giving all the elements in the figure their full weight, that the individual fancies himself ready for the Lord's coming because he belongs to the community of believers in Christ, and with it looks for the Lord's coming and sets himself to receive Him, whilst in forgetfulness of his personal responsibility for his own self-presentation before the Lord he neglects to procure as a personal possession the moral character, in whose pure glory he is to appear before the coming Lord and show himself His disciple. So true wisdom demands, as the example of the wise virgins put in contrast expressly shows. As they take oil within the vessels with their lamps, so that each one carries it with her, so every one who would wisely prepare himself for the Lord's coming must take care that he has with him as an inner possession what will enable him to stand before the coming Lord as a member of His Church. In the parable the oil is related to the festal light, which is to shine before the bridegroom, simply as the lighting material which any one carries with him to the radiance which by its means he makes to stream from him at a given moment, or, without figure, as the moral capital, which one carries in him, is related to the presentation of himself in this moral state before the coming Lord. We can now dispense with all further inquiry, what the oil is, what the lamps, and what the vessels, whether the oil is the Holy Spirit,[1] and the lamps the human heart, the vessels the body, soul, and spirit,[2] or lamps and vessels together the means of grace,[3] or, which at least approaches in substance the correct view, the oil faith, and the lamps outward Christianity.[4] The oil cannot here signify the Holy Spirit of God, as has been supposed with inconsiderate transference of the Old-

---

[1] Olshausen, de Valenti, Stier, Lange, Cremer, Thiersch, Keil.
[2] Stier.   [3] De Valenti.   [4] Lisco.

Testament symbol of the anointing oil, because in the parable the oil does not appear as a gift which one receives, but as a possession which one procures for himself. And directly the single ideas, "oil, lamps, vessels," are separated from the context in which they stand, and interpreted each one by itself, incongruities are the result. The oil, and lamps, and vessels are not opposed to each other; but within the taking of the lamps common to all, which is the formal setting of oneself to receive the coming Lord, is found the contrast, that the one class also take to themselves oil in their vessels, and the other class do not, which contrast can only be interpreted in the way indicated. The other divergence in our interpretation—making the want of self-preparation generally the object of rebuke, not the want of perseverance in readiness,[1] according to the usual interpretation, —needs no special justification, resting as it does on our divergent interpretation of the narrative. As little as the meaning there could be, that even the foolish virgins had taken oil enough to make their lamps burn without interruption the whole time of waiting, but not as much as the wise with their supposed extraordinary reserve, so little can the parable be meant merely to reprove want of perseverance in readiness. Moreover, this interpretation will always be in collision, hard to avoid, with the sleeping of the wise virgins in ver. 5. For although it will soon appear that this feature is not used to describe the *conduct* of the disciples, but is to be applied in the interpretation in another way, still it would be in too obvious contrast with the purpose of the parable, if the latter meant by the example of *slumbering* wise virgins to teach *infatigabilis* constantia.[2]

The second part of the narrative begins with ver. 5, not with ver. 6, and is meant to show how perilous the want of self-preparation will prove on the day of Christ's coming. The perilous effect of this want, because irreparable, is due to the suddenness of the Lord's coming in a moment least expected, and this suddenness is first figuratively described in the unexpected coming of the bridegroom. But in the figurative story, which exhibits a choir of bridemaids looking out with joyous eagerness for the bridegroom's coming, such unexpectedness is only possible by the bridemaids gradually passing from their first state of watching and waiting into the opposite state of sleeping through the length of the period of waiting, and in this new state ceasing

[1] Calvin, Meyer, Weiss.   [2] Calvin.

to expect his coming for the present. When, therefore, ver. 5 says that in consequence of the bridegroom's delay the virgins all slumbered and slept, this state gives the necessary condition of their being surprised by his coming. The statement, therefore, does not belong to what precedes, where the manner of the preparation of the virgins for the bridegroom's coming is treated of, but altogether to the sequel, which describes the manner of this coming itself. And in this case the meaning of this statement will not be, speaking under quite another figure, to add something respecting the manner of preparing for the Lord's coming, and then to predict a general failing of all believers in this respect,—which is yet strangely left without reproof, and has no ill consequences for the wise,—but it is only meant to show how unexpectedly the announcement of the Lord's coming will at last fall even on His disciples. Exactly the same relation is found here as in the figurative circumstances of the narrative. That believers look with joyous eagerness for their Lord's coming to set up His kingdom, and expect every moment the events announcing the hour,—this is the natural state at first. Therefore the announcement can only fall on them unexpectedly on the supposition that in consequence of long delay they have naturally become accustomed to this delay, and eager expectation from one moment to another has given place to the opposite state in which they cease to expect the coming of their Lord at present. But this is something happening to all without distinction, just as naturally as sleep gradually falls on the eyes of all the virgins in the long tarrying of the bridegroom, and has nothing to do with the absence or presence of the inner readiness of the individual every moment to stand before the Lord. The two things are as certainly different as it is a very different thing, whether anything finds me unprepared, or merely comes to me unexpectedly. It is true, sleep may serve as a figure of the one just as well as of the other, according to the context. But here it plainly expresses the state in which one does not look for an event at present, the state of unpreparedness having already found its representation under another figure. Accordingly vv. 5 and 6 are to be interpreted thus: Like as the bridegroom's coming was only announced when the virgins were sleeping in consequence of his long tarrying, and no longer expected his coming at present, and just at midnight, when they lay in the deepest sleep, and least looked for him, so with like unexpectedness will the hour of Christ's coming burst, when His Church has become accustomed to His long delay, and just in the moment when it least of all anticipates His coming. And, on the other hand, as the hour of His advent bursts unexpectedly, so will His coming itself be accomplished just as rapidly. As the shout: "Lo, the bridegroom," going immediately before him, announces him as already come, and the cry: "Go forth to meet him," requires the instant departure of the virgins to receive him, so in the hour of the Parousia the announcement of the Lord's coming will be such that He Himself will come immediately behind it, and every one will be required without delay to appear before the Son of man as he is. Thus each several element in the description serves in its place to paint the perilous manner of Christ's coming to the unprepared,—on one hand the unexpectedness of its occurrence, and on the other the rapidity, admitting no respite, with which it is accomplished. But there is no intention here to predict definite facts and events occurring at Christ's Parousia, as *e.g.* by the midnight the spiritual darkness that will then prevail upon earth,[1] whereas the notion of darkness is a self-evident condition in the story of a lamp-procession, or by the cry: "Lo, the bridegroom," some definite announcement of Christ's coming distinct from other signs and events proclaiming the hour of His advent, such as different expositors suppose according to their taste, the trumpet of the angels,[2] or a watchman-cry of human messengers,[3] or *physical* signs in heaven and on earth,[4]—all with equally little support in the text, and only practicable in applying and expounding the thought of the parable.

If the Lord comes so unexpectedly on the one hand and so rapidly on the other as was pictured in vv. 5 and 6, then on the one hand to the unprepared the folly and self-deception of their carelessness must be just as suddenly revealed to them when they are called on by the Lord's unexpected coming to appear before Him, and on the other this knowledge will come to them too late, because His rapid coming will preclude the possibility of repairing the neglect in the hour of the Parousia itself. These are the two things taught in the conclusion of the parable, first in vv. 8 and 9, and again in vv. 10–12. When in vv. 8 and 9 we read of a prayer which the foolish addressed to the wise, and of a refusal which the latter returned, this conversation cannot

[1] Nebe.   [2] So several of the ancients.   [3] Olshausen, Stier.   [4] Nebe.

be meant to predict a like transaction really taking place in the hour of Christ's advent between the unprepared and the prepared, just as little as the other conversation between the foolish virgins and the bridegroom himself is meant to predict a similar dialogue taking place after the Lord's advent and the final crisis between those excluded from God's kingdom and the Lord Himself. These conversations stand on the same footing as those found before at the close of other parables.[1] The Biblical dialogue is simply the vivid pictorial form in which the author of the parable expresses within its figurative circumstances what He desires to teach His hearers. And here especially, where the dialogue is composed of prayer and refusal, the refusal of what the foolish virgins ask teaches the hopelessness of a possibility corresponding to the object of request and refusal, a possibility on which a disciple without self-preparation perhaps thought he might reckon in the hour of Christ's advent. Just as the foolish virgins received in answer to their prayer for oil an unconditional refusal, so they who are found without the requisite qualifications for appearing before the Lord at the Parousia will learn that there is no possibility of supplying or concealing their want by the help of their better prepared fellow-disciples. As they have hitherto trusted to their belonging to the community of believers to stand them in stead without personal preparation, so they must now really stand before the Lord. And the answer of the wise not merely says that this possibility is excluded, but also why. For when they not merely decline the request of the foolish in general terms, but also state the reason: "it will by no means suffice for us and you," thus intimating that they have no more than each one needs for herself, it is taught that in the hour of Christ's coming no one will be able to answer for others, because no one will be or have more in respect of his inner state than just what he needs in order himself to be able to stand before the Lord. That, in addition, no moral possession is communicable in the sense that one might give something of his own to another, is a side of the question which could not be brought forward in a parable, where an outward must serve as an image of an inward possession, without injury to the image in the aspect in which it is used. Therefore, when the hour of Christ's coming unexpectedly breaks, there will be a sudden end to the self-deception of the careless, as if belonging to the Church of waiting believers apart from

[1] Cf. the Lost Son, the Rich Man, the Labourers in the Vineyard.

personal preparation could enable to stand before the Lord or qualify for participation in His kingdom; and, like the foolish virgins, the careless will learn with terror, what hitherto they have concealed from themselves, that there is no other way than the one figuratively expressed in the counsel of the wise: "Go to them that sell, and buy *for yourselves;*" therefore without figure the way of self-preparation, by obtaining that state of heart and life whose pure lustre enables to stand before the Lord. Our not attempting any special interpretation of the sellers—either the doctrines of the word,[1] which would still have to be sought within the Church, and therefore among the wise virgins themselves; or Holy Scripture, so that the sellers would be its human authors,[2] which is still more forced—needs no justification, after the exposition of the text has shown that the counsel of the wise really does not point to the assistance of some other definite persons, but, on the contrary, remits to the way of *self*-acquisition, which certainly, as the words "Go to them," etc., affirm, must first really be traversed and re-traversed.

And just in this lies the finally decisive element, that the knowledge of the unconditional necessity of this way of self-preparation forced itself on him who had hitherto closed his eyes to it, and forced itself on him in the hour of Christ's coming, when it came too late. For such an one there will be no possibility of repairing previous neglect, when for the first time he would tread this path of self-preparation. That this second possibility, which a foolish man thought always open in extremity, is in truth absolutely excluded,—this is what is taught by the final incidents of the narrative and the conversation between the foolish virgins and the bridegroom. Just as little as this final conversation is meant to foretell a like transaction between the Lord and the unprepared disciples, can the events to which it is joined—the going away of the foolish, the entrance of the bridegroom in their absence, and their return after the door is shut—be meant to foretell a series of like events on the day of the Lord, such as that then the unprepared will really take the way of self-preparation, that Christ will appear before they have attained their end, and they will seek admission to God's kingdom, but will find it closed against them. The series of events is simply intended to picture to the hearers of the

[1] So many.   [2] Olshausen.

parable with dramatic vividness how all possibility of obtaining the neglected self-preparation will be absolutely excluded in the hour of Christ's coming, because the rapidity with which His coming will be accomplished will leave no time for it, while the crisis entering with His appearance is the final one, whose issues are unchangeable. The former is pictured in the rapid entrance of the bridegroom, before the virgins gone to buy oil have returned, and the latter in their request afterwards for a reopening of the closed door, and its refusal. If, therefore, it is a truth known from other sources, that they whom nothing could move in this life to earnest repentance and moral transformation, and thus to personal preparation for Christ's appearance, will then be unable under the impression of His sudden coming to find the way of earnest repentance, the doctrine of the parable is in no way inconsistent with this truth; but that truth is only another side of the same thing, another reason for the hopelessness of the same possibility of a final repairing of former neglect, a reason which, instead of contradicting the doctrine of the parable, that no time will be left for this, on the contrary strikingly agrees and essentially coheres with it. Accordingly, vv. 10–12 are to be interpreted thus: As the foolish virgins, when the bridegroom was on the way, found no time to buy oil for themselves, but the bridegroom came in their absence, and, whilst conducting those who were ready into the marriage-feast, closed the door against the rest, ver. 10, so to those who foolishly reckon on the possibility of finally remedying neglected preparation in the last moment, the time necessary for doing this will be wanting in the hour of Christ's coming; but, unexpected as will be the announcement of His coming, so rapid also will be the coming of the Lord Himself, who will then receive into the kingdom of glory only those who are ready to receive and stand before Him, but will exclude all the unprepared. And finally, this exclusion will continue for ever. This and only this does the conversation between the bridegroom and the virgins expressly say to all careless in this life, without intimating that after Christ's appearance and the crisis then introduced those excluded will seek admission to God's kingdom, but will pray in vain. As the prayer of the virgins for a reopening of the door found no answer, but the bridegroom rejected it with the words: "Verily I say to you, I know you not," *i.e.* you are strangers to me, because you were not ready to receive me (vv. 11, 12), so the last hope of self-contentment, to which even after all that has been said any one may cling, namely, that an exclusion from God's kingdom, carried out so unexpectedly and rapidly, is not seriously meant, and cannot hold good for ever, will then prove empty and vain. On the contrary, it will remain unchangeably true, that all whom the Lord does not find ready at His coming He will never acknowledge as His, however long and certainly they belonged to the community of His disciples in this life, and hoped for participation in His kingdom. One sees how the parable shatters one support of self-contentment after another up to the last straw, to which folly would fain cling, and how deeply the souls of the hearers, providing they heard rightly, must have been pierced by the exhortation here uttered for the third and last time: γρηγορεῖτε οὖν, ὅτι οὐκ οἴδατε τὴν ἡμέραν οὐδὲ τὴν ὥραν.

The Talents in Trust.

(Matt. xxv. 14-30.)

Another parable follows, joined directly to the exhortation of ver. 13 (γρηγορεῖτε οὖν κ.τ.λ.) simply by γάρ, without anything between. On the other hand, it is to be observed that the exhortation to watchfulness because of the uncertainty of the time of Christ's coming, uttered in ver. 13 on the basis of the parable of the Ten Virgins for the third time, does not recur at the close of this new parable. Accordingly, only an examination of the new parabolic story itself can show whether it stands in the same close connection with the solemn declaration of the uncertainty of the day and hour of the Parousia in xxiv. 36 as everything which precedes, enforcing the γρηγορεῖτε with special reference to that declaration, or whether the γάρ, by which it is joined in a confirmatory sense to the exhortation of ver. 13, only refers generally to the demand to be ready for the Lord's coming. In the latter case the following parable, merely joined to the section beginning with xxiv. 36 as a sort of appendix, serves again to enforce the requirement of readiness for the Parousia, without, however, retaining as previously the special reference to the *uncertainty of its time*.

In any case, when the parable itself is introduced by the

words: ὥσπερ γὰρ ἄνθρωπος ἀποδημῶν ἐκάλεσεν τοὺς ἰδίους δούλους, in such a form that the narrative advances from this point uninterruptedly without express mention of the thing compared, we are remitted by the retrospective γάρ, as well as by the comparative ὥσπερ, to what goes before. And this backward reference so obviously gives the answer to the question, what is the object of comparison, that only the grammatical expositor, who studies construction *ex professo*, misses the express mention of the thing compared. The object of comparison, unexpressed because continuous from xxiv. 37, and therefore understood, is the Second Coming of Christ, to which also the idea ἄνθρωπος ἀποδημῶν placed at the head plainly alludes. On this account we need not suppose an anantapodoton, as if an apodosis with οὕτως, intended to form the conclusion of the whole parable, had been lost because of the further expansion of the narrative,[1]—an inconceivable view, because the intention to condense the entire narrative into a single protasis is incompatible with the extent which it must necessarily have reached, even according to its first plan, apart from further expansion. The ὥσπερ adduces a comparison related to the object in question, and for this reason consisting of a single member:[2] "*Like us* (it is with the Parousia of the Son of man as if) *a man, about to journey into another country, called his own servants,*[3] *and delivered unto them his goods.*" Τὰ ὑπάρχοντα αὐτοῦ is not necessarily the entire property of every kind, and in every place belonging to the householder,[4] but is limited by the context to the property he had in his possession and under his personal management in his residence so far. Being now about to take a journey, he is obliged to hand over this property of his, which he is unable personally to manage as before, to other faithful hands during the time of his absence. He therefore calls, not strange labourers, but his own servants, belonging to him as his servants; and as their master, since he may expect that they will regard his interest as their own, entrusts to them and their hands the property he leaves behind. Thus, the general outline of the following narrative has been already completely sketched: A householder taking a journey, and leaving behind both his property and servants, to return in due time; and over against him the servants left behind, who receive independent power over

---

[1] Meyer.   [2] Gal. iii. 6; Rom. v. 12 is different.
[3] τοὺς ἰδίους δούλους.   [4] Cf. vv. 21, 23.

his property during his absence, and will have to give account of its management on his return.

Here the dependence of the clauses on ὥσπερ ceases. Ver. 15, where the mode of distributing the property among the individuals is more minutely described, and the detailed narrative begins, proceeds independently: καὶ ᾧ μὲν ἔδωκεν πέντε τάλαντα, ᾧ δὲ δύο, ᾧ δὲ ἕν, ἑκάστῳ κατὰ τὴν ἰδίαν δύναμιν, i.e. "*and to one he gave five talents, to another two, to another one, to each one according to his own ability.*" Of course the three are only adduced by way of example, not as if his servants consisted only of these three. The handing over of the property to the servants individually was done very unequally,— this the three examples show first of all,—for they are sums of very unequal amount which are assigned to the individuals,[1] the extremes differing as five to one. But this diverse endowment of the individuals was not caprice in the householder, but each one received κατὰ τὴν ἰδίαν δύναμιν, i.e. each one according to the ability peculiar to him, namely, ability not merely to carry on business generally,[2] but more definitely to take charge of and manage a greater or smaller sum of money. Of the property to be managed by the servants during his absence, the householder gave each one exactly as much or as little as he was in a position to take charge of and deal with independently. "*And he* (the householder, after doing so) *went on his journey straightway.*" It has been attempted indeed to separate the εὐθέως from ἀπεδήμησεν and join it to the following πορευθείς,[3] to which there is no objection on formal grounds if the well-attested δέ of the Rec. after πορευθείς was originally absent and the following sentence should begin asyndetically: εὐθέως πορευθεὶς ὁ τὰ πέντε τάλ. λαβὼν κ.τ.λ. On the other hand, it cannot be maintained that εὐθέως in the present evangelist always comes first.[4] But if internal reasons must decide, the junction with ἀπεδήμησεν is to be preferred. For, joined with πορευθείς, where it serves to emphasize the zeal of the first servant, it is really superfluous, because the case itself there implies, without εὐθέως, that the servant spoken of was not dilatory, but zealous. On

---

[1] Respecting the value of the talent=6000 denarii, or about £225, cf. on xviii. 24.
[2] De Wette et al. [3] Weiss et al.
[4] Cf. iii. 16, where εὐθύς comes after (ἀνέβη εὐθὺς ἀπὸ τοῦ ὕδατος), and the variant reading, putting the words in the more common order (εὐθὺς ἀνέβη), must be deemed a correction. In the same way, e.g., Mark i. 31, v. 13, vi. 25 ; Luke xvii. 7.

the other hand, joined with ἀπεδήμησεν, it says, not indeed that the householder departed without giving any more express orders about the application of the money,—for this might have been done when handing it over, without the departure being delayed, —but that, after giving the money to the servants, he at once left them to their own responsibility. No sooner had they taken over the property than they were left by their master to themselves, and found themselves in circumstances to deal with it alone and independently, each one with the sum assigned to him according to his own ability.

It is then said of the first-mentioned servant, ver. 16: πορευθεὶς δὲ ὁ τὰ πέντε τάλαντα λαβὼν εἰργάσατο ἐν αὐτοῖς, καὶ ἐποίησεν ἄλλα πέντε τάλαντα. The first clause shows what he did with the money received: "*And he went that had received the five talents, and traded with them.*"[1] The element of industry, in opposition to indolence, lying in the fundamental meaning of the verb ἐργάζεσθαι, ought to be retained here in the special meaning "to trade,"[2] therefore: he seeks with busy activity to use what he has received profitably. The second clause then tells the result of his activity: "*and he acquired* (ἐποίησεν) *other five talents.*" The expression ἐποίησεν corresponds to the similar use of the Hebrew עשׂה[3] and the Latin *facere*, but is not altogether synonymous with κερδαίνειν used in its place in ver. 17, because it does not denote gaining in general, but in allusion to the εἰργάσατο, an acquiring by one's own effort. The amount of profit he made exactly corresponded, as expressly noted by the ἄλλα, to the amount of the capital received—to the first five talents received five *others*. And it is just this which is said also of the second servant, ver. 17: ὡσαύτως καὶ ὁ τὰ δύο ἐκέρδησεν[4] ἄλλα δύο, i.e. "*In like manner also he that* (received) *the two gained other two.*" Thus the equalizing ὡσαύτως refers simply to the result which this servant attained, namely, that just as the first servant to the five talents received gained *other* five, so this one to the two received gained *other* two. Hence, also, it is no longer said ἐποίησεν, but more generally ἐκέρδησεν, because attention is only directed to the amount of profit, no longer to the mode of acquisition, while, no doubt, resemblance even in the latter respect is tacitly assumed. The emphasis of the state-

---

[1] ἐν αὐτοῖς, because his trading rests on the talents as the basis; cf. Weiss here.
[2] So frequently in the classics.   [3] Gen. xii. 5.
[4] καὶ αὐτός (Rec.) is wanting in important witnesses.

ment rests entirely on the fact, that in the case of the second servant also the amount of gain exactly corresponded to that of the capital received, just as in the case of the first, so that despite the materially less amount of his gain, he stands on complete equality with the first one as regards the value of his service.

All the greater is the contrast which the conduct of the third one presents to that of the first two, ver. 18 : ὁ δὲ τὸ ἓν λαβὼν ἀπελθὼν ὤρυξεν γῆν,[1] καὶ ἔκρυψεν τὸ ἀργύριον τοῦ κυρίου αὐτοῦ, i.e., "*But he that had received the one went away, dug up earth, and hid the money of his master.*" Instead, therefore, of energetically working for his master with the money entrusted to him, as he was bound to do, he went away and buried the money of his master, as though it were the money of a stranger, to whom he owed nothing beyond the keeping of the deposit. Thus we have already shown how the phrase "of his master" must be taken here, which is all the more noteworthy, because at the first glance it seems superfluous. Certainly it emphasizes, as Meyer says generally, the forgetfulness of duty implied in the servant's conduct. But the wrong-doing intimated does not consist in his acting thus with money not belonging to himself, but to the householder, since the bare circumstance that the money was another's property seems rather adapted to justify a course like his; but the circumstance rendering him guilty is, that he to whom the money belonged was no stranger to him, but his master, to whom he was bound as a servant.[2] Only on this natural interpretation of the words "of his master" does the wrong-doing of the servant come clearly out, namely, that he separates his interest from his master's, dealing with his master's money as with a stranger's property, by which one may think he has done enough if he simply keeps it for the owner. Thus, in vv. 16–18, not only is the conduct of the servants characterized objectively, but it is already placed in the true light, inasmuch as in the case of the second servant it was emphasized, that even with the small sum of two talents, by gaining other two he was rendered equal to the first; and, on the other hand, in the case

---

[1] So we must read, according to weighty evidence, instead of ὤρυξεν ἐν τῇ γῇ (Rec.); the use of ὀρύσσειν τι is therefore different here from what it is in xxi. 33; Mark xii. 1.

[2] Cf. ver. 14 : τοὺς ἰδίους δούλους.

of the third servant, how, with the least sum of but one talent, by burying it, he was guilty of forgetting his duty to his master. And it now clearly appears that the relative amount of five, and two, and one, marking the sums assigned to the three servants, was not used by the narrator without special purpose. It is not an evenly diminishing relation that is chosen, such as five, and three, and one, simply contrasting with each other one who received a large sum, one who received a middle sum, and one who received a small sum; but to the one who received five talents the two others are opposed, each one indeed having received a different amount, but still both only a small one in comparison with the former, namely, only two and one talent. Thus, one of the two could serve as an example how one who received but little in comparison with others, proved equal to them in diligence and fidelity; and the other, how such an one, with the least which he received, became just as guilty as he could have done with the greatest.

So far the way has been prepared, at least in the form of intimation, for what the second part of the parable tells of the judgment passed on the servants by the master on his return. Vividly picturing the moment of return and the decisive hour of reckoning by the historic present,[1] the narrative proceeds, ver. 19: "*But after a long time the lord of those servants*[2] *comes and reckons with them.*" When it is expressly remarked that the master came *after a long time*, this can only mean, since the narrative supplies no means for determining the length of time, that the master's absence lasted considerably longer than the servants had expected, which is of importance for the tenor of the narrative, inasmuch as the unfaithful servants might be confirmed in their idleness by the long postponement of the householder's return, and tempted to drop the long-delayed hour of reckoning out of their thoughts altogether. Of course, wrongly. For, however long he delayed, the householder came and reckoned with the servants respecting the management of his property entrusted to them. Then appeared the three servants specially referred to, ver. 20: "*And he came who had received five talents, and brought other five talents, saying, Lord, five talents thou deliveredst to me; lo, other five talents I have gained to them*" (ἐπ'

---

[1] ἔρχεται . . . συναίρει λόγον.

[2] ἐκείνων applies not merely to the three mentioned by way of example, but to all the servants to whom, according to ver. 15, the property was delivered.

αὐτοῖς). The genuineness of the last words: ἐπ' αὐτοῖς, has been contested by Lachmann and Weiss on good authority. Nevertheless their superfluity may have caused their omission. In any case, the preposition ἐπί with the dative here as often = insuper ad;[1] and this signification ought not to be mixed up with the other quite different one, "on the ground of, by means of" (Lange). The very words of the servant imply that what he received was the groundwork of what he gained, and also, that he does not put forward the work that was his duty and the means of the gain as a special merit. For he does not even mention his ἐργάζεσθαι, or say ἐποίησα for ἐκέρδησα, as he might have done according to ver. 16; but, like a faithful servant who has quite entered into his master's interests, he simply expresses his joy at the rich gain which the money committed to him has produced: "Behold, five others I have gained in addition." And then he receives the answer stated in ver. 21: "*His lord said unto him*," Εὖ δοῦλε ἀγαθὲ καὶ πιστέ, ἐπὶ ὀλίγα ἦς πιστός, ἐπὶ πολλῶν σε καταστήσω· εἴσελθε εἰς τὴν χαρὰν τοῦ κυρίου σου. The εὖ standing at the head must be understood, with the majority of expositors, as an independent exclamation, and joined with the vocative δοῦλε ἀγαθὲ καὶ πιστέ. It stands, therefore, absolutely like εὖγε elsewhere.[2] This deviation from the usage of good Greek is at all events more tolerable than the junction with ἐπὶ ὀλίγα ἦς πιστός, thus passing over δοῦλε ἀγαθὲ καὶ πιστέ: "Thou wast admirably faithful in regard to a little,"[3] in which case, moreover, the emphasis in this clause would fall back entirely on εὖ, and the word ὀλίγα would lose the penetrating emphasis it is evidently meant to have as a preparation for the contrast, ἐπὶ πολλῶν σε καταστήσω. The householder rather first bestows his praise on the servant, and then promises him his reward, so that the words: ἐπὶ ὀλίγα ἦς πιστός, belong not so much to the preceding eulogy, as to the following promise of reward, giving its reason, therefore: "*Well done, thou good and faithful servant! Over a little thou wast faithful, over much will I set thee.*" The eulogy consists in this, that with the approving exclamation "Well done," he calls him a good and faithful servant, "*good*" not in the general moral sense,

---

[1] Winer, *Gram.* p. 490.
[2] Cf. Luke xix. 17, where the Recepta has εὖ, but where εὖγε seems the original reading.
[3] Meyer.

but in his character as servant, therefore a true servant; and since he has especially proved himself such by his fidelity, which is the most prominent virtue of a good servant, the specific "faithful" is combined with the general term "good." The promise of reward is to the effect, that because he has been faithful over *a little*,[1] he will set him over *much*, just as a servant who has proved his fidelity in the small is trusted with the great:[2] Thus, the comparatively large sum delivered to this servant was but little in comparison with the wealth of goods,[3] over which he is now to be set, set as controller, so that he may now deal with them just as independently, despite the householder's presence, as with the sum of money during the master's absence. But this, of course, supposes that from the mere position of servant, which he has hitherto held, he is raised to the position of a friend of his master, sharing his full confidence, and taking part in his authority. Hence, to the promise of reward a saying is added, expressive of this elevation: "*Enter into the joy of thy lord*," *i.e.* into the state of joy accruing to him in his character as lord and in virtue of his authority, so that the servant will have part and lot in his master's state. No doubt, in the sphere of natural life, in the relation between master and servant, this is a reward of rare and unusual good fortune, but it is not on this account a digression from the figure, and a trenching on the interpretation;[4] just as little as the far more unusual conception, in the parabolic language of Luke xii. 35–38, of the master making the servants sit down at table, and girding himself and waiting on them, can be called a digression from the figure into the interpretation. Even the expression "enter" does not need to be specially traced to the idea of the thing symbolized (the Messiah's kingdom), as Meyer supposes, since the metaphorical use of εἰσέρχεσθαι for entering into a state or condition like "life, temptation, glory, rest," is quite usual.[5] This being so, all reason is removed for converting the "joy of the lord," into which the servant is to enter, into a mere festival[6] or entertainment,[7] held to celebrate the lord's return, since such

---

[1] The unusual combination πιστὸς ἐπί τι, instead of the usual πιστὸς ἐν τινι, is due to the desire to approximate as closely as possible to the contrasted ἐπὶ πολλῶν.
[2] Cf. xxiv. 47 and Luke xvi. 10.   [3] Money is no longer specially thought of.
[4] Weiss, who for this reason explains the words as an addition of the evangelist.
[5] Cf. xviii. 8, xix. 17, xxvi. 41, and parallels; Luke xxiv. 26; Heb. iii. 11, 13, iv. 1 ff., 10.
[6] De Wette, Lange.   [7] Kuinoel.

a specializing of the literal sense of "joy" is required neither by the figurative circumstances of the parable, nor by the expression "enter," and, as regards its admissibleness, is by no means rendered certain by the appeal to the free translation of the Septuagint Esth. ix. 17 (מִשְׁתֶּה into χαρά).[1]

The same that is said of the account rendered by the first servant is then repeated of that rendered by the second, vv. 22, 23: "*And he also came that had received*[2] *the two talents, and said, Lord, two talents thou deliveredst unto me; lo, other two talents I have gained. His lord said unto him, Well done, thou good and faithful servant! Over a little thou wast faithful, over much will I set thee; enter into the joy of thy lord.*" Thus, not only are the same events repeated at the reckoning with the second servant as in vv. 20, 21, but they are recounted exactly in the same words and without abridgment. And this is not mere circumstantiality of narration, but the repetition of the entire transaction between master and servant in all its parts is meant to be well pondered; namely, on one side how this second servant, although he has but two new talents to bring, can say with the same cheerfulness as the first that he has gained *other* two (as the former five *others*), and on the other, how he receives from the householder the same praise and the same reward. Because he has shown equal fidelity in what he received, the apparently considerable difference between what he received and what the other received vanishes before the wealth of goods, over which the second like the first is set, and before the participation in the joy of his lord to which he like the former one is raised.

But how will it fare with the third servant, who had buried his master's money, ver. 18? The reckoning with him is related in the section, vv. 24–30, which also forms the conclusion of the parable: "*And he also came that had received*[2] *the one talent, and said:* Κύριε, ἔγνων σε ὅτι σκληρὸς εἶ ἄνθρωπος, θερίζων, ὅπου οὐκ ἔσπειρας, καὶ συνάγων, ὅθεν οὐ διεσκόρπισας, *i.e. Lord, I knew thee,*[3] *that thou art a hard man,*

---

[1] In opposition to Kuinoel.

[2] Here the participle perfect ὁ τὸ ἓν τάλαντον εἰληφώς, because in him who left what he received unused the receiving has become a permanent state, in which he is found now just as he was when he received.

[3] ἔγνων is not to be taken, with Kuinoel and de Wette, in the sense of the perfect, "I know thee," since it assigns the motive of the following: καὶ φοβηθεὶς ἀπελθὼν ἔκρυψα, in the narrative.

reaping where thou didst not sow, and gathering where thou didst not scatter." Some expositors [1] would understand διασκορπίζειν, only occurring here of agriculture, as sowing, like σπείρειν. But this would make the second participial clause pure tautology. And since the συνάγειν opposed to it, used of agriculture, according to the usage of the present Gospel elsewhere, is by no means synonymous with θερίζειν, but signifies the gathering of the fruit already reaped into the barn [2] from the threshing-floor,[3] διασκορπίζειν also cannot be synonymous with θερίζειν, but is the work of winnowing on the threshing-floor to separate the chaff from the wheat, which must precede the συνάγειν. The two participial clauses then say in what the master's supposed hardness consists. But the whole is not a mere proverbial phrase to characterize a man who makes altogether unjustifiable demands,[4] nor do the words imply a reproach against the master that he gave the servant too little,[5] or that he wishes to take more than he has a right to demand,[6] or that he demands more than one can do,[7] because there is no reference at all to the amount of what was sown, or of what was to be reaped in relation to what was sown, but to the fact that in the field where the master had not done the work of sowing he yet reaped the fruit, and from the threshing-floor, where he had not winnowed, he yet gathered home the wheat. The alleged hardness of the householder is more closely defined thus, that he appropriates the produce where he has not done the work, and therefore the produce of work which, not he, but others have done. And when the servant immediately proceeds, ver. 25: καὶ φοβηθεὶς ἀπελθὼν ἔκρυψα τὸ τάλαντόν σου ἐν τῇ γῇ, i.e. "*and, because I was afraid, I went away and hid thy talent in the earth,*" it is clear that the fear of the servant here mentioned corresponds to the hardness of the householder just mentioned. The servant feared the hardness of the householder, which made him reap where he had not sown. And in this case the object of his fear cannot be, that he might lose the money in trade, or that he cannot satisfy the householder's severe demands,[8] but simply that the master will exercise against him the hardness which he thinks he sees in him, and therefore deprive him of the produce

---

[1] Kuinoel, de Wette, Stier.   [2] Cf. iii. 12, vi. 26, xiii. 30.
[3] In the field under the open sky.   [4] So e.g. Keil.
[5] So often.   [6] De Wette.   [7] Stier.
[8] One or the other in the majority of expositors.

of his labour and appropriate it himself. This fear, he says, led him, instead of working with the money, simply to preserve it, and for the purpose of preserving it to hide it in the earth, where it remained secure to its owner,[1] without as a mere temporary incumbent troubling further about it. And he thinks he has thus done everything which the owner of the money can reasonably demand of him, so that he not merely holds himself free from blame in respect to his course, but also justified, as he says in the final words with which he gives back the money received: ἴδε ἔχεις τὸ σόν, i.e. "*Lo, thou hast thine own.*" Because he is able to return the owner of the money his own intact, he thinks he is without blame, for the owner cannot even demand back more than what is his. We see that the whole language as well as the whole action of this servant has its root in the circumstance that he does not as a true servant, like the two first, make his master's interest his own, but as a bad servant separates his own interest from his master's, and treats his master's cause as foreign to him.[2] Hence the householder seems to him a hard man, desiring to draw profit from the toil, which he leaves to others. Hence, too, the fear that he might himself be no better off for his labour, and, inspired by this selfish fear, the abstinence from all exertion, as expressed in the burial of the money. Hence, finally, the notion that he will be quite within his right if he restores intact to the owner of the money what is really his.

How much he mistakes his true relation to the householder as his servant, bound to work for his interest, is told him in the sharp reproof with which the master at once meets him, ver. 26: "*But his lord answered and said to him:*" πονηρὲ δοῦλε καὶ ὀκνηρέ. Whereas, therefore, the householder bestowed on the two first servants the high eulogy: "Thou good and faithful servant," he calls this third one *a bad and idle servant*, bad again not in the moral sense generally, but in his character as servant, proved a bad servant especially by the indolence he showed in his master's service. With this reproof is joined an appeal to the servant's first utterance, according to which he professed to know of his master that he claims the produce where he has not laboured: ᾔδεις, ὅτι θερίζω, ὅπου οὐκ ἔσπειρα, καὶ συνάγω, ὅθεν οὐ διεσκόρπισα. On the ground of this utterance he is at once reminded what course this conception of his

---

[1] Hence expressly ἔκρυψα τὸ τάλαντόν σου. [2] See on ver. 18.

master's character should have led him to. But in this case ᾔδεις is not to be taken as a question of surprise: "Knewest thou that I reap," etc., since such an expression of surprise would be out of accord with the instant drawing of a convicting inference (ἔδει οὖν σε κ.τ.λ.), nor do the words imply a concession[1] or anything ironical,[2] but they simply reproduce the servant's words, in order to base on them the above inference: "*Thou bad and idle servant, thou knowest* (thou sayest) *that I reap where I sowed not, and gather where I scattered not.*"[3] The inference alone kept in view in reproducing the servant's utterance runs, ver. 27: ἔδει οὖν σε[4] βαλεῖν τὸ ἀργύριόν μου τοῖς τραπεζίταις, καὶ ἐλθὼν ἐγὼ ἐκομισάμην ἂν τὸ ἐμὸν σὺν τόκῳ, *i.e.* "*Consequently thou shouldest have cast* (if thou thyself wert unwilling to work for me with my money) *my money to the money-changers, and at my return I* (ἐγώ, I on my part as one of whom thou knewest that I reap where *I sowed not*, etc.) *should have recovered mine own* (not unused and unincreased, as thou givest it me back, ver. 25, but) *with interest.*" The expression "*cast*" in this connection not merely emphasizes the easiness of the course required,[5] but affirms that he should have *relieved* himself of the money. Ἀργύριον βάλλειν is nowhere a mere depositing, but always includes a getting rid of the money.[6] The sense of the words, therefore, is not, as has been most generally understood, that the servant should at least have carried on a comparatively easy trade with the money, but that instead of retaining the money in his keeping he should have surrendered it into the hands of others. Only thus understood is the requirement a strict inference from the premisses given. For if he professed to know of the owner of the money, that it was his practice to appropriate the produce of the labour of others, then, since he was unwilling to work for the owner's benefit, he should not have retained his money in his own keeping, where it lay unused contrary to the owner's intention; but he was bound to hand it over to others willing to employ it for the owner's benefit, that is, the money-changers. These would have done the work he

---

[1] De Wette. [2] Lange.
[3] Cf. on Luke xix. 22, where in the parable of the Pounds in a similar transaction between master and servant the corresponding sentence: ᾔδεις ὅτι κ.τ.λ., is introduced by the words: ἐκ τοῦ στόματός σου κρινῶ σε, as a mere reproduction of the servant's declaration.
[4] Some authorities have σε οὖν. [5] Meyer, Weiss, Keil, *et al.*
[6] Cf. xxvii. 6, and similar passages; Mark xii. 41 ff.; Luke xxi. 1 ff.; John xii. 6.

was unwilling to do, and the householder might have received the profit of their work in accordance with his presumed character. Thus the σε in the first clause and ἐγώ in the second were not emphatically opposed to each other for the purpose of pointing out how *the master* would have gained his end if the servant had done *his part*.[1] For the meaning cannot be, that the servant would really have done his duty as a good and faithful servant by throwing the money to the exchangers, but only that he would have done what he owed his master, as the owner of the money, from the false, suspicious, and selfish standpoint he had assumed in relation to him. On the other hand, by retaining his master's money in his hands, without making use of it, he who professed to know how self-interested his master was had positively sinned against his interest.

Having convicted him of this from his own mouth, the master proceeds in the language of command (to whom he gives the command is not expressly said, in distinction from the servants named before the servants forming his personal retinue are to be supposed), ver. 28 : "*Take therefore the talent from him, and give it to him that hath ten talents.*" Really, therefore, the householder is not the hard man the servant supposed him to be, depriving good and faithful servants at last of the produce of their toil along with the capital lent to them. He not merely left both to the first two servants, but in addition promised to set them over much in comparison with the little in which they showed their fidelity. But from this servant, who brings back his talent unused, he now takes it away, not, however, to take it himself, but to give it to him who has ten talents. And this strange order, according to which the servants are to take the one talent from him who has nothing beside it and give it to him who has already ten talents, is justified by a proverbial maxim [2] belonging simply to the householder's language in the parable, and in no wise added to the parable by Jesus as an interpretation,[3] ver. 29 : "*For unto him that hath shall be given, and he shall be set in abundance ;* [4] *but as relates to him that hath not,*[5] *even what he hath shall be taken from him.*" This proverbial

---

[1] In opposition to Weiss; nor would the reading σι οὖν necessitate such an emphasizing of the σι.   [2] Cf. xiii. 12 ; Mark iv. 25 ; Luke viii. 18.

[3] In opposition to Weiss. Cf. Luke xix. 25, 26.

[4] περισσευθήσεται, as in Luke xv. 17.

[5] τοῦ δὲ μὴ ἔχοντος is to be read as a genitive absolute on decisive evidence, not ἀπὸ δὲ τοῦ μὴ ἔχοντος, with the Recepta.

saying lays it down as a general rule, that to the possessor (of much) more will be added to the much he already has, his rich possession thus passing into abundance; on the other hand, the (relatively) possessionless will lose even the little he has, his relative want passing into absolute. But this general rule could only serve to justify the command given in so far as it was obvious that in this case the "non-having" of the one was just as much a result of his indolence and unfaithfulness as the "having" of the other was a result of his diligence and fidelity, and therefore the application of the rule is an act of retributive justice. And to the retribution decreed is added the positive punishment which the householder orders to be inflicted on him, ver. 30 : καὶ τὸν ἀχρεῖον δοῦλον ἐκβάλετε εἰς τὸ σκότος τὸ ἐξώτερον, i.e. "*and the useless servant cast forth into the darkness without*" (outside the bright festive rooms [1]). Although, therefore, no festal celebration of the householder's return was expressly mentioned in the narrative before, since the "joy of the lord" (vv. 21, 23) cannot be referred to such a feast merely, still the thought of such a celebration, so natural and common in other parables, really floats before the narrator's mind. And whereas the first two servants' entrance into the joy of their lord evidently includes participation in this festal joy, so the idle servant is to be expelled from the bright rooms of his master's house into the gloomy, joyless darkness, an expulsion signifying just as evidently to him exclusion from the fellowship of his master's household. This doom, then, forms in fact the contrast to the eulogistic word to the first two servants : "Enter into the joy of thy lord." Respecting the words added by Jesus Himself as the narrator of the parable : "*There shall be the* (well-known) *wailing and gnashing of teeth*" (of the condemned), which refer as a standing interpretation exclusively to the figurative local idea (τὸ σκότος τὸ ἐξώτερον), what has been already said on chap. xxii. 13 may be consulted.

These words conclude the entire paragraph, whose contents form the present parable. For, without any further word of application or explanation, with ver. 31 begins the prophetic discourse of the judgment on all nations, forming the conclusion of the entire eschatological discourse. Since the account of the judgment says that the Son of man will justify or condemn men

[1] Cf. on xxii. 13, where the parable of the Royal Marriage-Feast concluded with the same doom.

according as they have been friendly or hostile to His disciples on earth, it is evident that the account is not a new exhortation to the disciples to be ready for Christ's Parousia, but a comforting assurance given to the disciples for the time of suffering up to the Parousia (similar to the one in x. 40-42), to tell them how dear they are in the eyes of the Lord, whilst apparently exposed to all the injustice of the world. And as an assurance of such a kind, this third and last section of the eschatological discourse (vv. 31-46) forms a thoroughly independent conclusion of the whole. Accordingly, the purpose of the present parable is shown by its context to be what we have already inferred from its connection with the exhortation of ver. 13, namely, it belongs to the preceding second section of the eschatological discourse, inasmuch as it is meant to supply a new justification for the exhortation to readiness for the day of Christ's coming. It was uncertain, however, before, whether here, as from xxiv. 36 onwards, the specific reference to the uncertainty of the time and hour of the Parousia obtains. The review of the course and contents of the narrative now teaches us that the latter is not the case. In one passage of the narrative, indeed (ver. 19), there was mention of long delay in the householder's return contrary to expectation, but only in a cursory way, so that this allusion might have been omitted without the course of the narrative materially suffering. Therefore our parable is merely to be regarded as an *appendix* to the second part of the eschatological discourse, inasmuch as while in common with that second part it has a hortatory purpose in relation to the Parousia, it has not the same pervading reference to the statement standing at the head: "But of the day and hour knoweth no one, not even the angels of heaven, but the Father only" (xxiv. 36).

What other and special form the exhortation to readiness for Christ's coming obtains, must be seen from a review of the course and contents of the narrative. But this can be determined without difficulty directly we realize the essential points in the narrative. We were told of the return from a journey of a householder, who on his departure gave his property and the care of his interests into the hands of his servants left behind, and who now on his return rewards in the highest degree the faithful diligence with which two servants have meantime used the goods they received for his interest, while severely punishing the selfish indolence with which another let what he received lie dead and useless. If, then, we are right in assuming from the context as provisionally certain that the Parousia of Christ corresponds to the return of a householder from a journey, the exhortation which a parable of this kind is meant to give the disciples in reference to the Parousia can be no other than this, *that in the times between the departure of their Lord and His second coming they are to work with what He committed to them on His departure for Him and His cause with faithful diligence, because the most glorious reward awaits such fidelity at the hour of Christ's return, while the heaviest punishment threatens the selfish indolence that would decline active employment of what it has received.* The first part of the narrative characterizes this twofold dealing with what has been received in its contrastedness, whereupon the second and chief part exhibits both the reward and the punishment awaiting individuals according to their conduct in this respect at the hour of Christ's coming.

From this standpoint we have once more to follow and interpret the course of the narrative.

When in ver. 14, as the basis of the narrative, a householder is spoken of who, about to go on a journey, delivered his property to his servants, it is certain from the context that Jesus points His disciples to His rapidly approaching departure from this world, which had hitherto been the scene of His abode and work. And it is just as certain that to the return of the householder from his journey, kept in view in the narrative from the first, corresponds the second coming of the Son of man, which forms the theme of this entire eschatological discourse.[1] But if the journeying householder is Jesus Himself, at present on the point of leaving the world, then to the property of the householder,

---

[1] The opposite assertion, that the parable has nothing to do with Christ's second coming, because the journeying of the master in the narrative simply furnishes the situation for testing the servants (Weiss), obviously requires as its supplement the opinion, that the parable here does not merely not stand in its original context in the eschatological discourse (and just so the similar parable in Luke), but also stands in a quite perverted and confusing connection, thus imputing to the evangelist a gross misunderstanding of the subject. Moreover, the evangelist must not only have spoilt the parable in vv. 21, 23, and 30 by his confusing interpolations, but also (which *Weiss* has forgotten to censure) already in ver. 19, since the words "Now after a long time" can only be meant to allude to the postponing of Christ's second coming (cf. xxiv. 48, xxv. 5). After expunging all the objectionable passages, Weiss supposes in a novel fashion that the present parable formed with that of the Unjust Steward in Luke xvi. a pair of parables. Similarly Holtzmann. This is a playing with possibilities.

which he on his departure delivers to his servants to manage in his stead and for his interest during his absence, there can only correspond the good (or property) which was the peculiar possession of Jesus and the groundwork of His labour during His abode on earth, but which on His departure He commits to His disciples, that they may manage it in His stead for the furtherance of His kingdom upon earth. Of course this cannot be earthly goods and gifts,[1] nor, as most generally interpreted,[2] the spiritual gifts of grace or charisms, which were first conferred on the Church by the exalted Jesus with the outpouring of the Holy Spirit. For even these cannot be regarded as the property of the Lord, which, when He Himself departs, He commits to His disciples to manage, but only as a subjective equipment imparted to them subsequently for the duty of managing the object of possession proper. Add to this, that if this were the right interpretation, a parable predicting Pentecost in an obscure figure would have been unintelligible to the disciples at that time, whereas another interpretation lay near them. His property rather is simply and exclusively the word of the Lord or the gospel,[3] the word of the kingdom, with whose administration Jesus entrusts His disciples when Himself leaving the world. Therefore also the word again not as an object of possession in the sense that one is made by faith partaker of the salvation offered in it, but in the sense that one has power and authority to preach and extend it. For to the act of handing over in the parable cannot correspond the work of Jesus by which He planted in His disciples' hearts faith in the word, thus first making them His disciples, but only the special authorization by which He appointed those who already were His disciples (" His own servants ") to preach that word in the face of the world. In 1 Tim. vi. 20 also the word of the Lord is called in this sense " the deposit," the gift (or property) entrusted to them.[4] Therefore the interpretation is: Just as a householder, when going on a journey, called his servants and delivered to them his property to manage during his absence, so Jesus, when leaving the world, delivers to His disciples, who are left alone in the world, that which was His peculiar possession in the world, the groundwork and means of His earthly toil—the word of God's

---

[1] Weiss.   [2] Stier, Meyer, Cremer, *et al.*
[3] So several ancient expositors; in recent times only Hofmann on Luke xix. 11 ff.
[4] Cf. Wiesinger, van Oosterzee, von Hofmann.

kingdom, that after His departure they may freely and independently use it in His stead and labour for His kingdom, as they have seen Him do hitherto.

But what can be the meaning when it is said further of the householder, that he gave to one servant five talents, to another two, and to a third one, to each one according to his ability? Let us observe the point on which the emphasis of the statement rests. Plainly not on this, that the entire property is divided into four parts, each one receiving a different part of the whole, but upon this, that the whole property given to the individual servants was differently assigned in each case as regards its amount, according as the receiver was able to manage a larger or smaller amount. So is it with the word of the Lord, which He entrusts to His disciples on His departure. So far as it is committed to the whole body of disciples, it is the word in its entire fulness and wealth, as Jesus Himself preached it. But in so far as it is entrusted to individual disciples, it is very different in amount according to the greater or less capacity of the individual to comprehend it in its depths and preach it in its fulness. As, therefore, the householder assigned the amount of property to each one of his servants according as he was in a position independently to manage it, one receiving a great amount, a second little, and a third least, so the Lord entrusts to each individual disciple so much of the rich treasures of saving truth existing complete in His word as he is able inwardly to comprehend, and thoroughly to master and teach. In the same degree in which he is able to master the treasures of the word in this sense, will the Lord commit to him power and authority to administer it, therefore to one in a far higher degree, to another in a much less, and to a third in the least, according to the greater or less or least measure of capacity belonging to each. And when, finally, it was said of the householder that after delivering the property to his servants he at once took his departure, which in the context of the narrative could only mean that he at once left them to their own responsibility, it is clear that the noting of this circumstance, which else might very well have been omitted, points to a corresponding relation in the thing symbolized. And in this case Jesus can only have meant to remind His disciples how soon and unexpectedly they would be called upon without Him to be the depositaries and preachers of His word upon earth. What remains for Him to do to His disciples is just to commit the gospel of the kingdom of God to their hands as His legacy. But directly He has done this He will no longer remain with them, and they will be left alone, confronted with the task of administering the treasures of the word entrusted to them with unlimited independence, but also with full responsibility. If the goods of the householder are interpreted of spiritual gifts, this trait must either be passed over in silence, as is done by most expositors, which is out of the question, or such a wonderful interpretation will be adopted as this, that here is the closest possible approximation to the fact "that Ascension and Pentecost nearly coincide, *certainly in inverted order*" (Lange).

After thus sketching the duty to which the disciples are called after their Lord's departure, the narrative shows in its first part the different course which the disciples entrusted with this duty may take. First, by the typical example of the first two servants —one who had received much, and another who had received little—it shows how the disciples are to discharge their duty according to their Lord's mind and will, so that we see it makes no difference whether one has been entrusted with much or little. Like the first servant who energetically traded with the five talents, and gained in addition a sum of like amount, those who received much are strenuously to put to use the treasures of the word entrusted to them, in order to secure gain for the kingdom of their Lord equal in amount to the treasure committed to them. And they who have received little are to do in the same way. Like as the second servant, although he had received but two talents, proved himself equal to the first in diligence and fidelity by also gaining in addition a sum equal to what he received, so they to whom little has been entrusted can and ought by using equal diligence and fidelity to prove themselves equal to those who received much, by securing gain, if not equally great in itself, yet just as fully corresponding to what was entrusted to them. Their success ought to be, if not as great outwardly, yet of like intrinsic worth. The gain here meant, since it is the product of labour with the word of the Lord, can only consist in the winning of souls for the Lord's kingdom. If we wish, we may then extend the comparison to the point, that in the narrative the gain is also an augmenting of the capital itself. "Whoever trades with the word of the Lord augments it, because it is multiplied in the degree in which hearts are gained to become its seat."[1] But whether so far-reaching a comparison was intended by the author of the parable, must at least remain doubtful. The chief point of the comparison in any case is simply this, that by diligent labour with the means given in trust gain is secured, and gain corresponding in worth to the worth of the means held in trust. But that this gain in the case of money-trading consists in nothing but money again, follows too clearly from the nature of the figure employed to necessitate the transference of this relation of resemblance between the means and product of the labour into the interpretation.

But if, as the example of the second servant taught, those disciples to whom only little was entrusted are none the less fitted for successful toil in the Lord's cause, it follows from this, as shown in the example of the third servant, that he to whom the least was entrusted is not on this account less responsible for a conscientious use of what he has received, and is rendered no less guilty by neglect of this obligation. For when in ver. 18 it was said of the third servant, who only received one talent, that he went away and buried it in the earth, and it was especially emphasized that the money with which he so acted was his master's money, there is an intimation of the guilt incurred by a disciple of Christ by like dealing with the word of his Lord entrusted to him. He would be just as forgetful of duty as that servant were he to withdraw even the least portion of the treasures of the word entrusted to him from its destined influence in and upon the world, and let it lie useless in secret,—just as forgetful of duty, because He who has given it to him is his Lord, who has a right to require from His servants, not the mere preserving, but the faithful, successful use of the gift entrusted to them. Here also the *tertium comparationis* of the burying in the earth is expressed. To bury a sum of money in the earth seems, indeed, the securest way of preserving it; but in reality the money is thus most completely withdrawn from the work in the world for which it exists, and is rendered a useless, worthless thing. On this ground it is a speaking figure of the conduct of one who thinks he is justified in keeping the word of the Lord entrusted to him in safe secrecy; for in withdrawing it from publicity he withdraws it from its destined aim, which is to be preached to the world, and, so far as he is concerned, makes it

[1] So Hofmann on Luke xix. 11 ff., appealing to Acts xii. 24: ὁ λόγος τοῦ Θεοῦ ηὔξανεν καὶ ἐπληθύνετο.

aimless and useless. The special explanations of the earth by itself, making it mean either the earthly mind and walk, into which the indolent one sinks,[1] or the earthly disposition by which he makes the heavenly gift unfruitful,[2] or the flesh in which the spirit is buried,[3] are allegorizing explanations, which should not be advanced as exposition.

On the presuppositions now stated is based the second and chief part of the narrative, which describes the glorious reward on the one hand, and the heavy punishment on the other, coming to the disciples at the hour of Christ's advent, according as they have done like the first and second, or like the third servant. As the householder's return only ensued after an unexpectedly long period, so the Lord's second coming will be put off longer than the disciples think. This is again expressly foretold,[4] that no one may grow lax in fidelity on this account, or be confirmed in unfaithfulness, taking what is only a postponement of Christ's coming for its failure. However long the Lord delay, He will as certainly return as the householder of the parable, and will then, like him, require an account from His disciples (ver. 19). And as the first servant came before his master with humble joy, that with the five talents received he had gained other five (ver. 20), so those who have laboured faithfully with the great amount entrusted to them will be able to appear before the Lord rejoicing at the success with which they have been permitted to work for the Lord and His kingdom. And as the praise of a true and faithful servant was given to the first servant, so then the praise of a true and faithful servant of Christ will be given to them by their Lord; and with the praise a reward as rich and glorious beyond all measure as the one promised to the servant in the words of the householder. Because he was faithful over a little, says the householder, he will set him over much. So to the disciples, who on earth have proved their unselfish fidelity to Him in administering His word, the Lord will give power over so much in the future kingdom of God then to be set up, that in comparison with it all they had hitherto received is little. But what is promised them is not that in God's future kingdom they shall be made partakers in great blessing as an object of enjoyment, but that in the organism of God's future kingdom they shall receive great power as the substratum of a new and more comprehensive sphere of work

[1] Stier.   [2] Thiersch.   [3] Lange.   [4] xxiv. 48, xxv. 5; Luke xvii. 22.

than was granted them on earth, where only the word was entrusted to them as a substratum and means of labour. But if such great things are committed to them, after the Lord Himself has come again to set up His kingdom, this presupposes their elevation to be participants in the independent dominion of their Lord. And it is precisely this elevation that is figuratively expressed in the saying: "Enter into the joy of thy lord," and not merely, as is usually explained, entrance into the blessedness of Christ's kingdom in general. As the householder of the parable in that saying bids the servant take part in the joyous state in which he himself is found as master, so Christ will then make His faithful disciples participate in the state of blissful life belonging to Him—their Lord—in virtue of His divine power and glory.

But all this applies not only to those who, like the first servant, with the rich gifts entrusted to them, have borne specially rich fruit, but also quite as much to those who, like the second servant, by showing like fidelity have secured gain just as fully corresponding to their gifts, although less rich in itself. This it is which is taught by the repetition without abridgment of the account of the like proceedings in the reckoning with the second servant, vv. 22, 23. The latter, too, will be able to appear before the Lord in the hour of His coming with like joy as the former, and will find with the Lord the same praise of a good and faithful servant, and receive the same rich and glorious reward beyond all measure figuratively expressed in the saying: "Over a little thou wast faithful, over much will I set thee; enter into the joy of thy lord." The distinction, therefore, existing in this life between them as regards the greatness or littleness of the gifts entrusted to them will vanish before the high position of power and honour to which they will then be both equally raised on account of the equal fidelity they have shown.

But great and glorious as is this reward, so heavy, on the other hand, is the punishment that will be inflicted on those who let the word entrusted to them lie dead and useless. This is shown, finally, in what takes place at the reckoning with the third servant. By putting a supposed justification of his conduct in the mouth of this servant, the parable exactly characterizes the selfish disposition forming the basis of such conduct. At the same time, the refutation which the servant's attempted justification receives from the householder dissipates the notion that he who thinks and does so is still within his rights as against his master. As the third servant attributes his inactivity itself to this, that the householder appeared to him a hard man, making others work in order to appropriate the produce of their labour, and that on this account he could not undertake labour whose fruits would go to the householder, not to himself; so, in the like inactivity of a disciple of Christ nothing would be revealed but the unsubdued selfishness of heart which makes him, while acknowledging Christ as his Lord, yet really remain a stranger to the Lord and His cause inwardly. Whoever stands aloof from the Lord in such unsubdued selfishness of heart must certainly feel it a hardship to devote the work of his life to the cause of Christ and the interests of His kingdom, instead of to himself and his temporal interests; and the selfish fear that he may have nothing for himself from all his toil in the Lord's service will make him shrink from all self-denying labour with the word entrusted to him. And as the servant even thinks himself justified in burying the money because he has kept it, and can restore to the owner what is his, so he who stands at this selfish standpoint may give way to the notion that he remains within his rights as against the Lord in hiding the word entrusted to him to preach, because he can return it at last into the hands of Him from whom he had it, without Christ's cause being positively injured by his inaction. The answer which the householder gives to the servant is meant to teach how perverse and self-deceiving is this notion, vv. 26, 27. If the servant—so ran the answer—professed to believe his master a hard man, making others labour to appropriate the produce of their labour, and for this reason refused to work with the money entrusted to him, then, instead of uselessly burying the money to the owner's loss, he was bound to hand it over to those willing to use it to profit, so that the owner might receive his interest. So also a disciple, to whom the requirement of self-denying labour in the Lord's service seems an unreasonable hardship, and who therefore cannot consent to join in the work of preaching and extending His word, is under obligation to withdraw from the ministry of the word, and, so far as it was entrusted to him, to hand it over to those ready to work with it, and bear to the Lord the fruit He desires. Here it is implied, that as people are always found in the sphere of earthly business willing to undertake the employment of money which the first possessors desire to get rid of, so in the sphere of labour in God's kingdom the word of the Lord, even when individual disciples renounce it, and give up the Lord's service, will always find willing hearts and hands enough, ready to take their place and do the work they have refused. Thus the cause of the Lord sustains no injury from this or that individual openly renouncing it, as though particular individuals were indispensable to it; but it suffers from one who thinks he has a right to keep his position as a confessor and advocate of Christ's word, whilst withdrawing from the work of preaching and extending it, and hiding it from the world, in which it is designed to work,—just as the owner of a large property is not injured by the withdrawal of one or another manager, for whom others can be found, but is injured when one buries in the earth the sum entrusted to him, instead of putting it to use. This is the only interpretation that solves the difficulty presented to exposition by this peculiar admonition of the householder to the servant, *i.e.* solves it in real correspondence with the sense of the words in the context of the narrative. For certainly we ought not in the interpretation to pass over this admonition in silence, as many expositors do, unless we are to suppose that the entire conversation between the third servant and the householder is really just as meaningless and purposeless as it is minute and peculiar. Nor is this improved by the remark, that the purpose is to show the inexcusableness of the inactivity of a servant of Christ in a concrete example.[1] For how could the author of the parable intend to show this inexcusableness in a conversation whose contents have no sort of application to the activity or inactivity of a servant of Christ? The admonition would be scarcely less meaningless if it merely meant to say to him to whom it applies, that he should have done something at least with what was entrusted to him,[2] for on this interpretation the chief question, what he should have set about, if he was unwilling to work with it, not only remains without answer, but is incapable of answer. The other expositors, who attempt a definite interpretation, go astray in thinking themselves bound to point out a course remaining open in the second instance to a disciple of Christ who is unwilling to employ his gifts in independent labour, so that he may be able to stand before the Lord on the day of reckoning. In this sense such foreign and incongruous notions have been imported as these,—that he who did not work

[1] Meyer on Luke xix. 20-23.   [2] Stier.

should at least have prayed,[1] or adhesion to the most active leaders and members of the Church has been supposed to be demanded,[2] or he who declines the responsibility of independent labour should at least place his gifts at the disposal of others.[3] But the one, like the other, could only have been expressed in the figurative story by the requirement to join the more gifted fellow-servants, not by the requirement to put the money to the exchangers, who would only have entered the householder's service by accepting the money offered to them. Hence Hofmann[4] has applied the thought too artificially: "He who shrinks from personal labour in extending the doctrine of Jesus may help those who are skilled in teaching, without having been taken by Jesus Himself into His service, to do what he himself has not confidence for." But here, as by all the expositors just named, it is overlooked, first of all, that according to Matthew the one talent was entrusted also to the idle servant "according to his own ability," that he is therefore just as able, and for this reason just as bound, to work spontaneously with his gifts, as all the other servants with theirs. So also in the sphere of God's kingdom, to every one is entrusted what answers to his ability, whether much or little. Therefore the duty of personal faithful labour is the same to every one; and it is an impossible notion, that a disciple would be justified in shifting the responsibility for what is entrusted to him to other shoulders, or transferring the work enjoined on him to others. And, in the second place, in all these interpretations it is left out of sight that the householder by no means intends in that admonition to tell the servant what his duty was as a true and faithful servant, but that he merely refutes his attempted justification from his own words, and from the false standpoint of his own selfish disposition. He that stands aloof from the Lord's cause as selfishly as the servant from the householder, to whom the claim of the Lord on His disciples to give up their whole time and strength in unselfish labour to His service seems an intolerable hardship, so that he cannot persuade himself to comply with such a demand,—he will be so little justified by continuing to pass for a confessor and advocate of Christ's word, and thus uselessly preserving the treasure entrusted to him, that, on the contrary, he would be less guilty were he to renounce that word, hand over his duty to others, and

---

[1] Godet on Luke xix. 23.
[2] Lange, similarly Olshausen.
[3] Cremer.
[4] On Luke xix. 23.

thus at least not positively injure the Lord's cause. This is the meaning of the refutation of the servant's attempt at self-justification. Of similar import are all those utterances of Jesus in which He lays stress on the gravity of the demands which He makes on His disciples, with the unmistakeable purpose of severing the half-hearted and selfish, to whom this must seem intolerable harshness, from the circle of His disciples. To this class especially belongs the section (Luke xiv. 25–33), where in the parabolic sayings of the cost of building a tower and the means of waging a war, the exhortation is plainly expressed, that it is better to abstain from being a disciple altogether than not to comply with the demand for complete self-denial inseparable from the disciple's position. The first would be better for man than the second.[1]

And thus the punishment which the Lord will inflict on such an idle and unfaithful servant will correspond to the wrong-doing involved in such selfish indolence. The supposed merit of having at least preserved what was entrusted to him will so little be imputed to him as such, that, on the contrary, this very gift will then be taken from him. As the householder, on the basis of the refutation he has given to the plea of the idle servant, at once causes the talent to be taken from him (ver. 28), so from those who have preserved the word of the Lord committed to them without turning it to account, it will be taken away at Christ's coming, and they will be stripped of the position in God's kingdom which they have hitherto only held to the injury of the Lord's cause. And as the householder commands that which was taken from the idle servant to be given to him who has already ten talents, so then what is taken from the indolent will benefit those who by diligence and fidelity have borne rich fruit to the Lord. For not merely will the Lord leave them the rich product of their earthly labour even in the future kingdom of God as their crown of rejoicing, their glory and joy,[2] but He will also over and above reckon to their glory what He takes from the indolent in false glory. By exposing the false glory of the latter, as though they had done their duty by merely preserving the word entrusted to them, and taking that glory from them along with the word that was theirs, He will still further augment to the faithful the glory and joy which is the result of their faithful labour, so that they will become just as much richer as the others became poorer.

[1] Cf. also Rev. iii. 15, 16.   [2] 1 Thess. ii. 19 f.; cf. Hofmann on Luke xix. 24.

In this sense then, in reference to the disciples of Christ at His coming as in reference to the servants on the householder's return, the general maxim (ver. 29) will find its application: "Whosoever hath, to him shall be given, and he shall have abundance; but he that hath not, from him shall be taken away even that which he hath," without this implying anything else than simply a just estimation and corresponding recompense of the fidelity of the one class, through which they became "those who have," in its distance from the unfaithfulness of the others, through which they became "those who have not," namely, have nothing but what they received. By thus giving its definite interpretation to this special feature, that what is taken from the indolent benefits the faithful, we have only done what is essential This regulation is far too strange and far too little demanded by the tenor of the narrative, to allow us to pass it by in the interpretation, as most expositors do; all the less so, that the appeal to the clause: "He that has, to him shall be given," simply refers in the connection of the figurative story to this increase of the ten talents by the one, and not, as is usually done in the interpretation, to the great reward given to the faithful servants according to vv. 21, 23. Certainly the circumstance that the talent taken from the indolent only benefits the one who had ten talents, not also the one who had four talents, cannot be applied in the interpretation. Nor does it require any application. For if the thought above expressed needed to be illustrated in one of the two, the holder of the ten talents offered himself for the purpose in the first line, because the addition of the one talent appears all the more striking the greater the number already present. To say this is by no means to deny that the doctrine here stated bears an application to all faithful, diligent servants, provided they bear fruit corresponding in amount to the gifts entrusted to them.

But if the idle, unfaithful disciple of Christ, instead of receiving new work in the future kingdom of God, is deprived even of that which he had in this life, it follows of course that there is no room for him in that kingdom. Hence in Luke's parable of the Pounds (xix. 24 ff.) no further punishment of the idle servant is mentioned. But in the present parable the expulsion from the kingdom of God finds at the close special figurative expression. As the householder in the parable adds to the order to deprive the idle servant of his talent the command to cast him forth from the bright festal rooms of the master's house into the darkness, thus expelling him from his household, so Christ in the hour of His coming, besides depriving every idle, unfaithful servant of what was entrusted to him, will also inflict on him the penalty of exclusion from His kingdom, the kingdom of light and joy, and consign him to the place of condemnation. "There shall be the wailing and gnashing of teeth."

THE POUNDS[1] IN TRUST.

(Luke xix. 11-27.)

The parable of the Pounds preserved in Luke, which has much in common with the parable of the Talents in Matthew, likewise belongs, according to Luke's account, to the last period of the life and teaching of Jesus. For it is found in the last section of his Gospel, beginning with xviii. 31, in which section, again pursuing the chronological order, he describes the issue of the life of Jesus. But according to Luke (chap. xix.) the parable of the Pounds was not spoken (like that of the Talents) in the Passion-week and in the course of the eschatological discourse, but on the journey through Jericho to Jerusalem to the Paschal feast, which was to issue in His death, more definitely before the departure of Jesus from Jericho,[2] where He lodged in the house of Zacchæus the publican. After Zacchæus had joyfully received Jesus in his house (ver. 6), Jesus had said to Zacchæus, in opposition to the general murmuring which His lodging with a publican had called forth among the people:[3] "*To-day is salvation come to this house, because he also is a son of Abraham. For the Son of man came to seek and to save that which was lost*" (vv. 9, 10). And to this saying, addressed to Zacchæus, the parable is then joined in the following manner, ver. 11 : Ἀκουόντων δὲ αὐτῶν ταῦτα προσθεὶς εἶπεν παραβολήν. Respecting the persons to whom the parable was spoken, nothing further is said than that they were those who had heard the saying to Zacchæus. For the pronoun αὐτῶν has no retrospective allusion to some persons more fully described before, nor is any necessary. It means simply those present at

---

[1] Minæ. [2] Cf. ver. 23.
[3] But no longer in presence of the whole multitude, as Meyer supposes, as though everything related in vv. 8-27 is to be regarded as transpiring on the threshold of Zacchæus' house.

the conversation between Zacchæus and Jesus, for whom that last saying of Jesus was just as much designed as for Zacchæus himself, since Jesus, although speaking "*to* Zacchæus" ("unto him"), spoke at the same time in the third person to the bystanders about him ("because *he also* is Abraham's son"). But what led Jesus to add to the declaration which they had heard, the following parable, apparently of such different import, is clearly explained by the two infinitive clauses introduced by διά: διὰ τὸ ἐγγὺς εἶναι Ἰερουσαλὴμ αὐτόν, καὶ δοκεῖν αὐτοὺς ὅτι παραχρῆμα μέλλει ἡ βασιλεία τοῦ Θεοῦ ἀναφαίνεσθαι, *i.e.* "*because He was near Jerusalem, and they think that the kingdom of God will immediately appear.*"[1] The two infinitive clauses are closely connected, the first being merely the basis of the second. That He was near Jerusalem, became to the Lord the occasion of His uttering the following parable, inasmuch as in the minds of those present, with this circumstance there was linked the thought that the appearance of the kingdom of God was soon to be expected. And how they came to this association of ideas just then and in consequence of the declaration to Zacchæus, is not hard to see. Let us transport ourselves vividly into the situation. Attended by dense crowds of people, Jesus, on entering Jericho, had heard with approval the Messianic name "Son of David," with which the blind man addressed Him in the road, and had rewarded the faith of the man who so addressed Him with a miraculous cure, upon which all the people burst into praise of God (xviii. 35-43), so that His entry into Jericho became a public event. Even in the murmur of dissatisfaction running through the crowd after His lodging in the house of Zacchæus (xix. 7) it is still apparent how all eyes were turned to Him, and all hearts filled exclusively with interest in His person. To all this was now added the solemn saying of Jesus to Zacchæus, in which He designated Himself the Son of man, the bearer of the salvation promised to the sons of Abraham. When, then, this Jesus, who not only received such homage as that of the blind man, but also spoke of Himself as He did to Zacchæus, after already entering Jericho amid the enthusiastic acclamations of the people, was about to go up to Jerusalem amid ever-increasing crowds of pilgrims, and was scarcely a day's journey from its gates, how natural to excited hearts was the expectation that His arrival in Jerusalem, as it actually took place afterwards, and is at once related in ver. 28 ff.,

[1] ἀναφαίνεσθαι, "come into visible manifestation."

will assume the shape of a public entry as the Messiah in the city of Zion, and that then from Jerusalem, the city of God, the visible establishment of the kingdom of God will immediately take place! And here it becomes more clearly evident that they to whom Jesus spoke the parable were such as already believed in Him as the Messiah, and were not shaken in this faith by His lodging with Zacchæus, a view which very well agrees with the situation, because the only persons who besides the Twelve entered the house of the publican with Jesus, and thus became ear-witnesses of His conversation with Zacchæus, were those who formed His immediate surrounding and constant attendants on the journey to Jerusalem. But if the expectation in the minds of His attendants of the speedy appearance of God's kingdom gave the Lord the occasion for narrating the following parable,—which leaves it uncertain whether the expectation was made known in express words or in some other way,—it is to be expected that the parable itself will oppose the error expressed in the $\pi\alpha\rho\alpha\chi\rho\hat{\eta}\mu\alpha$, and put in contrast with it what Christ's disciples are really to expect concerning the future development of the kingdom of God.

Newly introduced by an $\epsilon\hat{\iota}\pi\epsilon\nu$ $o\hat{\upsilon}\nu$, the narrative itself then begins: "*A man of noble birth journeyed into a far country, to receive for himself a kingdom, and* (then) *to return.*" According to the analogy of the existing political circumstances of the Roman Empire, in which a number of small vassal states were found under the supreme sway of the Emperor, a man of noble birth is set forth, on whom a kingdom is to be conferred. But in order to receive this investiture it is necessary for him to undertake a journey into a distant land, where the seat of the supreme monarch is; and only after returning from this journey, which implies a long absence, will he enter on the kingdom. Nothing is said of his being the king of the country by descent. This is obviously imported by expositors in prospect of the interpretation. The designation $\epsilon\hat{\upsilon}\gamma\epsilon\nu\acute{\eta}\varsigma$ only assigns him a place in the order from which ruling princes usually proceeded, and in this sense merely paves the way for the statement respecting the purpose of his journey. Whether in this arrangement of the narrative, as most expositors maintain, there is a definite reminiscence of the similar journeys made to Rome by Herod I. and Archelaus, and in the subsequent hostile embassy sent after the nobleman (ver. 14) of the embassay of the fifty Jews who followed Archelaus to Rome,—events the last of which only occurred three decennia before,— or whether these traits were only freely shaped in analogy with the political circumstances of the age, cannot be decided, and is of no importance. For even if the former were the case, such a reminiscence of particular historical facts would be nothing more than an external point of support for a similar shaping of the figurative story. In no case should we be warranted in saying that Jesus here " compared His Ascension to the journey of Herod to Rome," and in reckoning this circumstance " among the little observed features of the deep humility of the Son of man."[1]

But before his departure the future king did what is told in ver. 13 : "*And he called his ten servants,*[2] *and gave them ten minæ,*" which means, as is evident from the further course of the narrative, that each of the ten servants received one mina. The question whether the ten were the whole of his servants,[3] or not,[4] is not to be raised, because the narrative says neither the one nor the other, but only that they were *ten* servants whom he called, therefore, of course, not a fragment taken at random, but a united complete number, each one of whom received the like mina and the like charge in reference to it: καὶ εἶπεν πρὸς αὐτοὺς Πραγματεύσασθε, ἐν ᾧ[5] ἔρχομαι, i.e. " *Trade ye, whilst I come.*" The latter clause (ἐν ᾧ ἔρχ.) in its condensed mode of expression only really becomes intelligible when we consider the pregnant force lying in the ἔρχομαι here, uttered as it is by the nobleman on the eve of a journey having no other aim and meaning than this, *to initiate his coming as king.* Only by keeping this position of things given in the context in view, according to which the ἔρχομαι as an idea of purpose includes under it, in fact, the whole journey, can we stop at the simple literal translation " whilst I come," without foisting on the ἔρχομαι the impossible meaning " to be on the journey,"[6] or supposing a scarcely conceivable brachylogy, by which the end of the period of absence is put for the whole,[7] or, finally, making of the clause ἐν ᾧ ἔρχ. an artificial relative clause, meaning: " *during which* (your carrying on trade) *I come.*"[8] Moreover, nothing is gained by this inversion of the relation of the two

---

[1] So *e.g.* van Oosterzee.
[2] δέκα δούλους ἑαυτοῦ without article, properly therefore "ten servants of himself."
[3] Stier. [4] von Hofmann.
[5] Decidedly attested in place of ἕως ἔρχομαι (Rec.).
[6] Stier, van Oosterzee, *et al.* [7] von Hofmann. [8] Meyer.

clauses, because the difficulty, namely, the identifying of the final return (and therefore of a mere point of time) with the entire space during which trade is to be carried on, still remains. It has certainly been thought that this distribution of minæ to the servants in order to their trading with them, is in ill accord with the political position assigned to the nobleman in ver. 12. But we can only be surprised at the nobleman distributing money, instead of arms, to his servants by overlooking, that hitherto he was only their master, not their commander-in-chief. And his giving them so small a sum as one mina each [1] is only unintelligible, when we transfer the idea of the talents from the parable of the Talents,[2] as if the subject here were the management of the property which the nobleman leaves behind. But of this nothing at all is said. The motive for delivering the money to the servants, with the charge to trade with it, does not seem here to be the need of appointing managers to the nobleman's property during his absence, but is simply a device of political wisdom on the part of the future king. His only purpose is by this small sum given to his servants, and this insignificant task allotted to them, all the more plainly to test their fidelity, and thus ascertain their fitness for employment in his future kingdom.

But from the servants standing at the nobleman's service before he receives his kingdom the narrative now turns to his fellow-citizens, the citizens, therefore, of the same city of which he himself hitherto was a citizen, in order to state what attitude they assumed to him, ver. 14 : *"But his fellow-citizens hated him, and sent an embassy after him, saying, We will not that this*[3] *man rule over us."* Therefore it is only hate to his person which moves them to opposition against his kingship. And so great is their hate against the designated king, that they do not scruple to follow him even to the throne of the suzerain with their opposition, and before this supreme court assert their defiant self-will in impotent protest: *We will not* that he rule over us.

We next find ourselves transported forthwith to the period after the nobleman's return in regal majesty and power. What there may have been to say respecting the trading of the servants

---

[1] An Attic mina according to different calculations from £3 to £3, 15s. Cf. on Matt. xviii. 24.
[2] Matt. xxv. 14.   [3] τοῦτον, Bengel : istum, fastidiose loquuntur.

with the money during his absence is here passed over in silence,[1] because it will find expression in the account to be rendered by the servants of the execution of the charge they received. Hence, in ver. 15, it is said at once: "*And it came to pass, when he had returned, having received the kingdom, that he commanded these servants to whom he gave the money to be called to him that he might learn:*" τίς τί διεπραγματεύσατο, i.e., resolving the compressed construction which fuses two interrogative sentences predicated of one subject into one :[2] "*who had gained anything, and what he had gained.*" Such is the usual rendering of διεπραγματεύσατο. For since the verb πραγματεύεσθαι, which already had in ver. 13 the special sense of "to carry on trade," here recurs, only strengthened by διά in the sense of zeal achieving its end and joined with an object-accusative, the signification "to gain by trade," which is in keeping with the circumstances of the case, must be maintained, in opposition to the diluted rendering of Meyer: "what any one had undertaken." The ten servants then come one after another, ver. 16: "*And the first came, saying, Lord, thy mina hath gained ten minæ more.*" It is expressly said προσειργάσατο.[3] The meaning therefore is not: The one mina has become ten in all, but: The one mina has gained ten *other* minæ *in addition*.[4] The servant makes, not himself, but his master's mina, the subject of this προσεργάζεσθαι. Only of the mina does he boast, that it has proved fruitful in trade in so high a degree, his own labour—the means of this result—only seeming to him the fidelity due, of which he cannot boast.[5] But it is just this fidelity for which his master now bestows praise and reward on him in rich measure. First the praise, ver. 17: "*And he said to him:* Εὖγε[6] ἀγαθὲ δοῦλε, *i.e. Well done, thou good servant.*" And then the reward: "*Because thou hast become*[7] *faithful in a very little, have thou authority over ten cities.*"[8] The same number, therefore, that describes the amount of the gain made by him, describes also the amount of the reward allotted to him. Because the amount of the gain here, where every servant had received the

---

[1] Matt. xxv. 16–18.   [2] Winer, *Gram.* p. 784.
[3] According to another reading : προσηργάσατο.   [4] Cf. on ver. 24.
[5] Cf. xvii. 10 and on Matt. xxv. 20.
[6] The Recepta has the less well-attested εὖ, after Matt. xxv. 21.
[7] ἐγένου, any one only *becomes* and is faithful in the degree in which he practises fidelity.
[8] ἴσθι ἐξουσίαν ἔχων ἐπάνω δέκα πόλεων.

same,[1] expresses the degree of fidelity shown, the amount of the gain becomes the standard for measuring the reward. But substantially the reward consists in this, that to the servant who has shown fidelity in the little, power is given over the great, namely, over a district in his lord's kingdom embracing just as many cities as he gained minæ. We see here that the province of the kingdom which the nobleman received extends far beyond the bounds of the city of which he himself was a citizen, and whose citizens had opposed his kingship.

Upon the first servant follows the second, boasting with the same humble joy of the produce of the mina entrusted to him, only that here the gain is less by half, ver. 18: "*And the second came, saying, Lord, thy mina hath gained[2] five minæ.*" And so he receives the like answer from the master, but with the difference that the number of the cities over which he is set is reduced to the number of the minæ he had gained, ver. 19: "*And he said to this one also:*" καὶ σὺ ἐπάνω γίνου πέντε πόλεων, i.e. "*Be[3] thou also[4] over five cities.*" The circumstance that the apostrophe: "Well done, good servant," does not expressly recur in the case of the second servant, does not denote a withholding of this praise.[5] The apostrophe is understood as matter of course, just as much as the clause justifying the reward: "because thou wast faithful in the least." If in Matt. xxv. 21 the entire address of the master is repeated to the letter, this circumstantiality has its special reason there, the aim being to signalize the equality of the praise and reward in both cases,—a reason obviously absent here, where, alongside the general resemblance of the praise and reward sufficiently expressed in the repeated καί (καὶ τούτῳ ... καὶ σύ), the special stress lies on the distinction shown in the different amount of the reward allotted,—there, power over ten, here, only over five cities. From the example of these two servants we must then gather how the king dealt with the rest of the servants, so far as they had obeyed the charge given them. According to the degree of the fidelity shown by each one, as displayed in the amount of gain secured, he assigned to them a position of more or less comprehensive authority in his kingdom.

---

[1] It is different in Matt. xxv. 15.   [2] ἐποίησεν, cf. on Matt. xxv. 16.

[3] [The γίνου is of course imperfectly represented by "be." The author says "come," explaining it by "be set."]

[4] Not "and thou," with van Oosterzee, because the καὶ σύ plainly corresponds to the καὶ τούτῳ immediately preceding.

[5] So e.g. Stier. van Oosterzee.

But all the ten did not obey the charge of their master as good servants. One is still to be spoken of, who is opposed as "the other" to the entire class of good servants represented by the first two.[1] Of him it is said in vv. 20, 21: "*And the other came, saying, Lord, behold, here thy mina, which I kept laid up in a handkerchief: for I feared thee, because thou art an austere man* (ἄνθρωπος αὐστηρός): *thou takest up what thou layedst not down, and reapest what thou didst not sow.*" It is exactly the same logic as in the attempted justification on the part of the third servant in Matthew (xxv. 24, 25), only in the reverse order of thought. For whereas there the hardness of the householder is the starting-point, from which the fear of the servant is *derived*, and from this again the idle keeping of the money, upon which followed, in conclusion, the return of his property to the lord with the words: "Lo, thou hast thine own;" here, the corresponding "Behold thy mina" stands first, joined with the confession that he has merely kept the mina in a handkerchief, and this conduct is then *traced back* to the fear he had of the master, and this fear again to the harshness in virtue of which he made others work and appropriated the produce of the work. These differences of language make no difference of meaning. For when here the keeping of the mina in a handkerchief appears in place of the burying of the talent, it is clear that the former course has the same meaning and end as the latter, only that with so much smaller a sum it is the more natural course. And when here in characterizing the harshness of the master the συνάγων, ὅθεν οὐ διεσκόρπισας forming the second clause in Matthew (ver. 24) is omitted, and instead αἴρεις, ὃ οὐκ ἔθηκας as the first clause precedes the θερίζεις ὃ οὐκ ἔσπειρας, the fault found with the reaping without having sown, common to the two passages, guarantees the sameness of the meaning. On the other hand, this essential sameness of meaning in the language of the idle servant makes the very considerable difference in the wording of the two parables all the more singular, and ·this must not be left out of sight in defining the relation of the two parables to each other.

On the other hand, in the refutation given to the servant's attempted justification, the two parables coincide even in the wording, although not entirely; for it is said, vv. 22, 23: "*He*

[1] If ὁ ἕτερος is the reading (Lachmann, Tischendorf), not with the Recepta simply ἕτερος (Meyer).

saith unto him, Out of thine own mouth will I judge thee (this announcement is wanting in Matthew), *thou wicked servant! Thou knewest* (not: knewest thou?)[1] *that I am an austere man, taking up what I laid not down, and reaping what I did not sow. And wherefore,*[2] *then, gavest thou not my money to an exchanger's table,*[3] *etc., and I* (in keeping with my supposed character)[4] *at my coming should then* (in the case put by the preceding question, to which the ἄν before ἔπραξα alludes)[5] *have exacted it with interest?"* The latter strong expression, ἔπραξα = exegissem, corresponds to the presupposed austerity of the master. Therefore, from the servant's own mouth, as is here expressly remarked, the king takes the refutation of the attempted justification, just like the householder in Matthew, reminding him that the view of his master's character expressed by him should rightly have led him to a quite different course from the one he took. For if he professed to know that the master who gave him the mina only cared about deriving profit from the labour of others, how could he keep his money lying dead and useless? And if he were unwilling to work for the owner's benefit, why did he not give it to a money-changer's table, where it would have been readily used by others, so that the owner might have exacted from them the interest for which he was supposed mainly to care? Hence the circumstance, that he at least preserved his master's money and returned it intact, can by no means excuse, far less justify, him, but must be reckoned an aggravation of his fault. And instead of assigning him a place in the administration of the kingdom because of his preserving the mina, as he seems to expect, the king takes from him even the mina that had been entrusted to him, and terminates his relation of service, ver. 24: *" And to the bystanders* (surrounding him as his royal retinue) *he said, Take from him the mina, and give it to him that hath the ten minæ,"* namely, the ten gained in addition to the one (ver. 16), therefore different from the corresponding passage in the parable of the Talents,[6] where, in the number ten, the amount gained was combined with the amount received (5 + 5). Apart from this unimportant difference, there is exactly the same twofold com-

---

[1] Cf. on Matt. xxv. 26.

[2] καὶ διὰ τί; observe the instant entrance of the question with καί, expressing the stringency of the inference.

[3] The article before τράπεζαν (Recepta) is to be expunged, according to the best authorities.

[4] Cf. on Matt. xxv. 27.   [5] Cf. Winer, *Gram.* p. 378.   [6] Matt. xxv. 28.

mand as in Matthew. Its strange element lies in its second part, according to which, the money taken from the idle servant is to be added to him who already has the largest sum. And this strange regulation is then justified by an appeal to the same general rule, only with the difference, that the alleging of the rule, which took place in Matthew with a simple "for," is here specially introduced by an objection of surprise on the part of the bystanders to whom the previous command was given, ver. 25: "*And they said to him, Lord, he hath ten minæ.*" This objection is met by the appeal to the rule as the king's reply with λέγω ὑμῖν, which here renders superfluous an express notice of the king beginning to speak again, and therefore takes the place of an εἶπεν δὲ αὐτοῖς, ver. 26: "*I say unto you, To every one that hath shall be given; but from him that hath not, even what he hath shall be taken away.*"[1] Nothing is said here of any further punishment of the servant. Enough that he has no part in the kingdom of the lord, and, after the taking away even of the mina entrusted to him, has nothing more in common with it.

But the king has not merely to call his servants to account, but also to hold judgment upon those who, although his fellow-citizens, have set themselves from hatred in opposition to him. Hence, in ver. 27, the language of the king turns with πλήν (verumtamen) from his servants to these his enemies, in order to say what is to be done with them. As his fellow-citizens they would have been called to enjoy the blessings of his kingdom in the first rank. But they who were his fellow-citizens became his foes, and as such only he now knows and names them, saying expressly why he has no other name for them: πλὴν τοὺς ἐχθρούς μου τούτους τοὺς μὴ θελήσαντάς με βασιλεῦσαι ἐπ' αὐτούς. The reading ἐκείνους, which the Recepta has on the authority of several MSS., for τούτους is plainly a correction, τούτους seeming less suitable to absent persons who had to be summoned. But τούτους here does not point to persons present, in which case the pronoun would have retained its usual position before the substantive, but it serves, just as in ver. 15,[2] to pave the way for the more precise definition which follows, as there in a relative sentence, so here in a participial sentence: τοὺς μὴ θελήσαντάς με βασιλεῦσαι ἐπ' αὐτούς.[3] But τούτους ought not

---

[1] Respecting the meaning and application of this maxim, cf. on Matt. xxv. 29.
[2] τοὺς δούλους τούτους, οἷς ἔδωκεν τὸ ἀργύριον.
[3] Observe the verbal resumption from ver. 14: οὐ θέλομεν τοῦτον βασιλεῦσαι ἐφ' ἡμᾶς.

on this account to be grammatically separated from the substantive ἐχθρούς and joined with the following participle,[1] which is forbidden by the quite analogous parallel of ver. 15. As the householder there ordered these his servants to whom he gave the money to be brought before him, so here: "*But these my enemies, who would not that I should rule over them, bring hither!*" And their doom, which he joins with the command to bring them, runs just as briefly as severely: "*and slay them before me.*" Instead, therefore, of being permitted to enjoy the kingdom of him, to whom as fellow-citizens they were so nearly related, they have to expect no other fate than that of rebels, when the king, to whom they have impotently opposed themselves, comes upon them with his royal power, and calls them before his tribunal. They will be brought, dragged, so to speak, in chains before the tribunal of the royal conqueror, to receive in his presence [2] the just punishment of their treason in its full severity. The strong expression "slay" in the mouth of the royal judge, affirms that he will show such rebels no weak clemency, but will inflict the penalty of a violent death due to them without mercy.

In what sense, then, does a narrative of such import contradict the expectation of a speedy appearance of the kingdom of God, by which, according to ver. 11, it was occasioned? The narrative itself spoke of the setting up of a kingly rule, which, however, was preceded by a journey into a far country, and a consequent prolonged absence of the future king, during which the fidelity of his servants is to be proved on the one hand, and the hate of his fellow-servants will be revealed on the other. We may here then assume as undoubted, that by this journey of the nobleman Jesus means to represent His own approaching departure from the world, and by his return His own coming again in royal power and glory; and further, that by the nobleman's servants left behind He would have His own disciples understood, and by his fellow-citizens His own fellow-countrymen, the citizens of Israel. And in this case an answer is given to the inquiry as to the relation of the parable to the expectation of a speedy appearance of God's kingdom, and the purpose of the whole parable is made clear. By the parable Jesus teaches His disciples and followers, who had yielded to this false expectation, that, *instead of a speedy setting up of His Messianic kingdom, His*

---

[1] So von Hofmann.
[2] ἔμπροσθέν μου, therefore on the spot, without further delay.

departure from the world is at hand, and consequently a long period of absence on His part, during which His disciples have to prove their fidelity to Him, while His foes will show the inveteracy of their hatred against Him, so that the hour of the actual erection of His kingdom, which will only dawn with His second advent, will be to the former an hour of reckoning, and to the latter an hour of doom. Thus the first part (vv. 12–14) characterizes the impending intermediate period, when the Lord will be absent, as a time of test for the fidelity of His disciples and of revelation for the hatred of His enemies, whereupon the second part (vv. 15–27) shows the significance thus given to the hour of the actual erection of the kingdom for the one and for the other.

There scarcely needs any special allusion to the fact, that in this way the pervading twofold reference of the parable on one side to the disciples, and on the other to Christ's enemies, combines into a united whole. The view which regards the parables as an artificial welding together of two dissimilar parts not originally connected,[1] can only be explained by the undue influence which the critical interest has been allowed to exert on the exegesis in defining the relation of this parable to the similar one in Matthew. Certainly the question may be raised: If Jesus has to do here primarily with His disciples and followers, who believe in His Messiahship, and cherish the hope of a speedy establishing of the Messiah's kingdom,[2] what led Him to give His parable a twofold reference, and with the primary teaching respecting the test-time impending for His disciples and hearers before His kingdom is established, to join the other teaching respecting the attitude His fellow-countrymen will assume to Him and His kingship? But the answer to this question also is given in what was ascertained (ver. 11) respecting the precise nature of the erroneous expectation which the parable was meant to oppose. The expectation of the speedy appearance of God's kingdom attached itself to the circumstance that Jesus was already near Jerusalem. From this it is clear that the opinion assumed this definite shape, that when Jesus has entered Jerusalem, as He did Jericho before, from this metropolis of the theocracy He will speedily erect His Messianic kingdom, the present theocracy of Israel, and the present race of the theocratic

---

[1] Unger, Strauss, Bleek, Meyer.

[2] For the context contains no hint that secret enemies of Jesus were also present, as *e.g.* van Oosterzee supposes.

people will therefore supply Him with the ground on which to erect the kingdom and will constitute its centre. To show them, therefore, how very far wrong they were in this special form of the expectation, from which they cannot yet free themselves, and which had just now forced itself on them afresh under the impressions of the moment, Jesus takes pains to characterize the intervening period, which was to test their fidelity, under the other aspect, namely, that it will reveal the implacable hate of His fellow-countrymen against Him, and their obstinate opposition to His kingship, from which it then follows naturally that this twofold reference recurs in the second part of the parable, in the picture of the Parousia.

It will not be difficult now to interpret the course of the narrative in detail, by making use of what has been already ascertained, in expounding the parable of the Talents, respecting the meaning of the portions common to the two parables. First of all, the antithesis must not be overlooked between the journey εἰς χώραν μακράν (ver. 12) and the διὰ τὸ ἐγγὺς εἶναι Ἰερουσαλήμ (ver. 11), which plainly is no accidental contrast. As the nobleman selected for the throne was obliged, before entering on his rule, to journey into a far country, to receive at the seat of power the investiture with the kingdom designed for him, and then return thence as king, so must Jesus, instead of nothing more than His entrance into Jerusalem, now close at hand, being necessary to the erection of His kingdom, first go afar to Him who can alone confer the crown of the Messianic kingdom, *i.e.* away from this world into the distance of the heaven that is God's throne, in order then to return to set up the Messianic kingdom, when that kingdom has been conferred upon Him by God. To the receiving of the kingdom, then, in this connection corresponds not so much the glorification accruing to the person of Jesus on His going away to God, "the installation of Christ in His heavenly dominion,"[1] as rather the authority God will confer on Him on His second coming from heaven in kingly power and glory to establish the Messianic kingdom of the future. Further, as relates to the designation εὐγενής, so far as one keeps to the original sense of the parable apart from application, it is not to be expressly included in the comparison, as though Jesus had meant by it to allude " in figurative fashion " to His heavenly origin as God's Son, or to His earthly descent

[1] Olshausen.

from royal blood as David's Son, and so emphasize His hereditary right to the throne of God's kingdom,[1] because in the narrative this designation, neither figuratively nor unfiguratively, makes the man to whom it is applied a prince inheriting the throne by birth, but simply by a graphic use of familiar political relations makes him a magnate destined to receive a kingdom from his suzerain in the way of investiture.

From that retirement of their Lord arises for the disciples of Jesus, as for the servants of the nobleman, an intermediate period, during which they will be without His visible presence, and must wait for His coming. But the period is not given them for idle waiting. It is of the most critical importance for themselves, because it is appointed them as a test-time, on the use of which their own participation in the kingdom of Christ and their position in it will depend. As the nobleman on his departure delivered to ten servants one mina each, commanding them, whilst he is initiating his coming as king, to trade with these minæ, precisely that in dealing with so slight a sum the fidelity of each one, and his fitness for the royal service, may be seen; so will Jesus, for the intermediate period up to His second advent, hand over to the body of His disciples[2] an apparently inconsiderable gift, and appoint them the duty of working with it for their Lord, while He is far away. This, indeed, will be but an insignificant task for those who had dreamt already of an instantaneous appearing of God's kingdom, but precisely in it they will prove their fidelity to Jesus, and by the degree of their fidelity in the little, Jesus will learn the degree of their capacity for the position in God's future kingdom destined for them. The nature of the gift Jesus gives His disciples for the intermediate period up to the second advent has been already ascertained in the exposition of Matt. xxv. 14, 15. It is simply His word that He delivers to them, that they may preach and extend it in the world. But in the representation of Luke's parable it is placed under another point of view in several respects. What was emphasized in Matthew,[3] namely, that with His word Jesus delivered to the disciples what had been His own possession, the means and instrument of His own working in the world, is here left out of sight, because here the attention is solely directed to

---

[1] Stier, Lisco, van Oosterzee.
[2] This idea of unity lies in the number ten.
[3] "He delivered to them his goods."

the circumstance, that it is a slight, insignificant gift which Jesus commits with the word to His disciples,—slight and insignificant in relation to the premature expectations of the disciples, conferring no power and reputation in the world, but just for this reason designed and adapted to be a touchstone of fidelity to those to whom it is committed. It is also now explained why the value of the gift is only in Luke represented by a mina, whereas in Matthew, where it appeared as the property of the departing one, it was expressed in talents. And when finally, in Matthew, a different number of talents was assigned to the individual servants according to their ability, while here every one receives only one mina, here again it is left out of sight (what was emphasized there by the assigning of different sums), that so much of the treasures of saving truth wrapped up in the word is entrusted to each disciple to preach as corresponds to his ability. Here, on the other hand, it is pointed out, that it is one and the same word with the preaching of which all disciples are entrusted.

But the same intermediate period that will test the fidelity of the disciples of Jesus, will, on the other hand, reveal the inveteracy of the hate marking the true attitude of His Israelitish fellow-countrymen to Him. That "His citizens" (ver. 14) are the Israelitish countrymen of Jesus, and the "city" therefore to which they belong the Israelitish theocracy, is beyond doubt in the present context, and, moreover, is certified by the analogous representation of the Israelitish theocracy in two other parables.[1] Accordingly, ver. 14 is to be interpreted thus: As the fellow-citizens of the nobleman were so full of hate to him as themselves to send an embassy of protest after him to the seat of supreme authority, and therefore ventured even to assert their self-will against the supreme will that destined the kingdom for him ($o\dot{v}$ $\theta\acute{e}\lambda o\mu\epsilon\nu$ $\tauo\hat{v}\tau o\nu$ $\beta\alpha\sigma\iota\lambda\epsilon\hat{v}\sigma\alpha\iota$ $\dot{\epsilon}\phi'$ $\dot{\eta}\mu\hat{\alpha}\varsigma$); so Jesus here foresees and foretells that His Israelitish countrymen will persist in their hatred against Him even after He has gone away to God, and inspired by this hatred will oppose their will to the supreme will of God, who received Jesus to Himself in heaven to confer on Him the crown of the Messianic kingdom. Therefore ver. 14 does not merely contain a general characterization of the hostility of Israel to Christ's person and kingdom, which is all that is usually understood in the interpretation, in which case it would

[1] Cf. on Matt. xxii. 7; Luke xiv. 21.

be left quite unexplained why, in order figuratively to represent such a general relation, a feature so specific as the despatch of an embassy of protest to the seat of power is borrowed from the political circumstances of the age. But as such an embassy denotes in the political sphere an assertion on the part of the protesters of their own will against the intentions prevailing at the seat of power, so it is predicted that, despite the fact (attested in historical fulfilment by the outpouring of the Spirit and the apostolic preaching) that Jesus is exalted to God to receive the crown of the Messianic kingdom, His fellow-countrymen will not desist from their hostility against Him, and will not scruple to direct their resistance against God's supreme will. Thus their resistance will follow the Lord into heaven to God's throne, as the protest of the fellow-citizens followed the nobleman into the far country to the throne of the suzerain, certainly in the character of a protest as impotent as it is obstinate.

But if this is the character of the intermediate period which must precede the appearance of Christ's kingdom, it follows that the hour of the setting up of that kingdom will be one of reckoning for His disciples and of judgment for His enemies. For as the king in the parable, when he returned in the possession of regal power and dignity, summoned the servants to whom he had given the money, in order to learn what each one had gained by trading (ver. 15); so Christ in the hour of His kingly return will call to account His servants to whom He entrusted His word, that it may be known what gain each one has made for his Lord by the lowly ministry of the word. So far, then, as the following transaction with the faithful servants resembles that in Matthew's parable (xxv. 20 ff.), the latter is to be consulted in interpreting the present parable. But the more similar the account of the first two servants in the two parables, the more strange appears the very important difference in the teaching given here from the teaching there. For whereas in Matthew the emphasis of the teaching lay on this, that at Christ's second coming, along with very different results of labour in this life, the praise and reward will remain the same to individual disciples, so far, that is, as the difference in the results simply arose from the different endowment of the individuals, and corresponds to it; so the teaching of the present parable tends in precisely an opposite direction, namely, to the effect that a different amount of gain secured for the Lord's cause in this life will be the standard for assigning an equally different reward, so far, that is, as the difference in the service has its cause in a different degree of diligence and fidelity. As the king made the first servant, who was able to show a gain of ten minæ, a commander over ten cities of his kingdom, and the second servant, who had gained five minæ, over five only, and so with the rest; so in the hour of His second advent Christ will assign to His faithful disciples a position of joint authority in His kingdom, but in very different degrees, according to the amount of gain they have secured for the Lord's cause in this life by different degrees of fidelity. For the degree of capacity for the new sphere of activity opening to them in God's future kingdom, as sharers in Christ's dominion, is shown simply in the faithful diligence displayed in the lowly ministry of the word ($\dot{\epsilon}\nu$ $\dot{\epsilon}\lambda\alpha\chi\dot{\iota}\sigma\tau\omega$, ver. 17). But whilst the teaching of Luke's parable tends in quite a different direction from that of the corresponding section in Matthew's parable, it is clear, on the other hand, that the former by no means contradicts the latter, but merely supplements it on the opposite side; so that the two taken together give a complete picture of the rewards in God's kingdom of the future. The teaching of the parable in Matthew is: The reason of different degrees of reward in that kingdom is not the different amount of success in this life, depending mostly, so far as can be seen outwardly, on a difference of endowment; on the contrary, the slightly gifted, so far as they have borne fruit corresponding to their endowments, will have the same praise from the Lord, and bear off the same reward, as the richly gifted for their great success.[1] The teaching of the parable in Luke is: A different degree of reward in God's future kingdom will result from the different measure of fidelity with which individuals served their Lord in this life, and from the consequent difference in the success achieved in relation to the endowments received,[2] and in so far from the different value of the success in itself, the value of which is determined in the Lord's sight simply by this relation.

On the other hand, the two parables substantially coincide in the transaction which took place in Matthew between the householder and the third servant of the three set forth as examples, and in Luke between the king and the servant singled out from

---

[1] Cf. also the interpretation of the Labourers in the Vineyard, Matt. xx. 1 ff., and especially on ver. 16: "The last shall be first, and the first last."

[2] In the parable, ten to one in the one, five to one in the other.

the ten as "the other," and opposed to the faithful ones. The exposition of the wording of the parable has shown that the attempted justification of the idle servant preserves exactly the same line of thought as in Matthew's parable, only in reverse order, and that the master's reply is of exactly the same import as there. Consequently the attempted justification here (vv. 20, 21), as there, characterizes the selfish standpoint of an indolent disciple, who shuns all labour in the service of Christ, because he regards it as hardness on the Lord's part, and fears that the Lord will reap the benefit of the life's work of His disciples, and who yet thinks himself justified in such inactivity, provided he keeps the word to himself, and is able to restore it intact to His hands from whom he received it. It is self-evident that the preserving the mina in the handkerchief ($\epsilon \tilde{\iota} \chi o \nu$ $\dot{a}\pi o\kappa\epsilon\iota\mu\acute{e}\nu\eta\nu$ $\dot{\epsilon}\nu$ $\sigma o\upsilon\delta a\rho\acute{\iota}\omega$) here signifies nothing more than the hiding in the earth in Matthew ($\dot{\epsilon}\kappa\rho\upsilon\psi a$ $\dot{\epsilon}\nu$ $\tau\hat{\eta}$ $\gamma\hat{\eta}$), only that in the latter description the diligent hiding of the word from the world, in which its destiny is to work, is still more strongly apparent, whilst the former simply presents the indolent disciple as one who keeps the word to himself without publishing it.[1] And again, just as in Matthew, in the master's answer to the servant (vv. 22, 23), the notion that any one is justified in inactivity is dissipated by the admonition, that he to whom the Lord's claim on the labour of His disciples seems a hardship, and who refuses such self-denying labour as the Lord demands, is bound to retire from the ministry of the word, and leave it to those who are ready to use it and secure the fruit the Lord desires. By this course he would do less injury to the cause of Christ than by continuing to pass for an advocate of Christ's word, and yet by his inactivity letting it lie dead and useless.

Finally, in ver. 24, the retribution befalling such inactivity at the Parousia is figuratively represented just as in Matthew. Instead of such indolent preservation of his gifts being reckoned a merit in a disciple, and a new position being assigned him on that ground in God's future kingdom, even that which was committed to him will be taken away, every bond between him and the Lord being thus severed. And what is taken from the indolent will be added to the most faithful, inasmuch as the fruit

---

[1] Lange, *e.g.*, sees in the mention of the handkerchief (*Schweisstuch*, *perspiration-cloth*), "which, of course, he does not use in these circumstances," a quite special indication of laziness.

of their faithful toil will be accounted to them of higher value in the same degree in which the imaginary merit of the indolent turns to shame and their glory is scattered. To the *most faithful*, we say here, not to the *faithful* simply, as in interpreting Matthew's parable. For the feature that the one mina is added to him who attained the highest gain of ten minæ, has here a farther-reaching significance than the corresponding feature in Matthew, inasmuch as here the highest degree of fidelity is expressed in the highest gain, the special value of this service being enhanced by the dark foil of the worthlessness of the imaginary service of the indolent. For a detailed interpretation of the master's language in the parable, both of his refutation of the servant and of the judgment he pronounces on him, inclusive of the appeal to the maxim: "He that hath, to him shall be given," etc., the exposition of Matt. xxv. 26–30 may be consulted. There it has been already shown that when Luke, unlike Matthew, says nothing of a formal expulsion of the idle servant, this leads to no essential difference of meaning, because what Luke says of the punishment of the servant already implies that he has no share in the kingdom of his lord, and therefore that he who is like him will have no share in the kingdom of Christ.

And if the hour of Christ's second advent will be an hour of reckoning even for His disciples, how much more will it be an hour of judgment for His enemies! The citizens of Israel, who hated Jesus, although He lived and worked among them as His countrymen, and who were impelled by their hatred for Him to resistance against the counsel and will of the most high God,— what can they be to the Messiah returning from heaven but enemies, and what other fate can the erection of the Messiah's kingdom bring them than that of rebels, on whom a victorious king takes righteous vengeance? For this reason, as the king in the parable, on his return from the far country, only knows those who were his fellow-citizens as his enemies, and causes them to be brought before him, that the extreme penalty due to treason may be inflicted on the spot without mercy, so will Christ do on His coming to those who, from being His fellow-countrymen, have become His foes. Although members of the chosen nation, to which Christ Himself belonged, who as such would have been called in the first rank to enjoy the blessings of the Messianic kingdom, the manifested Messiah at the setting up of His kingdom will call them before His tribunal as His foes, and forthwith inflict on them the punishment due to hardened rebels against His divinely-ordained eternal kingship,— the punishment of condemnation to the eternal death, of whose pain and terrors even the slaying of the rebels in the parable is but a feeble image. When it is said that such an image is unlike the mind of Jesus,[1] this is simply an *à priori* assertion easily refuted by the numerous passages in which Jesus speaks of the punishment of damnation with no less menacing solemnity, and no less terrible images. That nothing can be meant by the extreme penalty inflicted on the rebels in the parable but the condemnation to eternal death, which Christ will inflict on His foes in the judgment of the Parousia, and therefore that this passage refers exclusively to the last judgment on the foes of Christ and His kingdom at His second coming, and not, like other prophetic words of Jesus in other passages, to the historical event of the destruction of Jerusalem falling in the intermediate period between His going away and His return,[2] ought not to have been called in question, considering the clearness and distinctness with which the parable distinguishes the period of the second advent as one of reckoning and judgment from the intermediate period preceding it as the time of the Lord's absence in the heavenly world, designed to leave scope to His friends and foes to manifest their love and hate.

In conclusion let us briefly sum up what has been ascertained in the exposition respecting the relation of this parable to Matthew's parable of the Talents. First, both have this in common, that they represent the departure of Jesus from the world as the going on a journey, and His second advent as a return from a journey. But within this common element appears at once the most general distinction, that Luke's parable draws the material of its figurative representation from the circumstances of public political life; Matthew's parable, on the other hand, from those of private life. Whereas in Luke the lord is a magnate going a long journey to receive a kingdom from the suzerain, and then to return as king, in Matthew it is simply a householder undertaking a private journey, whose purpose is not more precisely defined, and returning only after a long period.

[1] Unger *et al.*   [2] Godet, van Oosterzee.

Hence arises another difference, that Luke's parable is able to set over against the lord going to receive a crown a twofold category of persons left behind, without injuring the internal unity and harmonious coherence of the narrative,—namely, on one hand, those who, already in his personal service, hope to be allowed to serve him in his future kingdom; and on the other, such as are hostile to him and his rule,—whilst in Matthew's parable, of course, only the servants of the household stand over against the householder as those left behind. And so all that Luke's parable says of the enemies of the lord, and therefore all that it predicts respecting the enmity of the countrymen of Jesus against Him and His kingdom, and respecting the doom that the Parousia will bring to them, is wanting in Matthew.

On the other hand, the two parables seem all the more nearly to coincide in what they say of the duty assigned to the servants by their departing masters, and of the reward or punishment allotted to the servants on the master's return, according to the fidelity or unfaithfulness shown. In both parables it is a sum of money which the master delivers to the servants to employ in trade during the time of his absence, and then in both parables it is related how the master richly rewarded two faithful servants who had traded and made profit with the money received, setting them over the great, because they had been faithful in the little; and how, on the other hand, he convicted of guilt an unfaithful servant, who had left the money unused, and punished him by taking away what he had received. Thus far reaches the common portion in the two parables in the proceedings between master and servants, and within this common portion the interpretation of the two parables must be the same. Only by unduly pressing words can we find distinctions hidden in these quite similar features, necessitating different interpretations, and so arrive at such a conclusion as Lange: "The former parable (Luke's) throughout describes the external, social, official side of the Christian calling, the latter the inner, individual side." But, on the other hand again, even within this common portion, acknowledged as such and interpreted alike, appear very important distinctions. First, it is strange that in Matthew's parable, in the handing over of the money, talents are mentioned, and therefore very considerable sums, but in Luke minæ only; whereas in the giving of the reward, conversely in Matthew, the servants are merely set over much property in general ($\dot{\epsilon}\pi\grave{\iota}\ \pi o\lambda\lambda\hat{\omega}\nu$), but in Luke over the entire complex of city-regions. This diversity certainly only arises as an outcome of the general distinction between the circumstances of private life, which are the means of representation in Matthew, and those of political life, so used in Luke. For there the subject is the management of a property during the owner's absence, the owner rewarding the faithful managers merely by handing over still more property; here the subject is an experiment of the future king, in the course of which his servants first prove their fidelity in a little sum of money, and then for their reward take part in managing his kingdom. Hence result in the interpretation merely different points of view for the like teaching respecting the duty assigned to the disciples after their Lord's departure, and respecting the reward of fidelity awaiting them at His second coming. But it is otherwise with the other point of diversity, consisting in this, that in Matthew the sum of money allotted to the individual servants was very different in amount, while the praise and the reward given to the faithful were alike, because they had each laboured with equal fidelity; whereas, conversely in Luke, the sum of money given was the same to all servants, while the reward of fidelity was very different to the individuals, the one having shown greater and the other less fidelity. From this diversity in the figurative representation resulted an essentially different thought in the interpretation, namely, that here the teaching of the one parable is co-ordinate with that of the first, supplementing it in the opposite direction. With the teaching of Matthew, that despite unequal endowments and unequal success, like fidelity will receive like reward in God's kingdom, Luke co-ordinates the other teaching, that in God's future kingdom there is a corresponding difference of reward for different degrees of fidelity and the consequent different degrees of service. Only when the two parables come to speak of the conviction and punishment of an unfaithful servant do they again coincide really and completely, not indeed in the wording, which was strikingly different in the self-justification of an unfaithful servant, but in substance.

Such are the facts of the case as ascertained by exegesis in reference to the relation of the two parables to each other. For the critical judgment, which must base itself on these facts, the circumstance is also of importance, that Luke's parable, to which most critics deny originality, is placed as an independent discourse in a definite historical context. According to Luke, it was uttered by Jesus at Jericho, before His departure thence to Jerusalem, by way of instruction to His followers, who mistakenly expected the speedy appearance of God's kingdom from His approaching entry into Jerusalem. Matthew's parable, on the other hand, is merely inwoven into the great eschatological discourse of Jesus, being joined to its second part as an appendix of similar import. Like this whole part of the discourse, it also exhorts to readiness for the Parousia, but without the special reference to the uncertainty of its time being retained which has hitherto governed this part of the discourse throughout. From all these facts it would follow that if an original identity of the two parables is to be held, the original context, and in consequence substantially the original form, must not be sought in Matthew,[1] but in Luke,[2] and the inweaving of the parable into the eschatological discourse of Matthew's Gospel must be ascribed to the redactor of this Gospel. But in reality, considering the pervading diversity seen everywhere in the two parables, even within the common portions, with the exception of the passage relating to the unfaithful servant, the supposition itself, according to which one of the two parables arose out of the other by a process of remodelling, is without really certain foundation. Or how can the requisite proof be obtained for the asserted impossibility, that after a short period Jesus should again use the same figurative material, and transform it into a dress for another truth of the same import, by way of supplementing the teaching of the first parable? For example, are not the two parables of the Treasure and the Pearl far more alike in form and substance than those of the Talents and Pounds? And is it on this account impossible for them both to originate with Jesus, or for them both to be spoken in one breath, so to speak, as they are according to Matthew's account? Considering, therefore, the relation of the two parables of the Talents and Pounds, as stated above, the only conjecture deserving mention is, that perhaps the passage relating to the unfaithful servant may have come into Luke's parable by transference from Matthew's parable, in which it is an integral constituent, so that the second part of the former would have for its contents originally only the rewarding of the faithful disciples on the one hand, and the punishing of the enemies of Christ on the other. But even this conjecture not

[1] So Unger, Strauss, Ewald, Bleek, Meyer, Weiss.   [2] So Olshausen.

merely shares in the general uncertainty of all conjectures of this class, but is, moreover, made specially doubtful by the strange diversity of wording in the passage in question, which rather favours the natural supposition of a free reproduction of the same thought on the part of the author than the conjecture of a later transference of this passage from one parable into the other.

THE PARABLES IN SYSTEMATIC ORDER.

I. THE NATURE AND GROWTH OF THE KINGDOM OF GOD.

   1. *Founding of the Kingdom.*

		PAGE
The Sower, or Divers Soils: The success of preaching dependent on the hearers,	Matt. xiii. 3–8, and parallels,	37

   2. *Development of the Kingdom.*

      a. The Immediate Future.

The Fig-Tree: Last respite for Israel,	Luke xiii. 6–9,	159
The Great Supper: From the Jews to the heathen,	Luke xiv. 16–24,	169
The Wicked Vinedressers:	Matt. xxi. 33–44, and parallels,	324

      b. Entire Development to the End.

The Fruit-bearing Earth: Through the personal labour of the members of the kingdom,	Mark iv. 26–29,	80
The Tares: Mingling of impure elements,	Matt. xiii. 24–30,	57
The Mustard-Seed: Growth until the world is embraced,	Matt. xiii. 31, 32, and parallels,	93
The Leaven: Growth until the world is pervaded,	Matt. xiii. 33, and parallels,	99
The Fishing-Net: First gathering, then sifting,	Matt. xiii. 47–50,	115
The Royal Marriage-Feast: First called, yet rejected,	Matt. xxii. 1–14,	349

   3. *Consummation of the Kingdom*

The Ten Virgins: Exclusion of those not found ready in the hour of Christ's coming,	Matt. xxv. 1–13,	382
The Labourers in the Vineyard: Strange assessment of the reward of grace in God's future kingdom,	Matt. xx. 1–16,	298
The Talents in Trust: The rewarding of fidelity and punishing of unfaithfulness in God's future kingdom,	Matt. xxv. 14–30,	405
The Pounds in Trust:	Luke xix. 11–27,	432

II. THE RIGHT ATTITUDE OF MEMBERS OF THE KINGDOM.

   1. *Towards God.*

The Pharisee and the Publican: Humility before God,	Luke xviii. 9–14,	269

The Hidden Treasure:	Joy in God that sacrifices everything for the highest good,	Matt. xiii. 44,	107
The Costly Pearl:		Matt. xiii. 45, 46,	111
The Importunate Friend:	Perseverance in prayer to God,	Luke xi. 5–10,	140
The Unjust Judge:		Luke xviii. 1–8,	257

2. *Towards the World.*
  a. To Men.

The Merciful Samaritan: Active proof of love to one's neighbour by helping the needy,	Luke x. 25–37,	127
The Unmerciful Servant: Unlimited placability towards wrong-doers,	Matt. xviii. 21–35,	281
The Lost Sheep: ⎫ Unselfish sympathy in the conversion of the sinner,	Luke xv. 4–7,	191
The Lost Coin: ⎬	Luke xv. 8–10,	197
The Lost Son: ⎭	Luke xv. 11–32,	200

  b. To Earthly Goods.

The Rich Fool: Folly of trusting in perishing goods,	Luke xii. 16–21,	149
The Rich Man: Culpability of the selfish use of earthly riches,	Luke xvi. 19–31,	232
The Unjust Steward: Wise employment of temporal means in reference to eternity,	Luke xvi. 1–9,	215

SCRIPTURE SECTIONS TREATED OF.

OLD TESTAMENT.

JUDGES.	PAGE		2 KINGS.	PAGE
ix. 7–15,	9		xiv. 9,	9
2 SAMUEL.			**ISAIAH.**	
			v. 1–6,	10
xii. 1–6,	10		xxviii. 23–29,	12

THE GOSPELS.

MATTHEW.	PAGE		MATTHEW—*continued*.	PAGE
vii. 24–27,	13, 2		xxi. 45, 46,	349
xii. 22–50,	29		xxii. 1–14,	349
xiii. 1–3,	30		xxiv. 1–35,	379
xiii. 3–9,	37		xxiv. 36–51,	380
xiii. 10–17,	33		xxv. 1–13,	382
xiii. 18–23,	43		xxv. 14–30,	405
xiii. 24–30,	57		xxv. 31–46,	419
xiii. 31, 32,	93			
xiii. 33,	99			
xiii. 34, 35,	32		**MARK.**	
xiii. 36–43,	66		iv. 3–9,	37
xiii. 44,	107		iv. 14–20,	43
xiii. 45, 46,	111		iv. 21–25,	80
xiii. 47–50,	115		iv. 26–29,	80
xviii. 1–17,	282		iv. 30–32,	93
xviii. 12–14,	196		xii. 1–12,	324
xviii. 21, 22,	282			
xviii. 23–35,	284			
xix. 21,	298		**LUKE.**	
xix. 27–30,	299		vii. 41–47,	18
xx. 1–16,	14, 298		viii. 5–8,	37
xxi. 23–27,	324		viii. 11–15,	43
xxi. 28–32,	325		ix. 51,	125
xxi. 33–44,	11		x. 25–29,	127

SCRIPTURE SECTIONS TREATED OF.

LUKE—*continued.*		LUKE—*continued.*	
CHAP.	PAGE	CHAP.	PAGE
x. 30–37,	130	xv. 8–10,	197
xi. 5–10,	140	xv. 11–32,	200
xii. 13–15,	149	xvi. 1–9,	215
xii. 16–21,	151	xvi. 10–13,	230
xiii. 1–5,	159	xvi. 14–18,	232
xiii. 6–9,	160	xvi. 19–31,	232
xiii. 18, 19,	93	xvii. 11,	125
xiii. 20, 21,	99	xvii. 20–37,	257
xiii. 22,	125	xviii. 1–8,	258
xiv. 1–15,	169	xviii. 9–14,	269
xiv. 16–24,	170	xix. 1–11,	432
xv. 1–3,	190	xix. 12–27,	434
xv. 4–7,	191	xx. 9–19,	324

THE END.

www.ingramcontent.com/pod-product-compliance
Lightning Source LLC
Chambersburg PA
CBHW022104300426
44117CB00007B/585